Lecture Notes in Computer Science 13289

Ana-Lucia Varbanescu · Abhinav Bhatele ·
Piotr Luszczek · Baboulin Marc (Eds.)

High Performance Computing

37th International Conference, ISC High Performance 2022
Hamburg, Germany, May 29 – June 2, 2022
Proceedings

Springer

Editors
Ana-Lucia Varbanescu
University of Twente
Enschede, The Netherlands

Abhinav Bhatele
University of Maryland
College Park, MD, USA

Piotr Luszczek
University of Tennessee
Knoxville, TN, USA

Baboulin Marc
Université Paris-Saclay
Orsay, France

ISSN 0302-9743 ISSN 1611-3349 (electronic)
Lecture Notes in Computer Science
ISBN 978-3-031-07311-3 ISBN 978-3-031-07312-0 (eBook)
https://doi.org/10.1007/978-3-031-07312-0

This Springer imprint is published by the registered company Springer Nature Switzerland AG
The registered company address is: Gewerbestrasse 11, 6330 Cham, Switzerland

Preface

ISC High Performance Computing—formerly known as the International Supercomputing Conference—was founded in 1986 as the Supercomputer Seminar. Originally organized by Hans Meuer, Professor of Computer Science at the University of Mannheim, and former director of its computer center, the 1986 edition of the seminar brought together a group of 81 scientists and industrial partners who shared an interest in high-performance computing (HPC). Since then, the annual conference has become a major international event within the HPC community, growing beyond its humble beginnings, and moving out of Mannheim into other cities throughout the years: Frankfurt, Heidelberg, Dresden, Hamburg, Leipzig, and this year back to Hamburg. Prior to the coronavirus pandemic, the conference had seen a steady increase in the number of submissions of high-quality research papers and corresponding growth in the number of conference attendees. Benefiting from the improving health indicators, ISC-HPC 2022 was again held in person in Hamburg.

The call for papers to ISC-HPC 2022 was issued in Fall 2021, inviting the researchers, developers, and practitioners alike to submit their latest results for consideration for one of the five conference tracks: (1) Architecture, Networks, and Storage; (2) HPC Algorithms and Applications; (3) Machine Learning, AI, and Emerging Technologies; (4) Performance Modeling, Evaluation, and Analysis; and (5) Programming Environments and Systems Software. In all, 53 full submissions were received from authors all over the world. The Research Papers Program Committee consisted of 71 members from 18 countries. After initial reviews were completed, a rebuttal process offered authors an opportunity to respond to reviewers' questions and help clarify issues the reviewers might have had. A virtual Program Committee meeting was held to discuss all the papers and to finalize consensus on the papers. Finally, the committee selected 18 papers for publication.

For the past several years, the ISC-HPC conference has presented an ISC-sponsored award to encourage outstanding research in HPC and to honor the overall best research paper submitted to the conference. Four years ago, this annual award was renamed in memory of the late Dr. Hans Meuer, who was general chair of the ISC-HPC conference from 1986 through 2014, and a co-founder of the TOP500 project. This year, from all research papers submitted, the Best Paper Committee selected the best paper based on its technical merit, its novelty, and impact on the HPC community. During a live ceremony, the following paper was awarded the Hans Meuer Award: *Remote OpenMP Offloading* by Atmn Patel from University of Waterloo, Canada, and Johannes Doerfert from Argonne National Laboratory, USA. The paper extended the canonical scope of OpenMP, which is traditionally confined to a shared memory domain, by utilizing the standard's modern features to offload the computational workload to GPU accelerators housed in remote cluster nodes. The Best Paper Committee appreciated the paper's unique combination of OpenMP familiarity and ease of use with accelerated and distributed computing that were accompanied by analysis of scaling capabilities. The winning paper also showed the solution's versatility and how it could use multiple transport layers, each of which offers a different set of trade-offs between performance, portability, and scalability potential.

As the chairs of the Research Papers Committee, we would like to express our gratitude to our colleagues for submitting high-quality papers to all five ISC-HPC scientific tracks. Also, we wish to extend our thanks to the track, area, and conflict chairs, as well as the members of the Best Paper Committee, and finally to the Research Papers Committee that provided the reviews and manuscript evaluation throughout the submission stages. We hope to express our thanks in person during this year's meeting and upcoming ISC-HPC 2023.

May 2022

Ana Lucia Varbanescu
Abhinav Bhatele

Organization

Program Chair

Keren Bergman	Columbia University, USA

Program Deputy Chair

John Shalf	Lawrence Berkeley National Laboratory, USA

Research Papers Program Committee

Research Papers Chairs

Ana Lucia Varbanescu (Chair)	University of Amsterdam, Netherlands
Abhinav Bhatele (Deputy Chair)	University of Maryland, USA

Architecture, Networks, and Storage

Jay Lofstead (Chair)	Sandia National Laboratories, USA
Edson Borin	University of Campinas, Brazil
Elsa Gonsiorowski	Lawrence Livermore National Laboratory, USA
Mozhgan Kabiri Chimeh	NVIDIA, UK
Nectarios Koziris	National Technical University of Athens, Greece
Michael Kuhn	Otto von Guericke University Magdeburg, Germany
Jay Lofstead	Sandia National Laboratories, USA
Preeti Malakar	Indian Institute of Technology Kanpur, India
Dhabaleswar Panda	Ohio State University, USA
Guangming Tan	Institute of Computing Technology (ICT), China
Osamu Tatebe	University of Tsukuba, Japan
Carsten Trinitis	Technical University of Munich, Germany
Venkatram Vishwanath	Argonne National Laboratory, USA

HPC Algorithms and Applications

Didem Unat (Chair)	Koç University, Turkey
Sameh Abdulah	KAUST, Saudi Arabia
Mehmet Belviranli	Colorado School of Mines, USA
Xing Cai	Simula Research Laboratory and University of Oslo, Norway

Lin Gan	Tsinghua University and National Supercomputing Center in Wuxi, China
Clemens Grelck	University of Amsterdam, Netherlands
Fuerlinger Karl	Ludwig Maximilian University Munich (LMU), Germany
Kamer Kaya	Sabancı University, Turkey
Simon McIntosh-Smith	University of Bristol, UK
Gabriel Noaje	NVIDIA, Singapore
Lena Oden	Fernuniversität in Hagen and Forschungszentrum Jülich GMBH, Germany
Johann Rudi	Argonne National Laboratory, USA
Tuğba Torun	Koç University, Turkey
Miwako Tsuji	RIKEN, Japan

Machine Learning, AI, and Emerging Technologies

Theodore L. Willke (Chair)	Intel Corporation, USA
Nikoli Dryden	ETH Zurich, Switzerland
Gurbinder Gill	Katana Graph Inc., USA
Jiajia Li	William and Mary College, USA
Maryam Mehri Dehnavi	University of Toronto, Canada
Bogdan Nicolae	Argonne National Laboratory, USA
Mostofa Patwary	NVIDIA, USA
Shaden Smith	Microsoft, USA
Edgar Solomonik	University of Illinois at Urbana-Champaign, USA
Sofia Vallecorsa	CERN, Switzerland
Abhinav Vishnu	AMD, USA
Yang You	National University of Singapore, Singapore

Performance Modeling, Evaluation, and Analysis

Nathan Tallent (Chair)	Pacific Northwest National Laboratory, USA
Ivy B. Peng	Lawrence Livermore National Laboratory, USA
Alexandru Calotoiu	ETH Zürich, Germany
Marc Casas	Barcelona Supercomputing Center, Spain
Tom Deakin	University of Bristol, UK
Seyong Lee	ORNL, USA
Simon McIntosh-Smith	University of Bristol, UK
Xiaozhu Meng	Rice University, USA
Bernd Mohr	Juelich Supercomputing Centre, Germany
Scott Pakin	Los Alamos National Laboratory, USA
Xian-He Sun	Illinois Institute of Technology, USA
Jidong Zhai	Tsinghua University, China
Tianwei Zhang	Nanyang Technological University, Singapore

Programming Environments and Systems Software

Michele Weiland (Chair)	EPCC, University of Edinburgh, UK
Bilel Hadri	KAUST Supercomputing Laboratory, Saudi Arabia
Guido Juckeland	HZDR, Germany
Michael Klemm	AMD and OpenMP ARB, Germany
Pouya Kousha	Ohio State University, USA
John L. inford	Arm, USA
István Z. Reguly	Pázmány Péter Catholic University, Hungary
Harvey Richardson	Hewlett Packard Enterprise, UK
Martin Ruefenacht	Leibniz Supercomputing Centre, Germany
Roxana Rusitoru	Arm, UK
Thomas R. W. Scogland	Lawrence Livermore National Laboratory, USA
Simon Smart	ECMWF, UK
Hiroyuki Takizawa	Tohoku University, Japan
Christian Terboven	RWTH Aachen University, Germany
Justs Zarins	EPCC, University of Edinburgh, UK

Birds of a Feather Committee

Roman Wyrzykowski (Chair)	Czestochowa University of Technology, Poland
Iosif Meyerov (Deputy Chair)	Lobachevsky State University of Nizhni Novogorod, Russia
Michael Bader	Technical University of Munich, Germany
Claudia Blaas-Schenner	TU Wien, VSC Research Center, Austria
Dominik Göddeke	University of Stuttgart, Germany
Aleksandar Ilic	INESC-ID and Universidade de Lisboa, Portugal
Jacek Kitowski	AGH University of Science and Technology, Poland
Dieter Kranzlmueller	Ludwig Maximilian University Munich (LMU) and Leibniz Rechenzentrum, Germany
Carola Kruse	Centre Européen de Recherche et de Formation Avancée en Calcul Scientifique (CERFACS), France
Krzysztof Kurowski	Poznań Supercomputing and Networking Center, Poland
Marco Lapegna	University of Naples Federico II, Italy
Simon McIntosh-Smith	University of Bristol, UK
Iosif Meyerov	Lobachevsky State University of Nizhni Novogorod, Russia
Koji Nakano	Hiroshima University, Japan
Gabriel Oksa	Slovak Academy of Sciences, Slovakia
Dana Petcu	West University of Timisoara, Romania

Antonio J. Peña	Barcelona Supercomputing Center, Spain
Thomas Rauber	University of Bayreuth, Germany
Lubomir Riha	IT4Innovations National Supercomputing Center and Technical University of Ostrava, Czech Republic
Masha Sosonkina	Old Dominion University, USA
Vladimir Stegailov	Higher School of Economics and JIHT RAS, Russia
Dave Turner	Kansas State University, USA
Bora Ucar	CNRS and ENS-Lyon, France

Project Posters Committee

Christian Perez (Chair)	Inria, France
Are Magnus Bruaset (Deputy Chair)	Simula Research Laboratory, Norway
Marco Aldinucci	University of Torino, Italy
Bartosz Bosak	Poznań Supercomputing and Networking Center, Poland
Nick Brown	EPCC, University of Edinburgh, UK
Theodoros Christoudias	The Cyprus Institute, Cyprus
Andrew Ensor	Auckland University of Technology, New Zealand
Ana Gainaru	Oak Ridge National Laboratory, USA
Andra Hugo	Apple, France
Kamer Kaya	Sabancı University, Turkey
Francesc Lordan Gomis	Barcelona Supercomputing Center, Spain
Maciej Malawski	Sano Centre for Computational Medicine, Institute of Computer Science AGH, Poland
Kengo Nakajima	University of Tokyo and RIKEN, Japan
Bogdan Nicolae	Argonne National Laboratory, USA
Eric Petit	Intel, France
Phil Ridley	Arm, UK
Jonathan Rouzaud-Cornabas	Inria and INSA de Lyon, France
Kentaro Sano	RIKEN, Japan
Francieli Zanon Boito	Inria, France
Ameli Chi Zhou	Shenzhen University, China

Research Posters Committee

Aparna Chandramowlishwaran (Chair)	UCI, USA
Hartwig Anzt	Karlsruhe Institute of Technology, Germany and University of Tennessee, USA

Maryam Mehri Dehnavi	University of Toronto, Canada
Jee Choi	University of Oregon, USA
Ana Gainaru	Oak Ridge National Laboratory, USA
Lin Gan	Tsinghua University and National Supercomputing Center in Wuxi, China
Amal Khabou	Université Paris-Saclay, France
Mariam Kiran	Lawrence Berkeley National Laboratory, USA
Penporn Koanantakool	Google LLC, USA
Ronald Kriemann	MPI for Math. i.t.S., Germany
Ang Li	Pacific Northwest National Laboratory, USA
Jiajia Li	William and Mary College, USA
Piyush Sao	Oak Ridge National Laboratory, USA
Christian Terboven	RWTH Aachen University, Germany
Bo Wu	Colorado School of Mines, USA
Rio Yokota	Tokyo Institute of Technology, Japan
Rohit Zambre	AMD Research, USA

Tutorials Committee

Kathryn Mohror (Chair)	Lawrence Livermore National Laboratory, USA
Suren Byna (Deputy Chair)	Lawrence Berkeley National Laboratory, USA
Ritu Arora	University of Texas at San Antonio, USA
Rosa M. Badia	Barcelona Supercomputing Center, Spain
Wahid Bhimji	Lawrence Berkeley National Laboratory, USA
Philip Carns	Argonne National Laboratory, USA
James Dinan	NVIDIA, USA
Ann Gentile	Sandia National Laboratories, USA
Tanzima Islam	Texas State University, USA
Simon McIntosh-Smith	University of Bristol, UK
Diana Moise	Cray, and HPE, Switzerland
Sarah Neuwirth	Goethe-University Frankfurt, Germany
C. J. Newburn	NVIDIA, USA
Dhabaleswar Panda	Ohio State University, USA
Raghunath Raja Chandrasekar	Frau, USA
Michela Taufer	The University of Tennessee, USA
Michele Weiland	EPCC – University of Edinburgh, UK

Workshops Committee

Hartwig Anzt (Chair)	Karlsruhe Institute of Technology, Germany and University of Tennessee, USA
Amanda Bienz (Deputy Chair)	University of New Mexico, USA
Cody Balos	Lawrence Livermore National Laboratory, USA

Harun Bayraktar	NVIDIA, USA
Natalie Beams	University of Tennessee, USA
Luc Berger-Vergiat	Sandia National Laboratories, USA
George Bosilca	University of Tennessee, USA
Lisa Claus	LBNL, USA
Terry Cojean	Karlsruhe Institute of Technology, Germany
Anthony Danalis	University of Tennessee Knoxville, USA
Edoardo Di Napoli	Juelich Supercomputing Centre, Germany
Markus Goetz	Karlsruhe Institute of Technology, Germany
Aditya Kashi	Karlsruhe Institute of Technology, Germany
Sarah Knepper	Intel, USA
Andreas Knuepfer	Technische Universität Dresden, Germany
Martin Kronbichler	Technical University of Munich, Germany
Weifeng Liu	China University of Petroleum, China
Simone Pezzuto	Università della Svizzera italiana, Switzerland
Enrique S. Quintana-Orti	Universitat Politècnica de València, Spain
Estela Suarez	Jülich Supercomputing Centre, Germany
Nico Trost	AMD, Germany
Markus Wittmann	Friedrich-Alexander-Universität Erlangen-Nürnberg, Germany

HPC in Asia Committee

Kento Sato (Chair)	RIKEN, Japan
James Lin (Deputy Chair)	Shanghai Jiao Tong University, China

Inclusivity Committee

Laura Schulz (Chair)	Frau, Germany

Publicity Committee

Carsten Trinitis (Chair)	Technical University of Munich, Germany

Proceedings Chairs

Piotr Luszczek (Chair)	University of Tennessee, USA
Marc Baboulin (Deputy Chair)	Université Paris-Saclay, France

Contents

HPC Algorithms and Applications

Performance Modeling, Evaluation, and Analysis

Programming Environments and System Software

Architecture, Networks, and Storage

Accelerating MPI All-to-All Communication with Online Compression on Modern GPU Clusters

Qinghua Zhou(✉), Pouya Kousha, Quentin Anthony, Kawthar Shafie Khorassani, Aamir Shafi, Hari Subramoni, and Dhabaleswar K. Panda

The Ohio State University, Columbus, OH 43210, USA
{zhou.2595,kousha.2,anthony.301,shafiekhorassani.1,shafi.16, subramoni.1,panda.2}@osu.edu

Abstract. As more High-Performance Computing (HPC) and Deep Learning (DL) applications are adapting to scale using GPUs, the communication of GPU-resident data is becoming vital to end-to-end application performance. Among the available MPI operations in such applications, All-to-All is one of the most communication-intensive operations that becomes the bottleneck of efficiently scaling applications to larger GPU systems. Over the last decade, most research has focused on the optimization of large GPU-resident data transfers. However, for state-of-the-art GPU-Aware MPI libraries, MPI_Alltoall communication for large GPU-resident data still suffers from poor performance due to the throughput limitation of commodity networks. However, the development of GPU-based compression algorithms with high throughput can reduce the volume of data transferred. The recent research of point-to-point-based online compression with these compression algorithms has shown potential on modern GPU clusters.

In this paper, we redesign an MPI library to enable efficient collective-level online compression with an optimized host-staging scheme for All-to-All communication. We demonstrate that the proposed design achieves benefits at both microbenchmark and application levels. At the microbenchmark level, the proposed design can reduce the All-to-All communication latency by up to 87%. For PSDNS, a traditional HPC application, our proposed design can reduce the All-to-All communication latency and total runtime by up to 29.2% and 21.8%, respectively, while ensuring data validation and not affecting the application convergence time. For Microsoft's DeepSpeed, a DL optimization library, the proposed design reduces the MPI_Alltoall runtime by up to 26.4% compared to a state-of-the-art MPI library with point-to-point compression while ensuring data validation. To the best of our knowledge, this is the first work that leverages online GPU-based compression techniques to significantly accelerate MPI_Alltoall communication for HPC and DL applications.

*This research is supported in part by NSF grants #1818253, #1854828, #1931537, #2007991, #2018627, #2112606, and XRAC grant #NCR-130002.

A.-L. Varbanescu et al. (Eds.): ISC High Performance 2022, LNCS 13289, pp. 3–25, 2022.
https://doi.org/10.1007/978-3-031-07312-0_1

Keywords: All-to-All · GPU · Compression · GPU-Aware MPI · HPC · DL

1 Introduction

Emerging high-performance computing (HPC) and cloud computing systems are widely adopting Graphics Processing Units (GPUs) to support the computational power required by modern scientific and deep learning (DL) applications. By offering high-bandwidth memory, tensor processing, and massive parallelism, GPUs enable running complex applications such as weather forecasting, brain data visualization, and molecular dynamics. MPI is the de facto communication standard widely used in developing parallel scientific applications on HPC systems. To further enhance the high compute power of current generation of hardware, researchers are building large-scale GPU clusters to benefit from massive computation capabilities offered by these accelerators.

Due to the computing power offered by GPUs, a large range of applications have been adapted to scale on GPU-based systems by application developers. Communication performance plays a vital role in end-to-end application performance on such systems. In fact, at a large scale, the communication operations become the performance bottleneck for any massively parallel HPC and DL application. Over the last decade, researchers have significantly optimized data transfers in MPI for GPU-resident data [2,21,24]. Inter-node communication operations for large messages are highly optimized to saturate the bandwidth of the InfiniBand network by the state-of-the-art MPI libraries [9,24]. [32] has shown the saturated inter-node network bandwidth of the state-of-the-art MPI libraries. Although these MPI libraries are well optimized, the communication time at the application level is still a major bottleneck for many HPC and DL applications. Since the inter-node communication bandwidth is already saturated via optimizations implemented by major MPI libraries, we should seek other innovative ways to reduce the communication time of the HPC applications.

Thinking outside the box, we propose exploiting compression to aid with optimizing the performance of MPI stacks and HPC/DL applications, subsequently. Compression can reduce the amount of data that needs to be transmitted and/or stored helping to mitigate the cost of communication. Various compression techniques have been proposed in the literature diving into CPU-based algorithms and GPU-based algorithms. The common issue with CPU-based algorithms is the low throughput compared to GPU-based designs [14,31]. Existing GPU-based compression schemes such as MPC [31], SZ [3], and ZFP [14] are typically focused on achieving a high compression ratio and not absolute high performance.

1.1 Motivation

There are challenging aspects to consider when applying compression to the HPC domain. HPC requires low overhead while maintaining high throughput. Further, some HPC applications require that the underlying compression and decompression operations are handled by the MPI library, leaving the HPC/DL application unchanged. We refer to this qualifier as "Online" compression. Online compression means the message should be compressed and decompressed in real-time inside the MPI library during a communication operation without any modifications to the end applications. This implies that the online compression algorithms should be self-contained with low overheads. Meeting these requirements first before maximizing the compression ratio and revamping the communication pattern/algorithm to fully exploit the HPC system's available transfer bandwidth is a challenging task that we undertake in this paper.

Since most MPI users are domain scientists first and programmers second, modifying the application to use compression is often out of reach. Adding support often involves understanding compression techniques and when to apply them based on message features such as size. Therefore, using compression directly in HPC/DL applications is a daunting task for domain scientists. In this context, [32] proposed an online compression enabled MPI library for point-to-point operations—this is an initial work in this direction.

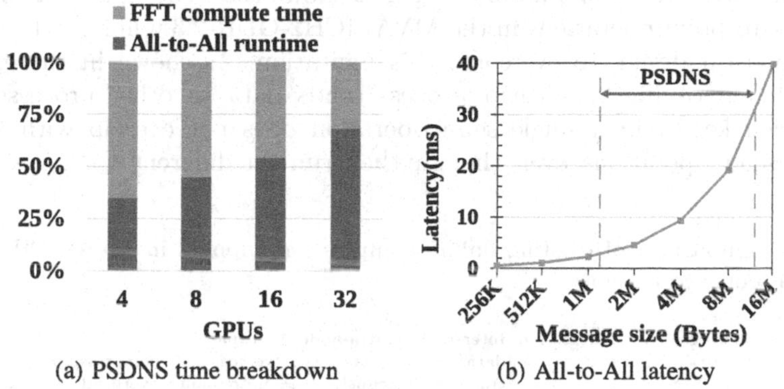

Fig. 1. Motivating Example: All-to-all communication time for 8 GPUs on 2 Longhorn nodes. The observed message range in PSDNS is 1.2 MB to 9.5 MB. With more GPUs, All-to-all communication time becomes dominant within the overall runtime of PSDNS application.

In this paper, we use the online compression idea to optimize the performance of MPI collective operations and improve HPC/DL application performance. One of the most communication-intensive operations is MPI_Alltoall which is used in many applications like PSDNS [23] and DeepSpeed [22]. DeepSpeed depends on MPI_Alltoall to support the addition of Mixture-of-Experts [10]. As shown in the Fig. 1(a), with larger scale, the MPI_Alltoall time dominates the overall execution time of the PSDNS application. Figure 1(b) shows the message size range of MPI_Alltoall operations observed in PSDNS application. In this context, the MPI_Alltoall operation is ideally suited to benefit from compression since it is the most dense communication operation used in various HPC and DL applications.

1.2 Challenges

To design an efficient online compression scheme for MPI_Alltoall operation, following research challenges need to be addressed.
Challenge-1: The Limitation of Point-to-Point Based Online Compression Technique: MVAPICH2-GDR-2.3.6 is the only public library that has support for online compression. Table 1 summarizes the representative MPI_Alltoall algorithms in the MVAPICH2-GDR-2.3.6 MPI library and existing support for online compression.

Both the Scatter Destination (SD) and Pairwise Exchange (PE) algorithms rely on the GPU-based point-to-point communication to transfer data between GPUs. With the current point-to-point based online compression, these algorithms can leverage compression for both inter-node and intra-node communication. However, there are limitations in the existing point-to-point based online compression design. For the PSDNS application, we use the NVIDIA profiler Nsight to monitor the compression behavior of the existing GPU-based Scatter Destination and Pairwise Exchange All-to-All algorithms in the state-of-the-art MVAPICH2-GDR-2.3.6 library. Figure 2 shows the existing design that utilizes point-to-point operations in the MVAPICH2-GDR-2.3.6 library. The figure also proposes a design to overcome this limitation. As shown in the existing design section of Fig. 2, when a process sends data to other processes, the compression kernel in a single send operation does not overlap with kernels in other send operations even though they run on different CUDA streams.

Table 1. Comparison of existing online compression support in MVAPICH2-GDR-2.3.6 with proposed design

Algorithms	Compression support	Compression level	Inter-node data transfer	Intra-node data transfer	Multiple streams compression	Hide compression overhead	Overlap opportunity
GPU-aware Scatter Destination [28]	Y	Point-to-Point	GPUDirect	IPC	Within single Send/Recv	N	N
GPU-aware Pairwise Exchange [29]	Y	Point-to-Point	GPUDirect	IPC	Within single Send/Recv	N	N
CPU Staged Scatter Destination [28]	N	N	RDMA	Shared Memory	N	N	N
CPU Staged Pairwise Exchange [29]	N	N	RDMA	Shared Memory	N	N	N
Proposed Design	Y	Collective level	Staging + RDMA		Across multiple Send/Recv	Y	Y

This limitation is similar for the decompression kernels in receive operations. This essentially becomes a bottleneck for implementing dense collective operations like MPI_Alltoall efficiently.

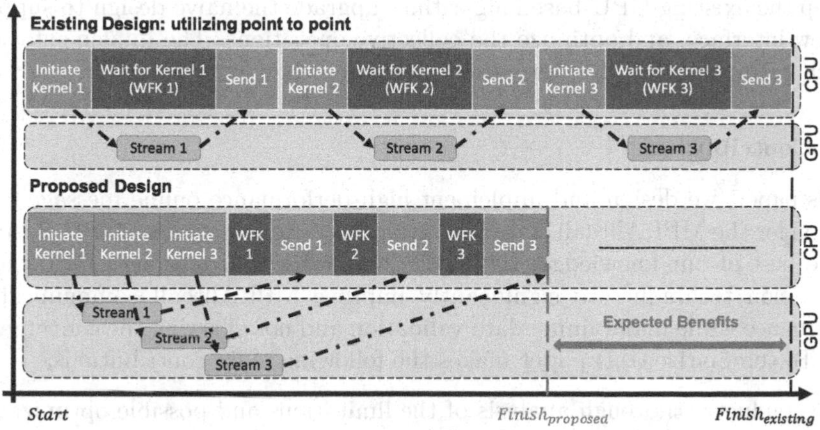

Fig. 2. Comparison between using existing compression method for point-to-point operations versus proposed design. The proposed design increases the overlap of kernel initialization and wait time by enabling compression at the collective level instead of the point-to-point level.

Challenge-2: Move the Point-to-Point Compression to the Collective-Level: The above limitation can be handled by utilizing compression at the collective level. In MPI libraries, collectives operations are typically built using point-to-point operations. In collective-level compression, the compression/decompression is done at the collective algorithm level before calling the underlying point to point send/receive operation to transfer data. This provides us the opportunity that CUDA kernels across multiple send/receive operations can be overlapped to reduce the compression overheads—this is depicted in Fig. 2 and forms the primary motivation of our proposed design in this paper. However, the underlying mechanism of Scatter Destination and Pairwise Exchange algorithms prevents us from moving the compression to the collective level efficiently. This pushes us to explore other MPI_Alltoall algorithms. The CPU Staging algorithm [28] moves the data from GPU to host and leverages the host-based Scatter Destination, Pairwise Exchange, or other MPI_Alltoall algorithms to transfer the data. Since the send and receive operations are host-based, we cannot merely use the existing GPU-based point-to-point compression. We need to co-design the GPU-based compression at the collective level (Sect. 3).

Challenge-3: Revamp and Optimize GPU-Based Compression for the Collective-Level Online Compression: While point-to-point compression focuses on reducing the inherent compression-related overheads, collective-level compression aims to further reduce the effective kernel computing time by co-designing the compression with the collective operations. This needs the enhancement of designing interfaces for the existing collective operations to support GPU-based compression. Furthermore, naive integration of the compression algorithms at the collective level may not achieve optimal performance (Sect. 3.1). We have to analyze the bottlenecks of such naive compression designs, revamp the existing GPU-based algorithm, upgrade the naive design to support the new interface, and optimize the collective operations. The implementations of each optimization will be proposed (Sect. 4).

1.3 Contributions

In this paper, we design and implement high-performance online message compression for the MPI_Alltoall communication operation on modern GPU clusters. To the best of our knowledge, this is the first work that leverages GPU-based compression techniques to significantly improve MPI_Alltoall communication performance while maintaining data validation and not affecting the convergence time. To summarize, this paper makes the following main contributions:

- We conduct a thorough analysis of the limitations and possible optimization opportunities for existing MPI_Alltoall algorithms with online compression support on modern GPU systems.
- We propose an online compression design that is integrated into the underlying communication libraries (e.g., MPI) for host-staging based MPI_Alltoall communication. Later, we analyze the limitations of naively integrating the existing ZFP compression library.
- We optimize the ZFP compression library to enable execution of compression/decompression kernels on multiple CUDA streams. These strategies reduce the overhead of compression/decompression kernels and improve overall performance.
- We use the OSU Micro Benchmark (OMB) suite to evaluate MPI_Alltoall communication and show that the proposed design can achieve up to 87% improvement in performance. We also enhance OMB to use real data sets and get up to 75% improvement in the MPI_Alltoall operation.
- We evaluate the effectiveness of the proposed design through application studies. In the PSDNS application, we can gain up to 29.2% and 21.8% reduced MPI_Alltoall runtime and total execution time, respectively, compared to the existing MVAPICH2-GDR-2.3.6 with point-to-point compression. In the Deep Learning framework DeepSpeed, the proposed design reduces the MPI_Alltoall runtime by up to 26.4% and improves throughput by up to 35.8%.

2 Background

In this section, we provide the necessary background knowledge including the recent development of GPU based compression algorithms, MPI_Alltoall algorithms in MPI libraries, GPUDirect technology, and GPU-aware communication middlewares.

2.1 Compression Algorithms for HPC Applications

In recent years, lossy compression libraries have shown acceptable error-bounds [6] for HPC applications. Among them, ZFP [14] is a well-known public compression library with user-friendly interfaces and supports CUDA-enabled fixed-rate compression. ZFP deconstructs a d-dimensional array into 4^d blocks. The resulting compression rate is the number of amortized compressed bits among these blocks. For example, for single-precision (32-bit) floating-point data, a compression rate of 8 bits/value can get a compression ratio of 4. In this work, we use the ZFP compression library.

NVIDIA recently proposed nvCOMP [19], a CUDA-based lossless compression interface to achieve high-performance compression kernels. nvCOMP supports Cascaded, LZ4, and Snappy compression methods. However, the burden of integrating nvCOMP APIs and using them for HPC applications requires changing application code. Since nvCOMP is a user-level library, we don't consider it for online compression.

2.2 Algorithms for MPI_Alltoall Communication

Different MPI libraries have their own implementations of MPI_Alltoall algorithms and often tune their library to pick up the most efficient MPI_Alltoall algorithm for a given system and message size at runtime. In existing MPI libraries, there are three representative MPI_Alltoall algorithms for large-message data transfers. (a) In the Scatter Destination algorithm [28], each process posts a series of MPI_Isend and MPI_Irecv operations and waits for these operations to complete. (b) In the Pairwise Exchange algorithm [29], each process runs MPI_Sendrecv to communicate with only one source and one destination. These send and receive operations will reply with GPU-based point-to-point communication schemes to transfer data between GPUs. (c) The CPU staging algorithm [28] leverages the host-based send and receive operations to transfer the data. The GPU data will be moved from GPU to host before the MPI_Isend operation, and will be copied back from host to GPU after MPI_Irecv.

2.3 GPU-Aware Communication Middleware

GPU-aware MPI libraries like SpectrumMPI [5], OpenMPI [20], and MVAPICH2 [17] can distinguish between host buffers and GPU buffers. These libraries have been optimized with GPU-based point-to-point communication schemes like CUDA Inter-Process Communication (IPC) [25] and NVIDIA GPUDirect technology [18] which supports direct reading and writing to host and device memory by the CPU and GPU. Such technologies provide optimal performance across varied communication paths.

3 Proposed Online Compression Design for MPI_Alltoall Communication

To tackle the limitation of using point-to-point based compression (Challenge-1) for MPI_Alltoall communication and move the point-to-point compression to collective level (Challenge-2), we redesign the host-staging based MPI_Alltoall algorithm in the MPI library to implement efficient MPI_Alltoall communication of GPU data with online compression. Figure 3 depicts the data flow of host-staging based MPI_Alltoall operations with compression. GPU data are exchanged among four GPUs. In GPU0, the device buffer sendbuf contains data A0, A1, A2, A3 which will be sent to the recvbuf in GPU0, GPU1, GPU2 and GPU3 respectively.

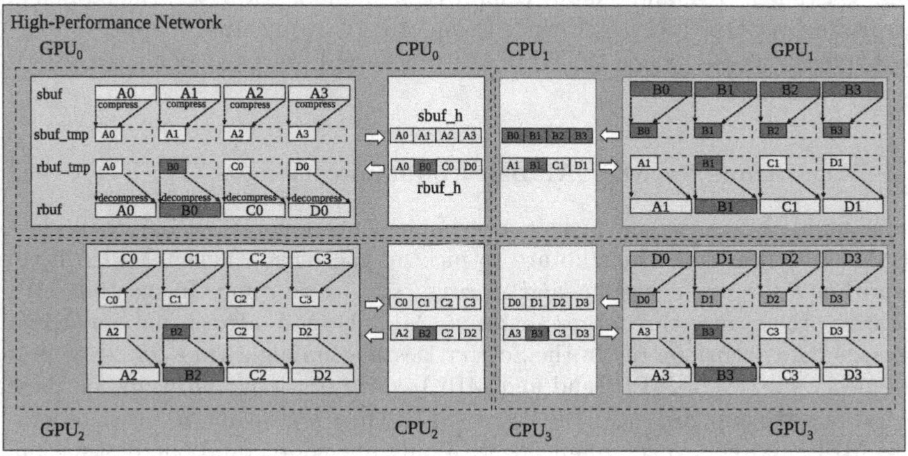

Fig. 3. Host-Staging based MPI_Alltoall with compression. GPU data will be compressed to the temporary device buffer sendbuf_tmp and copied by cudaMemcpyAsync to the host buffer sendbuf_host. MPI_Isend sends out the data in the host buffer to other CPUs. MPI_Irecv collects the data to the host buffer recvbuf_host from other CPUs. The received data will be copied by cudaMemcpyAsync to the temporary device buffer recvbuf_tmp and decompressed to the recvbuf.

Algorithm 1 provides a high-level overview of the compression design for host-staging based MPI_Alltoall. Before staging the GPU data to the CPU, a compression kernel will be launched on the send buffer for each process (Line 4). The compressed data will be stored into the corresponding part of a temporary device buffer sendbuf_tmp. Once the compression kernel finishes, the compressed data will be copied to the host buffer sendbuf_host using cudaMemcpyAsync on a specific CUDA stream *Stream*1 (Line 5). After each cudaMemcpyAsync, a CUDA event will be recorded on the same CUDA stream (Line 6).

With compression, the data size of the transferred data is changed. The MPI_Isend operation needs to specify the compressed data size instead of the original data size. We use a data size array B to record the data size of each compressed data after compression. For the peer processes on other GPUs, they also should specify the correct data size for the upcoming data in MPI_Irecv. To transfer such data size information before transferring the compressed data, we run an MPI_Alltoall to exchange the elements in the data size array between all the CPUs (Line 7). Since each element is only a 4 bytes integer, the overhead of such operation is negligible compared to the large data transfer.

The multiple MPI_Irecv operations for all the peer processes will be issued ahead of MPI_Isend (Line 9). Each MPI_Irecv is associated with a receive request. Before MPI_Isend, we use cudaEventSynchronize to indicate the completion of related cudaMemcpyAsync from device to host (Line 11). The MPI_Isend will be issued to send out data in the host buffer *S_H* to the buffer address in another CPU (Line 12).

Once a receive request is completed, the related compressed data is stored in the host buffer *R_H*. Similar to the send operation, the data will be copied to a temporary device buffer *R_tmp* using cudaMemcpyAsync on a specific CUDA stream (Line 14). The decompression kernel will be launched on the data of each process in *R_tmp* after the corresponding cudaMemcpyAsync is finished (Line 19). The compressed data will be restored to the receive buffer *R*.

Algorithm 1: Online Compression/Decompression Design for Host-Staging based MPI_Alltoall Communication

---

Input : Send buffer S, Control parameters A, Number of MPI processes N, Preallocated GPU buffer S_tmp, R_tmp, Preallocated Host buffer S_H, R_H, CUDA events for send E_S, CUDA events for receive E_R

Output: Receive buffer R, Compressed data size B for send buffer, Compressed data size C for receive buffer

1 **for** $i = 1$ *to* N **do**
2   Construct *zfp_stream* and *zfp_field*;
3   Attach A to *zfp_stream* and *zfp_field*;
4   (B_i, S_tmp_i)=zfp_compress(S_i, A_i); //Runs on default CUDA Stream0
5   cudaMemcpyAsync(S_tmp_i, S_H_i, B_i, cudaMemcpyDeviceToHost, Stream1);
6   cudaEventRecord(E_S_i, Stream1);
7 MPI_Alltoall(B, 1, MPI_INT, C, 1, MPI_INT, MPI_COMM_WORLD); // Exchange the compressed data size
8 **for** $i = 1$ *to* N **do**
9   MPI_Irecv(R_H_i, C_i, ...) //Receive compressed data;
10 **for** $i = 1$ *to* N **do**
11   cudaEventSynchronize(E_S_i);
12   MPI_Isend(S_H_i, B_i, ...); // Send compressed data;
13   **if** *MPI_Irecv finishes for* R_H_i **then**
14   cudaMemcpyAsync(R_tmp_i, R_H_i, C_i, cudaMemcpyHostToDevice, Stream2);
15   cudaEventRecord(E_R_i, Stream2);
16 **for** $i = 1$ *to* N **do**
17   cudaEventSynchronize(E_R_i);
18   Construct *zfp_stream* and *zfp_field* based on control parameter A;
19   R_i = zfp_decompress(R_tmp_i, C_i, A_i); //Runs on default CUDA Stream0

We define runtime parameters to enable/disable compression in the host-staging based MPI_Alltoall design. We also define several control parameters such as compression rate, dimensionality, and data type to run the ZFP compression library,

3.1 Analysis of the Benefits and Limitation for the Naive Compression Design

In this section, we analyze the compression-related benefits and costs to find out the bottleneck (Challenge-3) in the naive compression design. With compression, there will be less data movement by cudaMemcpyAsync between CPU and GPU in the staging operations. The run time of the staging operation will be reduced. MPI_Isend can send out the data in the host buffer much earlier. Similarly, the run time of transferring data between the CPUs will be reduced. On the receiver side, it will take less time to copy data from the host buffer to the device buffer. However, similar to the point-to-point based compression [32], there is also extra compression/decompression kernel execution time and related kernel launching overheads in the naive host-staging based compression. When the compression ratio is not high enough, the benefits brought by the reduced data size may not compensate for these extra running time costs. We need to optimize the compression design to reduce such costs.

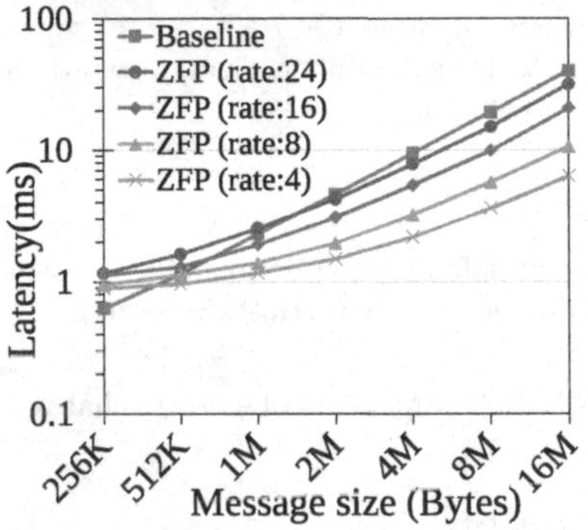

(a) Performance of MPI_Alltoall with naive compression design

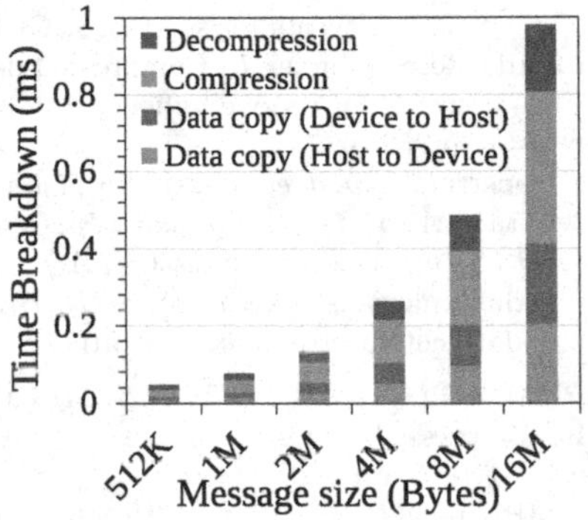

(b) Time breakdown of key operations with ZFP (rate:24)

Fig. 4. Performance of host-staging based MPI_Alltoall with naive compression design on 2 nodes (4 ppn) of the Longhorn cluster. Higher compression rate (16, 24) indicates a lower compression ratio. The design only starts to outperform the baseline from larger message size 1 MB for rate = 16 and 2 MB for rate = 24. The time breakdown shows the latency of single compression/decompression kernel, and data copy from host to device and device to host.

We evaluate the proposed compression design using the OSU Micro-Benchmark suite (OMB) on 2 nodes with 4ppn (4GPUs/node) of the TACC

Longhorn cluster. As shown in Fig. 4(a), the proposed host-staging based naive ZFP compression design can achieve benefits from 512 KB with low compression rates 8 and 4. However, with a higher compression rate (and consequently a lower compression ratio), it only starts to outperform the baseline for larger message size. Since ZFP is a lossy compression algorithm, this shortage will prevent the design from applying to those applications which need higher accuracy. Figure 4(b) depicts the time breakdown of some key operations in the naive compression design with ZFP (rate:24). The results show the latency of every single operation.

In the existing ZFP library, compression kernel cuZFP::encode runs on the default CUDA stream. In the naive compression design, although the cudaMemcpyAsync executing on a non-default stream with a non-blocking flag cudaStreamNonBlocking can achieve overlap with the compression kernels for other ranks, each cudaMemcpyAsync still needs to wait for the completion of compression kernel for its rank. As we can see in Fig. 5(a), since the compression kernels run serially in the default stream, there is a long waiting time for the MPI_Isend operation to send out the data since MPI_Isend must wait for the finish of compression kernel and memory copy from device to host.

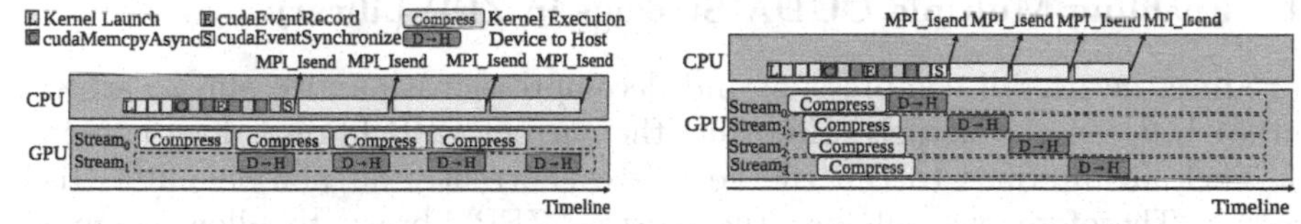

(a) Send operations with naive compression on default stream

(b) Send operations with optimized compression on multiple streams

Fig. 5. Comparison between compression on the default CUDA stream and multiple CUDA streams for send operations in the host-staging based All-to-All. Overall compression time is reduced due to the overlap between the compression kernels. The data will be sent out faster since the cudaMemcpyAsync and MPI_Isend can be executed much earlier.

There is also a similar limitation for the decompression phase. As shown in Fig. 6(a), the decompression kernel cuZFP::decode also runs on default CUDA stream. Although the cudaMemcpyAsync can be overlapped with the decompression kernel, it will cost a long operation time to restore data in the GPU due to the serial operations among the decompression kernels.

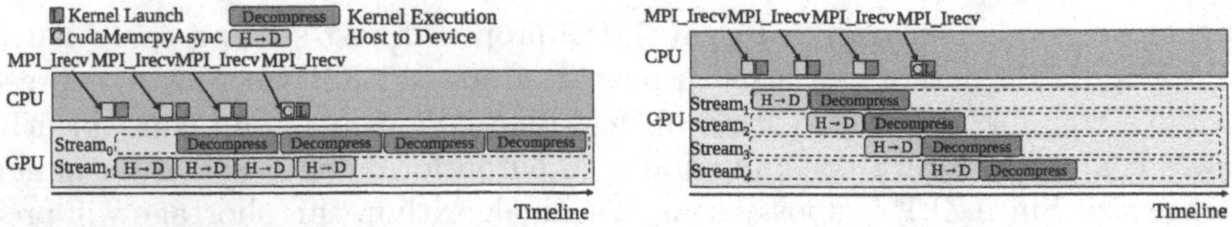

(a) Receive operations with naive decompression on default stream

(b) Receive operations with optimized decompression on multiple streams

Fig. 6. Comparison between ZFP decompression on the default CUDA stream and multiple CUDA streams. Explicit calling of cudaEventSynchronize is not needed. Overall decompression time is reduced due to the overlap between the decompression kernels.

4 Optimization Strategies in the Host-Staging Based MPI_Alltoall

Based on the previous analysis of the limitation of the naive compression design, we propose the following optimizations to address the Challenge-3.

4.1 Enabling Multiple CUDA Streams in ZFP Library

To reduce the overall compression and decompression time, we aim to achieve overlap between the kernels. However, the current ZFP library does not provide such an interface to run the kernels concurrently on non-default CUDA streams. Therefore, we enhance the existing ZFP library to allow compression and decompression kernels to run on multiple streams. We define two new functions, zfp_compress_multi_stream and zfp_decompress_multi_stream. A new parameter of CUDA stream object cudaStream_t is added to these functions. At the user level, we can assign a specific stream to the compression and decompression. ZFP uses a function table to select the correct low-level compression and decompression functions according to the execution policy (Serial, OpenMP, CUDA), stride, dimensionality, and scalar type. We extend the function table and introduce a new execution policy named zfp_exec_cuda_multi_stream to allow the selection of new lower-level APIs with a stream parameter. We add a new cudaStream_t parameter to all the related lower-level APIs.

In the proposed compression design, we use the 1D array type for ZFP compression with the number of floating-point values as the dimensionality. The compression kernel cudaEncode1 and decompression kernel cudaDecode1 will be launched to the CUDA stream specified by the new High-level APIs. In the existing compression kernel, launch function, and constant setup function, two synchronous CUDA memory copy functions (cudaMemset and cudaMemcpyToSymbol) are used to prepare for the compression and decompression on the default stream. We change them to cudaMemsetAsync and cudaMemcpyToSymbolAsync, respectively, with the same CUDA stream used for compression or decompression.

4.2 Proposed Optimization Metrics

With the enhanced ZFP library (ZFP-OPT), we use two new API calls in the compression design: zfp_compress_multi_stream and zfp_decompress_multi_stream.

Algorithm 2: Proposed optimized multi-stream compression/decompression for MPI_Alltoall Communication

---

Input : Send buffer S, Control parameters A, Number of MPI processes N, Preallocated GPU buffer S_tmp, R_tmp, Preallocated Host buffer S_H, R_H, CUDA events for send E_S, CUDA events for receive E_R
$[S_1, ..., S_N]$= Send buffers for peer processes in Send buffer S;
$[S\_tmp_1, ..., S\_tmp_N]$= Divided N partitions of S_tmp;
$[R\_H_1, ..., R\_H_N]$= Receive buffers for peer processes in R_H;
$[R\_tmp_1, ..., R\_tmp_N]$= Divided N partitions of R_tmp

Output: Receive buffer R, Compressed data size B for send buffer, Compressed data size C for receive buffer

1 Multi-stream compression for send operation:
2 **for** $i = 1$ *to* N **do**
3   Construct *zfp_stream* and *zfp_field* based on control parameter A;
4   zfp_stream_set_execution(*zfp_stream*, *zfp_exec_cuda_multi_stream*);
5   (B_i, S_tmp_i)=zfp_compress_multi_stream(S_i, A_i, $Stream_i$); //Runs on non-default CUDA Stream
6   cudaMemcpyAsync(S_H_i, M_i, B_i, cudaMemcpyDeviceToHost, $Stream_i$); //Run on the same CUDA stream
7   cudaEventRecord(E_i, $Stream_i$);
8 MPI_Isend, MPI_Irecv operations;
9 Multi-stream decompression for receive operation:
10 **for** $i = 1$ *to* N **do**
11   cudaMemcpyAsync(R_H_i, R_tmp_i, C_i, cudaMemcpyHostToDevice, $Stream_i$); // Runs on non-default CUDA stream
12   Construct *zfp_stream* and *zfp_field* based on control parameter A;
13   zfp_stream_set_execution(*zfp_stream*, *zfp_exec_cuda_multi_stream*);
14   R_i=zfp_decompress_multi_stream(R_tmp_i, A_i, $Stream_i$); //Runs on the same CUDA Stream

---

Algorithm 2 provides a high-level overview of the multi-stream compression and decompression for the for MPI_Alltoall operation. For the compression on send operation side, we set a new execution policy zfp_exec_cuda_multi_stream (Line 4). Then we launch the compression kernels to different CUDA streams (Line 5). Each corresponding cudaMemcpyAsync also runs on the same stream as the kernel (Line 6). The benefits of concurrent kernel execution are two-fold. Due to the overlap between the compression kernels, the overall compression time is reduced. Furthermore, since cudaMemcpyAsync can copy the compressed data to CPU earlier, MPI_Isend can send out the data from CPU in advance. Figure 5(b) depicts the optimized send operations with this mechanism. Note that, the overlapping situation among the kernels and data copy operations depends on the number of processes in the MPI_Alltoall operation and the compression rate.

Similarly, on the receive operation side, we optimize decompression using multiple CUDA streams. Once a receive request is finished, we run the cudaMemcpyAsync on a non-default stream to copy the compressed data from host to device (Line 11). To enable the multi-stream decompression, we also need to use the execution policy of zfp_exec_cuda_multi_stream (Line 13). The related decompression kernel will also run on the same stream (Line 14). In this way, we do not need to explicitly launch cudaEventSynchronize to wait for the completion of cudaMemcpyAsync. As shown in Fig. 6(b), the overlap between the decompression kernels will reduce the overall decompression time and thus, accelerate the data restoration phase in the GPU. In the proposed design, we define wrapper functions to execute the compression/decompression kernels. Such optimization metrics can be easily applied to compression/decompression kernels of other compression algorithms.

5 Microbenchmark Results and Analysis

We run the experiments on three GPU-enabled clusters: Longhorn [16] and the Liquid [15] subsystem at the Texas Advanced Computing Center, and the Lassen [13] system at Lawrence Livermore National Laboratory. Each computing node on the Longhorn and Lassen systems is equipped with IBM POWER9 CPUs and 4 NVIDIA V100 GPUs. They use RHEL operating system. Both systems enable NVLink2 interconnection between CPU and GPU, and Infiniband EDR between nodes. Each node on Frontera Liquid is installed with Intel Xeon E5-2620 CPUs and 4 NVIDIA Quadro RTX5000 GPUs. Frontera Liquid uses PCIe Gen3 interconnection between CPU and GPU, and Infiniband FDR between nodes. It installs CentOS operating system. More details about the system configurations can be found in their respective specification documents.

We used osu_alltoall in the OSU Micro-Benchmark suite (OMB) to evaluate the MPI_Alltoall communications of GPU data on multiple nodes. We also enhanced OMB to use real data sets for the MPI_Alltoall communication tests.

5.1 MPI_Alltoall Communication Latency on Micro-Benchmark

We run the OSU Micro-Benchmark suite (OMB) to evaluate the MPI_Alltoall communication latency. Figures 7(a) and 7(b) show the MPI_Alltoall communication latency of message size from 256 KB to 16 MB on the Frontera Liquid system. Since the proposed design is aimed at the transfer of large GPU messages, the performance results of smaller message sizes are not shown in the figures. We observe performance improvement with the optimized compression design in the 256 KB to 16 MB message range. With a lower compression rate, ZFP-OPT achieves a higher compression ratio and a further reduced communication latency. Compared to the baseline, ZFP-OPT (rate:4) can achieve up to 87.1% reduced latency at 16 MB on both 2nodes and 4nodes with 4ppn

(4 GPUs/node). Figures 7(c) and 7(d) show the MPI_Alltoall communication latency on the Longhorn system. On 2 nodes with 4ppn, ZFP-OPT starts to outperform the baseline from around 512 KB. Compared to Fig. 4(a), Fig. 7(c) demonstrates the performance improvement with the optimization strategies discussed in Sect. 4. On 4 nodes, except for rate = 24, ZFP-OPT has performance benefits starting from 256 KB. Similar to the Frontera liquid system, ZFP-OPT (rate:4) can achieve up to 87.1% reduced latency at 16 MB on 2 nodes and 4 nodes.

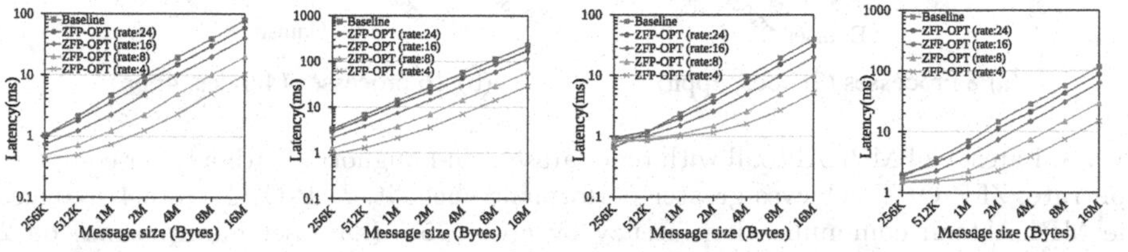

(a) Frontera: 8GPUs (2nodes, 4ppn) (b) Frontera: 16GPUs (4nodes, 4ppn) (c) Longhorn: 8GPUs (2nodes, 4ppn) (d) Longhorn: 16GPUs (4nodes, 4ppn)

Fig. 7. Latency of MPI_Alltoall on Frontera Liquid and Longhorn. On Frontera Liquid, ZFP-OPT starts to show benefits from 256 KB on both 2 nodes and 4 nodes. With a lower compression rate, ZFP-OPT achieves a higher compression ratio and reduces communication latency. On Longhorn, ZFP-OPT shows performance improvement from about 512 KB on 2 nodes. On 4 nodes, except for rate = 24, ZFP-OPT achieves benefits from 256 KB. On both systems, ZFP-OPT (rate:4) can achieve up to 87.1% reduced latency at 16 MB on 2 nodes and 4 nodes.

5.2 MPI_Alltoall Communication Latency with Real Data Sets

This section evaluates the impact of the proposed design on the MPI_Alltoall communication performance on the Longhorn system with real data sets from [31]. Figures 8(a) and 8(b) show the results of MPI_Alltoall communication latency on 2 nodes and 4 nodes respectively. In the fixed-rate compression mode, with the same compression rate, ZFP will have the same compression ratio it has in the micro-benchmark test. The proposed design achieves similar benefits as the Micro-benchmark test. With lower compression rate, it reduces communication latency further. ZFP-OPT (rate:4) reduces the MPI_Alltoall communication latency by up to 75% (num_plasma) on 2 nodes, 72% (obs_info) on 4 nodes respectively.

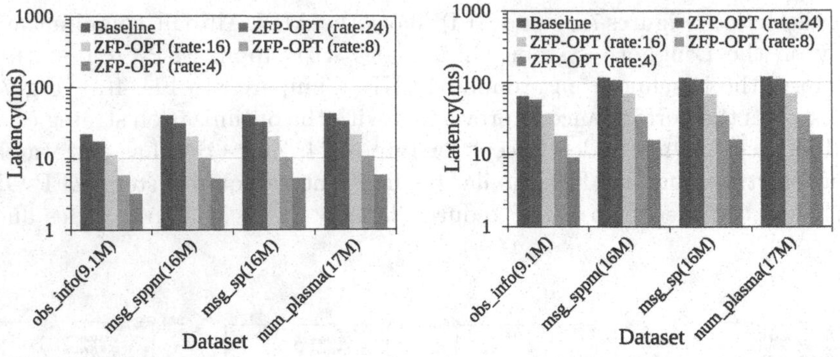

(a) 8 processes (2nodes, 4ppn) (b) 16 processes (4nodes, 4ppn)

Fig. 8. Latency of MPI_Alltoall with real datasets on Longhorn. With a lower compression rate, ZFP-OPT achieves greater performance benefit. ZFP-OPT (rate:4) reduces the MPI_Alltoall communication latency by up to 75% (data set num_plasma) on 2 nodes and 72% (data set obs_info) on 4 nodes, respectively.

5.3 Comparison of the Proposed Design and Existing MPI_Alltoall Algorithms with Point-to-Point Compression

In this section, we compare our proposed design with different algorithms: CPU Staging (No compression), Scatter Destination, and Pairwise Exchange in MVAPICH2-GDR-2.3.6. We use the runtime parameters provided by the MVAPICH2-GDR-2.3.6 to trigger the point-to-point compression for Scatter Destination and Pairwise Exchange.

On the Lassen system, for 8 GPUs on 2 nodes, our proposed design performs better than these algorithms starting from 1 MB as shown in Fig. 9(a) and 9(b). Figure 9(a) shows, for 16 MB data, the proposed design reduces the MPI_Alltoall latency by up to 11.2%, 17.8% and 26.6% compared to the Scatter Destination(zfp rate:24), Pairwise Exchange(zfp rate:24), and CPU Staging (No compression), respectively. In Fig. 9(b), with zfp compression (rate:4), the latency is reduced by up to 12.4%, 32.3%, and 85.4% compared to the Scatter Destination, Pairwise Exchange, and CPU Staging (No compression), respectively.

In application tests, we observe greater benefit compared to the Scatter Destination and Pairwise Exchange on larger scales.

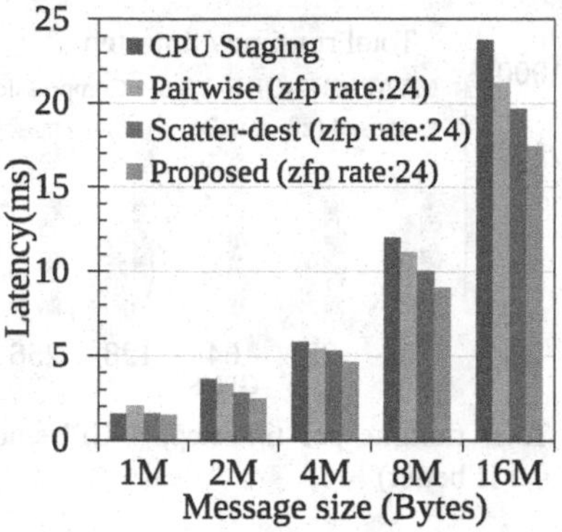

(a) Comparison with zfp (rate:24)

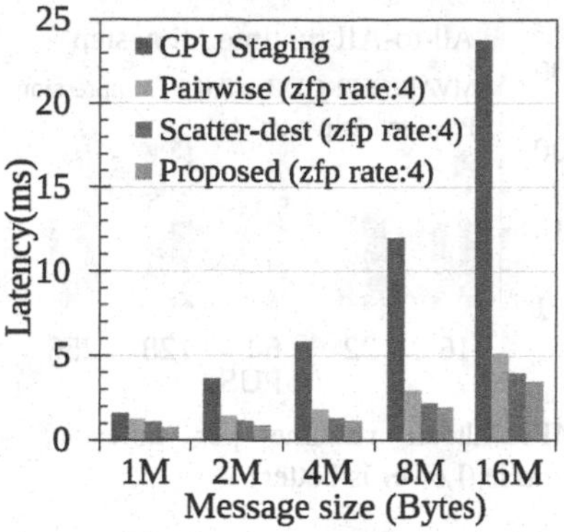

(b) Comparison with zfp (rate:4)

Fig. 9. MPI_Alltoall latency with different algorithms for 8 GPUs on 2 Lassen nodes. With zfp compression (rate:24), the proposed design reduces the MPI_Alltoall latency by up to 11.2%, 17.8%, and 26.6% compared to the Scatter Destination, Pairwise Exchange, and CPU Staging (No compression), respectively. With zfp compression (rate:4), the latency is reduced by up to 12.4%, 32.3%, and 85.4% compared to the Scatter Destination, Pairwise Exchange, and CPU Staging (No compression), respectively

6 Application Results and Analysis

6.1 PSDNS

We evaluate the proposed design with a modified 3D-FFT kernel of the Fourier pseudo spectral simulation of turbulence (PSDNS) application [23]. The code was written in Fortran with a hybrid MPI+OpenMP approach and compiled with the IBM XL compiler. We run PSDNS on the Lassen system which uses the IBM Power9 CPU architecture. In the 3D-FFT kernel, MPI_Alltoall is used to transfer the transposed data among the multiple GPUs. The kernel will also generate a timing report about the runtime per timestep of MPI_Alltoall operations, FFT computing, and other operations. It also checks the max global difference of the sinusoidal velocity field as an accuracy criteria. The underlying different algorithms of MPI_Alltoall can be triggered by runtime parameters. Note that the Scatter Destination and Pairwise Exchange algorithms are built on top of point-to-point operations. We compare our proposed design with the state-of-the-art MVAPICH2-2-GDR-2.3.6 with point-to-point compression.

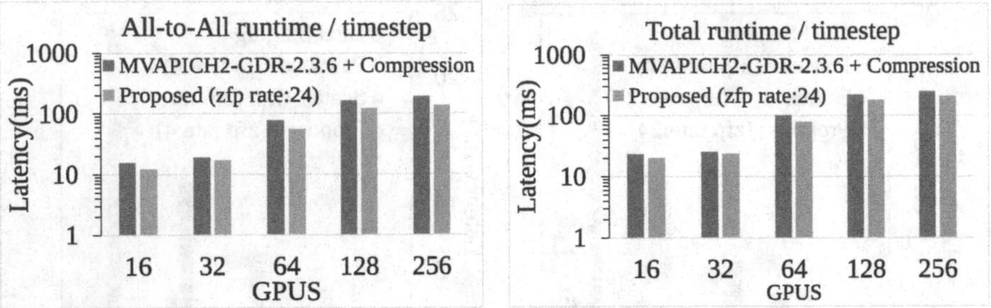

(a) MPI_Alltoall runtime per timestep, 4 GPUs/node (Lower is better)

(b) Total runtime per timestep, 4 GPUs/node (Lower is better)

Fig. 10. MPI_Alltoall runtime in the 3D-FFT kernel of the PSDNS application on the Lassen system. The proposed design with optimized ZFP(rate:24) can reduce the MPI_Alltoall runtime and total runtime by up to 29.2% and 21.8%, respectively, on 64 GPUs compared to the state-of-the-art MVAPICH2-GDR-2.3.6 with point-to-point compression.

As shown in Fig. 1(a), the MPI_Alltoall communication is dominant when the application runs on large scale. In this section, by increasing the grid size of nx, ny, nz along with the number of GPUs, we can evaluate our compression design on different problem scales. For 128 GPUs, the grid size (nx, ny, nz) is (1536, 1536, 1536).

Figure 10(a) depicts the MPI_Alltoall runtime per time step in the application. The proposed design with optimized ZFP (rate:24) is able to reduce the latency up to 29.2% on 64 GPUs(4 GPUs/node) compared to the state-of-the-art MVAPICH2-GDR-2.3.6 with point-to-point based compression. For MVAPICH2-GDR-2.3.6, we report the best result of either Scatter Destination or Pairwise algorithms with point-to-point based compression. Note that we set the same rate:24 for MVAPICH2-GDR-2.3.6. Since ZFP compression is lossy, we have ensured by working with application developers that the data generated with compression rate (>= 24) maintains acceptable precision for the FFT computation. Table 2 shows the max global difference of the proposed design reported in the 3D-FFT kernel. The tolerance of this value is 1.0E–05.

Table 2. Max global difference error

GPUs	No compression	Compression (rate:24)
16	3.492E–06	5.257E–06
32	3.721E–06	5.050E–06
64	3.275E–06	5.133E–06
128	2.943E–06	4.886E–06
256	3.218E–06	5.173E–06

Figure 10(b) depicts the total runtime per time step in the application. Despite the use of ZFP (rate:24) with low compression ratio for PSDNS, we are still able to show overall improvements in the application execution time. The proposed design with optimized ZFP (rate:24) reduces the total runtime by up to 21.8% on 64 GPUs compared to the MVAPICH2-GDR-2.3.6 with compression. These results demonstrate the scalability of the proposed design. The proposed design could be applied to larger scales due to the straightforward send/receive operations.

6.2 Deep Learning Application

Given DeepSpeed's addition of Mixture-of-Experts support [10] which depends on All-to-All operations, we have evaluated our compression designs at the PyTorch level. To measure potential deep learning training benefits, we have implemented a communication benchmark in PyTorch and DeepSpeed [22]. Specifically, our benchmark initializes MPI through DeepSpeed, initializes PyTorch tensors of varying sizes, and calls MPI_Alltoall on each tensor. We conduct the experiments on the Lassen system. For different numbers of GPUs, we use the following tensor sizes as shown in Table 3.

Table 3. Tensor size and message size

GPUs	Tensor size (Bytes)	Message size (Bytes)
8	$2097152 \times 8 \times 4$	8M
16	$1048576 \times 16 \times 4$	4M
32	$1048576 \times 32 \times 4$	4M
64	$524288 \times 64 \times 4$	2M
128	$524288 \times 128 \times 4$	2M

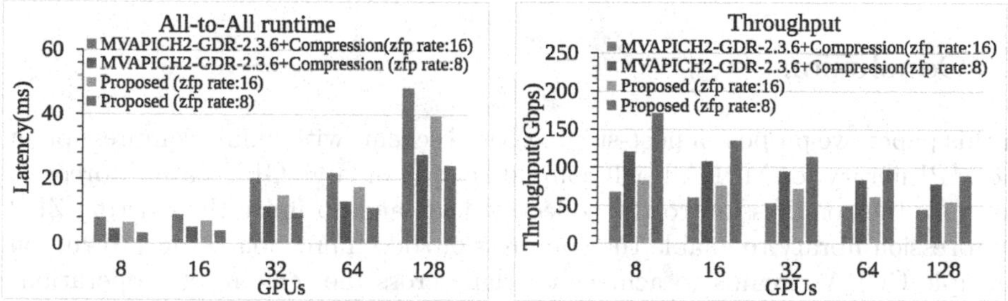

(a) MPI_Alltoall runtime (Lower is better)

(b) Throughput (Higher is better)

Fig. 11. MPI_Alltoall runtime and throughput in DeepSpeed benchmark on Lassen. The proposed design with optimized ZFP (rate:16) reduces the MPI_Alltoall latency by up to 26.4% and improves the throughput by up to 35.8% on 32 GPUs compared to the MVAPICH2-GDR-2.3.6 with point-to-point based compression.

Figure 11(a) shows MPI_Alltoall runtime in DeepSpeed on Lassen system with 4 GPUs per node. Figure 11(b) shows the throughput result. Similar to the PSDNS application, we compare our proposed design with the state-of-the-art MVAPICH2-GDR-2.3.6. The proposed design with optimized ZFP (rate:16) reduces the MPI_Alltoall latency by up to 26.4% and improves the throughput by up to 35.8% on 32 GPUs compared to MVAPICH2-GDR-2.3.6 with point-to-point based compression support. These results demonstrate the potential benefits for deep learning training.

7 Related Work

MPI_Alltoall communication operations [7] are data-intense operations in modern HPC and Deep Learning applications. In [1], Bruck et al. evaluate MPI_Alltoall collective algorithms, and propose efficient MPI_Alltoall operation implementations for multi port message-passing systems. In [26,27], Singh et al. utilize CUDA-aware MPI to implement the GPU-based MPI_Alltoall collective operations. More recently, with the advent of NVLINK interconnects on modern GPU clusters, additional design challenges are incorporated in the adaptive MPI_Alltoall design [8]. However, no work has been done to optimize GPU-based MPI_Alltoall operations using a GPU-based compression in MPI run-time. In previous work, Filgueira et al. [4] use CPU-based lossless compression algorithms for MPI communication, CoMPI, to show host-based benefits of compression. Jin et al. [6] show high compression throughput for large-scale HPC applications through using GPU-based lossy compression algorithms. Zhou et al. [32] proposed a framework to integrate the GPU-based compression algorithms MPC [31] and ZFP [14] into MPI library to realize online compression for point-to-point based GPU communication. Recently, Tian et al. proposed cuSZ [30] with dual-quantization schemes for NVIDIA GPU architectures. A recent lossless GPU-based compression library built by NVIDIA, nvCOMP [19], provides a compression interface for applications.

8 Conclusion

In this paper, we propose a host-staging based scheme with online compression in the MPI library for MPI_Alltoall communication of large GPU data. Moreover, we move the compression to the collective level and optimize the existing ZFP compression library to enable the compression/decompression kernels to run on multiple CUDA streams to achieve overlap across the send/receive operations and improve the performance of MPI_Alltoall while maintaining data validation and not affecting the convergence time. The proposed design demonstrates up to 87.1% reduced MPI_Alltoall communication latency at the benchmark-level. At the application level, we compare the proposed design to the state-of-the-art MPI library MVAPICH2-GDR-2.3.6 with point-to-point compression. In the PSDNS application, the proposed design yields up to 21.8% reduced overall running time. In the DeepSpeed benchmark, the proposed design reduces the MPI_Alltoall runtime by up to 26.4%.

As future work, we plan to study and incorporate more GPU-based compression algorithms, like cuSZ [30] and NVIDIA's nvCOMP [19]. To analyze the communication time in the compression design, we plan to utilize real-time monitor tools like OSU INAM [11,12]. Also, we plan to exploit the online compression design for various collective communications like All-Reduce and study the impact on more HPC and Deep Learning applications.

Acknowledgment. The authors would like to thank Kiran Ravikumar and Prof. P.K. Yeung from Georgia Institute of Technology for guiding conducting experiments with the 3D-FFT kernel of application PSDNS.

References

1. Bruck, J., Ho, C.T., Kipnis, S., Upfal, E., Weathersby, D.: Efficient algorithms for All-to-All communications in multiport message-passing systems. IEEE Trans. Parallel Distrib. Syst. **8**(11), 1143–1156 (1997)
2. Chu, C.H., Kousha, P., Awan, A.A., Khorassani, K.S., Subramoni, H., Panda, D.K.: NV-group: link-efficient reduction for distributed deep learning on modern dense GPU systems. In: Proceedings of the 34th ACM International Conference on Supercomputing (2020)
3. Di, S., Cappello, F.: Fast error-bounded lossy HPC data compression with SZ. In: International Parallel and Distributed Processing Symposium (IPDPS) (2016)
4. Filgueira, R., Singh, D., Calderón, A., Carretero, J.: CoMPI: enhancing MPI based applications performance and scalability using run-time compression. In: European Parallel Virtual Machine/Message Passing Interface Users' Group Meeting, pp. 207–218 (2009)
5. IBM: IBM Spectrum MPI: accelerating high-performance application parallelization (2018). https://www.ibm.com/us-en/marketplace/spectrum-mpi. Accessed 13 May 2022
6. Jin, S., et al.: Understanding GPU-Based Lossy Compression for Extreme-Scale Cosmological Simulations. ArXiv:abs/2004.00224 (2020)
7. Kale, L., Kumar, S., Varadarajan, K.: A framework for collective personalized communication. In: Proceedings International Parallel and Distributed Processing Symposium, p. 9 (2003). https://doi.org/10.1109/IPDPS.2003.1213166
8. Khorassani, K.S., Chu, C.H., Anthony, Q.G., Subramoni, H., Panda, D.K.: Adaptive and hierarchical large message All-to-All communication algorithms for large-scale dense GPU systems. In: 2021 IEEE/ACM 21st International Symposium on Cluster, Cloud and Internet Computing (CCGrid), pp. 113–122 (2021). https://doi.org/10.1109/CCGrid51090.2021.00021
9. Khorassani, K.S., Chu, C.H., Subramoni, H., Panda, D.K.: Performance evaluation of MPI libraries on GPU-enabled OpenPOWER architectures: early experiences. In: International Workshop on OpenPOWER for HPC (IWOPH 19) at the 2019 ISC High Performance Conference (2018)
10. Kim, Y.J., et al.: Scalable and efficient MOE training for multitask multilingual models (2021)

11. Kousha, P., et al.: Designing a profiling and visualization tool for scalable and in-depth analysis of high-performance GPU clusters. In: 2019 IEEE 26th International Conference on High Performance Computing, Data, and Analytics (HiPC), pp. 93–102 (2019). https://doi.org/10.1109/HiPC.2019.00022
12. Kousha, P., et al.: INAM: Cross-Stack Profiling and Analysis of Communication in MPI-Based Applications. Association for Computing Machinery, New York, NY, USA (2021). https://doi.org/10.1145/3437359.3465582
13. Lawrence Livermore National Laboratory: lassen—high performance computing (2018). https://hpc.llnl.gov/hardware/platforms/lassen. Accessed 13 March 2022
14. Lindstrom, P.: Fixed-rate compressed floating-point arrays. IEEE Trans. Visualiz. Comput. Graph. **20** (2014). https://doi.org/10.1109/TVCG.2014.2346458
15. Liquid Submerged System - Texas Advanced Computing Center, Frontera - Specifications. https://www.tacc.utexas.edu/systems/frontera
16. Longhorn - Texas Advanced Computing Center Frontera - User Guide. https://portal.tacc.utexas.edu/user-guides/longhorn
17. Network-Based Computing Laboratory: MVAPICH: MPI over InfiniBand, Omni-Path, Ethernet/iWARP, and RoCE (2001). http://mvapich.cse.ohio-state.edu/. Accessed 13 March 2022
18. NVIDIA: NVIDIA GPUDirect (2011). https://developer.nvidia.com/gpudirect. Accessed 13 March 2022
19. NVIDIA: nvCOMP (2020). https://github.com/NVIDIA/nvcomp. Accessed 13 March 2022
20. Open MPI: Open MPI: Open Source High Performance Computing (2004). https://www.open-mpi.org/. Accessed 13 March 2022
21. Potluri, S., Hamidouche, K., Venkatesh, A., Bureddy, D., Panda, D.K.: Efficient inter-node MPI communication using GPUDirect RDMA for infiniBand clusters with NVIDIA GPUs. In: 42nd International Conference on Parallel Processing (ICPP), pp. 80–89. IEEE (2013)
22. Rasley, J., Rajbhandari, S., Ruwase, O., He, Y.: Deepspeed: system optimizations enable training deep learning models with over 100 billion parameters. In: Proceedings of the 26th ACM SIGKDD International Conference on Knowledge Discovery and Data Mining, pp. 3505–3506. KDD 2020, Association for Computing Machinery, New York, NY, USA (2020). https://doi.org/10.1145/3394486.3406703
23. Ravikumar, K., Appelhans, D., Yeung, P.K.: GPU acceleration of extreme scale pseudo-spectral simulations of turbulence using asynchronism. In: Proceedings of the International Conference for High Performance Computing, Networking, Storage and Analysis. SC 2019, Association for Computing Machinery, New York, NY, USA (2019). https://doi.org/10.1145/3295500.3356209
24. Sharkawi, S.S., Chochia, G.A.: Communication protocol optimization for enhanced GPU performance. IBM J. Res. Develop. **64**(3/4), 9:1–9:9 (2020)
25. Shi, R., et al.: Designing efficient small message transfer mechanism for inter-node MPI communication on InfiniBand GPU clusters. In: 2014 21st International Conference on High Performance Computing (HiPC), pp. 1–10 (2014)
26. Singh, A.K., Potluri, S., Wang, H., Kandalla, K., Sur, S., Panda, D.K.: MPI All-toAll personalized exchange on GPGPU clusters: design alternatives and benefit. In: 2011 IEEE International Conference on Cluster Computing, pp. 420–427 (2011)
27. Singh, A.K.: Optimizing All-to-All and Allgather Communications on GPGPU Clusters. Master's thesis, The Ohio State University (2012)

28. Singh, A.K., Potluri, S., Wang, H., Kandalla, K., Sur, S., Panda, D.K.: MPI AlltoAll personalized exchange on GPGPU clusters: design alternatives and benefit. In: 2011 IEEE International Conference on Cluster Computing, pp. 420–427 (2011). https://doi.org/10.1109/CLUSTER.2011.67
29. Thakur, R., Rabenseifner, R., Gropp, W.: Optimization of collective communication operations in MPICH. Int. J. High Perform. Comput. Appl. **19**(1), 49–66 (2005). https://doi.org/10.1177/1094342005051521
30. Tian, J., et al.: CUSZ: an efficient GPU-based error-bounded lossy compression framework for scientific data. In: Proceedings of the ACM International Conference on Parallel Architectures and Compilation Techniques, pp. 3–15. PACT 2020, Association for Computing Machinery, New York, NY, USA (2020). https://doi.org/10.1145/3410463.3414624
31. Yang, A., Mukka, H., Hesaaraki, F., Burtscher, M.: MPC: a massively parallel compression algorithm for scientific data. In: IEEE Cluster Conference (2015)
32. Zhou, Q., et al.: Designing high-performance MPI libraries with on-the-fly compression for modern GPU clusters*. In: 2021 IEEE International Parallel and Distributed Processing Symposium (IPDPS), pp. 444–453 (2021). https://doi.org/10.1109/IPDPS49936.2021.00053

NVIDIA's Quantum InfiniBand Network Congestion Control Technology and Its Impact on Application Performance

Yuval Shpigelman(✉), Gilad Shainer, Richard Graham, Yong Qin, Gerardo Cisneros-Stoianowski, and Craig Stunkel

NVIDIA Corporation, Santa Clara, USA
{yuvals,shainer,richgraham,yongq,gcisneross,cstunkel}@nvidia.com

Abstract. Applications running on large scale systems often suffer from degraded performance and lack of reproducible run-times due to network-level congestion, whether caused by the application network traffic itself, or by unrelated background network traffic (i.e. other applications). This paper describes the hardware-based congestion control algorithm implemented in NVIDIA's Quantum HDR 200 Gb/s InfiniBand generation and the AI-based training used to obtain algorithm parameters. The hardware leverages NVIDIA's Data Center Quantized Congestion Notification (DCQCN) algorithm and protocol and applies it to the InfiniBand network layer. Congestion patterns described in the literature are studied and enhanced to create greater congestion and are used to study the impact of such patterns on three applications: Incompact3D, LAMMPS and VASP. The study shows that network congestion increases individual measured application run time by up to a factor of ten or greater, while introduction of the implemented congestion control on the Quantum HDR InfiniBand technology recovers most of the lost time for the tested applications and congestion.

Keywords: Infiniband congestion control · NVIDIA Quantum InfiniBand technology · Application performance

1 Introduction

Computer systems that execute High Performance Computing (HPC) and Artificial Intelligence (AI) applications typically run parallel workflows. As a result, data is exchanged over the network between workflow components. The data paths between such components tend to be shared between the elements of a workflow or between workflows, causing competition for those resources. Such competition often leads to a reduction in overall system efficiency and to unpredictable application performance. From a systems perspective, such platforms are costly and the reduction in system performance due to interference between different data flows reflects loss of available system resources. From an application performance perspective, lack of reproducible run-times makes it quite

A.-L. Varbanescu et al. (Eds.): ISC High Performance 2022, LNCS 13289, pp. 26–43, 2022.
https://doi.org/10.1007/978-3-031-07312-0_2

a challenge for code optimization as well as making it difficult to estimate the resources needed for a given task. Such losses are magnified when running parallel workflows, as the slowest component tends to determine the overall run-time due to tail-latency effects.

There are three different network-level mechanisms in common use that are used to reduce the network interference: (1) resource isolation, (2) data-path spreading and (3) data flow metering. Each of these addresses a different aspect of the challenge of using shared data paths efficiently.

Resource isolation, also known as Quality of Service (QoS), is used to separate resources associated with different classes of traffic and for managing data flow priority. Separate resources are used in the switches to keep different flows from interfering with each other due to resource sharing. While a very effective mechanism for avoiding overall system performance degradation, this suffers from the fact that the number of such resources that can be effectively supported is small. The InfiniBand specification defines 16 such levels, for example.

Data path spreading, also known as adaptive routing, is a mechanism used to leverage the plurality of data paths that may exist between two different endpoints. This is a very effective mechanism [1] for spreading and separating traffic by strategically utilizing all available parallel routes.

Data flow metering, a part of congestion control algorithms, is used to control the end-node data injection rate into the network to allow for efficient datapath sharing where such sharing cannot be avoided, such as in $N \rightarrow 1$ incast scenarios. Such mechanisms are applied to individual data flows and are designed to keep links on the network from saturating and applying indiscriminate data backpressure to avoid dropping traffic that can't be handled. Such back-pressure is draconian, and often results in congestion spreading to other parts of the network, because of head-of-line blocking [2,3] and the *parking lot* effect. Such congestion spreading can also result in impacting *victim flows* that are unrelated to the original source of the problem. This paper describes the mechanisms used in NVIDIA's Quantum InfiniBand network platforms to handle network congestion problems.

This paper briefly describes the hardware implementation of the NVIDIA DCQCN algorithm used by the Quantum InfiniBand hardware to implement congestion control. The DCQCN parameters are obtained using an AI training. The congestion patterns used by the GPCNet [4] benchmark are studied to setup traffic producing larger congestion effects. These network congestion patterns are used to study the impact of congestion on the run-time of randomly distributed parallel applications. Incompact3D, LAMMPS and VASP are the applications used, with the performance of each simulation measured when running in isolation using about 20% of the system nodes, when running with about 80% of the nodes generating background network congestion and finally with adding in congestion control to remedy the congestion effects.

This paper's contributions include a description of the implementation of the DCQCN algorithm in NVIDIA's Quantum HDR InfiniBand hardware technology. To our knowledge, This is the first attempt to apply DCQCN to a network with much lower latencies than Ethernet in conjunction with adaptive routing. This was applied to HPC workloads that don't typically exhibit long-lasting "flows", which necessitates algorithm parameters that respond more quickly to traffic changes. The paper also describes an AI-based methodology used to determine DQCQN algorithm parameters. Finally, the paper studies the impact of these capabilities on the performance under load of some widely used applications.

2 Previous Work

The importance of reducing congestion has been recognized since electronic networks were first developed. Solutions have included robust topologies [5] and accompanying routing techniques to avoid contention, dropping packets when excessive congestion occurs, utilizing multiple routes or adaptive routing [6] to spread traffic more evenly across network switches, use of virtual networks [7,13] to provide separate buffering resources for different classes of traffic or service/priority levels, and congestion control methods. Congestion control methods measure status of the network devices and properties of the network traffic to detect congestion, and then modify injection at traffic sources in order to reduce or avoid such congestion.

TCP was developed to handle both congestion and lossy or unreliable networks, and can handle networks that drop packets in response to congestion. This requires congestion control techniques that handle such packet drops or failures well. However, modern data centers and applications perform much more efficiently when the network latencies are more predictable and do not have long tail latencies. Therefore most data centers today use link-level flow control such as Ethernet's PFC [8] to avoid dropping packets. This has led to TCP congestion control algorithms that optimize traffic with this assumption, such as Data Center TCP (DCTCP) [9], which utilizes Explicit Congestion Notification (ECN) packets [10] that are now commonly supported in switches. More recently, the DCQCN protocol [11] builds upon DCTCP and ECN and leverages the Quantized Congestion Notification (QCN) algorithm [12] to guide flow decisions at the reaction point (the source).

The InfiniBand standard [13] was developed to provide high levels of performance while offloading much of the network stack to hardware, and also uses link-level flow control. When first architected, InfiniBand defined its own congestion control mechanisms [14,15]. In addition, other congestion control algorithms relying on PFC are interesting to consider for InfiniBand, although InfiniBand's much lower latencies necessitate the use of different parameters, and the algorithm must be offloadable. In this paper we apply NVIDIA's DCQCN [11] protocol to InfiniBand hardware, and we do not compare performance to other congestion control algorithms. However, congestion control remains a very active area of research, and we briefly overview other efforts here.

The most common congestion detection methods measure queue length or queue delay at a network device, and mark packets going through these queues. Network delay has also been used as a criteria for congestion detection, and a target for acceptable network delay can be utilized to regulate traffic flow

[16,17]. Combinations of queue length/delay and network delay have also been used to guide decisions [18]. Other congestion detection and response techniques are explored in recent work [19,20]. Congestion control continues to be a rich and important area of research, and these examples are not intended to fully represent recent advances in the field. Yang and Reddy provide an excellent early survey of congestion control strategies [21].

3 Congestion Control Implementation

Network congestion occurs when a network device (e.g., a switch or an adapter) receives traffic faster than it can forward it or consume it. This causes buffer occupancy to increase, and when a buffer is full, no more data can be received. Congestion control algorithms are designed to mitigate these effects. In lossless networks such as InfiniBand, this can quickly result in head-of-the-line blocking [2,3], as packets that could otherwise make progress are stuck behind packets that cannot do so.

Flow control can impact multiple flows running though a congested port, including flows that aren't being routed through the downstream source of the congestion, and therefore need not have their rate impacted to the same degree. These flows are known as victim flows. Figure 1a shows an example of such a situation, where the A flows cause congestion toward O_A. Flow control will cause the bandwidth allocation over the link between $S1$ and $S2$ to reduce flow V to 20% of the maximum line rate. Optimally, congestion control should provide flow V with an 80% bandwidth allocation.

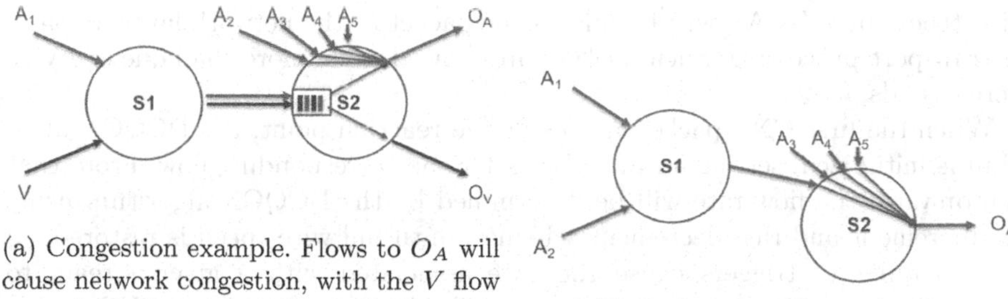

(a) Congestion example. Flows to O_A will cause network congestion, with the V flow towards O_V becoming the victim flow.

(b) Parking-lot effect example.

Fig. 1. Congestion illustration.

Another phenomenon caused by congestion is the "parking lot effect," wherein local flows gain more bandwidth than remote flows, because the remote flows share upstream network links. Figure 1b shows such an example, where arbitration in $S2$ will give 25% of the line rate to every ingress port. Therefore, A_1 and A_2 will get 12.5%, while the other 3 flows will get 25%. Congestion control can be used to give all five flows a similar bandwidth allocation, by providing the $S2$ ingress port coming from $S1$ 40% of the link bandwidth, and 20%

bandwidth to the other flows. These examples illustrate why congestion-control is critical for obtaining good efficiency and performance on large-scale networks.

To maintain the high-performance characteristics of networks under load, it is critical that congestion control algorithms react quickly to changing network conditions, to prevent quickly spreading the impact of full buffers. Therefore, InfiniBand HCAs offload the congestion control into the ASIC, rather than implementing it on the host as in TCP. This offloaded implementation provides reaction times on the order of magnitude of the network round trip, while in TCP algorithms the reaction time also includes the software stack latency, which tends to be much higher.

The end-to-end congestion control implementation includes several components: 1) a network injection rate-limiting component, or reaction point, 2) a congestion point (CP) and 3) a notification point. The rate-limiting algorithm is implemented in NVIDIA's ConnectX-6 InfiniBand HCA hardware, and uses NVIDIA's DCQCN [11] algorithm. Its congestion notification scheme is the Explicit Congestion Notification protocol (ECN) [10], informing the DCQCN algorithm via Congestion Notification Packets (CNPs). ECN is a standard capability supported by NVIDIA's Quantum InfiniBand HDR switches. The DCQCN algorithm builds upon QCN [12] and DCTCP [9], where the rate increase scheme is taken from the QCN algorithm and the rate decrease scheme is taken from the DCTCP algorithm.

When congestion starts to build at a switch in the network, it will mark the forwarded packets with a probability determined by the ECN protocol.

When an ECN-marked packet arrives at the notification point (the destination HCA), this HCA will send a CNP packet on a fast path (bypassing normal packet scheduling) and on a dedicated virtual network back to the reaction point (the source HCA), which handles the packet at the network layer, bypassing transport processing. Such packets are limited to no more than one every N microseconds.

When the first CNP packet arrives at the reaction point, the DCQCN algorithm is initialized, setting an *initial rate* for the corresponding flow. From that time onward, the flow rate will be determined by the DCQCN algorithm using rate-increment and rate-decrement schemes, until full wire speed is restored.

Two types of triggers cause the rate associated with a given stream to increase: 1) Time: After every time interval T that passes without a CNP packet arriving, and 2) Data: After every B bytes of data sent without a CNP packet arriving. Three types of rate increments are used: 1) fast recovery, 2) additive increase, with strength controlled by the DCQCN parameter AI, and 3) hyper increase, with strength controlled by the DCQCN parameter HAI.

The algorithm chooses the increment type based on the amount of successive intervals each increment trigger is triggered. Fast recovery is used for each time or data interval that passes without a CNP arrival, up to F successive intervals. At or above F intervals for either time or data, additive recovery is used. Finally, if both time and data intervals trigger more than F intervals in a row, the hyper rate increase algorithm is used.

A factor of α rate reduction is triggered by arriving CNP packets. The variable α's update is triggered by its own *alpha timer* and by CNP packets, as described in the DCQCN paper [11]. The rate computed by the DCQCN algorithm is adjusted using a mapping function from the computed rate to the applied rate. At low data rates α changes at a lower rate than the algorithm suggests, and at high data rates α changes more aggressively to recover full line rate sooner. The InfiniBand QP rate-limiting capabilities are used to control the data transmission rate.

DCQCN Parameter Optimization: InfiniBand networks pose additional challenges in comparison to Ethernet networks when determining the DCQCN algorithm parameters. InfiniBand adaptive routing capability can spray packets from the same source across multiple paths in the network, and therefore increases path diversity and creates a need for faster reaction times. These challenges force the reevaluation of DCQCN parameters, given that DCQCN has 12 parameters and the ECN protocol has another three parameters.

The ECN and DCQCN algorithm parameters are determined using the EVO [22] optimization package. EVO is a hybrid optimizer that employs evolutionary algorithms paired with other techniques such as ant colony optimizations that are controlled by internal reinforcement (meta) learning agents. EVO uses a user-defined cost function for optimization purposes, along with a set of constraints. The constraints are applied to ensure that the solution space will avoid values that provide unattainable system parameters, such as unattainable network bandwidth. An AI approach was chosen with the assumption that such a tool might analyze performance data in a more complete manner than manual methods. The results of the experiments are promising.

For this Evo cost function we use a metric with a max threshold parameter M_t. As shown in Fig. 2, the metric is linear between zero and M_t, where the cost of M_t is one. For results higher than M_t the function is linear with very steep slope, to avoid the high range of values.

The total cost function is the average of each of the contributing metrics. The metrics are defined such that lower is better.

Three network test codes are used to provide the cost function parameters. The tests include:

1. The b_effective test [23], with the normalized computed average bandwidth and its standard deviation from several measurements being the parameters contributing to the cost function.
2. A test code that generates an N to 1 incast traffic pattern, and with an additional victim flow. I.e., N servers A_1 to A_N send data to a single server O_A, while a separate server V sends data to a server O_V attached to the same destination/leaf switch as O_A. The path from V to the leaf switch overlaps at least one of the N server to O_A paths (see Fig. 1a). The test is run with several values of N. The metrics used include the normalized standard deviation of the measured bandwidth at the N servers, and the normalized available

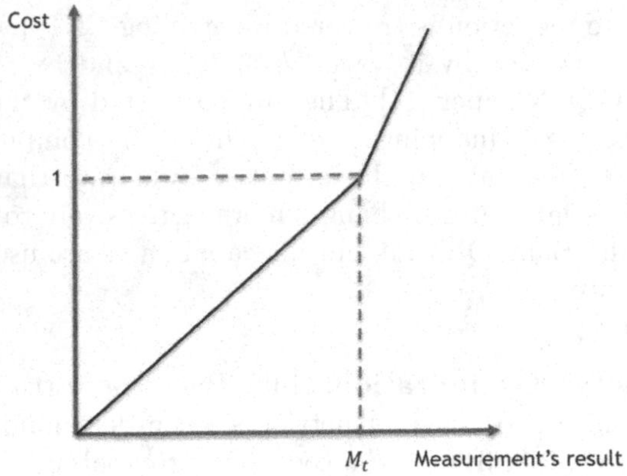

Fig. 2. Metric for measurement's cost function

bandwidth of the victim flow at O_V and of the incast receiver at O_A, where available bandwidth is the line rate minus the measured bandwidth.
3. The GPCNet benchmarks [4], where the metrics used are the GPGNet "key" results for the point-to-point latency test, the point-to-point bandwidth test, and the eight-byte allreduce latency test, for both the average and the 99th percentile measurements.

4 Experimental Setup

4.1 System Configuration

Table 1 describes the system configurations used in the testing.

4.2 Congestion Patterns

The four congestion patterns used to create background traffic include one-sided Remote Memory Access (RMA) $N \rightarrow 1$ incast (put_incast), point-to-point $N \rightarrow 1$ incast (p2p_incast), one-sided broadcast (get_bcast), and alltoall. These patterns are the ones used in the GPCNet benchmark. To generate more congestion, while maintaining medium-sized messages in the range frequently used by HPC applications, the GPCNet benchmark was run varying the data sizes used by the congestor patterns. For this set of tests congestion control was not used, as the goal is to measure the effect of the message size used by the GPCNet defined congestors on application performance. The default message size used by the test is 4 KBytes. Congestion impact (CI) values are reported, with CI for latency and bandwidth defined in Eqs. 1 and 2, respectively. Figure 3 shows the CI values for the test run on 96 nodes and 32 processes per node of the in-house cluster, with message sizes in the range of 4 to 16 KBytes.

Table 1. Test system details.

Feature	In-house cluster	Azure cluster
Operating system	Red Hat Enterprise Linux Server release 7.6 (Maypo)	Ubuntu 18.04.5 LTS (Bionic Beaver) VM under Microsoft Host Hypervisor
CPU	Intel Xeon E5-2697A v4	AMD EPYC 7V12 CPU
Number of Nodes		
Clock frequency	2.60 GHz	2.687 GHz
Sockets/node	2	2
Cores/socket	16	48 VM cores
InfiniBand driver	MLNX_OFED_LINUX5.4-1.0.3.0	MLNX_OFED_LINUX5.4-1.0.3.0
Subnet Manager	OpenSM 5.10.0	UFMAPL_4.6.1.4_UFM_6.7.0.12
HCA	NVIDIA ConnectX-6, HDR100	NVIDIA ConnectX-6, HDR
HCA Firmware	20.31.1014	20.28.4000
Storage	NFS	NFS

$$CI_l = Latency_{congested}/Latency_{isolated} \tag{1}$$

$$CI_b = Bandwidth_{isolated}/Bandwidth_{congested} \tag{2}$$

Note that the CI parameters are chosen to be unit-less, as a ratio of the isolated to congested measurements. With the application host configuration selected at random for each pair of measurements, congested and uncongested, some of the differences between the pairs of measurements are due to changes in the network topology. Using the ratio of the performance metric helps reduce the impact of application topology on the measurements and aids in exposing the impact of congestion control on application performance.

As Fig. 3 shows, for the message sizes used by the congestors, a message size of 8 KBytes impacts the key-results the most and is therefore the message size used to produce application background traffic.

The applications being studied were also used as congestors, replacing the congestors with both copies of the same application, as well as a mix of applications. This had minimal impact on application performance, and therefore was not further pursued.

4.3 Applications

Three applications are used to study the impact of congestion-control on the application: Incompact3D, LAMMPS and VASP. Incompact3D is chosen because it makes extensive use of FFTs, with about a third of the time for the test case spent in alltoall operations with message sizes of tens of KBytes each. LAMMPS and VASP are chosen because they are in wide use. The impact of congestion and congestion control on several other apps was also briefly examined, showing benefits similar to those of these three applications. However, resource constraints precluded these from the current study.

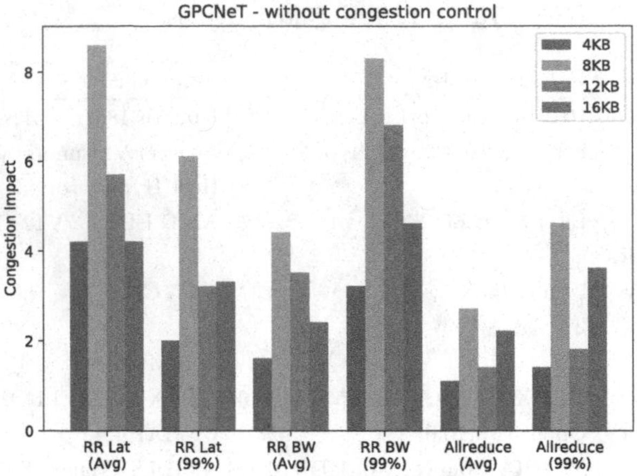

Fig. 3. Congestion Impact on 8-Byte random ring latency, 128-KByte random ring bandwidth, and 8-Byte multiple allreduce, average and 99th percentile for each benchmark without applying InfiniBand congestion control.

Application performance is measured with one copy run in isolation providing the baseline performance characteristics. In addition, each application is run with congestors executing in the background with and without congestion control. Congestion Impact values are reported for applications as well and the definition is similar to Eqs. 1 and 2 using the actual performance metrics defined in each application respectively. For VASP and Incompact3D the performance metric is wall-clock time in seconds, and for LAMMPS the performance metric is simulation speed in nanoseconds per day (ns/day).

Incompact3D. Xcompact3d is a Fortran 90, MPI-based, finite difference high-performance framework for solving the Navier-Stokes equations and associated scalar transport equations. Incompact3d is the flagship solver of the Xcompact3d ecosystem and is designed to study incompressible flows [24,25]. For the Cylinder input chosen for testing, when run with 608 processes on 19 nodes, Incompact3D spent over 90% of MPI communications time in MPI_Alltoall and MPI_Allreduce, as measured by an MPI profiling tool. This corresponds to about 40% of the runtime.

LAMMPS. The Large-scale Atomic/Molecular Massively Parallel Simulator (LAMMPS) is a classical molecular dynamics code. It runs on a single processor or in parallel using message-passing techniques with a spatial-decomposition of the simulation domain [26,27]. For the Rhodopsin input chosen when running LAMMPS, over 70% of the MPI time is spent in MPI_Send, and about 10% is spent in MPI_Allreduce, as measured by an MPI profiling tool. This corresponds to about 13% of the runtime.

VASP. The Vienna Ab initio Simulation Package (VASP) is a computer program for atomic scale materials modeling, e.g. electronic structure calculations and quantum-mechanical molecular dynamics, from first principles [28–32]. For the Pt_111 test input chosen, well over 80% of time spent in MPI communications in VASP is spent in collective operations, namely: MPI_Alltoall, MPI_Bcast, MPI_Allreduce, MPI_Alltoallv and MPI_Barrier, as measured by an MPI profiling tool. This corresponds to about 50% of the runtime.

5 Synthetic Congestion Bare-Metal Workload

To study the impact of congestion generated by synthetic congestors, a testing infrastructure was developed which coordinates running a single application along with congestors in a fully controlled environment. This infrastructure randomizes a given node list and divides it into two groups. The first group contains roughly 20% of the total number of nodes in the list, which are used to run the chosen application, and the remaining nodes are used to run the congestors, with a roughly equal number of hosts used for each congestor. Randomization of the node list affords the opportunity to simulate applications being run in a real HPC data center through a job scheduler. This avoids potential artifacts caused by using a fixed node allocation and/or a pre-selected network layout. The infrastructure collects the application performance metrics in three modes within the same node allocation. In the first mode the application is run in its node group without any congestors to collect baseline performance data. In the second mode both the application and congestors are run simultaneously and application performance is collected again to measure the impact of congestion on the application. The third mode is similar to the second one, but is executed using an InfiniBand service level that is configured to support congestion control.

As Sect. 4.2 describes, there are four basic congestion patterns. For a more comprehensive study of the impact of congestion on the applications, several combinations of these patterns are used. Because of the large amount of time required to collect all the data for a single congestion pattern, seven of the possible pattern combinations are used. Each of the individual congestors is used as the only congestor, and three more added, starting with the strongest congestor, and successively adding the next strongest congestor. Table 2 lists all the congestion patterns used in this paper. For each application and congestor combination, 50 jobs were run for each of the three test modes. The results are reported relative to the baseline runs, making it easier to compare results obtained from the different host layouts.

Figures 4, 5, and 6 show the results of the tests run to measure the impact of congestion and congestion control on the three applications and the seven data patterns used to generate congestion. This data was collected on the in-house bare-metal system. Table 3 lists the Congestion Impact values for these applications for reference. The first half are values without congestion control and the second half are values with congestion control.

Table 2. Congestion patterns

Congestor configuration	Activated congestor(s)
x11	put_incast
x12	p2p_incast
x13	get_bcast
x14	alltoall
x2	put_incast, p2p_incast
x3	put_incast, p2p_incast, get_bcast
x4	put_incast, p2p_incast, get_bcast, alltoall

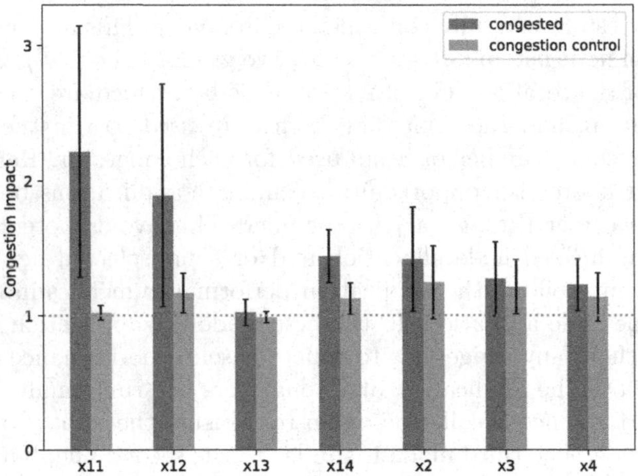

Fig. 4. Impact of congestion and congestion control as a function of congestor type for VASP. The average and standard deviation from 50 jobs per bar run on the 19 nodes for application and 74 nodes for the congestor are displayed.

Table 3. CI average and standard deviation as a function of congestor type for applications running on in-house cluster. Congestors are used for all runs. The top set of measurement do not use congestion control and the bottom set have congestion control activated.

	x11	x12	x13	x14	x2	x3	x4
VASP	2.21 ± 0.93	1.90 ± 0.82	1.02 ± 0.10	1.44 ± 0.20	1.42 ± 0.39	1.27 ± 0.28	1.23 ± 0.19
Incompact3D	1.20 ± 0.12	2.77 ± 1.55	1.01 ± 0.02	1.98 ± 0.24	1.11 ± 0.06	1.08 ± 0.07	1.05 ± 0.02
LAMMPS	2.09 ± 0.95	2.14 ± 1.02	1.00 ± 0.01	1.41 ± 0.26	1.79 ± 0.51	1.61 ± 0.38	1.51 ± 0.30
VASP	1.02 ± 0.05	1.17 ± 0.15	0.99 ± 0.04	1.13 ± 0.12	1.25 ± 0.27	1.21 ± 0.20	1.14 ± 0.18
Incompact3D	1.01 ± 0.01	1.06 ± 0.10	0.93 ± 0.06	0.97 ± 0.07	1.05 ± 0.05	1.04 ± 0.03	1.02 ± 0.02
LAMMPS	1.01 ± 0.01	1.17 ± 0.08	1.00 ± 0.01	1.12 ± 0.10	1.09 ± 0.06	1.06 ± 0.04	1.12 ± 0.07

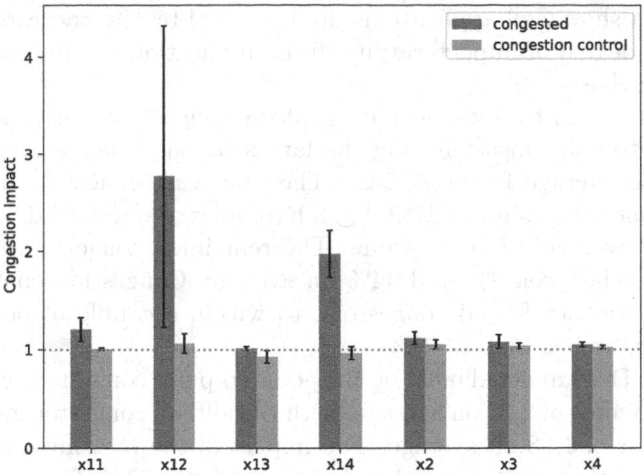

Fig. 5. Impact of congestion and congestion control as a function of congestor type for Incompact3D. The average and standard deviation from 50 jobs per bar run on the 19 nodes for application and 74 nodes for the congestor are displayed.

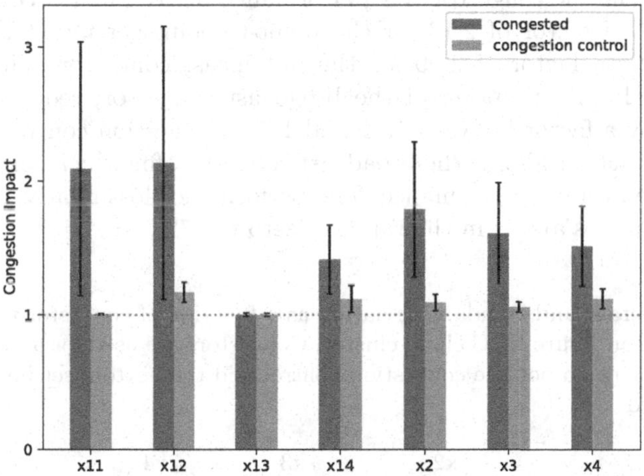

Fig. 6. Impact of congestion and congestion control as a function of congestor type for LAMMPS. The average and standard deviation from 50 jobs per bar run on the 19 nodes for application and 74 nodes for the congestor are displayed.

As the data shows, all applications are impacted by the background congestion, with the degree of impact varying from application to application and on a per-congestor basis.

VASP is impacted to some degree by all the congestors, with the put incast and the point-to-point incast having the largest impact, increasing the average run-time by an average factor of 2.21. The broadcast congestor increases the average run time by a factor of 1.89. Both have a large standard deviation, close to that of the average reference value. The remaining congestors increase run time much less, between 2% and 44% on average. Congestion control reduces the congestion impact for all congestors, to within a couple of percent of the reference value, and as high as 25%.

Incompact3D is impacted most by the point-to-point congestor, with run time increased by a factor of 2.77 on average, with the alltoall congestor increasing run time by a factor of 1.98 on average. The impact of the remaining congestors is small, increasing the average run-time between 1% and 11%. Congestion control reduces the congestion impact for all congestors, to within a single-digit percentage of the reference value, with some cases providing even better performance than that of the reference value.

LAMMPS is noticeably impacted by all of the congestors with the exception of the broadcast congestor. Its performance metric, nanoseconds per day, is decreased by a factor of 2.13 for the point-to-point get incast congestor on average, and by a factor of 2.09 for the put incast congestor. The remaining congestors, with the exception of the broadcast congestor, reduce application performance by a factor between 1.41 and 1.79. Congestion control reduces the congestion impact for all but the broadcast congestor, for which congestion does not change the average performance. The performance loss relative to the reference value improves and is in the range of zero to 17%.

Table 4. CI average and standard deviation as a function of congestor type for applications running on Azure HPC cloud cluster. Congestors are used for all runs. The top set of measurement do not use congestion control and the bottom set have congestion control activated.

	x2	x3	x4
VASP	10.22 ± 1.74	6.87 ± 1.45	6.58 ± 1.23
Incompact3D	9.47 ± 3.04	7.30 ± 3.03	5.52 ± 1.76
LAMMPS	4.63 ± 0.89	3.62 ± 0.66	2.90 ± 0.53
VASP	1.08 ± 0.02	1.07 ± 0.03	1.08 ± 0.02
Incompact3D	1.29 ± 0.44	1.26 ± 0.19	1.19 ± 0.17
LAMMPS	1.06 ± 0.05	1.08 ± 0.03	1.07 ± 0.04

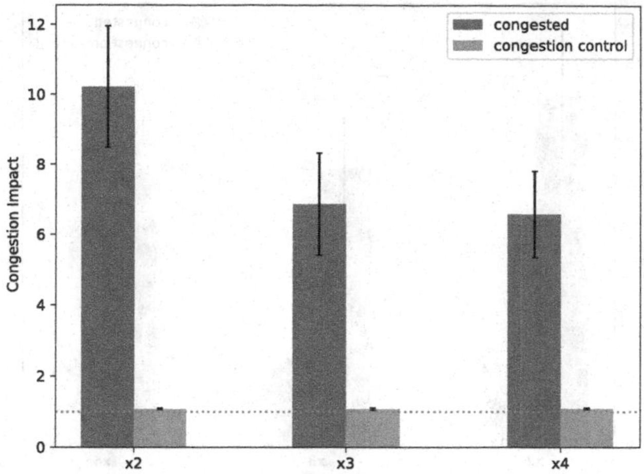

Fig. 7. Impact of congestion and congestion control as a function of congestor type for VASP. Average and standard deviation from 50 jobs per bar run with 80 nodes for application and 320 nodes for congestors.

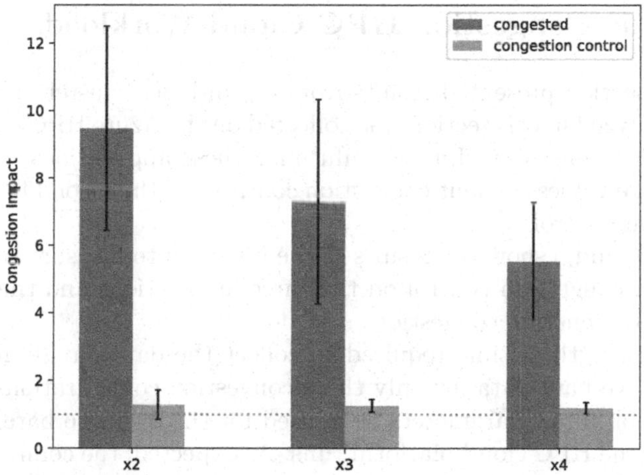

Fig. 8. Impact of congestion and congestion control as a function of congestor type for Incompact3D. Average and standard deviation from 50 jobs per bar run with 80 nodes for application and 320 nodes for congestors.

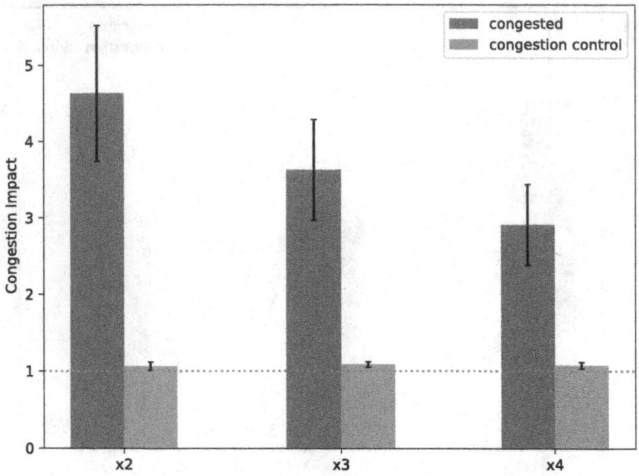

Fig. 9. Impact of congestion and congestion control as a function of congestor type for LAMMPS. Average and standard deviation from 50 jobs per bar run with 80 nodes for application and 320 nodes for congestors.

6 Synthetic Congestion HPC Cloud Workload

The previous section presented results from the in-house cluster. The data presented and analyzed in this section was collected on the Azure HPC cloud system. Table 4 lists the Congestion Impact values for these applications for reference. The first half are values without congestion control and the second half are values with congestion control.

Figures 7, 8, and 9 show the results of the tests run to measure the impact of congestion and congestion control on the three applications and the seven data patterns used to generate congestion.

Due to the length of time required to collect the data on 400 nodes of the Azure system, we have data for only three congestion configurations.

The same job input parameters were used for the in-house bare-metal platform runs and the HPC cloud platform runs. As expected, the communication to computation ratio increases between the 608-process runs on the bare-metal system and the 3,480-process runs on the HPC cloud system. For Incompact3D communication time increases from 40% to 81% of the total run time, for LAMMPS from 13% to 65% and for VASP from 50% to 93%.

Due to the larger communication to computation ratios, these cloud cluster results show noticeably more impact of congestion on the 3 base applications than for our in-house cluster, ranging to over a $10x$ execution multiple for VASP. However, when DCQCN congestion control is applied, for VASP and LAMMPS the application performance returns to within 10% of the baseline uncongested performance. For Incompact3D, the execution multiple ranges up to almost $1.3x$, but this still represents a recovery of over 95% of the extra execution time of the congested runs.

7 Discussion

This paper describes the congestion control algorithm used by NVIDIA's Quantum 200 Gbit/s InfiniBand network, the method used to optimize the algorithm's parameters, and its impact on the performance of three applications. The impact is measured with synthetic congestor patterns running simultaneously, but originating at and terminating at different network end points than those used by the applications. While the congesting communication patterns were taken from the GPCNet benchmark, the data transfer size was changed from the default 4-KByte setting to 8 KBytes to produce more congestion. This data size of 8 KBytes is in the range used by many applications.

The data collected for this paper shows that the synthetic congestors do indeed reduce application performance, anywhere from the rare case of no impact on the average performance of LAMMPS running with the broadcast congestor on the bare metal system, to an order of magnitude slowdown for VASP with the x2 congestor running on the HPC cloud platform. However, the congestion control algorithm recovers the vast majority of this performance loss, even for the worst case resulting performance penalty we encountered, which was almost $1.3x$ on average when running Incompact3D with the x2 congestor with congestion control on the Azure system. What is clear from this data is that the congestion control support provided by the end-to-end Quantum technology works well for these applications, and greatly improves performance for the communication patterns used in this study.

In conclusion, the congestion control technology deployed in NVIDIA's Quantum InfiniBand technology increases system throughput by significantly reducing the impact of congestion on the applications. In NVIDIA's Quantum-2 InfiniBand technology (400 Gbit/s), which is now in an early stage of its life-cycle, additional capabilities in support of congestion control have been added, such as the usage of further telemetry information, new time sensors, and innovative proactive traffic planners. It has been predicted in simulations to further reduce the impact of congestion on running applications, and these new capabilities will be evaluated with similar GPCNet testing in future work.

References

1. C. Zimmer, S. Atchley, R. Pankajakshan, et al.: An evaluation of the CORAL interconnects. In: Proceedings of the International Conference for High Performance Computing, pp. 1–18 (2019). https://doi.org/10.1145/3295500.3356166
2. Geoffray, P., Hoefler, T.: Adaptive routing strategies for modern high performance networks. In: 16th IEEE Symposium on High Performance Interconnects (Hot Interconnects), pp. 165–172 (2008). https://doi.org/10.1109/HOTI.2008.21
3. Mittal, R., et al.: Revisiting network support for RDMA. In: Proceedings of the 2018 Conference of the ACM Special Interest Group on Data Communication, pp. 313–326 (2018) https://doi.org/10.1145/3230543.3230557
4. Chunduri, S., Groves, T., Mendygral, P., et al.: GPCNeT: designing a benchmark suite for inducing and measuring contention in HPC networks. In: Proceedings of

the International Conference for High Performance Computing, Networking, Storage and Analysis (SC 2019), pp. 1–33 (2019). https://doi.org/10.1145/3295500.3356215
5. Clos, C.: A study of nonblocking switching networks. Bell Syst. Technol. J. **32**(2), 406–424 (1953). https://doi.org/10.1002/j.1538-7305.1953.tb01433.x
6. Ngai, J., Seitz, C.: A framework for adaptive routing in multicomputer networks. In: Proceedings of ACM Symposium on Parallel Algorithms and Architectures (SPAA), pp. 1–9 (1989). https://doi.org/10.1145/72935.72936
7. Dally, W.: Virtual-channel flow control. In: Proceedings of the 17th Annual International Symposium on Computer Architecture (ISCA), pp. 60–68 (1990). https://doi.org/10.1145/325164.325115
8. IEEE 802.11Qbb. Priority based flow control (2011)
9. Alizadeh, M., Greenberg, A., Maltz, D., et al.: Data Center TCP (DCTCP). In: ACM SIGCOMM (2010). https://doi.org/10.1145/1851275.1851192
10. Ramakrishnan, K., Floyd, S., Black, D.: The addition of explicit congestion notification (ECN). RFC 3168. https://doi.org/10.17487/RFC3168
11. Zhu, Y., Eran, H., Firestone, D., et al.: Congestion Control for Large-Scale RDMA Deployments. In: ACM SIGCOMM (2015). https://doi.org/10.1145/2829988.2787484
12. IEEE. 802.11Qau. Congestion notification (2010)
13. IBTA: InfiniBand Architecture Specification, Volume 1, Release 1.5. Available to IBTA members via. https://www.infinibandta.org
14. Gusat, M., Craddock, D., Denzel, W., et al.: Congestion control in infiniband networks. In: Hot Interconnects, pp. 158–159 (2005). https://doi.org/10.1109/CONECT.2005.14
15. Gran, E., Eimot, M., Reinemo, S.-A., et al.: First experiences with congestion control in InfiniBand hardware. In: International Parallel and Distributed Processing Symposium. (2010). https://doi.org/10.1109/IPDPS.2010.5470419
16. Mittal, R., Lam, V., Dukkipati, N., et al.: TIMELY: RTT-based congestion control for the datacenter. In: ACM SIGCOMM (2015). https://doi.org/10.1145/2785956.2787510
17. Kumar, G., Dukkipati, N., Jang, K., et al.: Swift: delay is simple and effective for congestion control in the datacenter. In: SIGCOMM 2020: Proceedings ACM Special Interest Group on Data Communication, pp. 514–528 (2020). https://doi.org/10.1145/3387514.3406591
18. Wang, Y., Lan, M., Zhao, T., et al.: Combining RTT and ECN for RoCEv2 protocol. In: HPCCT and BDAI 2020: Proceedings 2020 4th High Performance Computing and Cluster Technologies Conference and 2020 3rd International Conference on Big Data and Artificial Intelligence, pp. 158–164, Qingdao, China (2020). https://doi.org/10.1145/3409501.3409509
19. Li, Y., Miao, R., Liu, H., et al.: HPCC: high precision congestion control. In: SIGCOMM 2019: Proc. ACM Special Interest Group on Data Communication, pp. 44–58 (2019). https://doi.org/10.1145/3341302.3342085
20. Xue, J., Chaudhry, M., Vamanan, B., et al.: Dart: divide and specialize for fast response to congestion in RDMA-based datacenter networks. IEEE/ACM Trans. Networking **28**(1), 322–335 (2020). https://doi.org/10.1109/TNET.2019.2961671
21. Yang, C., Reddy, A.: A taxonomy for congestion control algorithms in packet switching networks. IEEE Network **9**(4), 34–45 (1995). https://doi.org/10.1109/65.397042

22. Saylor, D.: Evo: a hybrid optimizer employing evolutionary algorithms and reinforcement meta learning agents. [Unpublished manuscript]. Applied Machine Learning and Artificial Intelligence, NVIDIA (2013)
23. Effective Bandwidth Benchmark Homepage. https://fs.hlrs.de/projects/par/mpi/b_eff/b_eff_3.1
24. Incompact3D Homepage. https://www.incompact3d.com
25. Bartholomew, P., Deskos, G., et al.: Xcompact3D: an open-source framework for solving turbulence problems on a Cartesian mesh. SoftwareX **12**, 100550 (2020). https://doi.org/10.1016/j.softx.2020.100550
26. LAMMPS Homepage. https://www.lammps.org
27. Thompson, A., Aktulga, H., et al.: LAMMPS - a flexible simulation tool for particle-based materials modeling at the atomic, meso, and continuum scales. Comp. Phys. Comm. **271**, 10817, 100550 (2022). https://doi.org/10.1016/j.cpc.2021.108171
28. VASP Homepage. https://www.vasp.at
29. Kresse, G., Hafner, J.: Ab initio molecular dynamics for liquid metals. Phys. Rev. B **47**, 558 (1993). https://doi.org/10.1016/0022-3093(95)00355-X
30. Kresse, G., Hafner, J.: Ab initio molecular-dynamics simulation of the liquid-metal-amorphous-semiconductor transition in germanium. Phys. Rev. B **49**, 14251 (1994). https://doi.org/10.1103/PhysRevB.49.14251
31. Kresse, G., Furthmüller, J.: Efficiency of ab-initio total energy calculations for metals and semiconductors using a plane-wave basis set. Comput. Mat. Sci. **6**, 15 (1996). https://doi.org/10.1016/0927-0256(96)00008-0
32. Kresse, G., Furthmüller, J.: Efficient iterative schemes for ab initio total-energy calculations using a plane-wave basis set. Phys. Rev. B **54**, 11169 (1996). https://doi.org/10.1103/PhysRevB.54.11169

LLM: Realizing Low-Latency Memory by Exploiting Embedded Silicon Photonics for Irregular Workloads

Marjan Fariborz[1(✉)], Mahyar Samani[1], Pouya Fotouhi[1], Roberto Proietti[1], Il-Min Yi[2], Venkatesh Akella[1], Jason Lowe-Power[1], Samuel Palermo[2], and S. J. Ben Yoo[1]

[1] University of California Davis, Davis, CA 95616, USA
{mfariborz,msamani,pfotouhi,rproietti,akella,jlowepower, sbyoo}@ucdavis.edu

[2] Texas A&M University, College Station, TX 77843, USA
{ilmin.yi,spalermo}@tamu.edu

Abstract. As emerging workloads exhibit irregular memory access patterns with poor data reuse and locality, they would benefit from a DRAM that achieves low latency without sacrificing bandwidth and energy efficiency. We propose LLM (Low Latency Memory), a codesign of the DRAM microarchitecture, the memory controller and the LLC/DRAM interconnect by leveraging embedded silicon photonics in 2.5D/3D integrated system on chip. LLM relies on Wavelength Division Multiplexing (WDM)-based photonic interconnects to reduce the contention throughout the memory subsystem. LLM also increases the bank-level parallelism, eliminates bus conflicts by using dedicated optical data paths, and reduces the access energy per bit with shorter global bitlines and smaller row buffers. We evaluate the design space of LLM for a variety of synthetic benchmarks and representative graph workloads on a full-system simulator (gem5). LLM exhibits low memory access latency for traffics with both regular and irregular access patterns. For irregular traffic, LLM achieves high bandwidth utilization (over 80% peak throughput compared to 20% of HBM2.0). For real workloads, LLM achieves 3× and 1.8× lower execution time compared to HBM2.0 and a state-of-the-art memory system with high memory level parallelism, respectively. This study also demonstrates that by reducing queuing on the data path, LLM can achieve on average 3.4× lower memory latency variation compared to HBM2.0.

1 Introduction

Emerging applications, such as recommendation systems, mining large sparse graphs, etc., exhibit irregular memory access patterns with little data reuse and poor locality [17]. For these irregular workloads, the memory subsystem is increasingly becoming the bottleneck in modern computing architectures. The memory subsystem should not only provide high bandwidth but also low latency to

This work was supported in part by ARO award W911NF1910470.

A.-L. Varbanescu et al. (Eds.): ISC High Performance 2022, LNCS 13289, pp. 44–64, 2022.
https://doi.org/10.1007/978-3-031-07312-0_3

achieve high performance for irregular applications [9,14]. In addition, *variability* in memory latency is another concern as it limits the performance of computing systems [9] and increases the burden on the programmer. It is desirable that both the average memory access latency and its variability (e.g., as measured by the 95th percentile) are low.

To address these challenges, there has been a resurgence of interest in DRAM microarchitectures and memory system designs. With the emergence of silicon photonics technologies, and chiplet-based architectures with 2.5D/3D packaging, there are new opportunities to co-design the various components of the memory subsystem. Recent advances in DRAM architecture, such as wider I/O enabled by 2.5D/3D packaging (as in HBM and its derivatives [20,30]), higher data rates with serial links, and increased bank-level parallelism (again with HBM like technologies), have improved DRAM bandwidth significantly. However, often these bandwidth improvements come at the expense of additional latency and variability due to deeper queues in the memory controller to take advantage of the bank-level parallelism and serialization/deserialization (SerDes) latency [10]. There are also proposals [8,19,21,22] in literature that explicitly address the latency question in DRAM microarchitectures, and most of these proposals simply take advantage of *locality* to reduce latency.

We argue that the main source of latency for irregular workloads in the memory subsystem is **contention** caused by *sharing resources* such as buffers, ports, data/command/control buses, and the DRAM cells where the data actually resides. Increasing these resources comes at a significant cost and may have physical limits such as the number of pins (I/O pads) that can be placed in a given space. Thus, we must consider sources of contention in the *entire end-to-end path*, which includes the processor/memory interconnect, memory controller, and DRAM microarchitecture. In the past, end-to-end optimization of the memory subsystem was not feasible in commodity CPUs (though there has been a slow transition in this direction with integrated memory controllers and special-purpose processors with GDDR SDRAM). However, chiplet-based architectures such as AMD's EPYC and recently announced Intel's Sapphire Rapids offer the opportunity to **co-design** the off-chip(let) processor/memory interconnect, memory controller, and the DRAM microarchitecture [4].

This paper describes our co-design approach, which we call Low Latency Memory (LLM). LLM simultaneously optimizes latency, bandwidth, and energy efficiency by taking advantage of silicon photonics (SiPh) interconnects with optical parallelism and wavelength routing to reduce contention in the entire path from chiplet to the DRAM subarrays. This co-optimization is now possible because silicon photonics offers lower energy/bit [35], high bandwidth density ($Gb/s/mm^2$) with wavelength division multiplexing (WDM) [29], and all-to-all interconnectivity with chip-scale AWGRs (Arrayed Waveguide Grating Routers) [36].

2 Motivation

The primary source of performance degradation for irregular applications is contention among shared resources [14]. Figure 1a shows the high-level schematic of a generic chiplet-based architecture such as AMD EPYC [4]. There are four major components in this system: the interconnect fabric between each chiplet and the memory controllers, usually a complex crossbar-like structure with high bisection bandwidth; the memory controller, which consists of queues to buffer read/write requests bound for the particular memory channel; and finally the DRAM device, which consists of multiple banks, with each bank itself made up of subarray of cells. It is important to note that the interconnect fabric, the queues inside the memory controllers, data buses within the channel, global sense amplifiers, and global bitlines within the DRAM devices are *shared*, which introduces the potential for contention and additional latency due to arbitration, buffering, and serialization (time multiplexed sharing).

Figure 1b, shows the simulation results of end-to-end latency by adding parallelism only at the DRAM microarchitecture. Here we used eight random traffic generators connected to 4-Hi stack HBM2.0 (eight channels) in gem5 [26]. We used HBM as a baseline model of HBM2.0 working in the pseudo-channel mode, which divides each HBM2.0 channel into two pseudo-channels that share the

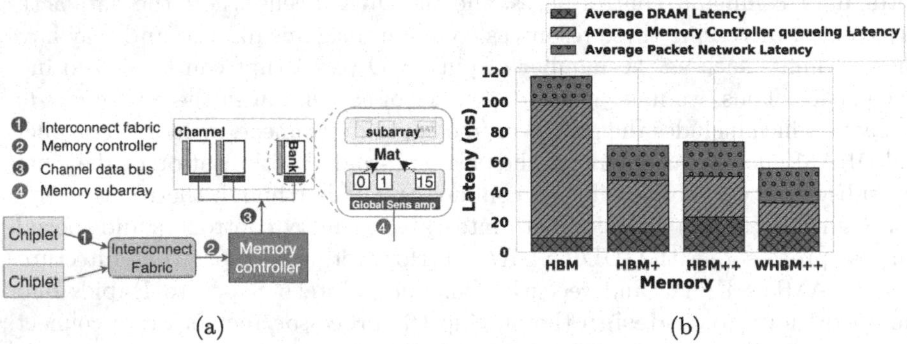

Fig. 1. (a) Generic high-level architecture of the memory subsystem. (b) Breakdown of end-to-end latency. HBM+ increase the pseudo-channels, HBM++ reduces the size of each bank, and WHBM++ increases the data bus width compared to HBM++.

Table 1. DRAM configuration

Category	HBM	HBM+	HBM++	WHBM++
Channels/stack	8	8	8	8
Pseudo-channel/channel	2	4	16	8
Banks/channel	16	16	32	32
Pins/pseudo-channel	64	32	8	64
t_{BURST}	4	8	32	4

channel's address/control (ADD/CMD) bus but have their own 64-bit wide I/O interface. Table 1 shows the specification of different memories. WHBM++ has an 8× number of pins compared to HBM++ while providing the same number of banks and pseudo-channels as HBM++.

We divided the end-to-end latency into three categories: network latency, the queuing latency at the memory controller, and DRAM access latency. Figure 1b shows that for HBM, most of the latency is in the queuing at the memory controller. When we increase resources without considering co-design, the memory controller bottleneck is alleviated. Still, the other components (the device and the network latency) begin to dominate the total latency, and there are diminishing returns. Thus, a high-performance memory, not only needs higher parallelism to reduce the memory controller queuing latency, but it must also reduce the device and interconnect latency. In fact, we propose to *re-architect the entire end-to-end system* to reduce the latency of the memory subsystem, specially as we scale the system to large number of compute units and run irregular workloads with poor data reuse and locality.

LLM makes the following ***contributions*** towards removing these sources of contention: **(a)** It proposes a ground up co-design of the entire path from the processor/memory interconnect to the DRAM microarchitecture. This co-design enables both bandwidth and latency improvement without sacrificing one for the other. LLM is composed of three pieces: a contention-less optical data plane, a low-bandwidth electrical control plane, and fine-grained memory banks with integrated photonics. **(b)** In the data plane (Fig. 2a), LLM provides a dedicated data path from every requestor to every memory bank. An LLM-like architecture is impractical with electrical interconnects because of the energy costs of data movement and the wiring complexity of providing these dedicated data paths. We propose using a passive and contention-less optical interconnect for the data plane with no intermediate buffering, thus reducing the queuing and the interconnect latency compared to other chiplet-based architectures. **(c)** The control plane (shown in Fig. 2b) communicates the address and command between chiplets and memory and coordinates the time that a chiplet sends or receives its data. A low bandwidth electrical network is used for carrying this control information. **(d)** LLM uses fine-grained memory units called μbanks that are exposed to the memory controller to exploit massive amounts of parallelism. LLM memory devices have integrated optics to allow low-latency high-bandwidth direct connections from the requestors to the memory μbanks.

3 Silicon Photonic Enabling Technologies

Over the past decade, optical interconnects have shown great potentials in overcoming the bandwidth bottlenecks that limit inter-processor and memory performance [5,15,44]. Commercial products (e.g., Ayar Labs in collaboration with Intel) leveraging foundry-enabled (e.g. GlobalFoundries offers SiPh-CMOS fabrication) SiPh fabrics and WDM SiPh transceivers have been announced, making SiPh technology feasible for chiplet-based communications [1].

The first SiPh device we use in this study is a microring resonator. Microrings are compact and energy efficient, WDM-compatible devices that are designed to resonate when presented with specific individual wavelengths and remain quiescent at all other times. Active microrings are designed to tune their resonance frequency as the amount of current in their base layer changes, enabling data modulation and demodulation. Microring modulators encode bits onto the optical medium (electrical-to-optical (EO) conversion), and microring filters extract the optical signal and send it to a photodetector performing optical-to-electrical (OE) conversion.

Earlier proposals used optical buses and large matrices of microrings (consisting of hundreds of microrings) for the memory-to-processor network [5,12,23]. In this proposal, we use AWGR [16,33,36,38] which is a passive silicon photonic fabric with a compact layout that offers scalable all-to-all connectivity through wavelength routing. Recent advances in the fabrication process of AWGRs now enable their integration with a significantly reduced footprint (1 mm^2), crosstalk (<–38 dB), and loss (<2 dB) [36]. This makes the AWGR a favorable candidate for energy-efficient, high bandwidth, all-to-all connectivity within HPC systems. Initial studies have shown AWGR to be promising choice for processor-to-memory network [15,16]. Figure 2d shows the wavelength routing in a 5×5 AWGR; all wavelengths inside a waveguide entering one input port of AWGR are evenly distributed over all the output ports, each to a unique output port.

A Vertical Optical Interconnect (VOI) is an optical waveguide that can potentially replace through-silicon vias (TSVs) in 3D stacked memories. Unlike previously demonstrated optical TSVs [32], VOIs have 1–2 μm pitch size [48] and they can provide higher bandwidth density compared to state-of-the-art TSVs (20 μm pitch size [31]).

4 Architecture

In this section we present the detailed design and implementation of LLM that harnesses the benefits of silicon photonics to reduce contention in the entire memory subsystem from the requestor (chiplet or group of chiplets) to the fine grain access units called μbanks inside the DRAM.

4.1 Processor-Memory Interconnect

LLM reduces contention by taking advantage of the lower energy consumption and the higher bandwidth density of optical interconnects for data communication. In addition, it uses a low bandwidth all-to-all electrical interconnect to manage bank conflicts and orchestrate the data movement.

Figure 2a shows the *optical data plane* with an AWGR provideing an all-to-all connection. On the memory-side, each channel is connected to a port of the AWGR using a waveguide. Each waveguide carries a wavelength for each μbank. Inside the memory channel, μbanks modulate/demodulate data on the waveguide through a tuned microring which is tuned to a specific wavelength. To

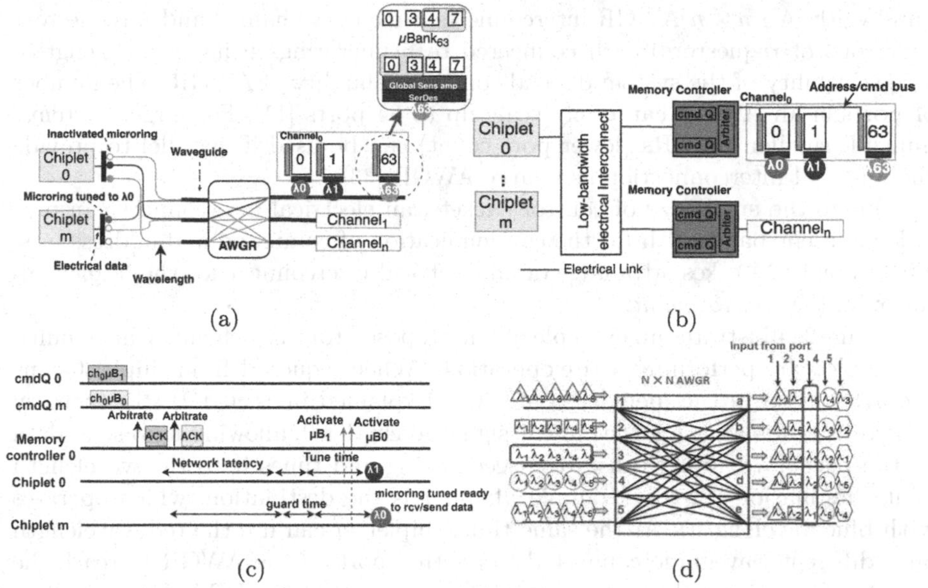

Fig. 2. High-level Overview of (a) data plane, and (b) control plane, (c) demonstrates an example of routing scheme in LLM, and (d) shows the wavelength routing property illustration of AWGR.

enable simultaneous reads/writes per channel we can assign two waveguides per channel to connect to two separate AWGRs (one for carrying read and another for write data).

While the AWGR can route the optical signal to the destination μbank, the requestors should modulate the data on the intended wavelength and send it to the correct AWGR port. Thus, each chiplet uses an array of tunable microrings where each microring in the array directly connects to a different input ports of the AWGR to send/receive the data. For an $n \times n$ AWGR, each chiplet requires n microrings.

The request's μbank address indicates the wavelength, and its channel address indicates which microring on which waveguide needs to be tuned to the corresponding wavelength. This configuration allows (a) single requestor to send requests to every bank within a single channel using a different wavelength on each of the waveguides connected to different input ports of the AWGR; (b) at a particular time, all the requestors can send requests to different channels using different wavelengths on a single waveguide connected to a single port of the AWGR; (c) at a particular time any combination of the above could occur. Note that the *only possible contentions are bank conflicts*, which cannot proceed in parallel anyway and are stalled at the memory controllers.

The choice of the number of waveguides, the number of wavelengths per waveguide, and the data rate in the waveguide are *design parameters* which dictate the maximum number of requestors, memory channels, μbanks, and μbank bandwidth. An $n \times n$ AWGR interconnects n memory channel and n requestors (or group of requestors) each connected to n microrings using n wavelengths. The scalability of the system depends on the scalability of AWGR. The number of ports in an AWGR can easily scale up to 64 ports [11]. For larger systems, multiple smaller AWGRs (lower port count) can be used in parallel to provide the all-to-all interconnection as a large AWGR [33].

Due to the small size of control packets, an electrical interconnect can provide sufficient bandwidth for the communication of command and address bits. Therefore, LLM takes advantage of an electrical interconnect for the implementation of the *control plane.*

Figure 2c illustrates an example of our proposed routing scheme, where multiple chiplets are performing write operations. When request 1 from chiplet 0 wins the arbitration in the memory controller (Explained in Sect. 4.2), the memory controller sends an acknowledgment signal to chiplet 0, allowing it to send data to the memory. Chiplet 0 uses the second ring and tunes it to the wavelength of its destination (in this example μbank 1 is the destination, which operates with blue wavelength). At the same time, chiplet m can use the red wavelength on a different waveguide connected to another port on the AWGR to reach the μbank 0 in the same channel. After issuing a request to the DRAM, data will be ready in the memory at a predefined time later (which is related to the memory access latency). The requestor uses this latency to tune the correct microring (the channel and μbank address indicate which microring must be tuned to which wavelength). Therefore, the memory device needs to have a deterministic response time. Hence, LLM uses a closed-page policy, where the DRAM row buffer is closed immediately after every read or write.

4.2 Memory Controller

LLM redesigns the memory controller to accomplish three main tasks- (i) issuing request at a high rate to increase throughput, (ii) manage arbitration in case of bank conflicts, and (iii) coordinate between requests and data signals (control flow scheme to enable processors to tune the microrings at a particular time).

To improve throughput, we propose reducing the head-of-line-blocking in memory controllers. In a standard memory controller, a bursty sender can overload the entire queue in the memory controller, forcing other processing units to stall. To avoid this, we assigned a single entry queue per requestor (a single or group of processing units) as shown in Fig. 3a. These single-entry queues only store the electrical command signals and the data is buffered at the requestor. Then, instead of requiring a complex priority queue (e.g., first-ready first-come-first-serve), we use a round robin arbiter to select an available request from one queue to a free memory μbank.

To maintain consistency between data and control signal, the memory controller must let the requestors know when to tune their microrings. On an LLC miss or write-back, the requestor sends a request to the memory controller. Then, every cycle, the arbiter selects a ready request from one of the command queues. For read requests, the memory controller asserts the appropriate command and address on the electrical command bus (shown in Fig. 3a in red). At the same time, the arbiter sends a notification back to the requestor to inform the requestor when the data will appear on the dedicated data bus for that μbank, allowing the requestor to tune its microring to an specific wavelength. We use electro-optically tunable microrings with few-nanosecond tuning speed [28, 40]. The requestor can tune its microring while memory is activating the corresponding row in the memory. The microring at the requestor needs to be tuned to the corresponding wavelength once the memory row is activated. To ensure this, memory controller delays the activation request by guard time of 10 ns.

4.3 Memory Microarchitecture

For irregular workloads, bank conflicts could cause long latency due to their random memory access pattern. Bank conflicts happen when multiple consecutive requests target different rows in the same bank. The impact of bank conflicts on latency is quite high. For instance, in HBM2.0 this latency is approximately 50 ns (precharge latency plus activation latency) [2].

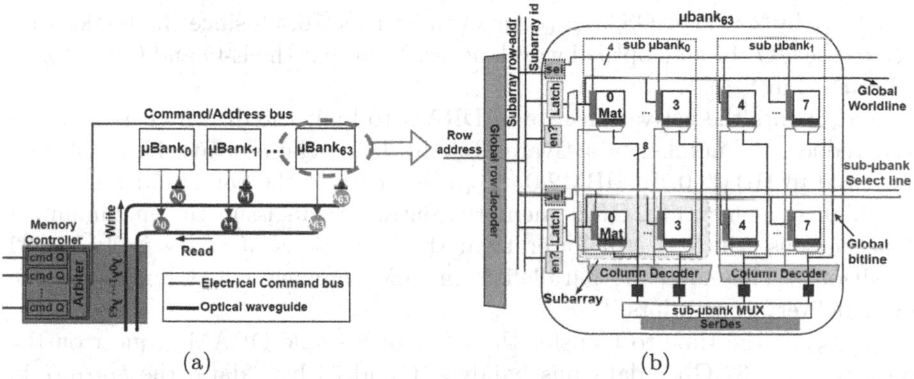

Fig. 3. (a) LLM channel organization. Data and commands are communicated through optical waveguide and electrical bus respectively. (b) μbank architecture which is divided into two sub-μbank that share the same optical data bus through a multiplexer. Each μbank is connected to a microring which is tuned to a certain wavelength.

LLM reduces the probability of bank conflicts by dividing HBM banks into smaller μbanks. In both HBM and LLM, groups of DRAM cells are combined into "mats" which are planar 2D arrays of 512×512 DRAM cells. Mats inside of a subarray are connected to a local sense amplifier and a global bitline connects local sense amplifiers to a global sense amplifier. In LLM μbanks, both the number and size of subarrays are $2\times$ smaller than HBM banks. Lower number of subarrays in LLM μbanks results in shorter global bitlines compared to HBM since each μbank is physically smaller than the HBM banks. LLM further reduces the size of the row buffer by splitting each μbank into two sub-μbanks. This design further reduces the activation energy in LLM which allows for more parallel accesses. Figure 3b shows the detailed architecture of μbank. The impact of our design decisions on the DRAM die size is discussed in Sect. 5.

In addition to the increased parallelism, this new bank organization also reduces the activation energy. A series of studies have shown that the activation row size directly impacts the DRAM activation energy [13,18,30,47]. Dividing the HBM banks into μbanks and sub-μbanks, reduces the activation row size and the activation energy by 75% compared to HBM2.0.

The second source of contention is the data bus shared by multiple banks inside of one channel. To remove this contention requests targeting different banks need to be t_{BURST} apart. LLM removes the contention on the shared data bus inside the channels by assigning a dedicated optical wavelength to each μbank. Each μbank uses a SerDes and a tuned microring to communicate data.

These microarchitectural changes in DRAM also affect the timing constraint of the memory system. t_{CAS} or t_{CL} defines the time between the column command and the appearance of the data at the memory interface I/O. This makes t_{CAS} the data movement latency within the memory die, which consists of pre-GSA (global sense amplifier) and post post-GSA latency. Reducing the length of the global bitline (2$\times$ smaller), lowers the capacitance which reduces the pre-GSA t_{CAS} by 2$\times$. Post-GSA t_{CAS} also will be 1 ns [16,43] since the banks send data to the I/O through optical wavelengths. Note that the E-O and O-E latency is discussed in Sect. 5.

t_{FAW} limits the activation rate in DRAM to limit the drawn current. Since LLM reduces the number of activated bits by 4$\times$, it can activate 4$\times$ more rows compared to HBM2.0. In HBM2.0, t_{FAW} is 12 ns. If the command bus works at a high frequency of 2 GHz, memory controller can issue the maximum of 24 activations which is still lower than the limitations of t_{FAW} in LLM (32 activations). Therefore, the parallelism in LLM channels is not limited by the power delivery constraints.

t_{BURST} is the time to transfer the data for a single DRAM request on the I/O bus. With 32 Gb/s data bus bandwidth and 64 byte data, the t_{BURST} in LLM is 16 ns. However, since each μbank in LLM has a dedicated data bus increasing t_{BURST} does not affect the requests targeting different μbanks in one channel. In a system with a shared data bus, the long t_{BURST} increases the serialization effect, enforcing all requests going to different banks in each channel to be t_{BURST} apart. The dedicated data bus eliminates the bus contention in LLM.

4.4 LLM Organization and Packaging

LLM dies can be organized as both 3D stacks (similar to HBMs) or non-stacked DRAMs (similar to GDDR memories). In this study, we assume that the LLM dies are organized in 3D stacks to offer increased capacity and bandwidth. To this end, we propose using the innovatively new enabling technology called Vertical Optical Interconnects (VOIs) [48] to replace the TSVs. These optical vias allow substantially higher bandwidth and scaling with number of channels, while keeping the area and number of I/O pins the same. In 3D stacked LLM, data can be moved between μbanks in different layers vertically through optical links. Thus VOIs can replace most of the electrical copper TSVs. Werner et al. explored the bandwidth and scalability advantages of VOIs in 3D stacked memories [45].

We place memory stacks, AWGR, and compute cores on the same package substrate and use a previously proposed technique for intra-package communication [15,41]. This approach uses dedicated processor node chiplets, and memory node chiplets with embedded SiPh transceivers. For instance the processor node chiplet consists of SerDes, SiPh transceivers, and the compute core dies. The dedicated SiPh transceivers are connected to the chiplets through Si bridges (which are ideal for short-distance electrical interconnection) and optically to AWGR through polymer waveguides. The memory node has SiPh transceivers embedded inside and can use polymer waveguides to connect to AWGR. The polymer waveguides are integrated on top of the organic package substrate and provide connectivity to AWGR. SiPh is ideal for long-distance, inter-package communication, enabling this system to scale out to multiple packages. The multipackage system uses a polymer waveguide for interconnecting separate packages for computing cores, AWGR, and memory stacks without performance and energy degradation.

5 Methodology

To evaluate the performance and latency of LLM, we used the gem5 simulator version 21.0 [26] with both synthetic workloads and full-system (with Linux kernel version 5.2.3). We modeled the network interconnect with Garnet3.0 and the cache hierarchy using Ruby to evaluate the system architecture.

We compared our design with high bandwidth memory systems such as HBM2.0. In addition, we used two state-of-the-art memory systems with more memory level parallelism. The first one is HBM2.0, with added subarray level parallelism for lower memory access latency. We augmented HBM2.0 by adding techniques from Kim et al. [22]. Throughout the paper, we refer to this as HBM-SALP. The second one is a highly concurrent memory system with 4× higher bandwidth than HBM2.0. In this architecture, the memory banks are finer and more independent. A narrow electrical bus with 4× higher datarate compared to HBM2.0 is assigned to these fine-grain memory banks. This design is our interpretation of Fine-Grained DRAM, and we refer to it as FGDRAM [30]. FGDRAM shows the benefits of incorporating μbanks without the contentionless optical data plane.

To be able to fully stress the bandwidth, we used *synthetic traffic* with different access patterns both with high and low locality. We used three different traffic patterns: *Stream*, *Random*, and *GUPS*. The Stream and Random traffic create a sequence of requests with linearly increasing and uniform random distributed addresses respectively. They both generate requests at user-specified frequencies. GUPS is a data dependent application [27] with a random distribution over memory addresses.

Using traffic generators is a *processor architecture agnostic* evaluation allowing these results to be portable whether LLM is used in a CPU, GPU, or accelerator platforms. Using traffic generators also enables experiments with different network injection rates to model memory intensive workloads that can fully stress the high bandwidth of our proposed memory system.

For the synthetic traffic simulation we used 32 traffic generators. For this experiment we scaled our high bandwidth baseline memories to reach the same peak bandwidth as LLM stack which is 4 TB/s (iso-bandwidth). In these iso-bandwidth experiments, both HBM and HBMSALP are given 8× the channels of LLM and FGDRAM 2× compared to LLM.

For latency and overall evaluation, we ran real workloads in the gem5 simulator. We used applications such as GAP benchmark suite (GAPBS) [7] as a representative for irregular workloads due to their random memory access pattern. Table 2 shows the system configuration. We used a multiple core CPU system, each with two levels of cache hierarchy.

Latency Parameters: The memory system needs to model both the network latency (which also includes the O-E and E-O and SerDes latencies) and the DRAM timing constraints. Both of these timings are included in our simulation platform. Due to the different bank and channel organizations, some timing constraints are different from LLM and HBM2.0. Table 2 illustrates the changed timing constraints between HBM, FGDRAM, and LLM. We assumed an optical

Table 2. Full system simulation parameters

Parameter	Description	Timing parameter (ns)	HBM2.0 [2]	FGDRAM [30]	LLM
CPU	16 cores; ×86 @ 4 GHz	tCAS	16	16	5
Caches	Private 32 kB L1I/D, 2/8-way per core	tBURST	4	16	16
	Private 512 kB, 8-way L2 per core	tFAW	12	12	12
	Directory coherence	Activates in tFAW	8	32	32
Memory	8 DRAM channels				

Table 3. Silicon photonic device parameters

Parameter	Value	Parameter	Value	Parameter	Value
VOI loss	1.3 dB	Photodetector loss	0.1 dB	Modulator Insertion loss	1 dB
Waveguide loss	0.5 dB/cm	Filter through loss	0.1 dB	Power margin	3 dB
Filter drop loss	1.5 dB	Receiver sensitivity	−17 dBm	Laser efficiency	14%
Coupler: Fiber-to-Package	3 dB	AWGR crosstalk	−20 dB	AWGR loss	1.8 dB

traversal of 1 ns [16,24]. We are using a low-power 16 Gb/s SerDes for seriliazing/deserializing 32 bits of data from global sense amplifiers, resulting in 2 ns latency. We assume that the E-O, O-E conversion latency takes 35 ns [28,40]. We also modeled the electrical control plane in LLM with a network latency of 20 ns, which is a conservative assumption in our system.

Power Model: For the power modeling of the optical interconnects, we used values for 65 nm CMOS [24,46] and scaled it down to 28 nm using SPICE models [24,46]. The laser efficiency is based on commercially-available comb lasers [3]. Table 3 illustrates the details of our silicon photonic devices.

Area: We compared the area of LLM stack based on both microarchitectural changes and the optical circuitry we have added to the memory microarchitecture design. We compared the area for a 4 die stack (4Hi) LLM and HBM. The dimensions of HBM dies are typically 5.5 mm × 7.7 mm [25].

Each μbank includes SiPh transmitter and receiver circuitry (5 µm pitch size), and a 16 Gb/s serializer-deserializer (SerDes) with an area of 0.0045 mm^2 (estimated using TSMC 28 nm CMOS process). Two waveguides are connected to each memory channel, each with 2 µm pitch size [48]. A 4Hi HBM requires 1024 TSVs for data but LLM requires only 32 VOIs. Overall, optical circuitry add 4.94% area overhead compare to a HBM stack.

LLM also requires 2× more column decoders and 4× more global sense amplifiers. Dividing each μbanks to sub-μbanks adds additional circuitry such as 4 bit wordline-select, and sub-μbank multiplexer. These area overhead are equal to FGDRAM and subchannel [10,30] which are 4.67%. LLM also requires latches to enable subarray level parallelism. Each latch requires 2 μm^2 area. In total microarchitectural changes to DRAM adds an additional 4.8% area overhead. A 4 stack-high LLM requires 9.74% area overhead compare to HBM2.0.

6 Evaluation

6.1 Synthetic Traffic Evaluation

In the first experiment, we ran stream and random synthetic traffic with different traffic rates to see how latency and throughput change as we increase the traffic rate. Figure 4 shows both the achieved throughput and the average access latency for read-only memory requests under varying injection rates. With stream traffic, all memories can achieve high throughput. However, under high injection rates, LLM has lower latency than the other designs due to its low latency interconnect and zero data queuing at the memory controller. At very low injection rates, HBMSALP has a lower average latency due to increased page hit rate and the SALP optimizations [22]. Since LLM uses closed-page policy for applications with high locality LLM will not show significant reduction in latency compered to HBMSALP. However, at all injection rates LLM has lower latency than FGDRAM and HBM.

For random traffic, Fig. 4b shows that LLM has much lower latency for all injection rates. The main reason HBM's latency increases even under a relatively low injection rate is due to DRAM row buffer misses which incur high latency. These row buffer misses cause contention in the memory controller which results in a high queuing delay. For LLM, reducing the size of the queues in the memory controller and using a closed-page policy leads to low latency under high injection rates. This low queuing is unlike HBM and FGDRAM which experience significant increase in latency as the traffic rate increases. Figure 4b shows the biggest difference between LLM and prior technologies. *LLM can achieve nearly the same throughput with random traffic as with streaming traffic.* In contrast, the best other technology, FGDRAM, can only achieve approximately 50% of its peak theoretical bandwidth under a random access pattern. The difference between LLM and FGDRAM, also shows that simply adding parallelism in the memory subsystem (μbanking) without re-architecting the entire datapath will not remove the contention in the system; it will simply move the contention to another point in the datapath.

To increase complexity in our synthetic traffic experiments, we applied the Giga Updated Per Second (GUPS) benchmark which has data dependent accesses. We measured the performance of these systems based on the GUPS as defined by the benchmark. Similar to Random and stream we used iso-bandwidth test for GUPS. Figure 4c show that even when given significantly more I/O (and cost) HBM and FGDRAM cannot match LLM's performance for this irregular workload.

Although HBMSALP adds more intra-bank parallelism compared to HBM, Fig. 4c shows it does not achieve considerable performance improvements. This result demonstrates the importance of optimizing the memory system for both bandwidth and latency. Even for latency-critical workloads like GUPS, the bandwidth can also be the limiting factor. Only optimizing for latency does not necessarily lead to the best performance.

6.2 Irregular Workloads

In a more realistic setup, we used gem5 21.0 full system mode to compare LLM with, HBM, HBMSALP, and FGDRAM in a system with 8 processing cores and 8 memory channels (iso-capacity configuration of different memory technologies) as opposed to the iso-bandwidth tests used in the synthetic traffic experiments. Though it is difficult for us to estimate the costs of each technology, this iso-capacity experiment compares the performance in a real system setting with each technology given approximately the same amount of resources. Due to the extensive time of simulation for each system configuration, we created traces for 8 core system and extended it to 16 core configuration. This enabled us to stress the bandwidth of the system under the same traffic pattern. We used 64×64 AWGRs with 64 wavelengths.

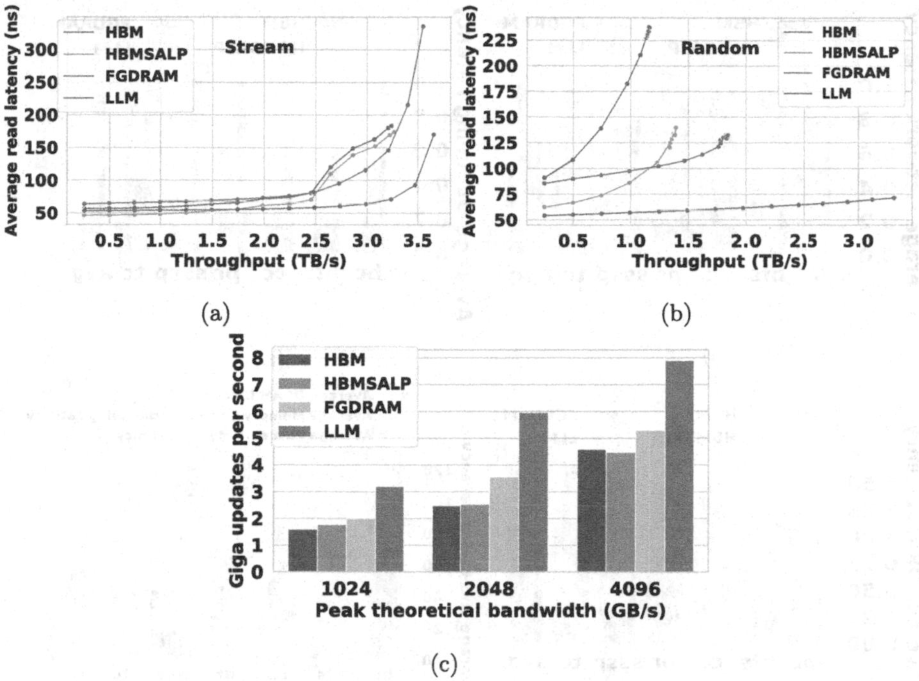

Fig. 4. Iso-bandwidth synthetic traffic with (a) Stream, (b) Random, and (c) GUPS traffic pattern. (a–b) Comparing the average read latency and throughput for different injection rates and access patterns. (c) GUPS traffic, shows even with the same peak bandwidth LLM provides more parallelism resulting in 2× improvement on average performance compared to HBM (with 8× more channels).

For the first experiment we compared the average latency for DRAM access, the queuing latency at the memory controller, and the average network latency. Figures 6(a–c) show the normalized comparison between these memory systems. For all workloads LLM has significantly lower queuing at the memory controller which is what we expected based on lack of data queuing at the memory controller. Also, the network latency for LLM remains smaller for all workloads because in large scale systems with higher crossbar radix electrical interconnect latency is higher. Compared to HBM, FGDRAM shows lower queuing latency which indicates the benefits of added parallelism at the memory microarchitecture without the optical datapath. Comparing LLM and FGDRAM, the queuing latency is on average 3× lower which shows the benefit of the co-design architecture of the memory controller, the interconnect design, and the all-optical data path. Finally, for the device latency (Fig. 5c), all systems have approximately the same latency except FGDRAM which is higher due to the larger t_{BURST}.

Figure 5d shows the total average latency of the three components (device, queuing, and network latency). This shows that for all systems except LLM, queuing latency is the dominant portion of the time (broken out in Fig. 5b).

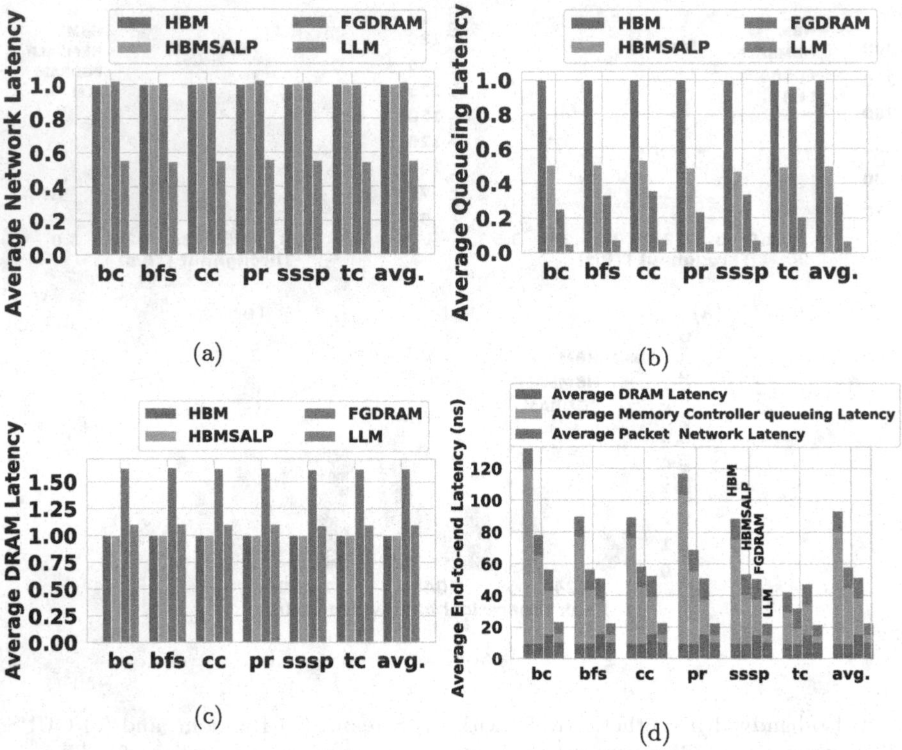

Fig. 5. Average latency normalized to HBM2.0 for (a) network (b) queuing (c) memory device, and (d) shows the average end-to-end latency. (a) shows LLM achieves in average 2× lower network latency, 1.1× higher DRAM latency due to the long bus latency, and (b) indicates 10× lower queuing latency compared to HBM2.0.

Figure 5d indicates the memory intensity of the workloads as well. For instance, *tc* has lower average end-to-end latency with lower queuing compared to the other workloads. Thus, optimizing just for throughput will not improve the execution time for this workload (e.g., FGDRAM does not improve performance for *tc* as shown in Fig. 6a since it sacrifices latency for bandwidth).

Figure 6a compares the execution time of GAPBS workloads for HBM, HBMSALP, FGDRAM, and LLM. Compared to HBM, LLM provides 3× reduction on average execution time. For the more memory intensive workloads, the increased bandwidth of LLM provides reduced execution time. Importantly, for the lower intensity workloads, LLM also provides an improvement over the other technologies (most notably FGDRAM running *tc*) due to its lower contention on the shared data bus.

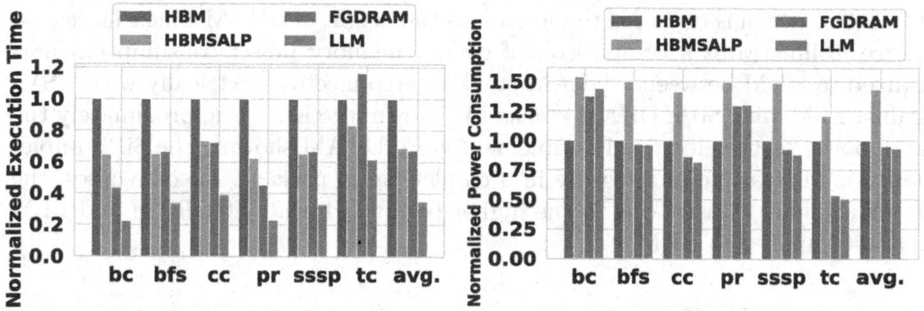

(a) (b)

Fig. 6. Execution time (a) and power consumption (b) normalized based on HBM2.0. LLM provides in average 3× lower execution time while maintaining same power consumption compared to HBM2.0.

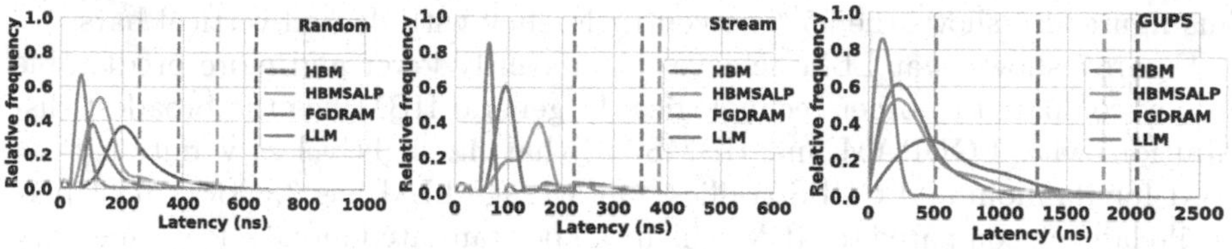

(a) (b) (c)

Fig. 7. The latency distribution for different memory systems under 3 types of synthetic traffic: (a) Random, (b) Stream, and (c) GUPS. LLM has a lower 95th percentile (shown as dashed lines) and therefore has lower latency variation. In (b) HBM and HBMSALP have the same distribution of latency.

6.3 Energy and Power Analysis

The DRAM access energy consists of activation energy, data movement energy, and I/O energy. We used the HBM2.0 energy values from O'Conner et al. [30]. The activation energy directly depends on the number of bits in a row that get activated. Similar to FGDRAM [30], LLM reduces the size of the row by a factor of 4×, and therefore, we reduce the activation energy to 227 pJ for LLM from 909 pJ in HBM 2.0. Pre-GSA energy is the energy of moving data from local and master bitlines to the global row buffer, and it depends on the length of bitline. Since we are reducing the size of the global bitlines, this energy will also be reduced to 0.755 pJ/bit from 1.51 pJ/bit in HBM2.0.

LLM uses optical links to move data between μbanks and processing cores. Therefore, both I/O and post-global sense amplifier energy values are equal and are independent of laser, SerDes, and modulation circuitry. For this SiPh stack, we used the parameters shown in Table 3 to match realistic current technologies. We found the total I/O energy (including laser, SerDes, modulation circuitry) to be 760 fJ/bit. In comparison, for conventional DRAM the I/O requires 800 fJ/bit [30], which is expected to increase as the height of DRAM stacks increases. Figure 6b illustrates a comparison of overall memory power consumption normalized to HBM between a DRAM stack interconnected electrically with TSVs against LLM with SiPh DRAM stacks. As shown, the LLM is approximately the same power as the electrically implemented FGDRAM showing the SiPh implementation is feasible to integrate in a chiplet-based package. In some cases, the power is higher, mostly due to the higher bandwidth that FGDRAM and LLM enable compared to HBM.

6.4 Latency Variation

Finally, we analyzed the latency variation in each memory system. In current systems, the main cause of latency variation in the system is queuing. Thus, one of the byproducts of our low contention memory system should be lower latency variation. Figure 7 shows the distribution of access times for each technology under stream, random, and GUPS synthetic traffics using 16 memory channels. This figure also shows the 95th percentile latency with dashed vertical bars.

Figure 7 shows that LLM achieves significantly lower and more predictable latency compared to other technologies. In general HBM has the broadest distribution, with FGDRAM and HBMSALP having slightly less variation than HBM for Random and GUPS traffics. On average LLM has 3× lower 95th percentile latency compared to HBM which can be translated into 3× lower memory latency variations. We see similar results for the full system graph workloads as well.

7 Related Work

Several studies have shown the benefits of using photonics to increase bandwidth and reduce data movement energy for processor/memory communication [5,6, 34,37,39,45]. Although these studies reduce contention at the interconnect, they did not contribute to increasing memory performance at the microarchitectural level. LLM extends these prior works by (a) reducing in-memory activation and data movement energy, allowing for higher parallelism, and (b) integrating optics inside of the memory channel and co-designing the memory controller to facilitate both bandwidth and *latency* improvements.

Previous work on DRAM energy [13,18,30,47] showed the benefits of reducing activation energy while maintaining a higher bandwidth than HBM2.0. These studies are still bounded by the processor/memory data movement energy. LLM extends these prior works by exploiting silicon photonic interconnects. Optical links do not suffer from the distance/bandwidth trade-off that impacts electrical interconnects. This allows LLM to achieve a low energy data movement in a chiplet based architecture while achieving higher peak bandwidth than the previous studies.

Creating smaller channels with narrower data bus and higher datarate is the technique used both in in the industry (with HBM2.0 and HBM2.0 pseudo-channel mode, and GDDR) and research [30] to enable high throughput memory systems. However, they do not consider optimizing the memory for latency. Furthermore, they use deep queues for bandwidth improvements which will result in higher latency. In contrast, LLM is a redesign of the complete memory subsystem. Decoupling data and control signals in the LLM allows for bandwidth and latency improvement at the same time.

Previous work, has explored many different avenues for decreasing DRAM latency including changing the DRAM controller [8], segmenting and shortening bitlines [22] and caching and paging policies [21]. Although these techniques proved to be effective in reducing the DRAM access latency, they are not optimized for irregular applications and in some cases can increase memory access latency variability. Wang et al. improved latency for irregular workloads by creating a low-cost DRAM substrate that enables data relocation [42]. Although effective for irregular workloads they have not shown any benefits for applications with high locality and the effects on memory latency variations. LLM reduces the amount of data queuing on the entire path and assigns a dedicated data path between each requestor and memory μbank. This technique reduces latency in both regular and irregular workloads but it also reduces memory access variability due to low queuing on the path.

8 Conclusion

In this paper, we investigated a new memory system that is optimized for applications with both regular and irregular access patterns with poor spacial locality. LLM introduces lower execution time compared to the baseline HBM2.0 systems. It also utilizes an all optical data communication fabric that provides a direct contention-free data link between processing cores and memory banks. The use of optical interconnects, optical links, and the new memory microarchitecture improve data movement, reduces activation energy and provides higher bandwidth/mm^2. By incorporating all these methods, LLM can reduce the execution time and energy with a modest area overhead. The cost increase for optoelectronic integrated LLM would be around 30% compared to electronic only HBM2.0. However, LLM achieves around 3$\times$ better execution time while maintaining the same power consumption as HBM2.0.

Due to low-contention data access in LLM, we believe that LLM-like designs can improve the performance in other computing systems. As future work we would like to evaluate the architectural impact and benefits of LLM in other systems such as graph accelerators.

References

1. Ayar Labs Realizes Co-Packaged Silicon Photonics - WikiChip Fuse. https://fuse.wikichip.org/news/3233/ayar-labs-realizes-co-packaged-silicon-photonics/
2. JEDEC. https://www.jedec.org/sites/default/files/docs/JESD212.pdf
3. Thermistor Specification Fiber Specification an exemplary Eye Diagram of one F-P mode Externally modulated at 2.5 GHz filtered-out single channel. www.innolume.com

4. Zen - Microarchitectures - AMD - WikiChip. https://en.wikichip.org/wiki/amd/microarchitectures/zen
5. Batten, C., et al.: Building many-core processor-to-dram networks with monolithic CMOS silicon photonics. In: International Symposium on Microarchitecture (MICRO), pp. 8–21 (2009)
6. Beamer, S., et al.: Re-architecting dram memory systems with monolithically integrated silicon photonics. In: Proceedings International Symposium on Computer Architecture (ISCA), pp. 129–140. IEEE (2010)
7. Beamer, S., et al.: The gap benchmark suite. arXiv preprint arXiv:1508.03619 (2015)
8. Carter, J., et al.: Impulse: building a smarter memory controller. In: Proceedings Fifth International Symposium on High-Performance Computer Architecture, pp. 70–79. IEEE (1999)
9. Chatterjee, N., et al.: Managing dram latency divergence in irregular GPGPU applications. In: Proceedings of the International Conference on High Performance Computing, Networking, Storage and Analysis (SC), pp. 128–139 (2014)
10. Chatterjee, N., et al.: Architecting an energy-efficient dram system for GPUS. In: IEEE International Symposium on High Performance Computer Architecture (HPCA), pp. 73–84. IEEE (2017)
11. Cheung, S., et al.: Ultra-compact silicon photonic 512× 512 25 GHZ arrayed waveguide grating router. IEEE J. Selected Top. Quant. Electron. **20**, 310–316 (2013)
12. Cianchetti, M.J., et al.: Phastlane: a rapid transit optical routing network. In: Proceedings of the International Symposium on Computer Architecture (ISCA), pp. 441–450 (2009)
13. Cooper-Balis, E., et al.: Fine-grained activation for power reduction in dram. In: International Symposium on Microarchitecture (MICRO), pp. 34–47 (2010)
14. Eklov, D., et al.: Bandwidth bandit: quantitative characterization of memory contention. In: Proceedings of the 2013 IEEE/ACM CGO, pp. 1–10 (2013)
15. Fotouhi, P., et al.: Enabling scalable chiplet-based uniform memory architectures with silicon photonics. In: Proceedings of the International Symposium on Memory Systems (MEMSYS), pp. 222–334 (2019)
16. Grani, P., et al.: Design and evaluation of AWGR-based photonic NOC architectures for 2.5 d integrated high performance computing systems. In: IEEE International Symposium on High Performance Computer Architecture (HPCA), pp. 289–300. IEEE (2017)
17. Gupta, U., et al.: The architectural implications of facebook's DNN-based personalized recommendation. In: IEEE International Symposium on High Performance Computer Architecture (HPCA), pp. 488–501. IEEE (2020)
18. Ha, H., et al.: Improving energy efficiency of dram by exploiting half page row access. In: International Symposium on Microarchitecture (MICRO), pp. 1–12. IEEE (2016)
19. Hassan, H., et al.: Chargecache: reducing dram latency by exploiting row access locality. In: IEEE International Symposium on High Performance Computer Architecture (HPCA). IEEE (2016)
20. JESD235A, J.: High Bandwidth Memory (HBM) Dram. JEDEC Solid State Technology Association (2015)
21. Kaseridis, D., et al.: Minimalist open-page: a dram page-mode scheduling policy for the many-core era. In: International Symposium on Microarchitecture (MICRO), pp. 24–35. IEEE (2011)

22. Kim, Y., et al.: A case for exploiting subarray-level parallelism (SALP) in dram. In: Proceedings of the International Symposium on Computer Architecture (ISCA), pp. 368–379. IEEE (2012)
23. Kirman, N., et al.: Leveraging optical technology in future bus-based chip multiprocessors. In: International Symposium on Microarchitecture (MICRO), pp. 492–503. IEEE (2006)
24. Li, H., et al.: A 25 Gb/s, 4.4 v-swing, ac-coupled ring modulator-based WDM transmitter with wavelength stabilization in 65 nm CMOS. IEEE J. Solid-State Circuits **50**, 3145–3159 (2015)
25. Li, L., et al.: 3d sip with organic interposer for ASIC and memory integration. In: IEEE 66th Electronic Components and Technology Conference (ECTC), pp. 1445–1450. IEEE (2016)
26. Lowe-Power, et al.: The gem5 simulator: Version 20.0+. arXiv preprint arXiv:2007.03152 (2020)
27. Luszczek, P.R., et al.: The HPC challenge (HPCC) benchmark suite. In: Proceedings of the 2006 ACM/IEEE Conference on Supercomputing, p. 213-es (2006)
28. Matsuo, S.A.O.: Microring-resonator-based widely tunable lasers. IEEE J. Select. Top. Quant. Electron. **15**, 545–554 (2009)
29. Nitta, C.J., et al.: On-chip photonic interconnects: a computer architect's perspective. Synthesis Lectures on Computer Architecture, pp. 1–111 (2013)
30. O'Connor, M., et al.: Fine-grained dram: energy-efficient dram for extreme bandwidth systems. In: International Symposium on Microarchitecture (MICRO), pp. 41–54. IEEE (2017)
31. Papistas, I., et al.: Bandwidth-to-area comparison of through silicon VIAS and inductive links for 3-d ICS. In: European Conference on Circuit Theory and Design (ECCTD), pp. 1–4. IEEE (2015)
32. Parekh, M.S., et al.: Electrical, optical and fluidic through-silicon VIAS for silicon interposer applications. In: IEEE Electronic Components and Technology Conference (ECTC), pp. 1992–1998. IEEE (2011)
33. Proietti, R., et al.: Experimental demonstration of a 64-port wavelength routing thin-clos system for data center switching architectures. J. Opt. Commun. Network. **10**, 49–B57 (2018)
34. Rumley, S., et al.: Silicon photonics for exascale systems. J. Lightwave Technol. **33**, 547–562 (2015)
35. Shacham, A., et al.: Photonic networks-on-chip for future generations of chip multiprocessors. IEEE Trans. Comput. **57**, 1246–1260 (2008)
36. Shang, K., et al.: Low-loss compact silicon nitride arrayed waveguide gratings for photonic integrated circuits. IEEE Photon. J. **9**, 1–5 (2017)
37. Shen, Y., et al.: Silicon photonics for extreme scale systems. J. Lightwave Technol. **37**, 245–259 (2019)
38. Takada, K., et al.: Low-crosstalk 10-GHZ-spaced 512-channel arrayed-waveguide grating multi/demultiplexer fabricated on a 4-in wafer. IEEE Photon. Technol. Lett. **13**, 1182–1184 (2001)
39. Udipi, A.N., et al.: Rethinking dram design and organization for energy-constrained multi-cores. In: Proceedings of the International Symposium on Computer Architecture (ISCA), pp. 175–186 (2010)
40. de Valicourt, et al.: Dual hybrid silicon-photonic laser with fast wavelength tuning. In: Optical Fiber Communications Conference and Exhibition (OFC), pp. 1–3 (2016)

41. Wade, M., et al.: Teraphy: a chiplet technology for low-power, high-bandwidth in-package optical I/O. In: International Symposium on Microarchitecture (MICRO), pp. 63–71 (2020)
42. Wang, Y., et al.: Figaro: Improving system performance via fine-grained in-dram data relocation and caching. In: International Symposium on Microarchitecture (MICRO), pp. 313–328. IEEE (2020)
43. Werner, S., et al.: Amon: an advanced mesh-like optical NOC. In: IEEE 23rd Annual Symposium on High-Performance Interconnects, pp. 52–59 (2015)
44. Werner, S., et al.: AWGR-based optical processor-to-memory communication for low-latency, low-energy vault accesses. In: Proceedings of the International Symposium on Memory Systems (MEMSYS), pp. 269–278 (2018)
45. Werner, S., et al.: 3d photonics as enabling technology for deep 3d dram stacking. In: Proceedings of the International Symposium on Memory Systems (MEMSYS), pp. 206–221 (2019)
46. Yu, K., et al.: A 25 Gb/s hybrid-integrated silicon photonic source-synchronous receiver with microring wavelength stabilization. IEEE J. Solid-State Circuits **51**, 2129–2141 (2016)
47. Zhang, T., et al.: Half-dram: a high-bandwidth and low-power dram architecture from the rethinking of fine-grained activation. In: Proceedings of the International Symposium on Computer Architecture (ISCA), pp. 349–360. IEEE (2014)
48. Zhang, Y., et al.: High-density wafer-scale 3-D silicon-photonic integrated circuits. IEEE J. Select. Top. Quant. Electron. **24**, 1–10 (2018)

SU3_Bench on a Programmable Integrated Unified Memory Architecture (PIUMA) and How that Differs from Standard NUMA CPUs

Jesmin Jahan Tithi[1](✉), Fabio Checconi[1], Douglas Doerfler[2], and Fabrizio Petrini[1]

[1] Parallel Computing Labs, Intel Corporation, Santa Clara, CA 95054, USA
{jesmin.jahan.tithi,fabio.checconi,fabrizio.petrini}@intel.com
[2] Lawrence Berkeley National Laboratory, Berkeley, CA 94720, USA

Abstract. SU3_Bench explores performance portability across multiple programming models using a simple but nontrivial mathematical kernel. This kernel has been derived from the Lattice Quantum Chromodynamics (LQCD) code used in applications such as Hadron Physics and hence should be of interest to the scientific community.

SU3_Bench has a regular compute and data access pattern and on most traditional CPU and GPU-based systems, its performance is mainly determined by the achievable memory bandwidth. However, this paper shows that on the new Intel Programmable Integrated Unified Memory Architecture (PIUMA) that is designed for sparse workloads and has a balanced flops-to-byte ratio with scalar cores, SU3_Bench's performance is determined by the total number of instructions that can be executed per cycle (pipeline throughput) rather than the usual bandwidth or flops. We show the performance analysis, porting, and optimizations of SU3_Bench on the PIUMA architecture and discuss how they are different from the standard NUMA CPUs (e.g., Xeon required NUMA optimizations whereas, on PIUMA, it was not necessary). We show iso-bandwidth and iso-power comparisons of SU3_Bench for PIUMA vs Xeon. We also show performance efficiency comparisons of SU3_Bench on PIUMA, Xeon, GPUs, and FPGAs based on pre-existing data. The lessons learned are generalizable to other similar kernels.

Keywords: SU3_Bench · SU3 · LQCD · QCD · PIUMA · Quantum chromodynamics

1 Introduction

SU3_Bench [2] is a microbenchmark developed at the Lawrence Berkeley National Laboratory (LBNL) to explore performance portability across multiple programming models and architectures using a simple, but nontrivial, mathematical kernel. This kernel has been derived from the (Multiple Instruction Multiple

A.-L. Varbanescu et al. (Eds.): ISC High Performance 2022, LNCS 13289, pp. 65–84, 2022.
https://doi.org/10.1007/978-3-031-07312-0_4

Data) MIMD Lattice Computation (MILC) Lattice Quantum Chromodynamics (LQCD) code [14]. The MILC Code is a body of high-performance software written in C for doing SU(3) (special unitary group of degree 3) lattice gauge theory on high-performance computers, as well as single-processor workstations. The SU3_Bench microbenchmark calculates an SU (3) matrix-matrix multiply using complex floating-point arithmetic. It operates over a lattice of dimension of L^4. The matrix-matrix and matrix-vector SU(3) operations are fundamental building blocks of LQCD applications. Most LQCD applications use domain-specific implementations (libraries) written in machine-specific languages and/or intrinsics. Hence, performance portable methodologies are of interest.

The SU3_Bench code available on GitHub [2] mainly focuses on performance portability on different GPUs. There is a recent attempt to port it to FPGAs [9] using OpenCL. SU3_Bench has different versions available for different platforms (CPU, GPUs, FPGAs) and different programming environments (CUDA, Intel dpcpp, hip, hipsycl, OpenACC, OpenCL, OpenMP, sycl). A common main driver routine is used for all programming models, with implementations specific to each model self-contained in respective C++ include files. This paper shows performance portability on two different architectures—the new Intel Programmable Integrated Unified Memory Architecture (PIUMA) and state-of-the-art Xeon NUMA Architecture. We share the step-by-step optimization methods and the insights we got from optimizing SU3_Bench on PIUMA and Xeon. We highlight how they are different architecturally, as we believe that this will be valuable to the community.

PIUMA is a Distributed Global Address Space (DGAS) architecture developed under the DARPA HIVE [3] program supporting native scale-out. Thus, the same program works for shared and distributed memory in the conventional sense. Although PIUMA targets sparse and irregular workloads, its design is centered on programmability (OpenMP-style programs can be easily adapted to run on PIUMA, with no difference between shared or distributed memory implementation), performance portability, and scalability. Mapping and analyzing the performance of any HPC workload on such a novel architecture is an interesting learning exercise on its own. Moreover, as a kernel, SU3_Bench is dense and poses a challenge, given how PIUMA is designed for sparse and irregular workloads. Unlike traditional architectures, where the "flops-to-byte" ratio is often a number in the range of 10 to 20 or even higher, on PIUMA this ratio is much smaller (1 to 2) and therefore, is not suitable for flop intensive workloads or kernels. SU_Bench has an arithmetic intensity of 1.35 for single precision (0.675 for double precision). Since PIUMA's arithmetic intensity is also less than 2, SU3_Bench's performance on PIUMA gives us some early insights on how a low flop intensive dense workload would perform on a low flop architecture that targets sparse workloads.

Contributions: We make the following contributions:

- This is the first paper showing the performance modeling of a dense workload on the recently proposed PIUMA [3] architecture.
- We show how to port and optimize SU3_Bench on PIUMA and contrast the optimization needs for PIUMA with Xeon. We show a roofline analysis of

SU3_Bench on PIUMA and Xeon and used that analysis to guide the optimization choices. We show step by step optimization on both platforms that allowed us to obtain close to the attainable peak performance for both platforms.
- We show comparative performance analysis (iso-bandwidth and iso-power) of SU3_Bench on PIUMA vs. Xeon.
- We also show a comparative analysis of performance efficiency with respect to the existing GPU [8] and FPGA [9] results of SU3.

2 Related Work

SU3_Bench development to date has been primarily focused on evaluating various programming models for acceleration using general-purpose GPU computing architectures [8]. Although most of the GPU programming models also support running on CPUs, optimization for NUMA architecture had not been a focus. The current SU3_Bench code has also not been tuned for a very wide SIMD architecture (e.g., AVX512 on Xeon CPUs) either. Tuning for wide SIMD primarily involves remapping the data structures to better expose vectorization opportunities to the compiler. While this has been extensively studied for popular LQCD domain-specific library implementations, for example [10], these implementations also rely on architecture-specific intrinsics that SU3_Bench avoids for portability. Davis [6] performed an extensive study of the OpenMP implementation using a wide variety of compilers, but only investigated the target offload performance on GPUs. Very recent work has shared experience in porting SU3 OpenCL code to FPGAs [9] and reported more than the expected amount of programming effort for the porting. We summarize the performance trends in different architectures in the results section.

Since PIUMA [3] is a relatively new architecture and the hardware is not yet available, all application performance reported on PIUMA used a cycle-accurate simulator. The original paper on PIUMA [3] reports application performance for several sparse workloads including Application Classification, Random Walks, Graph Search, Louvain Community Detection Algorithm, TIES Sampler, Graph2Vec, Graph Sage, Graph Wave, Parallel Decoding FST, Geolocation, SpMV, SpMSpV, and Breadth-First Search. The authors expect an order or two magnitudes of speedup over Xeon (iso-power comparison) for these workloads. PIUMA's large number of threads, 8-byte granularity data access, selective caching, global shared memory and offload engine (e.g., DMA) helped in achieving such speedup and scaling. Another recent research [15] shows how to port the Sinkhorn Word Movers Distance computation to PIUMA which is a mix of sparse and dense compute with relatively lower average arithmetic intensity and shows around 2× speedup for iso power comparison. Some of the optimizations the authors applied for this application on PIUMA are selective caching, use of faster scratchpads, remote atomics, DMAs, and use of build-in transcendental functions.

In contrast, in this paper, we consider a purely dense application and explore porting and optimization options to reach the peak performance.

3 Background on SU3_Bench

In this section, we share details about the SU3_Bench kernel. Figure 1 shows how the kernel looks in its sequential form. The i loop iterates over L^4 sites. Each site has four neighbors, or links, and loop j iterates over them. For each such link, it computes a $3 \times 3 \times 3$ general matrix multiplication (GEMM) among the complex numbers (real, img) representing the links using k, l, and m loops. There are 3×3 matrix elements per link and the innermost m loop is essentially doing a dot product, multiplying a row of $A[i]$'s element matrix with a column of $B[j]$'s link matrix.

```
for (i=0;i<total_sites;++i)     // L^4 sites, nominally L = 32
  for (j=0;j<4;++j)             // 4 "link" SU(3) matrices per site
    for(k=0;k<3;k++)            // 3x3 matrix elements per link
      for(l=0;l<3;l++) {
        cc = {0.0,0.0};
        for(m=0;m<3;m++)        // 3x1 matrix-vector per element
          cc += A[i].link[j].e[k][m] * B[j].e[m][l];
        C[i].link[j].e[k][l] = cc;
      }
```

Fig. 1. SU3_Bench core kernel.

In some sense, SU3_Bench is similar to the STREAM benchmark [7, 12] since it loads SU(3) matrices linearly from memory and stores the multiplication back to memory. This kernel has $\approx (L^4 \times 3 \times 3 \times 3 \times 2)$ compute and $\approx (L^4 \times 3 \times 3 \times 3)$ memory operations and hence is memory-bound on all (or most) modern architectures.

We first consider two key data structures used in the kernel. Figure 2 and Fig. 3 show the definitions for the *su3_matrix* and *site* data structures. An *su3_matrix* is a 3×3 matrix of complex type: for FP32 (single precision) data type, it requires 72 bytes (144 bytes for FP64, or double precision) of storage.

```
typedef struct { std::complex<float> e[3][3]; } fsu3_matrix;
typedef struct { std::complex<double> e[3][3]; } dsu3_matrix;
#if (PRECISION==1)
  #define su3_matrix    fsu3_matrix
#else
  #define su3_matrix    dsu3_matrix
#endif
```

Fig. 2. SU3_Matrix data structure.

The *site* definition (Fig. 3) is based on MILC [14], but reduced to the bare minimum. It contains four links of type *su3_matrix*, coordinates of this site, index in the large site array, and whether the parity is even or odd. It has some padding to make it a multiple of 64 and requires 320 bytes for FP32 or 640 bytes for FP64 type.

Next, we consider the sizes of the input and output arrays and their implications for performance. When $L = 32$ in Fig. 1, the size of site array A would be 320 MiB for FP32 ($32^4 \times 320 = 320$ MiB) and 640 MiB for FP64 data type. Similarly, the output array C would be of the same size as A.

```
typedef struct {
  su3_matrix link[4];  // the fundamental gauge field
  int x,y,z,t;         // coordinates of this site
  int index;           // my index in the array
  char parity;         // is it even or odd?
#if (PRECISION==1)
  int pad[2];          // pad out to 64 byte alignment
#else
  int pad[10];
#endif
} site __attribute__ ((aligned));
```

Fig. 3. Site data structure.

There is no expected cache re-use for A and C outside of the GEMMs. The size of B is 288 bytes for FP32, 576 bytes for FP64 data type, and this size is constant. B could stay in the cache and can be reused. Note that, in most state-of-the-art Xeon machines this data (A, B, and C) will not fit in the L3 cache, which is often of size 40 MiB or less per socket. A and C data would usually need to be streamed from/to memory.

According to Fig. 1, the number of floating point operations for each site is $4 \times (3 \times 3 \times 3)) \times (4 \text{ mul} + 4 \text{ add}) = 4 \times (108 \text{ mul} + 108 \text{ add}) = 4 \times 216 \text{ ops} = 4 \times 216 = 864$. The data size for each of A[i] and C[i] is 320 Bytes for FP32 (single precision) and 640 Bytes for FP64 (double precision) values. Therefore, the arithmetic intensity (AI) is $864/(320 \times 2) = 1.35$ for FP32 data and 0.675 for FP64 data. This calculation ignores reading from B.

The **key takeaway here** is, SU3_Bench is a dense kernel and has a low flops-per-byte requirement. It is expected to be memory bound in standard CPU/GPU architecture and it is interesting to explore whether that is also the case for the new PIUMA architecture that has a low flop-per-byte ratio.

4 Background on PIUMA

In this section, we give an overview of the PIUMA Architecture [3] and contrast that with Xeon.

The PIUMA architecture [3,5,13] consists of a collection of highly multi-threaded cores (MTC) and single-threaded cores (STC) as shown in Fig. 4. The MTCs are round-robin multi-threaded to address the lack of instruction-level parallelism in sparse workloads and incorporate latency hiding through thread-level parallelism instead of aggressive out-of-order or speculative execution models. Each thread can have one in-flight instruction, which simplifies the core design [3]. However, this also can be a limiting factor when an operation (e.g., fused multiply-add (FMA)) requires several data to be loaded before the operation can be executed. In contrast, on Xeon, we typically have only one type of core, that can execute instructions out of order and usually have large vector units to support single instruction multiple data (SIMD) executions as well.

While the MTCs are the data parallel engines in PIUMA, the STCs are used for single-thread performance-sensitive tasks, such as memory allocation and thread management. The cores are in-order stall-on-use scalar cores. Each core's offload region in Fig. 4 contains a direct memory access (DMA) engine that executes gather, scatter, copy, initialization, reduction, and broadcast operations. The DMA engine supports executing atomic operations at the remote destinations [3]. In contrast, Xeons typically do not have DMA engines or support for remote atomics.

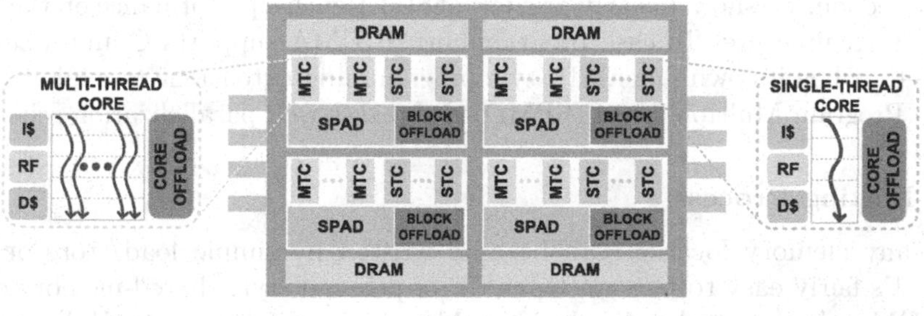

Fig. 4. High-level diagram of PIUMA architecture (collected from [3]).

All the cores have a local instruction cache (I$), data cache (D$), and register file (RF) and support selective data caching through the use of a unique bit in the address space. Caches are not coherent across the whole system to provide better scalability [3]. For correctness, a programmer may need to flush caches if shared data is modified.

The MTC and STC cores are grouped into blocks and each of them has a faster local scratchpad (SPAD) as low latency storage that can be used for optimizations such as double buffering. Data is not automatically cached (except thread-local stacks) and the programmers select which memory accesses to cache (e.g., local stack), which to put on SPAD (e.g., frequently reused data structures or the result of a DMA gather operation), and which to store on the shared global memory. There are no default prefetchers (to save bandwidth and energy and avoid wastage). Instead, the offload engines are used to efficiently fetch large chunks of data when needed [3]. In contrast, on Xeon, everything is automatically cached and prefetched. Xeon usually does not have SPAD, however, its last level cache is usually large. There is only one type of memory where everything gets allocated.

On PIUMA, there is no implementation difference between accessing local and remote memory [3]. However, PIUMA is not a large shared memory machine; rather, it's a collection of cores grouped hierarchically into blocks, dies, subnodes, and nodes, sharing a distributed global address space (DGAS). PIUMA implements the DGAS paradigm in hardware, giving each core a uniform view of the memory of the full system in one address space. This provides native hardware support for a wide variety of programming models. The memory controllers (one per block) can support native 8-byte accesses while supporting standard cache line accesses as well [3]. In contrast, Xeon only supports cache line width accesses.

PIUMA has a high-radix, low-diameter HyperX topology network which is optimized for 8-byte messages. PIUMA is designed to have higher/equal network bandwidth compared to the local DRAM bandwidth which is different from conventional architectures that assume higher local traffic than remote traffic [3].

PIUMA is a data accelerator and a Xeon works as a host to offload/launch the job to PIUMA in a seamless manner.

5 SU3_Bench on PIUMA

In this section, we show an early preview of SU3_Bench's performance on the new PIUMA architecture. To ease programming, PIUMA supports C and a subset of C++. It has its own OpenMP style programming extensions to exploit both Single Program Multiple Data (SPMD) and task-based parallelization schemes.

5.1 Porting Process

Since any memory location can be read/written by simple load/store operations, it's fairly easy to port an OpenMP or pthread style shared-memory code to PIUMA. We started with the OpenMP code available on GitHub [2] and simplified it to fit our needs. The most substantial changes were:

- We changed the main program to include PIUMA library header files and the Makefile to support PIUMA runtime.
- We used PIUMA specific memory allocation/free libraries which are specialized for DGAS allocations.

We split the workload equally among the MTC threads using an SPMD parallelization scheme by dividing the number of sites (i loop in Fig. 1). We used the STCs only for memory allocations/deallocations and the MTCs to initialize and execute the main kernel in parallel.

Since PIUMA supports a variety of memory allocation options, the porting process involves deciding how to allocate various data structures in memory and data gets allocated based on the instruction provided (no default first-touch policy [11]). By default, PIUMA uses an interleaved/striped memory allocation policy. For a program running on M blocks with M memory controllers, any memory allocation is striped in round-robin chunks across those memory controllers. This helps ensure even distribution of access pressure across the memory controllers and reduces queueing latency and conflicts for randomly accessed data. For our initial porting effort, we allocated everything in the main memory, striped across memory controllers. This default allocation does not appear to be the best allocation policy, since SU3_Bench has strictly sequential access. The best option would be to allocate data close to the memory controller where the accessing threads are. However, this research shows that since PIUMA is a DGAS system and the network bandwidth matches the local memory bandwidth, even when striping results in mostly remote accesses, we can achieve a substantial percentage of the peak memory bandwidth of the system.

Recall that PIUMA allows a program to selectively cache data by setting a given bit in its address. Caches are small in size. Additionally, data is not automatically prefetched. We initially chose to cache both A and B.

Simulation and Modeling. We have used a modified Sniper simulator [4] to simulate[1] the PIUMA system in a cycle-accurate manner. Since we run the code on a simulator that can be over $10,000\times$ slower compared to running on the actual hardware, it restricted our ability to simulate large problems and more iterations. The original code runs some warmup iterations (parameter -W) to warm up the caches. To reduce simulation time, we removed warmups on PIUMA while running the experiments. It had almost no impact on performance.

5.2 Roofline Analysis on PIUMA

To understand what to expect in terms of performance on PIUMA, we show the roofline analysis (Fig. 5) in the following section. In Sect. 3, we show that the arithmetic intensity of SU3_Bench for FP64 data type is 0.675 and PIUMA's effective flops-per-byte ratio is 1.25 (when only MTCs are used). Therefore, without further analysis, one can assume that for FP64 data, SU3_Bench's performance will

[1] We are in the power-on phase of a PIUMA system and we plan to update and integrate the simulated results with actual experimental data.

be bandwidth bound and for FP32 data, it will be compute-bound (needing 1.35 flops-per-byte). However, the details are a little more complicated. We focus on the FP64 case in the following.

If compute bound, the performance of SU3_Bench on PIUMA would be limited by the 8 GF/s peak (assuming 1 GHz clock) if all multiply-add operations were done using FMAs. If not using FMAs, the theoretical peak flop is 4 GF/s.

The upper bound imposed by memory bandwidth on performance on PIUMA is 4.32 GF/s ($\approx 0.675 \times MainMemoryBW$).

Apart from these two theoretical upper bounds, there is a third aspect of PIUMA that may dictate the performance of the SU3_Bench kernel and that is the rate of instruction issued per cycle. Since PIUMA has single-issue in-order scalar cores, the instruction mix limits how many cycles can be spent issuing FMAs, due to the need of loading and eventually storing data from the same scalar pipeline. For example, if we revisit the SU3_Bench kernel shown in Fig. 1, we see in the innermost dot product loop that for each element of C we need 12 FMAs and at least 12 loads for A and B in total and 2 stores for C. In other words, to produce 24 FLOPs, at least 12 loads, 2 stores, and 12 FMAs need to be executed. This leads to 24/(12 + 2 + 12) GF/s per pipeline and 3.7 GF/s per PIUMA core. Therefore, according to roofline analysis, we can only expect to get the minimum of the above three as the maximum performance, i.e., 3.7 GF/s from a single PIUMA core.

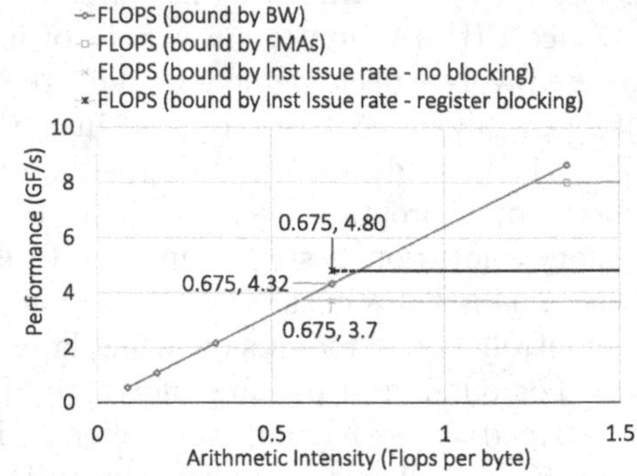

Fig. 5. Roofline model on PIUMA.

Thus, on PIUMA, the pipeline throughput or the instruction execution rate becomes the limiting factor. This is different from Xeon, where the performance is typically limited by FLOPs or Bandwidth. Since the performance on PIUMA is instruction throughput bound, we did not try SPAD optimizations or DMAs as it is unlikely that would improve performance.

5.3 Optimization on PIUMA

When we run our initial ported version of SU3_Bench on PIUMA simulator with L = 16, we obtained 2.14 GF/s, and an average DRAM bandwidth utilization of 74%, with an IPC (Instructions Per Cycle) of 3.7 for FP64 data. Thus, our initial implementation on PIUMA did not reach the roofline.

Register Blocking. We inspected the generated code and realized that it had a few extra instructions to handle register spilling and the compiler was unable to generate FMA instructions for all the updates. We realized that the $3 \times 3 \times 3$ complex GEMM might be too big for the simple MTC pipelines of PIUMA, causing frequent register spills. Instead, a tiled GEMM of size 2×3 of A times 3×3 of B followed by 1×3 of A times 3×3 of B could be a better approach.

The tiled multiplication of complex $A[2 \times 3]$ by $B[3 \times 3]$ requires 12 loads from A, 18 loads from B, and does 12 stores to C. Also, it requires $2 \times 3 \times 3$ complex multiplications, or 72 FMAs. A tiled multiplication of $A[1 \times 3]$ by $B[3 \times 3]$ requires 6 loads from A, 18 loads from B, and does 6 stores to C and requires $1 \times 3 \times 3$ complex multiplications, or 36 FMAs. Overall, the upper bound of FLOPs when limited by instruction issue rate in this case is $2 \times (72 + 36)/(12 + 18 + 12 + 72 + 6 + 18 + 6 + 36) = 1.2\,\text{GF/s}$ per pipeline and $4.8\,\text{GF/s}$ per MTC core. Thus, tiled GEMM improves the roofline bound compared to using dot product in the innermost loop and the achievable peak flop becomes $4.32\,\text{GF/s}$ bounded by the memory bandwidth.

FP32 Packed Store. Since PIUMA cores read/write at 8-byte granularity, for FP32 data types, we packed the real and the imaginary parts of a complex number into one 8-byte using bit shift and OR operators while storing them. This helped us to avoid the inefficiency of storing real and imaginary parts separately and saved one store operation and bandwidth.

Performance on PIUMA. We ran this tiled GEMM with L = 32 for FP64 (double precision) data type for 4 iterations.

We get 3.72 GF/s, and a bandwidth of 5.1 GB/s on one core (or block) of PIUMA. We strong scaled the problem up to 128 cores, where it obtains 244 GF/s and is around 70× faster than 1 PIUMA core for FP64 type and 105× faster for FP32 type. Figure 6 shows the strong scaling for L = 32, Iterations, I = 4, FP64, and FP32 data types. SU3_Bench appears to scale well up to 128 cores (16 dies and 8192 MTC threads).

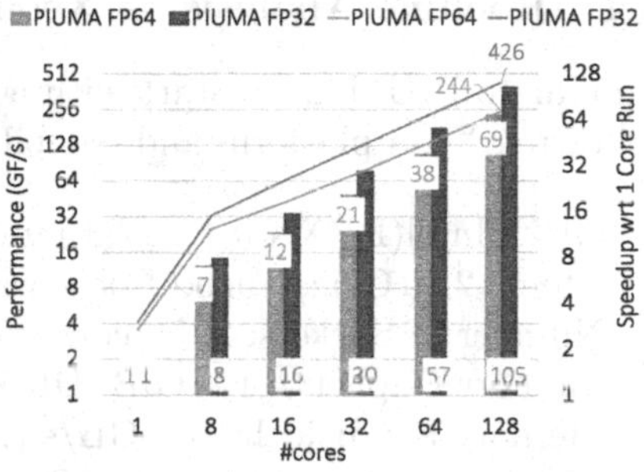

Fig. 6. Strong scaling on PIUMA.

Note that, there are 128 cores on 16 dies of PIUMA and these cores are distributed across those dies communicating using the inter die networks. Figure 6 suggests that, when running across multiple dies, the NUMA effects do not have a significant impact on performance, which is often a problem on multi-socket Xeon systems. There is a slightly better strong scaling for FP32, as its arithmetic intensity is higher and has 2× the cycles per load (compared to FP64) and also uses fewer cache lines with the 3×3 blocking. As we increase the number of cores, the uncore latency and imbalance/sync-delay gradually increase. For FP64, the barrier cost increased noticeably from 1 die to 2 dies (2% to 8%) in addition to the remote access latency. However, the impact on scaling is insignificant.

To **summarize**, what we learned from our exercise of porting SU3_Bench to PIUMA is as follows: on PIUMA where cores have simple scalar pipelines, the performance of the SU3_Bench kernel is limited by the effective instruction issue rate. PIUMA follows a non-conventional stripped allocation policy and both the memory and the network are optimized for 8-byte accesses granularity. With a few optimizations, the SU3_Bench kernel was able to obtain good performance up to 16 dies (8192 threads) of PIUMA distributed across the DGAS memory system. Considering performance portability, it was relatively easy to reach close to PIUMA's architectural peak for SU3_Bench, even though PIUMA has not been optimized for dense workloads.

6 Performance on Xeon

Originally, SU3_Bench had been mainly optimized for GPUs [8] (code available on GitHub [2]). It was missing an optimized version for Intel Xeon CPUs. The mainline OpenMP code failed to saturate the bandwidth of a Xeon socket.

In this section, we discuss the challenges in obtaining peak performance on a state-of-the-art Intel Xeon system, and show how the subtleties of variable definition, value initialization of C++ standard template library (STL), and the NUMA nature of the machine affect the performance of SU3_Bench. The NUMA optimization we discussed here has been integrated into the SU3_Bench GitHub repository [2].

6.1 Roofline Analysis on Xeon

Similar to PIUMA, we start with a roofline analysis. For analysis, we used the following Xeon platform and compiler:

- CPU: Intel(R) Xeon(R) Platinum 8280 CPU (CLX 8280)
- Clock: 2.70 GHz, Turbo Boost was ON by default
- Number of Sockets: 2, 56 cores, 56 threads
- Memory Capacity: 196 GiB (DRAM), 39.4 MiB (L3), 1 MiB (L2), 32 KiB (L1)
- Memory bandwidth: 105 GB/s (1 socket).
- STREAM bandwidth: 200 GB/s (2 sockets).
- Compiler: Intel(R) 64 Version 2020

Each core has 2 SIMD units with 8 lanes per unit and each of those lanes can execute two flops per cycle. Therefore, the maximum GFLOPS per second (GF/s) on this core is = 86.4 = 2.7 GHz $\times$ 2 SIMD units $\times$ 8 lanes/SIMD unit $\times$ 2 FLOPs/lane. On a single socket with 28 cores, maximum GF/s is 2150.4. The maximum bandwidth per single socket is = 105 GB/s. Therefore, the flops per byte ratio of this architecture is 20.5 = 2150.4/105 for FP64. The arithmetic intensity of the SU3_Bench kernel is 1.35 for FP32 data (0.675 for FP64 data) type and therefore, SU3_Bench should be bandwidth bound on Xeon.

Figure 7 shows the theoretical roofline analysis of SU3_Bench on this Xeon. Because of the way data structures have been implemented (see Fig. 2, 3), it is difficult for compilers to identify vectorization opportunities for the inner loop (see Fig. 1), especially for CPUs with wide SIMD units. Assuming only 1 lane per each of the 2 SIMD units are used, the peak performance for a single-core is 10.4 GF/s and for a single socket, it is 141.8 GF/s. The peak performance with 1 SIMD unit and 1 lane per unit utilization is 5.4 GF/s for a core and 141.8 GF/s for a socket. Lastly, the peak performance with 1 SIMD unit and 1 lane per unit without any FMA utilization is 2.7 GF/s for a core and 75.6 GF/s for a socket.

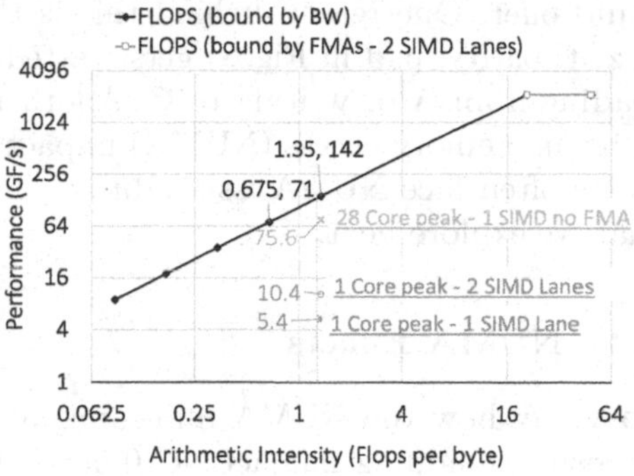

Fig. 7. Roofline model on Xeon.

6.2 SU3 Implementation

Since we are interested in performance on Xeon, we built on top of the existing OpenMP implementation. Originally, there were four OpenMP versions in the GitHub repository, each of which uses different "#pragma omp target teams" constructs on the i, j, k, and l loops. There is an additional outermost loop that runs the core kernel a given number of iterations (I) and warmup (W) times to provide stable performance data.

Despite having four versions, the SU3_Bench OpenMP implementation was missing a very basic OpenMP loop structure of "#pragma omp parallel for" on the i loop. The "#pragma omp target teams distribute num_teams (num_teams) thread_limit (threads_per_team)" directive used in the original four versions creates a league of teams each with (threads_per_team) threads to hierarchically distribute the threads which might be unnecessary for Xeon CPUs. We added a simple implementation of SU3_Bench with "#pragma omp parallel for" on the i loop and called it `VersionX`. VersionX is faster than all prior OpenMP versions of SU3_Bench, most likely due to not being burdened by the overhead of hierarchical threading of teams. In the rest of this section, we focus on VersionX.

6.3 Performance on Xeon

Table 1 shows the initial performance of VersionX on two sockets of CLX 8280. Since the CLX 8280 is a NUMA machine, to reduce NUMA impact, we set the thread affinity to be `compact`. Table 1 shows that the performance on two sockets is close to half of what we expected from the roofline analysis. The value of L, in this case, is 32, so, none of the arrays other than B would fit in the cache completely, and data should be streamed from memory. However, the maximum bandwidth obtained is only 75 GB/s which is lower than what even one socket could offer. One reason behind this is that some portion of each site data (x, y, z, t, parity, pad in Fig. 3) gets wasted (around 10% of the bandwidth) while reading from A or writing to C. Another reason could be the well-known non-uniform memory access (NUMA) impact – on two sockets of Xeon, unoptimized codes often face NUMA issues due to higher access latency to a remote socket that we explore next.

6.4 NUMA Effects

To verify how the NUMA imbalance affects performance, we rerun the above experiment adding numactl -C 0-55 -N 0,1 -m 0,1 to the command line while running the program to use both nodes 0 and 1 for the compute resources and memory allocation. The second row of Table 1 shows the performance data. Controlling NUMA allocation marginally improves performance for a single iteration (-I 1 -W 1). However, the obtained bandwidth is still 54.4 GB/s—only half of the single socket's streaming bandwidth. Also, notice that the performance degraded for 100 or 200 iterations compared to not using numactl. As a result, the maximum bandwidth obtained is reduced to only 56 GB/s and it did not change much by increasing the number of iterations (increased number of iterations usually makes the loop and OpenMP thread launching overhead negligible).

To get further information on the runs, we used the `Intel Vtune tool` to analyze the performance for the 200 iteration case without using numactl. We found that although the application reported bandwidth (effective bandwidth) was only ≈82 GB/s, the actual bandwidth noted by Vtune is around 182 GB/s—almost double of what the useful bandwidth was. This 182 GB/s is close to 210 GB/s, the maximum offered by the system. It also maxed out the system's UPI bandwidth (68.9 GB/s) indicating substantial cross-socket traffic.

6.5 Impact of Page Migration

In order to explain the dependency on the number of iterations and numactl, we looked at the impact of automatic page migration. The Linux memory management subsystem, unless directed otherwise, supports migrating pages between NUMA nodes to improve the locality of the accesses. The use of numactl prevents automatic page migrations, automatic NUMA balancing, and automatic NUMA placement of an application [1]. Therefore, whatever beneficial page migrations were happening with more iterations got stopped with the use of numactl flag.

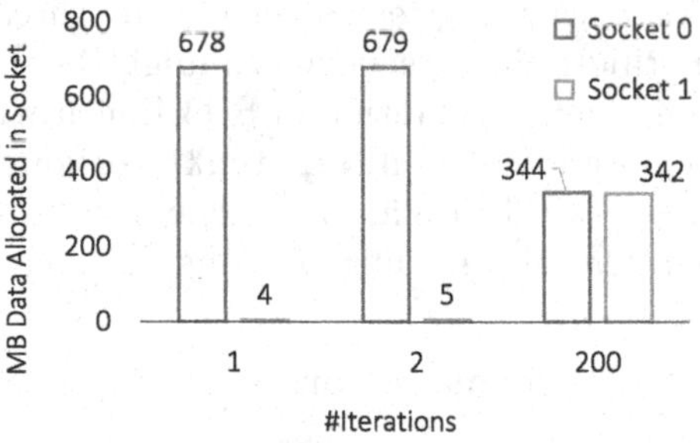

Fig. 8. Total page sizes at different sockets.

Table 1. Performance of VersionX, with and without using **numactl** to control affinity. I and W indicate number of total iterations and warmup iterations respectively.

Runs	-I 200 -W 1		-I 100 -W 1		-I 1 -W 1	
	GF/s	GB/s	GF/s	GB/s	GF/s	GB/s
Without numactl	100.8	74.7	76.4	56.6	73.3	54.3
With numactl	75.0	55.6	74.9	55.5	73.5	54.4

We developed a custom library to print the allocated memory in each socket and Fig. 8 shows that with an increased number of iterations, the distribution of the pages allocated to each socket becomes more balanced as Linux migrates pages closer to the node where the thread is. Since threads are pinned, each page is migrated at most once, and increasing the number of iterations amortizes the migration cost over a longer execution time. That is why with numactl off, performance improves with iterations. However, if numactl is on, the automatic page migration stops and as a result, the performance remains the same other than smoothing out the thread launching and cache warmup overheads.

The above results indicate that during allocation, the data is mainly placed in the first socket.

6.6 Parallel Initialization

As a commonly practiced solution, we parallelized the data initialization routine making sure the memory access pattern mirrored the ones used during time-sensitive compute phases. This allows us to take advantage of the first touch page allocation policy, guaranteeing that data is allocated with proper affinity to the NUMA node that will use it the most.

We added empty default constructors for *site* and *su3_matrix* objects, to prevent the STL containers from performing value initialization on them. The C++ standard mandates that upon construction, containers zero-initialize their elements under certain circumstances, including those that arise in SU3 (shown in Fig. 9). When this is applied to a global shared container, whose constructor is generally called before entering a parallel region, zero-initialization results in the main thread accessing all the elements, with the consequent slowdown and sub-optimal first-touch placement. We measured the imbalance resulting from not providing empty default constructors. Figure 10 shows that the data gets allocated and touched on socket 0 during the declaration of the variables itself when empty default constructors are not provided.

```
std::vector<site> a(total_sites);
std::vector<su3_matrix> b(4);
std::vector<site> c(total_sites);
```

Fig. 9. Variable declaration in SU3_Bench.

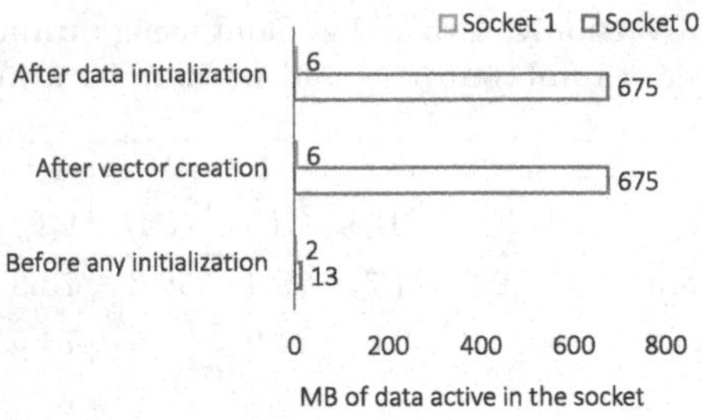

Fig. 10. Amount of data allocated on both sockets at different stages.

Ensuring proper data placement with STL containers, and consequently eliminating page migration (and subsequent bandwidth wastage) issues, improves performance by 2.6× over the naive implementation, resulting in 143.46 GB/s effective memory bandwidth and 193.54 GF/s floating-point performance on the 2 sockets (56 cores) of CLX8280—69% of 210 GB/s (close to peak considering 20% wastage in bandwidth for A and C).

How Xeon Optimizations are Different from PIUMA. If we contrast the above optimization efforts with the optimization efforts on PIUMA, it emerges that we did not pin threads or needed to resort to default constructors to obtain good performance across dies for PIUMA. The data was evenly distributed across memory controllers. The effect of data placement on PIUMA was negligible, making it a competitive option for performance portability. This result is also different from the experience in porting this benchmark to FPGAs [9] where the authors reported that interleaved data allocations across different memory channels led to poor performance.

6.7 Additional Optimizations and Performance

Strong Scaling. Figure 11 shows strong scaling of VersionX on Xeon. We see a linear increase in performance from 1 to 14 cores, minimal performance improvement from 14 to 28 cores since it had already saturated the single socket bandwidth with 14 cores), then a linear performance increase from 29 to 56 cores, albeit, with a smaller slope than 1 to 14 cores.

This strong scaling trend matches our expectation considering a non-NUMA software whose performance is not sensitive to NUMA issues. The speedup line in Fig. 11 shows that till 28 cores (i.e., within a single NUMA domain), the performance for both with and without the empty constructor is similar. However, beyond one socket, the version with an empty constructor is over 2× faster than the original one. The total speedup obtained using 56 cores (compared to one core run) is 32.4×.

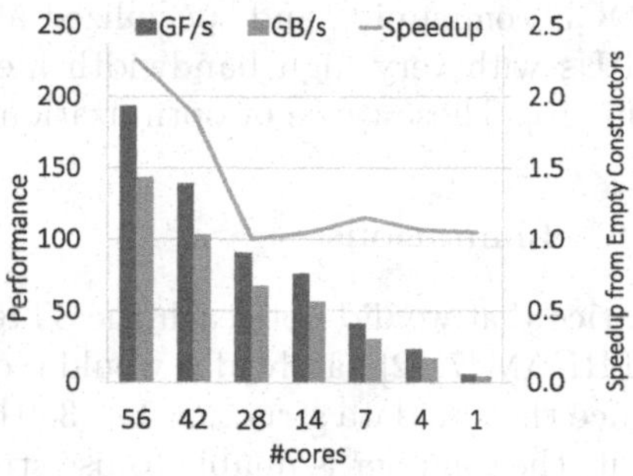

Fig. 11. Strong scaling (with and without empty constructor). Input, L = 32 -I 1 -W 1, data type: FP32

Note that for a bandwidth-bound kernel the expected maximum speedup from 56 cores is around 21× if one core can drive up to 10 GB/s STREAM bandwidth. This implementation of SU3_Bench obtaining 32.4× speedup indicates inefficiency of the single-core run which obtains 4.34 GB/s bandwidth in this case (recall that roofline shows single core can achieve 10.4 GF/s and hence, 8 GB/s of bandwidth).

Improving Single Core Performance. At this point, although the performance improvement on two sockets is satisfactory and relatively close to the peak, the single-core performance (5.85 GF/s) appeared to be indicative of the case where only 1 SIMD unit is used or the case where 2 SIMD units are used without any FMA. This motivated us to use explicit general matrix multiplication (GEMM) and FMA instructions instead of depending on the compiler to do so. We replaced the k, l, m loops with an explicit $3 \times 3 \times 3$ GEMM routine that manually called the FMA instructions after unrolling all products. This improved performance by 1.6×–1.8× up to 8 cores (see Fig. 12). However, at 28 cores, the performance improvement is only 11%, and at 56 cores, it is down to 0%. We observe a significant variance in performance from run to run at 56 cores for this version. Additionally, we had to use the compiler flag -xCORE-AVX512 and without this flag, the performance goes down below the original version.

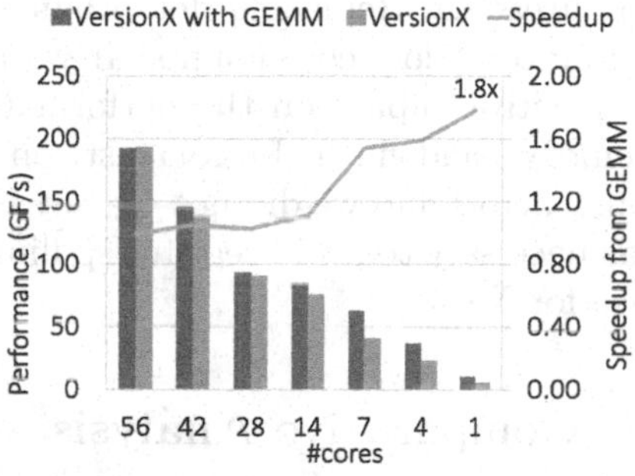

Fig. 12. Using GEMM instead of dot product. Input, L = 32 -I 1 -W 1, data type: FP32

This suggests that doing the manual GEMM allowed it to use AVX units. The single-core performance of this version reaches the peak performance of 2 SIMD units (10.4 GF/s). The total speedup with 56 cores, in this case, is 18.4× with respect to its one core run. Full SIMD utilization is a known issue in the

LQCD community, and specialized libraries have been developed for Intel Xeon CPUs with very high bandwidth memory subsystems, such as the Intel Xeon Phi [10]. Those types of optimizations are outside the scope of this paper.

6.8 Limitations

Notice that we did not reach the STREAM bandwidth of the system. Obtaining STREAM [7,12] bandwidth would require us to use streaming write instructions. Since the *site* data structure has 320 bytes size and we are only writing 288 bytes of it, the compiler is unable to use streaming writes because of the gaps between writes. Reading efficiency is also lowered by the same issue. Using arrays of structures of arrays (AOSOA) might help which is outside the scope of this paper since minimal changes in the code is desired.

6.9 Lessons Learned

From our porting effort to Xeon we learned that not providing a default constructor could create a potentially unexpected performance problem by allocating memory on single NUMA node at creation. Using an empty constructor and then initializing memory in parallel solves the issue. Simple OpenMP pragma provides good (and better) performance for SU3_Bench compared to hierarchical threading. Replacing dot products with a tiled GEMM only improves performance at low core counts. If we are running on the full system, tiling has no positive impact on the performance due to the increased saturation of the memory bandwidth. In contrast, on PIUMA, we did not have to add special constructors and we did not see any NUMA issue there. On PIUMA, 3×3 tiling was necessary to avoid register spilling and not for better vectorization (as is the case for Xeon).

7 Comparative Analysis

7.1 Comparison with Xeon

In this section, we compare the performance of PIUMA with that of Xeon. Figure 13 compares strong scaling of SU3_Bench on both platforms. With L = 32 for FP64 (double precision) data, and for 4 iterations, one PIUMA core is 1.57× slower than the CLX core and this difference is justified by the bandwidth difference among the two platforms. Eight PIUMA cores are 1.42× slower than 8 CLX cores. Again, this performance is consistent with the gap in bandwidth between the two. However, the speedup from 8 cores on PIUMA is 6.61× and for CLX, it is 6.04×. Sixteen cores of PIUMA are on par with 16 CLX cores because the bandwidths are on par too.

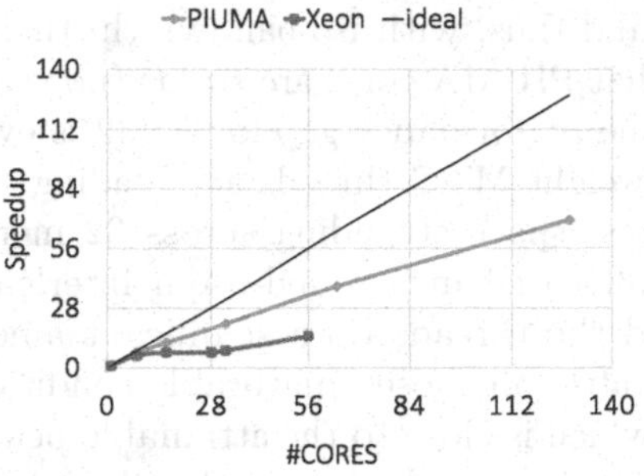

Fig. 13. Strong scaling, input: L = 32 -I 4 - W 1, data type: FP64.

At 32 cores, PIUMA is 1.48× faster than 32 cores of CLX. This happens mainly due to the difference between the effective bandwidth that each of these platforms can obtain and the fact that PIUMA supports 8-byte accesses and hence wastes less bandwidth than CLX. At 32 cores, PIUMA cores get 108 GB/s whereas Xeon gets 73.8 GB/s. PIUMA appears to strong scale better than Xeon as shown by Fig. 13. Although Xeon's architectural flops-per-byte ratio is 20.5 and PIUMA's effective flops-per-byte ratio is 1.25 (when only MTCs are used), PIUMA wins here in the effective usage of that flops-per-byte for a benchmark with 0.675 flops-per-byte need.

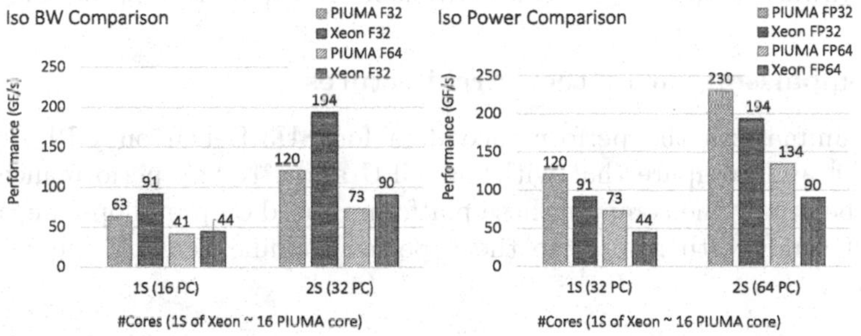

Fig. 14. PIUMA vs. Xeon iso comparison, input: L = 32 -I 4 - W 1, data type: FP64.

Instead of core-to-core comparison, next, we perform an iso-bandwidth comparison. In an ideal scenario, 32 cores of PIUMA should be able to drive the same bandwidth of 2 sockets of CLX8280, and 16 cores of PIUMA should be able to drive the same amount of bandwidth as one socket of Xeon. Figure 14 shows that 16 PIUMA cores are slower than 1 socket of Xeon (1 socket of Xeon is about 44% faster than 16 PIUMA cores for FP32 types) and 2 sockets of Xeon is about 60% faster than 32 cores of PIUMA. For FP64 type, on the other hand, 16 PIUMA cores are on par with Xeon, and 32 PIUMA cores are 24% slower than two sockets of Xeon. On PIUMA, the instruction issue rate is a limiting factor for SU3_Bench, and thus, with iso-bandwidth, there was still the performance gap. Also note that PIUMA cores are scalar (no vector units and in-order executions) and thus, the performance gap for FP32 is even higher than FP64. At 32 cores, 8192 lightweight MTC threads are reading and writing across the distributed global address space stranding across 32 memory controllers. Furthermore, the data is allocated in a round-robin interleaved format across all memory controllers and the threads do a significant amount of remote access while computing. Even after all those unfavorable conditions, the obtained performance is promising which is close to the attainable peak. The lessons learned from these comparison results and the potential architectural significance should be helpful.

Now, if we perform an iso-power comparison, PIUMA cores would be faster than Xeon ones on both FP32 and FP64 types as shown in Fig. 14 right side. For FP32 type, PIUMA cores are 20% to 33% faster and for FP64, PIUMA cores are about 49% to 64% faster than Xeon cores.

It appears that the best part of PIUMA for SU3_Bench is the native scale-out and ease of programming. Remember the minimal optimizations we had to do to port and optimize the code for PIUMA to get them close to the roofline performance. Despite not being architecturally designed for dense and flop-intensive workload, PIUMA was able to shine on the SU3_Bench microkernel showing hope for applicability for quantum chromodynamics HPC workloads.

As mentioned earlier, PIUMA hardware is not yet available and we hope that it will be available soon. We plan to verify our projected/simulated performance on the hardware as soon as it becomes available and share it with the community.

7.2 Comparison with Other Architectures

Table 2 summarizes the performance data for SU3_Bench on GPUs [8] and FPGAs [9] and compare that with our CPU and PIUMA performance. Since it would be unfair the compare these platforms based on pure flops, we can look at the efficiency with respect to the expected roofline peak on the respective platform.

Table 2. Comparison with other architectures. The data for GPU and FPGA is reprinted from [8] and [9].

Platform	Obtained GF/S	Efficiency %	Flops-per-byte
GPU: Nvidia V100	1111	86.9	16
GPU: AMD Vega 20	908	66.9	14
GPU: Intel Gen9	34.6	99	23
Xeon: Intel Xeon (CLX)	193.5	85	40
DGAS: Intel PIUMA	230.3	75	<2
FPGA: Intel Arria 10 GX	16.1	47.6	NA
FPGA: Xilinx Alveo U280	6.2	35.2	NA

On Intel Gen9, performance is close to 99% of the peak, on AMD Vega, it is 66.9%, on Nvidia V100, performance is close to 86.9% of the peak, on Xeon, performance is close to 85% of the peak and on PIUMA, performance is close to 75% of the peak. To put them in perspective of flops per byte ratio (single precision), V100 offers a sustained flop per byte ratio of 16, AMD Vega has 14, Gen9 has 23, Xeon (CLX) has 40 and PIUMA has less than 2. We believe that our study shows that PIUMA, based on an entirely different design paradigm and not based around compute throughput, can still be competitive on dense regular applications like SU3, once we take into account the scalability of the design, keeping the ease of programmability of a shared memory system.

8 Conclusion

To summarize, this paper talks about SU3_Bench, a microbenchmark derived from LQCD to test performance portability. We show its performance portability on two very different architectures—a state-of-the-art Xeon and the new Intel's Programmable Integrated Unified Memory Architecture (PIUMA). We show how to port the SU3_Bench to PIUMA with a few changes in the standard Xeon code to obtain good performance and how the effective instruction issue rate can impact application performance on PIUMA. Alternatively, this paper also serves as a use case study for porting "dense codes with low arithmetic intensity" to the PIUMA architecture that is primarily designed for sparse workloads. We learned that despite PIUMA's low architectural flop-per-byte capacity and non-conventional memory allocation policy, such a code (SU3_Bench) can obtain close to the peak performance in the system.

References

1. NUMA Balancing in RedHat. https://access.redhat.com/documentation/en-us/red_hat_enterprise_linux/7/html/virtualization_tuning_and_optimization_guide/sect-virtualization_tuning_optimization_guide-numa-auto_numa_balancing
2. SU3_Bench. https://gitlab.com/NERSC/nersc-proxies/su3_bench
3. Aananthakrishnan, S., et al.: PIUMA: programmable integrated unified memory architecture. arXiv preprint arXiv:2010.06277 (2020)
4. Carlson, T.E., Heirman, W., Eyerman, S., Hur, I., Eeckhout, L.: An evaluation of high-level mechanistic core models. ACM Trans. Archit. Code Optim. **11**(3), 1–25 (2014). https://doi.org/10.1145/2629677
5. David, S.: DARPA ERI: HIVE and Intel PUMA Graph Processor. WikiChip Fuse (2019). https://fuse.wikichip.org/news/2611/darpa-eri-hive-and-intel-puma-graph-processor/
6. Davis, J.H., Daley, C., Pophale, S., Huber, T., Chandrasekaran, S., Wright, N.J.: Performance assessment of OpenMP compilers targeting NVIDIA V100 GPUs. In: Bhalachandra, S., Wienke, S., Chandrasekaran, S., Juckeland, G. (eds.) WACCPD 2020. LNCS, vol. 12655, pp. 25–44. Springer, Cham (2021). https://doi.org/10.1007/978-3-030-74224-9_2
7. Deakin, T.: BableStream Benchmark (2017). http://uob-hpc.github.io/BabelStream/

8. Doerfler, D., Daley, C., Applencourt, T.: SU3_Bench, a micro-benchmark for exploring exascale era programming models, compilers and runtimes. In: 2020 Performance, Portability, and Productivity in HPC Forum (2020)
9. Doerfler, D., et al.: Experiences porting the SU3_bench microbenchmark to the Intel Arria 10 and Xilinx Alveo U280 FPGAs. In: International Workshop on OpenCL, pp. 1–9 (2021)
10. Jeffers, J., Reinders, J., Sodani, A.: Quantum chromodynamics. In: Intel Xeon Phi Processor High Performance Programming: Knights Landing Edition, 2nd edn. Morgan Kaufmann Publishers Inc., San Francisco (2016)
11. Lameter, C.: NUMA (non-uniform memory access): an overview. ACM Queue **11**(7) (2013). https://dl.acm.org/ft_gateway.cfm?id=2513149&ftid=1388705&dwn=1
12. McCalpin, J.D.: STREAM: Sustainable Memory Bandwidth in High Performance Computers. https://www.cs.virginia.edu/stream/
13. McCreary, D.: Intel's Incredible PIUMA Graph Analytics Hardware. Medium (2020). https://dmccreary.medium.com/intels-incredible-piuma-graph-analytics-hardware-a2e9c3daf8d8
14. MIMD Lattice Collaboration, Bernard, C., et al.: The MILC Code (2010)
15. Tithi, J.J., Petrini, F.: A new parallel algorithm for sinkhorn word-movers distance and its performance on PIUMA and Xeon CPU. CoRR abs/2107.06433 (2021). https://arxiv.org/abs/2107.06433

Machine Learning, AI, and Emerging Technologies

"Hey CAI" - Conversational AI Enabled User Interface for HPC Tools

Pouya Kousha(✉), Arpan Jain, Ayyappa Kolli, Saisree Miriyala, Prasanna Sainath, Hari Subramoni, Aamir Shafi, and Dhableswar K. Panda

The Ohio State University, Columbus, OH 43210, USA
{kousha.2,jain.575,kolli.38,miriyala.6,prasanna.11,shafi.16}@osu.edu, {subramon,panda}@cse.ohio-state.edu

Abstract. HPC system users depend on profiling and analysis tools to obtain insights into the performance of their applications and tweak them. The complexity of modern HPC systems have necessitated advances in the associated HPC tools making them equally complex with various advanced features and complex user interfaces. While these interfaces are extensive and detailed, they require a steep learning curve even for expert users making them harder to use for novice users. While users are intuitively able to express what they are looking for in words or text (e.g., show me the process transmitting maximum data), they find it hard to quickly adapt to, navigate, and use the interface of advanced HPC tools to obtain desired insights. In this paper, we explore the challenges associated with designing a conversational (speech/text) interface for HPC tools. We use state-of-the-art AI models for speech and text and adapt it for use in the HPC arena by retraining them on a new HPC dataset we create. We demonstrate that our proposed model, retrained with an HPC specific dataset, can deliver higher accuracy than the existing state-of-the-art pre-trained language models. We also create an interface to convert speech/text data to commands for HPC tools and show how users can utilize the proposed interface to gain insights quicker leading to better productivity.

To the best of our knowledge, this is the first effort aimed at designing a conversational interface for HPC tools using state-of-the-art AI techniques to enhance the productivity of novice and advanced users alike.

Keywords: Conversational AI · Performance tools · Speech recognition · Natural language processing

1 Introduction and Motivation

Recently, High-Performance Computing (HPC) has been empowering advances in Artificial Intelligence (AI) and Deep Learning (DL). Popular DL frameworks such as TensorFlow [1] and PyTorch [26] are adopting high-performance messaging libraries for scaling-out workloads on HPC platforms [29]. This trend has resulted in AI practitioners and enthusiasts attempting to utilize HPC software

The original version of this chapter was revised: The name of the fourth author was inserted. The correction to this chapter is available at https://doi.org/10.1007/978-3-031-07312-0_19

A.-L. Varbanescu et al. (Eds.): ISC High Performance 2022, LNCS 13289, pp. 87–108, 2022.
https://doi.org/10.1007/978-3-031-07312-0_5

and hardware resources for their applications. It is important for developers of HPC software subsystems to make this transition smoother by enhancing the productivity of HPC tools and libraries for the AI community where the expertise in traditional HPC technologies varies significantly.

One area where new and expert HPC users often struggle, alike, is understanding the performance of their parallel workloads. Analyzing performance bottlenecks for HPC and AI workload is a complicated task. This is, however, critical to improve performance and push boundaries of the state-of-the-art solutions. In this context, the challenge for traditional HPC software, tools, and frameworks is to provide *intuitive* and simple—yet efficient—interfaces to HPC software and hardware resources. *The goal here is to reduce the steep learning curves of HPC tools and libraries.*

There are various tools in HPC for monitoring, analyzing, and characterizing the performance of applications. Profiling tools can be categorized into user-level profiling and system-level profiling based on their usage and provided privileges. For example TAU [22], HPCToolkit [18], and mpiP [2] provide user-level profiling insights while Prometheus [4], TACC STATS [11], and LDMS [9] give us system-level monitoring insights. While HPC tool interfaces are comprehensive and extensive, they require a steep learning curve for learning terminologies and visual interfaces making them very hard to use for novice users with little HPC experience (depicted in Fig. 1). Consider the example of NVIDIA-Nsight [6] or TAU tools that give very detailed insights. Although their interfaces are excellent, navigating and using their interfaces by using keyboard and mouse still requires a lot of learning which includes referring to documentation and going over tutorials and instructional videos - all of which takes time and reduces overall productivity of end users.

This *steep* learning curve reduces the productivity of expert users while deterring new HPC users to even try these tools that are important for identifying and fixing performance bottlenecks. On the other side, most HPC tool users are intuitively able to express what they are looking for in words or text. Unfortunately, there is no user interface available to HPC tools that can accept such forms of user input.

There are alternative interfaces that the user can utilize. Surveys of end users done by firms like [5] and [7] indicate that users are more likely to use a conversational AI interface as opposed to using older keyboard/mouse style inputs. For example in mobile devices graphical user interface (GUI) exists but, over time the users are more interested to perform daily tasks through Alexa or Siri or similar conversational interfaces. This shows that once the capability is introduced the users are likely to benefit from it as part of future interface expansion as conversational interface is more intuitive. Unfortunately, no interface exists that allows end-users to interact with state-of-the-art HPC tools using speech/text.

1.1 Contributions

In this paper, we take up this challenge and attempt to minimize the learning curve and complexities needed to use state-of-the-art performance profiling tools.

Our proposed solution, titled **Conversational AI Interface (CAI)** exploits Automatic Speech Recognition (ASR) and Natural Language Understanding (NLU)—using DL behind the scenes. CAI has a novel Conversational User Interface (CUI) powered by AI/DL to provide relevant and contextual information to end users. In CUI, while ASR models convert spoken language to text, NLU classifies the text into an intent (the overall objective of the query like network topology) and assigns slots (optional arguments to customize the given intent) thereby allowing CAI to convert the conversational AI input to a format that is understood by the profiling tool. Thus, CAI uses a combination of ASR and NLU to realize a AI-based conversational interface for profiling tools that allows users to interact with these tools using ❶ text and ❷ speech. Both of these novel interfaces provide solutions to increase the productivity of users by reducing the learning curve and hiding the complexity of advanced tool interfaces. Note that the aim is not to replace existing GUI-based interfaces for HPC tools but to supplement t hem and enhance the overall user experience. Further, to demonstrate the feasibility of our approach, we take one HPC profiling tool, OSU INAM [8], and create a conversational AI interface for it as a sample case study. Figure 1 depicts a high-level overview and motivation for CAI. As depicted in Fig. 1, we believe such a solution will result in productivity benefits for novice and expert users alike.

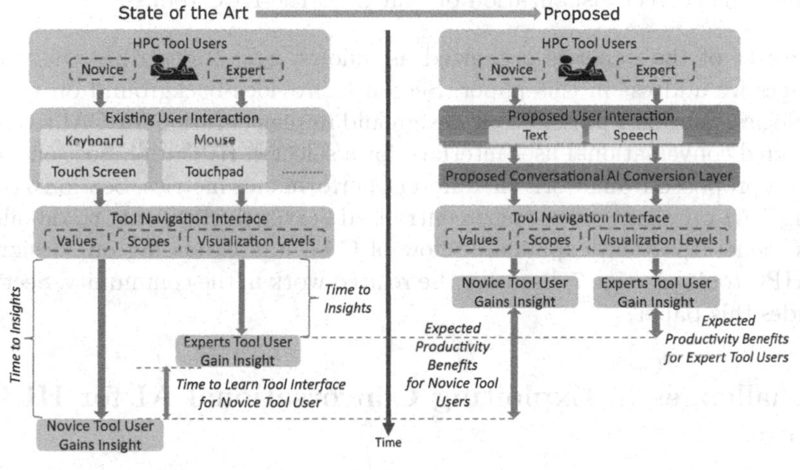

Fig. 1. Comparison HPC tool usage for state-of-the-art and CAI. Insight#1: On the left side, there is a different overhead in getting performance insight for expert vs novice users but the proposed designs would eliminate this overhead. Insight#2: By using text or speech interface the response time for both users will be lower.

To summarize, the key contributions of this paper are as follows:

1. Proposed an AI-based conversational interface for HPC profiling tools that allows users to interact using speech/text.

2. Designed and created the first speech and text datasets that contain HPC specific terminologies for training ASR and NLU models to be used by the HPC community.
3. Fine-tuned Speech2Text and Wav2Vec ASR models with the proposed HPC dataset to convert a speech command to a text command and trained Joint-Bert and StackPropagation NLU models to understand the context of text command.
4. Improved error rate for Speech2Text DL model from 64% to 2.8% for HPC dataset and 27% to 12% for HPC+TIMIT dataset.
5. Reported 93% accuracy for intent classification and 0.8773 score (F1 score) for slot detection using JointBert DL model for NLU on HPC dataset.
6. Compared the performance of DL inference on client/end user systems (e.g. laptops, desktops) that use HPC profiling tools. Also, implemented a centralized server for inferring on an in-house HPC cluster to reduce the latency for slower client/end user systems.
7. Implemented a simple web-based interface for a sample profiling tool and provided visibility into the intermediate results to better understand the data flow and final output.
8. Deployed and tested CAI and the CAI enhanced tool OSU INAM on a state-of-the-art production HPC system and evaluated the ability of CAI to correctly interpret speech/text input from multiple different volunteer users and display the correct visualization output from the HPC tool.

The rest of the paper is organized as follows: Sect. 2 describes the various challenges we address in this paper. Section 3 provides background on relevant technologies. Section 4 presents our design and implementation for CAI to enable AI-powered conversational user interface for a selected HPC tool. Section 5 evaluates our proposed framework via different performance metrics. Section 6 covers running CAI on client side versus centralized server deployment, trade-offs for speech model selection, explainable flow of CAI, and extending our designs to other HPC tools. Section 7 discusses the related work in the community. Section 8 concludes this paper.

2 Challenges in Exploiting Conversational AI for HPC Tools

We highlight the AI-specific and System-specific challenges associated with creating a conversational AI interface for HPC tools in this section.

AI-Challenge-1 (AI-#1): Creating Text and Speech Dataset with HPC Terminologies/Abbreviations—Each scientific field including HPC has its own terminologies and abbreviations—like Central Processing Unit (CPU), Host Channel Adapter (HCA)—that are typically well-understood in the community. We will refer to these as *HPC jargon* in the rest of the paper. Currently, available language datasets naturally do not provide coverage of HPC jargon. To develop

NLU/ASR DL models, the first step is to create such textual and speech-based datasets. To the best of our knowledge, these kinds of datasets do not exist today.

AI-Challenge-2 (AI-#2): Custom ASR Model for HPC—The performance, in terms of accuracy, of existing off-the-shelf ASR models degrades when the input contains HPC jargons. Figure 2 shows a real example of two sentences, representing a typical interaction of a user with an HPC profiling tool, being transformed to wrong texts by existing ASR models. Our evaluation of state-of-the-art ASR models, presented later in Table 2, depict that the Word Error Rate (WER) for such input data is 64.6 and 77.3. For natural languages, the WER is 2. This clearly motivates that need to retrain and fine-tune existing ASR models for HPC-specific dataset.

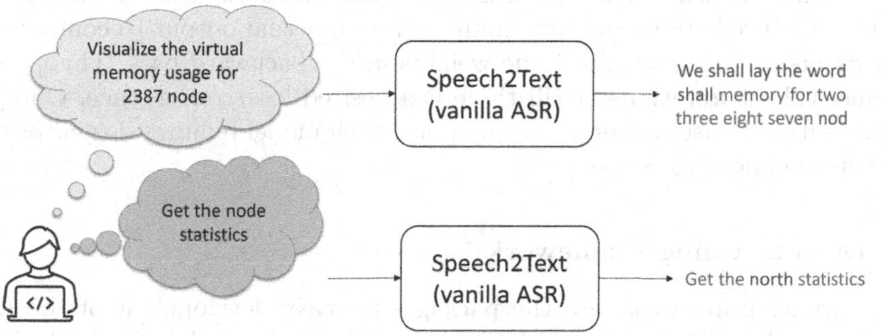

Fig. 2. Real Output of Automatic Speech Recognition (ASR) by Speech2Text model for two HPC phrases - By using original ASR model, HPC phrases on the left would transform to wrong text (in red) on the right (Color figure online)

AI-Challenge-3 (AI-#3): Custom NLU Model for HPC—Existing off-the-shelf NLU models do not have intents and slots required in HPC tools. In fact, there is no existing model nor dataset for NLU for HPC. This motivates the need to retrain off-the-shelf NLU models with hyper parameter tuning using HPC dataset capable of performing well for this kind of input data.

System-Challenge-1 (Sys-#1): Defining Interface between Conversational AI and HPC Tools—A conversational AI interface to a tool requires a layer that can translate and communicate the result of speech/text input from the user to a format the tool understands. This involves labeling missing arguments for specific user intents and proper mapping of these to the tool performance insight features. User input can have multiple values with different formats and the interface should correctly distinguish them. Considering that HPC tools are written in variety of programming languages and have their own framework, it is challenging to ascertain the communication interface, or standard, between the NLU module and the HPC profiling tool.

System-Challenge-2 (Sys-#2): Integration of Conversational AI to HPC Tools—Another system specific challenge is the integration of NLU+ASR models into existing profiling tools. The conversational interface component needs to be modular in order to accommodate better NLU and ASR models in future without a significant revamp. Also, we plan to evaluate the automation of this integration process for an existing profiling tool. A challenge here is to ascertain and minimize the changes needed to enable the end-to-end pipeline.

3 Background

3.1 Deep Neural Networks Training

Deep neural networks (DNNs) are multi-layer variants of traditional Artificial Neural Networks (ANNs). Each layer in DNN is a collection of basic mathematical functions like weighted summation, called neurons. The forward pass is used to make predictions that are compared with actual output to compute the error. Errors are used to adjust the weights in the backward pass. This process continues till set iterations or till there is a desired loss/convergence. One pass over the entire dataset is known as an epoch, each model requires dozens or even hundreds of epochs to converge.

3.2 Deep Learning Frameworks

Deep learning frameworks are the packages for easy development of the Deep Learning models. They support building and training models for both GPUs and CPUs with built-in libraries for model definition. PyTorch is a well-known open-source Deep Learning framework with define-by-run approach. It provides libraries for defining layers in deep learning models, which developers can use while building their model and it handles the remaining work in training and inferencing of the model.

3.3 OSU INAM

OSU INAM [23] is a HPC network communication profiling, monitoring, and analysis tool designed to provide a holistic online and scalable insight for the understanding of communication traffic on HPC interconnect and GPU through tight integration with MPI runtime, job scheduler, and MPI-based application [19]. INAM runs on one node in the cluster and remotely gathers information from HPC layers in scalable manner [8]. It provides insight and profiling for various HPC users like administrators, software developers, and domain scientists. INAM is capable of gathering and storing performance counters at sub-second granularity for very large clusters (≈2,500 *nodes*). It supports gathering metrics from the PBS and SLURM job schedulers. INAM has been deployed at various HPC clusters and downloaded more than 4,400 times from the project website [23].

4 Design and Implementation

In this Section, we elaborate our design and implementation to enable the conversational interface for HPC profiling tools. Our goal is to remain as modular as possible and integrate the proposed conversational interface for an existing profiling tool (Reference deleted to follow the double-blind policy). Although we choose one HPC tool, the design choices and implementations for NLU and ASR are portable to other tools. However, the interface and integration components require some adjustment to port it to another HPC profiling tool (refer to Sect. 6.4 for more info). Figure 3 shows the high level perspective of our design components that we describe in this section.

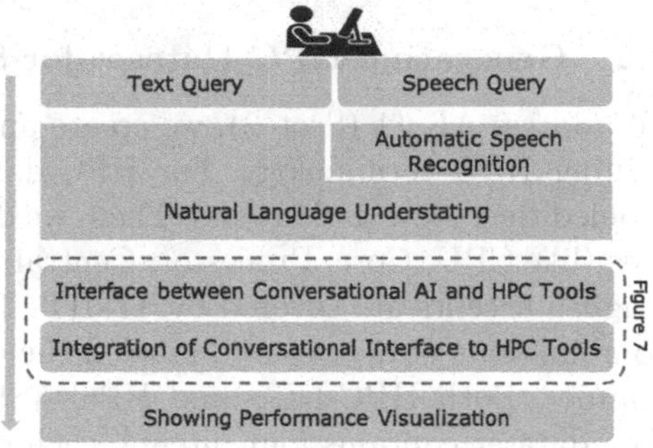

Fig. 3. High level design and flow of transforming HPC user query into performance visualization

4.1 Terminologies and Performance Metrics

Terms and legends used in this paper are explained below.

- **ASR**: Automatic Speech Recognition
- **NLU**: Natural Language Understanding
- **Intent**: An intent is high-level goal that the user is trying to accomplish
- **Slot**: Optional arguments that customizes the intent.
- **TIMIT Dataset**: A publicly available speech dataset consisting of 8 major American English dialects.
- **HPC-ASR Dataset**: An in-house ASR dataset created by us for HPC terminologies.
- **HPC-NLU Dataset**: Slots and Intents dataset created by us for training NLU models for HPC profiling tools.
- **Speech Query**: This is an audio that is passed to the ASR and NLU models to generate the visualization. This is spoken by the user. It is one of the ways in which the user can interact with CAI.
- **Text Query**: This is a text that is passed to the NLU model to generate the visualization. This is typed by the user on the web UI. This is the other way in which the user can interact with CAI.
- **WER**: Word Error Rate is the performance metric commonly used to evaluate the ASR models. WER is a metric that works by comparing words in the predicted text and the reference text.
  The formula is as follow:
  $WER = \frac{(S+D+I)}{N}$ where "S" is the number of substitutions, "D" is the number of deletions, "I" is the number of insertions, "C" is the number of correct words, and "N" is the number of words in the reference ($N = S + D + C$).

- **F1 score**: The performance metrics used to evaluate the NLU models for the slot accuracy and classification accuracy for intents.

$$F1_{score} = \frac{2 * (precision * recall)}{Precision + Recall} \quad Accuracy = \frac{number\ of\ correct\ predictions}{total\ number\ of\ predictions}$$

4.2 Generating HPC Dataset for Speech and Text

To address AI-#1 (Sect. 2), we create an HPC dataset for text and speech containing HPC terminology. For HPC-dataset, we generated basic queries and labeled their slots and intents. Then, we developed synonyms for HPC terminologies (like CPU, Core, Processor, Central-processor, host-processor for CPU) and English accents are covered by TIMIT. Then we used the synonyms to generate combinations of queries and labeled their slots and intents in human-supervised manner. Both HPC-NLU and HPC-ASR output has been human supervised. The dataset contains four intents, each corresponding to common profiling tool usages: 1) node_usage, 2) net_usage, 3) process_usage, and 4) statistics. The semantic label for each utterance is a dictionary with the intent and a number of slots. An example of a command and its corresponding semantics is shown in Fig. 13 under the slot detected box. The scripts are produced with a few variations of phrases in HPC terminology for each of the intents and recorded from 12 different people with 6 dialects by reading the scripts. The recordings are denoised and verified through human supervision for all of the HPC-ASR database. We labeled the intents and slots for the text in the dataset to create HPC-NLU dataset. We randomly divide the HPC-NLU and HPC-ASR datasets into two subgroups each, one for training (70% of total) and another for testing (30% of total).

4.3 Fine-Tuning Automatic Speech Recognition (ASR) for HPC

To address AI-#2 (Sect. 2) we need a DL model which can understand the audio and transcribe it to a meaningful sentence. We selected and trained two off-the-shelf models - Wav2Vec [12] and Speech2Text [30] where the vanilla (base) models were pre-trained on LibriSpeech ASR corpus, a dataset consisting of approximately 1,000 h of English speech for ASR. The architecture of the models is shown in Fig. 4. We train the models with hyper-parameters tuning on a combination of our in-house HPC-ASR dataset and TIMIT [15]. The TIMIT dataset is used to accommodate different dialects of users and enhance the speech utterance. For Speech2Text and Wav2Vec models, the texts are lower-cased, included with numbers, and tokenized using SentencePiece [20]. By using the HPC dataset create in Sect. 4.2, our models are able to handle complex HPC phrases for understanding HPC user query. Figure 5 shows the same example in Sect. 2 being transformed to the correct text after fine-tuning Speech2Text ASR model on HPC+TIMIT dataset. We tested our models in 4 configurations in Sect. 5.3 of the base vanilla model, the model trained on HPC dataset, the model trained on TIMIT dataset, and the model trained on a combination of HPC and TIMIT datasets.

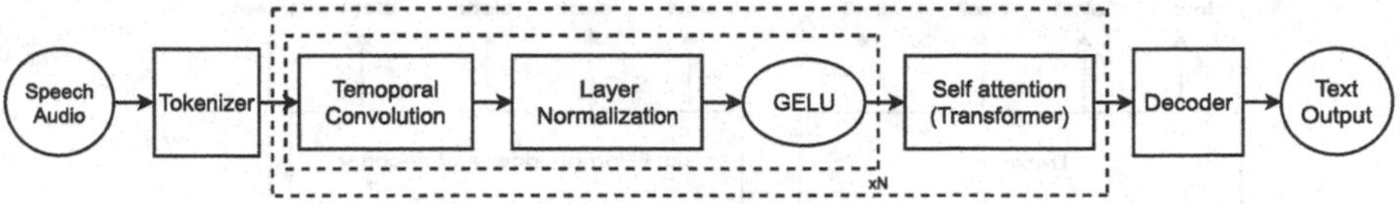

(a) Wav2Vec model architecture

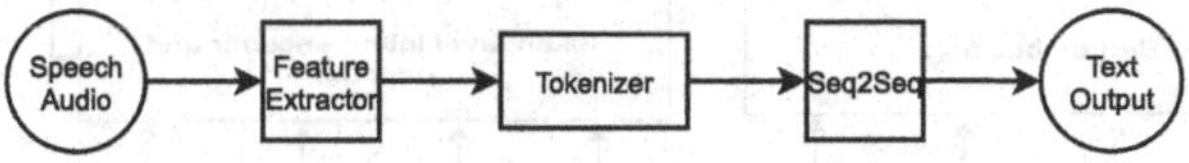

(b) Speech2Text model architecture

Fig. 4. Architecture of models used for ASR in our proposed design.

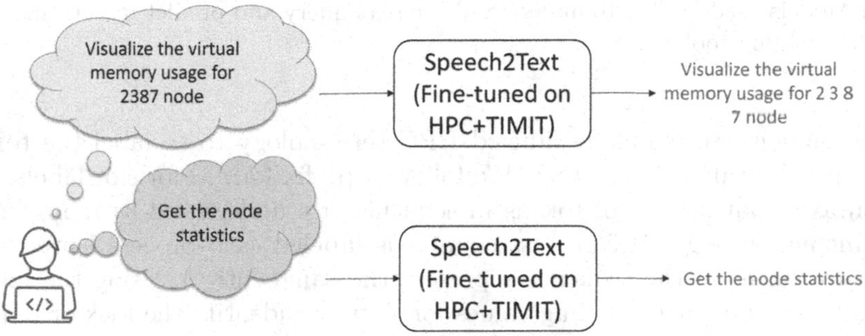

Fig. 5. Real Output of customized Speech2Text model with the two HPC phrases in Fig. 2 where the queries are transformed correctly

4.4 Designing a Natural Language Understanding (NLU) Scheme for HPC Tools

To address AI-#3 (Sect. 2) we train a DL model which can understand and extract the HPC-related information from the output of ASR as text or user's input. The important information to extract from the text is the intention of the user, HPC keywords, and numeric or identity values in the text that have different format. For example, the job number of "453" should not translate as "four five three" or "five hundred and fifty three". We trained two attention-based DL models (StackPropagation and JointBert) on HPC-NLU dataset. Figure 6 shows the architecture of StackPropogation and JointBert models for NLU. These models trained to perform intent detection and slot filling by taking a sentence as a sequence of tokens and assign a label to each token. Based on the tokens the models also detect the intention of the whole sentence. The output of NLU models is a list of Tokens with their assigned labels. This list enables us to extract the required keywords and values, and intent helps in identifying the corresponding visualization in the next modules.

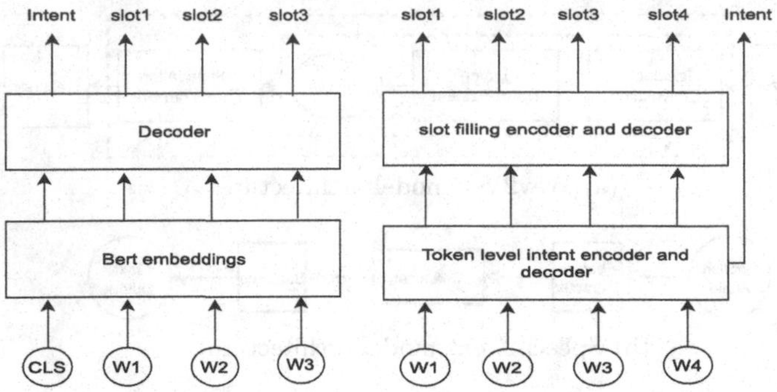

(a) JointBert architecture (b) StackPropogation architecture

Fig. 6. Models used in CAI to understand the text query and predict intents and slots for HPC profiling tools.

The models use manually labeled HPC terminology to to label the tokens along with the values in the text. We followed prefix format for slot labels, this way phrases that are set of tokens in sequence are understood as representing the same entity (e.g. MPI process counter is labeled as B-process I-process as these two tokens in the sequence represent the same entity). Using the intent, slots labeled, and corresponding values for slots, we identify the task or request in the sentence as discussed in Sect. 4.5.

4.5 Interface Between Conversational AI and HPC Tools

As mentioned in Sys-#1 (Sect. 2), we need to design an interface to map the processed user query to the corresponding HPC tool visualization. NLU handles and labels the existing slots and values for the given input based on the speech/text query. The output of NLU is an intent and a list of label-value pair for each word where the label is slot or utterance as shown in Fig. 13. The interface layer should process the intent and corresponding slots to generate a specific tool-related request to the HPC tool. Figure 7 shows the processing steps for transition from NLU outcome to visualization in green. Each box is a separate modules, implemented as a stand-alone python module shown in Fig. 7. We walk through the interface in the order of the boxes in Fig. 7.

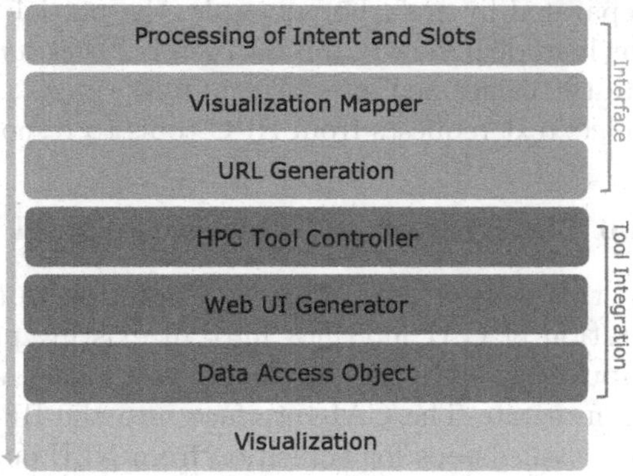

Fig. 7. Detailed modules of interface and interaction for our design

Processing of Intent and Slots: The first module handles three tasks for processing of intents and slots as follows: First, the interface layer handles missing slots and values as there could be missing slots when the user requests a profiling intent. For example, if a user asks for visualization of hardware counters but not specify the metric, considering we have several hardware counters then we assign unicast counters by the default. Second, this module handles incorrect slots and values for different queries and guarantees that from the tools perspective all arguments for decision making exist. Third, this module standardizes the format of different values like time, date, and various HPC measurements. For example, the user can request an insight for the last hour.

Visualization Mapper: This module decides on scope and level of visualization including the chart types and which HPC tool visualization we should select. The visualization level can be cluster, job, node, or process level. The scope could be the time frame that the user is requesting. For making the mapping of request to the corresponding visualizations, the visualization mapper needs input from available visualizations from the HPC profiling tool. Hence, the visualization mapper transforms intents and slots into corresponding performance visualizations. This encapsulates the time to train the user for navigating through different pages and sections of the tool. The alternative design choice would be to make the mapping at the tool level and pass the slots and intents to the tool. Our decision to do the visualization mapping in the interface helps to have fewer changes to the HPC profiler tool as fewer arguments would be passed to the tool by handling the decision at this level.

URL Generation: By this step of CAI the corresponding visualization and values are determined. The next step is to create a connection between the HPC tool and our python-based components. HPC profiling tools and the interface modules have different programming environments. The format and method to communicate between HPC tools and DL components is critical as it imposes the required changes to the HPC tool components to receive and process it. For our paper, the HPC tool supports web access and there are controller in place to handle different web pages and visualizations. Based on this, we decided to exploit this option and generate a Uniform Resource Locator (URL) to interact with the HPC tool. By passing the generated URL to the tool, the tool process the request and direct it to the corresponding web page to show the visualization. All visualization parameters required by the tool are merged into the URL as parameters separated by "&". For example, the partial URL for viewing cluster utilization for historical view of job ID 1456 is "$/network?view = historic\&jobid = 1456$". All the mentioned interface modules run as a python server listening to incoming voice/text requests from HPC tools to respond with appropiate URL.

4.6 Integration of Conversational AI to HPC Tools

In this section, we present our solution to address Sys-#2 that aims for integration of CAI interface into an existing profiling tool. By having a URL as input that gives the arguments and visualization selection for our tool, we aim to integrate The CAI Interface into the HPC profiler tool. Figure 7 shows the processing steps for transition from NLU outcome to visualization in blue.

The modifications to the tool are as follows: 1) The tool needs to record the voice and send it to CAI Interface 2) the tool needs to receive the URL respond and process it. We aim to support Web UI to allow users to benefit from CAI on different platforms and assures accessibility of CAI. For the second task, the flow is as follows: The HPC controller is a Spring Boot controller to redirect the response URLs to corresponding web pages inside the tool. Then, the web UI generator adjusts the values and scopes based on the user parameters extracted from URL for web page initialization. The Data Access Object generates the query to retrieve the profiling data from the time-series database and pass to visualization to plots the visualizations. *The Data Access Object and Visualization have not been changed. The only changes are required for the first two components of the HPC tool controller and Web UI Generator. In the case that the target HPC tool supports web-UI the changes are minimal.*

5 Performance Evaluation

5.1 Evaluation Platform

We conducted our experiments on a 58-node cluster with a combination of nodes of 28 Intel Xeon Broadwell CPU running at 2.40 GHz with NVIDIA Volta V100-32 GB or Skylake CPU running at 2.60 GHz with K80 nodes GPUs. Each node is equipped with a 35 MB L3 cache. The cluster is equipped with MT4119 ConnectX-5 HCAs and Interconnected using SB7790 InfiniBand EDR 100 Gb/s Switches, each having 36 ports.
MPI Library: MVAPICH2 v2.3 [3]
Deep Learning Framework: PyTorch [26] is used to define and train DNNs for ASR and NLU.
Deep Neural Networks: Speech2Text [30], Wav2Vec [12], JointBert [13], and StackPropagation [27].
Datasets: LibriSpeech [25] and TIMIT [15], HPC-ASR Dataset, HPC-NLU Dataset

Table 1. Hardware details of evaluation platform used to conduct the experiments

Architecture	Type	Cores	Speed (GHz)	Label
Broadwell (Server)	CPU	28	2.4	BDW
SkyLake (Server)	CPU	28	2.6	SKX
K80 (Server)	GPU	4992 (Dual socket)	-	K80
V100 (Server)	GPU	CUDA: 5120 Tensor: 640	-	V100
Intel Core i5 8th gen (Surface Pro)	CPU	4	1.8	Client-1
Intel Core i7 11th gen (HP Pavillion)	CPU	4	2.8	Client-2
Intel Core i5 (MacBook Pro)	CPU	4	1.4	Client-3

5.2 Experimental Methodology

In this section, we describe our evaluation methodology used to conduct experiments. In Sect. 5.3, we first individually test the performance of pre-trained vanilla ASR models (Speech2Text and Wav2Vec) on our HPC-ASR dataset and the publicly available TIMIT dataset. Then, we fine-tune ASR models using HPC-ASR and TIMIT training datasets to achieve better WER on the test set. Then we train NLU models (JointBert and StackPropagation) from scratch using our HPC-NLU dataset in Sect. 5.4 to predict the intents and slots for generating appropriate visualizations for the given query. We used two types of validation test, some new queries that did not exist in the training and the other queries are synonym versions of training queries. In Sect. 5.5, we evaluate the performance of both ASR and NLU models to get the end-to-end performance for a speech query. Section 5.6 provides the overhead of deep learning inference for a speech and text query for variable query length on client devices. To improve the performance of deep learning inference for slow client devices, we transfer the inference to a python server running on our in-house cluster with GPU nodes. In Sect. 6.2, we compare the inference time and overall request time for client and centralized python server running on RI2 cluster. In Sect. 6.3, we show the explainability of our proposed conversational UI by providing a detailed flow of information from speech to URL generation.

5.3 ASR Results

In these experiments, we evaluate the performance of pre-trained vanilla ASR models (Speech2Text and Wav2Vec) on our HPC-ASR dataset and publicly available TIMIT dataset. As discussed in Sect. 2, the existing ASR models are not suitable for CAI conversational needs as models do not recognize HPC terminologies. Our HPC-ASR dataset has HPC terminologies and the publicly available TIMIT dataset has different accents, which will make our proposed design available to a wide range of speakers. Figure 8(a) and 8(b) show the fine-tuning (training) of Speech2Text and Wav2vec on three combinations of two datasets (training on HPC, TIMIT, and HPC+TIMIT datasets). Final test WER on TIMIT and HPC test set is shown in Table 2.

Table 2. Evaluation of Automatic Speech Recognition (ASR) models using Word Error Rate (WER) - Lower WER is better

Train Dataset		Dataset used for Test			
HPC	TIMIT	Speech2Text		Wav2Vec	
		HPC WER	HPC+Timit WER	HPC WER	HPC+Timit WER
✗	✗	64.613	27.53	67.92	27.16
✗	✓	71.15	33.18	77.38	35.43
✓	✗	2.85	21.8	3.24	65.6
✓	✓	2.92	12.18	3.09	14.24

The first row of the table constitutes the base vanilla models which are publicly available trained versions of speech2text and Wav2Vec (trained on LibriSpeech). The lower WER shows that training on our HPC dataset increases the accuracy of the models to HPC terminologies and combining our training with the TIMIT dataset gives us a better-generalized model when comparing the WER of the same row of the table for different test datasets. As WER depends on the dataset being used, comparing the numbers on the same column shows that using the HPC dataset leads to better (lower) WER. TIMIT dataset has several accents; therefore, we see higher WER for the TIMIT+HPC dataset, but it makes the ASR model more general and applicable to a wide variety of users. Speech2text performs slightly better than Wav2Vec and hence we use speech2text as the default ASR model.

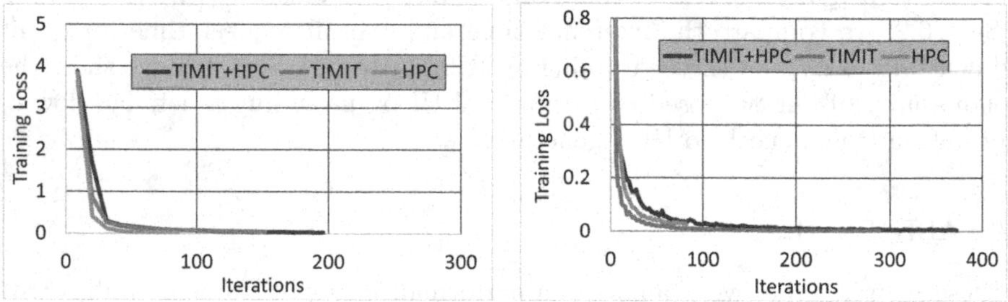

(a) Wav2Vec (b) Speech2Text

Fig. 8. Training loss for ASR models fine-tuned on different combinations of HPC ASR and TIMIT datasets. We show that both models are trained till the improvement in training loss is negligible.

5.4 NLU Results

As discussed in Sects. 2 and 4.4, no pre-trained NLU model is available for HPC profiling tools; therefore, we trained NLU models (JointBert and StackPropagation) from scratch using our HPC-NLU dataset. In this section, we evaluate the accuracy of predicting intents and filling slots for our trained NLU models versus human-supervised and labeled HPC-NLU dataset. The output of the model is compared to actual human-supervised HPC-NLU output, that contains synonyms, to calculate accuracy and F1-score. Figure 9 shows the training of JointBert and StackPropagation on HPC-NLU dataset. Table 3 shows the final test accuracy and F1 score for two StackPropagation and JointBert models on the HPC-NLU test set. These two models are trained on the dataset to understand the text and detect the intent and slots in it. We choose JointBert as our defualt model for NLU module as it gives better accuracy for both intents and slots.

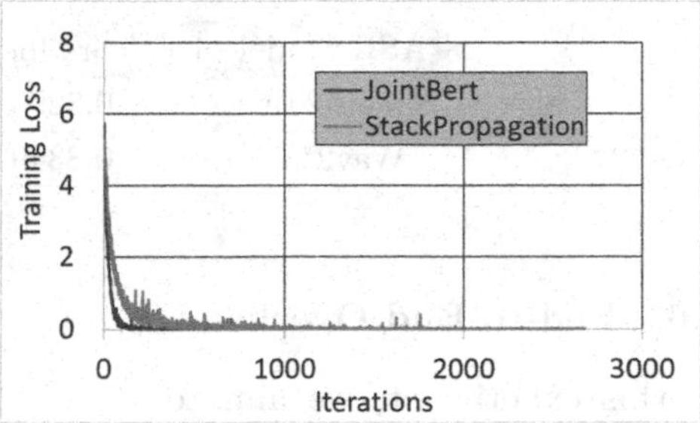

Fig. 9. Training loss of JointBert and StackPropogation models trained on HPC-NLU dataset for NLU. We train models till the improvement in training loss is negligible.

Table 3. Evaluation of natural language understanding deep learning models for labeling slots and intents - higher value is better

Model	F1 Score for slots	Intent Accuracy
StackPropagation	0.775	91.79%
JointBert	0.8773	93.36%

5.5 ASR + NLU Analysis

In this experiment, ASR and NLU modules are evaluated together as a pipeline to see if a user provides a speech query how accurately can we detect and assign slots and intents based on our models. Therefore, we use our trained NLU and ASR models to calculate inference accuracy. Table 4 shows the results on end-to-end inference. This shows the results of the chosen NLU model (JointBert) based on the output of our trained ASR models. From Table 4 it can be seen that the F1 score for slots is marginally better when Wav2Vec is used as the ASR model and the intent accuracy is marginally better when speech2text is used as the ASR model. In this work, we use Speech2Text with JointBert to make inference for speech queries. In future, we will use ensemble methods to get better accuracy by training multiple instances of the same model and taking majority decision to allot intent and slots.

Table 4. Evaluation of ASR+NLU pipeline with JointBert as the NLU model. Higher value is better

ASR Model	F1 Score for slots	Intent Accuracy
Speech2Text	0.8295	92.92%
Wav2Vec	0.8349	92.47%

5.6 End-to-End Overhead

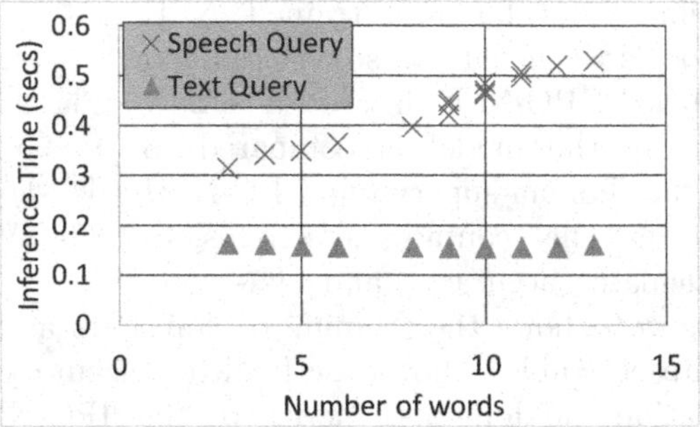

Fig. 10. Inference latency evaluation of ASR+NLU models on client side for 15 different queries consisting of different words

In this experiment, we aim to evaluate the overhead of our full pipeline: from user speech/text input in Sect. 5.5) to generating URL and passing it to the tool controller and Web UI generator. Since different visualizations vary in rendering time and it is tool-specific implementation, the numbers do not include the timing for rendering visualizations. Figure 10 showcases the time taken to process speech and text queries of varying lengths on an client device. In general, it can be seen that the time taken to process speech increases with an increase in the number of words in the query. This is expected as the ASR model takes an input of the varying size and hence bigger inputs take more time. The time taken to process a text query is more or less constant as the input size of the NLU model is fixed.

6 Discussion

6.1 Trade-Offs for Converting Speech to Intent

In our design, we use speech-to-text (ASR) followed by text-to-command (NLU) for processing user inputs and mapping them to the tool intents. The alternative approach for speech processing is to directly use speech-to-intent models. In this section, we discuss the trade-offs between the two approaches. We selected ASR + NLU approach since using speech-to-intent model proposes some problems. By having Speech-to-intent model working then any changes require the whole model to train again. In summary, our selection is due to the following reasons. First, speech-to-intent model requires creating a speech and intent dataset for all the tools and HPC applications and map each one to the output intent and slots which will affect modularity and portability of CAI as it limits replacing ASR and NLU models with state-of-the-art models for maintenance. Second, a different text-to-intent-model is required to be trained again for handling text inputs. Third, the speech-to-intent models are still upcoming as we discuss in related work section.

6.2 Comparison of Client-Side vs Server-Side Inference in CAI

In this section, we evaluate two choices of running CAI server on the client or server. If the server is running on client then the inference will be processed on the user computer to get the URL. In the other case, the inference will be done by sending the user's input to a centralized server.

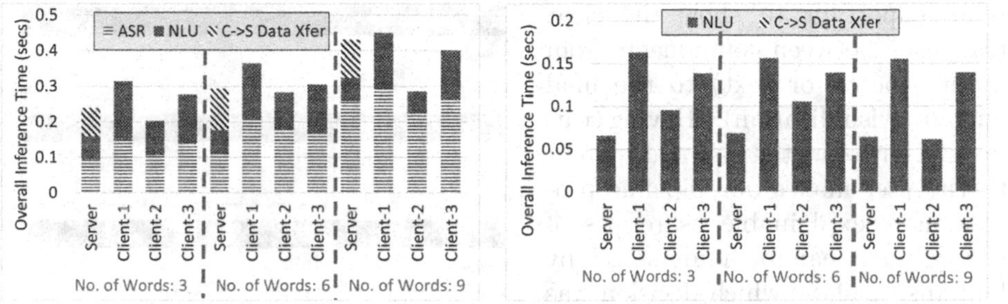

(a) Speech Query (b) Text Query

Fig. 11. Overall inference time comparing client and server configurations. Note that in Fig. 11(b) the transfer time for text is from client to server is and is thus hard to see. However, it is included

Figure 11 shows the end-to-end inference time versus the number of words in a query for both Speech Query and Text Query on Client devices and a Central Server. The Speech query end-to-end inference time on client device includes time taken by ASR to convert to transcript + time taken by NLU to extract intents and slots. Similarly total inference time for Text query is the time taken by NLU to extract intents and slots. End to end inference time for the server has time taken for transfer from client to the server in addition to that of time taken by client devices for both Text and Speech queries.

Table 5. Inference latency of CAI for user input processing comparing client versus central server for 100 iterations - the client nodes have a "Client" label

Type of device	Speech query (secs)	Text query (secs)
Client-1	1.2914	0.1243
Client-2	0.7409	0.0994
Client-3	0.7949	0.1406
BDW	0.4361	0.0320
SKX	0.4279	0.0291
K-80	0.2825	0.0195
V-100	0.2791	0.0121

Table 5 shows the inference time for speech query and text query on 3 Client devices and Central server nodes like BDW, SKX, K-80, and V-100. Speech query inference time includes time taken by ASR to convert to transcript + time taken by NLU to extract intents and slots+ time taken by python server to generate URL and for Text query, it is the time taken by NLU to extract intents and slots+ time taken by python server to generate URL. The inference time on the server is less compared to that of on client devices. We can see that the shortest inference time is obtained on V100 nodes of the server.

6.3 Insights for Getting Explainable Flow of CAI

It is important to show the clear transition between components from input (speech or text) to the final output (visualization). Having this insight implemented and transparent to the user makes our pipeline process more explainable as results of the solution can be understood by humans, to show which decision was made based on the input provided to each design module and enables understanding the decision making process.

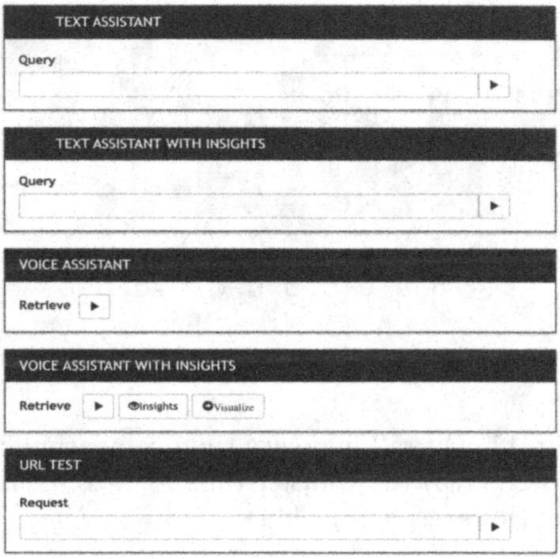

Fig. 12. Screenshot of developed UI for CAI showing various methods of getting the user input in different forms and presenting the option to get flow insight shown in Fig. 13

Figure 12 shows the web UI for the proposed approach where the user can choose to get insights into the flow of CAI by selecting text or voice query box with "insights" then the user gets Fig. 8 that shows the step by step flow with details of each step along with the performance visualization page. We can see that in the figure how CAI converts "show me the virtual memory usage for job 727384" as a voice to outputs for NLU and ASR including the intent and slots and finally make the visualization selection based on intermediate values (dark green). The final URL can be tested in the "URL Test".

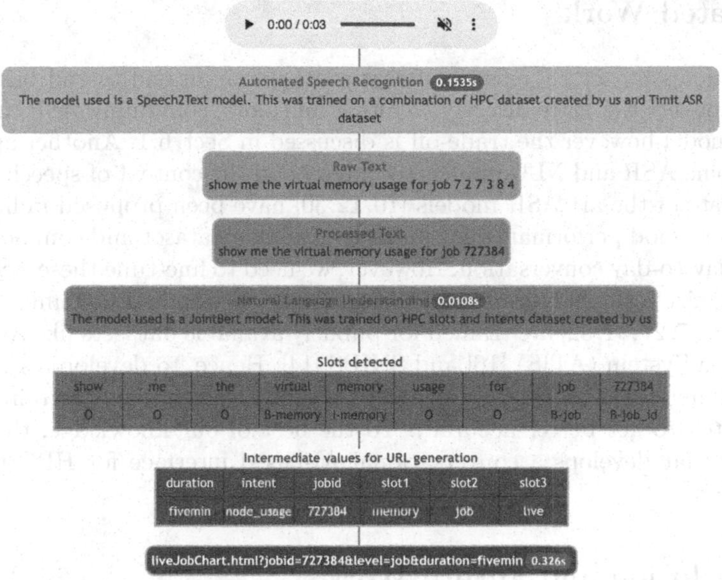

Fig. 13. Screenshot of the flow of information in proposed approach. The numbers show the latency of ASR and NLU modules and the final number in URL shows end-to-end latency.

6.4 Integrating Other HPC Tools with CAI

In this Section, we describe the changes required to make CAI work with other HPC tools. This can be used as take-away for integrating other HPC tools with CAI. Note that either steps 4 or 5 need modifications to the tool as a tool can be web-based (online) or stand-alone (offline) but not both.

1. If the tool uses tool-specific abbreviations and terminologies then the new samples containing those words need to be added to HPC-ASR and HPC-NLU dataset following step taken in Sect. 4.2 to add more intents and queries. Otherwise, step 2 can be skipped.
2. Use updated dataset to fine-tune ASR Sect. 4.3 and NLU Sect. 4.4 models to recognize new words in the queries.
3. Update interface layer of CAI to accommodate tool-specific variables and visualization types to provide the visualization mapper (Sect. 4.5) knowledge of different visualizations supported by the tool.
4. Web-based tool modifications: Tool needs to implement a unique URL for each visualization chart so that CAI can customize the charts through URL based on user's input.
5. Offline tool modification: The tool needs to parse the URL to get the values and pass them to the existing Data Access Object to fetch and visualize.

7 Related Work

Several studies [21,24,28] exist in literature that use an end-to-end based approach to convert the voice directly to intent and slots, combining ASR and NLU into one model however the trade-off is discussed in Sect. 6.1. Another approach is to combine ASR and NLU models to understand the context of speech sample. Several state-of-the-art ASR models [10,12,30] have been proposed in literature that provide good performance for publicly available dataset and common words found in day-to-day conversation. However, we need to fine-tune these ASR models to recognize technical terms found computer science and HPC. Similarly, NLU models [13,17,27,31,32] are trained for publicly available datasets like Air Travel Information System (ATIS) [16] and SNIPS [14]. Hence, to develop a system for HPC profiling tool, we need to generate our own dataset and retrain models from scratch to get better accuracy. To the best of our knowledge, this is the first work that develops a conversational AI-based interface for HPC profiling tools.

8 Conclusion and Future Work

In this paper, we explored the challenges associated with designing a conversational (speech/text) interface for HPC tools. We used state-of-the-art AI models for speech and text and adapted it for use in the HPC arena by retraining them on new HPC datasets we created. We demonstrated that our proposed model, retrained with an HPC specific dataset, delivers higher accuracy than the existing state-of-the-art pre-trained language models. We also created an interface to convert speech/text data to commands for HPC tools and show how users can utilize the proposed interface to gain insights quicker leading to better productivity. We also deployed and tested CAI and the CAI enhanced OSU INAM on a state-of-the-art production HPC system and evaluated the ability of CAI to correctly interpret speech/text input from multiple different volunteer users and display the correct visualization output from the HPC tool. To the best of our knowledge, this is the first effort aimed at designing a conversational interface using state-of-the-art AI techniques to enhance the productivity of novice and advanced users of HPC tools alike.

As part of future work, we plan on releasing various components developed as part of this paper including 1) the HPC-ASR and HPC-NLU datasets, 2) the retrained ASR and NLU models, 3) CAI, and 4) the enhanced OSU INAM profiling tool with support for CAI. We also plan to extend CAI to other popular profiling tools.

Acknowledgement. This research is supported in part by NSF grants #1818253, #1854828, #1931537, #2007991, #2018627, #2112606, and XRAC grant #NCR-130002.

References

1. Horovod: Distributed training framework for TensorFlow. https://github.com/uber/horovod
2. MPIP: Lightweight, Scalable MPI Profiling. http://www.llnl.gov/CASC/mpip/
3. MVAPICH: MPI over InfiniBand, Omni-Path, Ethernet/iWARP, and RoCE. http://mvapich.cse.ohio-state.edu/features/. Accessed 13 March 2022
4. Prometheus exporter. https://github.com/prometheus/node_exporter
5. The future of conversational AI (2021). https://www2.deloitte.com/us/en/insights/focus/signals-for-strategists/the-future-of-conversational-ai.html. Accessed 13 March 2022
6. Nvidia Nsight Developer Tools (2022). https://developer.nvidia.com/tools-overview. Accessed 13 March 2022
7. The impact of voice assistants (2022). https://www.pwc.com/us/en/services/consulting/library/consumer-intelligence-series/voice-assistants.html. Accessed 13 March 2022
8. Kousha, P., et al.: Accelerated real-time network monitoring and profiling at scale using OSU INAM. In: Practice and Experience in Advanced Research Computing (PEARC 2020) (2020)
9. Agelastos, A., et al.: The Lightweight Distributed Metric Service: A Scalable Infrastructure for Continuous Monitoring of Large Scale Computing Systems and Applications, pp. 154–165. SC 2014, IEEE Press, Piscataway, NJ, USA (2014). https://doi.org/10.1109/SC.2014.18, http://dx.doi.org/10.1109/SC.2014.18
10. Amodei, D., et al.: Deep Speech 2: End-to-End Speech Recognition in English and Mandarin. CoRR abs/1512.02595 (2015). http://arxiv.org/abs/1512.02595
11. Barth, B., Evans, T., McCalpin, J.: Tacc stats. https://www.tacc.utexas.edu/research-development/tacc-projects/tacc-stats
12. Baevski, A., Zhou, H., Mohamed, A., Auli, M.: Wav2vec 2.0: a framework for self-supervised learning of speech representations (2020). https://arxiv.org/abs/2006.11477
13. Castellucci, G., Bellomaria, V., Favalli, A., Romagnoli, R.: Multi-lingual intent detection and slot filling in a joint bert-based model. arXiv preprint arXiv:1907.02884 (2019)
14. Coucke, A., et al.: Snips voice platform: an embedded spoken language understanding system for private-by-design voice interfaces. CoRR abs/1805.10190 (2018). http://arxiv.org/abs/1805.10190
15. Garofolo, J., et al.: TIMIT Acoustic-Phonetic Continuous Speech Corpus (1993). 11272.1/AB2/SWVENO, https://hdl.handle.net/11272.1/AB2/SWVENO
16. Hemphill, C.T., Godfrey, J.J., Doddington, G.R.: The ATIS spoken language systems pilot corpus, pp. 96–101. HLT 1990, Association for Computational Linguistics, USA (1990). https://doi.org/10.3115/116580.116613
17. Hosseini-Asl, E., McCann, B., Wu, C., Yavuz, S., Socher, R.: A simple language model for task-oriented dialogue. CoRR abs/2005.00796 (2020). https://arxiv.org/abs/2005.00796
18. HPCToolkit: (2019). http://hpctoolkit.org/. Accessed 13 March 2022
19. Kousha, P., et al.: INAM: Cross-Stack Profiling and Analysis of Communication in MPI-Based Applications. Association for Computing Machinery, New York, NY, USA (2021). https://doi.org/10.1145/3437359.3465582

20. Kudo, T., Richardson, J.: Sentencepiece: a simple and language independent subword tokenizer and detokenizer for neural text processing. arXiv preprint arXiv:1808.06226 (2018)
21. Lugosch, L., Ravanelli, M., Ignoto, P., Tomar, V.S., Bengio, Y.: Speech model pre-training for end-to-end spoken language understanding (2019)
22. Malony, A.D., Shende, S.: Performance technology for complex parallel and distributed systems. In: Kotsis, G., Kacsuk, P. (eds.) Proceedings of DAPSYS 2000, pp. 37–46 (2000)
23. OSU InfiniBand Network Analysis and Monitoring Tool. http://mvapich.cse.ohio-state.edu/tools/osu-inam/
24. Palogiannidi, E., Gkinis, I., Mastrapas, G., Mizera, P., Stafylakis, T.: End-to-end architectures for ASR-free spoken language understanding. In: ICASSP 2020–2020 IEEE International Conference on Acoustics, Speech and Signal Processing (ICASSP), pp. 7974–7978 (2020). https://doi.org/10.1109/ICASSP40776.2020.9054314
25. Panayotov, V., Chen, G., Povey, D., Khudanpur, S.: Librispeech: an ASR corpus based on public domain audio books. In: 2015 IEEE International Conference on Acoustics, Speech and Signal Processing (ICASSP), pp. 5206–5210. IEEE (2015)
26. Paszke, A., et al.: PyTorch: An Imperative Style, High-Performance Deep Learning Library (2019)
27. Qin, L., Che, W., Li, Y., Wen, H., Liu, T.: A stack-propagation framework with token-level intent detection for spoken language understanding. arXiv preprint arXiv:1909.02188 (2019)
28. Serdyuk, D., Wang, Y., Fuegen, C., Kumar, A., Liu, B., Bengio, Y.: Towards end-to-end spoken language understanding. CoRR abs/1802.08395 (2018). http://arxiv.org/abs/1802.08395
29. Sergeev, A., Balso, M.D.: Horovod: fast and easy distributed deep learning in TensorFlow. CoRR abs/1802.05799 (2018). http://arxiv.org/abs/1802.05799
30. Wang, C., Tang, Y., Ma, X., Wu, A., Okhonko, D., Pino, J.: Fairseq s2t: fast speech-to-text modeling with fairseq (2020). https://arxiv.org/abs/2010.05171
31. Wen, T., et al.: A network-based end-to-end trainable task-oriented dialogue system. CoRR abs/1604.04562 (2016). http://arxiv.org/abs/1604.04562
32. Wu, D., Ding, L., Lu, F., Xie, J.: Slotrefine: a fast non-autoregressive model for joint intent detection and slot filling. CoRR abs/2010.02693 (2020). https://arxiv.org/abs/2010.02693

Hy-Fi: Hybrid Five-Dimensional Parallel DNN Training on High-Performance GPU Clusters

Arpan Jain(✉), Aamir Shafi, Quentin Anthony, Pouya Kousha, Hari Subramoni, and Dhableswar K. Panda

The Ohio State University, Columbus, OH 43210, USA
{jain.575,shafi.16,anthony.301,kousha.2}@osu.edu,
{subramon,panda}@cse.ohio-state.edu

Abstract. Recent advances in High Performance Computing (HPC) enable Deep Learning (DL) models to achieve state-of-the-art performance by exploiting multiple processors. Data parallelism is a strategy that replicates the DL model on each processor, which is impossible for models like AmoebaNet on NVIDIA GPUs. Layer parallelism avoids this limitation by placing one or more layers on each GPU, but still cannot train models like AmoebaNet on high-resolution images. We propose Hy-Fi: Hybrid Five-Dimensional Parallelism; a system that takes advantage of five parallelism dimensions—data, model, spatial, pipeline, and bi-directional parallelism—which enables efficient distributed training of out-of-core models and layers. Hy-Fi also proposes communication-level optimizations to integrate these dimensions. We report up to 2.67× and 1.68× speedups over layer and pipeline parallelism, respectively. We demonstrate Hy-Fi on up to 2,048 GPUs on AmoebaNet and ResNet models. Further, we use Hy-Fi to enable DNN training on high-resolution images, including 8,192 × 8,192 and 16,384 × 16,384.

Keywords: DNN · Model-parallelism · Distributed training · Hybrid parallelism · MPI · GPU

1 Introduction

In the last decade, Deep Learning (DL) has emerged as a viable approach to practice Artificial Intelligence (AI) in emerging disciplines including object recognition/detection, speech recognition, language translation, and emotion recognition. A typical DL model is capable of "learning" non-linear mathematical relationships between the input data and the corresponding output during training on sufficiently large datasets—this knowledge is later used to make predictions with new and unseen data. One of the main driving forces behind the success of complex and large-scale Deep Neural Networks (DNNs) is the availability of compute resources offered by modern High Performance Computing (HPC) hardware. Current state-of-the-art models like AmoebaNet [22] and

A.-L. Varbanescu et al. (Eds.): ISC High Performance 2022, LNCS 13289, pp. 109–130, 2022.
https://doi.org/10.1007/978-3-031-07312-0_6

GPT3 have become complex and computationally expensive—due to a large number of parameters—and cannot be trained on a single processing element (for e.g. a GPU). This fundamental limitation on training state-of-the-art DNNs is resolved by exploiting parallel and distributed training on HPC hardware. One popular and easy-to-use parallelization strategy for distributed DNN training is *data parallelism* [1]. This technique accelerates training by creating model replicas on multiple processing elements—including GPUs—and performs DNN training by dividing the input data into multiple *batches*. Each processing element is assigned a unique set of data, called a *batch*, which is used to perform parallel training steps, this assignment is followed by a synchronization step using an allreduce operation. This step incurs communication overhead in order to accumulate the gradients across all processing elements and ensure weights are synchronized after each training step.

While data parallelism offers near-linear scaling [3,17] for distributed DNN training, it incurs significant memory overhead since the entire model is replicated on each GPU. It therefore requires the entire model to fit inside the memory of a single GPU, which is not always possible especially for emerging large models. Even at the finest granularity of a training sample, most of the current state-of-the-art models like AmoebaNet [22] and GPT3 models cannot fit inside the memory of a single GPU; these models are hence known as *out-of-core DNNs or models.* The memory requirement of a DNN depends on its size (number of parameters) and the size of the input image. For this reason, a DL model that is trainable on a single GPU for a small-sized images may not be trainable on a single GPU for high-resolution (large-sized) images. This means that due to the inability to store a DL model replica on a single GPU, the data parallelism approach is only limited to the training of modestly-sized DNNs on low-resolution images like Cifar-100 (32×32 pixels) and ImageNet (244×244 pixels).

However, in modern scientific applications, image sizes can range from 512×512 pixels to $2{,}048 \times 2{,}048$ pixels [6]. For example, the 2D mesh-tangling problem represents hydraulic simulation and can be formulated as semantic image segmentation. The input data in mesh-tangling can range from $1{,}024 \times 1{,}024$ pixels to $2{,}048 \times 2{,}048$ pixels. In digital pathology, the advent of high-resolution scanners has led to the adoption of digital whole slide imaging (WSI) for diagnostic purposes. A typical application of WSI is measuring the degree of a tumor grade for diseases such as cancer. The detection problem [19] can be formulated as a classification task in which the input is a WSI and output is the presence or absence of cancer. Normally, WSIs are very high-resolution images.

To address this fundamental limitation of data parallelism, *layer-parallelism*—also known as inter-layer *model-parallelism*—is proposed in the literature [5] to enable training of the out-of-core DNNs. Here, the DNN is divided into smaller partitions, each consisting of one or more layers, that can fit inside a single GPU's memory. This approach—referred to as *basic model-parallelism*—has inherent scaling issues [10,11]. The reason is as follows: A DNN essentially is a directed acyclic graph where each node corresponds to a layer. As part of the forward pass, each layer takes inputs/activations from the previous layer and gives output to the next layer making this an inherently sequential process. This data dependency serializes parallel processing of layers in a DNN since only one GPU does the computation at any given time. In addition to basic model-parallelism, *pipeline-parallelism* [12] and *sub-graph parallelism* [13] are also instances of the inter-layer model-parallelism approach. A variant of model-parallelism is to exploit parallelism within layers. This approach is sometimes called intra-layer model-parallelism. Here, a single layer is divided across multiple GPUs. An instance of this technique is *spatial parallelism*, which partitions the images across multiple GPUs thereby distributing the layer. *Hybrid parallelism* combines data- and model-parallelism but also suffers from data dependency limitations.

1.1 Motivation

Several approaches have been proposed in the literature to address some of the limitations of model parallelism. However, most studies are performed for low-resolution images that exhibit different characteristics [12]. Compared to low resolution images, high-resolution images results in higher activation memory and larger tensors, which results in a larger communication overhead (Fig. 1).

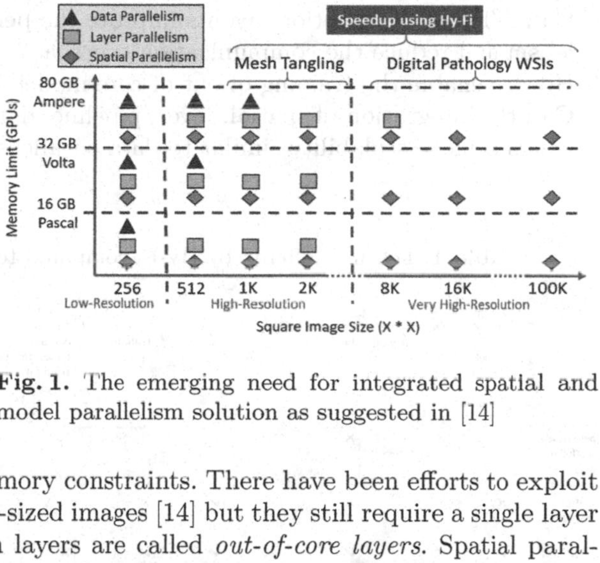

Fig. 1. The emerging need for integrated spatial and model parallelism solution as suggested in [14]

These approaches include pipeline, spatial, and bi-directional parallelism. Pipeline parallelism such as the schemes proposed in [10,12,21] exploits parallelism within training samples and accelerates the performance of model parallelism. However, pipeline parallelism is only possible when the model is trainable with batch size >1, which is typically impossible with high-resolution images due to memory constraints. There have been efforts to exploit pipeline parallelism for large-sized images [14] but they still require a single layer to fit inside the GPU—such layers are called *out-of-core layers*. Spatial parallelism, on the other hand, has performance issues due to high communication overhead and the inability to accelerate low-resolution images that are common in the latter half of DNNs. Bi-directional parallelism exploits the memory and compute available between the backward and forward passes of the first and second training iterations. It trains the model from both directions in order to use these potentially-wasted resources [14]. Therefore, existing solutions [12,14] limit the ability to train DNNs on very high-resolution images, which affects the DNN's accuracy and prohibits the training of complex DNNs.

To summarize, spatial parallelism distributes images across multiple GPUs, layer parallelism distributes the model, pipeline parallelism parallelizes the samples in a batch, and bi-directional parallelism employs memory-aware solutions to enhance the performance.

This paper focuses on efficiently utilizing distributed training for very high-resolution images that appear in real-world applications. These have unique requirements from the underlying DL training framework. Digital pathology, for example, uses a tiling mechanism to train Tall Cell Variant (TCV) classifiers on very high-resolution images, limiting the structural information and local/global context. Based on this, we seek to solve the following application-level requirements in this paper: 1) Enabling training on very high-resolution images, 2) Ability to train the model with any batch size on the same number of resources, and 3) provide speedup and support new emerging applications like TCV classifier. To address these requirements for training large-sized images, several design and system-level challenges need to be solved:

- How to efficiently integrate spatial, layer, pipeline, bi-directional, and data parallelism?
- How to reduce the communication overhead in an integrated distributed DNN training system?
- Can different distribution layouts improve the performance for spatial parallelism and reduce the communication overhead?
- How to enable the training of out-of-core models and out-of-core layers?
- Can the integration of spatial, layer, pipeline, data, and bi-directional parallelism achieve scalability similar to data parallelism?

Table 1. Features offered by Hy-Fi compared to existing frameworks

Studies	Features										
	Out-of-core model training (max batch size = 1)	Out-of-core layer training	Out-of-core batch size	Memory -aware solution	Pipelining support	Bidirectional training	Optimized communication for bi-directional training	Hybrid parallelism	Multi-node support	Speedup for out-of-core BS training	Speedup for CNN
Basic model parallelism (layer parallelism)	✔	×	×	×	×	×	N/A	×	✔	×	✔
Pipeline parallelism (Gpipe [12])	×	×	×	×	✔	×	N/A	✔	✔	×	✔
GEMS [14]	✔	×	✔	✔	✔	✔	×	✔	✔	✔	✔
TorchGipe [16]	✔	×	✔	✔	✔	×	N/A	×	×	✔	✔
PipeDream [10]	✔	×	×	×	✔	×	N/A	✔	✔	×	✔
LBANN (spatial [6]/domain parallelism [8])	✔	✔	×	×	×	×	N/A	✔	✔	×	✔
FlexFlow [15]	✔	✔	×	×	×	×	N/A	✔	✔	×	✔
Mesh-TensorFlow [23]	✔	✔	×	×	×	×	N/A	✔	✔	×	✔
Megatron [24]	✔	×	×	×	×	×	N/A	✔	✔	×	×
SUPER [13]	×	×	×	×	×	×	N/A	✔	✔	×	×
Proposed Hy-Fi	✔	✔	✔	✔	✔	✔	✔	✔	✔	✔	✔

1.2 Contributions

In this section, we highlight the major contributions of this study. To the best of our knowledge, no state-of-the-art distributed DNN training system supports out-of-core models, layers, and batch size with memory-efficient designs. Table 1 compares related data, model, pipeline, and spatial parallelism studies against the proposed Hy-Fi system. Section 6 provides an in-depth comparison of related studies. Major contributions of this study are as follows:

- We propose, design, and evaluate Hy-Fi: an integrated memory-efficient system that uses five dimensions of parallelism and provides scalable training.
- We overcome the limitations of individual parallelization techniques—spatial, layer, and bi-directional parallelism—by proposing communication optimizations and efficiently integrating all five dimensions of parallelism (spatial, layer, pipeline, bi-directional, and data) to use in tandem.
- Hy-Fi offers up to 2.02× speedup over pure layer parallelism and 1.44× speedup over pure pipeline parallelism for the spatial parallelism dimension. Using memory-efficient bi-directional parallelism, we increase speedup to 2.67× over pure layer parallelism and 1.68× over pure pipeline parallelism.
- We show near-linear scaling (94.5%) for distributed DNN training using Hy-Fi on 2,048 Volta V100 GPUs.
- We enable the training of next-generation deep learning models on very high-resolution images (8,192 × 8,192 and 16,384 × 16,384 pixels) and show up to 1.47× speedup over spatial parallelism.

2 Challenges in Exploiting Different Parallelism Dimensions in Distributed DNN Training

We highlight the challenges in implementing a multi-dimensional DNN training framework like Hy-Fi which has several communication optimizations and enables training on very high-resolution images.

Challenge-1: Halo Exchange in PyTorch
Spatial parallelism requires the halo exchange to implement distributed convolution and pooling layers. A halo exchange involves communication in different directions and differs in message size (Fig. 3). The message size and communication pattern depends on several parameters such as the kernel size, spatial parallelism size, partition position in the distributed image, and the number of neighbors, which exacerbates the challenge of implementing a halo exchange. A halo exchange can be implemented using non-blocking point-to-point communication provided by CUDA-aware MPI libraries, but they need to be synchronized with asynchronous execution in PyTorch [20] to ensure data validation.

Challenge-2: Exploitation of Different Parallelism Dimension
The proposed framework must be designed in a modular and user-transparent fashion to exploit different parallelism dimensions in tandem. Further, the system should be robust enough to take advantage of all parallelism dimensions

whenever possible. Spatial, layer, pipeline, bi-directional, and hybrid data parallelism offer compute parallelization in different dimensions and a potential to accelerate training of CNN. Hence, every parallelization dimension should be efficiently implemented and integrated with others in order to fully exploit the benefits of all the strategies in tandem.

Challenge-3: Scaling Integrated Hybrid Training Solutions
Training CNNs on high-resolution images is a compute-intensive task and requires a large numbers of GPUs to make it feasible. Hence, the proposed solution must be scalable to thousands of GPUs, which requires hybrid data parallelism. Integrating data parallelism into a multi-dimension parallelization framework like Hy-Fi is a non-trivial task since each parallelization dimension combines data parallelism differently. For example, spatial parallelism uses allreduce operations to synchronize weights across the distributed input, layer parallelism distributes the model and needs sub-communicators to implement hybrid parallelism, and bi-directional parallelism introduces extra replicas for data parallelism. Hence, designing a scalable solution exploiting multiple parallelism dimensions is a challenging task.

3 Limitations in Existing Approaches for Model Parallelism

We provide an overview of various existing model-parallelism approaches and discuss their limitations.

3.1 Layer Parallelism

The simplest model-parallelism scheme consists of placing DNN partitions (consisting of one or more *layers*) on separate GPUs before applying distributed forward and backward passes. These distributed forward and backward passes are implemented with simple Send and Recv operations. Layer parallelism has two primary drawbacks: 1) Under-utilization of resources and 2) A complex implementation compared to data parallelism. Given that only a single GPU can operate at once, layer parallelism suffers from poor scalability. Since DL frameworks do not provide distributed back-propagation implementations, layer parallelism is often challenging to implement. Manually partitioning a DNN is challenging in itself because not all layer connections preserve a simple ordering (e.g. skip or residual connections).

3.2 Pipeline Parallelism

Pipelining divides the input batch into smaller batches called micro-batches, the number of which we call *parts*. The goal of pipeline parallelism is to reduce under-utilization by overlapping micro-batches, which allows multiple GPUs to proceed with compute within the forward and backward passes. Pipeline parallelism has two primary drawbacks; 1) batch size limits the length of the pipeline, and 2) performance is poor compared to data or hybrid Parallelism. Pipelining also wastes GPU resources when the pipeline is not full. The only case with a full pipeline occurs when the number of parts equals the number of DNN splits *and* the batch size equals the pipeline length. These issues worsen at scale due to the pipelining *bubble* [12]. Further, it is not possible to use pipelining when the largest batch size is 1. Due to the above limitations, there is a need to further optimize both layer and pipeline parallelism.

3.3 Memory-Aware Synchronized Training (Bi-directional Parallelism)

Both basic and pipelining model parallelism suffer from under-utilization of resources. After completing the forward and backward passes for a given model partition, each GPU has free memory and compute resources available, which can be utilized to perform the forward and backward passes of a new model. GEMS-MAST [14] uses this free memory and compute resources by training a replica of the same DNN in an *inverted* manner. This design is called GEMS-Master. We call this bi-directional parallelism in the rest of the paper.

4 Proposed Hybrid Five-Dimensional Parallelism System

4.1 Spatial Parallelism

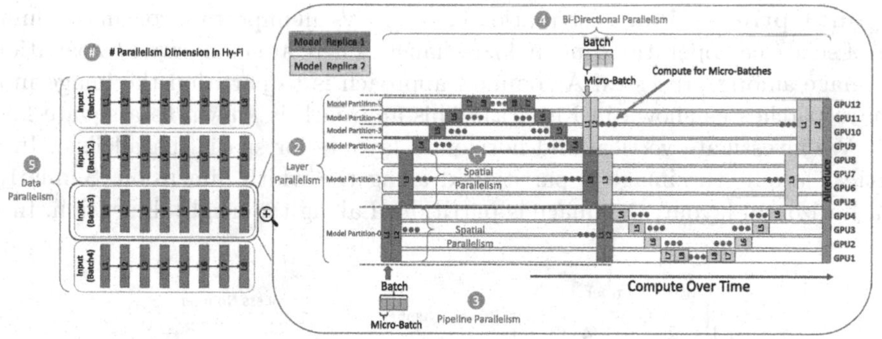

Fig. 2. High-level overview of proposed Hybrid Five-Dimensional Parallelism (Hy-Fi) where L# represents layer number. It shows the integration of different parallelism dimensions in Hy-Fi.

In spatial parallelism, the convolution layer is replicated across multiple GPUs, and image parts are partitioned across replicas. Specifically, the level of granularity in layer parallelism is a layer, while in spatial parallelism it is neurons. Convolution and Pooling layers can be distributed across multiple GPUs to work on the different regions of the image. Hence, unlike layer parallelism, this approach enables simultaneous computation on multiple GPUs while facilitating the training of the out-of-core convolution layer. There are two significant issues with the spatial parallelism approach; 1) Extra Communication is necessary and 2) Complex implementation. Spatial parallelism requires a halo exchange (shown in Fig. 3) at every convolution and pooling layer to compute the result for the pixels present on the boundary of image parts [6]. Parameters like stride, filter size, and padding affect the size of the halo exchange, which increases any spatial parallelism implementation's complexity compared to layer parallelism. In the backward pass, `allreduce` is required to synchronize the weights of the convolution layer for every process performing spatial parallelism (Fig. 2).

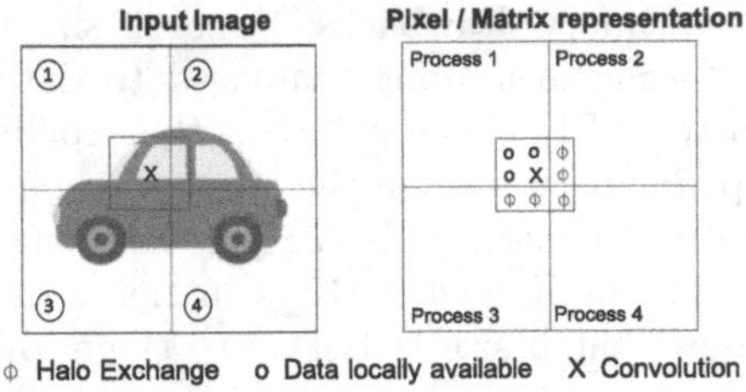

Fig. 3. Halo exchange in spatial parallelism. The input image is partitioned into four regions, and each region is given to the different processes. To calculate the convolution operation at X location, the value of nearby pixels is required.

To tackle communication overhead in spatial parallelism, we propose two optimization strategies.

Layout Optimization. Distribution layout plays an important role in the number of send/recv operations in a halo exchange. There are many ways to partition an image among processes. A common approach is to partition the image into square patches as shown in Fig. 4(a). This approach is known as a square layout. We investigate vertical and horizontal layouts for spatial parallelism. In a vertical layout, the image is partitioned along the width dimension. Similarly, in a horizontal layout, the image is partitioned along the height dimension. In a

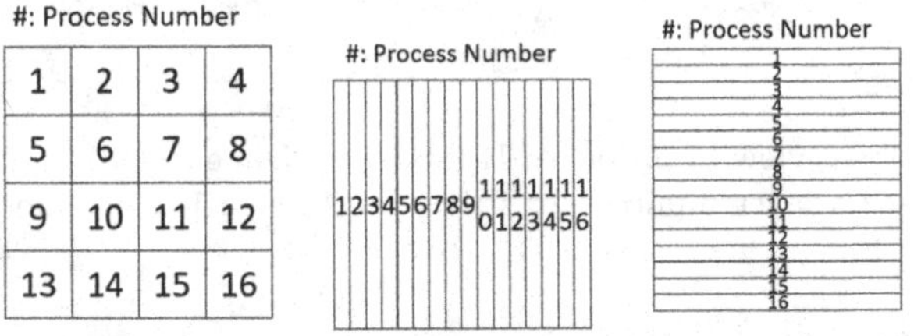

(a) Square Layout (b) Vertical Layout (c) Horizontal Layout

Fig. 4. Image distribution strategies

square layout, the maximum number of send/recv operations is 8. For example, process P6 will send/recv data from P1, P2, P3, P5, P7, P9, P10, and P11. However in horizontal and vertical layouts, the maximum number of send/recv operations is limited to 2 (can be inferred from Fig. 4(b) and 4(c)). Peculiar process placement in vertical and horizontal layout helps in reducing the inter-node communication by placing adjacent processes on the same node, which is not possible in a square layout. These factors help in reducing the communication.

Halo-D2: Reduced Communication Operations. A halo exchange is required at each layer in spatial parallelism in order to apply convolution/pooling operation in basic spatial parallelism. The main objective of the convolution operation is to produce an output of the same width and height. Normally in CNNs, several convolution operations of kernel size 3 are stacked together to efficiently implement a large kernel size [25]. This approach leads to several halo exchanges since it's required at every layer. We reduced the number of blocking communication operations by exchanging more pixels around the border. Spatial parallelism avoids the repeated computation on the border by exchanging data at every layer. However, in our evaluation, we found that the convolution operation takes the same time for images with a few more pixels due to the massively parallel computation provided by GPUs. For example, the computation time for a 256×256 image was the same as a 260×260 image. Therefore, by exchanging more data at one layer, we can avoid more halo exchanges in subsequent layers. Figure 5 shows an example of spatial parallelism with Halo-D2.

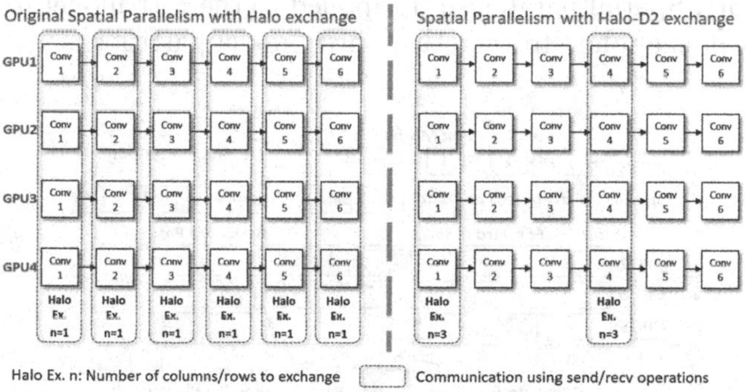

Fig. 5. Motivation for Halo-D2. Instead of exchanging only required data at every layer, additional data is exchanged to eliminate the need of exchanging data for subsequent layers.

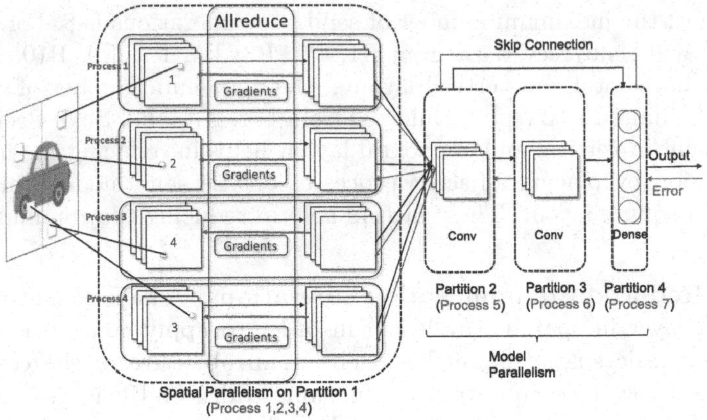

Fig. 6. Proposed spatial parallelism + layer parallelism design. CNN is sliced into four partitions. Spatial parallelism is applied to the 1st partition, and layer parallelism is used for the rest of the partitions.

4.2 Spatial Parallelism + Layer Parallelism

Due to the increased communication overhead, spatial parallelism is more suitable for large images, which makes this approach inappropriate for the latter half of CNNs where the image input size is usually few pixels. Layer parallelism can be used to compute this latter half. Figure 6 shows a combination of spatial parallelism and layer parallelism for a CNN partitioned into four partitions on layer granularity. Spatial parallelism is applied to the first model partition, and layer parallelism is applied to the other three model partitions.

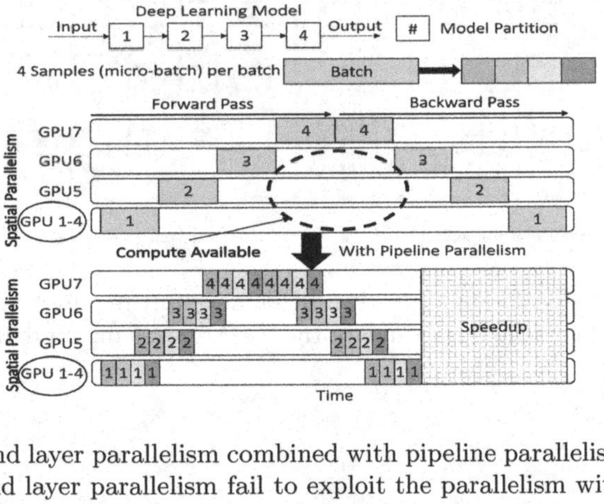

Fig. 7. Spatial and layer parallelism combined with pipeline parallelism. The combination of spatial and layer parallelism fail to exploit the parallelism within batches that can be used by pipeline parallelism to utilize more than one GPU at any given time.

4.3 Pipeline Parallelism

Spatial and Layer parallelism exploits parallelism within a layer and model. However, they fail to exploit parallelism within batches. Figure 7 shows the computational view of spatial and layer parallelism for the model shown in Fig. 6. As shown in the figure, compute is available between forward and backward pass. However, previous strategies fail to exploit this compute when the batch size is greater than 1. We use pipeline parallelism to exploit a third dimension of parallelism using micro-batches. Figure 7 shows the integration of pipeline parallelism with Spatial and Layer parallelism to exploit parallelism within batches, which improves the overall performance.

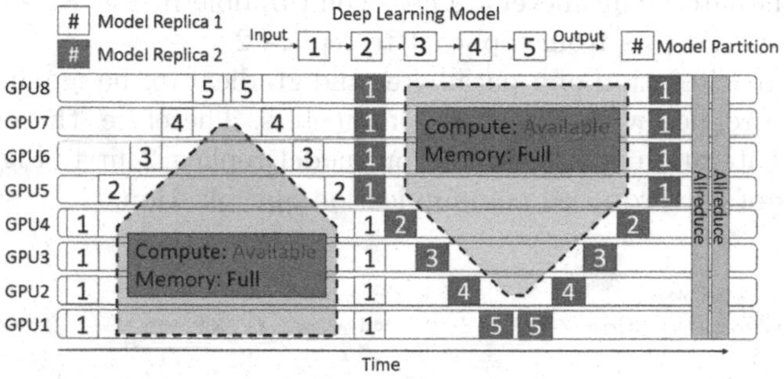

Fig. 8. Bi-directional with spatial and layer parallelism. A naive integration limits the performance because of blocking allreduce operations at the end. The available compute can be used to eliminate allreduce operation.

4.4 Spatial + Bidirectional Parallelism

To further improve the performance of spatial, layer, and pipeline parallelism, we explore a fourth dimension of parallelism i.e. the direction of forward and backward pass. By using bi-directional parallelism, we are able to overlap computation with different batches and therefore improve performance. This dimension is suitable when a DL researcher wants to train their model with larger batch size than the maximum feasible batch size (the maximum batch size is limited by GPU memory). Bi-directional parallelism increases the performance when the batch size is not possible under traditional parallelization strategies. In this section, we integrate first three dimension of parallelism with a fourth dimension (Bidirectional parallelism). Figure 8 shows the need for communication optimizations in the integration of spatial, layer, and pipeline parallelism with bi-directional parallelism.

Communication Optimization for Integration with Spatial Parallelism. To remove the necessary allreduce operation at the end, we use send/recv operations to communicate parameters and gradients of replica1 during the dotted bubble in Fig. 8. We divide our design into two steps: 1) Parameters exchange and 2) Gradient exchange.

Parameters Exchange: In this step, we assume that the first model replica has the latest DL model parameters and the second model replica does not have the latest parameters since we are not using an allreduce operation at the end to synchronize the training. Therefore, we will send the latest parameters from model replica 1 to model replica 2 during the first bubble.

Gradients Exchange: In an allreduce operation, gradients are averaged across all model replicas to synchronize the training and make sure parameters remain the same for all replicas. Since we are updating only the last replica, we need the gradients of the previous replica in order to synchronize the training and update replica 2 to the latest parameters. The second bubble in Fig. 8 can be used to exchange these gradients from replica 1 to replica 2.

After the first iteration of a parameter and gradient exchange, model replica 2 becomes the replica with the latest parameters. Therefore, the next forward and backward iteration will complete on model replica 2 first. Figure 9 shows two iterations of our proposed communication optimization.

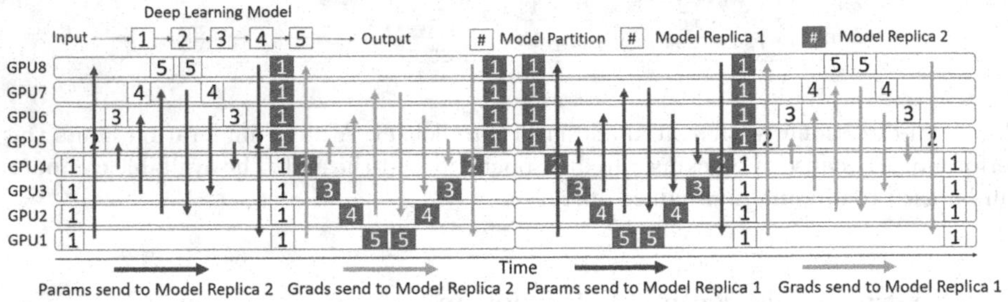

Fig. 9. Two iterations of communication optimized Hy-Fi master (spatial, layer, pipeline, and bi-directional)

4.5 Hybrid Data Parallelism

To scale proposed designs to a large number of GPUs, we exploit a fifth dimension of parallelism: data parallelism. We create clusters of GPUs, where each cluster implements the first four dimensions of parallelism in Hy-Fi and synchronizes each replica's parameters via allreduce operations. The integration with data parallelism allows our proposed design to scale to a large number of GPUs and provides better scaling efficiency.

Implementation Details: Our implementation of Hy-Fi is inspired by the pipeline parallelism fundamentals and APIs presented in the HyParFlow system [2]. For communication, we have used PyTorch's distributed module and created a wrapper communication class to create required communicators in proposed hybrid data parallelism (Sect. 4.5) and spatial parallelism (Sect. 4.1).

A model generator class is created to divide the model into partitions. *Trainer* class is created for every parallelism dimension to implement distributed forward and backward pass. For spatial parallelism, a wrapper class around *Conv2D* class is implemented to realize proposed designs for Halo communication.

5 Performance Evaluation

5.1 Evaluation Platform

All the experiments were conducted on LLNL/Lassen, which is an OpenPOWER system equipped with POWER9 processors and 4 NVIDIA Volta V100 GPUs. Each node of the cluster is a dual-socket machine, and each socket is equipped with 22-core IBM POWER9 processors and 2 NVIDIA Volta V100 GPUs with 16 GB HBM2. NVLink is used to connect GPU-GPU and GPU-Processor.

Softwares: Pytorch v1.7 and MVAPICH2-GDR 2.3.5.

Deep Neural Networks: We defined ResNet variants from Keras examples/applications in PyTorch and used the AmoebaNet model from TorchGpipe [16].

5.2 Evaluation Setup and Performance Metrics

We use images per sec as the main performance metric in this paper. Other terms and legends used in this performance evaluation are explained below.

- **Images per sec:** Number of images processed in training per sec.
- **BS:** Batch Size
- **LP:** Layer Parallelism (or Model-Parallelism Basic)
- **Pipeline:** Pipeline Parallelism.
- **SP and SP-Opt:** Hy-Fi's Spatial Parallelism and its optimized version (Layout Optimization and Halo-D2).
- **SP-#:** Hy-Fi's Spatial Parallelism with # Layout (Sq: Square, Hor: Horizontal, and Ver: Vertical)
- **SP-#-D2:** Hy-Fi's Spatial Parallelism with # Layout and Halo-D2 optimization.
- **Master-#:** Hy-Fi with four parallelism dimensions (Spatial, Layer, Pipeline, and Bi-Directional). # is the number of replications in Bi-Directional's Master design.
- **Master-#-Opt:** Master-# with communication optimization.

5.3 Evaluation Methodology

In this section, we describe the evaluation methodology used to conduct experiments and show Hy-Fi's benefits. Broadly, our experiments can be divided into four categories; 1) Performance analysis of different dimensions of parallelism in

Hy-Fi and their optimizations (Sect. 5.4 and 5.5) 2) Scaling Hy-Fi on a large number of GPUs (Sect. 5.6), 3) Comparison against existing frameworks (Sect. 5.7), and 4) Enabling training of very high-resolution images and speedup using Hy-Fi (Sect. 5.8). We use two variants of AmoebaNet and ResNet-218 v2 model. AmoebaNet-f214 and AmoebaNet-f416 have 18 cells and the number of initial filters is 214 and 416, respectively. AmoebaNet model variants are evaluated on $2{,}048 \times 2{,}048$ images. AmoebaNet-f214 is used since it can be trained on 8 GPUs with BS 2, making pipeline parallelism possible. AmoebatNet-f416 on $2{,}048 \times 2{,}048$ and ResNet-218-v2 on $1{,}024 \times 1{,}024$ can only be trained with BS = 1 on 8 GPUs, which makes pipeline parallelism impossible.

5.4 Performance Benefits of Spatial Parallelism

We start by demonstrating the benefits of Layout and Halo-D2 optimizations for Hy-Fi spatial parallelism and compare Hy-Fi's spatial parallelism with layer parallelism and pipeline-parallelism in the literature. Figure 10(a) shows the effect of number of fused layers in Halo-D2 (Sect. 4.1). The number of fused layers determines both the size of a halo exchange and how many layers can be skipped for a halo exchange. For the ResNet-218v2 model, we found that Halo-D2 gives the best performance for 4 fused layers. Proposed Halo-D2 optimization increases the training performance by up to 4.8%. Figure 10(b) shows the performance comparison of different proposed optimizations on spatial parallelism and compares them to LP. Hy-Fi's spatial parallelism is 1.94× faster than LP without optimizations for spatial parallelism.

By combining layout and Halo-D2 optimizations, we are able to improve the performance to 2.04×. Figure 11(a) and Fig. 11(b) show the performance comparison of spatial parallelism optimizations, LP, and pipeline parallelism (when possible). For AmoebaNet-f214, we use the first three dimensions of parallelism in Hy-Fi (spatial, model, and pipeline) when a batch size greater than 1 is possible. Hy-Fi is 2.2× faster than LP and 1.44× faster than existing pipeline parallelism. The proposed optimizations to spatial parallelism increases the performance improvement from 1.98× to 2.2×.

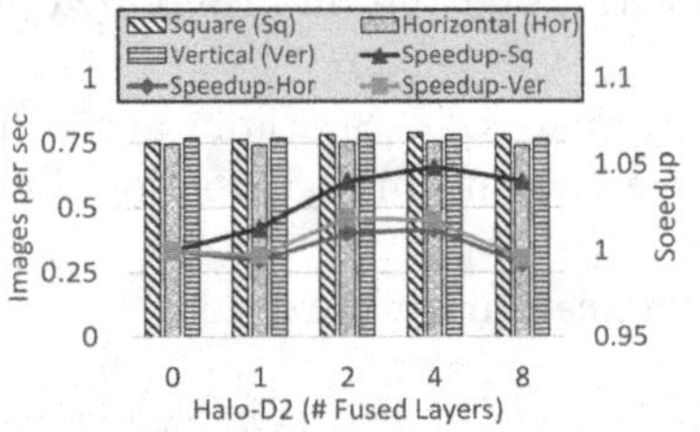

(a) Effect of number of fused layers in Halo-D2 for different layouts

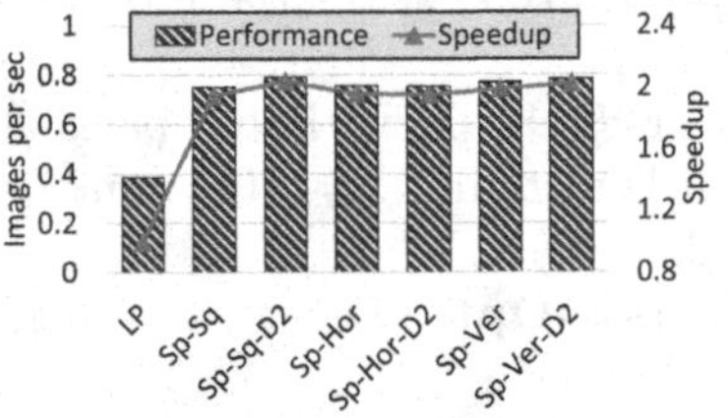

(b) Performance comparison of LP and spatial parallelism optimizations

Fig. 10. ResNet-218v2 on 8 GPUs using $1{,}024 \times 1{,}024$ images

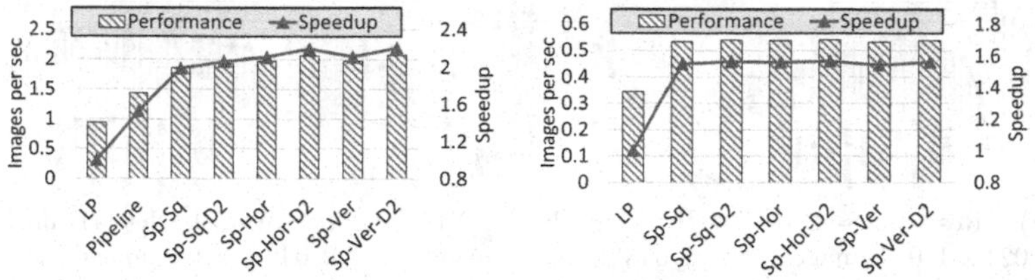

(a) AmoebaNet-f214 (b) AmoebaNet-f416

Fig. 11. Performance comparison of LP and different spatial parallelism optimizations for AmoebaNet on 8 GPUs using 2,048 × 2,048 images

5.5 Improving Performance Using Bi-directional Parallelism

The first three dimensions of parallelism do not exploit the free memory and compute resources available between training steps. Therefore we integrate bi-directional parallelism and increases its performance by removing the blocking allreduce operation at the end (Sect. 4.4). This enables the training of larger batch sizes on the same number of resources and improves the throughput, which was impossible earlier because of memory requirements. Figure 12 demonstrates the benefits of a fourth dimension of parallelism (GEMS-MASTER) in Hy-Fi. We compare our designs against existing layer and pipleine parallelism. Bi-directional parallelism uses a number of replications to stack more batches before the weight update. Therefore, we show performance improvements for up to 16 replications. The improvement in performance was negligible after 16 replications. In Fig. 12(a), we improve the performance from 2.04× to 2.67× using bi-directional parallelism. For AmoebaNet-f214 (Fig. 12(b)) and AmoebaNet-f416 (Fig. 12(c)), we show speedup improvement from 2.05× to 2.56× and from 1.56× to 1.78×. Using our proposed communication optimization (Sect. 4.4), we are able to improve speedup for replications = 1 from 2.28× to 2.34× and from 1.63× to 1.68× for AmoebaNet-f214 and AmobaNet-f416. For the ResNet-218v2 model, we observed that the improvement in speedup is 1.01× because of a small number of parameters compared to the AmoebaNet model, which translated into negligible allreduce time. As we tack more and more compute in MASTER by increasing the number of replications and batch size, the percentage of allreduce time decreases. Therefore, we see smaller and smaller speedup improvement for the communication optimization approach. However, we found that the communication optimized design always gave better performance than basic integration and proposed communication optimization improves the overall training performance by up to 7%. Therefore, Hy-Fi improves the performance for smaller batch sizes and enables researchers to use it without compromising on throughput.

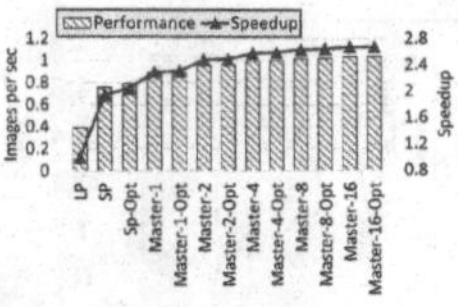

(a) ResNet218-v2 on 1,024 × 1,024 images

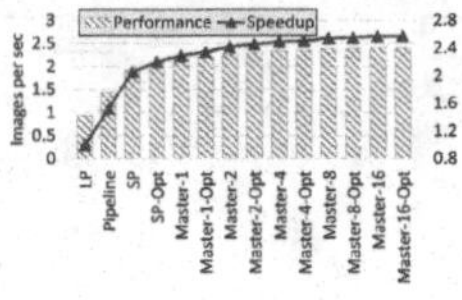

(b) AmoebaNet-f214 on 2,048 × 2,048 images

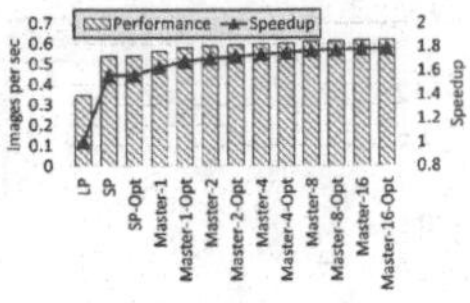

(c) AmoebaNet-f416 on 2,048 × 2,048 images

Fig. 12. Performance comparison of Hy-Fi's 4th dimension of parallelism (bi-directional) with and without communication optimization

5.6 Hybrid Parallelism

We demonstrate the proposed Hy-Fi system's scalability (Fig. 17) by scaling four CNNs. This experiment uses all five dimensions of parallelism and respective optimizations to scale Hy-Fi to 2,048 GPUs. All four evaluated Hy-Fi designs (Sp-Opt, Master-1-Opt, and Master-16-Opt) achieve near-linear speedup. For Hy-Fi's Master-1-Opt, we achieve 246× speedup for ResNet, 244× speedup for AmoebaNet-f214, and 242× speedup for AmoebaNet-f416 on 2,048 GPUs. The ideal speedup is 128× for 1,024 GPUs and 256× for 2,048 GPUs since models are partitioned across 8 GPUs. VGG16 achieves 199× speedup on 1,024 GPUs. The near-linear scaling of proposed designs can be attributed to the proposed communication optimization in Hy-Fi and its efficient implementation. Instead of doing allreduce operation twice in bi-directional parallelism, we do allreduce once in our proposed communication optimization (Fig. 13).

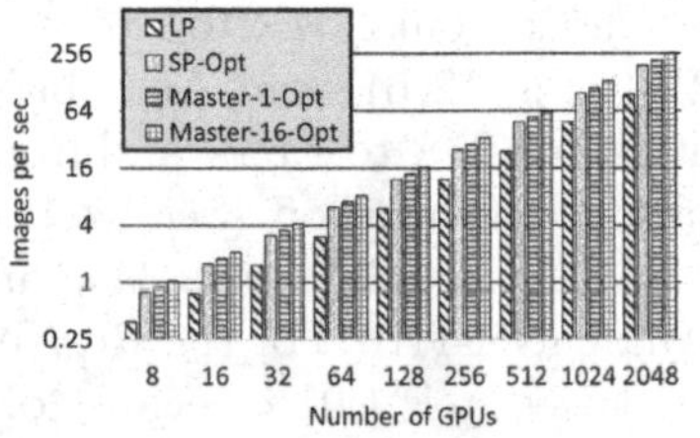

(a) ResNet218-v2 on 1,024 × 1,024 images

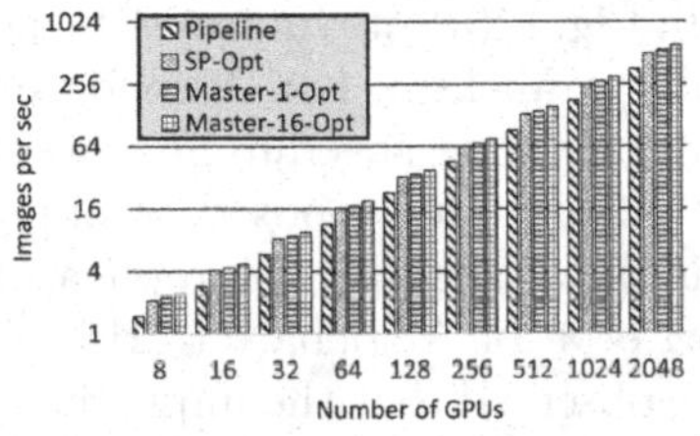

(b) AmoebaNet-f214 on 2,048 × 2,048 images

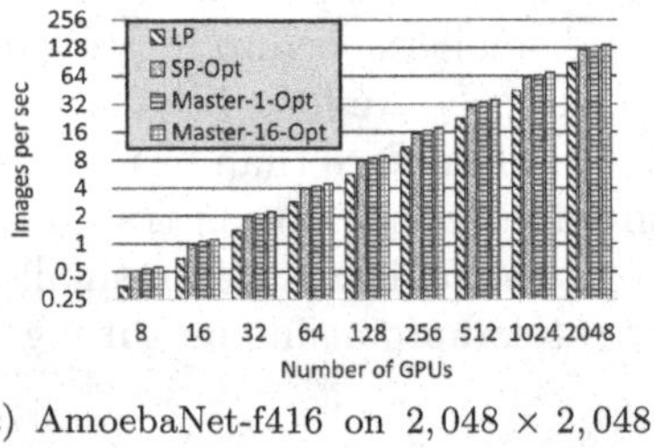

(c) AmoebaNet-f416 on 2,048 × 2,048 images

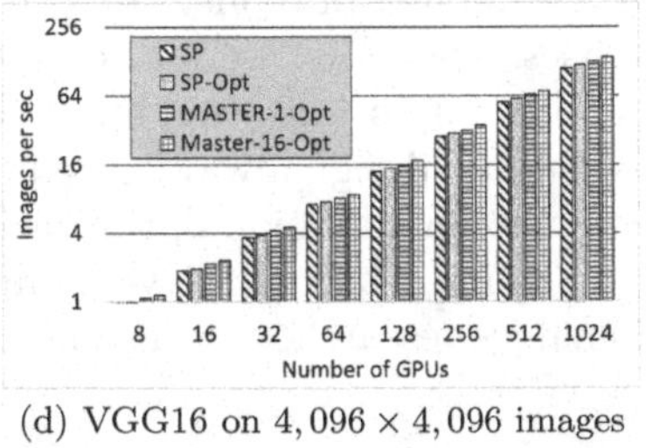

(d) VGG16 on 4,096 × 4,096 images

Fig. 13. Scaling Hy-Fi's optimized designs with all 5 parallelism dimensions on 2,048 GPUs

5.7 Hy-Fi vs Existing Frameworks

Comparison with TorchGPipe. We compare Hy-Fi against TorchGPipe for two primary reasons; 1) TorchGPipe has an efficient implementation of pipeline parallelism in PyTorch and 2) TorchGpipe has memory-level optimizations to enable the training of out-of-core batch sizes. Since TorchGpipe does not have multi-node support, we reduced the number of cells and initial filters in the AmoebaNet-f214 model to enable training on 4 GPUs. Figure 14(a) compares TorchGpipe's layer and pipeline parallelism implementations with ours and shows the benefits of Hy-Fi (1.2×) on the same batch size. It further validates the efficiency of our baseline implementation for layer and pipeline parallelism. Figure 14(b) compares the maximum performance attainable by both frameworks for any batch size and shows up to 1.06× speedup for Hy-Fi.

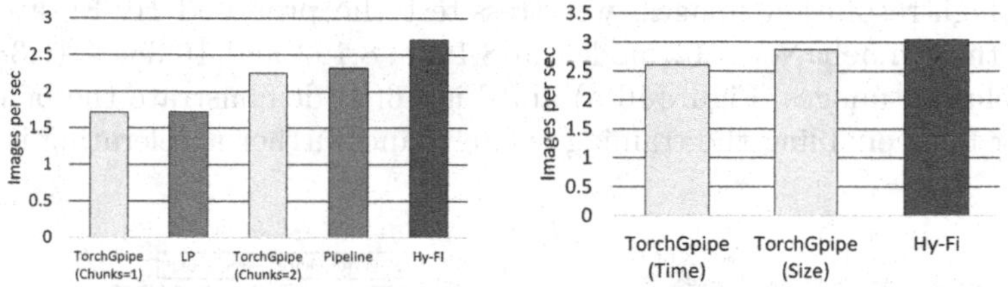

(a) Performance for Batch Size = 2 (b) Maximum Performance with any Batch Size

Fig. 14. Performance comparison of Hy-Fi and TorchGpipe for AmoebaNet on 4 GPUs using 2,048 × 2,048 images

Comparison with Mesh-TensorFlow and GEMS. To the best of our knowledge, there is no distributed training framework in PyTorch that implements spatial parallelism. Therefore, we use Mesh-TensorFlow since it is implemented in TensorFlow (TensorFlow and PyTorch are the two most popular DL frameworks). Since GEMS [14] conducted experiments on the same system, we use their Mesh-TensorFlow and GEMS numbers to compare our proposed designs.

Figure 15 compares Hy-Fi against state-of-the-art Mesh-TensorFlow and GEMS frameworks. We show 1.13× and 1.4× speedup for Hy-Fi over GEMS and Mesh-TensorFlow, respectively. We attempted to compare results with the FlexFlow framework, but encountered a number of issues with their PyTorch plugin. First, at the time of writing, many of the advanced operators/-modules in the Amoebanet PyTorch model are not interpretable by the base FlexFlow model transformation function. Further, we

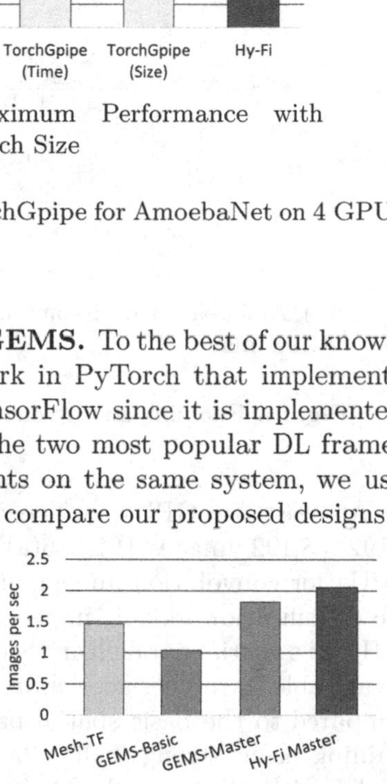

Fig. 15. Comparison with Mesh-TensorFlow and GEMS for ResNet-110 on 4 GPUs using 1,024 × 1,024 images

were unable to train on out-of-core batch sizes due to a conflict with the memory managers of FlexFlow and Legion [4] (which FlexFlow uses for intra-node communication).

5.8 Next-Generation DNN Designs on Very High-Resolution Images Using Hy-Fi

Today, Deep learning researchers develop models restricted by the number of layers for high-resolution images such as 8,192 × 8,192 and 16,384 × 16,384. Layer parallelism can be used to train out-of-core models, yet requires a single layer to fit inside a GPU's memory, which is a limitation for very high-resolution images. For example, a single channel 16,384 × 16,384 image consumes around 1GB of memory with FP32 representation. This makes the training impossible for CNNs using very high-resolution images. To illustrate the possibility of training models on very high-resolution images, we stress-test the proposed Hy-Fi system by training the AmoebaNet-f214 model on 8,192 × 8,192 and 16,384 × 16,384 very high-resolution images. Figure 16(a) and Fig. 16(b) demonstrate the benefits of Hy-Fi for both enabling the training entirely, and further accelerating it.

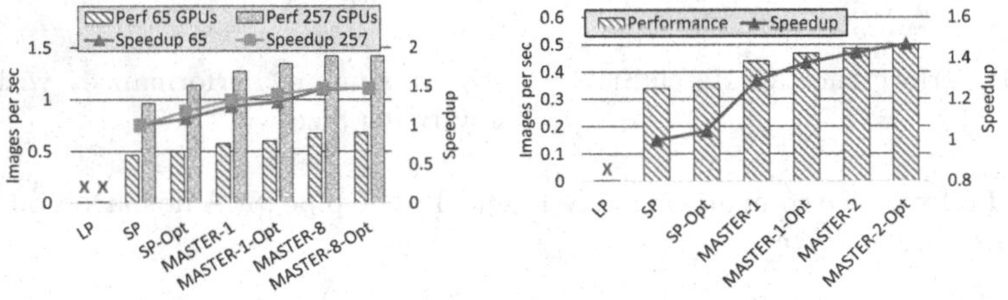

(a) AmoebaNet-f214 on 8,192 × 8,192 images

(b) AmoebaNet-f214 on 16,384 × 16,384 images

Fig. 16. Enabling and accelerating training on very high-resolution images

At least 16 GPUs are needed to train the AmoebaNet-f214 model on 8,192 × 8,192 images (Fig. 16(a)); therefore, we use spatial parallelism on 16 GPUs for convolution and pooling layers and layer parallelism on 1 GPU for the classification module in the AmoebaNet model. By using the optimizations in Hy-Fi's spatial parallelism (Sect. 4.1) and bi-directional parallelism (Sect. 4.4), we are able to further accelerate the training and achieve up to 1.476× speedup compared to the basic spatial parallelism approach. Further, we accelerate the training using strong scaling by increasing the number of GPUs to train the model with the same batch size. We are able to achieve a 2.26× speedup using strong scaling. In Fig. 16(b), we enable and accelerate the training for 16,384 × 16,384 images and achieve up to 1.47× speedup compared to basic spatial parallelism.

5.9 Verifying the Correctness of Hy-Fi

We have extended the PyTorch and implemented distributed training from scratch to support proposed designs. Therefore, it is important to show that Hy-Fi trains the model in the same number of epochs using proposed designs to give confidence to DL researchers. We trained ResNet-218 v2 CNN for a subset of Cifar-10 and Places-365 datasets. First, we provide results for the Cifar-10 dataset as it can be trained on a single GPU without distributed DNN training. Figure 17(a) shows trend of loss function for 100 epochs The objective of this experiment is to showcase the correctness of Hy-Fi's proposed designs with respect to sequential out-of-the-box training provided by PyTorch.

Figure 17(b) and Fig. 17(c) show trend of loss and accuracy functions for 30 epochs when training ResNet-218 v2 model on a dataset with larger image sizes (512×512). It cannot be trained on a single GPU as the model becomes out-of-core for 512×512 image size. We note that DNN training is a stochastic process; therefore, there can be variations in few epochs whether we use sequential training or distributed DNN training. However, the overall trend should remain the same. We ran these experiments multiple times to ensure that the loss function trend presented here is reproducible.

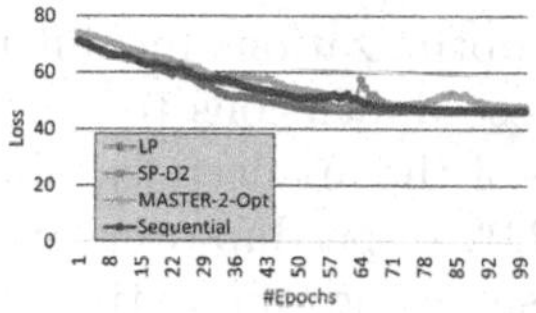

(a) On a subset of Cifar-10 dataset

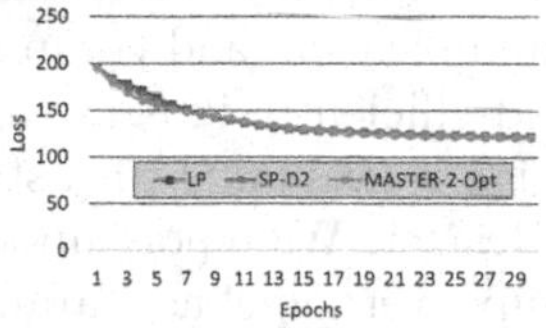

(b) On a subset of Places-365 dataset (Loss)

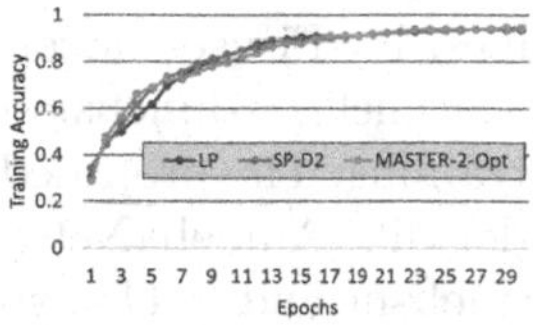

(c) On a subset of Places-365 dataset (Acc)

Fig. 17. Verifying the correctness of proposed designs in Hy-Fi by training ResNet-218 v2 on multiple datasets

6 Related Work

The growth of scientific and medical applications requiring massive data sample sizes [7] has led deep learning researchers to explore new parallelism techniques that train on such images without high accuracy and efficiency. Krizhevsky's work pioneered basic model parallelism techniques in [18]. GPipe [12] employs pipeline parallelism to enable the training of extremely large models like AmoebaNet [22]. Further, PipeDream [10] expands upon GPipe's pipelining idea by introducing pipeline parallelism, which combines inter-batch and intra-batch parallelism to increase overlap among GPUs. Torchgpipe [16] combined the overall design of GPipe (pipeline parallelism) with some of the eager execution and memory-aware enhancements of HyPar-Flow into a distributed PyTorch DL framework. GEMS [14] introduced memory-aware partition overlap for out-of-core models on GPUs, but does not support spatial parallelism. Spatial parallelism, however, is a more recent addition to model parallel techniques [9]. LBANN introduced spatial convolutions split across nodes in [6]. However, spatial parallelism support in LBANN doesn't include pipelining nor bidirectional training as in the GEMS design. FlexFlow [15] searches through all parallelization strategies with simulation algorithms and highlights different DNN parallelism dimensions. We attempted to compare our work with FlexFlow but ran into issues with the framework when handling large images on our system. Mesh-TensorFlow (MTF) [23] is a framework for distributed DNN training which partitions tensors across a processor mesh. We summarize these related studies and their features in Table 1.

7 Conclusion

Convolutional Neural Networks (CNNs) are making breakthroughs in the computer vision area, but are hard to train on very high-resolution images due to memory and compute constraints. In this paper, we present Hy-Fi - an integrated hybrid five-dimensional distributed DNN training system that uses different parallelism dimensions in tandem and accelerates training for very high-resolution images. Hy-Fi uses novel communication and compute optimizations for different parallelism dimensions and efficiently integrates these dimensions to speed up training. The proposed design is evaluated with state-of-the-art deep learning models like AmoebaNet and ResNet. We report up to 2.02× speedup over layer parallelism and 1.44× speedup over pipeline parallelism using our optimized spatial, layer, and pipeline parallelism. Further, we improve speedup using optimized memory-aware designs to 2.67× over layer parallelism and 1.68× over pipeline parallelism. We scale our designs to 2,048 GPUs and show up to 94.5% scaling efficiency. In the end, we demonstrate training on very high-resolution images and report up to 1.47× speedup over basic spatial parallelism. We believe that Hy-Fi will pave a way forward for solving complex and compute-intensive problems in scientific, digital pathology, and artificial intelligence areas.

Acknowledgement. This research is supported in part by NSF grants 1818253, 1854828, 1931537, 2007991, 2018627, 2112606, and XRAC grant NCR-130002.

References

1. Awan, A.A., Hamidouche, K., Hashmi, J.M., Panda, D.K.: S-Caffe: co-designing MPI runtimes and Caffe for scalable deep learning on modern GPU clusters. In: Proceedings of the 22nd ACM SIGPLAN Symposium on Principles and Practice of Parallel Programming, pp. 193–205. ACM, New York (2017)
2. Awan, A.A., Jain, A., Anthony, Q., Subramoni, H., Panda, D.K.: HyPar-Flow: exploiting MPI and Keras for scalable hybrid-parallel DNN training using TensorFlow (2019)

3. Awan, A.A., Subramoni, H., Panda, D.K.: An in-depth performance characterization of CPU- and GPU-based DNN training on modern architectures. In: Proceedings of the Machine Learning on HPC Environments, MLHPC 2017, pp. 8:1–8:8. ACM, New York (2017)
4. Bauer, M., Treichler, S., Slaughter, E., Aiken, A.: Legion: expressing locality and independence with logical regions. In: Proceedings of the International Conference on High Performance Computing, Networking, Storage and Analysis, SC 2012. IEEE Computer Society Press (2012)
5. Ben-Nun, T., Hoefler, T.: Demystifying parallel and distributed deep learning: an in-depth concurrency analysis. CoRR abs/1802.09941 (2018)
6. Dryden, N., Maruyama, N., Benson, T., Moon, T., Snir, M., Essen, B.V.: Improving strong-scaling of CNN training by exploiting finer-grained parallelism. CoRR abs/1903.06681 (2019). http://arxiv.org/abs/1903.06681
7. Farrell, S., et al.: Novel deep learning methods for track reconstruction (2018)
8. Gholami, A., Azad, A., Jin, P., Keutzer, K., Buluc, A.: Integrated model, batch, and domain parallelism in training neural networks. In: Proceedings of the 30th on Symposium on Parallelism in Algorithms and Architectures, SPAA 2018, pp. 77–86. ACM, New York (2018). https://doi.org/10.1145/3210377.3210394
9. Gholami, A., Azad, A., Jin, P., Keutzer, K., Buluc, A.: Integrated model, batch, and domain parallelism in training neural networks. In: Proceedings of the 30th on Symposium on Parallelism in Algorithms and Architectures, pp. 77–86 (2018)
10. Harlap, A., et al.: PipeDream: fast and efficient pipeline parallel DNN training. CoRR abs/1806.03377 (2018). http://arxiv.org/abs/1806.03377
11. Huang, Y., et al.: GPipe: efficient training of giant neural networks using pipeline parallelism. CoRR abs/1811.06965 (2018). http://arxiv.org/abs/1811.06965
12. Huang, Y., et al.: GPipe: efficient training of giant neural networks using pipeline parallelism. In: NeurIPS (2019)
13. Jain, A., et al.: SUPER: SUb-graph parallelism for transformers. In: 35th IEEE International Parallel and Distributed Processing Symposium (IPDPS), May 2021
14. Jain, A., et al.: GEMS: GPU-enabled memory-aware model-parallelism system for distributed DNN training. In: 2020 SC 2020: International Conference for High Performance Computing, Networking, Storage and Analysis (SC), pp. 621–635. IEEE Computer Society (2020)
15. Jia, Z., Zaharia, M., Aiken, A.: Beyond data and model parallelism for deep neural networks. CoRR abs/1807.05358 (2018). http://arxiv.org/abs/1807.05358
16. Kim, C., et al.: torchgpipe: on-the-fly pipeline parallelism for training giant models (2020)
17. Kousha, P., et al.: Designing a profiling and visualization tool for scalable and in-depth analysis of high-performance GPU clusters. In: 2019 IEEE 26th International Conference on High Performance Computing, Data, and Analytics (HiPC), pp. 93–102 (2019). https://doi.org/10.1109/HiPC.2019.00022
18. Krizhevsky, A.: One weird trick for parallelizing convolutional neural networks. CoRR abs/1404.5997 (2014). http://arxiv.org/abs/1404.5997
19. Lee, S., et al.: Interactive classification of whole-slide imaging data for cancer researchers. Cancer Res. **81**(4), 1171–1177 (2021). https://doi.org/10.1158/0008-5472.CAN-20-0668. https://cancerres.aacrjournals.org/content/81/4/1171
20. Paszke, A., et al.: Automatic differentiation in PyTorch (2017)
21. Petrowski, A., Dreyfus, G., Girault, C.: Performance analysis of a pipelined backpropagation parallel algorithm. IEEE Trans. Neural Netw. **4**(6), 970–981 (1993). https://doi.org/10.1109/72.286892

22. Real, E., Aggarwal, A., Huang, Y., Le, Q.V.: Regularized evolution for image classifier architecture search. CoRR abs/1802.01548 (2018)
23. Shazeer, N., et al.: Mesh-TensorFlow: deep learning for supercomputers. In: Advances in Neural Information Processing Systems, vol. 31. Curran Associates, Inc. (2018)
24. Shoeybi, M., Patwary, M.A., Puri, R., LeGresley, P., Casper, J., Catanzaro, B.: Megatron-LM: training multi-billion parameter language models using model parallelism. ArXiv abs/1909.08053 (2019)
25. Simonyan, K., Zisserman, A.: Very deep convolutional networks for large-scale image recognition. arXiv preprint arXiv:1409.1556 (2014)

HPC Algorithms and Applications

Efficient Application of Hanging-Node Constraints for Matrix-Free High-Order FEM Computations on CPU and GPU

Peter Munch[1,2(✉)], Karl Ljungkvist[3], and Martin Kronbichler[3]

[1] Helmholtz-Zentrum Hereon, Geesthacht, Germany
peterrmuench@gmail.com
[2] Technical University of Munich, Munich, Germany
[3] Uppsala University, Uppsala, Sweden

Abstract. This contribution presents an efficient algorithm for resolving hanging-node constraints on the fly for high-order finite-element computations on adaptively refined meshes, using matrix-free implementations. We concentrate on unstructured hex-dominated meshes and on multi-component elements with nodal Lagrange shape functions in at least one of their components. The application of general constraints is split up into two distinct operators, one specialized in the hanging-node part and a generic one for the remaining constraints, such as Dirichlet boundary conditions. The former implements in-face interpolations efficiently by a sequence of 1D interpolations with sum factorization according to the refinement configuration of the cell. We discuss ways to efficiently encode and decode such refinement configurations. Furthermore, we present distinct differences in the interpolation step on GPU and CPU, as well as compare different vectorization strategies for the latter. Experimental comparisons with a state-of-the-art algorithm that does not exploit the tensor-product structure show that, on CPUs, the additional costs of cells with hanging-node constraints can be reduced by a factor of 5–10 for a Laplace operator evaluation with high-order elements ($k \geq 3$) and affine meshes. For non-affine meshes, the costs for the application of hanging-node constraints can be completely hidden behind the memory transfer. The algorithm has been integrated into the open-source finite-element library `deal.II`.

Keywords: Adaptively refined meshes · Finite element methods · High order · Hanging-node constraints · Matrix-free operator evaluation · Node-level optimization · SIMD vectorization · Manycore optimizations

This work was supported by the Bayerisches Kompetenznetzwerk für Technisch-Wissenschaftliches Hoch- und Höchstleistungsrechnen (KONWIHR) through the projects "Performance tuning of high-order discontinuous Galerkin solvers for SuperMUC-NG" and "High-order matrix-free finite element implementations with hybrid parallelization and improved data locality". The authors gratefully acknowledge the Gauss Centre for Supercomputing e.V. (www.gauss-centre.eu) for funding this project by providing computing time on the GCS Supercomputer SuperMUC-NG at Leibniz Supercomputing Centre (LRZ, www.lrz.de) through project id pr83te.

A.-L. Varbanescu et al. (Eds.): ISC High Performance 2022, LNCS 13289, pp. 133–152, 2022.
https://doi.org/10.1007/978-3-031-07312-0_7

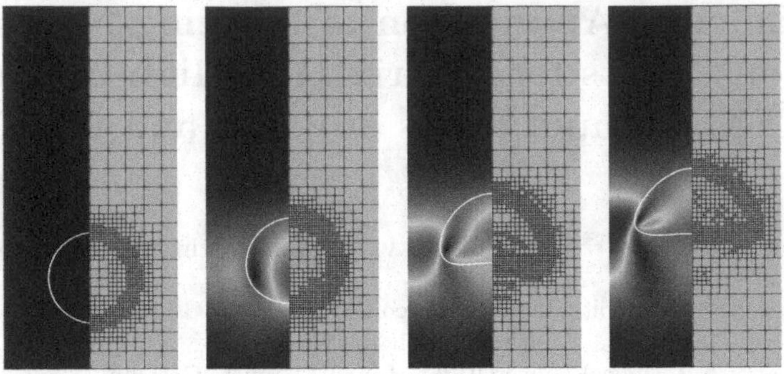

Fig. 1. The "rising-bubble" benchmark in 2D as an example of a simulation using AMR: left) velocity contour and zero level-set isoline and right) mesh resolving the resulting surface-tension forces at the interface accurately. The results have been obtained with the open-source two-phase solver `adaflo` [12].

1 Introduction

Matrix-free high-order finite element methods (FEM) are used to efficiently solve different types of partial differential equations (PDE) with applications in fluid mechanics [8,11], solid mechanics [7], mesh smoothing [1], or computational plasma physics [21]. The applicability of matrix-free methods to massively parallel computers has been demonstrated multiple times in the past [9].

In order to reduce the computational costs, one can adaptively refine meshes (AMR) to concentrate the work on the most relevant areas of the computational domain, where, e.g., the solution has high gradients or discontinuities (see Fig. 1). One of the ways to refine meshes, the non-conforming refinement strategy, refines cells independently by replacing parent cells by children cells (octants for hexahedral cells) and results in the occurrence of hanging nodes (see Fig. 2a). In order to guarantee the continuity, i.e., H^1 conformity, of the tentative solution at these places, hanging-node constraints have to be applied [25]. Although not strictly needed, many codes limit the difference in refinement of neighboring cells to one (1-irregular mesh), since a more abrupt transition in most cases does not lead to a significant reduction of time to solution to justify the implementation complexity.

Simulations with hanging nodes need iterative solvers that can cope with these nodes in a robust manner (e.g., geometric multigrid methods [13,20]) and algorithms to apply hanging-node constraints efficiently. Since matrix-free methods need to interpolate the constraints in each operator evaluation of each iteration, the efficient application of hanging-node constraints is a crucial HPC ingredient for the fast solution of PDEs with FEM on adaptively refined meshes and the core of the present publication.

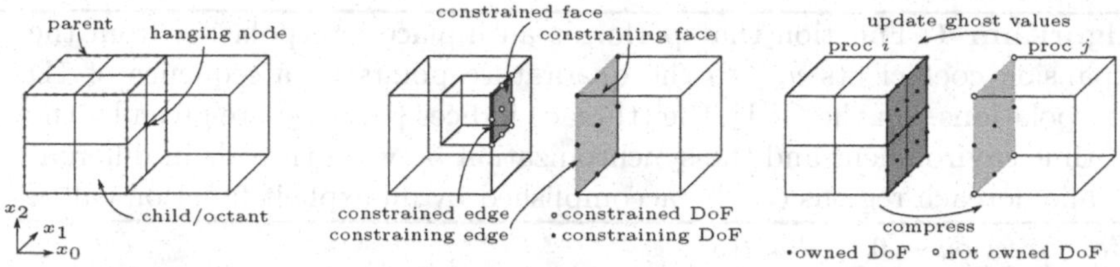

(a) Mesh (b) Degrees of freedom (c) Communication

Fig. 2. Definition of the most important terms of hanging-node constraints on a hexahedral mesh, incl. the communication pattern between two processes $i < j$, with one possessing only one unrefined cell and the other all children of a cell.

1.1 Matrix-Free Operator Evaluation

In this work, we consider matrix-free implementations for general meshes, which compute the integrals underlying a finite-element discretization on the fly. Here, the operator evaluation performs a loop over all cells and applies the effect of element stiffness matrices on a vector with the following basic steps [14]:

$$v = \mathcal{A}(u) = \sum_e \mathcal{G}_e^T \circ \mathcal{C}_e^T \circ \tilde{\mathcal{S}}_e^T \circ \mathcal{D}_e \circ \mathcal{S}_e \circ \mathcal{C}_e \circ \mathcal{G}_e \circ u. \tag{1}$$

In the first step, the degrees of freedom (DoFs) relevant for each cell e are gathered by $\mathcal{G}_e$ from the global source vector u. In the remainder of this study, these unknowns are called cell-relevant DoFs. The application of $\mathcal{C}_e$ interpolates from these cell-relevant DoFs to the cell-local values $u_{e,j}$ in the polynomial expansion of the finite-element solution $u_h|_e = \sum_j \varphi_j^{(e)} u_{e,j}$, consistent with all constraints due to hanging nodes and boundary conditions. Subsequently, values and/or gradients of u_h are evaluated at the quadrature points via $\mathcal{S}_e$ and the computed quantities are processed on each quadrature point by $\mathcal{D}_e$. The application of $\tilde{\mathcal{S}}_e^T$ represents the multiplication by the finite-element test functions and the summation over quadrature points. For simplicity of notation, we assume a symmetric (self-adjoint) PDE operator with $\tilde{\mathcal{S}}_e = \mathcal{S}_e$ in this work. Finally, $\mathcal{C}_e$ and $\mathcal{G}_e$ are applied in reverse order during multiplication by the finite-element test functions and the results are added into the global destination vector v.

The operator $\mathcal{G}_e$ is a Boolean matrix (DoF map) representing indirect addressing into the vectors u and v. In the past decades, significant efforts went into optimizing the evaluation operator $\mathcal{S}_e$. In particular, the exploitation of the structure of the shape functions and quadrature points allows replacing a general dense interpolation matrix by more efficient procedures. For example, sum factorization [19,22] (see Algorithm 1) performs a sequence of 1D interpolation steps to evaluate vectors at the quadrature points for tensor-product polynomials, reducing the computational complexity from $\mathcal{O}(k^{2d})$ to $\mathcal{O}(dk^{d+1})$ for scalar Lagrange elements of degree k. On a per-unknown metric, operation (1) with sum factorization implies an arithmetic complexity $\mathcal{O}(k)$ and a memory access complexity $\mathcal{O}(1)$. This makes the approach the most efficient way to compute the

Algorithm 1: Function that performs an inplace interpolation from the expansion coefficients $u_{e,i}$ to the quadrature points by a sequence of 1D interpolations. On the GPU, the (thread) indices $[i_0, i_1, i_2]$ are given by the runtime environment and the synchronization between threads in different parallel foreach regions can be accomplished by an explicit function call.

for *direction* $\leftarrow 0$ **to** *dim* **do**
  parallelforeach $index \in \{[i_0, i_1, i_2] \mid 0 \leq i_0, i_1, i_2 \leq k\}$ **do**
    /* interpolate along line (def. by *index* & *direction*) */
    value $\leftarrow$ $interp\_matrix[index[direction]].*\,data(index, direction)$
  parallelforeach $index \in \{[i_0, i_1, i_2] \mid 0 \leq i_0, i_1, i_2 \leq k\}$ **do**
    $data(index) =$ value

action of a discretized differential operator on vectors for higher-order finite elements with degree $k \geq 3$ on general (deformed) meshes [9,14]. On today's hardware, the boost in efficiency is primarily due to the reduction in memory access by skipping a memory-intensive assembled matrix in favor of on-the-fly computations on cached data. Implementations specialized for CPUs [1,14,15,21] and GPUs [1,16,18,26] are available in the literature.

Given the nested loop structures with different strides and data dependencies when interpolating in different directions with sum factorization, automatic vectorization leads to poor performance on modern CPUs and explicit outer-loop vectorization based on intrinsics either within a cell, i.e., across DoFs/quadrature points, or across cells, with each vector lane processing another cell, is necessary [15]. The latter is assumed for the CPU implementation, whereas in a GPU implementation, which runs parallel "threads" in a team, a thread works on an individual DoF within cells. Note that the algorithms and performance translate similarly to other alternatives [26], making the conclusions of this publication generic.

1.2 Application of Constraints

The constraint operator $\mathcal{C}_e$ relates cell-local DoFs to cell-relevant DoFs. Cell-local DoFs can be either constrained or not (○ vs. • in Fig. 2b). Constrained DoFs depend on constraining DoFs in the form of affine combinations $x_i = C_{ij}x_j + b_i$ with possible inhomogeneity $\boldsymbol{b}$. Examples of constraints are Dirichlet boundary conditions, periodic boundary conditions, and hanging-node constraints. Although $\boldsymbol{C}$ is generally sparse and can be efficiently stored in compressed row storage (CRS) format, it becomes locally dense for certain constraint types. For example, hanging-node constraints on faces relate all $n_{\text{dofs\_per\_face}}$ constrained DoFs of the subface on the fine side to the same number of constraining DoFs on the coarse side, see Fig. 2b. For the sake of brevity, we will call faces with DoFs with hanging-node constraints "constrained faces"; in a similar way, we will use the terms "constrained edges" and "constraining faces/edges". For tensor-product elements and scalar polynomial elements of degree k, the naive evaluation by a dense matrix of size $\mathcal{O}(n^2_{\text{dofs\_per\_face}})$ implies memory and arithmetic costs of $\mathcal{O}(k^{2(d-1)})$. These costs become the bottleneck of matrix-free algorithms of complexity $\mathcal{O}(dk^{d+1})$ for higher k.

1.3 Related Work

The interpolation of data to subcells or subfaces is a common operation in the context of FEM. For example, geometric multigrid methods [20] need to prolongate and restrict between cells and their children. In the case of discontinuous Galerkin methods and meshes with hanging nodes, data of neighboring cells have to be interpolated to subfaces for integration of fluxes on faces [15,17].

The development of adaptive solvers is a highly active field, as evidenced by the recent publication [23], necessitating advances in fast hanging-node algorithms. Recently, Cerveny et al. [6] presented a global operator $\mathcal{C}$ that can handle arbitrary irregular meshes obtained by anisotropic refinement. Kronbichler and Kormann [14] proposed a general way to process constraints during matrix-free loops in the context of FEM by a combined operator $(\mathcal{C} \circ \mathcal{G})_e$. Even though this approach identifies similar rows in the constraint matrix $\mathcal{C}$ to reduce memory access, it suffers from an exceeding complexity of the naive evaluation at higher orders $(\mathcal{O}(k^{2(d-1)}))$. In the context of spectral element methods [8,10] and FEM [16,18], a special-purpose hanging-node algorithm for 1-irregular meshes with only hypercube-shaped cells has been used that relies on the update of the DoF map $\mathcal{G}_e$ and efficient inplace interpolations. While the previous publications provide a clear understanding of the 2D case, this is not yet the case in 3D, in particular regarding recent advances in modern hardware, such as SIMD vectorization. The main difficulty are the 137 refinement configurations, as opposed to only 13 cases in 2D, and the appearance of constraints along edges.

1.4 Our Contributions

We present an algorithm to efficiently resolve constraints in the form of $\mathcal{C}_e$ and $\mathcal{C}_e^T$ of Eq. (1) with hanging-node contributions in the context of matrix-free FEM on CPUs and GPUs. The algorithm is built on the observation that, for Lagrange elements, the constraint matrix can be factored into a general-purpose operator and a special-purpose operator that can exploit the most efficient interpolation routines, e.g., sum factorization for tensor-product elements, and thus reduce the computational complexity to $\mathcal{O}((d-1)\cdot k^d)$, similarly to the operators developed in [8,10,16,18]. We give a detailed description of the special-purpose operator in 3D, which is crucial for the efficient implementation of our proposed algorithm. We assume that 1) the mesh has hypercube-shaped cells, 2) these cells have at most two children in each direction, and 3) the mesh is 1-irregular.

The algorithm presented in this publication has been integrated into the open-source C++-based FEM library `deal.II` [2,3]. The implementation is used by default in its matrix-free infrastructure; the correctness is checked by several hundreds of tests.

The remainder of this publication is structured as follows. In Sects. 2 and 3, we introduce the algorithm and discuss data structures and implementation details. In Sect. 4, we present performance results for serial runs and discuss the benefits of the given algorithm for parallel simulations. The results are obtained on Intel and AMD CPUs as well as on NVIDIA GPUs. Conclusions are given in Sect. 5.

2 Algorithm

We split $(\mathcal{C} \circ \mathcal{G})_e$ into three contributions $(\mathcal{C}^{\text{HN}} \circ \mathcal{C}^{\text{GP}} \circ \mathcal{G})_e$ with $\mathcal{C}^{\text{HN}}$ dedicated to the hanging-node constraints and $\mathcal{C}^{\text{GP}}$ to the remaining (general-purpose) constraints. The sequence of these contributions can be chosen arbitrarily. Two sequences have properties suitable for an HPC implementation and will be used in the following: (i) $\mathcal{C}_e^{\text{HN}} \circ \mathcal{G}_e^a \circ \mathcal{C}^{\text{GP}}$ and (ii) $\mathcal{C}_e^{\text{HN}} \circ \mathcal{C}_e^{\text{GP}} \circ \mathcal{G}_e^b$. Approach (i) applies the general-purpose constraints on the global vectors and then proceeds with operations on the element level, gathering the cell-relevant DoFs and applying the hanging-node constraints on the current cell. In practice, this approach involves a global pre- and postprocessing step ($\mathcal{C}^{\text{GP}}$, $(\mathcal{C}^{\text{GP}})^T$) before and after the matrix-free loop (1). In the literature, it is common to use $\mathcal{C}^{\text{GP}}$ for the application of homogeneous Dirichlet boundary conditions, for which it simplifies to zeroing out the entries constrained by Dirichlet boundary conditions. We use it also for more complex types of constraints, such as those constraining the normal or tangential components of a vector-valued solution. On a GPU, one would perform the preprocessing step, the matrix-free operator application, and the postprocessing step sequentially by three kernel calls. Approach (ii) applies the general constraints after gathering the cell-relevant DoFs within the loop (1). This approach accesses global vectors only once and operates exclusively on the fixed-size working set of a cell, assuming that caches are large enough to hold all cell-local values, which is the case on modern CPUs.

The operator $\mathcal{C}_e^{\text{HN}}$ independently applies the hanging-node constraints on the element level. The number of constrained and constraining DoFs is the same, i.e., $size(u_e) = size(\mathcal{C}_e^{\text{HN}} \circ u_e)$. By presorting the indices, this operation becomes a simple inplace line or face interpolation, which can be handled efficiently, e.g., by sum factorization. In approach 1), the presort can be accomplished by replacing the global indices of DoFs on constrained edges/faces by the constraining counterparts in the DoF map $\mathcal{G}_e^a$. For this operation, one needs to consider the orientation of the edges/faces within unstructured meshes, for which an extended version of the algorithm proposed in [24] can be used. In the case of approach (ii), $\mathcal{G}_e^b$ can be constructed by replacing the constrained indices in the DoF map $\mathcal{G}_e^a$ by their constraining counterparts in $\mathcal{C}_e^{\text{GP}}$.

Our algorithm can treat components of vectorial elements individually. However, some components might not be able or might not need to be treated by the proposed algorithm (e.g., non-nodal elements vs. mixed elements with discontinuous Galerkin components). The refinement configuration of a cell and the information on whether our fast hanging-node-constraint algorithm needs to be applied for the given component can be efficiently combined on the fly by a simple Boolean operation.

3 Implementation Details

In the following, we discuss how to encode the refinement configuration of a hypercube-shaped cell so that the information can be efficiently decoded during the interpolation phase. Furthermore, different vectorization strategies for the interpolation step are presented. Note that, at the time of writing, `deal.II` falls back to the general-purpose algorithm for non-hypercube cells on mixed meshes, which also contain cell shapes like simplices.

3.1 Data Structures

In this subsection, we discuss the data structures of $\mathcal{C}^{\mathrm{GP}}$, of $(\mathcal{C}^{\mathrm{GP}} \circ \mathcal{G})_e$, and of $\mathcal{C}_e^{\mathrm{HN}}$. By moving the hanging-node constraints to a special-purpose data structure, the global operator $\mathcal{C}^{\mathrm{GP}}$ is generally sparse so that a matrix-vector multiplication with a sparse matrix (as provided by `cuSPARSE`) is applicable. Data structures of the merged operator $\mathcal{C}_e^{\mathrm{GP}} \circ \mathcal{G}_e$ for CPUs have been proposed in [14]. They consist of an extended DoF map, indicators of constrained DoFs, and pointers to the rows of the constraint matrix. In order to minimize memory consumption, the value array of the sparse matrix is only stored for unique rows.

The hanging-node-constraint operator $\mathcal{C}_e^{\mathrm{HN}}$ requires information regarding the refinement configuration of each cell and appropriate face-subface interpolation matrices. For tensor-product elements, one only needs to store 1D interpolation matrices to the two 1D subfaces. As a result, we were able to derive—by exploiting the structure of $(\mathcal{C}^{\mathrm{HN}} \circ \mathcal{C}^{\mathrm{GP}} \circ \mathcal{G})_e$—an efficient and flexible algorithm whose memory consumption is $\mathcal{O}(N_{\mathrm{cells}})$ and is independent of the degree k.

3.2 Refinement Configuration

The refinement of a cell relative to the neighboring cells can be described as a pair (*subcell*, *face*) in 2D (not considered in the following) and as a triple (*subcell*, *face*, *edge*) in 3D. The first entry "subcell" indicates the octant within the parent cell, the second entry "face" the direction along which constrained faces (i.e., coarser neighboring cells) appear, and the third entry "edge" the direction of constrained edges. Note that, if a face is constrained, all its bounding edges are also constrained. Furthermore, we utilize the fact that only one of the faces/edges along a direction can be constrained as the other side necessarily belongs to the same leaf in the octree. Figure 3 visualizes all possible values of the entries of the triple. All 137 resulting valid refinement configurations are:

- the unconstrained case $(\{(0, 0, 0)\})$,
- 56 cases with at least one constrained face

$$\{(\mathit{subcell}, \mathit{face}, 0) \mid 0 \leq \mathit{subcell} < 8 \wedge 1 \leq \mathit{face} < 8\},$$

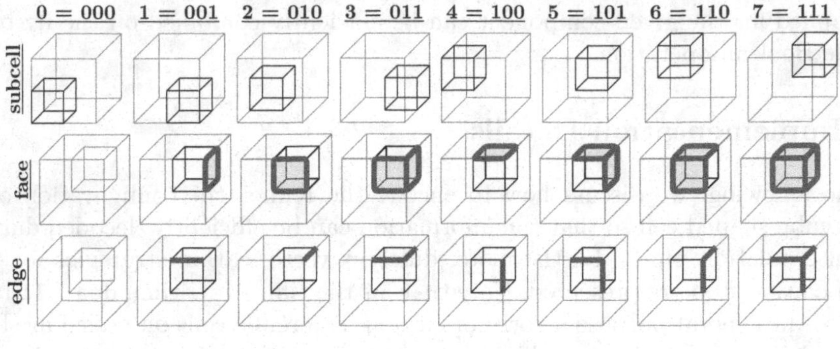

Fig. 3. Depiction of $0 \leq subcell, face, edge < 8$. The latter two refinement-configuration entries are plotted for subcell = 5. The resulting 137 configurations can be described by a triple (*subcell*, *face*, *edge*) or 8 bits.

- 56 cases with at least one constrained edge

$$\{(subcell,\ 0,\ edge) \mid 0 \leq subcell < 8 \ \wedge \ 1 \leq edge < 8\},$$

- and 24 cases in which a face and the edge orthogonal to it are constrained

$$\{(subcell,\ i,\ i) \mid 0 \leq subcell < 8 \ \wedge \ i \in \{1, 2, 4\}\}.$$

The triple could be encoded by a 9-bit integer. Alternatively, one could exploit the observation that the $face$ and $edge$ entries are either identical or one of them has the value zero to save a bit and to encode the information as a quadruple (containing: *subcell*, whether at least one face is constrained, whether at least one edge is constrained, non-zero entries of *face/edge*). The corresponding encoding/decoding routines between the triple $(a,\ b,\ c)$ and the quadruple $(\alpha,\ \beta,\ \gamma,\ \delta)$ are:

$$(\alpha, \beta, \gamma, \delta) \leftarrow \texttt{encode}(a, b, c) = (a, b > 0, c > 0, \texttt{max}(b, c))$$
$$(a, b, c) \leftarrow \texttt{decode}(\alpha, \beta, \gamma, \delta) = (a, \beta\ ?\ \delta : 1, \gamma\ ?\ \delta : 1)$$

3.3 GPU Interpolation

On the GPU, we use an extended version of Algorithm 1 for the application of hanging-node constraints, as presented in Algorithm 3. During the inplace interpolation (see Fig. 4a), threads need to determine whether 1) a DoF is constrained and if so 2) which 1D interpolation matrix should be used. The information can be extracted simply with bitwise operations from the refinement configuration, as shown in Algorithms 2 and 3. Our approach results in threads being idle during the interpolation if the DoFs processed by those threads are not constrained. Nevertheless, it turns out that this approach is very competitive, since it is approximately as expensive as the interpolation step from the nodal coefficients $u_{e,j}$ to the quadrature points as they have the same sequence of operations plus an additional instruction to compute the corresponding masks.

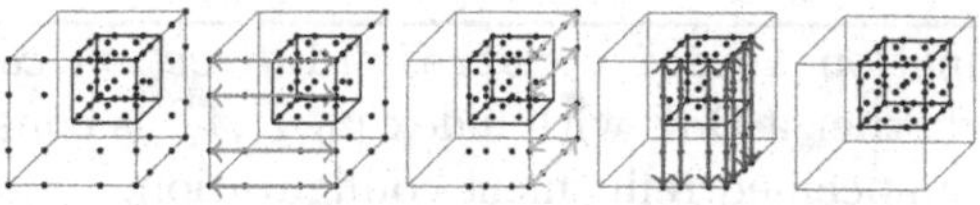

(a) Used on GPU with threads associated with unconstrained DoFs being masked out, i.e., corresponding threads being idle.

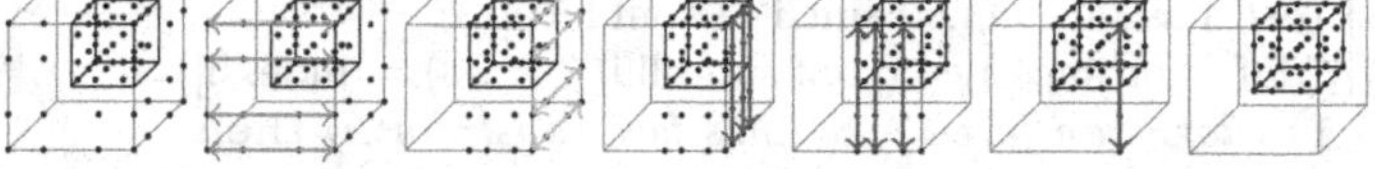

(b) Used on CPU. The interpolations in x_0- and x_1-direction are simply performed as in-face interpolations. The interpolation in x_2-direction is decomposed in three steps.

Fig. 4. Hanging-node-constraint application via sum factorization for 3D and $k = 3$ on GPU and CPU for a configuration with coarser neighbors at the right and in front of the highlighted cell.

3.4 CPU Interpolation

On the CPU, we use a different approach to perform the interpolations without checks on the DoF level. Motivated by the fact that only the pair (*face*, *edge*) determines the interpolation steps and these steps are additive, we can construct an algorithm that has a minimal number of if-statements (one switch-statement for face and one for edge, each with 8 specialized cases) and a limited number of starting points of faces/edges of the subcell, which can be precomputed at compile time. Figure 4b shows, as an example, the interpolation steps for refinement configuration (5,3,0). The interpolations in x_0- and x_1-direction are similar to the GPU version. In contrast, we decompose the interpolation in x_2-direction in three steps in order to prevent interpolating the values along the shared edges twice.

For the purpose of vectorization, `deal.II` provides a wrapper class with a `std::simd`-like interface, which is built around a fixed-size array and translates instructions into the right instruction-set extension [14]. In the vectorization strategy of `deal.II`, each lane of the array is associated with a distinct cell so that each operation on the wrapper class is performed with a single instruction for all cells in parallel. We will call the collection of cells that are processed at the same time a "cell batch". Implementations of operations $\mathcal{S}_e$ and $\mathcal{D}_e$ only operate on such vectorized data types; in `deal.II`, the merged operator $\mathcal{C}_e^{\text{GP}} \circ \mathcal{G}_e$ performs the laying out of the data in the right (vectorized, struct-of-arrays) format so that the input to $\mathcal{C}_e^{\text{HN}}$ already has this format.

Algorithm 2: Function `is_dof_constrained`(*direction*, *conf*, *index*) $\rightarrow$ *bool* that returns whether a DoF with index $[i_0, i_1, i_2]$ is constrained in the given direction for a specified refinement configuration.

```
rotate data structures conf and index to the right by (dim − direction − 1)
cell_has_edge_constraint ← conf.edge[2]
∀i ∈ {0,1}.(cell_has_face_constraint_i ← conf.face[i])
∀i ∈ {0,1}.(dof_is_on_face_i ← (conf.subcell[i] ? k : 0) = index[i])
if ∃i ∈ {0,1}.(dof_is_on_face_i ∧ cell_has_face_constraint_i) then
    return True ;                          /* DoF is constrained on face */
else if (∀i ∈ {0,1}.(dof_is_on_face_i)) and cell_has_edge_constraint then
    return True ;                          /* DoF is constrained on edge */
else
    return False ;                         /* DoF is not constrained */
```

Algorithm 3: Function that performs an inplace interpolation by a sequence of 1D interpolations for constrained DoFs, used on GPU. See also comments in Algorithm 1.

```
for direction ← 0 to dim do
    parallelforeach index ∈ {[i0, i1, i2] | 0 ≤ i0, i1, i2 ≤ k} do
        interp_matrix ← interpolation_matrices[conf.subcell[direction]]
        if is_dof_constrained(direction, conf, index) then
            value ← interp_matrix[index[direction]]. ∗ data(index, direction)
    parallelforeach index ∈ {[i0, i1, i2] | 0 ≤ i0, i1, i2 ≤ k} do
        if is_dof_constrained(direction, conf, index) then
            data(index) = value
```

However, the cells of a cell batch typically have different refinement configurations if no extra measures are taken, making vectorization of the considered algorithms more complicated. We will consider the following vectorization strategies in Subsect. 4.1: 1) `auto`: Cells with hanging-node constraints are processed individually. In this way, we completely rely on optimizing compilers, which is possible, since all if-statements and loop bounds are constant expressions. Data accesses from individual lanes of the struct-of-arrays storage of DoF values, while reading and writing, are necessary. 2) `grouping`: Cells with the refinement configuration are globally grouped together in a preprocessing step. As a result, all cells of a cell batch have the same refinement configuration. 3) `masking`: Here, we keep the sequence of the cells unmodified as in the case of `auto`, however, we process all geometric entities (6 faces and 12 edges) sequentially entity by entity and check whether they are constrained in any of the lanes of the cell batch. We apply a mask, e.g., using the instruction `vblendvpd` with x86/AVX or `vblendmpd` with x86/AVX-512 instruction-set extension, in order to only alter the relevant lanes.

3.5 Costs of Interpolation

We conclude this section by summarizing the number of floating-point operations that are needed to perform the interpolation for an arbitrary refinement configuration $(subcell, face, edge)$ in 3D:

$$\mathcal{K}((\bullet, face, edge)) = \mathcal{K}(face) + \mathcal{K}(edge) = \mathcal{O}(k^3).$$

This value is bounded by the costs of the interpolation from the support points to the quadrature points ($\mathcal{K}(cell) = 3(k+1)^3(1+2k)$). The terms are defined (with $|\bullet|$ counting bits) as:

$$\mathcal{K}(face) = \begin{cases} 0 & \text{for } |face| = 0 \\ \mathcal{K}(single\ face) & \text{for } |face| = 1 \\ 2\mathcal{K}(single\ face) - \mathcal{K}(single\ edge) & \text{for } |face| = 2 \\ 3(\mathcal{K}(single\ face) - \mathcal{K}(single\ edge)) & \text{for } |face| = 3 \end{cases}$$

and $\mathcal{K}(edge) = |edge|\mathcal{K}(single\ edge)$ with $\mathcal{K}(single\ edge) = (k+1)(1+2k)$ and $\mathcal{K}(single\ face) = 2(k+1)^2(1+2k)$, being the costs of the inplace interpolation of a single edge/face. The formulas evaluated for $k = 1, 4$ are shown in Table 1.

On the contrary, the arithmetic cost of the general-purpose algorithm for applying the hanging-node constraints on a single face is $\mathcal{O}(k^4)$. Both the hanging-node algorithm and the general-purpose algorithm have—under the assumption that the 1D interpolation matrices and the compressed constraint matrix are in cache for moderate k—a memory cost of $\mathcal{O}(1)$. As a consequence, the difference in performance is due to a different number of floating-point operations and differences in code generation. For the latter, the proposed specialized algorithm can use the polynomial degree and hence loop lengths as a compile-time constant, whereas the generic implementation can not, which on its own causes a 2x-3x difference in performance [15].

4 Experiments and Results

In this section, we investigate the suitability of the proposed algorithm on modern hardware. As a metric, we use the cost η of a cell that is either edge- or face-constrained. We define the cost as $\eta = (T_{\text{HN}} - T_{\text{NO}})/T_{\text{NO}}$, i.e., the ratio of the additional time to process a cell with hanging-node constraints and the time to process a cell without hanging-node constraints. For this purpose, we use two approaches to determine the value of η independently in Subsects. 4.1 and 4.2. The code of our experiments can be found online.[1]

Our experiments perform operator evaluations (also referred to as "matrix-vector product" or "vmult") of a scalar Laplace operator with homogeneous Dirichlet boundaries on two classes of locally refined 3D meshes. The meshes

[1] https://github.com/peterrum/dealii-matrixfree-hanging-nodes with the `deal.II` master branch retrieved on March 26 2022, with small adjustments to disable the automatic choice of the vectorization type by the library.

Table 1. Number of FLOPs for edge (e) and face (f) constraints as well as for interpolation from solution coefficients $u_{e,i}$ to values at quadrature points (cell). The numbers in the header indicate the count of constrained faces or edges. The numbers of FLOPs have been verified with hardware counters.

k	1e+0f	2e+0f	3e+0f	0e+1f	1e+1f	0e+2f	0e+3f	cell
1	6	12	18	24	30	42	54	72
4	45	90	135	450	495	855	1215	3375

Table 2. Runtime analysis in terms of memory transfer and GFLOP/s, as measured with the Likwid tool for $k = 4$ and affine/non-affine `shell` mesh ($L = 7/6$). Run on Intel Cascade Lake Xeon Gold 6230 (2560 GFLOP/s, 202 GB/s).

	No constraints			General-purpose algo			Hanging-node algo		
	s	GB/s	GF/s	s	GB/s	GF/s	s	GB/s	GF/s
Affine	0.028	122	437	0.057	86	252	0.034	107	386
Non-affine	0.016	194	174	0.021	162	149	0.016	191	183

are constructed by refining a coarse mesh consisting of a single cell defined by $[-1, +1]^3$ according to one of the following two solution criteria: 1) `shell`: after $L - 3$ uniform refinements, perform three local refinement steps with all cells whose center $\boldsymbol{c}$ is $|\boldsymbol{c}| \leq 0.55$, $0.3 \leq |\boldsymbol{c}| \leq 0.43$, and $0.335 \leq |\boldsymbol{c}| \leq 0.39$ or 2) `octant`: refine all mesh cells in the first octant L times. Figure 5 shows, as an example, the resulting meshes. Simulations are run with polynomial degrees $1 \leq k \leq 6$ to cover all cases from low- to high-order FEM.

Unless noted otherwise, the numerical experiments are run on a dual-socket Intel Xeon Platinum 8174 (Skylake) system of the supercomputer SuperMUC-NG.[2] It supports AVX-512 (8-wide SIMD). The 48 CPU cores run at a fixed frequency of 2.3 GHz, which gives an arithmetic peak of 3.5 TFLOP/s. The 96 GB of random-access memory (RAM) are connected through 12 channels of DDR4-2666 with a theoretical bandwidth of 256 GB/s and an achieved STREAM triad memory throughput of 205 GB/s. We use `GCC 9.3.0` as compiler with the flags `-march=skylake-avx512 -std=c++17 -O3`. Furthermore, the CPU code uses the vectorization strategy `auto` by default, computations are run with double-precision floating-point numbers and results are reported in 64-bit FLOPs.

4.1 Experiment 1: Serial Simulation

In the first experiment, we execute the program serially to rule out influences of MPI communication and potential load imbalances. In order to nevertheless obtain a realistic per-core memory bandwidth, we execute an instance of the program on all cores of a compute node simultaneously.

[2] https://top500.org/system/179566/, received on November 15, 2021.

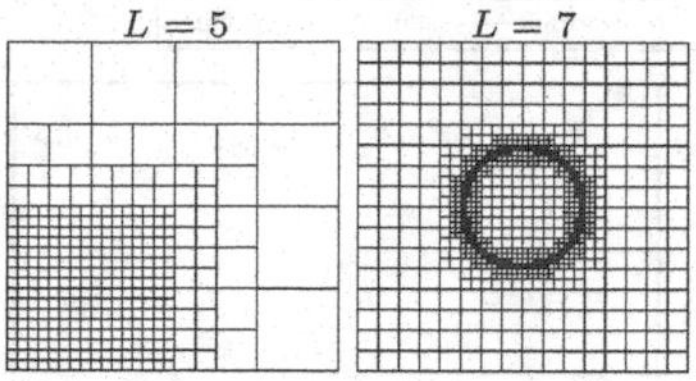

L	octant #cells	octant HN	shell #cells	shell HN
5	4.7E+3	23.0%	1.2E+3	68.9%
6	3.5E+4	12.2%	6.8E+3	78.4%
7	2.7E+5	6.2%	3.7E+4	69.9%
8	2.1E+6	3.1%	2.7E+5	38.3%
9	1.7E+7	1.6%	2.2E+6	19.3%

Fig. 5. Cross section of the `octant` geometry (left) and of the `shell` geometry (right) simulation for specified number of refinements. In addition, the number of cells (#cells:=$N_{\text{NO}} + N_{\text{HN}}$) and the share of cells with hanging-node constraints (HN:=$N_{\text{HN}}/(N_{\text{NO}} + N_{\text{HN}})$) are given for the considered refinement numbers.

In the context of such serial experiments, the total simulation time is the sum of the time spent on cells with hanging-node constraints and on cells without hanging-node constraints: $T = N_{\text{HN}}T_{\text{HN}} + N_{\text{NO}}T_{\text{NO}} = (N_{\text{NO}} + (1+\eta_1)N_{\text{HN}})T_{\text{NO}}$. From this formula, we derive an experimental definition of the cost:

$$\eta_1 = (T/T_{\text{NO}} - N_{\text{NO}})/N_{\text{HN}} - 1. \tag{2}$$

The cell counts N_{NO} and N_{HN} are given by the geometry (see Fig. 5), the total simulation time T can be measured, and the time to process a cell without hanging-node constraints T_{NO} can be approximated by running the simulations artificially without hanging-node constraints with runtime $\hat{T}$, i.e., $T_{\text{NO}} \approx \hat{T}/(N_{\text{NO}} + N_{\text{HN}})$.

Figures 6a and 6b show the throughput of a single operator application (processed number of DoFs per time unit) and the cost η_1 for different degrees k in the `shell` case for the general-purpose algorithm (all constraints, incl. hanging-node constraints, are processed by $\mathcal{C}_e^{\text{GP}}$) and for the specialized hanging-node algorithm. As a reference, the throughput of the simulation without application of any hanging-node constraints is presented. One can observe an overall drop in throughput by 32–63% in the case of the general-purpose algorithm and by 11–34% in the case of the specialized algorithm. This translates into an increase in runtime for evaluating the discrete PDE operator on a cell with hanging nodes by 125–215% and 20–136%, respectively. While the costs are increasing in the case of the general-purpose algorithm, the costs in the specialized case are decreasing to a value of approx. 20%. This difference in behaviors is related to the difference in complexities and to the overhead in the low-degree case $k = 1$.

Furthermore, Figs. 6a and 6b show the results for (high-order) non-affine meshes (dashed lines). In order to deform the analyzed geometries, the transformation function $x_i \leftarrow x_i + \Delta \sin(\pi \cdot x_i)$ with $\Delta = 10^{-8}$ is applied. This transformation makes the matrix-free cell loops memory-bound in the current implementation, since the code loads a 3×3 Jacobian matrix for each quadrature point. In such cases, additional work on cached data can be hidden behind the memory transfer [15], as is verified to be the case for the additional hanging-node interpolations in our simulations: for linear elements, the costs of the proposed implementation are reduced from 136% to 58% and, for all higher degrees, no

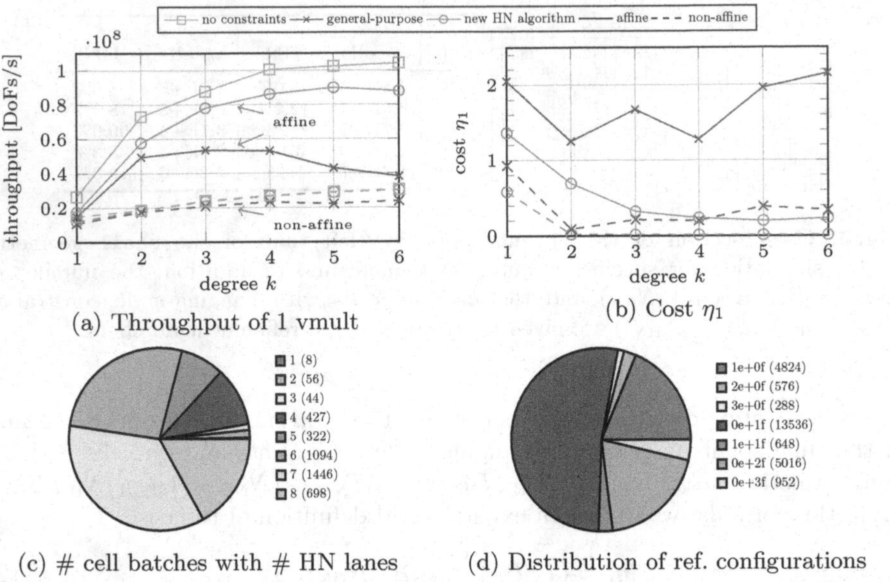

Fig. 6. a–b) Experimental results of the `shell` simulation on the CPU for degrees $1 \leq k \leq 6$ (for $L = 8/8/8/7/7/6$ in the affine case and one less for the non-affine case). c–d) Hanging-node statistics: count of cell batches with the given number of lanes with hanging-node constraints ($L = 7$); distribution of refinement-configuration types (grouped together by the number of edge and face constraints).

overhead can be observed with $\eta_1 \approx 1\%$. In contrast, one can still observe costs of up to 34% in the general-purpose case.

Figure 7a presents the results for the `octant` case. Since the number of hanging nodes is significantly less in this case, the penalty of applying the general-purpose algorithm leads to a throughput reduction of a mere 7–18%, and, in the case of the specialized algorithm, the throughput is comparable to the case without hanging nodes. The fact that the cost η_1 for processing cells with hanging-node constraints is similar to the one in the `shell` case makes us confident that the definition (2) to measure overhead and the experimental results presented here are transferable to other meshes and other refinement configurations.

We also analyzed the algorithm with hardware counters (for a broad overview see Table 2). We could observe an increase in scalar operations both in the case of the special-purpose and the general-purpose algorithm. While, however, the additional scalar operations per DoF decrease with increasing k in the case of the special-purpose algorithm, this is not the case for the general-purpose algorithm. Furthermore, the special-purpose algorithm can be fed with the required data from the fast L1 cache, while the general-purpose algorithm needs to access higher memory levels (incl. main memory) for the entries of the matrix $\boldsymbol{C}$. In the case of the special-purpose algorithm, the number of branch mispredictions per operation decreases for increasing k.

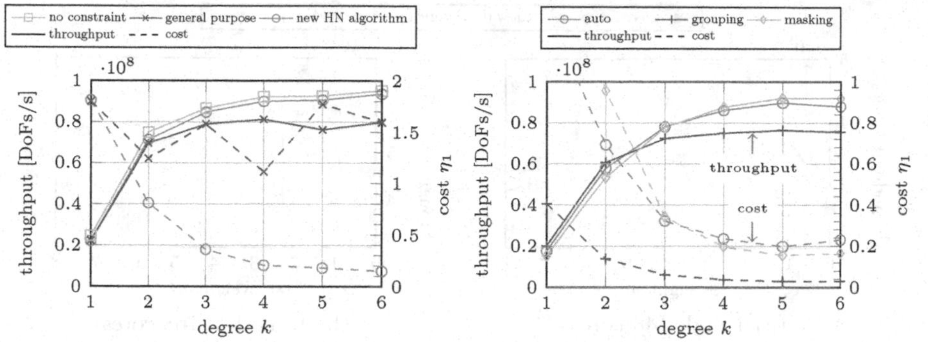

(a) Octant

(b) Vectorization (shell)

Fig. 7. a) Experimental results of the `octant` simulation for degrees $1 \le k \le 6$ (for $L = 7/7/7/6/6/6$). See also the comments in Fig. 6. b) Comparison of experimental results with different vectorization strategies for an affine `shell` mesh. Setup as in Fig. 6.

Figure 7b shows throughput and cost η_1 for the three vectorization strategies presented in Subsect. 3.4 (`auto`, `grouping`, and `masking`) for the `shell` case. One can observe that the strategy `grouping` can significantly reduce the value of the cost η_1: for degrees $k \ge 2$, it appears as if cells with hanging-node constraints would be similar in cost to regular cells. This is not surprising, since performing one packed operation in contrast to 5–8 scalar operations is significantly cheaper (see Fig. 6c regarding the number of lanes with hanging-node constraints). For low degrees, the reduced costs indeed lead to a (slight) increase in throughput, compared to the (default) `auto` strategy. For higher degrees, the strategy `grouping` reaches a throughput that is 15% lower than the one of the strategy `auto` in the `shell` case. This is related to the fact that the grouping results in discontinuous partitions, which lead—in combination with $\mathcal{O}(k^d)$ working sets of the cells during cell integrals—to a worse cache-locality behavior of the whole matrix-free loop (1) and an increase in cell batches, since a growing number of lanes might not be filled. The vectorization strategy `masking` adds costs by setting up the masks for 18 geometric entities and by increasing the number of conditional branches in contrast to the two switches in `auto`. While, for linear and quadratic elements, these additional costs are dominating, leading to $96\% < \eta_1 < 192\%$, they amortize and higher throughputs than in the case of `auto` are reached for higher degrees ($k \ge 4$). Our experiments (not presented here) have shown that, by switching to single-precision computations and hereby doubling the number of lanes processed by a cell batch, the turning point towards the vectorization strategy `masking` is shifted to lower degrees.

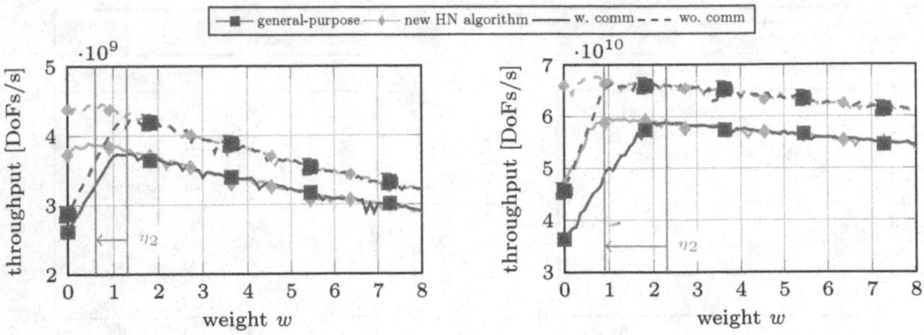

(a) 1 node (48 cores)

(b) 16 nodes (768 cores)

Fig. 8. Time of an operator application with either the general-purpose or the hanging-node algorithm and with communication either enabled or disabled. We used `octant` with $L = 7$ and $L = 9$ number of refinements as geometry and $k = 4$.

4.2 Experiment 2: Parallel Simulation

In this experiment, we distribute the mesh and the work among all processes of a compute node. The time spent on the operator evaluation by process i is proportional to $N_{\text{NO},i} + (1+\eta)N_{\text{HN},i}$ with $N_{\text{NO},i}$ and $N_{\text{HN},i}$, being the number of cells without and with hanging nodes possessed by that process. The overall time spent by the whole application is $\sim \max_i(N_{\text{NO},i} + (1+\eta)N_{\text{HN},i})$. If the same number of cells $N_{\text{NO},i} + N_{\text{HN},i}$ is assigned to each process i and additional costs $\eta \gg 1$ are ignored, this leads to load imbalances and to a decreased total throughput. In such situations, one would not distribute the number of cells but the work by assigning each cell a user-specified weight, e.g., the weight of 1.0 to cells without hanging-node constraints and the weight of $w+1 \geq 1$ to cells with hanging-node constraints. Such weights need to be determined by a tuning process. Small costs are desirable, on the one hand, as the throughput is acceptable without tuning of additional parameters and, on the other hand, because other code regions in the same application might have different—contradicting—requirements for the weights.

The goal of this experiment is to determine a factor η_2 that is given as the weight w for which the execution time is minimal in the `octant` case for $k = 4$. In the optimal case, the value η_2 should be comparable to η_1 from the first experiment.

Figure 8 shows the time of an operator application for different weights w on 1 and 16 compute nodes. As expected, the specialized hanging-node treatment is able to shift η_2 from 130% to 60% and from 230% to 90%. At the same time, it also reaches overall higher throughputs.

Comparing the values η_1 and η_2, one can observe that $\eta_1 < \eta_2$. Our investigations have revealed that this is related to the communication. The matrix-free operator evaluation (1) updates the ghost values during $\mathcal{G}$ and collects partial results from neighboring processes during a "compress" step in $\mathcal{G}^T$. The library `deal.II` assigns DoFs to cells/processes in the order of a space-filling curve [4,5];

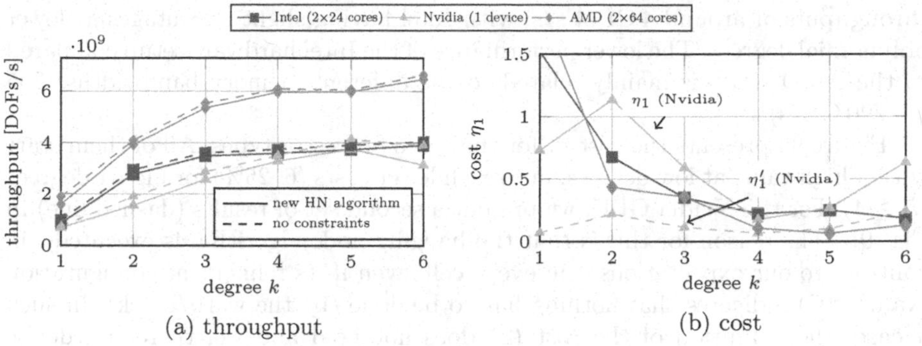

Fig. 9. Experimental results of the `shell` simulation for degrees $1 \leq k \leq 6$.

in particular, all the leaf children of a cell are assigned to the same process. This leads to communication patterns, as indicated in Fig. 2c, in which only the constraining cells need to send data during the update of the ghost values, while during the compression step only constrained cells are sending data. In many cases, constraining and constrained cells are well distributed, but not in the `octant` case. This can be verified by turning off the communication (dashed lines in Fig. 8), for which indeed $\eta_1 \approx \eta_2$. We defer the development of an algorithm for smarter assignment of DoFs to future work.

4.3 Experiment 3: Cross-Platform Validation

In the following, we present the results of parallel experiments for affine `shell` meshes for $1 \leq k \leq 6$ additionally on a dual-socket AMD Epyc 7742 CPU compute node and a single GPU device on Summit[3] (Nvidia Tesla V100). The AMD CPU consists of 2×64 cores running at 2.25 GHz and uses codes compiled for the AVX2 instruction-set extension (4-wide SIMD). This gives an arithmetic peak performance of 4.61 TFlop/s. The memory configuration uses 2×8 channels of DDR4-3200, resulting in a peak bandwidth of 410 GB/s and a measured STREAM triad bandwidth of 290 GB/s. The performance specifications of the V100 GPU in terms of GB/s and GFLOP/s are more than twice as high as the ones of the two CPU systems (arithmetic peak performance of 7.8 TFlop/s, peak memory bandwidth of 900 GB/s, and measured bandwidth of 720 GB/s), but with a less sophisticated cache infrastructure. On the AMD CPU, we use `gcc-7.5.0` as compiler with the flags `-O3 -march=znver2 -funroll-loops`, and, on the Nvidia GPU, we use `nvcc 11.0.3/gcc 9.1.0` as compiler with the flags `-O2`. We have chosen the number of refinements to the maximal memory capacity of the given hardware. We did not perform any tuning of the weight parameter w (see Subsect. 4.2) and set its value to zero.

Figure 9a presents the obtained throughput. The AMD system reaches the highest throughput of around 6 GDoFs/s. Nvidia and Intel show similar maximal

[3] https://www.top500.org/system/179397/, retrieved on November 15, 2021.

throughputs of around 4 GDoFs/s, with Intel having slight advantages at lower polynomial degrees. The lower performance of the Intel hardware setup compared to the AMD setup is mainly related to the different memory bandwidths (205 vs. 290 GB/s).

Figure 9b presents the cost η_1 for the three processor types. All of them start with a high value at low degrees, but reach lower costs (6–25%) for higher degrees ($k \geq 4$). For the Nvidia GPU, we present a second set of results (dashed line) in Fig. 9b. The reason for this is that the hanging-node algorithm is executed—in contrast to our expectations—on every cell, even if its refinement configuration (value "0") indicates that nothing has to be done (by the warp/block). In such a case, the definition of the cost (2) does not hold and we, therefore, define $\eta_1' = (T - \hat{T})/\hat{T}$, i.e., as the ratio of the additional time to run a simulation with hanging-node constraints and the time to run the same simulation artificially without hanging-node constraints. The values $6\% \leq \eta_1' \leq 24\%$ are reasonable, but implicate that simulations with any number of cells with hanging-node constraints have to pay this overall penalty, even if they only have ≈1% such cells, as is the situation in the `octant` case.

5 Conclusions and Outlook

We have presented an algorithm for the efficient evaluation of the continuity constraints at hanging nodes for matrix-free high-order FEM computations on unstructured, hex-dominated, mixed meshes and for multi-component elements that contain a Lagrange element in one of their components. The algorithm splits up the application of constraints into a hanging-node part and a general part, using efficient inplace interpolations for the former. For this purpose, the DoF map of the cells has to be updated and the configurations of cell refinements have to be determined as well as efficiently encoded and decoded. In 3D, we require 8 bits to encode all 137 possible configurations. The algorithm is applicable for both CPUs and GPUs with two distinct differences: 1) for the GPU, the application of non-hanging-node constraints, like Dirichlet boundary conditions, can not be merged into the cell loop, but needs to be applied separately and 2) specialized interpolation routines have to be used due to different vectorization strategies.

Experiments have shown that, for high-order finite elements, the costs of cells with hanging-node constraints can be reduced significantly for affine meshes. For low-order elements, we also obtain improvements, but the costs remain noticeable due to conditional branches required for checking the refinement configurations. For high-order non-affine meshes, the application of hanging-node constraints can be completely hidden behind memory access. For the CPU, we have discussed different vectorization strategies and identified that processing cell by cell is the most efficient approach in the context of matrix-free algorithms that are based on vectorization across cells for lower degrees $k \leq 3$, whereas masking is superior for $k > 3$. The benefits of our node-level optimization on parallel applications are significantly reduced load imbalances and higher throughput with a more moderate cell-weighting function.

Future work will extend the algorithm towards the support of more cell shapes (e.g., simplex, wedge, pyramid) in the context of mixed meshes and *hp*-adaptive FEM so that one does not need to fall back to a slower general-purpose algorithm in these cases. Moreover, we intend to perform further performance optimizations, which will target the reduction of overhead in the case of low-order elements, alternative vectorization strategies, and improved parallel distribution of degrees of freedom in order to minimize the communication overhead in the context of hanging-node constraints.

Acknowledgment. The authors acknowledge collaboration with Momme Allalen, Daniel Arndt, Magdalena Schreter, Bruno Turcksin as well as the `deal.II` community.

References

1. Anderson, R., et al.: MFEM: a modular finite element methods library. Comp. Math. Appl. **81**, 42–74 (2021)
2. Arndt, D., et al.: The `deal.II` library, version 9.3. J. Numer. Math. **29**(3) (2021)
3. Arndt, D., et al.: The `deal.II` finite element library: design, features, and insights. Comp. Math. Appl. **81**, 407–422 (2021)
4. Bangerth, W., Burstedde, C., Heister, T., Kronbichler, M.: Algorithms and data structures for massively parallel generic adaptive finite element codes. ACM Trans. Math. Softw. **38**(2), 14/1-28 (2011)
5. Burstedde, C., Wilcox, L.C., Ghattas, O.: p4est: scalable algorithms for parallel adaptive mesh refinement on forests of octrees. SIAM J. Sci. Comput. **33**(3), 1103–1133 (2011)
6. Cerveny, J., Dobrev, V., Kolev, T.: Nonconforming mesh refinement for high-order finite elements. SIAM J. Sci. Comput. **41**(4), C367–C392 (2019)
7. Davydov, D., Pelteret, J.P., Arndt, D., Kronbichler, M., Steinmann, P.: A matrix-free approach for finite-strain hyperelastic problems using geometric multigrid. Int. J. Num. Meth. Eng. **121**(13), 2874–2895 (2020)
8. Deville, M.O., Fischer, P.F., Mund, E.H.: High-order methods for incompressible fluid flow. Cambridge University Press (2002)
9. Fischer, P., et al.: Scalability of high-performance PDE solvers. Int. J. High Perf. Comp. App. **34**(5), 562–586 (2020)
10. Fischer, P.F., Kruse, G.W., Loth, F.: Spectral element methods for transitional flows in complex geometries. J. Sci. Comput. **17**(1), 81–98 (2002)
11. Krank, B., Fehn, N., Wall, W.A., Kronbichler, M.: A high-order semi-explicit discontinuous Galerkin solver for 3D incompressible flow with application to DNS and LES of turbulent channel flow. J. Comp. Phy. **348**, 634–659 (2017)
12. Kronbichler, M., Diagne, A., Holmgren, H.: A fast massively parallel two-phase flow solver for microfluidic chip simulation. Int. J. High Perform. Comput. Appl. **32**(2), 266–287 (2018)
13. Kronbichler, M., et al.: A next-generation discontinuous Galerkin fluid dynamics solver with application to high-resolution lung airflow simulations. In: SC 2021 (2021)
14. Kronbichler, M., Kormann, K.: A generic interface for parallel cell-based finite element operator application. Comput. Fluids **63**, 135–147 (2012)

15. Kronbichler, M., Kormann, K.: Fast matrix-free evaluation of discontinuous Galerkin finite element operators. ACM Trans. Math. Softw. **45**(3), 29/1-40 (2019)
16. Kronbichler, M., Ljungkvist, K.: Multigrid for matrix-free high-order finite element computations on graphics processors. ACM Trans. Parallel Comput. **6**(1), 2/1-32 (2019)
17. Laughton, E., Tabor, G., Moxey, D.: A comparison of interpolation techniques for non-conformal high-order discontinuous Galerkin methods. Comput. Methods Appl. Mech. Eng. **381**, 113820 (2021)
18. Ljungkvist, K.: Matrix-free finite-element computations on graphics processors with adaptively refined unstructured meshes. In: SpringSim (HPC), pp. 1–1 (2017)
19. Melenk, J.M., Gerdes, K., Schwab, C.: Fully discrete hp-finite elements: fast quadrature. Comput. Methods Appl. Mech. Eng. **190**(32), 4339–4364 (2001)
20. Munch, P., Heister, T., Prieto Saavedra, L., Kronbichler, M.: Efficient distributed matrix-free multigrid methods on locally refined meshes for FEM computations. arXiv preprint arXiv:2203.12292 (2022)
21. Munch, P., Kormann, K., Kronbichler, M.: hyper.deal: an efficient, matrix-free finite-element library for high-dimensional partial differential equations. ACM Trans. Math. Softw. **47**(4), 33/1–34 (2021)
22. Orszag, S.A.: Spectral methods for problems in complex geometries. Journal of Computational Physics **37**(1), 70–92 (1980)
23. Saurabh, K., et al.: Scalable adaptive PDE solvers in arbitrary domains. In: SC 2021 (2021)
24. Scroggs, M.W., Dokken, J.S., Richardson, C.N., Wells, G.N.: Construction of arbitrary order finite element degree-of-freedom maps on polygonal and polyhedral cell meshes. ACM Trans. Math. Softw. (2022). https://doi.org/10.1145/3524456
25. Shephard, M.S.: Linear multipoint constraints applied via transformation as part of a direct stiffness assembly process. Int. J. Num. Meth. Eng. **20**(11), 2107–2112 (1984)
26. Świrydowicz, K., Chalmers, N., Karakus, A., Warburton, T.: Acceleration of tensor-product operations for high-order finite element methods. Int. J. High Perf. Comput. Appl. **33**(4), 735–757 (2019)

Dynamic Task Fusion for a Block-Structured Finite Volume Solver over a Dynamically Adaptive Mesh with Local Time Stepping

Baojiu Li[1], Holger Schulz[2], Tobias Weinzierl[2,3](✉), and Han Zhang[1]

[1] Institute for Computational Cosmology, Durham University, Durham DH1 3FE, UK

[2] Department of Computer Science, Durham University, Durham DH1 3FE, UK
tobias.weinzierl@durham.ac.uk

[3] Institute for Data Science, Large-Scale Computing, Durham University, Durham DH1 3FE, UK

Abstract. Load balancing of generic wave equation solvers over dynamically adaptive meshes with local time stepping is difficult, as the load changes with every time step. Task-based programming promises to mitigate the load balancing problem. We study a Finite Volume code over dynamically adaptive block-structured meshes for two astrophysics simulations, where the patches (blocks) define tasks. They are classified into urgent and low priority tasks. Urgent tasks are algorithmically latency-sensitive. They are processed directly as part of our bulk-synchronous mesh traversals. Non-urgent tasks are held back in an additional task queue on top of the task runtime system. If they lack global side-effects, i.e. do not alter the global solver state, we can generate optimised compute kernels for these tasks. Furthermore, we propose to use the additional queue to merge tasks without side-effects into task assemblies, and to balance out imbalanced bulk synchronous processing phases.

Keywords: Task-based programming · Block-structured dynamic adaptive mesh refinement · Local time stepping · Wave equation solvers

---

The authors acknowledge the support through the embedded CSE programme of the ARCHER2 UK National Supercomputing Service (http://www.archer2.ac.uk) under grant no ARCHER2-eCSE04-2, Durham's oneAPI Academic Centre of Excellence made by Intel, ExCALIBUR's Phase Ia grant ExaClaw (EP/V00154X/1) and ExCALIBUR's cross-cutting project EX20-9 Exposing Parallelism: Task Parallelism (grant ESA 10 CDEL). They furthermore received support through the European Research Council via grant ERC-StG-716532-PUNCA, the STFC Consolidated Grants ST/T000244/1 and ST/P000541/1, and the China Scholarship Council (CSC) studentship at Durham University. This work has made use of the Hamilton HPC Service of Durham University.

A.-L. Varbanescu et al. (Eds.): ISC High Performance 2022, LNCS 13289, pp. 153–173, 2022.
https://doi.org/10.1007/978-3-031-07312-0_8

1 Introduction

Dynamic adaptive mesh refinement (AMR) and local time stepping (LTS) are algorithmic key ingredients behind many efficient simulation codes, i.e. codes that invest compute resources where they pay off most. We focus on the simulation of waves, i.e. hyperbolic partial differential equations (PDEs), from astrophysics which are solved via block-structured Finite Volumes with explicit time stepping. The combination of AMR plus LTS makes it challenging to load balance, as the workload per subdomain changes per time step. These changes are often difficult to predict and are not spatially clustered. Any geometric data decomposition thus has to yield (temporal) imbalances. Modern supercomputer architectures however exhibit and will exhibit unprecedented hardware parallelism [9], which we have to harness in every single simulation step.

Task-based programming promises to ride to the programmers' rescue. Tasks [3, 8] allow the programmer to oversubscribe the system logically, i.e. to write software with a significantly higher concurrency compared to what the hardware offers. A tasking runtime can then efficiently schedule the work modelled via tasks, i.e. map the computations onto the machine. The task runtime and its task stealing eliminate imbalances per rank [8]. In practice, tasking as exclusive overarching parallelisation paradigm however often yields inferior performance compared to traditional domain decomposition with bulk-synchronous processing (BSP). There are three main reasons for this: First, tasking introduces significant administrative overhead if tasks become too fine grained. Yet, if programmers reduce the task granularity, they sacrifice potential concurrency. This is problematic in our context: If too few Finite Volumes are clustered into a task, the task becomes too cheap. If too many Finite Volumes are clustered, we lose concurrency and constrain the AMR and LTS. The dilemma becomes particularly pressing for non-linear PDEs where eigenvalues and, hence, admissible time step sizes per task change—we hence can not cluster multiple tasks that are always triggered together [23]. Second, assembling the task graph quickly becomes prohibitively expensive and introduces algorithmic latency if the graphs are not reused, change at runtime, or are massive. Yet, if codes issue exclusively ready tasks, we deny the runtime information and any scheduling decision thus might, a posteriori, be sub-optimal. Finally, generic task code is often not machine-portable. Indeed, we find that different machines require different task granularities. CUDA or KNL-inspired architectures for example prefer larger tasks with limited data transfer compared to a mainstream CPU [17, 21, 25, 27] and they penalise too many kernel launches [27].

We study a generic Finite Volume code for wave equations that can handle different PDEs via functors: It spans a mesh and provides generic numerical kernels, while the actual PDE terms are injected via callback functions [24]. Our code is based upon the second generation of the ExaHyPE engine which inherits all fundamental principles from the first generation [18]. It is similar to others solver in the field such as SpECTRE [15] as it relies on generic Riemann solvers. The code features unconstrained dynamic AMR which can change the mesh in each and every time step, and patch-local LTS, and a combination of traditional non-overlapping domain decomposition and a task formalism.

Our novel idea is that the tasks are classified into urgent, i.e. potentially along the critical path, and non-urgent. The latter are called enclave tasks [6]. The urgent tasks are embedded into the actual BSP code, i.e. the mesh traversal of the non-overlapping domains. They are executed immediately. Enclave tasks can be held back in a user-defined task queue and are not instantaneously passed on to the tasking runtime. Instead, we analyse where BSP imbalances arise and just take as many tasks from the user queue as we need to compensate for them. Alternatively, we can spawn them as native tasks on top of the BSP parallelism and rely on the runtime to compensate for imbalances. Furthermore, we label the enclave tasks that have no global side-effects, i.e. do not alter the global solver's state. These tasks are processed by specialised, optimised compute kernels and can be batched into task sets which are processed en bloc. Different to other approaches, our code does not geometrically cluster or combine tasks, and it does not rely on a priori knowledge of the task creation pattern. We retain all flexibility and yet obtain compute-intense batches of tasks, while we do not assemble any task graph at all.

To the best of our knowledge, such a flexible approach has not been proposed before. Our working hypothesis is that the batching allows us to work with small tasks and still get high performance compute kernels, that a task graph assembly is not necessary and actually inadequate for LTS plus AMR, and that task-based programming plus domain decomposition outperforms plain BSP. We study the impact of our ideas for two astrophysical problems, though the principles apply to a lot of mesh-based PDE solvers and even Lagrangian methods which typically suffer from too fine-granular tasks.

The remainder of the paper is organised as follows: We briefly sketch our application area of interest and our benchmarks (Sect. 2) before we introduce our numerical ingredients and the resulting software architecture (Sect. 3). In Sect. 4, we discuss the four different levels of parallelisation applied, highlight the rationale behind these levels and the arising challenges. The key ideas of the present paper are sketched in the introductory paragraph of Sect. 5 before we provide details on their realisation. Section 6 hosts some numerical experiments. A brief outlook and summary (Sect. 7) close the discussion.

2 Applications

Our equations of interest are hyperbolic PDEs given in first-order formulation:

$$\frac{\partial Q}{\partial t} + \nabla \cdot F(Q) + \sum_{i=1}^{d} B_i(Q) \frac{\partial Q}{\partial_{x_i}} = S(Q) \qquad \text{with } Q : \mathbb{R}^{3+1} \mapsto \mathbb{R}^N. \tag{1}$$

They describe time-dependent wave equations. Conservative PDE formulations comprise a term $\nabla \cdot F(Q)$, otherwise non-conservative product (ncp) terms enter the equation. These B_is act on the directional derivatives. We implement two astrophysics scenarios on top of (1):

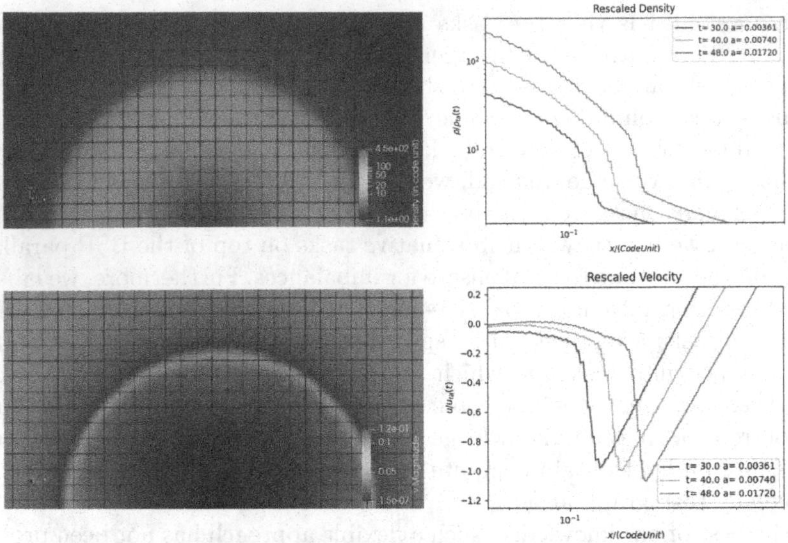

Fig. 1. Left: Characteristic density and velocity fields from the collisional secondary infall simulation. Due to the gravitational infall of mass, an outer-propagating shock appears. Right: Rescaled density and velocity profiles in radial direction.

2.1 Modified Euler Equations: Secondary Infall

Our first simulation is a secondary infall test in a hydrodynamic system on an expanding (cosmological) background, driven by Newtonian gravity. It studies spherically-distributed mass (collisional baryonic or collisionless dark matter) collapsing under self-gravity, which is an important testing scenario in galaxy formation. One property of interest is the theoretically predicted self-similarity after rescaling in the solution [5]: The density, pressure and velocity profiles depend exclusively on time, i.e. preserve their shape (Fig. 1). Our own studies with the present software suggest that this property is even preserved (approximately) for a set of non-standard graviational models [26]. The underlying equations are modified compressible Euler equations over five unknowns $\rho, E \in \mathbb{R}$ and $\mathbf{j} \in \mathbb{R}^3$. ρ, $\mathbf{j}$, E represent the density of mass, momentum and energy respectively. The self-gravitation enters the equations via a source term $S(Q)$ which depends upon $\rho\mathbf{g}$. $\boldsymbol{g}$ is the gravitational acceleration, which is proportional to $m_{<r}/r^2$ where $m_{<r}$ is the total (overdensity) mass within a given radius r around the infall's centre. This system is a flavour of (1) with $N=5$, where $B_i=0$.

The F term is independent of the global solution behaviour. This does not hold for the right-hand side: The value of the mass function $m_{<r}$ requires global information from all volumes within r. We construct a mass array $\{m_i\}_{0\leq i\leq \max}$ storing the total mass within radii $\{r_i\}_{0\leq i\leq \max}$. The m_i values are calculated by accumulating the mass within r_i per time step. During the subsequent time step, we feed the following interpolation into the source term $S(Q)$:

$$m_{<r} = \begin{cases} m_0 r^3/r_0^3, & r \leq r_0 \\ m_i \frac{r_{i+1}-r}{r_{i+1}-r_i} + m_{i+1} \frac{r-r_i}{r_{i+1}-r_i}, & r_i < r \leq r_{i+1} \\ m_{\max} + \frac{4\pi}{3}\rho(r_{\max})\left(r^3 - r_{\max}^3\right), & r > r_{\max} \end{cases} \tag{2}$$

The interpolation works with bucketing, i.e. the $m_{<r}$ is discretised, while the modifications in (2) near and far from center allow us to accumulate only the mass values within a finite area around the centre. We work with a finite number of shells or spheres for which we calculate the actual mass. In a Finite Volume setting, volumes far away from the centre do not feed into the subsequent S evaluations. Their behaviour is local , i.e. the time stepping's update of such volumes has no global side-effect. As the solution Q evolves smoothly in time, we can evolve $\{r_i\}_{0\leq i\leq \max}$ smoothly in time, too, such that the error due to the discretisation into spheres remains bounded.

2.2 CCZ4 GR Equations: Gauge Waves

Our second tested scenario solves a complete numerical relativity system based upon the CCZ4 formalism in vacuum [2]. The equations simulate strong gravity in regions where the Newtonian approximation is invalid. The textbook version of the vacuum CCZ4 system involves 25 variables and is second order in space. It also is subject to constraints. We follow [12] and recast the equations into first order by introducing auxiliary variables. This expands the whole system to $N = 59$ variables in (1). The auxiliary variables allow us to eliminate the second-order terms. They also map the constraints onto Lagrangian parameters, i.e. the Einstein constrain equations are enforced weakly.

Our code is a complete C++ rewrite of the equations (12a)-(12m) as published in [12] which absorbs the flux terms within the ncp, i.e. $F(Q) = 0$. Both the eigenvalue and ncp calculation are phrased as dense tensor products (like $2\alpha\tilde{\Gamma}^i_{jk}\tilde{A}^{jk}$), i.e. yield a high arithmetic intensity.

In this paper, we assess the code performance through the gauge wave test from [1]. This setup is derived from a time dependent coordinate transformation of the flat Minkowski metric: The spacetime is trivial, which is a property we do not exploit further. We expect a standing wave which travels through the domain and enters on the other side. The eigenvalues are invariant, and the wave's amplitude and frequency do not change over time subject to numerical dissipation. Different to the previous setup, we need periodic boundary conditions.

3 Software and Solver Architecture

We solve both challenges with first-order explicit time stepping (explicit Euler) on block-structured adaptive meshes. Finite Volumes with a generic Rusanov solver for the arising Riemann problema deliver our spatial discretisation.

3.1 Dynamically Adaptive AMR

We discretise the computational domain Ω_h through an octree or spacetree formalism, as it is state-of-the-art in the field [7,10,11,14,20,22,24]. Let the cubic domain Ω_h represent the root of a tree data structure. Equidistant, axis-aligned cuts through the cube along each Cartesian coordinate axis yield children of the tree and span a mesh. For each of these cubes, we decide independently whether we continue to refine recursively or not. We end up with an adaptive Cartesian mesh of *cells*, where each cell is a cube. The cells can have different sizes and hanging vertices are allowed, i.e. the mesh is non-conformal. We do not impose any balancing [14,20].

Each unrefined cell, i.e. cell which is not refined further, hosts a $p \times p \times p$ Cartesian grid. $p \geq 2$ is globally fixed. The elements within this embedded grid are called *volumes*. All the volumes within one cell form a *patch*. The resulting computational mesh of volumes is adaptive and block-structured. The patch formalism can also be read as a non-overlapping domain decomposition, where the patches of different sizes tessellate the computational domain.

The terminology around block-structured adaptive mesh refinement (AMR) is ambiguous. Different to other papers in the field [11], we employ the phrase "block-structured" but make all patches within our mesh host the same number of volumes. Different cardinalities for the subdivision within the tree are popular: Splitting into two parts along each coordinate axis yields the classic quadree or octree scheme [14,20], while splitting into $k > 2$ parts yields shallower trees. For $p = k$, our overall formalism results in a tree with fixed branching factor. For $p > k$, we can read our mesh as inhomogeneous tree using the same branching factor of k^d everywhere besides the very last level, where the branching factor suddenly becomes p^d. It becomes a hybrid combination of the ideas behind cell-by-cell refinement and patch-based AMR [22]. To match a given spatial accuracy, different choices of k and p can yield volumes of sufficiently small size yet with different topologies. Our code uses $k = 3$ [24] but leaves p as free parameter.

3.2 Finite Volumes

Let every volume carry a constant shape function. This defines our *finite volumes*. We apply an explicit Euler discretisation with time step size T, i.e. assume that all shape functions per patch remain constant over a time interval of length T. A weak formulation of (1) allows an integration by parts and the Gauss divergence theorem to yield a textbook Finite Volume scheme. Along the volume interfaces, our implementation uses the Rusanov flux

$$\begin{aligned}\text{flux}_n^{\pm}(Q)|_{\partial v} = \frac{1}{2}F_n(Q^+) + \frac{1}{2}F_n(Q^-) \mp \frac{1}{2}(Q^+ - Q^-)B_n(\frac{Q^+ + Q^-}{2}) \\ - \max(\lambda_{\max}(Q^+), \lambda_{\max}(Q^-))(Q^+ - Q^-)\end{aligned}$$

with left/right values $Q^{\pm}$ and maximum eigenvalues over the Jacobian.

The generic numerical scheme is tailored towards a particular application by specifying the number of unknowns N in (1) and by providing implementations of a source S and the maximum eigenvalue. As we work in a Cartesian world, we furthermore inject a flux F and the B_i for each of the three coordinate axes.

3.3 Compute Kernels

Let each patch be surrounded by a halo layer of width one. If two face-connected patches host volumes of exactly the same size, such a halo layer is a copy of the volumes from the face-connected neighbouring patch. If a neighbouring patch hosts a coarser mesh, the halo volumes are filled with a linear interpolation of coarser data. If a neighbouring patch hosts a finer mesh, the halo volumes host the averaged data of finer meshes.

With the notion of a halo layer, we can phrase the Finite Volume update of a patch as a *compute kernel*: It accepts the patch data plus the halo and yields the next time step's solution via the PDE term realisations passed in by the user. The kernel requires an epilogue code which updates the kernel's halo layer for the subsequent time step. This is a functional programming approach: We have some generic numerical code which is passed functors that realise the actual physics. Our code uses virtual function calls for the functors. These virtual functions belong to a global solver object which hosts all global solver attributes.

3.4 Time Stepping Variants

We realise four different time stepping schemes. The simplest scheme is *fixed time stepping* which consists of two logical steps per time step and works with a given, time-invariant ΔT: (i) Update all Finite Volumes. For this, we run over all cells aka patches that host them. (ii) Analyse adaptive mesh refinement (AMR) criteria, i.e. refine and coarsen the mesh, and update all halo layers with the correct information from adjacent patches.

Our *adaptive time stepping* adds an additional epilogue to the kernel invocation and reduces ΔT: (i.a) Update all Finite Volumes. (i.b) Determine the maximum eigenvalue $\lambda_{\max}$ over all volumes within the patch and compute a patch-local admissible next time step size $\Delta T^{(\text{adm})} = Ch/\lambda_{\max}$. (ii.a) Realise the AMR and initialise the halo layers. (ii.b) Reduce a global admissible time step size and use this one for the next time step. Due to the global reduction, the adaptive time stepping ensures that the CFL condition is never violated even if the wave propagation speed changes over time.

Subcycling accepts that volumes of different size are subject to different (local) CFL conditions: (i.a) Augment each patch with a patch-local time stamp $T(v)$. (i.b) Run over all patches. Update the Finite Volumes within a patch if and only if all face-connected patches either carry the same time stamp or are ahead in time. Otherwise skip the patch. Use the time step size $\Delta T = \Delta \hat{T} \cdot h/h_{\max}$. $h_{\max}$ is the global coarsest volume size and h is the local patch's volume size. (i.c) Determine the normalised admissible patch-local time step size $\Delta \hat{T}^{(\text{adm})}(v) = Ch_{\max}/\lambda_{\max}$ (ii.a) Realise the AMR and initialise the halo layers. (ii.b) Reduce a global normalised admissible time step size $\Delta \hat{T}(v)$.

The *local time stepping* eliminates the strict coupling between neighbouring patches: (i.a) Augment each patch with a patch-local time stamp $T(v)$ and time step size $\Delta T(v)$. (i.b) Run over all patches. Update the Finite Volumes within a patch if and only if all face-connected patches either carry the same time stamp or are ahead in time. Use the local time step size $\Delta T(v)$. (i.c) Determine a new local time step size if the patch has been updated. (ii) Realise the AMR and initialise the halo layers.

Subcycling requires linear interpolation in time along mesh resolution boundaries. Local time stepping requires linear interpolation for each halo layer update. For linear PDEs, it would yield subcycling. In our case, we solve non-linear PDEs. There is no clear $1{:}k^i$ time step relation between patches of different resolution, and even patches of the same mesh size are allowed to advance in time with different speed if their eigenvalues differ.

Some literature in the field [22] uses the term adaptive for subcycling. This is a reasonable decision once we observe that too small time step sizes introduce numerical diffusion and thus pollute the simulation result. In this context, one can argue that both our fixed time stepping and adaptive time stepping are inappropriate for dynamically adaptive meshes over non-linear PDEs.Larger volumes or volumes with small eigenvalues should advance in time faster.

3.5 Concurrency Analysis

Once we have made a decision to update a patch, we are able to process it independently of other patches as we supplement each patch with a halo layer. The patch update becomes a task. In a regular mesh with $P \times P \times P$ volumes, we obtain a best-case concurrency level of $(P/p)^3$. Within our tree formalism, we know $\exists \ell : k^\ell \cdot p = P$ and we consequently could obtain the same mesh with patch sizes $\ldots, k^2p, kp, p, p/k, p/k^2, \ldots$, too. Larger p reduce the concurrency of the patch updates yet increase the arithmetic weight per task. Smaller p yield higher concurrency yet increase the cost per Finite Volume update due to (time step) bookkeeping per patch and data movements for the halos, even though the arithmetic intensity per volume is independent of the choice of p.

Larger p also reduce the AMR cardinality. If shocks arise, smaller values of p allow us to resolve these features with fewer volumes. Finally, large p constrain the time step adaptivity, since all Finite Volumes within a patch advance in time with the same time step size. In the context of subcycling and the local time stepping, we see that both schemes yield permanently changing concurrency levels, as the number of patches that are updated per time step changes per step. This even holds if the AMR grid remains static or we have a regular mesh in the local time stepping scheme.

The halo data exchange between patches of the same size is embarrassingly parallel. In a distributed memory context, it however requires MPI data exchange. The halo data projections from coarse to fine impose no concurrency constraints either. The restriction, i.e. the averaging, requires some local synchronisation, as no two neighbouring patches may restrict into the same halo volume at the same time.

4 Parallelisation

4.1 Domain Decomposition

In our code, the computational domain's adaptive mesh of cells is split along a space-filling curve (SFC) [4,13]: Curve segments of similar cell count are first distributed over the compute nodes (ranks), before we split each rank's subpartition once again along the SFC into one chunk per thread. Fewer chunks are used if the subpartitions would become too small. We end up with two levels of data parallelism: A distributed memory one and a shared memory one. Both realise the same SFC decomposition paradigm yet differ in the way they exchange data: The top level sends MPI messages around, while the shared memory domain decomposition copies memory segments.

Rationale 1. *The two-level domain decomposition maps directly onto plain SPMD and BSP programming: All MPI ranks run through the same code, spawn one large parallel region (parallel for) and make each thread run through one chunk of the domain.*

The two-level balancing yields a chains-on-chains problem [13]: The SFC linearises all patches into one long sequence of patches which we cut first into chunks per MPI rank and then into chunks per thread. We employ a uniform cost model which is a strong simplification for subcycling. More sophisticated chains-on-chains approaches tackle this aspect [16]. However, they intrinsically fail for local time stepping if the underlying PDE is non-linear. A uniform cost model also fails to reflect that adaptive mesh refinement with non-conformal meshes requires inter-resolution transfer operators at patch boundaries where the mesh resolution changes. These induce additional cost.

Challenge 1. *The BSP programming model applied to a geometric domain decomposition is inherently ill-suited to handle local time stepping codes with dynamic AMR for non-linear hyperbolic PDEs.*

4.2 Task Decomposition

The update of the individual patches is embarrassingly parallel. This statement however ignores data dependencies along mesh refinement transitions, ignores that dynamic AMR is expensive due to memory allocations which do not arbitrarily scale up, and it ignores that the halo data exchange via MPI requires deterministic messaging, while periodic boundary conditions typically involve some sorting or mapping. Some patch update tasks might belong to the critical path of the overall task graph as they are more expensive than others or feed into data transfer.

We therefore realise the concept of enclave tasking [6] and map each time step onto two mesh sweeps: Let a skeleton cell be a cell which is flagged to be refined or coarsened, is adjacent to a coarser cell, adjacent to a subdomain boundary or adjacent to a periodic boundary. The code sweeps through the domain. Per skeleton cell, it invokes the compute kernel, triggers all halo data exchange along the domain boundaries and realises the adaptive mesh refinement. In a second sweep, the code receives this boundary data, and updates all halo data.

The non-skeleton cells are treated differently: The first, primary sweep spawns a task for the corresponding patch and memorises the task's number within the cell. In the secondary sweep, each thread waits for the corresponding task to terminate once it hits a non-skeleton cell. It subsequently works in the task's result into the mesh before it updates the halo layers.

Rationale 2. *We do not explicitly assemble a task graph. Instead,we spawn only ready tasks. These tasks should overlap with boundary data transfer, adaptive mesh refinement operations or mesh administration.*

Challenge 2. *The scheme bursts large numbers of ready tasks. These have to be held back until they can be used to compensate for BSP imbalances.*

Challenge 3. *To gain maximum flexibility to compensate imbalances, the patches (tasks) have to be small.*

4.3 Intra-patch Concurrency

Finite Volume schemes spend the majority of their runtime on patch updates. Each patch update is a sequence of nested for loops with known cardinality. In the innermost loop, we invoke the user functions. Our code refrains from exploiting any patch-internal concurrency for the cores. A patch is an atomic task which is not subdivided further.

Rationale 3. *The patch updates have to yield the MFLOP/s, i.e. aggressive vectorisation has to result from the patch updates unless the user function itself is costly and vectorised.*

Challenge 4. *The compiler cannot vectorise over virtual function calls.*

5 Performance Optimisation

5.1 Optimised C++ Kernels

Our implementation hides complexity from the domain code, as domain experts only write code for the PDE terms. They feed into generic compute kernels. Our per-patch optimisation efforts focus on those non-skeleton tasks which have no side-effects. A user-defined flag per cell indicates whether the patch kernel evaluation alters global variables, i.e. the m_i values, or not. For the remaining tasks, we use our generic compute kernel.

Exploit Lack of Side-Effects. We extract our Rusanov patch update into a C++ template function over the solver type and replicate all PDE terms in the user code by specialisations: For every PDE term within a solver class, we establish a second variant which is static, i.e. has class-bindings instead of object-bindings. This static flavour is stripped off all global data access routines, aka the $\{m_i\}$ accumulation. For (2), we hence optimise only patches outside of $r_{\max}$. Our patch update for side-effect free cells calls the static PDE term variant, i.e. we eliminate virtual function calls (cmp. Challenge 4).

Next, we remove all C++ expressions from the template kernels which prohibit the compiler to inline. This involves the elimination of initialisation lists which are internally mapped onto for or while loops by C++. As we know the exact loop ranges for all constructs through the template arguments, we can replace such loops, i.e. manually unroll them. It also implies moving the PDE term definitions into headers, annotating them with `__attribute__((always_inline))` and removing explicit template instantiations. Explicit template instantiations enable the compiler to generate object files and thus speed up the translation while the library sizes are reduced. However, once machine code is "hidden away" within object files, our compiler struggles to inline. Aggressive inlining allows the compiler to unroll the loops, to vectorise, and it enables us to store all temporary data on the call stack rather than the heap which we use in our generic kernel implementations accepting functors and any data cardinality.

Finally, we realise a patch update kernel which computes all the fluxes per volume, all eigenvalues and all ncp terms before it updates the image, as well as a kernel which updates all volumes in-situ. The former variant requires temporary arrays which can be realised in different storage formats (AoS or SoA). The in-situ approach runs over the faces, computes the flux/ncp contribution per face and immediately updates both adjacent volumes. Similar to a red-black Gauss-Seidel, we update the columns, rows and layers of the patch in an interleaved fashion such that no race conditions arise. As the Rusanov flux requires averaging between two cell fluxes plus left and right eigenvalues, many terms are calculated twice. Yet, we need no massive temporary data structures.

Batched Kernels. So far, we have two semantically different patch update routines: The standard routine is a generic numerical scheme which accepts N and p as parameters and is given one functor per PDE term plus the eigenvalue invocation. Each functor can alter the state of the underlying PDE solver. It can, for example, aggregate global data views. A second routine is used for cells hosting patches that do not alter the global solver state.

This second flavour can be extended into a third, batched variant: Assume we have $\hat{P}$ patches not causing side-effects, each with its own time stamp and time step size yet the same patch dimensions and PDE terms. We can then update all $\hat{P}$ patches in parallel. The lack of side-effects implies that there are no race conditions. This adds an additional loop over the patches to our compute kernels. The batched kernel variant takes the $\hat{P}$ patches and first computes the flux, e.g., of one volume of the first patch, then the second patch, and so forth, before it continues with the second volume. Despite small patches, the vectorisation now operates over a large iteration space (cmp. Challenge 3) which can be collapsed.

5.2 Task Queues

We propose an optimised threading architecture, where each rank issues one OpenMP thread per rank-local subpartition. This is BSP. To compensate for the intrinsic imbalances (cmp. Challenge 1), we employ our task-based parallelism on top: When a traversal encounters a non-skeleton cell, i.e. a patch update that is not algorithmically latency-sensitive, it creates a task.

This task is not passed into the underlying task runtime. Instead, we store it in an application queue. Once ready tasks are spawned into a task system, they are typically "lost" to the application code, i.e. it is difficult to manipulate them anymore. Furthermore, a fundamental principle of task systems is that the application code hands the responsibility for when a task is executed over to the runtime. With the application queue, we keep control over the tasks: If tasks within the queue are required in a subsequent BSP traversal, i.e. if there's a task dependency, and if this task has not yet completed, our BSP code runs through the user queue, processes one task, and checks again for completion. It polls the queue. If the queue becomes empty, the underlying BSP thread yields. This architecture allows us to realise the following tasking schemes:

- *BSP tasking.* All tasks in the application queue remain there until they are polled by a subsequent BSP section. This realises a lazy evaluation scheme, where tasks are evaluated upon demand. We postpone their execution.
- *Native tasking.* Our native tasking scheme maps all tasks that hit the application queue directly onto OpenMP tasks. They are not buffered.
- *Fill.* This extension of BSP uses an atomic counter within the BSP section. It is initialised with the number of SFC partitions per rank and decremented once a BSP thread has finished its thread-local mesh traversal. Each BSP thread thus sees how many companion threads are still working. As long as some other BSP threads are still active, a thread does not close the BSP section but grabs a task from the user queue and executes it directly. It "releases" tasks if and only if we spot imbalances on the BSP side (cmp. Challenge 2).
- *Specialise late.* In this extension of the fill variant, a thread waiting for companion BSP threads first checks if the next task in the queue causes no side-effects. If so, it invokes the optimised kernel. Otherwise, it calls the generic kernel.
- *Batch(#t) late.* If a BSP thread recognises that companion BSP sections run longer, it takes up to #*t* consecutive tasks from the queue if they all have the same task type and lack side-effects. It then invokes the batched, optimised kernel over this set of #*t* tasks. Tasks are fused into one large task (cmp. Challenge 3).
- *Specialise immediately or batch immediately.* In this variant of the fill strategy, we immediately check if we can invoke a specialised kernel on one task or over a sequence of tasks, respectively, whenever a task is spawned.

6 Results

We run our experiments on Durham's Hamilton 8 cluster. It hosts AMD EPYC 7702 64-Core processor, i.e. the AMD K17 (Zen2) architecture. The 2×64 cores are spread over two sockets, but they are organised in 8 NUMA domains. Each core has access to 32 kB exclusive L1 cache, and 512 kB L2 cache. The L3 cache is (physically) split into chunks of 16 MB associated with four cores.

We use the Intel oneAPI software stack with icpx 2021.4.0. Intel's MPI (version 2021.4) is used for the distributed memory parallelisation, though we disable MPI for the single-node measurements. The tasking and vectorisation are realised through OpenMP. We use the most aggressive generic compiler optimisation level (`-Ofast`) and native code generation (`-mtune=native -march=native`).

6.1 Single Task (Kernel) Optimisations

Table 1. Single patch kernel performance for the modified Euler equations (top) and CCZ4 (bottom) for various patch sizes $p \times p \times p$. We compare the plain kernel with virtual functions (baseline) against kernels without side-effects which either run through the patches one by one or batch the operations. Three different realisations w.r.t. the data organisation and computation orchestration are studied. Per measurement, we present the time ($[t] = s$) per Finite Volume update incl. the subsequent CFL computation, while the fastest configuration and those slower than the baseline run are set in bold.

p	Baseline	Patch-wise			Batched		
		AoS	SoA	In-situ	AoS	SoA	In-situ
3	$1.12 \cdot 10^{-6}$	$8.28 \cdot 10^{-7}$	$8.81 \cdot 10^{-7}$	$\mathbf{4.27 \cdot 10^{-7}}$	$7.85 \cdot 10^{-7}$	$7.91 \cdot 10^{-7}$	$6.52 \cdot 10^{-7}$
4	$9.11 \cdot 10^{-7}$	$8.07 \cdot 10^{-7}$	$8.10 \cdot 10^{-7}$	$\mathbf{3.93 \cdot 10^{-7}}$	$7.35 \cdot 10^{-7}$	$7.34 \cdot 10^{-7}$	$6.21 \cdot 10^{-7}$
7	$7.91 \cdot 10^{-7}$	$7.43 \cdot 10^{-7}$	$7.85 \cdot 10^{-7}$	$\mathbf{3.54 \cdot 10^{-7}}$	$7.00 \cdot 10^{-7}$	$7.09 \cdot 10^{-7}$	$5.62 \cdot 10^{-7}$
8	$7.84 \cdot 10^{-7}$	$7.67 \cdot 10^{-7}$	$7.70 \cdot 10^{-7}$	$\mathbf{3.52 \cdot 10^{-7}}$	$6.90 \cdot 10^{-7}$	$6.87 \cdot 10^{-7}$	$5.63 \cdot 10^{-7}$
15	$7.99 \cdot 10^{-7}$	$7.48 \cdot 10^{-7}$	$7.72 \cdot 10^{-7}$	$\mathbf{3.44 \cdot 10^{-7}}$	$6.92 \cdot 10^{-7}$	$6.80 \cdot 10^{-7}$	$5.47 \cdot 10^{-7}$
16	$7.95 \cdot 10^{-7}$	$7.41 \cdot 10^{-7}$	$7.62 \cdot 10^{-7}$	$\mathbf{3.45 \cdot 10^{-7}}$	$6.85 \cdot 10^{-7}$	$6.87 \cdot 10^{-7}$	$5.47 \cdot 10^{-7}$
3	$1.84 \cdot 10^{-5}$	$1.73 \cdot 10^{-5}$	$1.70 \cdot 10^{-5}$	$\mathbf{1.17 \cdot 10^{-5}}$	$1.60 \cdot 10^{-5}$	$1.60 \cdot 10^{-5}$	$1.26 \cdot 10^{-5}$
4	$1.68 \cdot 10^{-5}$	$1.65 \cdot 10^{-5}$	$1.65 \cdot 10^{-5}$	$\mathbf{1.12 \cdot 10^{-5}}$	$1.50 \cdot 10^{-5}$	$1.53 \cdot 10^{-5}$	$1.22 \cdot 10^{-5}$
7	$1.56 \cdot 10^{-5}$	$\mathbf{1.57 \cdot 10^{-5}}$	$1.56 \cdot 10^{-5}$	$\mathbf{1.02 \cdot 10^{-5}}$	$1.45 \cdot 10^{-5}$	$1.45 \cdot 10^{-5}$	$1.10 \cdot 10^{-5}$
8	$1.55 \cdot 10^{-5}$	$\mathbf{1.70 \cdot 10^{-5}}$	$\mathbf{1.68 \cdot 10^{-5}}$	$\mathbf{1.03 \cdot 10^{-5}}$	$1.44 \cdot 10^{-5}$	$1.44 \cdot 10^{-5}$	$1.11 \cdot 10^{-5}$

We first assess the impact of our kernel optimisations in isolation. For this, we focus only on the runtime of the patch update routines without any time stepping, mesh administration, halo updates, and so forth, and compare the generic FV patch update implementation using functors with the optimised versions which are used for tasks without side-effects. Our results present data for various patch sizes on one core. The compiler optimisation report clarifies that the translator succeeds in vectorising the user functions themselves (baseline) or vectorises over the patch entries or the batch of patches respectively.

The inlining pays off for the Euler equations (Table 1). A tuning of the intermediate data formats (AoS vs. AoS) however is irrelevant. Instead, avoiding the storage of intermediate results and computing the eigenvalues and fluxes twice gives the best performance. For CCZ4, the evaluation of a single source, ncp or eigenvalue is already expensive and utilises all vector capabilities according to the compiler feedback. The aggressive inlining, collapsing and vectorisation of the patch loops harms the performance unless we use the in-situ updates or batching. In-situ without batching continues to yield the best performance overall. We have not been able to identify significant runtime differences between AoS, SoA and in-situ for the baseline code using virtual function calls.

Lessons Learned 1. *With a distinction of patch updates with side effects from kernels without them as well aggressive inlining and vectorisation, the small patches manage to match the throughput of large regular patches of volumes.*

If we first compute all fluxes in one direction, then in the other, then all ncps, then all eigenvalues, until we eventually combine these ingredients to update the outcome, the compiler vectorises all calculations once we inline the function calls. Yet, it suffers from many memory accesses. It is better to compute the eigenvalues, flux and ncp feeding into the Rusanov flux redundantly and to update all unknowns in-situ, i.e. to minimise the memory accesses. With this update scheme plus the exploitation of no side effects, we speed up our code by a factor of two for a memory-bound, simplistic PDE. For complex PDE terms, the approach still reduce the runtime robustly by roughly 30%. It remains an open question if a switch of the intermediate data structures or the elimination of redundant calculations would be the method of choice for other architectures or PDE choices. Furthermore, we do not exploit the fact that the arising equation system is sparse due to the flat Minkowski metric. Our generic kernel evaluates many terms which degenerate to zero. It is unclear how such domain knowledge can help to improve the performance further.

6.2 Single Node Studies on Regular Grid

We next study the scaling behaviour on one node. Our first subject of interest is the performance of the code on a regular grid. Here, subcycling equals the global adaptive scheme. Our benchmarks use a patch size of $p = 4$, i.e. each patch hosts 64 volumes. The runs span a total time of $(0, 10^{-3})$ which allows the solution to unfold reasonably such that we find a whole spectrum of eigenvalues over the domain for the modified Euler equations, while the regular grid hosts 34,012,224 (Euler) or 6,751,269 (CCZ4) volumes.

For Euler, the adaptive time stepping outperforms a fixed time stepping, as it dynamically adopts the time step size to the actual solution's needs while the fixed time stepping has to be conservative (Fig. 2): We have to set the fixed time step to the minimum of admissible step sizes over the whole simulation time span. Due to the absence of any clustering [23] in our local time stepping, i.e. the opportunity for every patch to march with its very own ΔT, the individual patches get "out of sync" and only few patches can advance in time per grid sweep. Typically, we update around 0.2% of all patches at one point in time. Local time stepping hence does not pay off. Adaptive time stepping equals the fixed time stepping for CCZ4 once we pick the same, time-invariant time step size for both. We typically do not know the admissible time step sizes for such complex PDEs a priori and thus have to build in some slack. It manifests in translated speedup curves. Due to the time invariance, the local time stepping yields the same performance patterns, too.

All schemes scale reasonably up to half a socket. After that, their scaling deteriorates. The runtime eventually increases if we use too many cores. Even though the mesh is perfectly balanced and does not change, we have slight runtime imbalances between the BSP sections—we use one SFC subpartition per core—which the native tasking on top of BSP can mitigate. Holding back tasks in an application queue on top of the OpenMP runtime introduces overhead. The fill strategy is thus slower than native tasking. Our CCZ4 setups are smaller than the Euler experiments and thus run into the strong scaling earlier, while the more expensive patch updates imply that any BSP imbalance—due to periodic boundary conditions, e.g.—manifests in stronger performance differences. Consequently, any fill-up decision runs risk to delay the termination of the BSP section further. Once we identify tasks without side-effects and invoke specialised, optimised kernels, we get the better performance than for all other strategies. For reasonably small core counts, both the immediately spawning of specialised kernels and the holding back of kernels and (late) specialising upon-demand yield comparable performance.

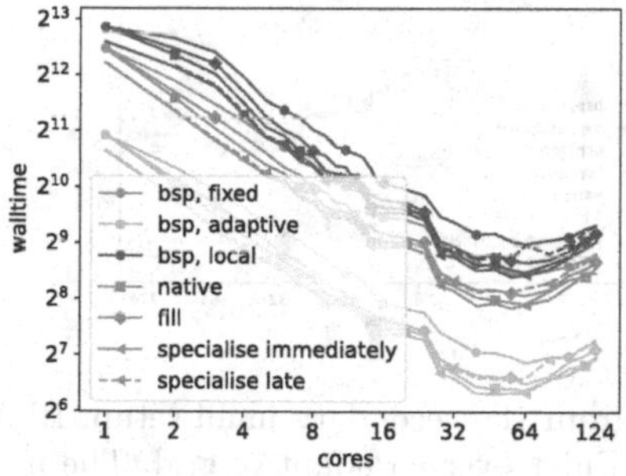

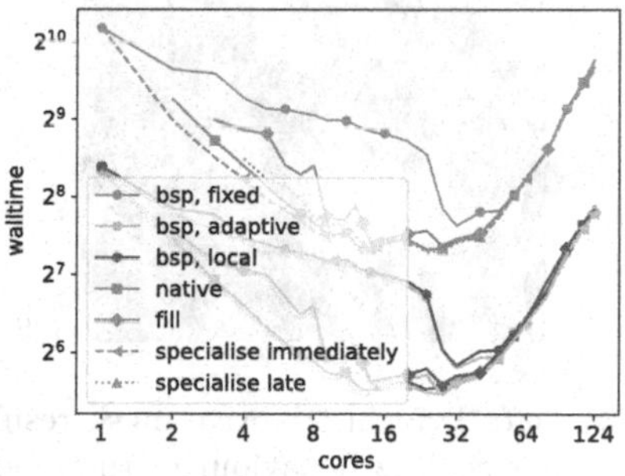

Fig. 2. Single node scaling behaviour of the modified Euler (left) and CCZ4 (right) with different time stepping and task orchestration schemes.

Lessons Learned 2. *A task parallelisation on top of classic BSP re-stabilises the code suffering from non-uniform load per BSP partition.*

We manage to preserve the positive impact of the kernel specialisations, though the tasking is responsible for the major runtime improvement. In total, we speed up the code by a factor of two. Our development experience suggests that this is possible if and only if we work with one additional user queue per core into which enclave tasks are "parked". This queue is merged into the global task queue once the corresponding BSP section producing tasks has terminated. If one global application queue is used right from the start, too many threads hit this queue and synchronise each other.

While the batching does not yield improved performance, it does not penalise the performance either as long as the ratio of work to cores remains high. On an EPYC, we have limited vectorisation potential. Furthermore, OpenMP tasks are tied to one core. It is thus not a surprise that we do not benefit from the batching, but the observation is encouraging for other systems, future runtimes and accelerators where individual tasks have to span multiple cores. This is facilitated by fused, large tasks.

6.3 Single Node Studies for Adaptive Grids

We continue with the Euler equations and 4^3 patches and let the AMR refinement follow the outer-propagating shock (Fig. 1). This is a challenging setup given the low arithmetic cost and high communication demands. All of our tests use a domain decomposition which is 90% accurate when the simulation starts, i.e. we compute the optimal load balancing and ensure that no rank is more than ±10% off. We do not rebalance subpartitions throughout the test.

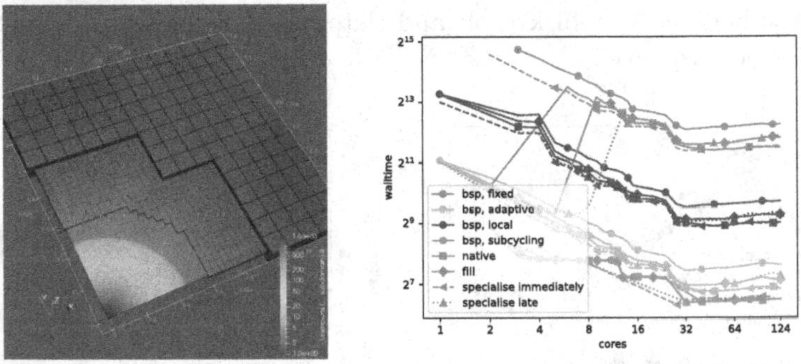

Fig. 3. Left: Typical adaptive mesh resulting from the secondary infall setup. Right: Single node scaling behaviour of the modified Euler over an adaptive grid. The mesh has three levels of adaptive refinement.

For an adaptive mesh, the task-based approach on top of BSP continues to outperform its BSP counterpart (Fig. 3). The latter suffers from AMR: As long as we use up to four cores and hence four partitions only, the BSP partitions might be imbalanced, but they produce many tasks which help to keep the cores busy. For more subdomains, fewer tasks are labelled as enclaves. The code fails to overlap expensive, "unpredictable" calculations for the mesh resolution transitions with plain compute tasks corresponding to regular grid subregions.

It continues to be advantageous to check if we can use a specialised compute kernel for a task. Compared to the kernel benchmarking or the regular grid calculations, the specialisation however does not yield the full factor of two in runtime improvements anymore. Finally, subcycling pays off performance-wisely, while local time stepping is slower than its adaptive algorithmic cousins.

Lessons Learned 3. *Our manual task specialisation and scheduling allows us to preserve reasonable on-node scaling even if we use adaptive mesh refinement. It can also handle subcycling and local time stepping.*

6.4 Multi-node Runs

Our techniques focus on the single node performance of PDE solvers with AMR and LTS. Yet, they have impact on MPI: The idea to add tasks on top of BSP implies that we also have tasks which can be used to overlap data exchange which typically is triggered after a rank's BSP sections have terminated. This overlap is the more powerful the more tasks we have relative to any urgent rank work and data exchange. Therefore, AMR and many MPI ranks challenge the scheme. At the same time, the balancing with tasks runs risk to suffer from NUMA effects.

We stick to setups from the previous sections. They have reached a strong scaling saturation already. As we use one BSP section per core, all experiments rely on the same geometric partitioning yet distribute the SFC segments differently between threads and ranks. Our benchmarks suggest that it is advantageous to stick to SPMD/BSP parallelism for regular grids with up to 32 MPI ranks per node (Fig. 4). It is not clear if the good performance is due to NUMA effects or other machine characteristics. We however observe that the specialisation gains are diminished. For adaptive meshes, it is better to work with smaller rank counts per node.

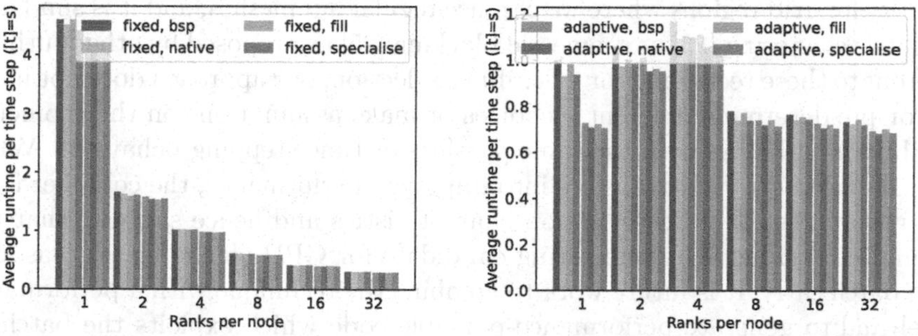

Fig. 4. Different arrangements of ranks-per-node (rpn) for a four-node (512 core) simulation run with the modified Euler equations over a regular (left) or adaptive (right) grid. The setups equal those of the previous sections.

Lessons Learned 4. *Splitting up NUMA nodes into logically separated processors is usually advantageous from a performance point of view, yet reduces the number of non-urgent tasks which we can reschedule, optimise or batch. It hence makes the code performance less robust w.r.t. AMR.*

We emphasise that application task queues sitting on top of the tasking system have to be used carefully in an MPI context if they prevent tasks from overlapping with MPI data exchange. As soon as the problem size relative to the core count becomes larger again, we retain the qualitative statements of the single node studies and the specialisation starts to pay of again (not shown).

7 Conclusion and Outlook

Task-based programming is not omnipresent in large-scale PDE solvers. Our data suggests that it can significantly improve the performance of classic BSP-style parallelism realised via parallel fors, if tasks can step in to compensate for BSP imbalances. We do not propose to use tasks as alternative to classic BSP parallelism but as a complementing technique. For the realisation of this concept, we avoid assembling any task graph, i.e. focus on the production of ready tasks, and add an additional task queue on top of the OpenMP task queue. It allows us to release work into the computation such that BSP imbalances are mitigated. We get the best of both worlds, i.e. BSP and tasking. While the tasking on top of BSP helps us to scale better, we also propose to distinguish tasks with global side-effects from low-priority tasks without side-effects and to handle the latter with specialised compute kernels that exploit their intrinsically higher internal concurrency level. In many cases, this doubles the code performance, even though we do not impose any constraints on the LTS or AMR or require any a priori analysis of the patch behaviour.

While a batched handling of assemblies of tasks without side-effects is an appealing concept, it does not robustly translate into an improved performance in our applications. Such a task fusion is conceptionally close to approaches that work with different p values for different blocks to keep the administration overhead low for grid regions where we can use regular submeshes, and it is similar to geometric clustering [23] or geometric blocking [25] as proposed by other authors. Different to these techniques or a flexible p selection, our approach does not hard-wire or pre-determine different p choices or make assumptions on the geometric distribution of blocks with the same p values or time stepping behaviour. While the task fusion does not translate into improved performance, the compiler feedback reports excellent vectorisation characteristics and hence suggests that the automatic batching is an interesting candidate for GPU offloading, e.g., as long as we batch early. It is future work to combine the technique with a performance model and to generate performance-portable code which exploits the batching similar to dynamic choices of p for different components of a supercomputer.

Our manual postponing of task spawns through the application task queue can be interpreted as an approach which implicitly prioritises BSP code segments over tasks. The hierarchy of parallelisation approaches in our code translates into a task prioritisation. It is hence reasonable to assume that carefully chosen task priorities would allow us to obtain similar runtime characteristics within an exclusively task-based programming model. Overall, the data suggests that a task graph assembly is not required as long as the prioritisation works. To meet our goal, our implementation replicates some OpenMP features such as queues on the user level. If future OpenMP generations provided options such as automatic task fusion or a careful prioritisation of tasks, it would be reasonable to eliminate our added tasking code layers to reduce the code complexity.

Next steps of our work comprise the analysis of the impact of the time stepping scheme on the quality of the solution. Our studies suggest that local time stepping is slower than global adaptive time stepping or subcycling. However, these measurements do not assess the impact of these schemes on the solution quality. In theory, local time stepping should introduce less numerical dissipation than the other schemes and hence yield better results. In this context, we also have to study more more sophisticated Riemann solvers [15]. This improved quality has to be assessed against the proposed runtime improvements. Finally, the generality of our concepts implies that a our approach might be advantageous for very flexible, task-based Lagrangian codes such as [19], too, as well as other solver components such as linear algebra subsystems.

References

1. Alcubierre, M., et al.: Towards standard testbeds for numerical relativity. Class. Quantum Gravity **21**(2), 589–613 (2004)
2. Alic, D., Bona-Casas, C., Bona, C., Rezzolla, L., Palenzuela, C.: Conformal and covariant formulation of the Z4 system with constraint-violation damping. Phys. Rev. D **85**(6), 064040 (2012)
3. Ayguade, E., et al.: The design of OpenMP tasks. IEEE Trans. Parallel Distrib. Syst. **20**(3), 404–418 (2009)
4. Bader, M.: Space-Filling Curves: An Introduction with Applications in Scientific Computing. Texts in Computational Science and Engineering, vol. 9. Springer, Heidelberg (2013). https://doi.org/10.1007/978-3-642-31046-1
5. Bertschinger, E.: Self-similar secondary infall and accretion in an Einstein-de Sitter universe. Astrophys. J. Suppl. Ser. **58**, 39–65 (1985)
6. Charrier, D., Hazelwood, B., Weinzierl, T.: Enclave tasking for dg methods on dynamically adaptive meshes. SIAM J. Sci. Comput. **42**(3), C69–C96 (2020)
7. Daszuta, B., Zappa, F., Cook, W., Radice, D., Bernuzzi, S., Morozova, V.: GR-Athena: puncture evolutions on vertex-centered oct-tree adaptive mesh refinement. Astrophys. J. Suppl. Ser. **257**(2), 25 (2021)
8. Demeshko, I., et al.: TBAA20: task based algorithms and applications. DOE report LA-UR-21-20928 (2021)
9. Dongarra, J., et al.: The international exascale software project roadmap. IJHPCA **25**, 3–60 (2011)

10. Dubey, A., et al.: A survey of high level frameworks in block-structured adaptive mesh refinement packages. J. Parallel Distrib. Comput. **74**(12), 3217–3227 (2016)
11. Dubey, A., Berzins, M., Burstedde, C., Norman, M.L., Unat, D., Wahib, M.: Structured adaptive mesh refinement adaptations to retain performance portability with increasing heterogeneity. Comput. Sci. Eng. **23**(05), 62–66 (2021)
12. Dumbser, M., Guercilena, F., Köppel, S., Rezzolla, L., Zanotti, O.: Conformal and covariant Z4 formulation of the Einstein equations: strongly hyperbolic first-order reduction and solution with discontinuous Galerkin schemes. Phys. Rev. D **97**, 084053 (2018)
13. Harlacher, D.F., Klimach, H., Roller, S., Siebert, C., Wolf, F.: Dynamic load balancing for unstructured meshes on space-filling curves. In: 26th IEEE International Parallel and Distributed Processing Symposium Workshops & PhD Forum, IPDPS, pp. 1661–1669. IEEE Computer Society (2012)
14. Isaac, T., Burstedde, C., Ghattas, O.: Low-cost parallel algorithms for 2:1 octree balance. In: IEEE 26th International Parallel and Distributed Processing Symposium, pp. 426–437 (2012)
15. Kidder, E., et al.: SpECTRE: a task-based discontinuous Galerkin code for relativistic astrophysics. J. Comput. Phys. **335**, 84–114 (2017)
16. Meister, O., Rahnema, K., Bader, M.: Parallel memory-efficient adaptive mesh refinement on structured triangular meshes with billions of grid cells. ACM Trans. Math. Softw. **43**(3), 1–27 (2016)
17. Peterson, B., et al.: Automatic halo management for the Uintah GPU-heterogeneous asynchronous many-task runtime. Int. J. Parallel Program. **47**(5–6), 1086–1116 (2018). https://doi.org/10.1007/s10766-018-0619-1
18. Reinarz, A., et al.: ExaHyPE: an engine for parallel dynamically adaptive simulations of wave problems. Comput. Phys. Commun. **254**, 107251 (2020)
19. Schaller, M., Gonnet, P., Chalk, A., Draper, P.: SWIFT: using task-based parallelism, fully asynchronous communication, and graph partition-based domain decomposition for strong scaling on more than 100,000 cores. In: Proceedings of the Platform for Advanced Scientific Computing Conference, PASC 2016. Association for Computing Machinery (2016)
20. Sundar, H., Sampath, R.S., Biros, G.: Bottom-up construction and 2:1 balance refinement of linear octrees in parallel. SIAM J. Sci. Comput. **30**(5), 2675–2708 (2008)
21. Sundar, H., Ghattas, O.: A nested partitioning algorithm for adaptive meshes on heterogeneous clusters. In: Proceedings of the 29th ACM on International Conference on Supercomputing, ICS 2015, pp. 319–328 (2015)
22. Teyssier, R.: Cosmological hydrodynamics with adaptive mesh refinement–a new high resolution code called RAMSES (2002)
23. Uphoff, C., et al.: Extreme scale multi-physics simulations of the tsunamigenic 2004 Sumatra megathrust earthquake. In: Proceedings of the International Conference for High Performance Computing, Networking, Storage and Analysis, SC 2017 (2017)
24. Weinzierl, T.: The Peano software–parallel, automaton-based, dynamically adaptive grid traversals. ACM Trans. Math. Softw. **45**(2), 14 (2019)
25. Weinzierl, T., Wittmann, R., Unterweger, K., Bader, M., Breuer, A., Rettenberger, S.: Hardware-aware block size tailoring on adaptive spacetree grids for shallow water waves, pp. 57–64 (2014)

26. Zhang, H., Weinzierl, T., Schulz, H., Li, B.: Spherical accretion of collisional gas in modified gravity I: self-similar solutions and a new cosmological hydrodynamical code. Monthly Notices of the Royal Astronomical Society (2022). Submitted
27. Zhang, W., Myers, A., Gott, K., Almgren, A., Bell, J.: AMReX: block-structured adaptive mesh refinement for multiphysics applications. Int. J. High Perform. Comput. Appl. **35**(6), 508–526 (2021)

Accelerating Simulated Quantum Annealing with GPU and Tensor Cores

Yi-Hua Chung, Cheng-Jhih Shih, and Shih-Hao Hung(✉)

Department of Computer Science and Information Engineering,
National Taiwan University, No. 1, Sec. 4, Roosevelt Rd.,
Taipei 10617, Taiwan (R.O.C.)
{r09944072,r09922028,hungsh}@ntu.edu.tw

Abstract. Inspired by quantum annealing, simulated quantum annealing (SQA) mimics quantum tunneling effects on classical computers to perform annealing through a path-integral Monte Carlo simulation, which increases the potential to find the global optima faster than traditional annealing algorithms for large-size combinatorial optimization problems while today's quantum annealing systems are of a limited number of qubits'. As previous studies have accelerated SQA with Graphics Processing Unit (GPU) and specialized hardware such as Field Programmable Gate Array (FPGA), we propose an innovative parallelizing strategy called hierarchical update to vastly improve the efficiency of parallel computing, which is capable of accelerating state-of-the-art SQA implementations further by 7X-47.2X based on our case studies. Furthermore, we develop a tensorizing scheme to leverage the Tensor Cores on modern GPUs to deliver up to 1.83X of additional speedup. Overall, our work solves fully-connected Ising models faster than any previous SQA work. Our solution outperforms existing GPU-based solutions by 86.6X and FPGA-based solutions by 14X.

Keywords: High performance computing · GPU acceleration · Tensor Cores · Simulated quantum annealing · Optimization problems

1 Introduction

Quantum annealing (QA) is a metaheuristic method to solve combinatorial optimization problems [1], such as portfolio optimization [2], protein folding [3], and traveling salesman problem [4], which are often NP-hard problems. These combinatorial optimization problems can be converted into Ising models [5] and solved with QA and traditional simulated annealing (SA) [6]. Unlike SA, QA could potentially solve large problems as it owns the property not subject to the combinatorial explosion. While SA uses thermal excitations, QA uses quantum tunneling [7] to tunnel through the tall but narrow barriers, which may help escape from local minima and find the global best solution for the combinatorial optimization problems. However, QA systems such as D-Wave are very expensive today with limited qubits to model the problems.

A.-L. Varbanescu et al. (Eds.): ISC High Performance 2022, LNCS 13289, pp. 174–191, 2022.
https://doi.org/10.1007/978-3-031-07312-0_9

Simulated quantum annealing (SQA) [8] is inspired by QA and tries to mimic the quantum tunneling effect on classical computers through a path-integral Monte Carlo simulation. By mimicking the quantum tunneling effect, SQA has the potential to find the global minima quicker than traditional SA. It is also possible to solve large-size combinatorial optimization problems with SQA, while state-of-the-art QA systems are of limited qubits. To further accelerate SA and SQA, several studies have employed hardware accelerators, such as Application Specific Integrated Circuits (ASICs) [9,10], Field Programmable Gate Array (FPGA) [11–13], as well as Graphics Processing Unit (GPU) [14–16].

Some annealing platforms require an Ising model to be mapped restrictively onto special topologies, as their processors have limited connectivity. For example, D-Wave demands Chimera graph [17] or Pegasus graph [18], which requires an additional transformation procedure called minor embedding [19] and may affect the solution quality with additional computation overhead. In this work, we utilize GPU memory to support a fully-connected Ising model to improve solution quality and avoid the overhead of embedding. Meanwhile, high-performance GPUs are widely available today to provide the most cost-effective solutions.

To perform SQA on a GPU, a fully-connected Ising model is transformed into a matrix form, so that the computing cores on the GPU can operate on the elements of the matrices in parallel. Among the aforementioned accelerated solutions, GPU provides a cost-effective, scalable approach, not only because SQA can compute with thousands of cores on a GPU chip, but it can also run with thousands of GPU chips in a modern supercomputer [20].

In this work, we further exploit the Tensor Cores [21] that are available on modern GPU chips to give 7X-86X speed over the previous work [22] for solving fully-connected Ising models, which is the most efficient SQA implementation as far as we know. We have developed several tensorizing and parallelizing schemes to utilize the Tensor Cores and increase the parallelism for the GPU code. With our optimization, running SQA on GPU with Tensor Cores is even faster than FPGA-accelerated SQA [12]. Moreover, since Tensor Cores have been actively developed to support neural network applications, we expect that the proposed method continues to benefit significantly from this trend.

The remainder of this paper is organized as follows. Section 2 explains the Ising Model, describes the algorithm and implementations of SQA and introduces the Tensor Cores. Section 3 proposes a new parallelization scheme to improve the utilization of GPU cores and further optimizes the code with the Tensor Cores. Section 4 compares our work to previous works to reveal the performance advantage of the proposed methods. Finally, we conclude this paper and point out some potential research directions in the future in Sect. 5.

2 Background and Previous Works

This section first mentions the basics of Ising models for solving combinatorial optimization problems. Then, we explain how simulated quantum annealing (SQA) solves on Ising models, and survey the previously proposed hardware methods for accelerating SQA. Finally, we introduce the Tensor Cores.

2.1 Ising Model

An Ising model is one of the simplest systems that exhibits a phase transition of the thermodynamic system [23–26]. In the Ising model, the total energy of the system for a lattice with N spins is given as:

$$H(\sigma) = -\sum_{i<j} J_{i,j}\sigma_i\sigma_j - \sum_i h_i\sigma_i \tag{1}$$

where binary spin $\sigma_i \in \{1, -1\}$, $J_{i,j}$ indicates the strength of the coupled interaction between σ_i and σ_j, and h_i is the external magnetic field. Besides, the sign of the coupling term $J_{i,j}$ tells us whether the σ_j prefers to align or to anti-align with the σ_i. The size of the external magnetic field h_i represents how strong its field is, revealing how much higher the energy of the σ_i is than the others. And the sign of h_i tells whether it's spin up or spin down that's preferred. Moreover, h_i also represents the external field trying to align all the spins in one direction.

Solving Ising models is NP-complete [5], which means that the solution of many NP-hard problems, e.g. the traveling salesman problem, can be obtained by solving Ising models. Hence, many works have focused on solving Ising models to establish the solution of combinatorial optimization problems [2–4].

2.2 Simulated Quantum Annealing (SQA)

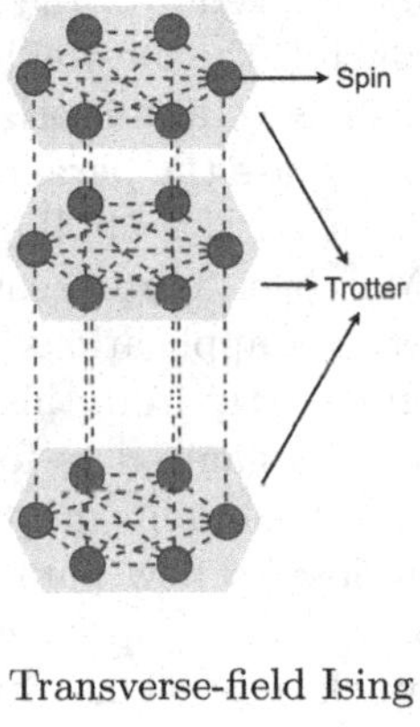

Fig. 1. Transverse-field Ising model

Stoquastic Hamiltonian is applied to various simulation algorithms based on the classical Markov chain. And these algorithms are collectively referred to as Quantum Monte Carlo (QMC) methods [28,29]. Different QMC methods can be applied to the QA Hamiltonian equation [30,31]. The version based on the path-integral [29] representation of the thermal state is considered in this paper. Proved by Suzuki, Masuo [8], it is known that the partition function of the m-dimensional quantum Ising model in the traversed field is mapped to the partition function of the classical Ising model with (m+1)-dimension as shown in Fig. 1, and expressed by [14]:

$$H(\sigma) = -\sum_{k=1}^{M}(\sum_{i<j}\frac{J_{i,j}}{M}\sigma_{i,k}\sigma_{j,k} + \sum_{i}\frac{h_i}{M}\sigma_{i,k} + J^{\dagger}\sum_{i}\sigma_{i,k}\sigma_{i,k+1}) \quad (2)$$

where $J^{\dagger} = T/2 \cdot \ln \coth(\Gamma(t)/(MT))$ indicates the strength of couplings between replicas, T is a controlled temperature, M is the number of replicas, and $\Gamma(t)$ is the controlled transverse field. By reducing the temperature T and transverse field $\Gamma(t)$, the system is expected to have the lowest energy. As the temperature T becomes close to zero at the end of the annealing process, the strength of the coupling $J^{\dagger}$ will approach infinity and each replica will have the same spin configuration with high probability. When M is large enough, the behavior of SQA resembles that of QA. However, it doesn't mean that the larger M has a higher probability to achieve the ground state energy [7].

For an Ising model formulated by Eq. (1), the local-field energy of each spin on the fully-connected graph is the cross dot between all the coupling coefficients and the corresponding spins on the same trotter, as shown in Eq. (3):

$$\text{local\_field}_{i,m} = \sum_{j=1}^{N} J_{i,j}\sigma_{j,m} \quad (3)$$

where $\sigma_{j,m}$ is the j-th spin in the m-th trotter. The couplings, spins, and local-field energy are mapped to the following three matrix forms:

- **Coupling matrix:** As shown in Fig. 2a, the corresponding coupling coefficient between σ_i and σ_j is placed in the location in the coupling matrix with column i and row j. Since the interaction relations between σ_i and σ_j are equal, the coupling matrix is symmetric. Hence, the matrix size is $N * N$.
- **Spin matrix:** As displayed in Fig. 2b, the spins on the same trotter are placed in the same column of the spin matrix. That is, for example, if there is an i-th spin on the j-th trotter, then the spin is notated as $\sigma_{i,j}$, and it is placed on the location where row $= i$ and column $= j$. So, with spin number $= N$ and trotter number $= M$, the matrix size will be $N * M$.
- **Local-field energy matrix:** Exhibited in Fig. 2c, the matrix elements of the local-field energy matrix are in the same order as the spin matrix. Hence, the local-field energy $\text{local\_field}_{i,j}$ of $\sigma_{i,j}$ is positioned in the place where row $= i$ and column $= j$. Also, the size of the matrix is equal to $N * M$.

Algorithm 1 shows the SQA algorithm. The algorithm first sets up the Ising model and the initial condition by (1) loading the coupling data derived by the Ising problem into the coupling matrix (J) in Line 1, (2) initializing the elements in the spin matrix (σ) randomly with either –1 or 1 in Line 2, and then (3) constructing the local-field matrix based on Eq. (3) in Lines 3–11.

The construction of the local-field matrix is basically done with matrix multiplication, the entry $\text{local\_field}_{i,j}$ of the local-field matrix is derived by multiplying

$$\begin{pmatrix} J_{1,1} & J_{1,2} & \cdots & J_{1,N} \\ J_{2,1} & J_{2,2} & \cdots & J_{2,N} \\ \vdots & \vdots & \ddots & \vdots \\ J_{N,1} & J_{N,2} & \cdots & J_{N,N} \end{pmatrix}_{N*N}$$

(a) Coupling matrix

$$\begin{pmatrix} \sigma_{1,1} & \sigma_{1,2} & \cdots & \sigma_{1,M} \\ \sigma_{2,1} & \sigma_{2,2} & \cdots & \sigma_{2,M} \\ \vdots & \vdots & \ddots & \vdots \\ \sigma_{N,1} & \sigma_{N,2} & \cdots & \sigma_{N,M} \end{pmatrix}_{N*M}$$

(b) Spin matrix

$$\begin{pmatrix} local\_field_{1,1} & \cdots & local\_field_{1,M} \\ \vdots & \ddots & \vdots \\ local\_field_{N,1} & \cdots & local\_field_{N,M} \end{pmatrix}_{N*M}$$

(c) Local-field matrix

Fig. 2. The matrices form satisfy the input constraints of Tensor Cores

---

Algorithm 1: SQA Algorithm

---

1 Coupling Matrix ← Couplings Data
2 Randomly initialize $\sigma \in \{-1, 1\}$
3 local_field ← 0
4 *// Construct local-field energy*
5 **for** *m = 1 to M* **do**
6   **for** *i = 1 to N* **do**
7   **for** *j = 1 to N* **do**
8             $\text{local\_field}_{i,m} \mathrel{+}= J_{i,j} * \sigma_{j,m}$
9   **end**
10   **end**
11 **end**

12 **for** *t = 1 to MC-STEP* **do**
13   **for** *i = 1 to N* **do**
14   **for** *m = 1 to M* **do**
15             $\Delta H = \sigma_{i,m}(\text{local\_field}_{i,m} - J^{\dagger}(\sigma_{i,m+1}+\sigma_{i,m-1}))$

16   // Judge_to_Flip
17   **if** $e^{\frac{-\Delta H}{T}}$ >*random()* **then**
18                 $\sigma_{i,m}=-\sigma_{i,m}$

19   // Update local-field energy
20   **for** *j = 1 to N* **do**
21                     $\text{local\_field}_{j,m} \mathrel{+}= 2 * J_{i,j} * \sigma_{i,m}$
22   **end**
23   **end**
24   **end**
25   **end**
26 **end**

---

term-by-term the entries of the i-th row of coupling matrix and the j-th column of the spin matrix, and summing these N products as shown in Eq. (3).

Line 12 to Line 26 of Algorithm 1 is the main algorithm of SQA. The temperature of the system will decrease during each MC-STEP in Line 11. Besides, a larger MC-STEP usually produces a better result closer to the global optimum. The loop in Line 13 and Line 14 executed all spins on all trotters of the Ising model of SQA. If making a flip of the queried spin will cause a decrease in the system energy, then the spin will be flipped. After one spin-flip happens, the local-field energies of the spins on the same trotter will be updated from Line 20 to Line 22. Suppose the k-th spin on m-th trotter is flipped, $\text{local\_field}_{i,m}, i \in \{1, ..., N\}$ should be updated as follows:

$$\begin{aligned} \text{local\_field}'_{i,m} &= J_{i,1}\sigma_{1,m} + ... + J_{i,k}\sigma'_{k,m} + ... + J_{i,N}\sigma_{N,m} \\ &= \text{local\_field}_{i,m} + J_{i,k}\sigma'_{k,m} - J_{i,k}\sigma_{k,m} \\ &= \text{local\_field}_{i,m} + J_{i,k}\sigma'_{k,m} - J_{i,k}(-\sigma'_{k,m}) \\ &= \text{local\_field}_{i,m} + 2 * J_{i,j}\sigma'_{k,m} \\ &= \text{local\_field}_{i,m} + J_{i,j}(2 * \sigma'_{k,m}) \end{aligned} \tag{4}$$

where the $\sigma'_{k,m}$ is the new state of the flipped spin, and the $\text{local-field}'_{i,m}$ is the new local-field energy of the corresponding spin.

Many previous attempts at using specialized hardware to accelerate the annealing processing of SQA were proposed. References [11–14] provide FPGA implementation on SQA. Among these attempts, [14] focuses on solving king-graph Ising models with limited connectivity, while the others solve fully-connected Ising models. Since the spins without connections can be updated simultaneously, different topologies of SQA may affect the time to sweep all the spins. However, not-fully-connected SQA requires an additional minor embedding process [19], which may deeply affect not only the spins required to do the annealing process but also the solution quality [32] due to additional constraints to fit the target problems into the desired topology.

Several works [15,16,22] make use of GPUs to accelerate the SQA algorithm. While [15,16] target sparse-connectivity Ising models, [22] uses GPUs to solve fully-connected Ising models. Compared to using FPGAs as an accelerator, GPUs provide an easier programming interface and have plenty of computational resources. Besides, GPU can accommodate large-scale Ising models.

In [22], the authors proposed a GPU-based SQA accelerator for fully-connected Ising models. They used parallel reduction to perform spatial parallel processing of local-field computation and used concurrent kernel execution to implement temporal parallel processing for multiple-spin-flips.

2.3 Tensor Cores

NVIDIA introduced *Tensor cores* [21] as a specialized hardware accelerator for performing matrix operations in deep learning applications. The Tensor Cores introduced in the Volta GPU architecture can perform matrix-multiply-and-accumulate on 4×4 matrices per clock cycle, as shown in Fig. 3, for low-precision inputs represented in FP16 or INT8. In the latest Ampere GPU architecture, the Tensor Core supports more low-precision data representations such as TF32 and BFLOAT16 as well as sparse matrix operations [33].

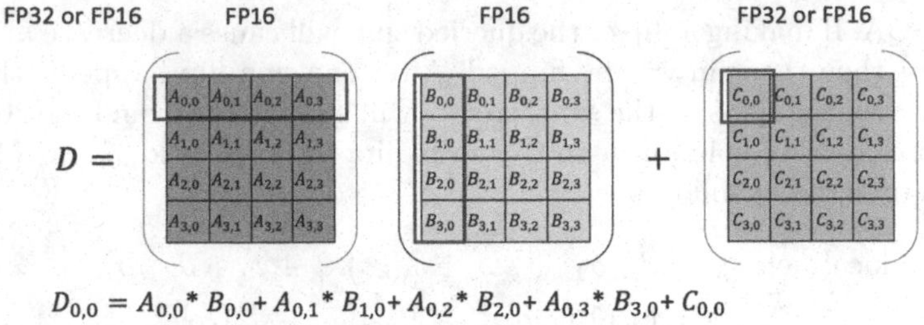

Fig. 3. In the Volta GPU, a tensor core performs a matrix-multiply-and-accumulate on 4×4 matrices per clock cycle.

We use the NVIDIA cuBLAS [34] library to program Tensor Cores for *General Matrix to Matrix Multiplication* (GEMM). The cuBLAS library calls the CUDA Warp Matrix Multiply and Accumulation (WMMA) API [39,40] to perform 16×16 matrix-multiply-and-accumulate using a warp (32 threads). The cuBLAS library dynamically decides the number of WMMA warps to spawn based on the matrix size and the GPU resources. The annealing process of SQA involves lots of multiply-and-accumulate operations during the update of local-field energies, which can be transformed to run on the Tensor Cores. To our knowledge, this work is the first published work to accelerate annealing algorithms with Tensor Cores.

3 Methodology

In the previous work, [22], while the loop which does Judge_to_Flip (Lines 14–24 in Algorithm 1) can be parallelized, it does not offer a high degree of parallelism as the loop is bounded by the number of trotters (M), nor can it utilize the Tensor Cores. When M is small, we have to find a way to increase the degree of parallelism to fully utilize the GPU. However, since the input is a fully-connected Ising model, any two spins can be connected so that the computation for the spins on the same trotter cannot be further parallelized within this loop. Thus, we propose a *hierarchical update* strategy and modify the algorithm, as shown in Algorithm 2, to increase the number of GPU threads and let each thread forward computation results to the affected threads to remove the data dependency as soon as possible, which is discussed in Sect. 3.1. Matrix operations can be accelerated directly with cuBLAS [34], as mentioned in Sect. 2.3. However, while the SQA algorithm appears to manipulate matrices, it is still necessary to modify the algorithm in order to solve fully-connected Ising problems effectively with the Tensor Cores. Thus, we need to convert the operations of SQA into matrix forms and use cuBLAS, which is discussed in Sect. 3.2.

3.1 Hierarchical Update

In a fully-connected Ising problem, if the flipping takes place for one spin, the local-fields for all the spins must be updated to calculate ΔH in Lines 20–22 of

Algorithm 1, which prohibits it from flipping multiple spins before updating the entire local-field energies. Since the cost of updating the entire local-field energies is high, we propose to perform *hierarchical update* in Algorithm 2, which has the loop indexed by k (Lines 20–22) calculate the local-field energy in advance only for the block i to keep ΔH updated, so the judgment ($e^{\frac{-\Delta H}{T}} > random()$) in Line 18 could proceed for the later iterations without updating the entire local-field energies. However, this strategy introduces additional overhead, which increases with blk_sz, so it is important to adjust the blk_sz for best performance.

Performance-wise, the execution time of Algorithm 2 is dominated by the Monte Carlo simulation performed in Lines 12–36. We apply *blocking* to the loop indexed by i (Line 13) to reduce the number of CUDA kernel launches and increase the data locality as well as the opportunity for tensorizing. Within the loop, there are two program regions: *Judge_to_Flip* (Lines 15–26) and *Update_Local-Field_Energy* (Lines 28–34).

In **Judge_to_Flip**, the spins on each trotter (m) have to be judged sequentially to decide whether they should be flipped, while all the trotters can be processed in parallel. In our implementation, the iterations in the loop indexed by m are parallelized to run across the streaming multiprocessors (SMs) in the GPU, but the loop indexed by j has to be executed sequentially. The judgment ($e^{\frac{-\Delta H}{T}} > random()$) in Line 18 decides to flip a spin if the energy reduction caused by the flipping is larger than the random number.

There are $blk\_sz * M$ spins to be queried in each sub-task. blk_sz is called block size. Due to the dependency of the upper and lower trotters to the proposed spin, the spins in the same worldline cannot be updated simultaneously from different parities. We propose to update all the spins with two rounds as shown in Fig. 4, where the spins framed in the same color can be queried simultaneously. For example, assume blk_sz = 128, the spins numbered from (k+1) to (k+64) on the odd trotters and the spins numbered from (k+65) to (k+128) on the even trotters will be queried to flip sequentially in the orange block. After that, the spins numbered from (k+65) to (k+128) on the odd trotters and the spins numbered from (k+1) to (k+64) on the even trotters will be queried to flip sequentially in the blue block. Within two rounds, all the spins in the sub-task will be judged completely.

The loop indexed by (m), highlighted in red in Line 15 of Algorithm 2, is executed by multiple streaming processors (SMs). That is, each trotter is handled by one SM. The loop indexed by (k), highlighted in blue (Line 20), updates the local-field energies with multiple threads on a SM. If the spin is flipped, the spin state will be updated and the related local-field energies will also be updated to fully utilize the resources of the GPU in Lines 20–22. After each thread has updated its corresponding local-field energies into local memory, the values are used to determine whether the next spin will be flipped when the program revisits Line 17. The call to `__syncthreads()` is needed to enforce that the threads on a SM are synchronized. With sufficient GPU resources, the implementation pre-calculates the related local-fields with k = 1-blk_sz when updating the related spins located in the assigned block. Note that the random numbers used in Line

Algorithm 2: Proposed Algorithm

```
1  Coupling Matrix ← Coupling Data
2  Randomly initialize σ ∈ {−1, 1}
3  local_field ← 0
4  // Construct_local_field_Energy, using Tensor Cores
5  for m = 1 to M do
6      for i = 1 to N do
7          for j = 1 to N do
8              local_field_{i,m} += J_{i,j} * σ_{j,m}
9          end
10     end
11 end
12 for t = 1 to MC-STEP do
13     for i = 1; i ≤ N / blk_sz; i++ do
14         // Judge_to_Flip (ii = i * blk_sz)
15         for m = 1; m ≤ M; m++ do
16             for j = 1; j ≤ blk_sz; j++ do
17                 ΔH = σ_{ii+j,m} (local_field_{ii+j} − J†(σ_{ii+j,m+1}+σ_{ii+j,m−1}))
18                 if e^{−ΔH/T} >random() then
19                     σ_{ii+j,m} = −σ_{ii+j,m}
20                     for k = 1; k ≤ blk_sz; k++ do
21                         local_field_{ii+k} += 2 * J_{ii+j,i+k} * σ_{ii+j,m}
22                     end
23                 end
24                 __syncthreads()
25             end
26         end
27         // Update local_field Energy, using Tensor Cores
28         for m = 1; m ≤ M; m++ do
29             for j = 1; j ≤ N; j++ do
30                 for k = 1; k ≤ blk_sz; k++ do
31                     local_field_{j,m} += 2 * J_{j,k} * σ_{k,m}
32                 end
33             end
34         end
35     end
36 end
```

18 are pre-calculated with log($random()$) in the CPU and transferred to the GPU for every spin in each step. Since the time to generate and transfer random numbers on the CPU is overlapped with the computation on the GPU, it reduces the workload for the GPU without increasing the time for each annealing step.

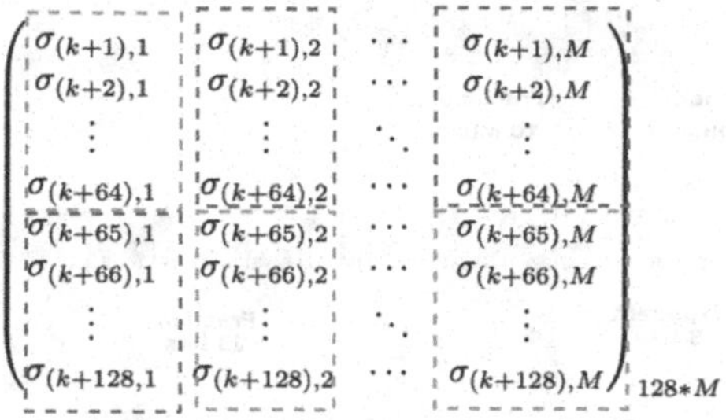

$$\begin{pmatrix} \sigma_{(k+1),1} & \sigma_{(k+1),2} & \cdots & \sigma_{(k+1),M} \\ \sigma_{(k+2),1} & \sigma_{(k+2),2} & \cdots & \sigma_{(k+2),M} \\ \vdots & \vdots & \ddots & \vdots \\ \sigma_{(k+64),1} & \sigma_{(k+64),2} & \cdots & \sigma_{(k+64),M} \\ \sigma_{(k+65),1} & \sigma_{(k+65),2} & \cdots & \sigma_{(k+65),M} \\ \sigma_{(k+66),1} & \sigma_{(k+66),2} & \cdots & \sigma_{(k+66),M} \\ \vdots & \vdots & \ddots & \vdots \\ \sigma_{(k+128),1} & \sigma_{(k+128),2} & \cdots & \sigma_{(k+128),M} \end{pmatrix}_{128*M}$$

Fig. 4. Update order of spins

Finally, **Update_local-field_energy** can be expressed by matrix multiplication of the coupling matrix and the resulting matrix of judged spin plus the previous local-field energy matrix. This region can be performed well by the GPU with the cuBLAS library. It can be further accelerated with Tensor Cores, as discussed in the following subsection.

3.2   Utilizing the Tensor Cores

To utilize the Tensor Cores, we re-implement the update of local-field energy (Lines 28–34) in Algorithm 2 by calling `cublasGemmEx` in the cuBLAS library as shown in Listing 1.1, where M is the number of trotters, N is the number of spins and K is set to blk_sz. The value of $alpha$ (Line 4) is set to $1.0f$, which is the scalar used for multiplication, and the value of $beta$ (Line 7) is also set to $1.0f$, which is the scalar utilized for accumulation. In Lines 5–6, $couplings\_matrix$ and $spin\_matrix$ are both declared as FP16 with the `CUDA_R_16F` data type for best performance. If needed, these matrices can be declared as other data types supported by Tensor Cores, such as FP32, TF32, BF16, etc. The $local\_field$ matrix is declared FP32 with `CUDA_R_32`, which provides the needed range to accumulate the multiplication results of the $couplings$ and $spin$ $matrices$.

```
1  K = blk_sz
2  cublasErrCheck(cublasGemmEx(cublasHandle,
3      CUBLAS_OP_N, CUBLAS_OP_N,
4      N, M, K,
5      &alpha,
6      couplings, CUDA_R_16F, N,
7      judged_spin, CUDA_R_16F, K,
8      &beta,
9      local_field, CUDA_R_32, N,
10     CUBLAS_COMPUTE_32F,
11     CUBLAS_GEMM_DEFAULT_TENSOR_OP));
```

Listing 1.1. Updating local-field energy

As shown in Fig. 5, compared to FP32, the number of bits of FP16 is reduced in half. The benefits of using FP16 include reduced usage for GPU device memory, less time to transfer data from the GPU device memory to the GPU cores,

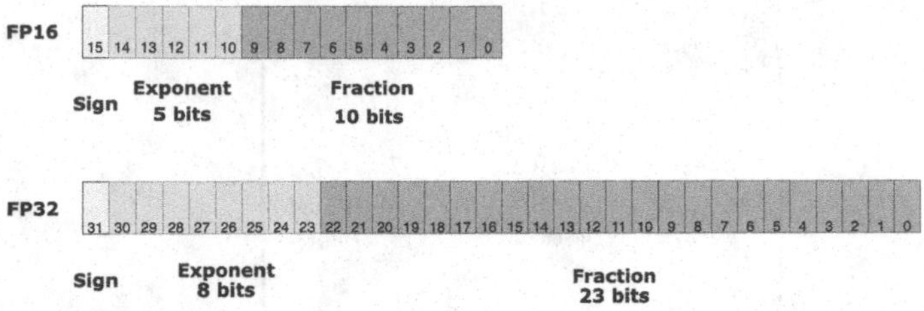

Fig. 5. The format of half precision (FP16) and single precision (FP32)

and a higher peak FLOPS rate. However, the maximum integer range of consecutive without precision loss of FP16 is $[-1024, 1024]$, which limits the range of the coupling values. Since the *couplings_matrix* and *spin_matrix* can be represented well with FP16 in our case studies, and the intermediate results of matrix multiplication are stored without loss in the *local_field* matrix with FP32, the precision of the proposed system should not be affected by this optimization.

4 Performance Evaluation

We evaluate the proposed method by measuring its performance in solving the MAX-CUT problem [36], which basically aims to split a graph into two mutually exclusive subgraphs with maximum number of inter-subgraphs edges. The MAX-CUT problem is a representative combinatorial problem that can be solved by SA and SQA. Several previous works have chosen it for performance evaluation and reported the results [22,37,38]. In these experiments, as discussed in Eq. (2), the temperature T the magnetic field $\Gamma(t)$ are gradually reduced, as we schedule $\frac{1}{T} = t * (1 - \frac{1}{8})/(\text{MC-STEP})$, and $\Gamma(t) = G_0 * (1 - t/\text{MC-STEP})$ during the annealing process, where G_0 is initially set to 8. We measure the time required to complete each annealing step and the number of inter-subgraph edges reported by the annealers at the end. Section 4.1 evaluates the benefits of the proposed hierarchical update strategy. Section 4.2 compares the processing time of previous work and our work. Section 4.3 discusses the choice of *blk_sz*, which affects the task granularity and impacts the performance significantly. To further break down the execution time, we examine our proposed method in accelerating the update of local-field energy by using the Tensor Cores in Sect. 4.4. Finally, we examine the quality of solutions provided by the proposed method in Sect. 4.5.

4.1 Benefits of Hierarchical Update

The hierarchical update strategy adopted in our work calculates the local-field energy of the spins in the block so that judgment can proceed continuously in the later iterations without updating whole local-field energies. We perform 100 annealing steps with and without the hierarchical update strategy on an Intel(R) Core(TM) i9-9900KF CPU running at 3.60 GHz with Ubuntu 18.04.5 LTS OS

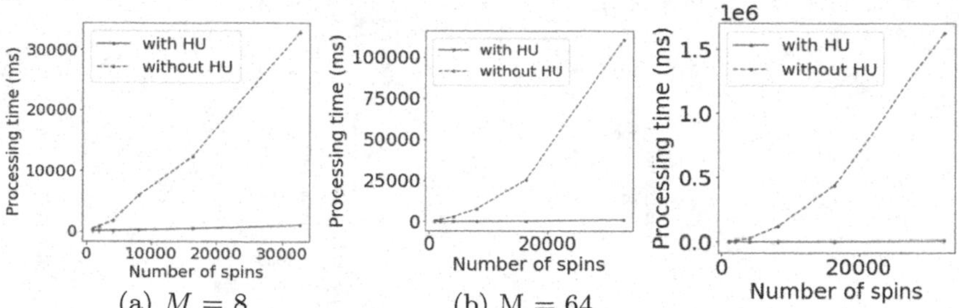

(a) $M = 8$ (b) M = 64 (c) $M = 512$

Fig. 6. The processing time for 100 annealing steps

Table 1. Latency of per annealing step (ms). Tohoku_GPU and Tohoku_FPGA are from [22] and [12] respectively, while HU w/o TC is the setting using hierarchical update without Tensor Cores and HU w/ TC with Tensor Cores.

Method	N	M = 4	M = 16	M = 64	M = 256	M = 512
Tohoku_GPU	4096	12.0 (1X)	15.0 (1X)	32.0 (1X)	215.0 (1X)	826.0 (1X)
Tohoku_FPGA		4.61 (2.6X)	5.11 (2.9X)	N/A	N/A	N/A
HU w/o TC		1.7 (6.9X)	1.8 (8.3X)	2.1 (15.1X)	4.4 (48.6X)	**6.9 (119.5X)**
HU w/ TC		1.7 (6.9X)	1.7 (8.8X)	1.8 (17.7X)	3.3 (65.2X)	**5.3 (156.0X)**
Tohoku_GPU	8192	35.0 (1X)	44.0 (1X)	75.0 (1X)	269.0 (1X)	898.0 (1X)
Tohoku_FPGA		17.45 (2.0X)	18.7 (2.4X)	N/A	N/A	N/A
HU w/o TC		3.4 (10.3X)	3.9 (11.2X)	4.7 (15.9X)	11.3 (23.9X)	18.6 (48.4X)
HU w/ TC		3.6 (9.8X)	3.5 (12.4X)	3.7 (20.1X)	8.1 (33.3X)	13.5 (66.7X)
Tohoku_GPU	16384	151.0 (1X)	169.0 (1X)	239.0 (1X)	1009.0 (1X)	2130.0 (1X)
Tohoku_FPGA		65.77 (2.3X)	70.33 (2.4X)	N/A	N/A	N/A
HU w/o TC		7.5 (20.3X)	9.3 (18.1X)	13.2 (18.1X)	32.1 (31.4X)	56.8 (37.5X)
HU w/ TC		7.4 (20.3X)	7.7 (22.0X)	8.9 (26.9X)	20.9 (48.4X)	36.6 (58.1X)
Tohoku_GPU	32768	1003.0 (1X)	1069.0 (1X)	1301.0 (1X)	4754.0 (1X)	8732.0 (1X)
Tohoku_FPGA		264.93 (3.8X)	N/A	N/A	N/A	N/A
HU w/o TC		19.7 (50.8X)	27.5 (38.9X)	37.1 (35.1X)	104.0 (45.7X)	**184.8 (47.2X)**
HU w/ TC		19.3 (52.0X)	20.6 (51.8X)	24.9 (52.2X)	59.8 (79.5X)	**100.9 (86.6X)**
Tohoku_GPU	65536	N/A	N/A	N/A	N/A	N/A
Tohoku_FPGA		N/A	N/A	N/A	N/A	N/A
HU w/o TC		54.1	82.8	129.6	376.6	683.1
HU w/ TC		54.2	62.0	81.9	203.2	352.8

and a GeForce RTX 3080 GPU with CUDA 11.3 library to compare the total processing time for various numbers of trotters (M), as shown in Fig. 6. It is clear that the proposed hierarchical update strategy effectively accelerates the annealing process, especially when the number of spins (N) is large.

4.2 Per-Step Annealing Time

In this subsection, we compare the proposed method against the state-of-the-art GPU-based and FPGA-based quantum annealing simulators published by

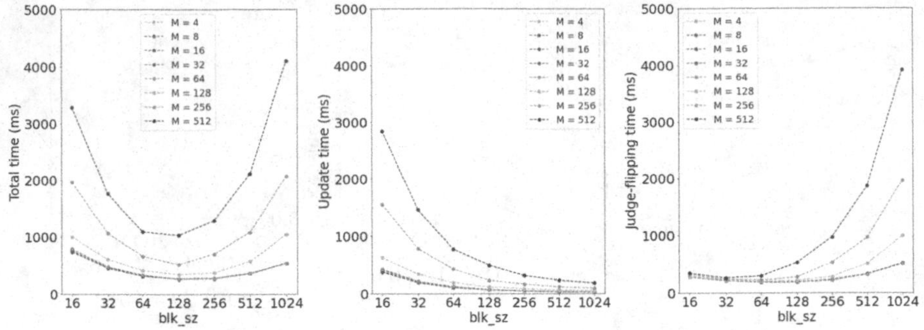

(a) Total-annealing time (b) Update_Local-field time (c) Judge_to_Flip time

Fig. 7. Processing of the update function, as $N = 8192$

Tohoku University in [12,22].[1]. For a fair comparison, we perform the experiments on a setup that consists of an Intel(R) Xeon(R) Gold 6154 CPU chip running at 3.00 GHz with CentOS Linux release 7.8.2003(Core) and a Tesla V100-SXM2 GPU with the CUDA 11.3 library. The setup in [22] uses Quadro GV100 GPU, which adopts the same Volta architecture as the Tesla V100 and performs single-precision FP operations at 14.8 TFLOPS/s, while the V100-SXM2 delivers 15.7 TFLOPS/s. Our setup has a 6% advantage over Tohoku's.

Table 1 shows the processing time cost per MC-STEP for each solution as N increases from 4096 to 65536 and M increases from 4 to 512. The table also calculates the relative performance using Tohoku's GPU implementation running on a Quadro V100 GPU (Tohoku_GPU) as the baseline. The baseline implementation can solve up to 32768 spins due to the constraint of GPU local memory. The FPGA solution proposed by Tohoku (Tohoku_FPGA), running on an Intel Arria 10 FPGA chip outperforms the baseline by 2-3.8X, but the FPGA solution could not solve large problems due to the memory limitation, and thus some of the data are missing in the table. Notice that the per-step annealing time grows linearly with M and N^2 in theory, but it may not be the case when M or N is too small to fully utilize the GPU or the FPGA. Also notice that when $(N,M) = (4096,512)$, Tohoku_GPU takes an unusually long time to execute, so we treat this data point as an anomaly and exclude it from the following discussions.

Our proposed hierarchical update strategy enables our GPU solution to outperform both solutions provided by Tohoku. Even without using the Tensor Cores, our solution (HU w/o TC) is 7× to 48× faster than Tohoku_GPU[2]. With the Tensor Cores, our solution (HU w/ TC) provides 7× to 86× speedup over the baseline. When N or M increases, the proposed solutions provide greater acceleration over the baseline as the degree of parallelism becomes higher and it appears that our solution utilizes the parallelism more efficiently than Tohoku's GPU solution does. The Tensor Cores version is especially effective for

[1] We acknowledge the authors for sending us the experiment results.
[2] The speedup is up to 120× if $(N,M) = (4096,512)$ is included.

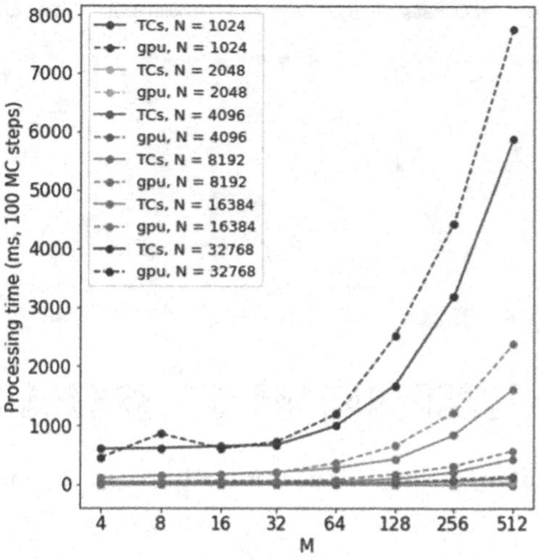

Fig. 8. Tensor Cores impact on Update_local-field_Energy

solving large problems. For example, when $N = 32768$, it provides an extra 1.8× speedup over the non-TC version. Notice that our solution does not exhibit the anomaly for $(N,M) = (4096,512)$. As far as the problem size is concerned, our GPU implementation can solve Ising problems up to 65536 spins if the coupling matrix is represented with FP16 with 32 GB GPU memory.

Table 2. The Gset benchmarks and their best known solutions

Gset	N	#Edges	Best known	Gset	N	# Edges	Best known
G5	800	19176	11631	G41	2000	11785	2405
G9	800	19176	2054	G42	2000	11779	2481
G13	800	1600	582	G43	1000	9990	6660
G18	800	4694	992	G44	1000	9990	6650
G19	800	4661	906	G47	1000	9990	6657
G20	800	4672	941	G48	3000	6000	6000
G21	800	4667	931	G49	3000	6000	6000
G26	2000	19990	13328	G50	3000	6000	5880
G31	2000	19990	3309	G51	1000	5909	3848
G34	2000	4000	1384	G53	1000	5914	3850
G38	2000	11779	7688	G54	1000	5916	3852
G39	2000	11778	2408	G63	7000	41459	27045

4.3 The Choice of *blk_sz*

As mentioned in Sect. 3.1, the choice of *blk_sz* impacts the effectiveness of the performance with the hierarchical update, and the aforementioned experimental

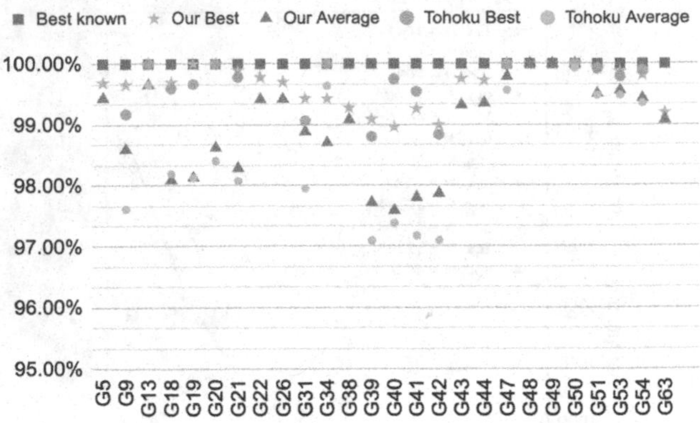

Fig. 9. The solution quality of our work, relative to the previous works

results were done by setting *blk_sz* to 128, which was chosen after a series of experiments. To evaluate the impact of *blk_sz*, we profile the annealing time under various *blk_sz*. Figure 7a shows the total annealing time under different *blk_sz* and M, which basically decreases when *blk_sz* increases from 16 to 128 and then increases when *blk_sz* increases beyond 128, so it is obvious that the performance is best when *blk_sz* is set to 128. To further investigate the impact of *blk_sz*, we break down the total annealing time into two dominating parts: Update_Local-field_Energy and Judge_to_Flip. As shown in Fig. 7b, the time required to update the local-field energies decreases as *blk_sz* increases, as the larger *blk_sz* enables more efficient utilization of the Tensor Cores to perform the matrix multiplication. On the other hand, Fig. 7c shows that the time required by Judge_to_Flip decreases initially, but increases when *blk_sz* becomes large.

The time required by Judge_to_Flip decreases initially when *blk_sz* increases from 16 to 128 because the larger block size reduces the number of launches of the Judge_to_Flip kernel to the GPU and utilizes more GPU cores to perform the computation. However, when *blk_sz* keeps increasing, the larger block size requires each Judge_to_Flip kernel to examine more spins and causes additional overhead, which dominates the execution time when *blk_sz* increases beyond 128. The choice of *blk_sz* depends mainly on the system architecture, i.e. the GPU and the GPU memory, but is independent of N and M. Thus, we set *blk_sz* to 128 to produce most of the experimental results in this paper.

4.4 The Impact of Tensor Cores

In order to utilize the Tensor Cores, the update of local-field energy is done in a mixed-precision fashion, where the data types of the two matrices (coupling and spin) for matrix multiplication are half precision (FP16) while the local-field energy matrix is single precision (FP32). We run the experiments with N from 1024 to 32768 and M from 1 to 50 and record the time to process. The *blk_sz* is set to 128 (the selection of *blk_sz* is discussed in Subsect. 4.3) in the experiment and the annealing step is set to 100. Under different N and M, we ran each experiment 10 times and averaged all the outcomes as the results.

As shown in Fig. 8, the solid-line and dashed-line represent the processing time of Update_Local-field_Energy with and without using Tensor Cores respectively, and the experiments with the same M are presented in the same color. The results show that the processing time grows around 4× as N is doubled when $M = 512$ in both cases, as its computational complexity, is $O(N^2)$ according to Algorithm 1. Since the GPU resources are effectively utilized, when the size of M is smaller than 512, the required time increases less than 4× as N grows twice. Moreover, in those cases of $M \geq 32$, the programs accelerated by Tensor Cores are faster than those which only use the GPU.

4.5 The Quality of Solution

The proposed hierarchical update strategy may have slight effects on the results, as it alters the order of data accesses and computations, so we examine the quality of the solution by comparing our results to previous works to reveal how close the solutions were delivered by our work. The benchmarks are listed in Table 2 with the best known results reported by [22]. As shown in Fig. 9, our best results are within 99.66% of the best known solutions listed in Table 2, while our average results are within 98.97% of the best known results, exhibiting good stability while solving the problems much faster than the previous methods.

5 Conclusion

Our experimental results show that the proposed hierarchical update strategy effectively accelerates SQA on modern GPUs and outperforms the previous works by far due to efficient parallelization and tensorization. We show that Tensor Cores can be used to further speed up the proposed solutions, especially for problems with a large number of spins or many trotters. In particular, increasing the number of trotters allows SQA to impose more of the quantum tunneling effect and can lead to higher solution quality for certain Ising problems, although it is not guaranteed as the algorithm is heuristic. Our experiments also show that the proposed algorithm delivers stable solutions that are very close to the best Known results from previous work. The memory capacity of today's GPUs has limited the problem size which can be solved on one GPU. As shown in Fig. 8, the Tensor Cores accelerate more effectively with large M at the cost of increased memory usage. This limitation could be relaxed with more GPU memory capacity in the future or multiple GPUs. Even though this paper mainly focuses on GPU implementations, the proposed hierarchical update strategy is a general approach that works to accelerate SQA and SA[3]. It can be extended to make use of multiple CPUs/GPUs/accelerators to scale the performance, which also enlarges the solvable problems with larger distributed memories.

[3] SA can be treated as a special case of SQA with $M = 1$.

References

1. Kadowaki, T., Nishimori, H.: Quantum annealing in the transverse Ising model. Phys. Rev. E **58**(5), 5355 (1998)
2. Venturelli, D., Kondratyev, A.: Reverse quantum annealing approach to portfolio optimization problems. Quantum Mach. Intell. **1**(1), 17–30 (2019)
3. Perdomo-Ortiz, A., Dickson, N., Drew-Brook, M., Rose, G., Aspuru-Guzik, A.: Finding low-energy conformations of lattice protein models by quantum annealing. Sci. Rep. **2**(1), 1–7 (2012)
4. Papalitsas, C., Andronikos, T., Giannakis, K., Theocharopoulou, G., Fanarioti, S.: A QUBO model for the traveling salesman problem with time windows. Algorithms **12**(11), 224 (2019)
5. Cipra, B.A.: The Ising model is NP-complete. SIAM News **33**(6), 1–3 (2000)
6. Metropolis, N., Rosenbluth, A.W., Rosenbluth, M.N., Teller, A.H., Teller, E.: Equation of state calculations by fast computing machines. J. Chem. Phys. **21**(6), 1087–1092 (1953)
7. Heim, B., Ronnow, T.F., Isakov, S.V., Troyer, M.: Quantum versus classical annealing of Ising spin glasses. Science **348**(6231), 215–217 (2015)
8. Suzuki, M.: Relationship between D-dimensional quantal spin systems and (d+1)-dimensional Ising systems: equivalence, critical exponents and systematic approximants of the partition function and spin correlations. Prog. Theor. Phy. **56**(5), 1454–1469 (1976)
9. Abdel-Aty, A.H., Khedr, A.N., Saddeek, Y.B., Youssef, A.A.: Thermal entanglement in quantum annealing processor. Int. J. Quantum Inf. **16**(01), 1850006 (2018)
10. Yamaoka, M., Yoshimura, C., Hayashi, M., Okuyama, T., Aoki, H., Mizuno, H.: A 20k-spin Ising chip to solve combinatorial optimization problems with CMOS annealing. IEEE J. Solid State Circ. **51**(1), 303–309 (2015)
11. Waidyasooriya, H.M., Hariyama, M., Miyama, M.J., Ohzeki, M.: OpenCL-based design of an FPGA accelerator for quantum annealing simulation. J. Supercomput. **75**(8), 5019–5039 (2019). https://doi.org/10.1007/s11227-019-02778-w
12. Waidyasooriya, H., Hariyama, M.: Highly-parallel FPGA accelerator for simulated quantum annealing. IEEE Trans. Emerg. Topics Comput.**9**, 2019–2029 (2019)
13. Liu, C.Y., Waidyasooriya, H.M., Hariyama, M.: Data-transfer-bottleneck-less architecture for FPGA-based quantum annealing simulation. In: 2019 Seventh International Symposium on Computing and Networking (CANDAR), pp. 164–170. IEEE, November 2019
14. Okuyama, T., Hayashi, M., Yamaoka, M.: An Ising computer based on simulated quantum annealing by path integral monte carlo method. In: 2017 IEEE International Conference on Rebooting Computing (ICRC), pp. 1–6. IEEE, November 2017
15. Weigel, M.: Performance potential for simulating spin models on GPU. J. Comput. Phys. **231**(8), 3064–3082 (2012)
16. Cook, C., Zhao, H., Sato, T., Hiromoto, M., Tan, S.X.D.: GPU based parallel Ising computing for combinatorial optimization problems in VLSI physical design. arXiv preprint (2018). arXiv:1807.10750
17. Dwave, https://www.dwavesys.com/
18. Dattani, N., Szalay, S., Chancellor, N.: Pegasus: the second connectivity graph for large-scale quantum annealing hardware (2019). arXiv preprint arXiv:1901.07636
19. Choi, V.: Minor-embedding in adiabatic quantum computation: I. The parameter setting problem. Quantum Inf. Process. **7**(5), 193–209 (2008)

20. JUQCS-G. https://www.fz-juelich.de/portal/DE/Home/home_node.html
21. Markidis, S., Der Chien, S.W., Laure, E., Peng, I.B., Vetter, J.S.: Nvidia tensor core programmability, performance & precision. In: 2018 IEEE International Parallel and Distributed Processing Symposium Workshops (IPDPSW), pp. 522–531. IEEE, May 2018
22. Waidyasooriya, H.M., Hariyama, M.: A GPU-based quantum annealing simulator for fully-connected Ising models utilizing spatial and temporal parallelism. IEEE Access **8**, 67929–67939 (2020)
23. Heim, B., Rønnow, T.F., Isakov, S.V., Troyer, M.: Quantum versus classical annealing of Ising spin glasses. Science **348**(6231), 215–217 (2015)
24. Isakov, S.V., Zintchenko, I.N., Rønnow, T.F., Troyer, M.: Optimised simulated annealing for Ising spin glasses. Comput. Phys. Commun. **192**, 265–271 (2015)
25. Steinberg, A.P., Kosowsky, M., Fraden, S.: Simulations: the Ising Model (2013)
26. Gould, H., Tobochnik, J.: Statistical and Thermal Physics. University Press, Princeton (2010)
27. Kirkpatrick, S., Gelatt, C.D., Jr., Vecchi, M.P.: Optimization by simulated annealing. Science **220**(4598), 671–680 (1983)
28. Suzuki, M., Miyashita, S., Kuroda, A.: Monte Carlo simulation of quantum spin systems. I. Prog. Theor. Phys. **58**(5), 1377–1387 (1977)
29. Bravyi, S.: Monte Carlo simulation of stoquastic Hamiltonians (2014). arXiv preprint arXiv:1402.2295
30. Crosson, E., Harrow, A.W.: Simulated quantum annealing can be exponentially faster than classical simulated annealing. In: 2016 IEEE 57th Annual Symposium on Foundations of Computer Science (FOCS), pp. 714–723. IEEE, October 2016
31. Bravyi, S., Divincenzo, D.P., Oliveira, R.I., Terhal, B.M.: The complexity of stoquastic local Hamiltonian problems (2006). arXiv preprint quant-ph/0606140
32. Bernal, D.E., Booth, K.E.C., Dridi, R., Alghassi, H., Tayur, S., Venturelli, D.: Integer programming techniques for minor-embedding in quantum annealers. In: Hebrard, E., Musliu, N. (eds.) CPAIOR 2020. LNCS, vol. 12296, pp. 112–129. Springer, Cham (2020). https://doi.org/10.1007/978-3-030-58942-4_8
33. NVIDIA ampere. https://images.nvidia.com/aem-dam/en-zz/Solutions/data-center/nvidia-ampere-architecture-whitepaper.pdf
34. cuBLAS. https://docs.nvidia.com/cuda/cublas/index.html
35. cutlass. https://github.com/NVIDIA/cutlass
36. Gset. https://web.stanford.edu/~yyye/yyye/Gset/
37. Benlic, U., Hao, J.K.: Breakout local search for the max-cutproblem. Eng. Appl. Artif. Intell. **26**(3), 1162–1173 (2013)
38. Goto, H., et al.:High-performance combinatorial optimization based on classical mechanics. Sci. Adv. **7**(6), eabe7953 (2021)
39. CUDA-9. https://developer.nvidia.com/blog/programming-tensor-cores-cuda-9/
40. WMMA. https://docs.nvidia.com/cuda/cuda-c-programming-guide/index.html#wmma

m-CUBES: An Efficient and Portable Implementation of Multi-dimensional Integration for GPUs

Ioannis Sakiotis[1(✉)], Kamesh Arumugam[2], Marc Paterno[3], Desh Ranjan[1], Balša Terzić[1], and Mohammad Zubair[1]

[1] Old Dominion University, Norfolk, VA 23529, USA
isaki001@odu.com
[2] Nvidia, Santa Clara, CA 95051-0952, USA
[3] Fermi National Accelerator Laboratory, Batavia, IL 60510, USA

Abstract. The task of multi-dimensional numerical integration is frequently encountered in physics and other scientific fields, e.g., in modeling the effects of systematic uncertainties in physical systems and in Bayesian parameter estimation . Multi-dimensional integration is often time-prohibitive on CPUs. Efficient implementation on many-core architectures is challenging as the workload across the integration space cannot be predicted a priori. We propose *m*-CUBES, a novel implementation of the well-known VEGAS algorithm for execution on GPUs. VEGAS transforms integration variables followed by calculation of a Monte Carlo integral estimate using adaptive partitioning of the resulting space. *m*-CUBES improves performance on GPUs by maintaining relatively uniform workload across the processors. As a result, our optimized CUDA implementation for NVIDIA GPUs outperforms parallelization approaches proposed in past literature. We further demonstrate the efficiency of *m*-CUBES by evaluating a six-dimensional integral from a cosmology application, achieving significant speedup and greater precision than the CUBA library's CPU implementation of VEGAS. We also evaluate *m*-CUBES on a standard integrand test suite. Our approach yields a speedup of at least 10 when compared against publicly available Monte Carlo based GPU implementations. In summary, *m*-CUBES can solve integrals that are prohibitively expensive using standard libraries and custom implementations.

Work supported by the Fermi National Accelerator Laboratory, managed and operated by Fermi Research Alliance, LLC under Contract No. DE-AC02-07CH11359 with the U.S. Department of Energy. The U.S. Government retains and the publisher, by accepting the article for publication, acknowledges that the U.S. Government retains a non-exclusive, paid-up, irrevocable, world-wide license to publish or reproduce the published form of this manuscript, or allow others to do so, for U.S. Government purposes. FERMILAB-CONF-22-043-LDRD-SCD.
We acknowledge the support of Jefferson Lab grant to Old Dominion University 16-347. Authored by Jefferson Science Associates, LLC under U.S. DOE Contract No. DE-AC05-06OR23177 and DE-AC02- 06CH11357.
We thank Mahsa Sharifi for contributing to the initial implementation of *m*-Cubes.
code available at https://github.com/marcpaterno/gpuintegration.

A.-L. Varbanescu et al. (Eds.): ISC High Performance 2022, LNCS 13289, pp. 192–209, 2022.
https://doi.org/10.1007/978-3-031-07312-0_10

A modern C++ interface header-only implementation makes m-CUBES portable, allowing its utilization in complicated pipelines with easy to define stateful integrals. Compatibility with non-NVIDIA GPUs is achieved with our initial implementation of m-CUBES using the Kokkos framework.

1 Introduction

The task of multi-dimensional numerical integration is often encountered in physics and other scientific fields, e.g., in modeling the effects of systematic uncertainties in physical systems and Bayesian parameter estimation. However, multi-dimensional integration is time-prohibitive on CPUs. The emerging high-performance architectures that utilize accelerators such as GPUs can speed up the multi-dimensional integration computation. The GPU device is best suited for computations that can be executed concurrently on multiple data elements. In general, a computation is partitioned into thousands of fine-grained operations, which are assigned to thousands of threads on a GPU device for parallel execution.

A naive way to parallelize the multi-dimensional integration computation is as follows: divide the integration region into "many" (m) smaller sub-regions, estimate the integral in each sub-region individually (I_i) and simply add these estimates to get an estimate for the integral over the entire region ($\Sigma_{i=1}^{m} I_i$). The integral estimate in each sub-region can be computed using any of the traditional techniques such as quadrature or Monte Carlo based algorithms. If we use a simple way of creating the sub-regions, e.g., via dividing each dimension into g equal parts, the boundaries of the sub-regions are easy to calculate, and the estimation of the integral in different sub-regions can be carried out in an "embarrassingly parallel" fashion. Unfortunately, this approach is infeasible for higher dimensions as the number of sub-regions grows exponentially with the number of dimensions d. For example if $d = 10$ and we need to split each dimension into $g = 20$ parts the number of sub-regions created would be $g^d = 20^{10}$ which is roughly 10^{13}. Moreover, uniform division of the integration region is not the best way to estimate the integral. The intuition is that the regions where the integrand is "well-behaved" do not need to be sub-divided finely to get a good estimate of the integral. Regions where it is "ill-behaved" (e.g. sharp peaks, many oscillations) require finer sub-division for a reliable, accurate estimate. However, when devising a general numerical integration method, we cannot assume knowledge of the behavior of the integrand. Hence, we cannot split up the integration region in advance with fewer (but perhaps larger in volume) sub-regions where the integrand is "well-behaved" and a greater number of smaller sub-regions in the region where it is "ill-behaved". To summarize, efficient implementation of multi-dimensional integration on many-core architectures such as GPUs is challenging due to two reasons: (i) increase in computational complexity as the dimension of the integration space increases, and (ii) the workload across the integration space cannot be predicted.

The first challenge, "curse of dimensionality", can be addressed to some extent by using a Monte Carlo based algorithm for multi-dimensional integration, as the convergence rate of such methods is independent of the dimension d. The convergence rate can sometimes be further improved by utilizing low-discrepancy sequences (Quasi-Monte Carlo) instead of pseudo-random samples [3,8]. When utilizing Monte Carlo based approaches, the second challenge of consolidating sampling efforts on the "ill-behaved" areas of the integration space, is addressed through "stratified" and/or "importance" sampling, which aim to reduce the variance of the random samples. Stratified sampling involves sampling from disjoint partitions of the integration space, the boundaries of which can be refined recursively in a manner similar to adaptive quadrature. Importance sampling integration methods, use Monte Carlo samples to approximate behavior of the integrand in order to sample from a distribution which would significantly reduce the variance and accelerate convergence rates. This is accomplished by an initially uniform weight function that is refined across iterations, and results in more samples in the location where the magnitude of the integrand is either large or varies significantly.

The sequential VEGAS algorithm is the most popular Monte Carlo method that makes use of importance sampling [10,11]. There are several implementations and variants, including Python packages, C++-based implementations in the CUBA and GSL libraries, and the R Cubature package. Unfortunately, while VEGAS can often outperform standard Monte Carlo and deterministic techniques, sequential execution often leads to prohibitively long computation times. A GPU implementation of the original VEGAS algorithm was proposed in [9], but is not packaged as a library though an implementation exists in [2]. VegasFlow is a Python library based on the TensorFlow framework, providing access to VEGAS and standard Monte Carlo implementations that can execute on both single and multi-GPU systems [4,5]. Another Python package with support for GPU execution was proposed in [14], incorporating stratified sampling and a heuristic tree search algorithm. All GPU implementations demonstrate significant speedup over serial versions of VEGAS but impose restrictions on the required computing platforms and programming environments, e.g., the CUDA implementation of [9] requires an NVIDIA GPU.

We propose m-CUBES, a novel implementation of the well-known VEGAS algorithm for multi-dimensional integration on GPUs. m-CUBES exploits parallelism afforded by GPUs in a way that avoids the potential non-uniform distribution of workload and makes near-optimal use of the hardware resources. Our implementation also modifies VEGAS to make the computation even faster for functions that are "fully symmetric". Our approach demonstrates significant performance improvement over [2,14]. Our initial implementation was targeted for NVIDIA GPUs utilizing CUDA, but the m-CUBES algorithm is applicable to any many-core system. Utilization of the Kokkos programming model allows execution on various parallel platforms including non-NVIDIA GPUs and even CPU-clusters. Our goal is to make publicly available a robust, portable and easy-to-use, implementation of VEGAS in CUDA and Kokkos that will be suitable for the execution of challenging integrands that occur in physics and other scientific fields.

The remainder of the paper is structured as follows. In Sect.2, we describe various Monte Carlo based algorithms. In Sect. 3, we describe the VEGAS algorithm. In Sect. 4 we describe the m-CUBES algorithm. In Sect. refexperimentalresults, we discuss the accuracy and performance of our implementation, comparing its execution time against publicly available Monte Carlo based methods. In Sect. 6 we discuss the interface and portability features used on an complex integral utilized in parameter estimation in cosmological models of galaxy clusters. Section 7 presents results on an initial Kokkos implementation.

2 Background

We summarize here the previous work related to our research. We first summarize the previously developed sequential Monte Carlo Methods and libraries. Thereafter we summarize the research on parallel VEGAS based methods.

2.1 Monte Carlo Methods

The GSL library provides three Monte Carlo based methods, standard Monte Carlo, MISER, and VEGAS. Standard Monte Carlo iteratively samples the integration space of volume V, at T random points x_i to generate an integral estimate in the form of $\frac{V}{T}\sum_{t=i}^{T} f(x_i)$, whose error-estimate is represented by the standard deviation.

VEGAS is an iterative Monte Carlo based method that utilizes stratified sampling along with importance sampling to reduce standard Monte Carlo variance and accelerate convergence rates. The stratified sampling is done by partitioning the d-dimensional space into sub-cubes and computing Monte Carlo estimates in each sub-cube. For importance sampling, VEGAS samples from a probability distribution that is progressively refined among iterations to approximate the target-integrand. VEGAS uses a piece-wise weight function to model the probability distribution, where the weight corresponds to the magnitude of the integral contribution of each particular partition in the integration space. At each iteration VEGAS adjusts the weights and the corresponding boundaries in the integration space, based on a histogram of weights. The piece-wise weight-function is intentionally separable to keep the number of required bins small even on high-dimensional integrands. Existing implementations of VEGAS, are also found within the CUBA and GSL libraries. A Python package also exists, with support for parallelization through multiple processors.

MISER is another Monte Carlo based method, which utilizes recursive stratified sampling until reaching a user-specified recursion-depth, at which point standard Monte Carlo is used on each of the generated sub-regions. MISER generates sub-regions by sub-dividing regions on a single coordinate-axis and redistributing the number of sampling points dedicated to each partition in order to minimize their combined variance. The variance in each sub-region is estimated at each step with a small fraction of the total points per step. The axis to split for each sub-region, is determined based on which partition/point-redistribution will yield the smallest combined variance.

CUBA is another library that provides numerous Monte Carlo based methods (VEGAS, Suave, Divonne). Suave utilizes importance sampling similar to VEGAS but further utilizes recursive sub-division of the sub-regions like MISER in GSL. The algorithm first samples the integration space based on a separable weight function (mirroring VEGAS) and then partitions the integration space in two similar to MISER. Suave then selects the sub-region with the highest error for further sampling and partitioning. This method requires more memory than both VEGAS and MISER.

Divonne uses stratified sampling, attempting to partition regions such that they have equal difference between their maximum and minimum integrand values. It utilizes numerical optimization techniques to find those minimum/maximum values. Divonne can be faster than VEGAS/Suave on many integrands while also providing non-statistically based error-estimates if quadrature rules are used instead of random samples.

2.2 Parallel Programming Models

CUDA is a popular low-level programming model, allowing the execution of parallel computations on NVIDIA GPUs and has been used extensively in scientific computing. The NVIDIA GPU restriction can be avoided by utilizing Kokkos, a C++ library that implements an abstract thread parallel programming model which enables writing performance portable applications for major multi- and many-core HPC platforms. It exposes a single programming interface and allows the use of different optimizations for backends such as CUDA, HIP, SYCL, HPX, OpenMP, and C++ threads [6,13]. Parameter tuning in the parallel dispatch of code-segments, allows for both automatic and manual adjustments in order to exploit certain architectural features.

2.3 Parallel GPU Methods

The *g*VEGAS method is a CUDA implementation of VEGAS that allows execution on a GPU [2,9]. This method parallelizes the computation over the sub-cubes used in VEGAS for stratification. It uses an equal number of samples in each sub-cube as proposed in the original VEGAS algorithm. It assigns a single thread to process each sub-cube, which is not very efficient and is discussed in Sect. 4. The importance sampling that requires keeping track of integral values in each bin (explained in the next section) is done on the CPU which slows down the overall computation. Additionally, the number of possible samples is limited due to their allocation on GPU memory which imposes performance limitations. These design choices are a product of their time as the implementation was developed in the early stages of the CUDA platform. A modernized version exists in [1] but does not meet the statistical requirements related to the returned χ^2 as indicated in [10]. For that reason, Sect. 5 includes comparison with the implementation of [2].

Non-C++ implementations are available as well. ZMCintegral is a Python library for performing Monte Carlo based multi-dimensional numerical integration on GPU platforms, with support for multiple-GPUs. The algorithm uses stratified sampling in addition to a heuristic tree search that applies Monte Carlo computations on different partitions of the integration space [14].

3 The VEGAS Algorithm

VEGAS is one of the most popular Monte Carlo based methods. It is an iterative algorithm, that attempts to approximate where the integrand varies the most with a separable function that is refined across iterations. The main steps of a VEGAS iteration are listed in Algorithm 3. The input consists of an integrand f which is of some dimensionality d, the number of bins n_b on each dimensional axis, the number of samples p per sub-cube, the bin boundaries stored in an d-dimensional list B, and the d-dimensional list C which contains the contributions of each bin to the cumulative integral estimate.

Initially the integration space is sub-divided to a number of d-dimensional hyper-cubes, which we refer to as sub-cubes. VEGAS processes each sub-cube independently with a for-loop at line 2. At each sub-cube, the algorithm generates an equal number of samples[1], which are processed through the for-loop at line 3. To process a sample, VEGAS generates d random numbers in the range $(0, 1)$ at line 4, corresponding to one point per dimensional-axis. Then at line 5, we transform the point y from the domain of the unit hyper-cube $(0, 1)$ to actual coordinates in the integration space. At line 6, we evaluate the integrand f at the transformed point x, yielding the value v which contributes to the cumulative integral estimate. Before proceeding to the next sample, we identify at line 7 the bins that encompass each of the d coordinates in x. We use the indices of those bins ($b[1 : d]$) to increment their contribution (v) to the integral at line 8. Once the samples from all sub-cubes have been processed, we exit the twice-nested for-loop. At line 9, we use the bin contributions stored in d, to adjust the bin boundaries B in such a way that bins of large contributions are smaller. This approach results in many small bins in the areas of the integration space where the integrand is largest or varies significantly, resulting in more samples being generated from those highly contributing bins. Finally, the contribution of each sample must be accumulated at line 10, to produce the Monte Carlo integral estimate and to compute the variance for the iteration.

The most desirable features of VEGAS are its "importance sampling" which occurs by maintaining bin contributions and adjusting the bin boundaries at the end of each iteration. The use of sub-cubes introduces "stratified sampling" which can further reduce the variance of the Monte Carlo samples. Those two variance reduction techniques make VEGAS successful in many practical

[1] Here, we focus on the original VEGAS algorithm which uses equal number of samples in each sub-cube. The later versions of the algorithm deploy adaptive stratification that adjust the number of integral estimates used in each sub-cube.

cases and the independence of the sub-cubes and samples make the algorithm extremely parallelizable.

Algorithm 1. VEGAS

1: **procedure** VEGAS(f, d, n_b, p, B, C) ▷ Each iteration consists of the steps below
2:     **for all** sub-cubes **do**
3:         **for** $i \leftarrow 1$ to p **do** ▷ f is evaluated at p points in each sub-cube
4:             $y_1, y_2, ..., y_d \leftarrow$ generate d points in range $(0, 1)$ uniformly at random
5:             $x_1, x_2, ..., x_d \leftarrow$ map vector y to vector x ▷ f is evaluated at x
6:             $v \leftarrow f(x_1, x_2, ..., x_d)$
7:             let b_i denote the index of the bin to which x_i belongs in dimension i
8:             increment $C[1][b_1]$, $C[2][b_2]$, ..., $C[d][b_d]$ by v ▷ Store bin contributions
9:     $B[1:d][1:n_b] \leftarrow$ adjust all bin boundaries based on $C[1:d][1:n_b]$
10:     $I, E \leftarrow$ compute integral estimate/variance by accumulating v
11: **return** I, E

---

4 The Algorithm m-CUBES

The main challenges of parallel numerical integrators are the "curse of dimensionality" and workload imbalances along the integration space. While high-dimensionality is made manageable by the use of the Monte Carlo estimate in VEGAS (Algorithm 3), workload imbalances need to be addressed. This is particularly true for newer variations of the VEGAS algorithm, which involve a non-uniform number of samples per sub-cube. Parallelization of VEGAS poses additional challenges from the need to accumulate the results of multiple samples from different processors. In Algorithm 3, line 10 involves such an accumulation which requires processor synchronization. Furthermore, a race condition can occur at line 8, where the contributions of a bin may need to be updated by different processors.

To parallelize VEGAS, m-CUBES (Algorithm 4) assigns a batch of sub-cubes to each processor and generates a uniform number of samples per sub-cube. This solves the work-load imbalance issue and further limits the cost of accumulating results from various processors. The integrand contributions from all sub-cubes of each processor (Algorithm 3, line 6), are processed serially. As a result, those values can be accumulated in a single local variable, instead of synchronizing and transferring among processors. This does not eliminate the cost of accumulation, as we still need to collect the contributions from the sub-cube batches in each processor at line 10, but the extent of the required synchronization is reduced significantly.

The input of the m-CUBES algorithm consists of the integrand f and its dimensionality d, the number of bins per coordinate axis n_b, the maximum number of allowed integrand evaluations $maxcalls$, and the upper/lower boundaries of the integration space in each dimension, represented in the form of two arrays L, H. The user must also supply the required number of iterations $itmax$ and

Algorithm 2. m-CUBES

1: **procedure** m-CUBES($f, d, n_b, maxcalls, L, H, itmax, ita, r$)
2: I, $E \leftarrow 0$ ▷ Integral/Error estimate
3: $g \leftarrow (maxcalls/2)^{1/d}$ ▷ Number of intervals per axis
4: $m \leftarrow g^d$ ▷ Number of cubes
5: $s \leftarrow$ SET-BATCH-SIZE($maxcalls$) ▷ Heuristic
6: $B[1:d][1:n_b] \leftarrow$ INIT-BINS(d, n_b) ▷ Initialize bin boundaries
7: $C[1:d][n_b] \leftarrow 0$ ▷ Bin contributions
8: $p \leftarrow maxcalls/m$ ▷ number of samples per cube
9: **for** $i \leftarrow 0$ to ita **do**
10: r, $C \leftarrow$ V-SAMPLE()
11: I, $E \leftarrow$ WEIGHTED-ESTIMATES(r)
12: $B \leftarrow$ ADJUST-BIN-BOUNDS(B, C)
13: CHECK-CONVERGENCE()
14: **for** $i \leftarrow ita$ to $itmax$ **do**
15: $r \leftarrow$ V-SAMPLE-NO-ADJUST()
16: I, $E \leftarrow$ WEIGHTED-ESTIMATE(r)
17: CHECK-CONVERGENCE()

the number of iterations that will involve bin adjustments (ita). We also use the array r to store the results which consist of the integral estimate and standard deviation.

In line 2, we initialize the cumulative integral estimate and error-estimate (standard deviation) to zero. In line 3 we compute the number of intervals per axis; the boundaries of the resulting sub-cubes remain constant for the duration of the algorithm. In contrast, the bin boundaries B are adjusted across iterations. At line 4 we determine the number of sub-cubes m, while we also compute the batch size s, referring to the number of sub-cubes that each thread will process iteratively. Then the bin boundaries are generated on line 6, by equally partitioning each axis into n_b bins, and storing their right boundaries in the list B.

Then we proceed with the m-CUBES iterations. The first step is to compute the result r and bin contributions C, by executing the V-SAMPLE method (Algorithm 4) at line 10. V-SAMPLE produces the Monte Carlo samples, evaluates the integrals and updates the bin contributions. This method requires almost all data-structures and variables as parameters, so we omit them in this description. At line 11, the estimates are weighted by standard VEGAS formulas that can be found in Eqs. (5) and (6) of [11]. We then adjust the bin boundaries B based on the bin contributions C. If the weighted integral estimate and standard deviation produced at line 11, satisfy the user's accuracy requirements, execution stops, otherwise we proceed to the next iteration. Before proceeding to the next iteration, the bin boundaries B are adjusted at line 12. The only difference between an m-CUBES and a VEGAS iteration from the original algorithm, are the parallelized accumulation steps and mappings between processors and sub-cubes.

A second loop of iterations (lines 14 to 17) is invoked once *ita* iterations are completed. In this set of iterations, we perform the same computations with the exception of bin adjustments and their supporting computations which are omitted. This distinction is introduced due to the common occurrence of the boundaries B converging after a number of iterations and remaining unchanged. In those cases, the costly operations of keeping track of bin contributions and updating them has no positive effect. As such, the user can mandate a limit of iterations with that will involve bin adjustments, and sub-subsequent iterations will execute faster by avoiding redundant operations.

V-SAMPLE and V-SAMPLE-NO-ADJUST are the only methods that involve parallelization, encompassing the functionality of lines 2 to 8 from Algorithm 3. To facilitate the accumulation steps needed to yield the integral contributions from multiple sub-cube batches, V-SAMPLE utilizes hierarchical parallelism, where each processor launches many groups of cooperative threads (CUDA thread-blocks/Kokkos teams) of size x, requiring a total $\frac{m}{x}$ such groups. Each thread within a group is independent and processes its own sub-cube batch of size s (see Algorithm 4, line 5). The benefit of this approach, is that group-shared memory and group-synchronization capabilities allow for more efficient accumulation of the integral estimates v local to each thread. The race condition involved with incrementing the bin contributions from multiple threads, is solved through atomic addition operations. The same operation is used to accumulate the integral estimate from all groups.

The input of the V-SAMPLE method, consists of the integrand f of dimensionality d, the number of sub-cubes m, sub-cube batch size s, number of samples per sub-cube p, bin bounds B, bin contributions C, and result r. Once finished, V-SAMPLE will return an estimate for the integral, variance, and updated bin contributions C.

The for-loop at line 2, indicates the sequential processing of s sub-cubes from each thread. At line 3 we initialize a random number generator. Each thread has local integral and error estimates I and E (line 4) respectively, which encompass the contributions from all s sub-cubes. Each thread processes its assigned sub-cubes with the serial for-loop at line 5. As the sub-cubes are processed, the local estimates I_t and E_t of each sub-cube are accumulated in I and E. This involves yet another for-loop at line 7, to serialize the p samples generated per sub-cube. Similar to the accumulation of I_t to I, we accumulate the estimates I_k and E_k (local to the sample) to I_t and E_t.

For each sample, we generate an d-dimensional point x where we will evaluate the integrand f. This yields estimates for the sample that are used to increment the sub-cubes estimates at lines 10 and 11. Then, based on the bin IDs that are determined in line 12. we update the bin contributions in line 14. The atomic addition guarantees serial access for each thread updating C at each index $b[1 : s]$, avoiding race conditions. The actual bin-contribution is the square of the integral estimate I_k. Then, we update the variance at line 16, followed by the updating of the thread-local estimates for the entire batch of sub-cubes in lines 16 and 17.

Once the for-loop at line 5 is finished, we accumulate the I, E from each thread in parallel. This is accomplished by a group-reduction that utilizes shared memory and warp-level primitives if available. Finally, once each group has accumulated estimates from all its sub-cubes across all its threads, a final atomic addition in lines 23 and 24 accumulates the estimates from all groups and can return them as the result r.

The V-SAMPLE-NO-ADJUST method is almost identical to V-SAMPLE, with the distinction that the loop at lines 13-14 are not needed which yields a boost in performance.

Algorithm 3. V-SAMPLE

```
 1: procedure V-SAMPLE(f, d, m, s, p, B, C, r)
 2:     for m/b threads parallel do
 3:         SET-RANDOM-GENERATOR(seed)
 4:         I, E ← 0                                  ▷ cumulative estimates of thread
 5:         for t = 0 to s do
 6:             I_t, E_t ← 0                          ▷ estimates of sub-cube t
 7:             for k ← 1 to p do
 8:                 x[1 : d] ← GENERATE()
 9:                 I_k, E_k ← EVALUATE(f, x)
10:                 I_t ← I_t + I_k                   ▷ Accumulate sub-cube contributions
11:                 E_t ← E_t + E_k
12:                 b[1 : d] ← GET-BIN-ID(x)
13:                 for j ← 1 to d do                 ▷ Store bin contributions
14:                     ATOMICADD(C[b[j]], I_k^2)
15:             E_t ← UPDATEVARIANCE(E_t, I_t, p)
16:             I ← I + I_t                           ▷ update cumulative values
17:             E ← E + E_t
18:         I ← REDUCE(I)
19:         E ← REDUCE(E)
20:         if thread 0 within group then
21:             ATOMICADD(r[0], I)
22:             ATOMICADD(r[1], E)
```

5 Experimental Results

We performed two separate series of experiments to compare against the GPU methods gVegas and ZMCINTEGRAL. Our experiments utilized a standard integrand test suite (Eqs. 1 to 6) which consists of several integrals with different characteristics such as corner/product peaks, Gaussian, C^0 form, and oscillations. We used a single node with a 2.4 GHz Xeon R Gold 6130 CPU, v100 GPU with 16 GB of memory and 7.834 Tflops in double precision floating point arithmetic, and compiled with GCC 9.3.1 and CUDA 11.

$$f_{1,d}(x) = \cos\left(\sum_{i=1}^{d} i\, x_i\right) \tag{1}$$

$$f_{2,d}(x) = \prod_{i=1}^{d}\left(\frac{1}{50^2} + (x_i - 1/2)^2\right)^{-1} \tag{2}$$

$$f_{3,d}(x) = \left(1 + \sum_{i=1}^{d} i\, x_i\right)^{-d-1} \tag{3}$$

$$f_{4,d}(x) = \exp\left(-625 \sum_{i=1}^{d} (x_i - 1/2)^2\right) \tag{4}$$

$$f_{5,d}(x) = \exp\left(-10 \sum_{i=1}^{d} |x_i - 1/2|\right) \tag{5}$$

$$f_{6,d}(x) = \begin{cases} \exp\left(\sum_{i=1}^{d} (i+4)\, x_i\right) & \text{if } x_i < (3+i)/10 \\ 0 & \text{otherwise} \end{cases} \tag{6}$$

5.1 Accuracy

In the m-CUBES algorithm, we use relative error as a stopping criteria for achieving a specified accuracy, which is the normalized standard deviation (see Algorithm 4 for the error computation). The required accuracy associated with numerical integration, can vary significantly across applications depending on the context. To our knowledge no numerical integration algorithm can claim a zero absolute error on all integrands or even guarantee integral/error estimates that satisfy the various relative error tolerances τ_{rel}. As such, it is important to evaluate the degree of correctness for specific challenging integrands whose integral values are known *a priori*. It is equally important to demonstrate how an algorithm adapts to increasingly more demanding precision requirements and whether the yielded integral/error estimates truly satisfy the user's required τ_{rel}. This is especially true for Monte Carlo based algorithms, whose randomness and statistically-based error-estimates make them less robust than deterministic, quadrature-based algorithms. In our evaluation of m-CUBES, we adopt the testing procedures of [7] in selecting the target integrands but preselect the various integrand parameter constants as in [12]. We deviate from [12], in that we omit the two box-integrands that were not challenging for VEGAS. We also do not report results on $f_{1,d}$ in our plots, as no VEGAS variant could evaluate it to the satisfactory precision levels. The various tolerances are the same on all experiments as each integrand is evaluated on increasingly smaller τ_{rel}. We start evaluating all integrands with a τ_{rel} of 10^{-3}. Upon each successful execution, we divide τ_{rel} by five until either surpassing the minimum value of 10^{-9} (maximum accuracy) or failing to achieve the required error tolerance.

We investigate the quality of the m-CUBES error-estimates in Fig. 1, where we display multiple 100-run sets of results on each different level of precision for each integrand. The user's requested digits of precision are represented in the x-axis, while the true relative error is mapped to the y-axis. To make our plots more intuitive, with the x-axis representing increasing accuracy requirements, we perform the $-log_{10}(\tau_{rel})$ transformation on the x-axis of all plots; this translates "roughly" to the required digits-of-precision. We still plot the user's τ_{rel} for each experiment as the orange point. Since we only plot results for which m-CUBES claimed convergence with appropriately small χ^2, comparing against the orange point indicates whether the algorithm is as accurate as it claims.

Due to the randomness of the Monte Carlo samples, there is a wide range of achieved relative error values for the same digits-of-precision. This is to be expected as the error-estimate is interpreted as the standard deviation of the weighted iteration results. Deviation in the results can be more pronounced when generating smaller number of samples which is typical in low-precision runs. In most cases, the number of samples must be increased for higher precisions runs. This leads to a smaller deviation in the results, demonstrated in the figure by the increasingly smaller boxes on the right side of the x-axis. This smaller deviation yields improved accuracy, as we observe the box boundaries encompassing the target relative error. We observed similar behavior from GSL, CUBA, and the VEGAS 5.0 Python package on which we performed single-run experiments.

5.2 Performance

m-CUBES generates the random numbers and evaluates the integrand within two GPU kernels, V-SAMPLE which additionally stores bin contributions in order to better approximate the distribution of the integrand, and V-SAMPLE-NO-ADJUST which does not update bin contributions. The execution time of the two kernels, is directly dependent on the number of required function calls per iteration which in turn determines the workload (number of sub-cubes) assigned to each thread. The required number of iterations tends to increase for higher precision runs. For low-precision runs, the same number of samples and iterations can result in convergence. This is why for some integrands ($f_{4,8}$, $f_{5,8}$, $f_{3,3}$, $f_{2,6}$), the three, four, and five digits of precision runs display similar execution time. Missing entries indicate that the corresponding algorithm did not convergence to the required τ_{rel} in a reasonable amount of time.

We compare m-CUBES and gVEGAS by evaluating integrands 1 to 6 for various τ_{rel}. We observe that m-CUBES can be more than one order of magnitude faster. This is attributed to the additional data movement (function evaluations) gVegas requires between CPU and GPU, the smaller number of samples per iteration that are imposed by required memory allocations. By contrast, m-CUBES accumulates bin contributions and function evaluations within the GPU and only performs their adjustment on the CPU while the bin boundaries and their contributions are the only data moved between CPU and GPU.

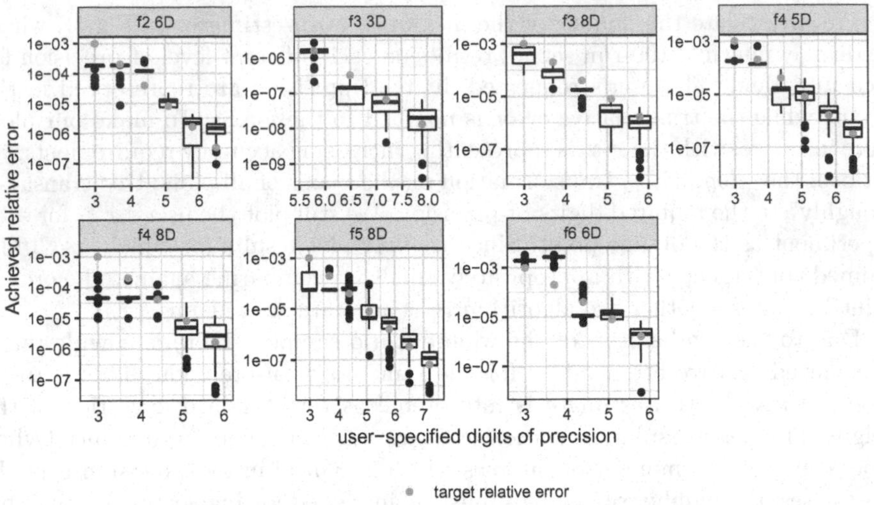

Fig. 1. This box plot displays the user-requested relative error tolerance (orange dot) and the achieved relative errors of m-CUBES algorithm on the y-axis. Each box is a statistical summary of 100 runs. The top and bottom box boundaries indicate the first and third quartiles. The middle line is the value of the median while the vertical lines protruding from the top and bottom box boundaries indicate the minimum and maximum values. The individual points displayed are outliers. (Color figure online)

$$f_A\left(x\right) = \sin\left(\sum_{i=1}^{6} x_i\right) \tag{7}$$

$$f_B\left(x\right) = \frac{1}{(\sqrt{(2\cdot\pi\cdot .01)})^2}\exp\left(-\frac{1}{2\cdot(.001)^2}\sum_{i=1}^{9}(x_i)^2\right) \tag{8}$$

The results of ZMCINTEGRAL presented in [14] did not include integrands 1 to 6 and our experiments showed that ZMCINTEGRAL performed slower than serial VEGAS in those cases; as we are not aware of the "best"configuration parameters for those integrands, we do not include such results on the grounds of unfair comparison. Instead, we use the same parameters on the same integrals reported in [14] (integrands 7 and 8). The f_A integrand was evaluated over the range $(0,10)$ on all dimensions, while the integration space of f_B was the range $(-1,1)$ on all axes. Since ZMCintegral does not accept τ_{rel} as parameter, we try to match the achieved standard deviation of ZMCintegral for a fair comparison by using a τ_{rel} of 10^{-3} and setting the maximum iterations of 10 and 15 respectively. We report our results in Table 1, where we observe a speedup of 45 and 10 respectively, though in both cases m-CUBES reported significantly smaller error-estimates than ZMCintegral (Fig. 2).

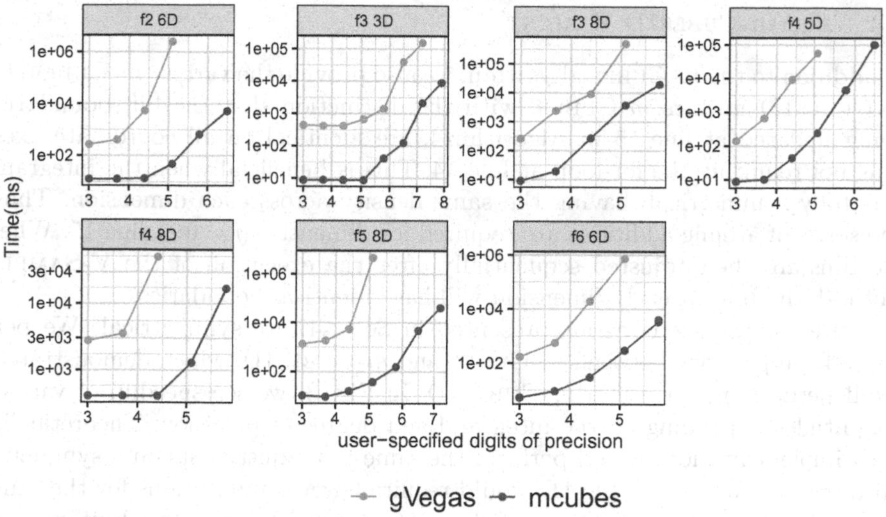

Fig. 2. gVegas comparison

Table 1. Comparison with ZMCintegral

Integrand	Alg	True value	Estimate	Errorest	Time (ms)
f_A	zmc	−49.165073	−48.64740	1.98669	4.75×10^4
f_A	m-CUBES		−49.27284	1.19551	1.07×10^3
f_B	zmc	1.0	0.99939	0.00133	8.30×10^3
f_B	m-CUBES		1.00008	0.00005	9.80×10^2

5.3 Cost of Function Evaluation

One of the fundamental operations of m-CUBES and all Monte Carlo integration methods is the evaluation of the samples after randomly generating their location in the region space. The execution time for the sample evaluations of the closed-form integrands 1 to 8 was typically negligible compared to the total execution time (typically less than 1% and at most 18% in the case of f_A). "Real-world" integrands can be more costly due to often required non-trivial operations or even expensive memory accesses to look-up tables. In such cases, additional parallelism at the sample evaluation level could provide performance improvement. For example, we could use multiple threads to evaluate a single sample instead of having each thread compute a sample independently. Such operations could involve the parallel generation of the points in each dimensional axis, or even the parallelization of computations requiring multiple look-up operations, such as interpolation, to minimize serial memory accesses.

5.4 The m-CUBES1D VARIANT

In addition to the m-CUBES algorithm, we also provide the variant m-CUBES1D. m-CUBES1D mirrors m-CUBES, with the distinction that the bin boundaries being updated at line 15 in Algorithm 4, are identical on all coordinate axes, thus not requiring the for-loop at line 14. This is beneficial when the integrand f is fully symmetrical, having the same density across each dimension. Thus, one series of atomic additions are required for dimension $j = 0$ at line 15. When the bins are then adjusted sequentially after the execution of the V-SAMPLE method, the bins at each dimension will have identical boundaries.

Three of the six integrals presented in Sect. 4, are symmetrical. We performed comparisons between m-CUBES and m-CUBES1D, which demonstrate a small performance boost in m-CUBES1D. In Fig. 3, we see speedup of various magnitudes depending on the integrand and degree of precision. Theoretically, both implementations would perform the same bin-adjustments on a symmetrical integrand, and m-CUBES1D would require fewer computations for the same effect. We expect that execution of this variant on non-symmetrical integrands, will severely hinder the bin adjustments.

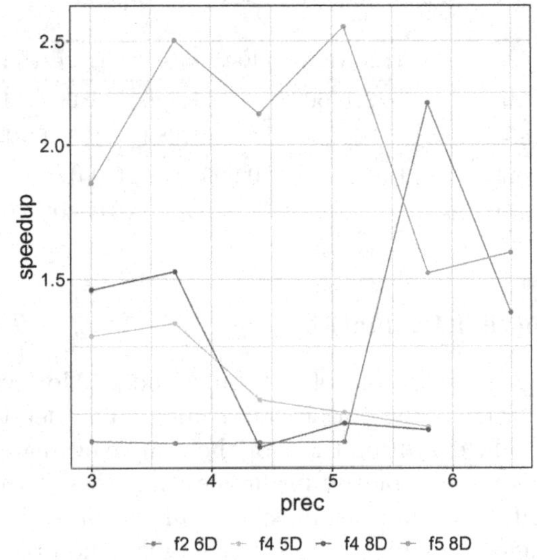

Fig. 3. Speedup of m-CUBES1D over m-CUBES on symmetrical integrands.

6 Portability

There are two aspects related to portability: restrictions on the execution platform, and maintaining flexibility when defining an integrand.

6.1 Defining Integrands in CUDA

Ideally, an integrator should be "easy" to incorporate into existing codes and the integrand definitions should be suitable for execution on various platforms, whether that is CPUs or GPUs regardless of architecture (NVIDIA, INTEL, AMD, etc.) Additionally, a user should have minimum restrictions when defining the integrand, being allowed to use dynamically created data-structures within the integrand, maintain an integrand state (persistent variables, tabular data, etc.), and define boundaries in the integration space.

The different memory spaces utilized by a GPU pose a challenge in regards to defining integrands with complex states (non-trivial structures). While the user could potentially interface with m-CUBES through the appropriate use of CUDA to handle the different memory spaces, this would severely hinder its ease-of-use and require sufficient knowledge of GPU programming. Additionally, a user who wishes to maintain the option of which platform (CPU, GPU) to execute on, would be forced to write multiple, potentially very different implementations of the same integrand to accommodate the requirements of each platform. To solve this problem, we require the user to define an integrand as a functor to interface with m-CUBES. We also supply our own data-structures such as interpolator objects and array-like structures, that handle the GPU related data manipulations internally, but are set and accessed similar to standard library or GSL equivalents. This allows the user to initialize such objects and structures in a familiar fashion and use them in their defined integrands without having to worry about allocating and transferring data to GPU memory and without having to write any complicated CUDA code. Finally, in regards to "easily" using integrators in existing code-bases, m-CUBES is implemented as a header-only library.

A use-case demonstrating these features, involves an integrand required for a cosmological study in an astrophysics application. The integrand is six dimensional and requires the utilization of numerous interpolation tables that must be read at run-time and consists of several C++ objects. We evaluated that integrand and compared execution times against the serial VEGAS implementation of CUBA. m-CUBES returns similar results to those of the CUBA implemenation with appropriate performance. This demonstrates that our solutions pertaining to portability are functional and do not induce any prohibitive costs that would make m-CUBES is unsuitable for computationally expensive "real-world" integrands.

6.2 Execution Platform Portability Using Kokkos

We have completed an initial implementation of m-CUBES in Kokkos with minimal algorithmic changes to the original CUDA version. The hierarchical parallelism constructs of Kokkos, allow the specification of the same thread-block configuration as required by the CUDA kernels. This makes "translation" to Kokkos easy to perform but further optimization is required to maintain performance across architectures.

We present results on the f_A and f_B integrands in Table 2, which displays the kernel time (time executing on GPU) and total time (CPU and GPU time). We evaluated both integrands with the Kokkos version, for three digits of precision on an NVIDIA V100 GPU. This demonstrates the minimum expected overhead in the range 10–15% for the parallel segments of the code, which are expected to cover the majority of execution time. We note that Kokkos can in some cases be faster on the serial code execution. This leads to the low-precision runs on the two integrands being slightly faster in Kokkos. Additional experiments on other integrands show that this is not the case when computational intensity increases. For example, when we compare the running times for the integrand $f_{4,5}$ with 100 runs for each precision level, Kokkos incurs 20–50% overhead.

Table 2. Confusion matrix of one of the folds for the final classification of DGCNN-MS-T-W, with $W = 150$

(a) Execution Time (ms) on f_A

platform	kernel	total
CUDA	829.760	1280.318
Kokkos	968.880	1001.035

Execution Time (ms) on f_B

platform	kernel	total
CUDA	664.977	1126.529
Kokkos	726.766	767.343

7 Conclusion

We presented m-CUBES, a new parallel implementation of the widely used VEGAS multi-dimensional numerical integration algorithm for execution on GPUs. m-Cubes is a portable header-only library, with a modern interface and features that allow easy interfacing and requires no knowledge of GPU programming to use. We also supply infrastructure to facilitate the definition of complex and stateful integrands. Our experiments on a standard set of challenging integrals and a complex stateful integrand consisted of numerous C++ objects, demonstrate superior performance over existing GPU implementations. Furthermore, We supply the variant m-CUBES1D to accelerate evaluation of symmetrical integrals. We also provide an initial Kokkos implementation to allow execution on non-NVIDIA GPUs.

Acknowledgment. This manuscript has been authored by Fermi Research Alliance, LLC under Contract No. DE-AC02-07CH11359 with the U.S. Department of Energy, Office of Science, Office of High Energy Physics.

References

1. https://github.com/lbiedma/gVegascp
2. https://xgitlab.cels.anl.gov/whopkins/MadgraphGPU
3. Borowka, S., Heinrich, G., Jahn, S., Jones, S., Kerner, M., Schlenk, J.: A GPU compatible quasi-monte carlo integrator interfaced to pySecDec. Comput. Phys. Commun. **240**, 120–137 (2019). https://doi.org/10.1016/j.cpc.2019.02.015

4. Carrazza, S., Cruz-Martinez, J.M.: VegasFlow: accelerating Monte Carlo simulation across multiple hardware platforms. Comput. Phys. Commun. **254**, 107376 (2020). https://doi.org/10.1016/j.cpc.2020.107376
5. Cruz-Martinez, J., Carrazza, S.: N3pdf/vegasflow: vegasflow v1.0, February 2020. https://doi.org/10.5281/zenodo.3691926
6. Edwards, H.C., Trott, C.R., Sunderland, D.: Kokkos: Enabling manycore performance portability through polymorphic memory access patterns. J. Parall. Distrib. Comput. **74**(12), 3202–3216 (2014). https://doi.org/10.1016/j.jpdc.2014.07.003, http://www.sciencedirect.com/science/article/pii/S0743731514001257, domain-Specific Languages and High-Level Frameworks for High-Performance Computing
7. Genz, A.: Testing multidimensional integration routines. In: Proceedings of International Conference on Tools, Methods and Languages for Scientific and Engineering Computation, pp. 81–94. Elsevier North-Holland Inc., USA (1984)
8. Goda, T., Suzuki, K.: Recent advances in higher order quasi-monte carlo methods. arXiv: Numerical Analysis (2019)
9. Kanzaki, J.: Monte carlo integration on GPU. The Eur. Phys. J. **71**(2), 1–7 (2011)
10. Lepage, G.P.: Adaptive multidimensional integration: VEGAS enhanced. J. Comput. Phys. **439**, 110386 (2021). https://doi.org/10.1016/j.jcp.2021.110386,https://www.sciencedirect.com/science/article/pii/S0021999121002813
11. Peter Lepage, G.: A new algorithm for adaptive multidimensional integration. J. Comput. Phys. **27**(2), 192–203 (1978). https://doi.org/10.1016/0021-9991(78)90004-9, https://www.sciencedirect.com/science/article/pii/0021999178900049
12. Sakiotis, I., Arumugam, K., Paterno, M., Ranjan, D., Terzić, B., Zubair, M.: PAGANI: a parallel Adaptive GPU algorithm for numerical integration. Association for Computing Machinery, New York, NY, USA (2021), https://doi.org/10.1145/3458817.3476198
13. Trott, C.R., et al.: Kokkos 3: Programming model extensions for the exascale era. IEEE Trans. Parallel Distrib. Syst. **33**(4), 805–817 (2022). https://doi.org/10.1109/TPDS.2021.3097283
14. Wu, H.Z., Zhang, J.J., Pang, L.G., Wang, Q.: Zmcintegral: a package for multi-dimensional monte carlo integration on multi-GPUS. Comput. Phys. Commun. **248**, 106962 (2020). https://doi.org/10.1016/j.cpc.2019.106962, https://www.sciencedirect.com/science/article/pii/S0010465519303121

Performance Modeling, Evaluation, and Analysis

Comparative Evaluation of Call Graph Generation by Profiling Tools

Onur Cankur(✉) and Abhinav Bhatele

Department of Computer Science, University of Maryland,
College Park, MD 20742, USA
ocankur@umd.edu, bhatele@cs.umd.edu

Abstract. Call graphs generated by profiling tools are critical to dissecting the performance of parallel programs. Although many mature and sophisticated profiling tools record call graph data, each tool is different in its runtime overheads, memory consumption, and output data generated. In this work, we perform a comparative evaluation study on the call graph data generation capabilities of several popular profiling tools – Caliper, HPCToolkit, TAU, and Score-P. We evaluate their runtime overheads, memory consumption, and generated call graph data (size and quality). We perform this comparison empirically by executing several proxy applications, AMG, LULESH, and Quicksilver on a parallel cluster. Our results show which tool results in the lowest overheads and produces the most meaningful call graph data under different conditions.

Keywords: Profiling tools · Call graph · Performance analysis · Parallel performance · Measurement

1 Introduction

Analyzing and optimizing the performance of parallel programs is critical to obtaining high efficiency on high performance computing (HPC) architectures. The complexity in hardware architectures and system software makes measuring and recording performance data challenging. At the same time, the complexity in HPC applications and compiler transformations can make analyzing and attributing performance to source code and external libraries challenging [23]. Even so, a plethora of performance analysis tools exists for gathering and analyzing performance data [1,5,9,13,22]. One category of performance tools collects performance data that is aggregated over time. In this work, we refer to these as profiling tools to distinguish them from tracing tools that gather more detailed time-series data or full execution traces. Specifically, we focus on profiling tools that record contextual information about the performance data such as calling context, file and line numbers in the source code, etc., which can help users in attributing performance to source code.

Although several profiling tools exist in the HPC community, they differ in their profiling methods and capabilities, which affects their efficiency and the

A.-L. Varbanescu et al. (Eds.): ISC High Performance 2022, LNCS 13289, pp. 213–232, 2022.
https://doi.org/10.1007/978-3-031-07312-0_11

quality of generated performance data. Broadly, profiling tools use one of two methods for collecting information – instrumentation and sampling. Instrumentation involves adding extra instructions to the source or binary code that are used to measure the execution time of different parts of a program. In contrast, sampling does not require adding instructions. It periodically samples the program counter, uses that to identify the code being executed, and aggregates the performance measurements of a code block across multiple samples. These different profiling methods can lead to varying overheads and capabilities in different profiling tools. For example, an instrumentation-based profiling tool might cause more overhead than a sampling-based tool while providing more accurate output. Besides, two different profiling tools that use the same method might have different capabilities depending on how well they are implemented. For instance, a sampling-based tool might work better than others under low sampling intervals. Since end-users have many choices when using a profiling tool, a systematic study is needed to understand the impact of different profiling techniques on data generation.

Performance data gathered by profiling tools consist of different kinds of information about the program such as the call graph, communication patterns, and MPI process topology. In this study, we focus on the call graph data generation capabilities of profiling tools since the call graph provides critical information about program structure, which can be quite useful in performance analysis. There are many factors that come into play when comparing call graph data generation. Runtime overhead and memory consumption are two comparison metrics that naturally come to mind since they directly impact the application being profiled. In addition, profiling complex parallel applications on a large number of processes can result in a large amount of call graph data being generated, which can also be an important factor to consider when comparing tools. The quality and usefulness of the data generated in terms of its correctness (e.g., correctly measuring and attributing execution time) and ability to attribute performance to source code are also important. In this paper, we consider runtime overhead, memory usage, and quality of the call graph data to compare the data generation capabilities of profiling tools.

We compare several popular tools that are used in the HPC community to profile parallel programs – Caliper [5], HPCToolkit [1], Score-P [9], and TAU [22] – in terms of their capabilities, performance, and generation of meaningful call graph data. More specifically, we compare their runtime overheads, memory usage, and the size, correctness and quality of the generated call graph data. We conduct these experiments on a parallel cluster by profiling three different proxy applications, AMG, LULESH, and Quicksilver, using both instrumentation and sampling under different sampling intervals and different numbers of processes. To the best of our knowledge, this is the first comparative evaluation study on call graph data generation capabilities of profiling tools for parallel programs. In addition, we extend and use Hatchet [4], a Python-based tool that enables analyzing the output from profiling tools programmatically, to compare call graph data. We show which tools are more efficient in terms of measurement overheads and memory consumption, and generate more meaningful call graph data under different conditions and for different proxy applications. Specifically, this study makes the following contributions:

- Comparatively evaluate the call graph generation capabilities of profiling tools considering their measurement and memory overheads, and quality of the generated data.
- Extend the Hatchet performance analysis tool to support output data generated by Score-P and TAU, enabling the comparison of data from several popular profiling tools.
- Provide feedback to tool developers for the improvement of various aspects of the performance data gathering process.

2 Background and Related Work

In this section, we provide an overview of the profiling tools used in this paper and give detailed background information about profiling methods and the output of profiling tools. We also introduce Hatchet, using which we perform our analyses. Finally, we present related work on the evaluation of profiling tools.

2.1 Different Methods for Profiling

Performance measurement tools can be divided into two categories: profiling and tracing. In this work, we only consider profiling which can be done using sampling or instrumentation. Instrumentation can be classified along two dimensions: the method of instrumentation and where is the instrumentation added. The method can be manual (by the developer) or automatic (by the tool, compiler, library interposition, etc.) and it can be performed by adding additional instructions in the source code, byte code, or binary code [18]. These additional instructions allow measuring the performance of a code section.

On the other hand, sampling-based profiling tools take periodic snapshots of the program, check the location of the program counter and collect the function call stack by performing stack unwinding [23] and then aggregate this data that they gathered periodically. It also allows to change sampling interval, hence, provides controllable overhead.

2.2 Information Gathered by Profiling Tools

The data generated by profiling tools usually contains contextual information (the function name, file name, call path, process or thread ID, etc.) and performance metrics such as time, cache misses, communication information, and the total number of instructions along with the callpath information on the program. Some profiling tools collect individual callpaths (i.e. calling contexts) on the program and represent it in a tree format called calling context tree. Other tools aggregate that information and generate call graphs which show aggregated information in which a procedure that is called in multiple distinct paths is represented as a single node. Profiling tools typically have their own custom output formats to store the calling context tree (CCT) or call graph. In this paper, we use call graph as a general term for both CCT and call graph.

2.3 Profiling Tools Used in This Study

All profiling tools in this study, which are introduced below, support C, C++, and Fortran programs and MPI, OpenMP, and pthreads programming models (see Table 1).

Table 1. Salient features of different profiling tools

Tool	Samp.	Instr.	Languages	Output format
Caliper	Yes	Yes	C, C++, Fortran	.json and custom
HPCToolkit	Yes	No	C, C++, Fortran	XML and custom
Score-P	Partially	Yes	C, C++, Fortran, Python	XML and custom
TAU	Yes	Yes	C, C++, Fortran, Java, Python	custom

Caliper is a performance analysis toolbox that provides many services for users to measure and analyze the performance, such as tracing and profiling services [5]. It allows users to activate these capabilities at runtime by annotating the source code or using configuration files. It provides *json* or custom file formats and generates CCT data.

HPCToolkit is a toolkit for performance measurement and analysis [1]. It supports both profiling and tracing and uses sampling instead of instrumentation. It generates a performance database directory that contains *XML* and custom file formats that store CCT information.

Score-P is a measurement infrastructure that supports both profiling and tracing [9]. It is primarily an instrumentation-based tool that supports source, compiler, and selective instrumentation, but it also supports sampling for instrumented executables. Score-P supports Python in addition to C, C++, and Fortran. It generates `.cubex` [20] output tarballs which are in *CUBE4* format and contain files in *XML* and custom formats and generates CCT information.

TAU is also a performance measurement and analysis toolkit and supports profiling and tracing [22]. TAU also primarily uses instrumentation but it also supports sampling. It supports different types of instrumentation such as source instrumentation using PDT [11], compiler instrumentation, and selective instrumentation. It supports C, C++, Fortran, Java, and Python and generates profile.<rank>.<>.<thread> files which are in custom format and stores CCT as its default profiling output format.

2.4 Post-mortem Analysis of Profiling Data

Most of the profiling tools we evaluate provide their own analysis and visualization tools such as HPCViewer [15], ParaProf [3], and CubeGUI [20]. Visualization tools usually provide a graphical user interface (GUI) that allows the visualization of one or two call graphs at the same time. These GUIs provide limited call graph analysis capabilities since they do not provide a programmable interface. In this study, we used and improved Hatchet [4] to compare the call graph data generated from different profiling tools on the same platform.

Hatchet is a Python-based performance analysis tool that provides a programmable interface to analyze the call graph profiling data of different tools on the same platform [4]. It reads in the profiling data and generates a data structure called *graphframe* which stores numerical (e.g. time, cache misses) and categorical (callpath, file and line information, etc.) information along with the caller-callee relationships on the program.

2.5 Related Work

All tools used in this paper have some kind of prior performance evaluation. For example, some of them study the overhead of TAU using tracing, profiling, sampling, and instrumentation [14,17,21]. There is a similar study on HPCToolkit [12] which includes runtime overhead evaluation. Score-P and Caliper include similar runtime overhead evaluation studies in their corresponding papers [5,9]. Although each tool has been evaluated for performance, these past studies only cover the runtime and memory overhead of a tool, different profiling methods a tool supports, or include a simple overhead comparison with another tool that is not currently state-of-the-art. Therefore, the only criteria considered in these papers are the runtime and memory overheads, and they do not evaluate the quality of the call graph data generated by profiling tools.

Other evaluation studies on profiling tools only include functional comparisons [8,16]. The closest related work to our paper is published in 2008 [10]. However, it is more like a case study and a generic user experience comparison of profiling tools that were widely used at that time and it does not contain empirical experiments. Our study is the first empirical comparative study on call graph data generation by state-of-the-art profiling tools, considering their runtime overhead, memory usage, and output quality.

3 Methodology for Comparative Evaluation

In this study, we consider runtime overhead, memory usage, size, richness and correctness of the generated call graph data. We do not consider information such as communication volume and process topology. Below, we present the various axes along which call graph data generation capabilities are compared and describe the metrics used for comparison.

3.1 Comparison of Runtime Overhead

One of the most important factors to consider when comparing call graph data generation is the runtime overhead incurred when using them. The execution time of an application should not be perturbed significantly by the profiling tool. Different profiling methods can incur different overheads. For example, sampling causes less overhead than instrumentation methods because it is less intrusive. Similarly, one instrumentation method can cause more overhead than another instrumentation method. Hence, we evaluate the runtime overhead by conducting experiments using both sampling and instrumentation techniques separately. In addition, sampling-based methods have the flexibility to adjust the runtime overhead by increasing or decreasing the sampling interval. We also compare the tools by varying the sampling intervals wherever supported.

We run each application without any profiling and measure the execution time by calling `MPI_Wtime()` at the start and end of the program. Dividing these two timings gives us the relative execution time of a program. We then run each application with different profiling tools to calculate the increase in execution time due to profiling overheads.

3.2 Comparison of Memory Consumption

Ideally, performance tools should not consume large amounts of memory. Hence, it is important to compare the additional memory consumption of different profiling tools. We compare the amount of memory consumed by profiling tools during application execution. We perform the same experiments using the default and varying sampling intervals and using instrumentation.

We measure the memory usage of a program using the `getrusage()` function call and obtain the largest memory usage at any point during program execution. We calculate the additional memory consumed by a tool by gathering memory usage information for two runs – one with and one without profiling.

3.3 Comparison of the Quality of Call Graph Data

We expect profiling tools to provide useful information without generating unnecessary or repetitive information. In this study, we evaluate the quality of the call graph profiling data recorded by each tool considering the data size, correctness and richness of the data with the assumption that if the data generated by multiple tools is nearly identical, it should be close to the ground truth.

Size of Call Graph Data: A significant amount of call graph data can be generated when profiling HPC applications, which can make post-mortem analysis challenging. We evaluate the size of the data generated when using different tools for the same experiments by using default and varying sampling intervals and instrumentation. We use default settings for each tool without changing the number of metrics collected and collect per-process data without aggregating it. We also observe how the data size increases with an increase in the number of processes since some tools generate a separate file per MPI process while others represent this data in a more compact output format.

Correctness of Call Graph Data: The correctness of the generated call graph data is critical in order to perform meaningful analysis. We consider the information to be correct if different tools generate the same results with correct contextual information. We follow two different strategies for this analysis. First, we load the profiling data from different tools in Hatchet and identify the top 5 slowest call graph nodes in the call graph by inclusive and exclusive time and investigate if the tools identify the same slowest nodes. We also compare the file, line numbers, and callpaths reported by each tool for the slowest nodes. Second, we identify the hot path in each dataset. The hot path refers to a call path in the graph in which all nodes account for 50% or more of the inclusive time of their parent [2]. The node at the end of a hot path is called a hot node. Therefore, hot path analysis gives us the most time-consuming call path in the execution. Our hot path analysis implementation in Hatchet makes it possible to perform the same analysis for each tool.

Richness of Call Graph Data: The richness of call graph profiling data refers to having detailed information in the CCT such as caller-callee relationships, and contextual information (file and module information, line number, etc.). To evaluate richness, we take the following parameters into account: the maximum and average callpath lengths, the number of nodes, the number of identified .so files (dynamically loaded modules), and the number of MPI routines. The callpath length provides insight into how detailed the caller-callee relationships are. In addition, examining the number of total and unique nodes in the call graph tells us if a tool is missing some information or generating excessive data that is not required. We also compare the information generated by different tools about dynamically loaded libraries and MPI routines. Similar to the correctness evaluation, these comparisons are performed using Hatchet. For example, we filter the Hatchet dataframe by node names to get the MPI functions or .so files. We traverse the graph to calculate the maximum and average callpath length.

3.4 Extensions to Hatchet

We have improved Hatchet by implementing TAU and Score-P readers to use in this study. Below, we explain how we implement these readers.

Score-P Reader: Score-P stores profiling data in CUBE4 tar files (extension: `.cubex`) [20]. These tar files in turn contain `anchor.xml`, `.index`, and `.data` files. The `anchor.xml` file contains metadata information about metrics and processes along with caller-callee relationships. The `.index` and `.data` files contain information about metric measurement and metric values. To implement a Python reader in Hatchet, we use pyCubexR which is a Score-P reader that can read `cubex` files. After implementing the reader, we compared the generated Hatchet graphframe with the CubeGUI visualization provided by Score-P to confirm the correctness of our implementation.

TAU Reader: TAU generates profiles in its custom format. It generates a separate file for each process and thread. In addition, it generates a separate directory for each metric (time, cache misses, etc.). We combine all this information gathered from different directories and files, and create a single CCT which is stored as a graphframe in Hatchet. Finally, we validate our reader implementation by comparing the Hatchet graphframe with ParaProf output which is a visualization tool for TAU outputs.

4 Experimental Setup

In this section, we describe each experiment in detail. We used three HPC applications written in C/C++ and four profiling tools in our experiments: AMG [6], LULESH [7], and Quicksilver [19] proxy applications and Caliper, HPCToolkit, Score-P, and TAU profiling tools. We chose LULESH because it is a simple code (lines of code = ~5.5k), which can help us illustrate differences between tools. Quicksilver is more complex than LULESH in terms of lines of code (~10k), and AMG (~65k) uses external libraries such as Hypre which makes its call paths more complex. In addition, all the profiling tools we used in this study are actively and widely used in many supercomputers and they are still being improved. We used the latest release versions of these tools: Caliper 2.6.0, HPCToolkit 2021.05.15, Score-P 7.1, and TAU 2.30.1. We compared their sampling and instrumentation capabilities by running experiments accordingly. We separately built each of the applications with these tools using GCC 8.3.1 and Open MPI 3.0.1. We only used MPI, so multithreading using OpenMP or Pthreads was not enabled. We ran the applications on a parallel cluster which has x86_64 architecture with 36 cores on each node and performed weak scaling experiments using 64, 128 (125 for LULESH), 256 (216 for LULESH), and 512 processes using 1 through 16 nodes and 32 cores on each node in all experiments.

4.1 Experiment 1: Comparison of Sampling Capabilities

In this experiment, we used Caliper, HPCToolkit, Score-P, and TAU using their default sampling intervals. However, it should be noted that Score-P supports sampling of instrumented programs, while other tools directly perform sampling on executables without instrumenting them. The default sampling interval for Caliper, HPCToolkit, Score-P, and TAU is 20, 5, 10, and 30 ms, respectively. We evaluated the runtime overhead, memory usage and the size, richness, and correctness of the generated data.

4.2 Experiment 2: Impact of Sampling Intervals

Similar to Experiment 1, we only used the tools that support sampling and evaluated the same comparison metrics. However, for this experiment, we used varying sampling intervals as follows: 1.25, 2.5, 5, 10, 20 ms. Sampling interval refers to the milliseconds spent between two samples (Caliper uses Hertz as a unit). For example, sampling interval with a value of 5 ms refers that the profiling tool samples the program for every 5 ms. This experiment shows whether tools can properly work when the sampling interval is low and how the performance and the generated data change as we change the interval.

4.3 Experiment 3: Comparison of Instrumentation Capabilities

In this experiment, we compared the instrumentation capabilities of Caliper, Score-P, and TAU since HPCToolkit does not support instrumentation. We tried to use the default instrumentation method that the tools support. By default, Caliper supports manual source instrumentation, Score-P supports compiler instrumentation, and TAU supports automatic source instrumentation. During the experiments, we realized that TAU's automatic source instrumentation, which uses PDT, gives errors for almost all of the runs because it is not fully updated. Therefore, we decided to use compiler instrumentation for TAU which works for all applications. Caliper requires manual annotations to perform the source instrumentation. We used annotated versions of LULESH and Quicksilver which are publicly shared by Caliper developers on Github and we annotated AMG by ourselves learning from the already available annotations. We evaluated the same comparison metrics also in this experiment and this experiment shows which tool or instrumentation method causes more overhead or can generate better data and how well these tools can perform an instrumentation method.

5 Evaluation

In this section, we present the findings of our empirical comparison of call graph data generation by different profiling tools.

5.1 Runtime Overhead

We first evaluate the runtime overhead of the profiling tools by performing experiments using instrumentation and sampling with default and varying intervals.

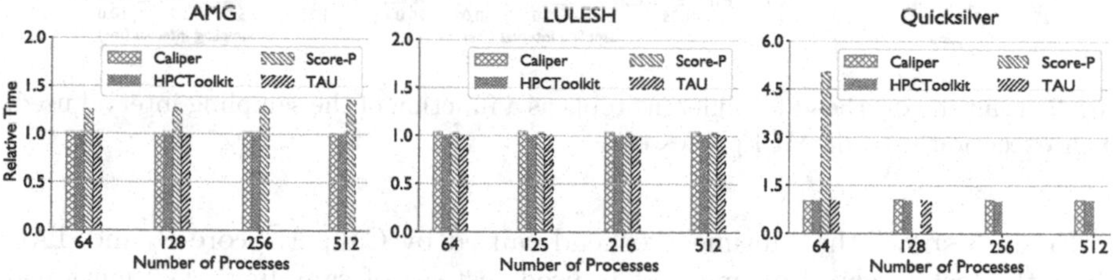

Fig. 1. Runtime overhead for different tools when the sampling method is used. Default sampling intervals (20, 5, 10, and 30 ms) were used for Caliper, HPCToolkit, Score-P, and TAU respectively.

Figure 1 shows runtime overheads caused by Caliper, HPCToolkit, Score-P, and TAU when we sample the programs using default sampling intervals. We can see that most tools have a small overhead (slightly over 1×) except Score-P. Score-P has ~1.25× overhead for AMG, ~1.02× for LULESH, and ~5× for

Quicksilver. We think that the significant difference between the overhead caused by Score-P and other tools is because Score-P samples instrumented executables while others can directly perform sampling on uninstrumented executables. Caliper, HPCToolkit, and TAU do not have a significant overhead. The overhead increases as we increase the number of processes but the increase is small. In addition, TAU fails to produce output when we use it with AMG and Quicksilver on 256 and 512 processes. Similarly, Score-P does not work when we run Quicksilver using 128, 256, and 512 processes. Both TAU and Score-P give segmentation faults in some runs. We tried to fix these errors by debugging, running the applications multiple times, and contacting the developers but could not find a solution.

In Fig. 2, we show the runtime overhead of the tools under varying sampling intervals (1.25–20.0 ms). It can be observed that the runtime overhead does not change significantly under different sampling intervals and the results are similar to what we see in Fig. 1. Hence, we can say that the sampling interval does not have a significant impact on the runtime overhead. We realized that Caliper, Score-P, and TAU do not work at all when the sampling interval is 1.25 ms on AMG and Quicksilver runs, and TAU and Score-P do not work deterministically under some sampling intervals. For example, sometimes three of five experiments run to completion while at other times, only one of them works. HPCToolkit works under all samplings intervals and its runtime overhead is stable in all settings.

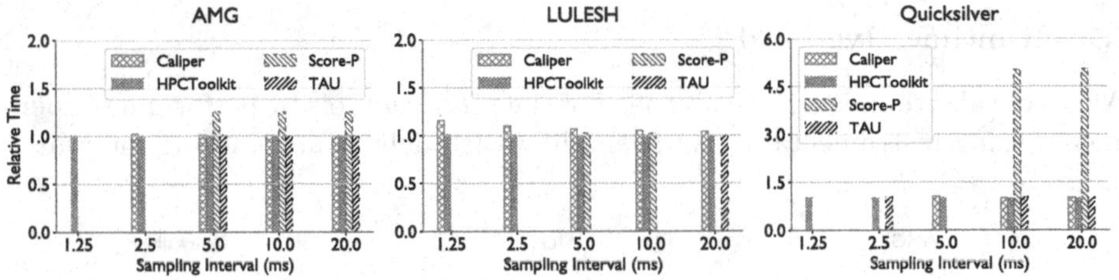

Fig. 2. Runtime overhead for different tools as a function of the sampling interval used. Each execution used 64 MPI processes.

Figure 3 shows the runtime overhead caused by Caliper, Score-P, and TAU when the instrumentation method is used instead of sampling. As mentioned before, we used automatic compiler instrumentation for both TAU and Score-P and manual source instrumentation for Caliper. All three plots in Fig. 3 show that Caliper results in lower runtime overhead. Interestingly, TAU has the highest runtime overhead (~2×) for LULESH while Score-P has the highest overhead for Quicksilver (~10×) although the same compiler version and same compiler wrappers that the tools provide are used. We believe this is related to the implementation details of each tool and how they handle some specific cases (e.g. inlining and loop optimizations). Therefore, we can say that compiler instrumentation is not stable under different conditions and is highly dependent on the application. We also note that TAU and Score-P's compiler instrumentation of Quicksilver causes more overhead compared to sampling (Fig. 1).

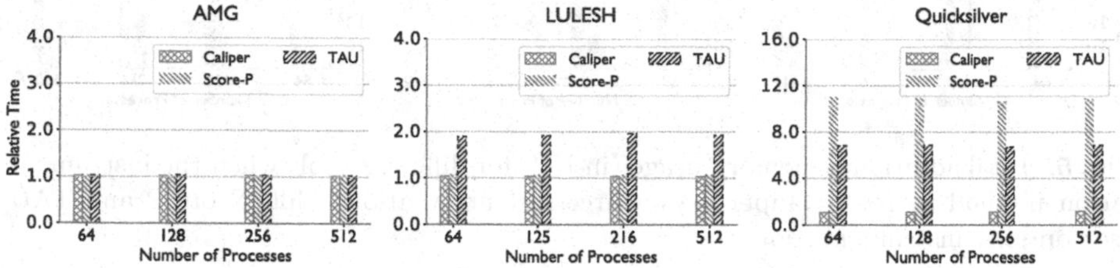

Fig. 3. Runtime overhead for different tools when the instrumentation method is used. Caliper uses source instrumentation, while Score-P and TAU use compiler instrumentation.

5.2 Memory Consumption

In this section, we evaluate the memory usage of each tool but we do not report the results under default sampling intervals because we observed that it does not change significantly depending on the sampling interval.

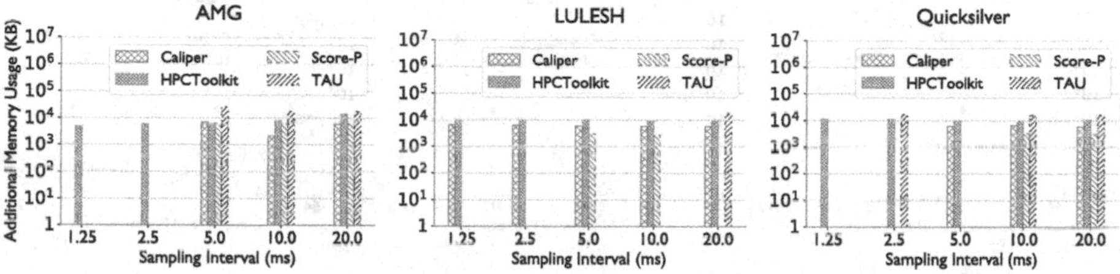

Fig. 4. Total additional memory usage (in KB) for different tools as a function of the sampling interval used. Each execution used 64 MPI processes.

Figures 4 and 5 show that the total memory usage for each tool typically does not change drastically with different applications, different numbers of processes, and different sampling intervals. It can be observed in both figures that TAU uses more memory in all of the runs where it works (~10 MB in sampling and ~100 MB in instrumentation) compared to the other tools. Score-P has the least memory usage except in AMG runs using 10 ms and 20 ms sampling intervals (see left plot in Fig. 4). HPCToolkit has the second-highest memory usage while Caliper has the third-highest. It can also be seen that TAU uses more memory when compiler instrumentation is used (~100 MB, Fig. 5) versus sampling (~10 MB, Fig. 4). Because of this significant difference between tools, we can say that memory usage is an important comparison metric to evaluate call graph data generation.

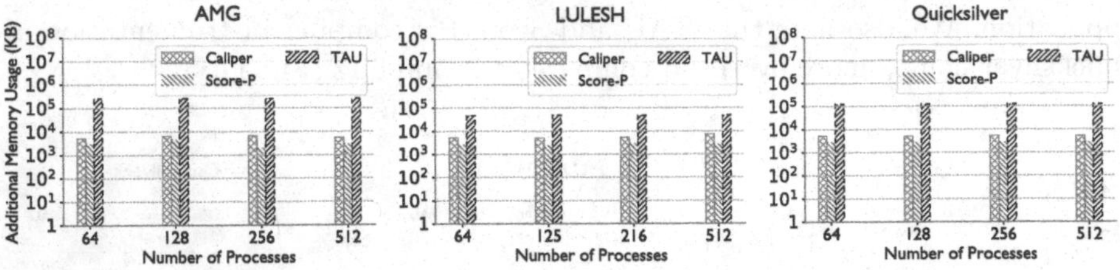

Fig. 5. Total additional memory usage (in KB) for different tools when the instrumentation method is used. Caliper uses source instrumentation, while Score-P and TAU use compiler instrumentation.

Next, we evaluate the quality of the generated call graph data considering the size, richness, and meaningfulness of the data.

5.3 Size of Call Graph Data

We compared the size of the generated call graph data while performing the same experiments. We observed that there is a significant difference between tools in terms of the size of the generated data.

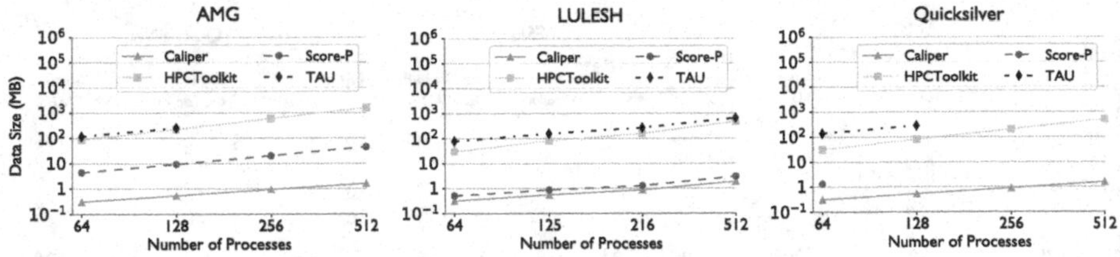

Fig. 6. Size of the profiling data (in MB) for different tools when the default sampling method is used. Default sampling intervals (20, 5, 10, and 30 ms) were used for Caliper, HPCToolkit, Score-P, and TAU respectively.

Figure 6 shows the increase in the data size when the default sampling method is used for each tool. The size of the generated data increases with an increase in the number of processes since data for more processes is being recorded. We can see that TAU generates the largest amount of data for all applications (from ~100 to ~1000 MB). In addition, TAU and HPCToolkit generate much more data compared to Score-P and Caliper because they generate a separate file for each process while Score-P and Caliper generate more compact data. For example, Caliper generates only a single *json* file that contains information about all the processes. In contrast, Fig. 7 shows the decrease in the data size under varying sampling intervals. In this case, the size of the data decreases as we increase the sampling interval since less data is being recorded as we increase the time between two samples. Interestingly, Caliper has an opposite behavior and it generates slightly more data as the sampling interval is increased. We examined the Caliper data and realized that it generates more nodes as we increase the interval up to 5.0 ms and then, it starts generating fewer nodes again.

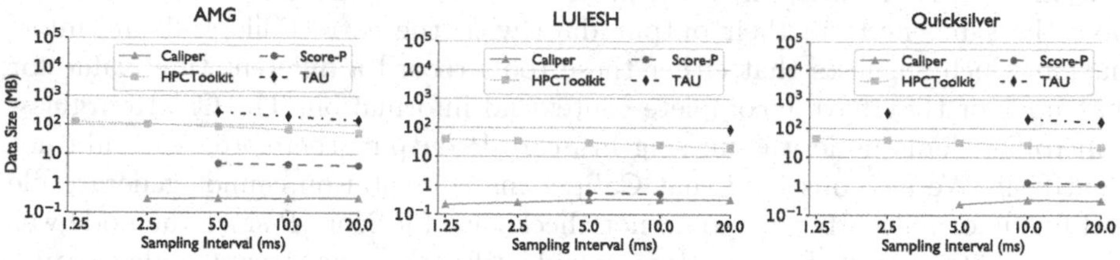

Fig. 7. Size of the profiling data (in MB) for different tools as a function of the sampling interval used. Each execution used 64 MPI processes.

Similar to Fig. 6, we see the increase in data size when using instrumentation in Fig. 8. As the number of processes is increased, TAU generates the largest amount of data. In addition, it can be also seen from LULESH plots in Figs. 6 and 8 that TAU generates more data when sampling is used instead of compiler instrumentation because it generates additional information such as `[CONTEXT]` and `[SAMPLE]` nodes. `[CONTEXT]` nodes do not store useful information and they can be removed from the data.

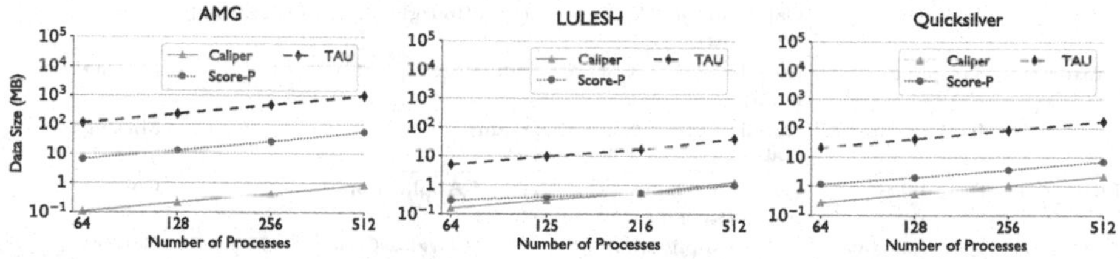

Fig. 8. Size of the profiling data (in MB) for different tools when the instrumentation method is used. Caliper uses source instrumentation, while Score-P and TAU use compiler instrumentation.

5.4 Correctness of Call Graph Data

In order to evaluate the correctness of the call graph data, we compare the two slowest nodes and their identified callpaths and summarize the other findings. We only report results for LULESH since we get similar results with other applications. First, we identified the slowest and the hot node for each tool and checked if the file and line information of the slowest node is correct. Table 2 shows the identified slowest nodes, hot nodes, and the correctness of file and line information for the slowest node. We assume that if the majority of the tools provide the same output, it should be close to the ground truth. As it can be seen from the table, Caliper instrumentation, HPCToolkit sampling, and TAU instrumentation can identify the same node, CalcHourglassControlForElems, as the slowest node with the correct file and line information. Caliper and TAU sampling cannot identify the same node as the slowest node although they also have the same node in their output data with the correct file and line information which suggests that either these tools record a different time value for that node or they have incomplete contextual information. The CalcHourglass-ControlForElems node was missing in Score-P output, therefore, we could not identify it. We also observed that Caliper instrumentation cannot generate file and line information but we could not check that for Score-P since the node was missing in its output. Score-P does not identify the same slowest node because it does not record information for inlined functions by default but provides an option to enable it.

Table 2. Comparison of the correctness of the generated call graph data for different tools when the default sampling interval and instrumentation method are used. The data was generated by executing LULESH using 64 MPI processes.

Tool	Method	Slowest node (inc. time, exc. time)	Hot node	File & line correctness
Caliper	Sampling	(main, syscall)***	main***	Correct**
	Instrumentation	(main, CalcHourglassControl-ForElems)	lulesh.cycle	Missing
HPCToolkit	Sampling	(main, CalcHourglassControl-ForElems)	Loop in lulesh.cc at line 1048 (CalcHourglassControlForElems)	Correct Correct
Score-P	Sampling	(lulesh-scorep2.0 (main), main)	lulesh-scorep2.0 (main)	Missing
	Instrumentation	(lulesh-scorep2.0 (main), main)	main	Missing
TAU	Sampling	(progress_engine, progress_engine)***	.TAU Application***	Correct**
	Instrumentation	(.TAU Application (main), CalcHourglass-ControlForElems)	CalcHourglassControlForElems	Correct

Figure 9 shows the callpath for the commonly identified slowest node, CalcHourglassControlForElems. We confirm that TAU and Caliper sampling outputs (Fig. 9(b), 9(a)) contain information about that node and can generate its callpath although they cannot identify it as the slowest node. We can see from TAU and Caliper sampling callpaths that they do not aggregate the measured time values for that node and they connect the nodes related to it directly to the main node which results in having many related nodes with low time values. In addition, Caliper sampling cannot generate the name of the node as seen in Fig. 9(a), and the only way to find it is to use the line information on the output for that node. Score-P is missing that node in its output, therefore, it is

```
21.939 _start
└─ 21.939 __libc_start_main
   └─ 21.939 main
      ├─ 4.264 lulesh.cc:1062
      ├─ 4.283 lulesh.cc:1063
      ├─ 4.502 lulesh.cc:1064
      ├─ 4.450 lulesh.cc:1065
      └─ 4.439 lulesh.cc:1066
```

(a) Caliper (sampling)

```
78.569 .TAU application
└─ 10.140 [CONTEXT] .TAU application
   ├─ 0.003 [UNWIND] lulesh.cc.1048
   │  └─ 0.003 [SAMPLE] CalcHourglassControlForElems
   ├─ 0.053 [UNWIND] lulesh.cc.1053
   │  └─ 0.053 [SAMPLE] CalcHourglassControlForElems
   ├─ 1.468 [UNWIND] lulesh.cc.1061
   │  └─ 1.468 [SAMPLE] CalcHourglassControlForElems
   ├─ 1.659 [UNWIND] lulesh.cc.1062
   │  └─ 1.659 [SAMPLE] CalcHourglassControlForElems
   ├─ 1.658 [UNWIND] lulesh.cc.1063
   │  └─ 1.658 [SAMPLE] CalcHourglassControlForElems
   ├─ 1.721 [UNWIND] lulesh.cc.1064
   │  └─ 1.721 [SAMPLE] CalcHourglassControlForElems
   ├─ 1.678 [UNWIND] lulesh.cc.1065
   │  └─ 1.678 [SAMPLE] CalcHourglassControlForElems
   ├─ 1.742 [UNWIND] lulesh.cc.1066
   │  └─ 1.742 [SAMPLE] CalcHourglassControlForElems
   ├─ 0.050 [UNWIND] lulesh.cc.1069
   │  └─ 0.050 [SAMPLE] CalcHourglassControlForElems
   ├─ 0.109 [UNWIND] lulesh.cc.1072
   │  └─ 0.109 [SAMPLE] CalcHourglassControlForElems
   └─ 0.000 [UNWIND] lulesh.cc.1082
      ├─ 0.000 [SAMPLE] CalcHourglassControlForElems
      └─ 0.000 [UNWIND] CalcHourglassControlForElems
```

(b) TAU (sampling)

```
10.482 <program root>
└─ 10.482 main
   └─ 10.482 Loop@lulesh.cc:2881
      └─ 10.482 2887:LagrangeLeapFrog
         └─ 10.482 2720:LagrangeNodal
            └─ 10.482 1285:CalcForceForNodes
               └─ 10.046 1168:CalcVolumeForceForElems
                  └─ 9.951 1135:CalcHourglassControlForElems
```

(c) HPCToolkit

```
77.760 main
└─ 77.667 lulesh.cycle
   └─ 77.661 LagrangeLeapFrog
      └─ 77.652 LagrangeNodal
         └─ 71.833 CalcForceForNodes
            └─ 70.575 CalcVolumeForceForElems
               └─ 68.212 CalcHourglassControlForElems
```

(d) Caliper (instrumentation)

```
132.265 .TAU application
└─ 132.229 main
   └─ 132.226 LagrangeLeapFrog
      └─ 132.221 LagrangeNodal
         └─ 132.206 CalcForceForNodes
            └─ 130.930 CalcVolumeForceForElems
               └─ 130.752 CalcHourglassControlForElems
```

(e) TAU (instrumentation)

Fig. 9. Callpath of the CalcHourglassControlForElems node obtained by different tools for LULESH running on 64 processes.

not included in this figure. In summary, TAU and Caliper sampling and Score-P generate incomplete call graphs for LULESH compared to TAU instrumentation, Caliper instrumentation, and HPCToolkit.

We also investigated the top five slowest nodes and observed that Caliper instrumentation, HPCToolkit, and TAU instrumentation identify almost the same nodes as the top five but the order of the top five list is somewhat different in each tool. Score-P sampling and instrumentation also find similar top five slowest nodes with greater differences. Caliper and TAU sampling do not identify the same slowest nodes. We present the call paths of the second slowest node in Fig. 10. The leaf node in each call path is the second slowest node. It can be seen that the leaf nodes are usually different from each other except for a few similarities. Score-P instrumentation (Fig. 10(f)) identifies the same second slowest node as TAU instrumentation (Fig. 10(g)). However, their callpaths are not identical since they handle inlined functions differently. Similarly, Score-P sampling (Fig. 10(d)) identifies the same second slowest node as HPCToolkit (Fig. 10(b)) but the callpaths are different. In addition, Caliper instrumentation (Fig. 10(e)) does not identify the same slowest node but the node identified by Caliper is also in the top five list of HPCToolkit and TAU instrumentation. Caliper sampling (Fig. 10(a)) and TAU sampling (Fig. 10(c)) do not provide as meaningful results. Note that we do not have Score-P results in Fig. 9 because Score-P identifies the main node as the slowest node and the slowest node that is commonly identified by other tools does not exist in the Score-P output.

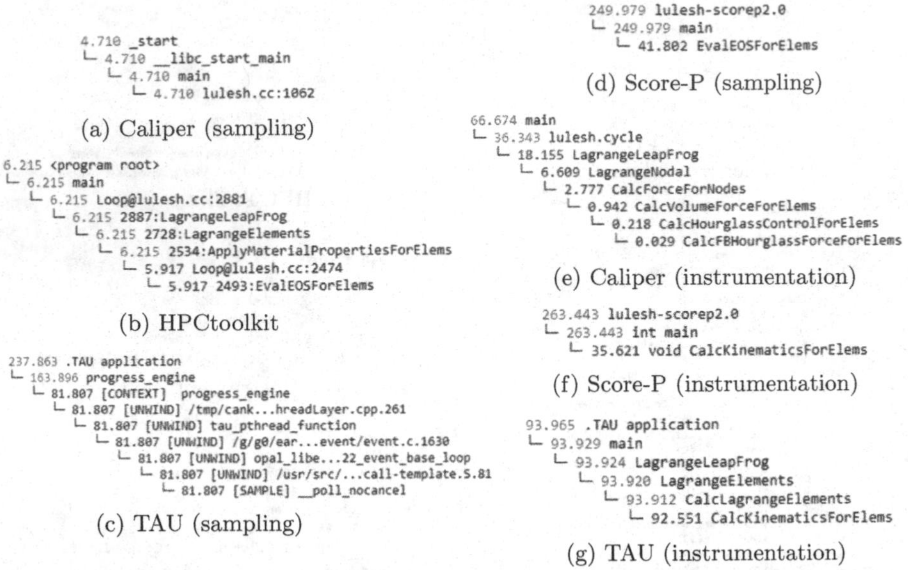

(a) Caliper (sampling)

(b) HPCtoolkit

(c) TAU (sampling)

(d) Score-P (sampling)

(e) Caliper (instrumentation)

(f) Score-P (instrumentation)

(g) TAU (instrumentation)

Fig. 10. Callpath of the second slowest node obtained by different tools for LULESH running on 64 processes.

However, it identifies the same second slowest node as some other profiling tools, hence, we included Score-P in Fig. 10.

5.5 Richness of Call Graph Data

We compared the richness of the call graph data generated by the profiling tools considering the maximum and average callpath depth, the number of nodes, the number of dynamically loaded libraries (.so files), and the number of MPI functions. The data is gathered by running each application on 64 processes.

Table 3 shows the richness of the data generated by each tool using their default method. The fourth and fifth columns show the maximum and average callpath lengths in the call graph data. The callpaths generated by HPCToolkit and Caliper sampling usually have similar depths. TAU and Score-P compiler instrumentation abnormally generate very long callpaths for a node called `hypre_qsort0` which is a recursive sorting function. Interestingly, they keep creating a new callpath for that function every time it calls itself instead of aggregating its information. The other tools usually generate callpaths that have fewer than ten nodes. The length of the callpaths might be related to how well a tool can handle inlined functions, but generating unnecessary data might also result in longer callpaths. Therefore, we cannot infer that a longer callpath is richer. In addition, some of these tools allow the user to set the maximum callpath length to be recorded, so expert users could adjust it depending on their needs. Therefore, this comparison gives insights on tools' and profiling methods'

Table 3. Comparison of the richness of the generated data for different tools when a fixed sampling interval (20.0 ms) and the instrumentation method are used. Each execution used 64 MPI processes.

App.	Tool	Method	Max depth	Avg depth	No. of nodes (all, unq)	No. of .so files (all, unq)	No. of MPI functions (all, unq)
AMG	Caliper	Sampling	30	9.724	(1414, 739)	(363, **36**)	(37, 17)
		Instrumentation	3	2.384	(50, 22)	0	(38, 10)
	HPCToolkit	Sampling	**35**	**13.931**	(12112, **2528**)	(**4616**, 25)	(585, 66)
	Score-P	Sampling	63	10.859	(1470, 199)	0	(668, 52)
		Instrumentation	163*	31.428*	(3117, 332)	0	(676, 51)
	TAU	Sampling	12	8.416	(**13645**, 1976)	(2010, 20)	(**1036**, **91**)
		Instrumentation	111*	10.12*	(1956, 334)	0	(683, 52)
LULESH	Caliper	Sampling	19	3.984	(832, 729)	(96, **47**)	(7, 6)
		Instrumentation	7	5.115	(71, 31)	0	(40, 7)
	HPCToolkit	Sampling	**23**	**10.412**	(4546, **1775**)	(**1496**, 22)	(96, **81**)
	Score-P	Sampling	5	3.0	(97, 65)	0	(19, 11)
		Instrumentation	4	2.656	(43, 34)	0	(19, 11)
	TAU	Sampling	12	5.473	(**4999**, 1281)	(915, 12)	(**236**, 32)
		Instrumentation	8	4.408	(114, 78)	0	(36, 11)
Quicksilver	Caliper	Sampling	**30**	10.703	(1495, 807)	(413, **25**)	(17, 8)
		Instrumentation	8	3.937	(122, 84)	0	(36, 7)
	HPCToolkit	Sampling	29	**14.376**	(5253, **2392**)	(**1307**, 22)	(24, 15)
	Score-P	Sampling	10	5.05	(343, 206)	0	(40, 15)
		Instrumentation	9	5.184	(418, 267)	0	(80, 29)
	TAU	Sampling	12	7.802	(**7776**, 1779)	(731, 16)	(**230**, **41**)
		Instrumentation	9	4.831	(401, 246)	0	(47, 18)

capabilities for generating sufficient call graph data with enough caller-callee relationships.

The next column shows the number of all and unique nodes. HPCToolkit data usually contains more unique nodes although TAU sampling usually has the largest number of nodes. We believe that it is related to how `[UNWIND]` nodes are stored in TAU data format since we realized that they include unnecessary information (confirmed by TAU developers). This suggests that the information is not stored as efficiently in TAU. Caliper and Score-P usually generate call graphs with fewer nodes since they generate less data.

The difference between the number of all `.so` files generated by different tools is larger than the difference between the number of unique `.so` files. For example, while HPCToolkit output contains a much larger number of `.so` files compared to Caliper sampling, the number of unique `.so` files in Caliper sampling is larger. The reason is that HPCToolkit can identify more dynamically loaded libraries while Caliper can identify only some of them so the number of all `.so` files is much higher in HPCToolkit data. We also realized that the number of unique `.so` files are is significantly different from each other when sampling is used. However, Score-P does not provide information about `.so` files when we use sampling. The table also shows that `.so` files cannot be identified when using instrumentation which is expected since they are dynamically loaded libraries.

We emphasize that it does not imply that the instrumentation method provides poor call graph data compared to the sampling method since information about `.so` files might not be necessary for some analyses.

The last column shows the number of MPI functions. We investigated how many MPI functions can be detected by each tool since it is a commonly used programming model. TAU sampling generates a significantly large number of MPI functions in all applications compared to other tools. As mentioned before, the reason might be that TAU generates unnecessary `[CONTEXT]` nodes that do not contain useful information and these nodes are mostly related to MPI functions.

In summary, all the information about runtime overhead, memory usage, and data size should be connected to the quality of output to have a more complete evaluation of call graph data generation. We emphasize that we cannot conclude that a tool provides richer call graph data by only looking at Table 3. However, this comparison shows some characteristics, abnormalities, and sufficiency of call graph data generated by different tools.

6 Discussion

Our comparative evaluation shows that the runtime overhead when using profiling tools is similar, except in the case of Score-P for some applications. Additional memory consumed by a tool does not vary significantly with the application being profiled. In general, we can order the memory usage of tools from highest to lowest as TAU, HPCToolkit, Caliper, and Score-P. Also, TAU typically generates the largest amount of data with HPCToolkit being a close second. The size of the data generated by Score-P and Caliper is notably lower compared to TAU and HPCToolkit because their representation of output data is more compact. The top five slowest nodes identified by the profiling tools are usually similar to each other except when using sampling in Caliper and TAU. However, although different tools identify the same nodes as slow, the relative ordering of the top five slowest nodes is usually different from each other. In terms of call path completeness, Caliper instrumentation, TAU instrumentation and HPCToolkit generate more complete call graphs in default mode.

After extensively using and evaluating the tools, we are also in a position to provide some feedback to their respective developers. From all the figures in Sect. 5.3, it can be seen that TAU usually generates the largest amount of data. The reason for this is that it stores repetitive information such as `[CONTEXT]` nodes. These nodes do not have useful metric values and could be removed from the generated data. In addition, TAU stores the same metric information twice – in a separate line by itself and at the end of each callpath. This can be optimized by storing the information only once. When we implemented a reader for TAU output in Hatchet, we realized that TAU generates a separate file for each metric that contains exactly the same callpath information when more than one metric is measured. The size of the output data can be further reduced by storing the call graph only once.

When using the instrumentation method in Caliper, we observed that Caliper does not generate file and line number information in instrumentation only mode. Although we perform manual source instrumentation in this study, it would be helpful for the end user if file and line number information was in the output. Finally, when using sampling in Caliper and TAU and either method in Score-P, the generated call graphs are relatively incomplete on the experiments performed in this study. We believe that their callpath generation capabilities can be improved.

In summary, we performed the first empirical study to compare call graph data generation capabilities of profiling tools considering many different aspects. We used these tools as per their official documentation and contacted the tool developers when needed. This study shows that more comprehensive evaluation studies on profiling tools considering their scalability and other performance analysis capabilities may reveal interesting information and could be helpful for the community. In the future, we plan to extend this work by using production applications, collecting other structural information, and performing more empirical and analytical analyses on the output data.

Acknowledgments. This work was supported by funding provided by the University of Maryland College Park Foundation.

References

1. Adhianto, L., et al.: HPCTOOLKIT: tools for performance analysis of optimized parallel programs. Concurr. Comput. Pract. Exp. **22**(6), 685–701 (2010)
2. Adhianto, L., Mellor-Crummey, J., Tallent, N.R.: Effectively presenting call path profiles of application performance. In: 2010 39th International Conference on Parallel Processing Workshops, pp. 179–188. IEEE (2010)
3. Bell, R., Malony, A.D., Shende, S.: *ParaProf*: a portable, extensible, and scalable tool for parallel performance profile analysis. In: Kosch, H., Böszörményi, L., Hellwagner, H. (eds.) Euro-Par 2003. LNCS, vol. 2790, pp. 17–26. Springer, Heidelberg (2003). https://doi.org/10.1007/978-3-540-45209-6_7
4. Bhatele, A., Brink, S., Gamblin, T.: Hatchet: pruning the overgrowth in parallel profiles. In: Proceedings of the ACM/IEEE International Conference for High Performance Computing, Networking, Storage and Analysis, SC 2019, November 2019. https://doi.org/10.1145/3295500.3356219. lLNL-CONF-772402
5. Boehme, D., et al.: Caliper: performance introspection for HPC software stacks. In: SC 2016: Proceedings of the International Conference for High Performance Computing, Networking, Storage and Analysis, pp. 550–560 (2016). https://doi.org/10.1109/SC.2016.46
6. Henson, V.E., Yang, U.M.: BoomerAMG: a parallel algebraic multigrid solver and preconditioner. Appl. Numer. Math. **41**(1), 155–177 (2002). https://doi.org/10.1016/S0168-9274(01)00115-5. https://www.sciencedirect.com/science/article/pii/S0168927401001155. Developments and Trends in Iterative Methods for Large Systems of Equations - in Memorium Rudiger Weiss
7. Karlin, I., Keasler, J., Neely, R.: Lulesh 2.0 updates and changes. Technical report LLNL-TR-641973, August 2013

8. Knobloch, M., Mohr, B.: Tools for GPU computing-debugging and performance analysis of heterogenous HPC applications. Supercomput. Front. Innov. **7**(1), 91–111 (2020)
9. Knüpfer, A., et al.: Score-p: a joint performance measurement run-time infrastructure for periscope, Scalasca, TAU, and Vampir. In: Brunst, H., Müller, M.S., Nagel, W.E., Resch, M.M. (eds.) Tools for High Performance Computing 2011, pp. 79–91. Springer, Heidelberg (2012). https://doi.org/10.1007/978-3-642-31476-6_7
10. Leko, A., Sherburne, H., Su, H., Golden, B., George, A.D.: Practical experiences with modern parallel performance analysis tools: an evaluation. In: Parallel and Distributed Processing, IPDPS 2008 IEEE Symposium, pp. 14–18 (2008)
11. Lindlan, K.A., et al.: A tool framework for static and dynamic analysis of object-oriented software with templates. In: SC 2000: Proceedings of the 2000 ACM/IEEE Conference on Supercomputing, p. 49. IEEE (2000)
12. Liu, X., Mellor-Crummey, J.: A tool to analyze the performance of multithreaded programs on NUMA architectures. ACM Sigplan Not. **49**(8), 259–272 (2014)
13. Madsen, J.R., et al.: Timemory: modular performance analysis for HPC. In: Sadayappan, P., Chamberlain, B.L., Juckeland, G., Ltaief, H. (eds.) ISC High Performance 2020. LNCS, vol. 12151, pp. 434–452. Springer, Cham (2020). https://doi.org/10.1007/978-3-030-50743-5_22
14. Malony, A.D., Huck, K.A.: General hybrid parallel profiling. In: 2014 22nd Euromicro International Conference on Parallel, Distributed, and Network-Based Processing, pp. 204–212. IEEE (2014)
15. Mellor-Crummey, J., Fowler, R., Marin, G.: HPCView: a tool for top-down analysis of node performance. J. Supercomput. **23**, 81–101 (2002). https://doi.org/10.1023/A:1015789220266
16. Mohr, B.: Scalable parallel performance measurement and analysis tools-state-of-the-art and future challenges. Supercomput. Front. Innov. **1**(2), 108–123 (2014)
17. Nataraj, A., Sottile, M., Morris, A., Malony, A.D., Shende, S.: *TAUoverSupermon*: low-overhead online parallel performance monitoring. In: Kermarrec, A.-M., Bougé, L., Priol, T. (eds.) Euro-Par 2007. LNCS, vol. 4641, pp. 85–96. Springer, Heidelberg (2007). https://doi.org/10.1007/978-3-540-74466-5_11
18. Nethercote, N.: Dynamic binary analysis and instrumentation. Technical report, University of Cambridge, Computer Laboratory (2004)
19. Richards, D.F., Bleile, R.C., Brantley, P.S., Dawson, S.A., McKinley, M.S., O'Brien, M.J.: Quicksilver: a proxy app for the monte Carlo transport code mercury. In: 2017 IEEE International Conference on Cluster Computing (CLUSTER), pp. 866–873. IEEE (2017)
20. Saviankou, P., Knobloch, M., Visser, A., Mohr, B.: Cube v4: from performance report explorer to performance analysis tool. Procedia Comput. Sci. **51**, 1343–1352 (2015)
21. Shende, S., Malony, A.D.: Integration and application of TAU in parallel Java environments. Concurr. Comput. Pract. Exp. **15**(3–5), 501–519 (2003)
22. Shende, S.S., Malony, A.D.: The TAU parallel performance system. Int. J. High Perform. Comput. Appl. **20**(2), 287–311 (2006)
23. Tallent, N.R., Mellor-Crummey, J.M., Fagan, M.W.: Binary analysis for measurement and attribution of program performance. ACM Sigplan Not. **44**(6), 441–452 (2009)

MAPredict: Static Analysis Driven Memory Access Prediction Framework for Modern CPUs

Mohammad Alaul Haque Monil[1,2](✉), Seyong Lee[2], Jeffrey S. Vetter[2], and Allen D. Malony[1]

[1] University of Oregon, Eugene, OR, USA
{mmonil,malony}@cs.uoregon.com

[2] Oak Ridge National Laboratory, Oak Ridge, TN, USA
{monilm,lees2}@ornl.gov, vetter@computer.org

Abstract. Application memory access patterns are crucial in deciding how much traffic is served by the cache and forwarded to the dynamic random-access memory (DRAM). However, predicting such memory traffic is difficult because of the interplay of prefetchers, compilers, parallel execution, and innovations in manufacturer-specific micro-architectures. This research introduced MAPredict, a static analysis-driven framework that addresses these challenges to predict last-level cache (LLC)-DRAM traffic. By exploring and analyzing the behavior of modern Intel processors, MAPredict formulates cache-aware analytical models. MAPredict invokes these models to predict LLC-DRAM traffic by combining the application model, machine model, and user-provided hints to capture dynamic information. MAPredict successfully predicts LLC-DRAM traffic for different regular access patterns and provides the means to combine static and empirical observations for irregular access patterns. Evaluating 130 workloads from six applications on recent Intel micro-architectures, MAPredict yielded an average accuracy of 99% for streaming, 91% for strided, and 92% for stencil patterns. By coupling static and empirical methods, up to 97% average accuracy was obtained for random access patterns on different micro-architectures.

1 Introduction

Recent innovations in computing have been shaped by the end of Dennard scaling and the need to address the memory wall problem. As a result, multicore

---

This manuscript has been authored by UT-Battelle LLC, under contract DE-AC05-00OR22725 with the US Department of Energy (DOE). The US government retains and the publisher, by accepting the article for publication, acknowledges that the US government retains a nonexclusive, paid-up, irrevocable, worldwide license to publish or reproduce the published form of this manuscript, or allow others to do so, for US government purposes. DOE will provide public access to these results of federally sponsored research in accordance with the DOE Public Access Plan (http://energy.gov/downloads/doe-public-access-plan).

A.-L. Varbanescu et al. (Eds.): ISC High Performance 2022, LNCS 13289, pp. 233–255, 2022.
https://doi.org/10.1007/978-3-031-07312-0_12

and manycore processors with multilevel memory hierarchies on heterogeneous systems are becoming increasingly common [1]. With increasing hardware complexity, designing analytical models becomes a nontrivial task. With the rise of heterogeneous systems, the importance of such a modeling approach for prediction has increased significantly. Because executing an application on an ill-suited processor may result in nonoptimal performance [2], the runtime system must quickly decide where to execute kernels on the fly. Predicting a kernel's performance and energy consumption can enable runtime systems to make intelligent decisions. For such predictions, floating-point operations (FLOPs) and memory traffic (last-level cache [LLC]-dynamic random-access memory [DRAM] traffic) are important metrics to determine. Although calculating the number of FLOPs is fairly straightforward, statically predicting memory traffic is complex because the memory access request can be served by the cache or DRAM.

Statically predicting LLC-DRAM traffic is vital for three reasons. First, a heterogeneous runtime system can make intelligent scheduling decisions if it can statically identify compute and memory-bound kernels based on the Roofline model [3]. A study named MEPHESTO [2] demonstrated that energy performance–aware scheduling decisions can be made based on operational intensity (FLOPs per LLC-DRAM bytes) of kernels. Tools such as Intel Advisor and NVIDIA Nsight Compute can generate the operational intensity of a kernel. However, a runtime system needs this information before executing the kernel to make better placement decisions. Although static analysis tools can provide the FLOP count at compile time [4], statically predicting LLC-DRAM traffic must be explored. Simulation frameworks can provide LLC-DRAM traffic, but they are not fast enough to be integrated into a runtime system [5]. Second, developing a framework to predict the energy and performance of modern CPUs requires predicting LLC-DRAM memory transactions because LLC-DRAM transactions incur a significant amount of energy and time [6]. Finally, a static approach for predicting the LLC-DRAM traffic enables simulation-based design space exploration to determine the best memory configuration. For these reasons, this study aims to build a framework capable of predicting the LLC-DRAM traffic statically. However, a static analysis approach for predicting the LLC-DRAM traffic encounters three main challenges: (1) it must keep up with the continuous innovation in the processors' memory hierarchy, (2) it must deal with the complex memory access patterns and different execution models (sequential and parallel), and (3) it does not have access to the dynamic information needed to obtain high prediction accuracy.

This research presents MAPredict, a framework that predicts the LLC-DRAM traffic for applications in modern CPUs. To the best of the authors' knowledge, this is the first framework that simultaneously addresses all of the aforementioned challenges. This paper presents systematic experimentation on different Intel microarchitectures to elicit their memory subsystem behavior and build the analytical model for a range of memory access patterns. Through static analysis at compile time, MAPredict creates Abstract Scalable Performance Engineering Notation (Aspen) [7] application models from annotated source code, captures the dynamic information, and identifies the memory access patterns. It then couples the application and machine models to accurately predict the LLC-DRAM traffic.

Table 1. Machines and micro-architectures.

Name	Year	Processor detail. Here, L3 = LLC
BW	2016	Xeon E5-2683 v4, 32 cores, L2 - 256 KiB, L3 - 40 MiB
SK	2017	Xeon Silver 4114, 20 cores, L2 - 1 MiB, L3 - 14 MiB
CS	2019	Xeon Gold 6248, 40 cores, L2 - 1 MiB, L3 - 28 MiB
CP	2020	Xeon Gold 6348H, 96 cores, L2 - 1 MiB, L3 - 132 MiB

This paper reports the following contributions:

- a systematic unveiling of the behavior of Intel CPUs for read and write strategies that accounts for prefetchers, compilers, and multithreaded executions;
- a formulation of a cache- and prefetching-aware analytical model using application, machine, and compiler features;
- a static analysis-driven framework named MAPredict to predict LLC-DRAM traffic at compile time by source code analysis, dynamic information, and analytical modeling; and
- an evaluation of the MAPredict using 130 workloads (summation of number_of_functions * input_sizes) from six benchmarks in four micro-architectures of Intel in which higher prediction accuracy was achieved for regular access patterns compared with the models from literature. MAPredict also provides means to combine static and empirical observation for irregular access.

2 Understanding Memory Reads and Writes in Intel Processors

This section introduces the hardware, LLC-DRAM traffic measurement strategy, and the factors that trigger an LLC-DRAM transaction. From the application's viewpoint, the memory access pattern is crucial. The two most common memory access patterns—sequential streaming access and strided memory access—were considered. Cache line size, page size, initialization, and prefetching mechanism were identified as important factors. This section also explores the effects of the evolution of CPU micro-architectures.

2.1 Hardware Description

Intel CPUs were considered in this study because they are the most widely available processors in high-performance computing (HPC) facilities [8]. Table 1 depicts the four recent micro-architectures that were a part of this study: Broadwell (BW), Skylake (SK), Cascade Lake (CS), and Cooper Lake (CP). The introduction of the noninclusive victim L3 cache and the larger L2 cache (starting from the SK processors) is the most important change concerning the memory subsystem [9]. The findings from this work can also be extended for other manufacturers, including GPUs [10].

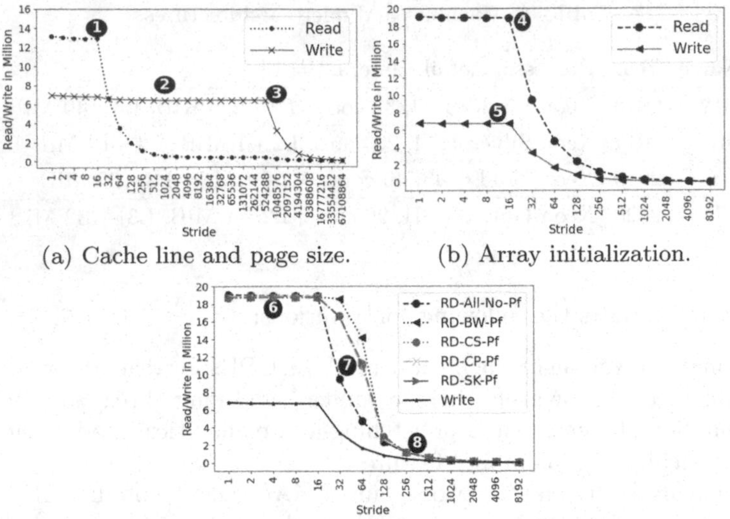

(a) Cache line and page size. (b) Array initialization.

(c) Prefetchers.

Fig. 1. LLC-DRAM traffic for different read and write scenarios in Intel processors. LLC-DRAM traffic is shown at the y-axis. Here, *RD-All-No-Pf* = read traffic for all micro-architectures with prefetching disabled and *RD-BW-Pf* = read traffic for Broadwell micro-architecture with prefetching enabled.

2.2 A Tool for Measuring the LLC-DRAM Traffic

All the LLC-DRAM traffic measurements reported in this study were gathered through a script-based dynamic analysis tool. The dynamic analysis tool uses Tuning and Analysis Utilities (TAU) [11] and Performance Application Programming Interface (PAPI) [12] to measure function-wise LLC-DRAM traffic from uncore counters (imcX::UNC_M_CAS_COUNT) of the integrated memory controllers. This tool provides LLC-DRAM traffic measurement in the unit of cache line (64 bytes), and this unit was followed throughout this study.

2.3 Different Read and Write Strategies

To investigate the application-cache interplay, a variant of vector multiplication code that exhibits sequential streaming (stride = 1) and strided access pattern (stride > 1) was considered. The code has three arrays (100 million 32 bit floating points). The cache line length of these Intel processors is 64 bytes and an array size of 100 million should generate 6.25 million writes and 12.5 million reads (two reads and one write per index). However, Fig. 1 indicates otherwise, as discussed in the following sections.

Effect of Cache Line Size. In Fig. 1a, the read-write traffic is shown where the read traffic is near 12.5 million for stride 1. This trend continues until stride 16

(64 bytes/size_of_32bit_float = 16), referenced by ❶. Because a cache line is 64 bytes long, while fetching one 32 bit floating-point data, the memory subsystem fetches 15 (60 bytes' worth) additional neighboring data. After stride 16 at ❶, the read traffic halves every time the stride is doubled. Write traffic for stride 1 is also near 6.25 million. However, for the write traffic, region ❷ stretches up to a stride of 524,288. For a stride of one (100 million access) and a stride 524,288 (only 190 access), the same number of cache lines (6.25 million) are transferred.

Effect of Page Size. In Fig. 1a, the effect of page zeroing is visible because of uninitialized write array. The write traffic in Fig. 1a is unaffected by the cache line size and depends instead on the page size. The default page size on Intel processors is 4 KiB (i.e., a stride of 1,024 for a 32 bit floating point). Linux supports "transparent huge pages," which allows for larger page sizes. Intel processors support large pages of 2 MiB and 1 GiB. In this case, a page size of 2 MiB was selected by the OS. This explains why there is a transition at ❸ on a stride of 524,288 (524,288 * size_of_32bit_float = 2 MiB).

Effect of Initialization. Figure 1b shows traffic when the write array is initialized. The write traffic is near 6.25 million at stride 1, and at this point, the effect of the cache line size is visible at ❺. Specifically, the impact of page zeroing is not observed like Fig. 1a. After a stride of 16, the traffic is reduced by half when the stride is doubled. However, the read traffic is near 18.75 million for stride 1, indicating the effect of "allocating store" (i.e., the region indicated by ❹).

Effect of Hardware Prefetching. Intel implements aggressive prefetching, but not all the details are openly available to the community. In the experimental results shown in Fig. 1a and Fig. 1b, prefetching is disabled. Three regions in read traffic are shown in Fig. 1c. The regions ❻ (strides 1–16) and ❽ (strides 128 and onward) show no visible difference with prefetching enabled. Further investigation by experimenting with a smaller stride confirmed that the effect of prefetching vanishes after a stride of 80 (indicated by ❽). The region ❼ (from strides 32–128) shows that extra cache lines were fetched. Because of Intel's prefetchers, for a stride of 64, each access could result in three cache lines being fetched. Moreover, the prefetching behavior in region ❼ is not the same for all micro-architectures. Read traffic is 10% higher in BW than in SK, CS, and CP, which show the same level of read traffic. This observation could be attributed to the change in the cache subsystem design following the BW micro-architecture.

Effect of Compiler and Multithreaded Execution. The GNU compiler was used to generate Fig. 1. However, using the Intel compiler can provide a different result because of the default "streaming store" or "nontemporal store" for a stride of 1. For streaming store, data are not read from the DRAM for a store miss. Instead, the data are written to DRAM through a write-combining buffer. When experimenting with a multithreaded version, the authors found no difference when one thread and 16 thread executions were compared.

3 Modeling Different Types of Access

A static analysis framework needs analytical models for different types of memory access patterns to predict the LLC-DRAM traffic. This section builds on the findings from Sect. 2 to formulate analytical models for different access patterns. This section discusses three kinds of regular access patterns. First, the model is formulated for the sequential streaming access pattern to predict LLC-DRAM cacheline transfer. Then, models are prepared for other access patterns by using the model for streaming access patterns. Finally, irregular random access patterns are discussed.

3.1 Sequential Streaming Access Pattern

The sequential streaming access pattern (i.e., stride = 1) is one of the most common access patterns found in applications. Prefetching does not affect the amount of traffic transferred between LLC and DRAM for this pattern. However, the effect of the cache line and page size must be considered.

Read Traffic. Because the LLC-DRAM read transaction is performed in a unit of cache lines, the amount of read traffic can be expressed using Eq. (1). In Eq. (1), a data structure size is $\text{Element}_{\text{count}}$, and the size of each element is $\text{Element}_{\text{size}}$ bytes. $\text{Read}_{\text{count}}$ is the number of LLC-DRAM transactions for reading a data structure. Data structure initialization has no effect on $\text{Read}_{\text{count}}$. Because alignment is uncertain, the ceiling is considered.

$$\text{Read}_{\text{count}} = \left\lceil \frac{\text{Element}_{\text{count}} * \text{Element}_{\text{size}}}{\text{Cacheline}_{\text{size}}} \right\rceil. \tag{1}$$

Write Traffic. The initialization of the data structures is crucial for write traffic. At first, the case in which the data structure is not initialized but only memory is allocated is discussed. For such a case, the page size becomes the deciding factor because of page zeroing, as shown in Sect. 2.3. In Eq. (2), $\text{Write}_{\text{not\_init}}$ is the number of cache line transfers when the data structure is not initialized. Because the machines in Table 1 support transparent huge pages by default, the page size picked by the operating system (OS) depends on the data structure size. (In this work, no changes were made in the OS.) The ceiling is considered to capture the extra traffic from the fragmented access on the last page.

When a data structure is initialized, page zeroing does not occur, the cache line becomes the deciding factor, and the write-allocate policy is used. One write operation also causes one read operation. The write traffic ($\text{Write}_{\text{init}}$) is shown in Eq. (3). The extra read traffic ($\text{Read}_{\text{for\_write}}$) generated for the write operation is shown in Eq. (4).

$$\text{Write}_{\text{not\_init}} = \left\lceil \frac{\text{Element}_{\text{count}} * \text{Element}_{\text{size}}}{\text{Page}_{\text{size}}} \right\rceil * \frac{\text{Page}_{\text{size}}}{\text{Cacheline}_{\text{size}}}, \tag{2}$$

$$\text{Write}_{\text{init}} = \left\lceil \frac{\text{Element}_{\text{count}} * \text{Element}_{\text{size}}}{\text{Cacheline}_{\text{size}}} \right\rceil, \tag{3}$$

$$\text{Read}_{\text{for\_write}} = \begin{cases} 0 & \text{if data structure is not initialized} \\ \text{Write}_{\text{init}} & \text{if data structure is initialized} \end{cases}. \tag{4}$$

Thus, total read traffic for streaming access, $\text{Read}_{\text{stream}} = \text{Read}_{\text{count}} + \text{Read}_{\text{for\_write}}$, and total write traffic for streaming access, $\text{Write}_{\text{stream}} = \text{Write}_{\text{not\_init}}$ or $\text{Write}_{\text{init}}$, are based on data structure initialization. Because streaming store operations do not cause extra read traffic for initialized write data structure, $\text{Read}_{\text{for\_write}}$ is set to zero when Intel compilers are used.

3.2 Strided Access Pattern

The strided access pattern is another common pattern. Based on the observation in Fig. 1c, there are three regions. Read and write traffic formulation for each region is presented as follows.

Streaming Region. When the $(\text{Stride} * \text{Element}_{\text{size}})$ is smaller than the $\text{Cacheline}_{\text{size}}$, both reads and writes are the same as streaming access (region ❻ in Fig. 1c). In this region (strides 1–16), read and write traffic are same as streaming access because the whole cache line is transferred. For this reason, total read and write traffic for this region is presented by $\text{Read}_{\text{stream}}$ and $\text{Write}_{\text{stream}}$.

No Prefetching Region. As discussed in Sect. 2.3, the effect of prefetching vanishes after stride 80, and thus this is the starting point of a "no prefetching" region, which is indicated by ❽ in Fig. 1c. For this reason, when $(\text{Stride} * \text{Element}_{\text{size}})$ is larger than $(5 * \text{Cacheline}_{\text{size}})$, no prefetching region is considered because $(5 * \text{Cacheline}_{\text{size}})$ = stride 80 for 32 bit floating point.

Write traffic is considered first. If the data structure is initialized, then the write traffic is decided by the cache line size and stride size. It also causes extra read traffic. This case is expressed in Eq. (5).

$$\text{Write}_{\text{init}} \text{ or } \text{Read}_{\text{for\_write}} = \text{Write}_{\text{stream}} / \left(\frac{\text{Stride} * \text{Element}_{\text{size}}}{\text{Cacheline}_{\text{size}}} \right). \tag{5}$$

If the data structure is not initialized, then the write traffic is decided by the $\text{Page}_{\text{size}}$. If $(\text{Stride} * \text{Element}_{\text{size}}) > \text{Page}_{\text{size}}$, then Eq. (6) expresses write traffic; otherwise, write traffic is equal to $\text{Write}_{\text{stream}}$. Read traffic is expressed as Eq. (7).

$$\text{Write}_{\text{non\_init}} = \text{Write}_{\text{stream}} / \left(\frac{\text{Stride} * \text{Element}_{\text{size}}}{\text{Page}_{\text{size}}} \right), \tag{6}$$

$$\text{Read}_{\text{count}} = \text{Read}_{\text{stream}} / \left(\frac{\text{Stride} * \text{Element}_{\text{size}}}{\text{Cacheline}_{\text{size}}} \right). \tag{7}$$

Prefetching Zone. Only when ($Stride * Element_{size}$) is larger than the cache line and smaller than five times the cache line does the effect of prefetching becomes visible, as denoted by region ❼, which ranges from stride 16 to stride 80 in Fig. 1c). In this region, if prefetching is disabled, write and read traffic can be expressed as Eq. (5), Eq. (6), and Eq. (7). However, the main difference is observed when prefetching is enabled, and in that case, only read traffic is affected. Intel prefetching suggests fetching an adjacent cache line and an additional cache line if all model-specific register bits are set. For this reason, the data access number is multiplied by three in the prefetching zone. This is expressed in Eq. (8). Because prefetching has no effect on write traffic, the write traffic is expressed as the non-prefetching formula given in Eqs. (5) and (6).

$$Read_{count} = 3 * \left(\frac{Element_{count}}{Stride}\right). \tag{8}$$

Moreover, SK, CS, and CP show a 10% read traffic drop compared with BW (Fig. 1c), which was considered in the model.

3.3 Stencil Access Pattern

Stencil access patterns are also common in scientific applications. The write operation in a stencil access pattern usually follows a sequential streaming pattern, and thus the equations for streaming access are followed. However, read operations must be considered for different dimensions.

1D Stencil. In a 1D stencil pattern, consecutive elements are usually accessed in each operation. Because adjacent elements can be served by the cache, the read operations follow a sequential streaming pattern.

2D and 3D Stencils. Like a 1D stencil, if the elements are adjacent, a streaming access pattern is followed. When the distance is larger than the cache line size, individual accesses are counted. However, if the distance between stencil points is high for a large dataset, then the cache size becomes a limiting factor by causing capacity misses. Old data may need to be brought to the cache more frequently for a large 2D or 3D stencil when there are multiple iterations.

3.4 Random Access Pattern and Empirical Factor

The random access pattern is found in applications with irregular access [5]. Moreover, modern CPUs introduce randomness in data reuse because of their replacement policies, and the cache cannot retain all data for further use. Therefore, LLC-DRAM traffic prediction for random access must consider the randomness derived from applications and machines. The number of total access in irregular cases is expressed by $Access_{random}$. This section first discusses randomness in applications, then discusses randomness derived from machines.

Data Structure Randomness. In data structure randomness, the reuse behavior becomes uncertain because of how the data structures are accessed; for example, A[B[i]] (A's memory access can be random). In this case, the randomness has one dimension because only the location of access is random, and the total number of access, $Access_{random}$ is known. In such cases, cache reuse is nondeterministic at compile time because the access depends on another data structure at run time. Furthermore, prefetchers may fetch extra cache lines, which adds more uncertainty. Thus, machine randomness must be considered for this case.

Algorithmic Randomness. The worst case of randomness is algorithmic randomness, which has two dimensions: (1) randomness in the number of total access, $Access_{random}$, and (2) randomness in which locations are accessed. Although the first randomness depends on the data structure size, the second may introduce data reuse in the cache. Complex branching usually exists in this kind of randomness. An example of algorithmic randomness is searching algorithms, such as binary search. For such cases, algorithmic complexity analysis provides an upper bound of memory access on a data structure and is considered to define $Access_{random}$. The second dimension is captured through machine randomness.

Machine Randomness and Empirical Factor. Machine randomness depends on cache size, replacement policies, and memory access location. In recent Intel processors since SK, replacement policies are dynamically selected from a set of policies at run time, and the policy chosen for a given scenario is not disclosed [9]. Moreover, in the cases of algorithmic and data structure randomness, the access location is random. So, multiple dimensions of randomness from the machine and the application make statically determining the LLC-DRAM traffic a complex problem. The undisclosed mapping of dynamic replacement policies from Intel makes it even more complicated. To the best of the authors' knowledge, statically determining LLC-DRAM traffic in modern CPUs for irregular cases is an unsolved problem. This study does not

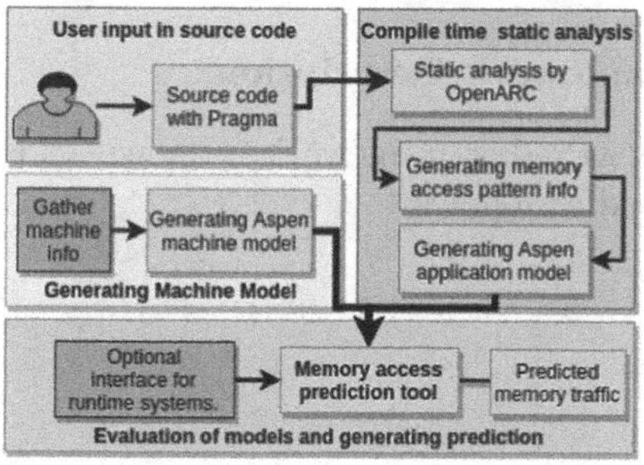

Fig. 2. Workflow of MAPredict framework.

claim to solve this problem statically; rather, it combines static analysis and empirical observation. At this point, an empirically obtained $Empirical_{factor}$ is introduced to represent machine randomness. The $Empirical_{factor}$ is calculated from memory access obtained from the dynamic analysis tool (Sect. 2.2) and statically obtained total access ($Access_{random}$) where $Empirical_{factor}$ = measured_access/statically_obtained_access. This ratio captures the randomness of the application and the underlying machine.

4 MAPredict Framework

This section describes the MAPredict framework. MAPredict statically gathers information from an application and a machine to invoke the appropriate model presented in Sect. 3 and generates a prediction for LLC-DRAM traffic. MAPredict depends on the Open Accelerator Research Compiler (OpenARC) [13] for static analysis of the code and on the COMPASS [4] framework for expressing an application in the Aspen [7] domain-specific modeling language. This section presents an overview of OpenARC, Aspen, and COMPASS, then describes the MAPredict framework.

4.1 Aspen, OpenARC, and COMPASS

Aspen [7] is a domain-specific language for analytical performance modeling in a structured fashion. Aspen's formal language and methodology provide a way to express applications and machines' characteristics abstractly (e.g., Aspen application model and machine model). Aspen tools can provide various predictions, such as predicting resource counts (e.g., number of loads, stores, FLOPs, and so on). OpenARC [13] is an open-source compiler framework for various directive-based programming research that provides source-to-source translation, which is a desired feature for creating Aspen application models. COMPASS [4] is an Aspen-based performance modeling and prediction framework built on OpenARC. COMPASS provides a set of Aspen pragma-based directives that can be used in source code. MAPredict extends COMPASS by adding new Aspen directives to enable cache-aware memory access prediction.

4.2 MAPredict Framework Description

The workflow of the MAPredict framework is shown in Fig. 2. Four phases of MAPredict are described as follows.

```
model matmul {
param N = 512
data a [((4*N)*N)]
kernel Matmul_openmp {
  execute [N] "block_Matmul" {
    loads [((1*sizeof_float)*N)] from b as stride(1)
    loads [((1*sizeof_float)*N)] from c as stride(N)
    stores [(1*sizeof_float)*N] to a as stride(1)
}}}
```

Listing 1.1. Application model: matrix multiply (partial view).

Source Code Preparation Phase. The primary purpose of MAPredict is to prepare a source so that when the preparation is complete, MAPredict can statically provide memory access prediction. This one-time effort of source code preparation (i.e., phase 1) is necessary for capturing the dynamic information unavailable at compile time. First, COMPASS-provided Aspen compiler directives (i.e., pragmas) identify the target model region in the code to capture information at compile time. MAPredict introduces new traits that must be included in the directives to specify memory access patterns, where necessary. Access pattern traits, such as sequential streaming and strided access patterns, are automatically generated; however, user input through pragmas is needed for stencil and random access patterns. User inputs are also needed for specifying dynamic (e.g., malloc) input sizes of data structures and $\text{Empirical}_{\text{factor}}$ for random access patterns because of their unavailability at compile time.

Compile Time Static Analysis Phase. In phase 2, MAPredict gathers the application information required to execute the model presented in Sect. 3. MAPredict invokes OpenARC's compile time static analysis capability, which generates an intermediate representation of the code and captures variables, variable sizes (i.e., $\text{Element}_{\text{size}}$), instruction types (i.e., load or store), FLOPs, loop information, access pattern information, machine-specific $\text{Empirical}_{\text{factor}}$, and so on from source code. After gathering the needed information, the source-to-source translation feature of OpenARC is invoked to generate the Aspen language's abstract application model by following Aspen's grammar [7]. An application model combines different types of statements in a graph of kernels with one or more execution blocks. An example of an application model is given in Listing 1.1, which shows load and store information of matrix multiplication. Every load and store statement shows the access pattern of that data structure.

Machine Model Generation Phase. The machine model is manually prepared by gathering information about the machine, following the Aspen grammar, which is a one-time effort. The machine model contains information unavailable in the application model and is required to execute the model presented in Sect. 3. MAPredict gathers information about the micro-architecture,

$\text{Cacheline}_{\text{size}}$, $\text{Page}_{\text{size}}$, prefetching status, compiler, and so on from the machine model.

Prediction Generation Phase. MAPredict's prediction engine is invoked by passing the application and machine models. MAPredict invocation can also be made from a runtime system by using the optional runtime invocation feature of COMPASS. When MAPredict is invoked, it traverses the call graph of the Aspen application model in a depth-first manner. In this graph, each node represents an execution block (i.e., a part of a function). MAPredict walks through every load and store statement of the application model, collects the access pattern, and evaluates the expression to obtain $\text{Element}_{\text{count}}$, $\text{Element}_{\text{size}}$, Stride, and so on. Then, MAPredict uses the machine model information to invoke the appropriate prediction model to generate memory access prediction for that statement. MAPredict performs this evaluation for each statement and generates a prediction for the execution block, which is recursively passed to make a kernel/function-wise prediction. When the graph traversal finishes, MAPredict provides a total memory access prediction for the application. MAPredict can provide kernel-wise memory access and execution block-wise memory access. In a debug mode, it offers a statement-wise detailed analysis.

4.3 Identifying Randomness and $Empirical_{Factor}$

MAPredict combines static and empirical approaches to address randomness. In a large code base, identifying randomness is challenging because randomness usually exists only in certain functions. MAPredict facilitates identifying randomness in source code. First, the source is annotated with basic MAPredict traits without any $\text{Empirical}_{\text{factor}}$. When MAPredict is executed, it provides function-wise memory access prediction. Then, the dynamic analysis tool is run on real hardware to obtain the same function-wise data. Comparing the results from both tools shows which functions provide low accuracy, indicating a potential source of randomness. However, a function can be large. MAPredict provides execution block-level and statement-wise detailed analysis to pinpoint the randomness. After identification, as described in Sect. 3.4, the $\text{Empirical}_{\text{factor}}$ is calculated by comparing the output from the dynamic analysis tool (i.e., measured value) and MAPredict (i.e., statically obtained value). Then, the $\text{Empirical}_{\text{factor}}$ is annotated in the source code for that statement or execution block. When MAPredict is rerun, it uses the $\text{Empirical}_{\text{factor}}$ to generate the prediction.

5 Experimental Setup

This section discusses the experiment environment. The processors listed in Table 1 were used in the experiments. The OS of these processors was CentOS 7, which supports transparent huge pages by default. The applications and their input sizes and access patterns are listed in Table 2. Forty-four functions from these applications were evaluated for different input sizes, creating 130 workloads. GCC-9.1 and Intel-19.1 compilers were used for experimentation. For parallel execution, the OpenMP programming model was used. In the graphs, *BW* stands for *Broadwell without prefetching*, and *BW_pf* stands for *Broadwell with prefetch enabled.* A similar convention was used for others. All graphs in the experiment section show accuracy in the y-axis.

5.1 Accuracy Calculation

Relative accuracy was considered in which accuracy = [100 - Absolute {(measured-predicted)/measured * 100}]. The measured value was generated by the dynamic analysis tool described in Sect. 2.2. The predicted values were generated using MAPredict. Both MAPredict and the dynamic analysis tool provide function-wise traffic, making function-wise accuracy calculation possible.

Table 2. Benchmarks. Here, R = region, M = million, and B = billion.

Name	Pattern	Input sizes
STREAM Triad [14]	Sequential streaming access pattern	50M, 100M, 150M
Jacobi [13]	Stencil pattern without initialization	67M, 268M, 1B
Laplace2D [13]	Stencil pattern with initialization	16M, 64M, 100M
Vecmul for R - ❼ [13]	Strided pattern in prefetching zone	50M, 100M, 200M
Vecmul for R - ❽ [13]	Strided pattern in no prefetching zone	100M, 200M, 400M
XSBench [15]	Algorithmic randomness	Large
Lulesh [16]	Mixed patterns	15M, 27M, 64M

5.2 Comparison with Literature

Prediction accuracy of MAPredict was compared with a model from literature [17]. Although the study [17] investigated data vulnerability, its main contribution was the analytical model for LLC-DRAM traffic prediction by considering application and machine characteristics. Two other studies investigated memory access prediction for static analysis [4,5]. The main reason they were not considered for comparison is the lack of a detailed analytical model with equations. Moreover, one of these studies depends on cache simulation [5], and another depends on instruction counts without considering machine properties [4].

6 Experimental Results

The accuracy of the MAPredict framework was evaluated in two steps. In the first step, the prediction accuracy of different applications with regular memory access patterns was evaluated. In the second step, irregular access patterns and a large application with mixed access patterns were investigated.

6.1 Regular Access Patterns

Regular access patterns were investigated for various micro-architectures, input sizes, compilers, and execution models.

Sequential Streaming Access Pattern. To evaluate the model for sequential streaming memory access pattern, the Triad kernel of STREAM [14] was used. The data structure was initialized, and the size was 50 million 64 bit floating points. The total traffic, which was the summation of read and write traffic, was measured for all the micro-architectures with prefetching disabled and enabled. The prediction accuracy from MAPredict and the model from the literature [17] are compared in Fig. 3a. MAPredict invoked Eq. (3) and provided 99.1% average accuracy in all processors when prefetching was disabled and 99.1% average accuracy in all processors when prefetching was enabled. For the same cases, the model from literature provided 75.0% and 75.4% average accuracy when prefetching was disabled and enabled, respectively.

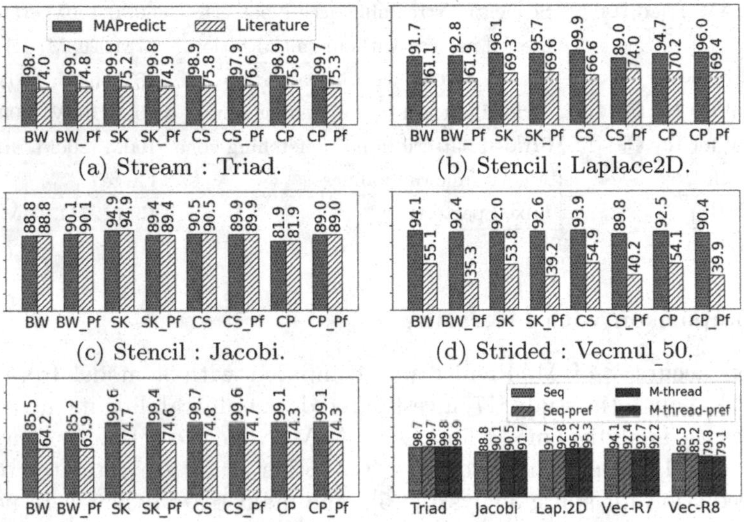

(a) Stream : Triad.

(b) Stencil : Laplace2D.

(c) Stencil : Jacobi.

(d) Strided : Vecmul_50.

(e) Strided : Vecmul_200.

(f) Single vs. multithreaded.

Fig. 3. Accuracy comparison of different regular access patterns. Y-axis is accuracy, and x-axis is micro-architectures with prefetching disabled and enabled. Blue is MAPredict, white is the literature, and green is multithreaded. (Color figure online)

Stencil Memory Access Pattern. MAPredict's accuracy for stencil pattern was evaluated by using two benchmark kernels: Laplace2d and Jacobi [13]. Both kernels have a 2D stencil access pattern with adjacent points. However, Laplace2D has the write array initialized, and Jacobi has the write array noninitialized. Laplace2D operates on a 4,000 × 4,000 matrix of 64 bit floating points, whereas Jacobi operates on an 8,912 × 8,912 matrix of 32 bit floating points. Figure 3b shows the comparison for Laplace2D. Because the data structure is initialized, allocating-store causes extra read, which the model from literature does not consider. MAPredict provided 95.9% and 92.5% average accuracy when prefetching is disabled and enabled, respectively. However, the model from literature provided 65.7% and 68.5% average accuracy when prefetching was disabled and enabled, respectively. The prediction accuracy of Jacobi is portrayed in Fig. 3c. Because the write data structure is noninitialized, page zeroing occurred. Although the model in the literature did not consider page zeroing, the equation remained the same. Thus, the same accuracy was observed.

Strided Memory Access Pattern. To evaluate strided access patterns of prefetching and non-prefetching regions (indicated by ❼ and ❽ in Fig. 1c), vector multiplication of 100 million was used with strides 50 and 200. A stride size of 50 was used with a noninitialized write array to evaluate the page zeroing effect. Initialized write array was considered for stride 200. For the prefetching zone, traffic is significantly different across micro-architectures. Moreover, for stride 50, the whole array was written to the memory instead of one in 50. Figure 3d shows that MAPredict captured the prefetching differences between different micro-architectures successfully and provided 93.3% and 91.6% average accuracy when prefetching was disabled and enabled, respectively. However, the model from literature provided 54.6% and 38.2% average accuracy when prefetching was disabled and enabled, respectively, because it did not account for prefetchers and page-zeroing. For stride 200, the initialized data structure causes allocating-store. The comparison is shown in Fig. 3e in which MAPredict and the model from literature provided 88.5% and 66.2% average accuracy when prefetching was disabled and enabled, respectively.

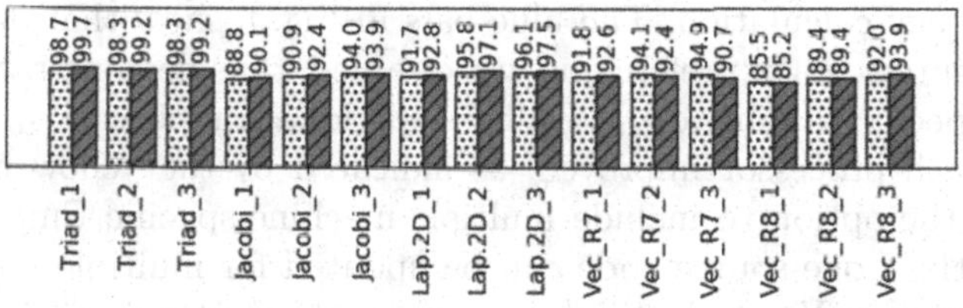

Fig. 4. Accuracy of various input sizes. White is prefetching disabled, and blue is prefetching enabled. (Color figure online)

Multithreaded Execution and Effect of Compiler. Multithreaded and single-threaded executions are compared in Fig. 3f. Eight threads of BW were used for experimentation, and OpenMP from GCC was used. No significant difference was observed for sequential streaming, stencil, and strided access patterns. Moreover, MAPredict captured the streaming store operation by Intel compiler and provided better accuracy (93%) than the model from the literature (74%). All the micro-architectures showed a similar trend.

Comparison of Different Input Sizes. MAPredict's accuracy was evaluated for different input sizes for each application with the regular access patterns given in Table 2. Triad was tested with array sizes of 50 million, 100 million, and 150 million. Matrix sizes for Jacobi were $8,192 \times 8,192$, $16,384 \times 16,384$, and $32,768 \times 32,768$. Laplace2D was tested with $4,000 \times 4,000$, $8,000 \times 8,000$, and $10,000 \times 10,000$ matrix sizes. Strided vector multiplication was tested with vector sizes of 50 million, 100 million, and 200 million for the prefetching region and 100 million, 200 million, and 400 million for the no prefetching region. The prediction accuracies of each dataset for prefetching enabled and disabled cases are presented in Fig. 4. The accuracy of different input sizes demonstrates that MAPredict provides consistent accuracy for varied input sizes. The BW processor was used for this evaluation, and a similar trend was observed for others.

6.2 Irregular Access and Large Application with Mixed Patterns

To evaluate MAPredict's capability to combine static and empirical data for irregular access and mixed patterns, XSBench and Lulesh were considered.

Algorithmic Randomness. XSBench [15] is a proxy application that calculates the macroscopic neutron cross section by randomly searching for energy and material. The energy search was done by employing a binary search on a unionized energy grid, an example of algorithmic randomness (total access = $\text{Access}_{\text{random}}$ * $\text{Empirical}_{\text{factor}}$). As discussed in Sect. 3.4, the access number and location are random. Because it follows a binary search, algorithm complexity ($\log n$) was used to measure $\text{Access}_{\text{random}}$. The $\text{Empirical}_{\text{factor}}$ was calculated for BW with prefetching disabled and used for all other processors ($\text{Empirical}_{\text{factor}}$ = the ratio of measured value and $\text{Access}_{\text{random}}$). The predicted value was then compared with the average of five measurements (up to 5% standard deviation) for accuracy calculation. The blue bars in Fig. 5 show that only BW provided high accuracy when prefetching was disabled, thus demonstrating the need for machine-specific $\text{Empirical}_{\text{factor}}$. When individual $\text{Empirical}_{\text{factor}}$ is used, the accuracy of each processor improved, as indicated by the yellow bar. MAPredict provides the option to include multiple machine-specific $\text{Empirical}_{\text{factor}}$ in one pragma; thus, one source code can be updated for multiple machines. The method presented in Yu et al. [17] did not calculate the total number of random access and rather focused on the access location, which makes the comparison irrelevant. Algorithmic randomness is an extreme case, and it is only present in

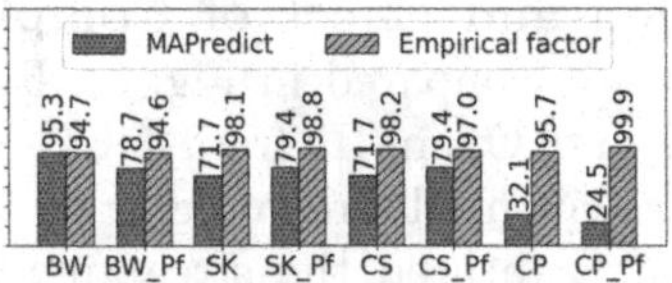

Fig. 5. Accuracy of algorithmic randomness for XSBench.

a certain function. For this reason, a large application with mixed patterns is investigated next for different input sizes.

Large Application with Mixed Patterns: Lulesh. Lulesh [16] was considered to demonstrate that MAPredict can work with a large application with different memory access patterns. Lulesh is a well-known application with different memory access patterns for a 3D mesh data structure. It has 38 functions with a complex call graph and 4,474 lines of code, making it a large and complex example. Three large data structure sizes ($250 \times 250 \times 250$, $300 \times 300 \times 300$, and $400 \times 400 \times 400$) were used. The SK machine was selected for experimentation because it has the smallest cache and thus stresses the capability of MAPredict by increasing the probability of machine randomness.

Lulesh Function Categorization. Out of 38 functions in Lulesh, 24 functions provide significant memory transactions (>1 million LLC-DRAM transactions, which have different memory access patterns). Most memory-intensive functions are shown at Table 3 in which the second column shows access patterns. Here, *St* is the stencil (eight-point nonadjacent 3D stencil), *S* is the stream, *DR* is the data structure randomness, *I* is noninitialized arrays, *N* is nested randomness (DR with branches), and *All* is all the above patterns.
Empirical$_{factor}$. Lulesh has data structure randomness in three functions. The Empirical$_{\text{factor}}$ is calculated by comparing the static and dynamic data to address this randomness, which is a one-time effort. So, three Empirical$_{\text{factor}}$ values were used in three functions out of 38.

Table 3. Analysis of Lulesh (selected functions). Here, *d1* = input size 1 without prefetching, *p-d1* = input size 1 with prefetching, *M* = million, and *B* = billion.

Function name (shortened)	Access pattern	MAP redict	TAU PAPI	Accuracy - 3 input sizes					
				d1	p-d1	d2	p-d2	d3	p-d3
IntegrateStressF.Elm	St,S	81M	83M	99.0	97.4	88.5	88.9	91.8	91.7
CFBHour.ForceF.Elm	St,S	239M	241M	96.9	99.1	97.0	96.5	82.2	82.6
CHourg.Cont.F.Elm	St,I,DR	604M	647M	92.8	93.1	93.0	92.7	76.2	77.9
LagrangeNodal	All	824M	874M	94.2	94.2	95.3	95.1	85.4	86.5
CKinematicsF.Elm	S,St	99M	100M	98.7	99.7	96.0	96.6	98.3	98.7
CLagrangeElements	St,S,I	126M	130M	98.3	97.5	99.7	99.9	98.5	98.3
CMon.QGrad.F.Elm	S,St	99M	105M	95.2	94.4	95.6	95.6	94.6	94.5
CMon.QReg.F.Elm	DR,N,S	141M	150M	94.9	94.6	95.4	93.2	94.3	93.2
CEnergyF.Elm	S	249M	261M	97.7	95.6	94.0	98.6	99.9	93.4
EvalEOSF.Elm	DR,S	429M	451M	99.1	95.1	95.7	97.9	98.4	93.0
UpdateVol.F.Elm	S	10M	10M	99.9	99.9	99.7	99.9	99.9	99.9
LagrangeElements	All	824M	869M	98.4	95.0	99.3	96.7	96.9	93.7
Overall	All	1.6B	1.7B	95.0	93.0	96.6	94.3	95.8	99.2

Traffic: Number of LLC-DRAM Transactions. The third and fourth columns of Table 3 show the LLC-DRAM transaction obtained for MAPredict and TAU + PAPI (dynamic analysis tool). The last function, which is the parent of all functions, shows a total of 1.7 billion LLC-DRAM transactions. However, for the largest data size, Lulesh exhibits 3.5 billion LLC-DRAM transactions.

Lulesh Scaling and Accuracy. Scaling in terms of input sizes provides a measure of success for a one-time calculation of the $\text{Empirical}_{\text{factor}}$. The fifth through tenth columns of Table 3 show the accuracy of different functions for different input sizes for prefetching enabled and disabled cases. Because some functions are parents to other functions and the last function is the parent to all (total traffic), inaccuracy in one function affects the overall accuracy. MAPredict showed more than 93% accuracy for all input sizes, which demonstrates the scalability of the model and $Empirical_{factor}$. However, when multithreaded experiments were used, the overall accuracy dropped but still provided more than 80% accuracy.

6.3 Discussion

For regular access patterns, MAPredict's static analysis provides higher accuracy than the literature model and can handle different input sizes, microarchitectures, cache sizes, compilers, and execution models. However, MAPredict requires empirical observation for irregular patterns.

Overhead of MAPredict. One objective of MAPredict is for it to be usable from runtime systems for fast decisions. The evaluation of Lulesh takes 28.3 ms (38 functions), averaging to less than 1 ms per function. For source code preparation, 249 lines of Aspen directives (79 MAPredict directives) were used for 4,474 lines of code in Lulesh, which is 5.5% source code overhead. However, smaller benchmarks needed fewer directives; for example, Triad needed one, Vecmul needed four, Jacobi needed six, and Laplace2D needed six directives.

Usability of $Empirical_{Factor}$. The calculation of $\text{Empirical}_{\text{factor}}$ is needed for irregular accesses. However, the $\text{Empirical}_{\text{factor}}$ calculation is a one-time effort. Once calculated, it becomes a part of the source code and can provide prediction statically. Moreover, randomness usually occurs in only a small portion of an application because regular access patterns are more commonly found. So, the $\text{Empirical}_{\text{factor}}$ calculation is needed only where randomness exists.

7 Related Works

This section presents related works, which are divided into two categories.

7.1 Memory Access Prediction

Several studies investigated memory access patterns to make reasonable predictions. Yu et al. [17] used analytical models of different memory access patterns for investigating application vulnerability. Peng et al. [5] used data-centric abstractions in Tuyere to predict memory traffic for different memory technologies. Unlike MAPredict, application models in these aforementioned studies were manually prepared. Moreover, MAPredict goes beyond these work by including the effect of page size, prefetchers, and compilers in machine models. Moreover, the Tuyere framework showed the benefit of using ASPEN application models over trace-based or cycle-accurate simulators (e.g., Ramulator [18], DRAMSim [19]) in terms of time and space. MAPredict further improved upon Tuyere by providing predictions in 1–3 ms per function and considering different micro-architectures. Allen et al. [20] investigated the effect of two memory access patterns (sequential streaming and strided) on GPUs. Some previous works used load and store instruction counts to measure memory access and used that count to predict performance (e.g., COMPASS by Lee et al. [4]). Compile time static analysis tools—such as Cetus [21], OpenARC [13], and Caascade [22]—were also used to measure instruction counts at compile time and can provide a prediction. MAPredict does not solely depend on instruction counts; it captures the effect of cache hierarchy through analytical models. In contrast to MAPredict's near-accurate prediction, analytical models such as the Roofline Model [3] and Gable [23] provide an upper bound for a system.

7.2 Understanding Intel Processors

Some studies delved into Intel processors to understand their performance by using benchmarks. Using the Intel Advisor tool, Marques et al. [25] analyzed the performance of benchmark applications to understand and improve cache performance. Alappat et al. [9] investigated Intel BW and CS processors to understand the cache behavior using the likwid tool suite [28]. Hammond et al. investigated the Intel SK processor [26] by running different HPC benchmarks. Hofmann et al. also investigated different Intel processors to analyze core and chip-level features [29,30]. Molka et al. [27] used a micro-benchmark framework to analyze the main memory and cache performance of Intel Sandy Bridge and AMD Bulldozer processors. Performance evaluation using benchmarks was also done in Saini et al. for Ivy Bridge, Haswell, and Broadwell micro-architectures [31,32]. These studies investigated Intel micro-architectures using benchmarks; however, unlike MAPredict, they did not develop strategies for predicting memory traffic.

Table 4. Comparison with other works. Here, $A = all$ and $P = partial$.

Studies by	Static analysis	Analytical model	Access pattern	Diff. micro-architecture	Diff. compilers	Multi-threaded	Pref-etcher
Peng et al.[5]	✓	✗	A	✗	✗	✓	✗
Yu et al. [17]	✓	✓	A	✗	✗	✗	✗
Monil et al. [24]	✗	✗	P	✓	✗	✗	✓
Lee at al. [4]	✓	✗	P	✓	✗	✓	✗
Marques et al. [25]	✗	✗	P	✗	✗	✓	✗
Alappat et al. [9]	✗	✗	P	✓	✓	✓	✓
Hammond et al. [26]	✗	✗	P	✓	✗	✓	✗
Molka et al. [27]	✗	✗	P	✓	✗	✓	✗
MAPredict	✓	✓	A	✓	✓	✓	✓

7.3 Comparing MAPredict with Other Studies

Table 4 compares MAPredict with other literature in which the first four rows represent the study of memory access patterns and static analysis. The next four rows represent studies that focused on understanding Intel micro-architectures. Table 4 shows that MAPredict addresses the missing parts from both domains to provide a unique framework.

8 Conclusion and Future Work

This paper presents the MAPredict framework, which predicts memory traffic for Intel processors. This study investigated the interplay between an application's memory access pattern and Intel micro-architectures' cache hierarchy. Based on the observation from Intel processors, an analytical model was derived that considers memory access patterns of an application, processor properties, and compiler choice. MAPredict generated an application model for a given application through compile time analysis. The application was combined with a target machine model to synthesize the appropriate analytical model and predict LLC-DRAM traffic. Through experimentation with benchmarks on processors from Intel BW, SK, CS, and CP micro-architectures, the analytical model's validity was verified by achieving an average accuracy of 99% for streaming, 91% for strided, and 92% for stencil patterns. MAPredict also provided hints in the source code to capture dynamic information and randomness from the application or machine to obtain better accuracy. By combining static and empirical approaches, MAPredict achieved up to 97% average accuracy on different micro-architectures for random access patterns. Future work will investigate MAPredict on AMD, ARM, and IBM processors.

Acknowledgments. This research used resources of the Experimental Computing Laboratory at Oak Ridge National Laboratory, which are supported by the US Department of Energy's Office of Science under contract no. DE-AC05-00OR22725.

This research was supported by (1) the US Department of Defense, Brisbane: Productive Programming Systems in the Era of Extremely Heterogeneous and Ephemeral Computer Architectures and (2) DOE Office of Science, Office of Advanced Scientific Computing Research, Scientific Discovery through Advanced Computing (SciDAC) program.

References

1. Jalby, W., Kuck, D., Malony, A., Masella, M., Mazouz, A., Popov, M.: The long and winding road toward efficient high-performance computing. Proc. IEEE **106**(11), 1985–2003 (2018)
2. Monil, M.A.H., Belviranli, M., Lee, S., Vetter, J., Malony, A. In: International Conference on Parallel Architectures and Compilation Techniques (PACT), (2020)
3. Williams, S., Waterman, A., Patterson, D.: Roofline: an insightful visual performance model for multicore architectures. Commun. ACM **52**(4), 65–76 (2009)
4. Lee, S., Meredith, J., Vetter, J.: Compass: a framework for automated performance modeling and prediction. In: 29th International Conference on Supercomputing (ICS15), pp. 405–414 (2015)
5. Peng, I., Vetter, J., Moore, S., Lee, S.: Tuyere: Enabling scalable memory workloads for system exploration. In: International Symposium on High-Performance Parallel and Distributed Computing, pp. 180–191 (2018)
6. Umar, M., Moore, S.V., Meredith, J.S., Vetter, J.S., Cameron, K.W.: Aspen-based performance and energy modeling frameworks. J. Parallel Distrib. Compu. **120**, 222–236 (2018)
7. Spafford, K.L., Vetter, J.S.: Aspen: a domain specific language for performance modeling. In: SC12: International Conference for High Performance Computing, Networking, Storage and Analysis, pp. 1–11, Salt Lake City (2012)
8. Top 500 supercomputers published at sc20. https://www.top500.org/
9. Alappat, C., Hofmann, J., Hager, G., Fehske, H., Bishop, A., Wellein, G.: Understanding HPC benchmark performance on Intel Broadwell and Cascade Lake processors. arXiv preprint arXiv:2002.03344 (2020)
10. Monil, M.A.H., Lee, S., Vetter, J.S., Malony, A.D.: Comparing LLC-memory traffic between CPU and GPU architectures. In: 2021 IEEE/ACM Redefining Scalability for Diversely Heterogeneous Architectures Workshop (RSDHA), pp. 8–16 (2021)
11. Shende, S., Malony, A.: The TAU parallel performance system. Int. J. High Perform. Comput. Appl **20**(2), 287–311 (2006)
12. Terpstra, D., Jagode, H., You, H., Dongarra, J.: Collecting performance data with PAPI-C. In: Muller, M., Resch, M., Schulz, A., Nagel, W. (eds.) Tools for High Performance Computing 2009, pp. 157–173. Springer, Berlin (2010). https://doi.org/10.1007/978-3-642-11261-4_11
13. Lee, S., Vetter, J.S.: OpenARC: open accelerator research compiler for directive-based, efficient heterogeneous computing. In: ACM Symposium on High-Performance Parallel and Distributed Computing (HPDC), Vancouver, ACM (2014)
14. McCalpin, J.D.: Stream benchmarks (2002)
15. Tramm, J., Siegel, A., Islam, T., Schulz,M.: XSBench-the development and verification of a performance abstraction for Monte Carlo reactor analysis. In: Conference: PHYSOR 2014 - The Role of Reactor Physics toward a Sustainable Future (PHYSOR) (2014)

16. Karlin, I.: Lulesh programming model and performance ports overview. Technical report, Lawrence Livermore National Lab. (LLNL), CA, USA (2012)
17. Yu, L., Li, D., Mittal, S., Vetter, J.S.: Quantitatively modeling application resiliency with the data vulnerability factor. In: ACM/IEEE International Conference for High Performance Computing, Networking, Storage, and Analysis (SC) (2014)
18. Kim, Y., Yang, W., Mutlu, O.: Ramulator: a fast and extensible DRAM simulator. IEEE Comput. Archit. Lett. **15**(1), 45–49 (2015)
19. Rosenfeld, P., Cooper-Balis, E., Jacob, B.: DRAMSim2: a cycle accurate memory system simulator. IEEE Comput. Archit. Lett. **10**(1), 16–19 (2011)
20. Allen, T., Ge, R.: Characterizing power and performance of GPU memory access. In: Internatopnal Workshop on Energy Efficient Supercomputing (E2SC), pp. 46–53 (2016)
21. Dave, C., Bae, H., Min, S., Lee, S., Eigenmann, R., Midkiff, S.: Cetus: a source-to-source compiler infrastructure for multicores. Computer **42**, 36–42 (2009)
22. Lopez, M.G., Hernandez, O., Budiardja, R.D., Wells, J.C.: CAASCADE: a system for static analysis of HPC software application portfolios. In: Bhatele, A., Boehme, D., Levine, J.A., Malony, A.D., Schulz, M. (eds.) ESPT/VPA 2017-2018. LNCS, vol. 11027, pp. 90–104. Springer, Cham (2019). https://doi.org/10.1007/978-3-030-17872-7_6
23. Hill, M., Reddi, V.J.: Gables: a roofline model for mobile SoCs. In: International Symposium on High Performance Computer Architecture (HPCA), pp. 317–330 (2019)
24. Monil, M.A.H., Lee, S., Vetter, J., Malony, A.: Understanding the impact of memory access patterns in Intel processors. In: MCHPC 2020: Workshop on Memory Centric High Performance Computing. IEEE (2020)
25. Marques, D.: Performance analysis with cache-aware roofline model in Intel advisor. In: International Conference on High Performance Computing & Simulation, pp. 898–907 (2017)
26. Hammond, S., Vaughan, C., Hughes, C.: Evaluating the Intel Skylake Xeon processor for HPC workloads. In: International Conference on High Performance Computing & Simulation (HPCS18), pp. 342–349 (2018)
27. Molka, D., Hackenberg, D., Schöne, R.: Main memory and cache performance of Intel Sandy Bridge and AMD Bulldozer. In: Proceedings of the Workshop on Memory Systems Performance and Correctness, pp. 1–10 (2014)
28. Treibig, J., Hager, G., Wellein, G.: LIKWID: a lightweight performance-oriented tool suite for x86 multicore environments. In: 2010 39th International Conference on Parallel Processing Workshops, pp. 207–216. IEEE (2010)
29. Hofmann, J., Fey, D., Eitzinger, J., Hager, G., Wellein, G.: Analysis of Intel's Haswell microarchitecture using the ECM model and microbenchmarks. In: Hannig, F., Cardoso, J.M.P., Pionteck, T., Fey, D., Schröder-Preikschat, W., Teich, J. (eds.) ARCS 2016. LNCS, vol. 9637, pp. 210–222. Springer, Cham (2016). https://doi.org/10.1007/978-3-319-30695-7_16
30. Hofmann, J., Hager, G., Wellein, G., Fey, D.: An analysis of core- and chip-level architectural features in four generations of intel server processors. In: Kunkel, J.M., Yokota, R., Balaji, P., Keyes, D. (eds.) ISC High Performance 2017. LNCS, vol. 10266, pp. 294–314. Springer, Cham (2017). https://doi.org/10.1007/978-3-319-58667-0_16

31. Saini, S., Hood, R., Chang, J., Baron, J.: Performance evaluation of an Intel Haswell-and Ivy Bridge-based supercomputer using scientific and engineering applications. In: 2016 IEEE 18th International Conference on High Performance Computing and Communications (HPCC), pp. 1196–1203. IEEE (2016)
32. Saini, S., Hood, R.: Performance evaluation of Intel Broadwell nodes based supercomputer using computational fluid dynamics and climate applications. In: 2017 IEEE 19th International Conference on High Performance Computing and Communications Workshops (HPCCWS), pp. 58–65. IEEE (2017)

Rapid Execution Time Estimation for Heterogeneous Memory Systems Through *Differential Tracing*

Nicolas Denoyelle[1], Swann Perarnau[1], Kamil Iskra[1], and Balazs Gerofi[2](✉)

[1] Argonne National Laboratory, Lemont, USA
{ndenoyelle,swann,iskra}@anl.gov
[2] RIKEN Center for Computational Science, Kobe, Japan
bgerofi@riken.jp

Abstract. As the complexity of compute nodes in high-performance computing (HPC) keeps increasing, systems equipped with heterogeneous memory devices are becoming paramount. Efficiently utilizing heterogeneous memory-based systems, however, poses significant challenges to application developers. System-software-level transparent solutions utilizing artificial intelligence and machine learning approaches, in particular nonsupervised learning-based methods such as reinforcement learning, may come to the rescue. However, such methods require rapid estimation of execution runtime as a function of the data layout across memory devices for exploring different data placement strategies, rendering architecture-level simulators impractical for this purpose.

In this paper we propose a differential tracing-based approach using memory access traces obtained by high-frequency sampling-based methods (e.g., Intel's PEBS) on real hardware using of different memory devices. We develop a runtime estimator based on such traces that provides an execution time estimate orders of magnitude faster than full-system simulators. On a number of HPC miniapplications we show that the estimator predicts runtime with an average error of 4.4% compared to measurements on real hardware.

Keywords: Memory management · Heterogeneous memory · Machine learning

1 Introduction

As dynamic random-access memory (DRAM) approaches its limits in terms of density, power, and cost, a wide range of alternative memory technologies are on the horizon, with some of them already in relatively large-scale deployment: 3D NAND flash [32], non-volatile memories such as 3D-XPoint [16], spin-transfer torque magnetic RAM [45], and phase-change memory [27]. Moreover, high-performance volatile memories, such as Hybrid Memory Cube [19], high-bandwidth memory (HBM) [21], and Graphics Double Data Rate 6 [22], are

A.-L. Varbanescu et al. (Eds.): ISC High Performance 2022, LNCS 13289, pp. 256–274, 2022.
doi.org/10.1007/978-3-031-07312-0_13

actively being developed and deployed. Resource disaggregation [4], an emerging compute paradigm that has been receiving a lot of attention recently, will further expand the heterogeneous memory landscape.

While these technologies provide opportunities for improving system utilization and efficiency through better matching of specific hardware characteristics with application behavior, at the same time they pose immense challenges to software developers. Management of such heterogeneous memory types is a major challenge for application developers, not only in placing data structures into the most suitable memory, but also in adaptively moving content as application characteristics change over time. Operating system and/or runtime level solutions based on artificial intelligence (AI) and machine learning (ML) that optimize memory allocations and data movement by transparently mapping application behavior to the underlying hardware are therefore highly desired.

Although a large body of existing work explores various ML approaches for heterogeneous memory management [12,18,43,44], to the best of our knowledge none of this work applies nonsupervised learning such as reinforcement learning (RL) [41]. This gap exists despite RL's enormous potential that has been demonstrated in a wide range of fields recently [31]. RL evolves an agent to refine its policy through repeatedly interacting with the environment. Hence it requires rapid and low-overhead estimation of application execution time as a function of memory layout over heterogeneous memory devices. Cycle-level full-system simulators such as gem5 [8] and cycle-accurate memory simulators such as Ramulator [25] and NVSIM [11] incur slowdowns that are prohibitive for such a scenario. Additionally, restricting the simulation to memory devices only, namely by feeding memory access traces (captured by tools such as PIN [28] or DynInst [9]) into memory simulators, loses timing information about the computation, in turn degrading the accuracy of the overall simulation. Furthermore, these tools are still orders of magnitude slower than execution on real hardware.

This paper explores an alternative approach to rapid execution time estimation over heterogeneous memory devices, a method we call *differential tracing*. The basic idea is to obtain high-fidelity memory access traces running on real hardware using different memory devices; matching the traces to identify differences in runtime; and, based on this information, providing an estimate for execution time as a function of the virtual memory to device mapping. To this end, we utilize Intel's precise event-based sampling (PEBS) [20] mechanism and propose a number of extensions (e.g., the notion of *application phasemarks*) to the tracing mechanism that enables high-accuracy matching of memory traces. Using the matched traces, we develop an estimator that provides a runtime estimate substantially faster than cycle-level simulators.

Specifically, in this paper we make the following contributions.

- We address the issue of providing an execution time estimator for hybrid memory systems without incurring unacceptable slowdowns that would otherwise be prohibitive in iterative machine learning methods such as RL.

- We introduce a number of novel extensions to sampling-based memory access tracing (e.g., application phasemarks) that improve our ability to match memory traces.
- We evaluate our proposal on four HPC miniapplications across a wide range of memory layouts and compare the estimates with real hardware execution.

We find that the proposed method provides an average estimation error of 4.4% compared with execution on real hardware, while it runs orders of magnitude faster than gem5 and Ramulator.

The rest of the paper is organized as follows. We begin with further motivation in Sect. 2. Section 3 provides background information on memory access tracing and lightweight kernels. Our custom PEBS driver and the estimator are detailed in Sect. 4, and evaluation is provided in Sect. 5. Section 6 provides additional discussion, Sect. 7 surveys related work, and Sect. 8 concludes the paper.

2 Motivation

Before getting into the details of our proposal, we provide a high-level overview of the approach we are pursuing. Our aim is to further clarify the motivation for this work. Figure 1 outlines the idea of RL-based heterogeneous memory management.

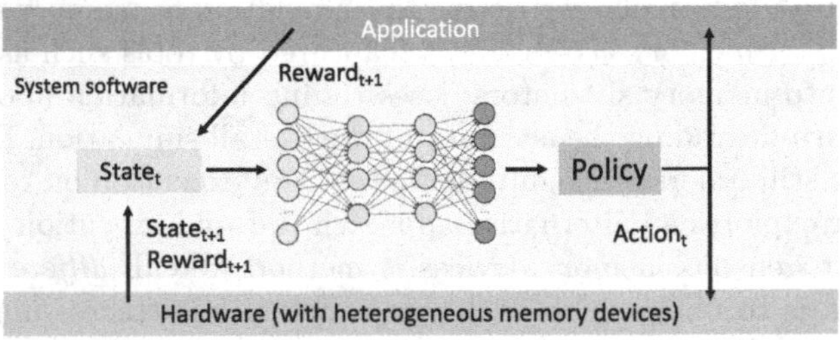

Fig. 1. Reinforcement-learning-based heterogeneous memory management.

In essence, the system software runs an RL agent that periodically observes application behavior through low-level hardware metrics such as memory access patterns, the current utilization of memory bandwidth, and the measured arithmetic intensity. Subsequently, it feeds this state information into a policy network that infers an action for potentially rearranging the memory layout of the application, that is, moving data across memory devices. In turn, the application (optionally in cooperation with the hardware) provides feedback on progress in the form of rewards, for example, inverse proportionally with execution time. The agent's goal is to maximize rewards and thus to minimize execution time.

Ideally, one would train such agents in a real execution environment on actual hardware. However, RL requires a large number of iterations for exploring the environment, which renders real-hardware-based training extremely resource demanding. Therefore, a better approach is to train the agent offline with a surrogate hardware model faster than the actual hardware. In the remainder of the paper, we call this model an *estimator*. While existing hardware simulators can provide accurate runtime estimation, they are impractical because of the immense slowdown they incur (see Sect. 5 for a quantitative characterization of the overhead). Instead, what we need is a simulation environment that provides swift estimation of application execution time as a function of the memory layout.

In summary, we emphasize that the goal of this study is not to optimize the memory layout of the particular applications considered for evaluation but, rather, to provide a simulation environment that can be used to train machine learning models for memory management in a general context.

3 Background

3.1 Precise Event-Based Sampling

PEBS is a feature of some Intel microarchitectures that builds on top of Intel's Performance Counter Monitor (PCM) facility [20]. PCM enables the monitoring of a number of predefined processor performance counters by monitoring the number of occurrences of the specified events[1] in a set of dedicated hardware registers.

PEBS extends the idea of PCM by transparently storing additional processor information while monitoring a PCM event. However, only a small subset of the PCM events actually support PEBS. A "PEBS record" is stored by the CPU in a user-defined buffer when a configurable number of PCM events, named the "PEBS reset", occur. The actual PEBS record format depends on the microarchitecture, but it generally includes the set of general-purpose registers as well as the virtual address for load/store operations.

A *PEBS assist* in Intel nomenclature is the action of storing the PEBS record into the CPU buffer. When the number of records written by the PEBS assist events reaches a configurable threshold inside the PEBS buffer, an interrupt is triggered. The interrupt handler is expected to process the PEBS data and clear the buffer, allowing the CPU to continue storing more records. The smaller the threshold, the more frequent the interrupt requests (IRQs). We note that the PEBS assist does not store any timing information. Timestamping the PEBS data, however, can potentially occur in the IRQ handler.

3.2 Lightweight Kernel-Based Development Environment

Lightweight multikernels have emerged as an alternative operating system architecture for HPC, where the basic idea is to run Linux and a lightweight kernel (LWK) side-by-side in compute nodes to attain the scalability properties of

[1] The exact availability of events depends on the processor's microarchitecture.

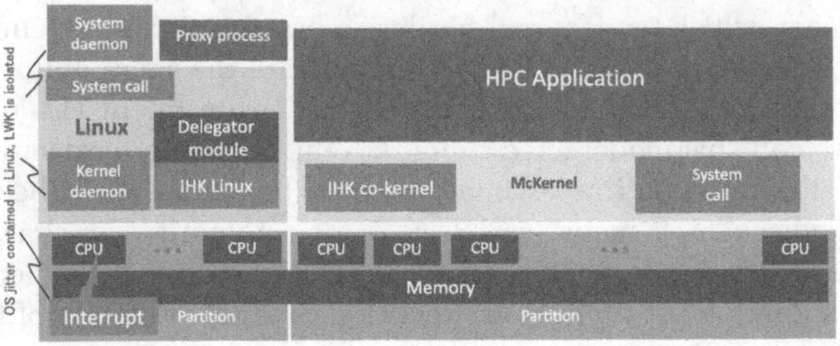

Fig. 2. Overview of the IHK/McKernel architecture.

LWKs and full compatibility with Linux at the same time. IHK/McKernel is a multikernel OS whose architecture is depicted in Fig. 2. A low-level software infrastructure, called Interface for Heterogeneous Kernels (IHK) [40], provides capabilities for partitioning resources in a many-core environment (e.g., CPU cores and physical memory), and it enables management of lightweight kernels. IHK can allocate and release host resources dynamically. No reboot of the host machine is required when altering its configuration, thus enabling relatively straightforward deployment of the multikernel stack on a wide range of Linux distributions.

McKernel is a lightweight co-kernel developed on top of IHK [15]. It is designed explicitly for HPC workloads, but it retains a Linux-compatible application binary interface so that it can execute unmodified Linux binaries. McKernel implements only a small set of performance-sensitive system calls; the rest of the OS services are delegated to Linux. Specifically, McKernel provides its own memory management, it supports processes and multithreading, it has a simple round-robin cooperative (tickless) scheduler, and it implements standard POSIX signaling. It also implements interprocess memory mappings, and it offers interfaces for accessing hardware performance counters.

McKernel has a number of favorable properties with respect to this study. First, it is highly deterministic. Not only does it provide predictable performance across multiple executions of the same program, but it also ensures that the same virtual memory ranges are assigned to a process when executed multiple times, assuming that the application itself is deterministic. As we will see, this significantly simplifies comparing memory access traces obtained from multiple executions.

Second, McKernel's relatively simple source code provides fertile ground for developing custom kernel-level solutions. For example, it provides a custom PEBS driver [29] that we extend with an API to capture higher-level application information (e.g., the application phasemarks discussed in Sect. 4.1), as well as another custom interface that enables selectively binding parts of the application address space to specific memory devices without changing the application code (detailed in Sect. 4.2).

4 Design and Implementation

This section discusses the design of our proposed execution time estimator along with its most relevant implementation details.

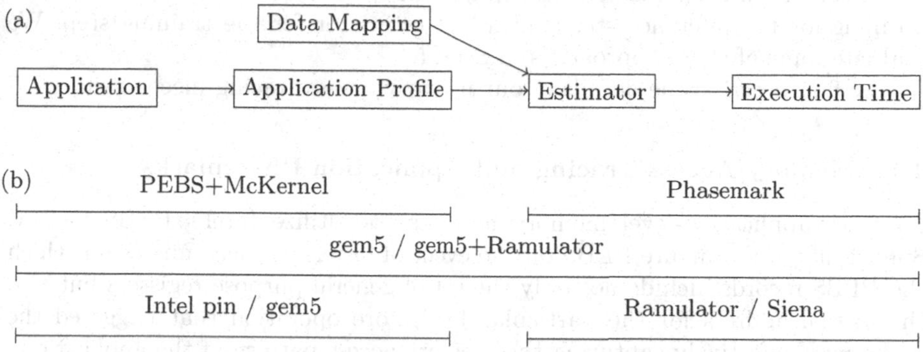

Fig. 3. High-level representation of the steps needed to build the proposed estimator (a) and the tools that assist with the implementation (b).

Figure 3(a) gives an overview of the steps to build the proposed estimator. The system comprises two main pieces: the application profiler and the estimator. First, we collect memory access traces of the target application (*Application Profile* in the figure). Since we want to train an agent offline, trace collection may be slow for the purpose of training. However, the profiling step must have a low overhead once the agent is deployed (i.e., during inference), and the estimator has to be fast for training. Thus, it is desired that both pieces be fast, incur low overhead, and attain high accuracy.

In our implementation of this system (*PEBS+McKernel* in Fig. 3(b)), we collect high-frequency memory access traces from a real, heterogeneous memory-equipped hardware environment where we place application content into different memory devices. Therefore, the application profile is composed of sampled memory access traces annotated with timing information, once for each memory device of the target computing system. Using sampling hardware counters is effectively the lowest-overhead, application-oblivious way to collect an application's memory access trace.

The estimator, which we will describe in more detail below, matches the traces and identifies execution phases (*Phasemark* in the figure) along with the accessed memory regions that impact performance. Taking into account the discrepancy between traces from different memory devices, it estimates execution time based on input that describes the layout of application data with respect to the underlying memory devices, the mapping between virtual memory ranges to the corresponding memory devices that back those mappings (*Data Mapping* in Fig. 3(a)).

Different approaches exist for implementing such a system, as outlined in Fig. 3(b). It can be implemented with a different profiling method and/or a different estimator (*Intel pin/gem5* and *Ramulator/Siena* in the figure, respectively) or even combining the profiling and estimation steps into a single step (*gem5/gem5+Ramulator*). We found that existing approaches are impractical in the context of reinforcement learning because RL requires both low-overhead profiling for the inference step and a fast estimator for the training step. We evaluate some of these approaches in Sect. 5.

We first describe the details of our memory access tracing mechanism.

4.1 Memory Access Tracing and Application Phasemarks

To track application-level memory accesses, we utilize Intel's PEBS facility. Specifically, we configure PEBS on the event of last-level cache misses for which the PEBS records include not only the set of general-purpose registers but also the virtual address for the particular load/store operation that triggered the cache miss, effectively capturing the memory access pattern of the application.

It has been reported previously that standard PEBS drivers incur nontrivial overhead and have limited configuration flexibility [1,26,30]. For example, in both the Linux kernel's PEBS driver and the one provided by Intel's vTune software, no interface is available for controlling the internal PEBS assist buffer size, which implicitly controls the frequency of PEBS interrupts that enable the annotation of PEBS records with high-granularity timestamps. Olson et al. also reported that decreasing the PEBS reset value below 128 on Linux caused the system to crash [30]. For these reasons we utilize McKernel's custom PEBS driver, which has been shown to have negligible runtime overhead even at very high-granularity tracing, for example, by capturing memory accesses with a PEBS reset counter as low as 16 [29].

In addition to high-frequency tracing, we extend the kernel device driver to annotate PEBS records with two extra pieces of information. First, we introduce the notion of *application phases*, for which we add a dedicated `phasemark()` system call in McKernel. The call simply increments a counter in the PEBS driver, which is in turn appended to each PEBS record. Second, we automatically record the number of retired instructions elapsed since the beginning of the last application phase, which again is attached to the PEBS record. As we will see below, this extra information enables us to match memory access traces from different memory devices with very high accuracy. We note that phasemark calls can be inserted into the application source code either manually or through compiler-level code transformation.

Figure 4 highlights the impact of phasemarks in two memory access traces captured from DDR4 and high-bandwidth memory, respectively, when running the Lulesh miniapplication [23]. For more information on the hardware platform used for this experiment as well as on the specifics of how we execute the application, see Sect. 5. The x-axis of the figures indicates elapsed time, while the y-axis shows virtual page indices (i.e., virtual addresses divided by the page size).

The width of the two plots is proportional to the execution time, while the red vertical lines pinpoint application phasemarks captured by the PEBS driver. The two plots show the same four phases of the application, with the only difference being that the application was running on different memory devices.

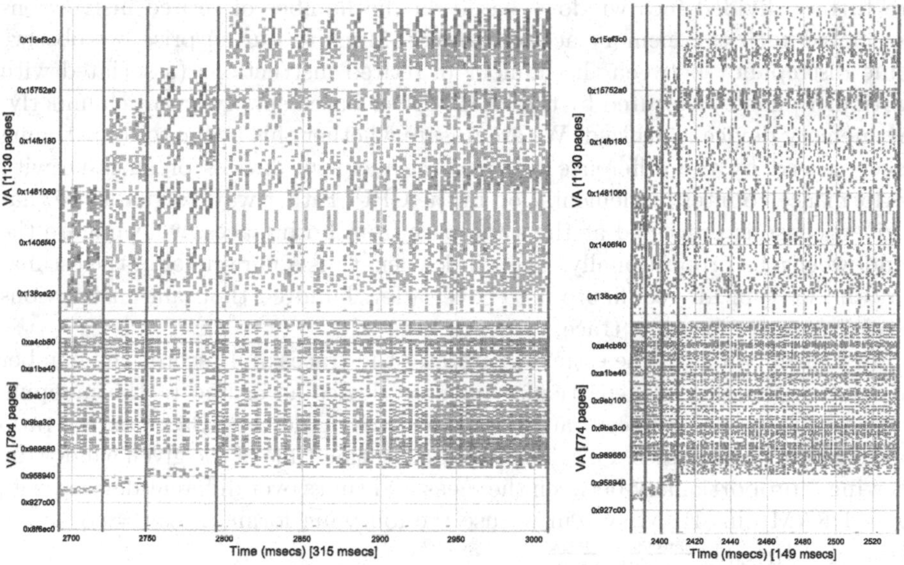

(a) DDR4 (b) MCDRAM

Fig. 4. Lulesh memory traces from DDR4 vs. MCDRAM, annotated with application phasemarks.

As shown, the virtual memory ranges of the two executions are almost identical. This is due to the deterministic behavior of McKernel's memory management subsystem. In addition, phasemarks help determine how much a given application phase is impacted by the fact that memory content is placed into a particular memory device. This information is especially important because not all phases experience the same effect. For example, the execution time of the fourth phase in the figure is reduced by 44% when using MCDRAM; the first phase, however, becomes almost 4× faster. Had we not marked the different phases, trace matching would become significantly more complex, since it would need to identify parts of the trace where the application proceeds at a different pace from that of others when executed out of a different memory device. In contrast, with the presence of phasemarks, we have stable anchors for periodic synchronization while processing the traces. In Sect. 5 we quantitatively characterize the impact of phasemarks on runtime estimation accuracy.

4.2 Execution Time Estimation and Verification

Estimation. The mechanism of the execution time estimator is remarkably simple. The algorithm processes memory traces of a given application obtained from different memory devices by iterating through the individual phases supplemented by the phasemark annotation. In a given phase, the memory access traces are further divided into windows based on the number of retired instructions associated with the memory access samples. Much to our surprise, we observe some discrepancy between the number of retired instructions (associated with particular phases) captured by the PEBS driver based simply on which underlying memory device is utilized. We are unsure whether this is due to some timing effect caused by the difference between the memory devices or an issue with performance counter implementation in the CPU. Either way, to guarantee that a given phase is processed at the same pace from both traces, we configure the window lengths proportionally. The window length is a parameter of the estimator, and we typically configure it to cover a few hundred thousand instructions according to the baseline trace.

In a given window, the estimator iterates the traces and records the number of accesses that hit each particular memory device according to the mapping between the virtual memory ranges and the backing devices. Based on the ratio of the number of accesses, we calculate the execution time of the given window by skewing it proportionally between the measured times over different devices, e.g., for a DRAM plus HBM system we use the following formula: $t_{est} = t_{DRAM} - (t_{DRAM} - t_{HBM}) \cdot \frac{\#accesses_{HBM}}{\#accesses_{all}}$.

As one may notice, this mechanism completely disregards data dependencies among memory accesses and greatly simplifies the interpretation of memory access traces. Nevertheless, as we will see in Sect. 5, this simple approach (in combination with phasemarks) proves to be surprisingly accurate. We also note that utmost accuracy is not required for the ML training process to be successful; rather, it is sufficient if it is expressive enough to guide the learning algorithm to the right optimization path.

Verification. To verify the accuracy of the estimator, we extend McKernel's memory management code with two custom APIs. One allows the specification of a list of virtual memory ranges along with their target memory device; the other makes it possible to indicate a percentage that is interpreted as the fraction of application pages that are to be mapped to a given memory device. The kernel automatically places the memory of the calling process on the target device irrespective of whether it covers the stack, heap, data/BSS sections, or anonymous memory mappings in the process's address space.

As opposed to standard POSIX calls such as `set_mempolicy()` or `mbind()` that need to be invoked at the application level, this memory placement mechanism is carried out in an application-transparent fashion. This approach greatly simplifies experimentation because we do not need to make modifications to individual applications. Using the APIs, we can easily verify the accuracy of the proposed estimator against measurements on real hardware.

5 Evaluation

All of our experiments were performed on an Intel® Xeon Phi™ 7250 Knights Landing (KNL) processor, which consists of 68 CPU cores, accommodating 4 hardware threads per core. The processor provides 16 GB of integrated, high-bandwidth MCDRAM, and it is accompanied by 96 GB of DDR4 RAM. We configured the KNL processor in Quadrant flat mode; in other words, MCDRAM and DDR4 RAM are addressable at different physical memory locations. We used 64 CPU cores for applications and reserved the rest for OS activities. While we acknowledge that the KNL platform has come of age, we emphasize that our proposal is orthogonal to the underlying hardware. We use KNL because it is currently the only generally available CPU architecture supporting both high-bandwidth memory and regular DDR4. Note that Intel has already announced its upcoming Sapphire Rapids CPU model that will provide a similar hybrid memory environment [3]. For the wall-clock measurements of the estimator, we use an Intel® Xeon™ Platinum 8280 (Cascade Lake) CPU equipped platform.

5.1 Application Benchmarks

To evaluate the proposed estimator, we chose the following miniapplications primarily because they are the subject of a substantial runtime difference when executed out of high-bandwidth memory.

- **MiniFE** is a proxy application for unstructured implicit finite element codes. It is similar to HPCCG and pHPCCG but provides a much more complete vertical covering of the steps in this class of applications [17].
- **Lulesh** is the Livermore Unstructured Lagrangian Explicit Shock Hydrodynamics benchmark, which is part of the Shock Hydrodynamics Challenge Problem. It was originally defined and implemented by Lawrence Livermore National Laboratory, and it is a widely studied proxy application in U.D. Department of Energy co-design efforts [23].
- **LAMMPS** is an acronym for Large-scale Atomic/Molecular Massively Parallel Simulator. LAMPPS is a classical molecular dynamics code [36].
- **Nekbone** solves a standard Poisson equation using a conjugate gradient iteration with a simple preconditioner on a block or linear geometry. Nekbone exposes the principal computational kernel that is pertinent to Nek5000 [5].

All our measurements are performed in flat MPI configuration, that is, running 64 MPI ranks on a single node with a dedicated CPU core for each process. This setup enables us to achieve two important goals. First, we make sure that we exercise the entire chip and measure a practical application deployment. Second, the single-threaded execution of each rank ensures deterministic behavior with respect to memory mappings, which in turn enables us to easily measure configurations where only specific ranges of the address space are mapped to high-bandwidth memory. We also note that we observe negligible performance variation across multiple executions on McKernel, and thus we omit error bars on measured data points. As for PEBS, we configure the reset value to 16.

5.2 Results

We provide two sets of experiments with respect to estimation accuracy. In the first setup we gradually increase the fraction of the application address space that is mapped to high-bandwidth memory from 0% (i.e., running entirely out of DDR4) all the way up to 100%, where all memory is allocated out of MCDRAM. We increase the ratio in steps of 10%. Figure 5 summarizes the results.

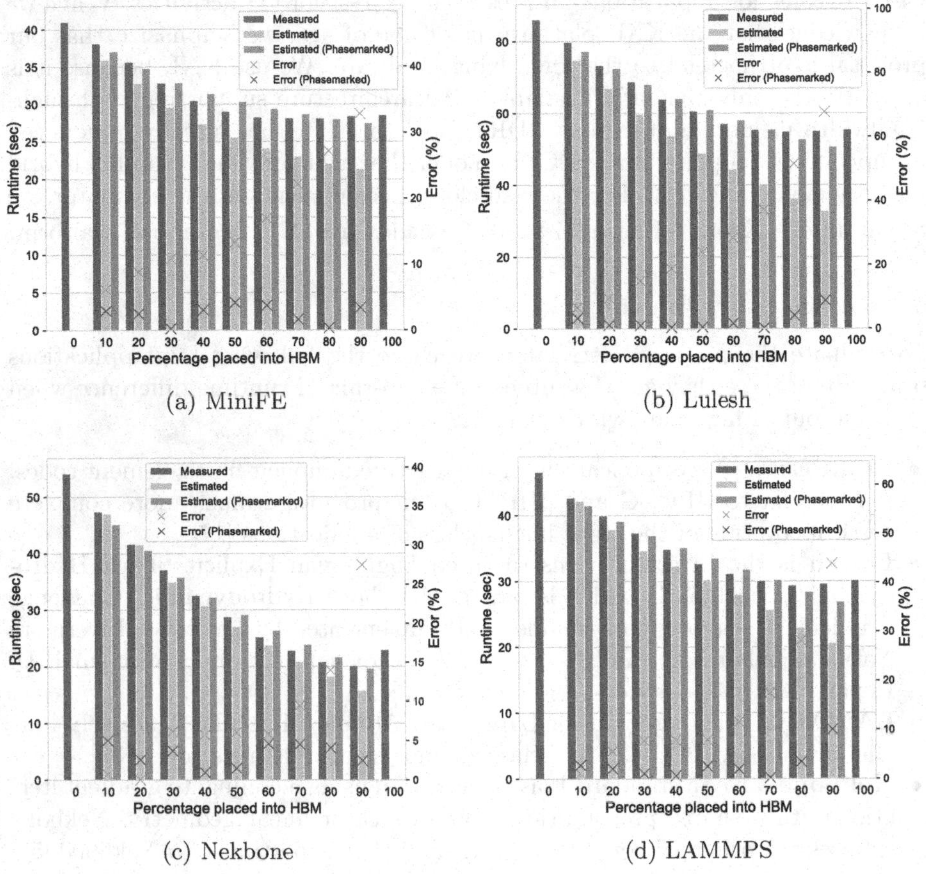

(a) MiniFE (b) Lulesh

(c) Nekbone (d) LAMMPS

Fig. 5. Runtime estimations vs. measurements as a function of data fraction placed in high-bandwidth memory.

On each plot the x-axis indicates the fraction of application memory that is mapped to HBM. The left y-axis shows execution time, where the blue, orange and green bars indicate runtimes as measured, estimated w/o phasemarks, and estimated with phasemarks, respectively. We do not estimate values for full DDR4 and MCDRAM executions. The right y-axis covers estimation error (against the measured values). The actual values are shown by the blue and red crosses, for with and w/o phasemarks, respectively.

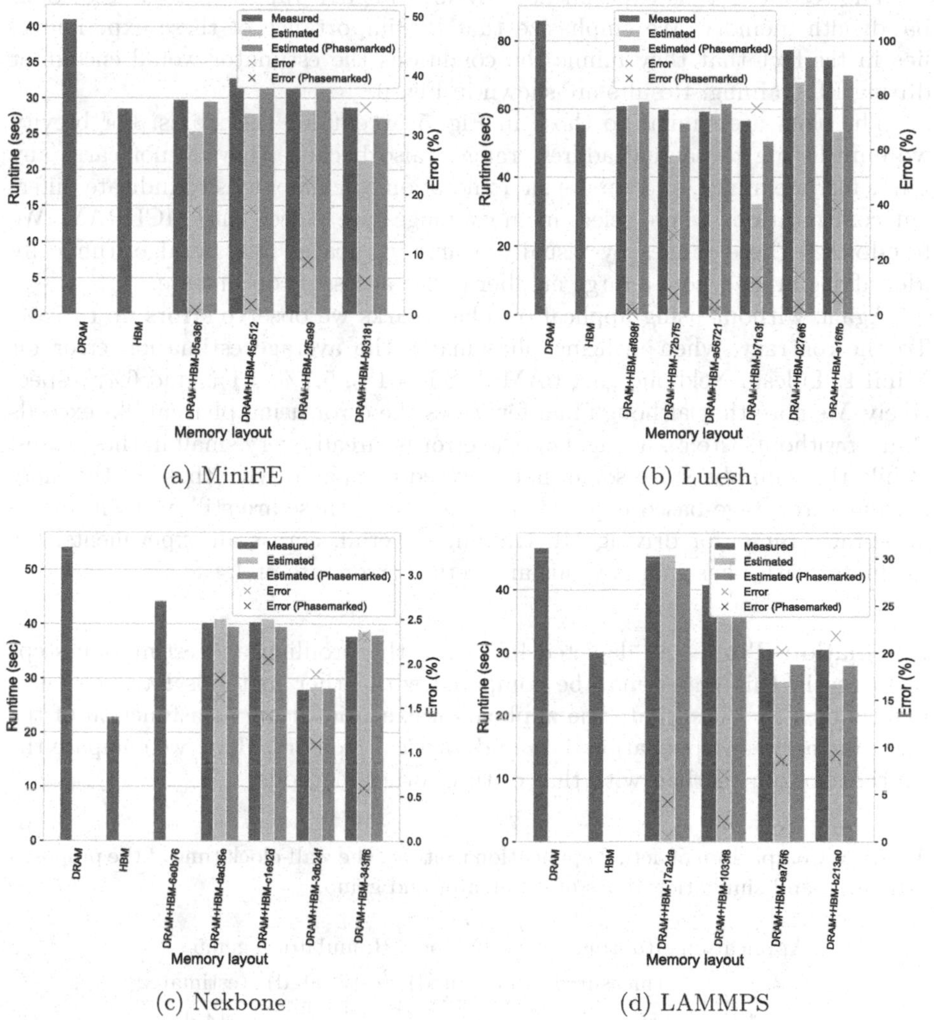

(a) MiniFE (b) Lulesh

(c) Nekbone (d) LAMMPS

Fig. 6. Runtime estimations vs. measurements as a function of data ranges placed in high-bandwidth memory.

As shown, without using phasemarks we endure estimation errors up to over 60%, while with the incorporation of phasemark information the proposed mechanism provides a remarkably accurate estimation of runtimes. Specifically, the average estimation error when using phasemarks for MiniFE, Lulesh, Nekbone, and LAMMPS is 2.4%, 2.3%, 3.2%, and 2.7%, respectively. The largest error (while using phasemarks) we observe across all the experiments is for LAMMPS at 90% of the memory placed into HBM where we see approximately a 10% error. We find this particular result counterintuitive because most pages are in HBM already; we are still investigating the root cause of it.

The second set of experiments covers arbitrary ranges placed into high-bandwidth memory. We emphasize that the importance of these experiments lies in the fact that they mimic the conditions the estimator would encounter during RL training. Results are shown in Fig. 6.

The plots are similar to those in Fig. 5 except for the x-axis. For brevity we omit listing the actual address ranges (also because they do not carry any particular meaning), and we use short notations on the x-axis to indicate different configurations where select memory ranges are placed into MCDRAM. We handpicked these ranges by visually examining traces and by algorithmically identifying areas where a large number of the accesses concentrate.

Again, without using application phasemarks we observe errors up to 75%. To the contrary, when utilizing phasemarks the average estimation error for MiniFE, Lulesh, Nekbone, and LAMMPS is 4.1%, 5.7%, 3.1%, and 6%, respectively. We note that although in a few cases the error using phasemarks exceeds that of without it (e.g., in Fig. 6c), the error is already very small in these cases. While these numbers are somewhat elevated compared with those of the more regular percentage-based experiments, we believe these are still well within the acceptable range for driving ML training. Overall, across all experiments, the estimator with phasemarks yields an average error rate of 4.4%.

Estimation Time. As depicted in Fig. 3, the profiling and estimation steps proposed in this paper may be compared with other methods having similar utility, that is, to estimate the application execution time as a function of the mapping between application data and physical memory. Here, we compare the overhead of our method with that of three other methods.

Table 1. Comparison of actual application runtime, the wall-clock time of the proposed estimator, and simulation times of Ramulator and gem5.

Application	Runtime (measured)	Estimator (measured)	Ramulator (estimated)	gem5 (estimated)
MiniFE	41 s	~9 s	~1 h	~14 days
Lulesh	86 s	~54 s	~2 h	~29 days
Nekbone	54 s	~66 s	~1 h	~18 days
LAMMPS	46 s	~39 s	~1 h	~15 days

Based on measurements, we report the upper limit of application runtime (i.e., running out of DRAM) and the wall-clock time it takes the proposed mechanism to give an estimate. In addition, we estimate the simulation times of Ramulator and gem5. Ramulator [25] is a memory simulator capable of simulating multiple memory technologies. In our experience, using Ramulator to process a memory access trace obtained with the Intel Pin [28] binary instrumentation tool was about 100 to 1,000 times slower than running the actual application. We estimate wall-clock times based on these values. The gem5 [8] simulator is a cycle-level simulator, modeling several components of a hardware platform including CPUs, caches, and the memory hierarchy. We estimate gem5 runtimes based on the approximate 30,000 times slowdown reported by Sandberg *et al.* [38], which is also in line with our own experience running smaller benchmarks.

Results are shown in Table 1. As seen, the runtimes of both gem5 and Ramulator are prohibitive for our purpose. In contrast, the proposed estimator provides runtime estimates several orders of magnitude faster. In fact, except for Nekbone, it runs faster than the application itself. We note that the slowdown in Nekbone is related to the large number of memory accesses that impacts the speed of the simulation. We leave further performance optimization of the estimator for future work. Nevertheless, we point out that the estimator runs on a single CPU core as opposed to the application that occupies at least an entire chip. Taking into account RL's ability to utilize multiple agents concurrently, our solution provides efficiency improvements proportional to the number of CPU cores even if compared with actual application runs. Moreover, since the application profile used in the proposed mechanism is based on sampled memory access traces, we can adjust the trade-off between the trace resolution and the estimator accuracy to speed up the profiling and estimation.

6 Discussion

This section provides additional discussion on various aspects of the proposal.

The ultimate goal of this study is to train ML agents that will guide memory placement in heterogeneous memory environments in an application transparent fashion. Phasemarking is used exclusively for building the environment to train the agent (i.e., for generating training data) and the expectation is that ML agents will generalize enough to work on unseen access patterns.

We emphasize that at the time of deployment an RL agent only needs to observe memory accesses (e.g., through PEBS) and there is no need for phasemarking each application when the system is deployed. Furthermore, our special-purpose OS is only utilized for the creation of training data. Once an RL agent is trained, it can be deployed in any standard OS/runtime environment with the only requirement for being able to sample memory accesses.

One might recognize the possibility to directly utilize phasemark information for memory management. While this may be feasible, it is outside the scope of this study and we leave it for future exploration. Our goal is to derive an application-transparent solution that does not require code instrumentation.

7 Related Work

A significant amount of research has been done over the years on improving page placement for complex memory architectures.

Focusing on modern memory architectures and profiling-based methods, we identify several works of interest. The first set of research studies can be characterized by the focus on designing a system or runtime using different memory tiers as a stage-in/stage-out cache. These studies can predict which pages of memory should be migrated from large and slow to small and fast memory devices ahead of time, either in a system with NVRAM and DRAM or a system with DRAM and HBM. We highlight the works of Doudali *et al.* [12–14] that showcase ML methods to predict which pages to migrate next or how often to perform migration. These works are difficult to adapt to our objective, however, since they operate under the assumption that any application page would benefit from being in fast memory at the right time, which is not necessarily the case in the HPC context [33,37]. Indeed, we aim here to select the right placement for each page and not to design a paging scheme that would move the working set of an application in and out of a hierarchy of devices. We also note that many of the above-mentioned studies consider only single CPU core execution, which we think is unrealistic in an HPC setting. We can also differentiate these works with respect to the profiling method used: whether it is based on estimating locality metrics (e.g., reuse distance) [2,12,24] or a form of memory pressure (e.g., access count per region) [6,30,39].

We further highlight studies providing heuristics or software facilities for data migration between heterogeneous memories [7,35], either through the use of the same metrics as above or through more knowledge of the application. Phase detection is also an extensive field of study, surveyed in [10]. We note that most phase detection methods, in particular architecture-supported ones, tend to be used for reconfiguration purposes (make a change in a policy) and not as much for comparison of traces of the same application in different setups. Nevertheless, we will investigate the use of other lightweight phase detection systems in our future work.

Binary instrumentation tools can also be used to track memory accesses, filter them between the last-level cache and memory, and model the timing of the instructions. Such solutions could be used as profilers for our trace-based estimator. However, the overhead of binary instrumentation-based methods for memory analysis tools has been shown to increase the number of instructions to execute by 10 times [42]. Intel Pin [28] (3.21) is a binary instrumentation framework shipped with a single-level cache emulator tool. Although it could be used here as a profiler, in our experience the overhead of the tool is more on the order of 100 to a 1000 times.

Ramulator [25], the memory simulator we used for evaluation, can also be combined with other tools such as Siena [34] to simulate heterogeneous memory systems. These tools can be used as an estimator to evaluate the impact of data mapping on applications in a fashion similar to our own estimator. Unlike with our tool, however, where we can rely on sampled memory access traces, these tools require a complete trace to provide an accurate timing estimation.

8 Conclusion and Future Work

As architectural complexity grows in HPC systems, it becomes increasingly challenging to efficiently utilize these platforms. Therefore, intelligent application-transparent solutions are greatly desired. In particular, ML/AI techniques that can discover solutions without labeled data may come to the rescue. However, techniques such as reinforcement learning require a large number of interactions with the environment; and thus, when applied to heterogeneous memory management, they require rapid execution time estimation of the application running on a hybrid memory platform.

This paper has proposed a novel execution time estimation mechanism that relies on comparing sampled memory access traces obtained on real hardware from different memory devices. This relatively simple mechanism achieves remarkably accurate runtime predictions (with an average error rate of 4.4%) while running orders of magnitudes faster than high-fidelity architectural simulators. Thus, the proposed mechanism opens up the opportunity to be deployed in nonsupervised machine learning frameworks such as in RL.

Our immediate future work entails integrating the proposed estimator into an RL framework to explore the feasibility of its application to heterogeneous memory management. With respect to gem5, while it is not a suitable solution for high-speed and low-overhead runtime estimation, we intend to use it in the future as a validation platform for new architectures.

Acknowledgment. This research was supported by the Exascale Computing Project (17-SC-20-SC), a collaborative effort of the U.S. Department of Energy Office of Science and the National Nuclear Security Administration. The material was based upon work supported by the U.S. Department of Energy, Office of Science, under contract DE-AC02-06CH11357. This research was also supported by the JSPS KAKENHI Grant Number JP19K11993.

References

1. Akiyama, S., Hirofuchi, T.: Quantitative evaluation of Intel PEBS overhead for online system-noise analysis. In: Proceedings of the 7th International Workshop on Runtime and Operating Systems for Supercomputers ROSS 2017 (2017)
2. Alvarez, L., Casas, M., Labarta, J., Ayguade, E., Valero, M., Moreto, M.: Runtime-guided management of stacked DRAM memories in task parallel programs. In: Proceedings of the 2018 International Conference on Supercomputing (2018)
3. AnandTech: Intel to launch next-gen Sapphire Rapids Xeon with high bandwidth memory (2021). https://www.anandtech.com/show/16795/intel-to-launch-next-gen-sapphire-rapids-xeon-with-high-bandwidth-memory
4. Angel, S., Nanavati, M., Sen, S.: Disaggregation and the Application. USENIX Association, Berkeley (2020)

5. Argonne National Laboratory: Proxy-apps for thermal hydraulics (2021). https://proxyapps.exascaleproject.org/app/nekbone/
6. Arima, E., Schulz, M.: Pattern-aware staging for hybrid memory systems. In: International Conference on High Performance Computing (2020)
7. Benoit, A., Perarnau, S., Pottier, L., Robert, Y.: A performance model to execute workflows on high-bandwidth-memory architectures. In: Proceedings of the 47th International Conference on Parallel Processing (2018)
8. Binkert, N., et al.: The gem5 simulator. SIGARCH Comput. Archit. News (2011). https://doi.org/10.1145/2024716.2024718
9. Buck, B., Hollingsworth, J.K.: An API for runtime code patching. Int. J. High Perform. Comput. Appl. (2000), https://doi.org/10.1177/109434200001400404
10. Dhodapkar, A.S., Smith, J.E.: Comparing program phase detection techniques. In: Proceedings. 36th Annual IEEE/ACM International Symposium on Microarchitecture, 2003. MICRO-36 (2003)
11. Dong, X., Xu, C., Xie, Y., Jouppi, N.P.: NVSim: a circuit-level performance, energy, and area model for emerging nonvolatile memory. IEEE Trans. Comput. Aid. Des. Integr. Circ. Syst. **31**, 994–1007 (2012)
12. Doudali, T.D., Blagodurov, S., Vishnu, A., Gurumurthi, S., Gavrilovska, A.: Kleio: A hybrid memory page scheduler with machine intelligence. In: Proceedings of the 28th International Symposium on High-Performance Parallel and Distributed Computing (2019)
13. Doudali, T.D., Zahka, D., Gavrilovska, A.: The case for optimizing the frequency of periodic data movements over hybrid memory systems. In: The International Symposium on Memory Systems (2020)
14. Doudali, T.D., Zahka, D., Gavrilovska, A.: Cori: dancing to the right beat of periodic data movements over hybrid memory systems. In: 2021 IEEE International Parallel and Distributed Processing Symposium (IPDPS) (2021)
15. Gerofi, B., Takagi, M., Hori, A., Nakamura, G., Shirasawa, T., Ishikawa, Y.: On the scalability, performance isolation and device driver transparency of the IHK/McKernel hybrid lightweight kernel. In: 2016 IEEE International Parallel and Distributed Processing Symposium (IPDPS), May 2016
16. Hady, F.T., Foong, A., Veal, B., Williams, D.: Platform storage performance with 3D XPoint technology. In: Proceedings of the IEEE (2017)
17. Heroux, M.A., et al.: Improving performance via mini-applications. Tech. rep, Sandia National Laboratories (2009)
18. Hildebrand, M., Khan, J., Trika, S., Lowe-Power, J., Akella, V.: AutoTM: automatic tensor movement in heterogeneous memory systems using integer linear programming. In: Proceedings of the Twenty-Fifth International Conference on Architectural Support for Programming Languages and Operating Systems (2020). https://doi.org/10.1145/3373376.3378465
19. HMC Consortium: Hybrid Memory Cube Specification 2.1. (2015). http://www.hybridmemorycube.org/files/SiteDownloads/HMC-30G-VSR_HMCC_Specification_Rev2.1_20151105.pdf
20. Intel Corporation: Intel 64 and IA-32 Architectures Software Developer Manuals (2021). https://www.intel.com/content/www/us/en/developer/articles/technical/intel-sdm.html
21. JEDEC Solid State Technology Association: High Bandwidth Memory (HBM) DRAM (2015)
22. JEDEC Solid State Technology Association: Graphics Double Data Rate 6 (GDDR6) SGRAM standard (2017)

23. Karlin, I., Keasler, J., Neely, R.: LULESH 2.0 updates and changes. Tech. rep., Lawrence Livermore National Laboratory (2013)
24. Kim, J., Choe, W., Ahn, J.: Exploring the design space of page management for multi-tiered memory systems. In: 2021 USENIX Annual Technical Conference (USENIX ATC 21) (2021)
25. Kim, Y., Yang, W., Mutlu, O.: Ramulator: a fast and extensible DRAM simulator. IEEE Comput. Archit. Lett. **15**, 45–49 (2016)
26. Larysch, F.: Fine-grained estimation of memory bandwidth utilization. Master's thesis (2016)
27. Lee, B.C., Ipek, E., Mutlu, O., Burger, D.: Architecting phase change memory as a scalable DRAM alternative. SIGARCH Comput. Archit. News (2009). https://doi.org/10.1145/1555815.1555758
28. Luk, C.K., et al.: Pin: building customized program analysis tools with dynamic instrumentation. In: Proceedings of the 2005 ACM SIGPLAN Conference on Programming Language Design and Implementation (2005)
29. Nonell, A.R., Gerofi, B., Bautista-Gomez, L., Martinet, D., Querol, V.B., Ishikawa, Y.: On the applicability of PEBS based online memory access tracking for heterogeneous memory management at scale. In: Proceedings of the Workshop on Memory Centric High Performance Computing (2018)
30. Olson, M.B., Zhou, T., Jantz, M.R., Doshi, K.A., Lopez, M.G., Hernandez, O.: MemBrain: automated application guidance for hybrid memory systems. In: IEEE International Conference on Networking, Architecture, and Storage (2018)
31. Padakandla, S.: A survey of reinforcement learning algorithms for dynamically varying environments. ACM Comput. Surv. **54**(6) (2021). https://doi.org/10.1145/3459991
32. Park, K.-T., et al.: 19.5 three-dimensional 128Gb MLC vertical NAND flash-memory with 24-WL stacked layers and 50MB/s high-speed programming. In: 2014 IEEE International Solid-State Circuits Conference Digest of Technical Papers (ISSCC) (2014)
33. Parsons, B.S.: Initial benchmarking of the Intel 3D-stacked MCDRAM. Tech. rep, ERDC (2019)
34. Peng, I.B., Vetter, J.S.: Siena: exploring the design space of heterogeneous memory systems. In: SC18: International Conference for High Performance Computing, Networking, Storage and Analysis (2018)
35. Peng, I.B., Gioiosa, R., Kestor, G., Cicotti, P., Laure, E., Markidis, S.: RTHMS: a tool for data placement on hybrid memory system. ACM SIGPLAN Notices **52**, 82–91 (2017)
36. Plimpton, S.: Fast parallel algorithms for short-range molecular dynamics. J. Comput. Phy. **117**, 1–19 (1995)
37. Pohl, C.: Exploiting manycore architectures for parallel data stream processing. In: Grundlagen von Datenbanken, pp. 66–71 (2017)
38. Sandberg, A., Diestelhorst, S., Wang, W.: Architectural exploration with gem5 (2017). https://www.gem5.org/assets/files/ASPLOS2017_gem5_tutorial.pdf
39. Servat, H., Peña, A.J., Llort, G., Mercadal, E., Hoppe, H.C., Labarta, J.: Automating the application data placement in hybrid memory systems. In: 2017 IEEE International Conference on Cluster Computing (CLUSTER) (2017)
40. Shimosawa, T., et al.: Interface for heterogeneous kernels: A framework to enable hybrid OS designs targeting high performance computing on manycore architectures. In: 21st International Conference on High Performance Computing (2014)
41. Sutton, R.S., Barto, A.G.: Reinforcement Learning: An Introduction (1998). http://www.cs.ualberta.ca/~sutton/book/the-book.html

42. Uh, G.R., Cohn, R., Yadavalli, B., Peri, R., Ayyagari, R.: Analyzing dynamic binary instrumentation overhead. In: WBIA Workshop at ASPLOS. Citeseer (2006)
43. Wu, K., Ren, J., Li, D.: Runtime data management on non-volatile memory-based heterogeneous memory for task-parallel programs. In: SC18: International Conference for High Performance Computing, Networking, Storage and Analysis (2018)
44. Yu, S., Park, S., Baek, W.: Design and implementation of bandwidth-aware memory placement and migration policies for heterogeneous memory systems. In: Proceedings of the International Conference on Supercomputing, pp. 1–10 (2017)
45. Zambelli, C., Navarro, G., Sousa, V., Prejbeanu, I.L., Perniola, L.: Phase change and magnetic memories for solid-state drive applications. In: Proceedings of the IEEE (2017)

Understanding Distributed Deep Learning Performance by Correlating HPC and Machine Learning Measurements

Ana Luisa Veroneze Solórzano(✉) and Lucas Mello Schnorr(✉)

Informatics Institute (PPGC/UFRGS), Porto Alegre, Brazil
{alvsolorzano,schnorr}@inf.ufrgs.br

Abstract. Frameworks for Distributed Deep Learning (DDL) have become popular alternatives to distribute training by adding a few lines of code to a single-node script. From a High-Performance Computing (HPC) perspective, traditional profiling tools for researches in Machine Learning (ML) fail to expose details about distributed training performance, such as identifying synchronization points, communication and computing time, and devices usage throughout the training. Moreover, these results are usually considered independently. We present a methodology for performance analysis of DDL frameworks that combines HPC and ML tools to apply intrusive and non-intrusive tracing to enrich the findings for a strong scaling in three clusters with different GPU models. We selected two modern DDL frameworks: Horovod and Tarantella. Using spatial and temporal analysis, we identify bottlenecks in the frameworks, such as a long initialization time for Horovod, the non-distribution of data during the testing phase for Tarantella. We extract performance measurements using temporal aggregation considering the training phases, which can benefit DDL frameworks' developers to improve their tools. Horovod presented the best scaling efficiency for 4 GPUs or more, with up to 84.6% scaling efficiency for 4 GPUs and large batch size, while Tarantella achieves 54.7% for the same case. Using our temporal aggregation approach, we identified this result origins from Horovod processing an epoch faster than Tarantella.

Keywords: Distributed Deep Learning · Performance analysis · HPC

1 Introduction

Training a Deep Neural Network (DNN) using big datasets can take days. Distributed Deep Learning (DDL) frameworks take advantage of large-scale hybrid systems to accelerate the training by rapid prototyping [17]. The more user-friendly tools run over popular Machine Learning (ML) frameworks, such as TensorFlow [2] and PyTorch [25], can distribute a single-device training to a cluster of multi-GPU nodes, requiring only a few extra lines of code [5,28].

A.-L. Varbanescu et al. (Eds.): ISC High Performance 2022, LNCS 13289, pp. 275–292, 2022.
https://doi.org/10.1007/978-3-031-07312-0_14

The increase of DDL frameworks and the complexity of distributed training strategies generate new performance characteristics for evaluation on scalable distributed systems. Comprehensive literature reviews that compare DDL frameworks consider the parallelization strategy employed, programming language support, efforts to overlap communication with computation, if it is easy to use, and portability to other architectures [3,10,22]. Practical evaluations for DDL usually measure the execution time and the training accuracy. Both aspects are typically covered by single-node training evaluations, as well as the training speedup when adding more devices, the performance of weak and/or strong scaling, throughput, and the framework's usability verifying if they are easy to use [11,17,21]. Other works go a step further and also evaluate the memory usage of devices, the overhead of data communication, I/0 behavior, the training phases (i.e., forward and back propagation), and data copies from host to devices [15,20,29]. These works present independent results from an ML and an HPC perspective and give overall measurements. To tackle the performance of modern DDL frameworks, a methodology to correlate and understand the performance impact of using such frameworks requires more attention.

We propose a new methodology to evaluate and compare DDL frameworks' performance correlating measurements obtained with state-of-the-art HPC and ML tools, using spatial and temporal visualizations. We use two modern DDL frameworks: Horovod [28] and Tarantella [5]. They share similarities in their installation, usage, and distribution strategy, but they use different all-reduce algorithms and communication libraries. Both frameworks are compiled as a standard-alone Python package and with a C++ back-end implementation for distributed computing. Therefore, it is challenging to perform an in-depth analysis of their distributed approach performance using methodologies as applied on standard parallel and distributed applications. Our main contributions are:

- A practical comparison and performance evaluation of Horovod and Tarantella on three multi-GPUs clusters with different GPU cards using strong-scaling for a CNN using a full-factorial design. We evaluate the framework's scalability efficiency and execution time considering resources usage.
- Analysis of Horovod using code instrumentation with Score-P to gather detailed information about its MPI implementation.
- A new strategy to present the results using spatial and temporal visualizations. We depict the exact computing time within GPUs for the training iterations and reveal more detailed information than usual ML profilers that do not correlate temporally high-level programming language measures with GPUs usage. Our approach can prevent users from excluding the first iterations for performance analysis [20,29].
- Performance evaluation of the overall computing time in the host and devices using temporal aggregation considering the training epochs.
- Identify frameworks bottlenecks by using our new methodology. Based on our comparison between frameworks with the same parallel strategy, we can indicate along the training time where the frameworks could be improved.

This paper is organized as follows: we present the DDL frameworks and tracing and profiling tools for DL that motivated our research approach (Sect. 2), the selected frameworks Tarantella and Horovod (Sect. 3), our methodology and tools (Sect. 4), our results comparing the performance of Horovod and Tarantella and contributions using our temporal visualizations (Sects. 5 and 6), a discussion about the results (Sect. 7), and finally our conclusion (Sect. 8). We endeavor to make our analysis reproducible. A public companion hosted at https://gitlab.com/anaveroneze/isc2022-companion contains the dataset and analysis to reproduce our results. A perennial archive is also available in Zenodo at https://zenodo.org/record/6349605.

2 Related Work

Several frameworks are being implemented in recent years due to the fast innovations in Deep Learning (DL). They are targeted to specific scenarios, specific devices, or to be less or more user-friendly. Frameworks more user-friendly prevent users from acquiring a deep knowledge of high-performance systems to improve their training performance. They run on top of popular ML libraries and abstract the system configurations to quickly transform a single-node training into a multi-node training. For being very recent, there is a lack of studies evaluating and comparing the performance of these frameworks.

DDL Frameworks. Horovod uses data parallelism on top of TensorFlow, Keras, Apache MXNet, or PyTorch, with MPI in the back-end for distributed computing [28]. LBANN is a toolkit for accelerating the training using data, model, and pipelining parallelism, developed at the Lawrence Livermore National Laboratory [30]. It uses libraries most developed by their team (e.g. Hydrogen and Aluminum). Due to that, instructions and documentation are focused on the laboratories' facilities. Whale is another DDL framework targeting large models using data, model, and pipelining parallelism on top of TensorFlow, but it is not available online for usage [13]. Orca is part of the BigDL 2.0 project for distributing big data to run on Apache Spark and Ray [7]. Tarantella applies data parallelism using the Global Address Space Programming Interface (GASPI) standard for distributed computing on top of TensorFlow and Keras [5].

Tracing and Profiling Tools for DL. TensorBoard is a tool to trace and profile TensorFlow and visualize in a browser [1]. It started supporting multi-GPUs at the end of 2020 in version 2.4. NVIDIA System Management Interface (NVSMI) is a command-line tool to monitor NVIDIA GPUs usages [23]. It can output the measurements in a CSV file. NVIDIA Visual Profiler (NVProf) is a profiling and tracing tool for events running in NVIDIA GPUs [24]. It outputs an SQLite to be open in the NVProf interface, which must be locally installed, and can output a CSV. Profiling at the Python level can gather training information about training duration and status at runtime. Python cProfile reports statistics about the training time and efficiency [26]. Keras callbacks provide a set of functions to get events about training during runtime [14]. TensorFlow offers a more easy-to-use abstraction of the Keras callbacks to get events about the accuracy, loss, training, testing, and validation phases. Horovod offers a native profiler tool called Horovod Timeline that generates a JSON file compatible with the Google Chrome Tracing Viewer [28]. It facilitates the identification of epochs, MPI, and NVIDIA Collective Communication Library (NCCL) operations during training.

Discussion. Horovod and Tarantella are implemented using the same programming languages (C++ and Python) and offer the same parallel strategy. They are both open-source and have support for TensorFlow and CUDA. Adding Tensorboard to the Python script of Horovod generates one trace file per node, but it only shows one CPU and one GPU per node, even when using more resources. Adding the same for Tarantella only generates traces for the node from where we launch the script. Also, Tensorboard does not provide a visualization of workers in different nodes, in the same panel. Python cProfile model profiles the performance of the training and the execution time for TensorFlow only as a whole, without details of the framework behavior at runtime [31]. NVProf visualization API opens one file for each worker at a time, preventing us from contrasting the worker's execution. However, NVProf measurements give insightful information to analyze DDL behavior. Keras callbacks are easy to use and offer important insights on specific aspects of the training. Still, there is a lack of details on how the model uses the devices during the time frame representing an epoch duration. Horovod Timeline presents limitations to opening and navigating large log files in the browser. For example, training with four workers in 100 epochs and 100 batch size generated a trace with more than 300 MB.

Novelty of Our Work. We compare and evaluate the performance of two modern frameworks to facilitate DDL. We use tracing and profiling tools and correlate the results, to understand the impact of using the frameworks considering the training steps. As far as we are aware, no previous comparison of such frameworks or temporal correlation of these tools was previously proposed in the literature. Furthermore, we implement data analysis and visualizations strategies that are independent of proprietary GUIs for visualization.

3 Frameworks Overview

We selected Horovod and Tarantella since they are both open-source, implemented in Python and C++, and support TensorFlow and CUDA. Both use the data parallelism strategy, which consists of distributing chunks of the dataset among workers. Each worker stores the entire model in memory to process its chunk, and at the end of an epoch, the workers update their gradients based on the training of the entire dataset.

Horovod is a framework developed by Uber in 2017 and hosted by the Linux Foundation AI & Data Foundation [28]. It can be downloaded as a stand-alone Python package or compiled via source code. It uses MPI to distribute training between host and devices and NCCL to perform collective communication between NVIDIA GPUs and multi-nodes over PCIe and NVLink interconnections. Horovod carries out all reduce operations asynchronously, interleaving communication with computation. To improve performance, it also employs the Tensor Fusion technique to combine small all-reduce tensors operations into larger ones. Such techniques improve the training performance when combined with TensorFlow to compute operations in the backward propagation step to advance the reductions processing [17]. Distributing training with Horovod requires a few lines of code to import and initialize Horovod, pin each GPU available to a process, and wrap the optimizer to use Horovod optimizer. To guarantee the parameters and weights are correctly initialized, we use a Horovod callback function to broadcast global the initial parameters from rank 0.

Tarantella is a framework developed at the Fraunhofer Institute for Industrial Mathematics [5]. It uses the GPI-2[1] communication library, which implements the GASPI specification. The GPI-2 has a C++ interface to implement collective operations [9], supporting one-sided asynchronous communication that can allow applications to overlap the communication with computation. Tarantella also implements the Tensor Fusion technique, but it has a synchronous communication pattern. Tarantella usage is simpler than Horovod. It automatically broadcast the initial weights to all workers without user intervention. It also identifies the available GPUs and makes them visible to TensorFlow during the framework initialization. It only requires importing the library and wrapping the Keras model to use the Tarantella model.

4 Methodology

4.1 System Configuration and Software Tools

Table 1 presents Chifflot, Chifflet, and Gemini clusters, part of the Grid'5000 [4]. They have the Debian 4.19.160-2 operating system, GCC version 8.3.0, OpenMPI 4.5.0, GPI-2 1.5.0, which is an open source implementation of the GASPI standard, CUDA 11.3.1, and Python 3.7.3. NVLink is available in Gemini, with a link speed of 25 GB/s. We use TensorFlow 2.4.0, which includes the Keras API, Horovod 0.22.1, and Tarantella 0.7.0. For data processing and analysis, we use the R language coupled with the tidyverse package[2], and the ggplot2 package to create all visualizations.

Table 1. Specifications for the clusters used, all with Intel CPUs and NVIDIA GPUs.

Configuration	Chifflot	Chifflet	Gemini
Nodes	6	8	2
CPU/node	2x(Xeon Gold 6126)	2x(Xeon E5-2680v4)	4x(E5-2698v4)
GPU/node	2x(Tesla P100)	2x(GTX 1080Ti)	8x(Tesla V100)
CUDA cores	3,840	3,584	5,120+640 Tensor
Frequency	1190 MHz	1481 MHz	1230 MHz
Memory	12 GB GDDR5	11GB GDDR5X	16 GB HBM2

[1] https://github.com/cc-hpc-itwm/GPI-2.
[2] https://cran.r-project.org/web/packages/tidyverse/index.html.

4.2 Evaluation Setup

Our approach consisted in comparing the frameworks and correlating results obtained with different measurement tools to evaluate their performance during the training. We selected the well-known Lenet-5 model for the MNIST dataset, composed of 60,000 handwritten digits images plus 10,000 specifically for testing. Each image has a 28 × 28 dimension (784 pixels), divided in 10 classes [18,19]. We use 54,000 images for training, 6,000 images for validation, and 10,000 for testing. We use strong scaling by fixing the work size when adding more devices, which can achieve the same accuracy as the sequential training when using a small dataset, as MNIST, for example [6]. We use the Keras callbacks, NVSMI, and NVProf tools to collect the measurements and have a temporal evolution of the frameworks' behavior. Additionally, we used Score-P 6.0 tool to trace the MPI communication for Horovod [16].

Our experiments follow a full-factorial design using Jain's methodology for computer systems performance analysis [12]. The factors are grouped into two categories depending to what they are related to: (i) the training itself and (ii) hardware resources. For the first, we consider the DL frameworks, models, datasets, and batch sizes. For the second, we consider the number of nodes and GPUs. Different from most works that analyze a single experiment, we performed a total of 84 experiments as a result of 10 repetitions for each case. Each experiment has 100 epochs, which was sufficient for achieving high accuracy.

4.3 Challenges

Tracing the Frameworks. Horovod uses MPI, which could be traced with Score-P, but still presented some challenges to install and use properly. Tarantella uses GPI-2, whereas MPI has become the most used communication interface for frameworks with native training distribution support, like TensorFlow, MXNET, Keras, and PyTorch [21]. We found a branch of the Extrae instrumentation package[3], but we were unable to trace Tarantella properly using Extrae. Our analysis has been possible anyway for correlating results from NVProf and Keras callbacks, which brought the main contributions of this work. We evaluate the time with MPI operations for Horovod with Score-P, but future research is required to extract the same from Tarantella.

Correlating Tools Output. NVProf can output traces in the CSV file format or its default file format, with a `.nvvp` extension, which stores the CUDA operations as an SQLite file, interpreted by the NVProf visualization tool. Considering our data analysis using R, our first approach was to output CSV files. However, it shows the relative time of each event without revealing what they are relative to. It is essential to use the same base timestamp for all measurement tools to correlate information as we collected for the Keras callbacks. We found it is a limitation of the CSV output, so our solution was to also output a `.nvvp`

[3] https://github.com/bsc-performance-tools/extrae/tree/GASPI.

file and use the RSQLite package[4] to process the data with R and get absolute timestamps.

Generate Temporal Visualizations. Real-world ML training took hundreds of epochs to achieve the desired accuracy. For our model, training for 100 epochs converges and can be representative enough of the distributed training performance. Nevertheless, fitting large amounts of data on small screens is a challenge in the performance visualization of parallel applications [27]. Since our goal was also to evaluate the DDL frameworks' behavior during the training steps, we found that tracing fewer epochs can already reveal valuable insights and fit in temporal visualization panels.

5 The Horovod and Tarantella Comparison

Figure 1 presents the average execution time (in the Y axis) for Horovod (red color) and Tarantella (blue) when scaling up until 12 GPUs (on the X axis), with a 99.97% confidence interval. We show results for a number of batch sizes (facet rows) and underlying resource configurations (facet columns). Horovod presents the best performance using 4 or more GPUs compared to Tarantella for all cases. It also scales until 12 GPUs, different from Tarantella, which perform similarly when increasing from 6 to 12 devices. The frameworks achieve similar results in different GPU models, except with the 100 batch size. The Horovod execution time increases with batch size 100, when going from one node with one GPU to two nodes, one GPU each, which can be explained by Horovod start applying its reduction algorithm and NCCL operations when distributing the training.

The experiments with one device in Fig. 1 were executed with the frameworks set-up in the script. We expected they achieved a similar execution time without overhead in single-device training. However, Tarantella presented a higher execution time than Horovod in all cases. Figure 2 presents the frameworks' overhead (the Y axis) for a non-distributed training with one GPU compared to the pure TensorFlow implementation as a function of the batch size (the X axis). Horovod presents negligible overhead compared to the pure TensorFlow experiment, which was expected since Horovod launches a copy of the script for each worker, and with one worker, it will launch one process. Tarantella adds a significant overhead of up to 160 s for the smaller batch size in the Gemini cluster. Tarantella launches one copy of the script and implements its data partitioning and distribution by subclassing the Keras fit function used to train the model for a fixed number of epochs. Investigating the Tarantella source code, we observed the lack of verification if the training uses more than one GPU before distributing the training, which can cause this overhead.

We think this extra time in Tarantella could affect other experiments if related to an initialization phase, especially when scaling for more devices. Figure 3 presents the total time between the training script initialization and the beginning of the first batch for an experiment with 100 images, as a function

[4] https://db.rstudio.com/databases/sqlite/.

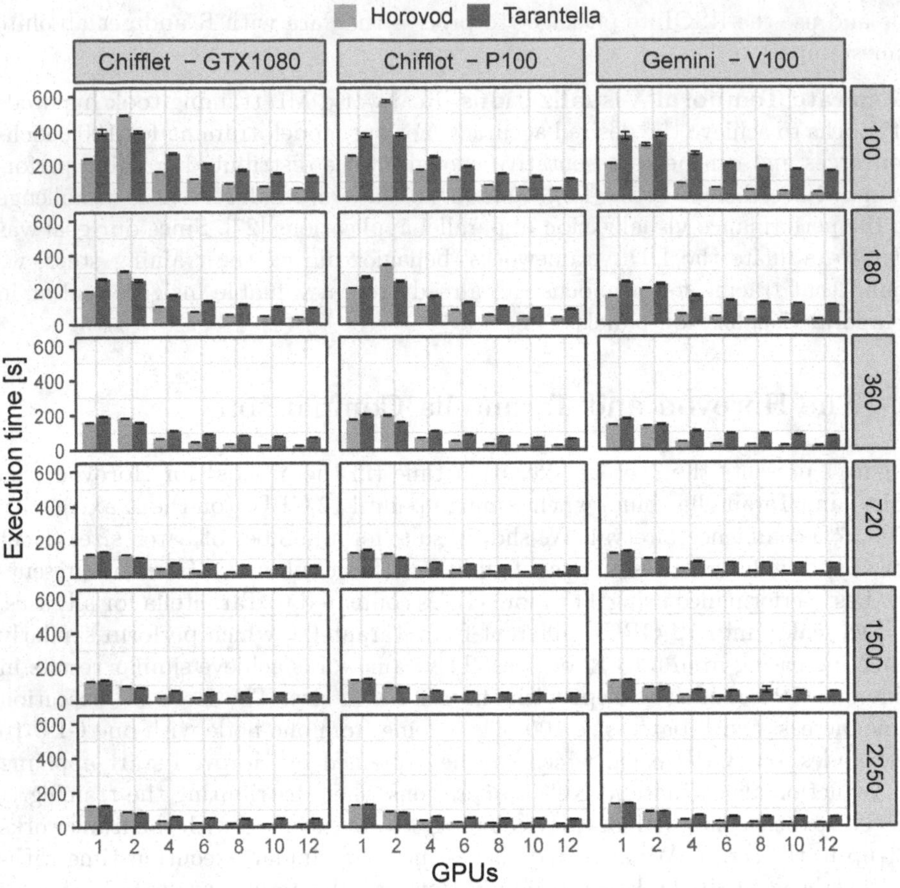

Fig. 1. Average execution time for LeNet-5 over MNIST for Horovod (red bars) and Tarantella (blue bars). Each horizontal facet represents a batch size, and each vertical facet represents a cluster. (Color figure online)

of the number of GPUs (X axis). The frameworks' initialization before starting the script was measured separately, around 0.14 s for Horovod and 0.33 for Tarantella. The percentage values above the bars represent the percentage of time of initialization over the execution makespan. Horovod and Tarantella spent similar time before training. Horovod had 7.7% of the time with initialization for 12 GPUs at Gemini, which is a significant value percentage, since the training time was very small, as shown in Fig. 1. Our interpretation of these results indicates that Tarantella's extra execution time compared to Horovod is unrelated to its initialization.

Figure 4 compares the scaling efficiency using the Eq. 1, where T_1 is the execution time with one GPU, and T_n with n GPUs. In our strong scaling approach, as we show in the Figure, Horovod achieves higher efficiency for all cases with

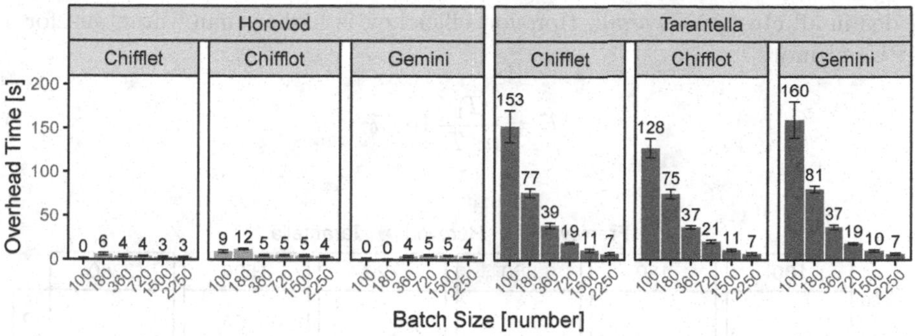

Fig. 2. Overhead time of using the DDL frameworks compared to a single GPU training with TensorFlow. The average overhead is written above the error bars.

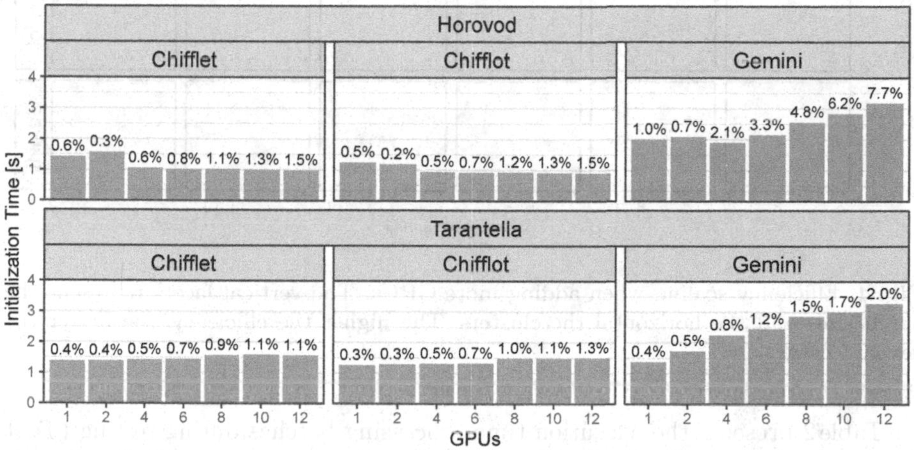

Fig. 3. Time spent with initialization for an experiment with batch size 100, and the percentage of time it represents over the execution makespan for each case.

more than 6 GPUs, with a difference of almost 50% between Tarantella and Horovod. This difference indicates Tarantella could potentially improve its performance since they use the same parallel strategy. Horovod efficiency improves when increasing the batch sizes, 80% for Chifflet and Chifflot for 2250 batch size, and 76% for 1500 batch size. The same happens for Tarantella, but more slightly, with ≈41% for Chifflet and Chifflot, 2250 batch size, and ≈39% for 1500 batch size. Both frameworks achieve lower scaling efficiency for more than 6 GPUs for batch sizes of 100 and 180 since the batches are not large enough to enable further gains. Horovod is ≈84% faster for 4 GPUs in all clusters for 2250 batch size, the highest efficiency, and for 12 GPUs achieved 68% in Chifflot, 65% for Chifflet, and 53% in Gemini. Tarantella's maximum scaling efficiency is 78% for Chifflot with 1500 batch sizes with 2 nodes, and it is only ≈23% faster for 12 nodes in all clusters. Overall, Horovod efficiency is higher than Tarantella for 4 GPUs or more.

$$E = \frac{T_1}{n \cdot T_n} 100\% \quad (1)$$

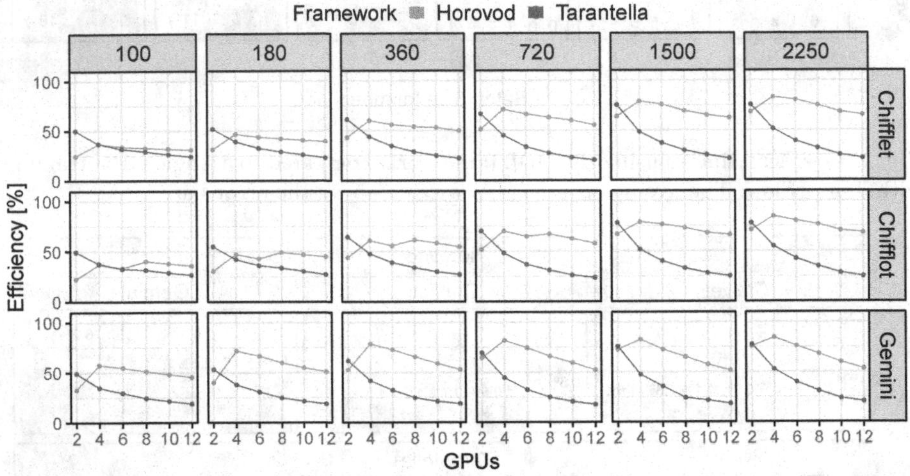

Fig. 4. Efficiency scaling when adding more GPUs. The vertical facets represent the batch sizes and the horizontal the clusters. The higher the efficiency, the better the devices' usage.

Table 2 presents the execution time processing batches during testing (**Test Batches**), training (**Train Batches**), the overall execution time (**Total Time**), and the time difference (**Difference**) between the Total Time, not considering the Train and Test Times. We selected results for the Chifflot cluster for 2250 batch size, which represents the performance behavior of the other GPU cards when scaling from 2 to 12 GPUS. Our goal was to understand if Horovod is faster than Tarantella for processing the batches faster or if the time processing batches are similar, so the difference comes from other reasons.

In Table 2, both frameworks decrease their total execution time when scaling for more workers, in the Total Time column. Horovod's time computing batches is 5.84 times faster, going from 2 GPUs to 12, while Tarantella is only 2.54 times faster. The time testing drops when scaling the training for all cases in Horovod, but it remains similar for Tarantella. It indicates that Tarantella does not distribute the testing batches as it does for the training batches, which can improve its performance. In general, Horovod spends fewer time communicating than Tarantella (column Difference). Processing larger batches in more GPUs in parallel finishes the training faster and results in lower time with communication to pass through all the dataset, as we see for the Difference column of almost 9 s from 2 to 12 GPUs.

Table 2. Execution time in **seconds** processing batches during training (**Train Batches**), testing (**Test Batches**), the total execution time for the experiment (**Total Time**), and the time the experiment is not computing batches (**Difference**).

Framework	GPUs	Train batches (Tr)	Test batches (Te)	Total time (TT)	Difference TT − (Tr + Te)
Horovod	2	**76.42**	2.68	90.96	**11.86**
Horovod	12	**13.09**	0.61	16.6	**2.9**
Tarantella	2	**66.7**	4.44	84.85	13.71
Tarantella	12	**26.25**	4.42	45.29	14.62

6 Breaking the Frameworks Black-Box

Distributed training adds new strategies to take advantage of the computing resources and minimize the communication overhead, when adding more workers. We use execution traces, profiling, and visualization to get further insight about the internal behavior of the Horovod and Tarantella during the performance analysis. The overhead collecting Keras callbacks and NVSMI traces was up to 4% of the total execution time for the smaller batch size for Tarantella and up to 2.5% for Horovod. Due to the variability in the overhead, in practice, this difference remains unnoticeable for larger batch sizes.

Instrumenting Horovod with Score-P requires installing Score-P with support to the `gcc-compiler plugin`, scorep-binding-python [8], and configuring Horovod with support to Score-P tracing. We configured the Horovod compilation to replace the framework's compiler and linker with the corresponding wrapper for MPI and Score-P[5]. We converted the Score-P trace file to CSV using otf2utils[6], to easily process with R.

Table 3 presents the total training time duration, and the total time spent with the `MPI_Allreduce` operation for each node in one Horovod run with batch size 720. The percentage of time with `MPI_Allreduce` represents 73.62% to 82.30% of the total training time in the respective ranks. These high values come from the asynchronous all reduce operations, but still, overlapping the computations with communications needs to be well used since spending more than 80% of the time with reductions can indicate a performance bottleneck.

Figure 5 presents a space/time view of the reduction operations that took place along one epoch for the training phase with 4 workers and batch size 1500. The blue color in the background represents the batches process captured with Keras callbacks. The `MPI_Allreduce` operations are executed throughout all batches with small and bigger data volumes. We zoomed in a time slice to investigate the reductions inside two batches. The vertical green dashed lines represent the time beginning and ending a batch, which occurs subsequently.

[5] https://scorepci.pages.jsc.fz-juelich.de/scorep-pipelines/docs/scorep-6.0/html/scorepwrapper.html.

[6] https://github.com/schnorr/otf2utils.

Table 3. Training duration for each MPI rank for Horovod using a batch size 720 (Training), time with reductions for each rank (MPI_Allreduce), and the percentage of time it represents over the complete training (Percentage of Time).

MPI rank	Training (seconds)	MPI_Allreduce (seconds)	Percentage of time
0	84.84	62.46	73.62%
1	85.19	70.11	82.30%
2	84.97	65.34	76.89%
3	85.12	69.63	81.80%

This figure exposes the challenge of fitting one epoch training in a visualization, even for a small dataset, and zooming into a few batches. We identify a pattern where `MPI_Allreduce` processes bigger messages inside each batch, starting around the middle of its execution. Right after the batch beginning and end, all ranks process faster reductions, making them narrow in the plot.

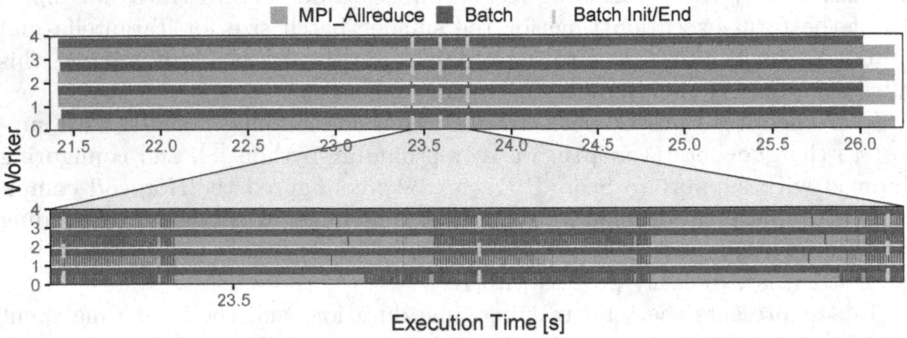

Fig. 5. Correlating Keras callbacks and Score-P traces to investigate the training for Horovod in one epoch. In red, the pattern of reduction operation during each batch for the four ranks involved in this analysis (on the Y axis). (Color figure online)

Figures 6 (Horovod) and 7 (Tarantella) present a correlation between the results obtained with Keras callbacks and NVProf for 10 epochs in the Chifflet cluster. The panel on the top shows the epochs with Keras callbacks and the NVProf events for the whole execution. Below, the NVProf panel zooms into the first epoch, and the last panel zooms into one batch of this epoch, where we characterize the NVProf operations shown in the legend. The vertical lines in red mark the zoomed parts. Looking at the top panel, we identify the computing time at the devices during what is considered an epoch to Keras. The callbacks encompass more than the actual training time for the first epoch for both frameworks. Works that only use tracing at the high-level programming language skip the first iterations or the first epoch of the training to avoid measuring the initialization time [20,29]. This correlation confirms we can identify the actual training time using the NVProf and consider the entire training duration.

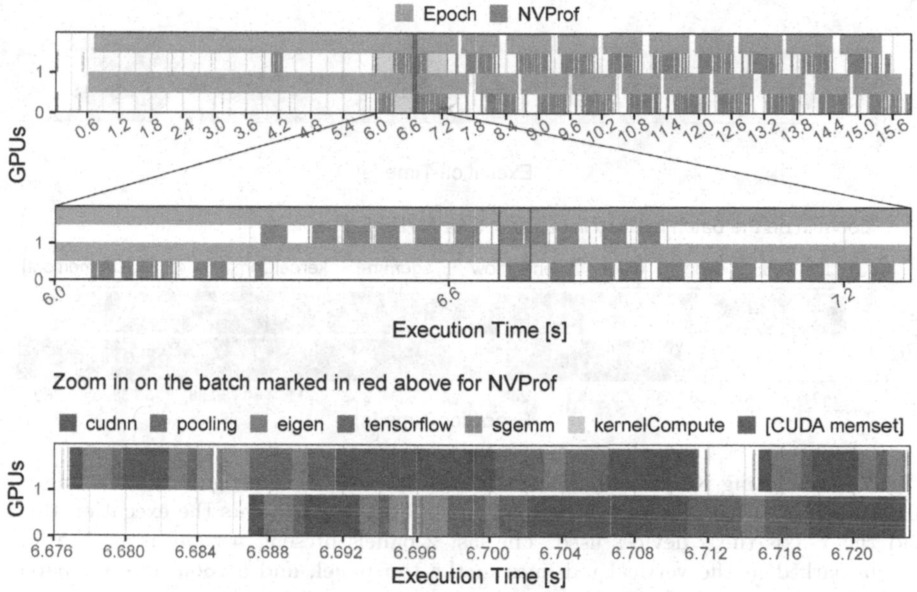

Fig. 6. Correlating Keras callbacks and NVProf traces to investigate the training for **Horovod** in 10 epochs in the top panel. The X-axis represents the execution time, and the Y-axis the 2 devices used. The last 2 panels present: a zoom in on the first epoch marked in the vertical red lines in the top panel; and a zoom in on a batch, marked in the second plot. (Color figure online)

In the top panel for Horovod (Fig. 6), we notice the origin of the longer initialization time. For the first epoch, most of the ≈7.7 s are performed in the host, with a more extended initialization than Tarantella, which leaves space for investigating if initialization in Horovod could be improved. For the other epochs, we notice the time computing in the GPUs with an interval between epochs to average gradients among all workers. Zooming in the first epoch, we notice the asynchronous execution of the batches. Zooming in one batch in the last panel, we identify the operations performed per batch. They are mostly cuDNN operations, followed by pooling operations, Eigen operations, a library to perform linear algebra operations, TensorFlow operations, SGEMM for matrix-matrix operations in single precision, and computations inside the kernel.

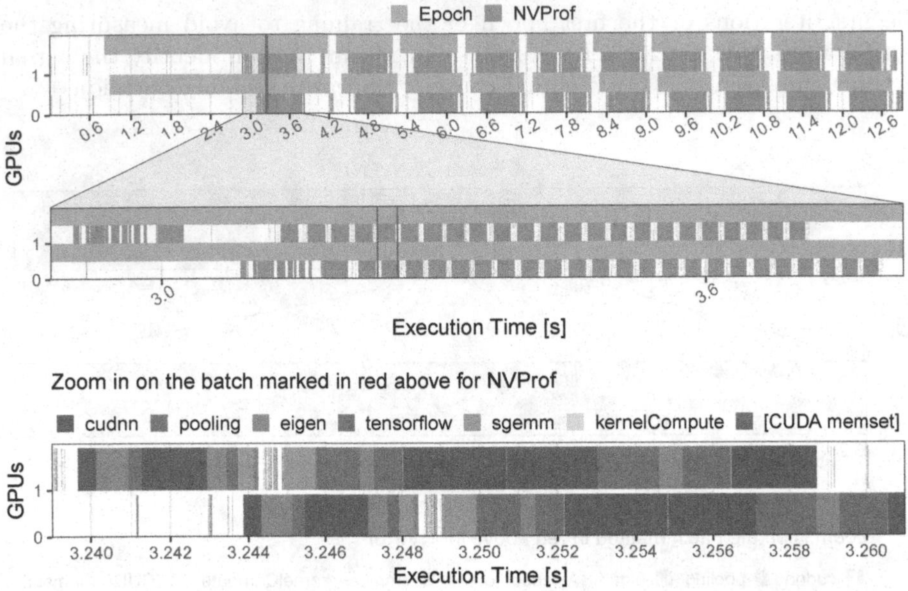

Fig. 7. Correlating Keras callbacks and NVProf traces to investigate the training for **Tarantella** in 10 epochs in the top panel. The X-axis represents the execution time, and the Y-axis the 2 devices used. The last 2 panels present: a zoom in on the first epoch marked in the vertical red lines in the top panel; and a zoom in on a batch, marked in the second plot. (Color figure online)

Tarantella's experiment (Fig. 7) shows in the first panel a shorter initialization time than Horovod but a longer time interval between epochs. The epochs process is also more synchronized between devices. Zooming into one epoch, we again notice a constant execution of operations inside the devices, even for the initialization phase. Zooming into one batch, we identify the same operations performed inside a batch for Horovod, as expected for the training using the same model.

We used the Keras callbacks and the NVProf measurements to perform a temporal aggregation considering the time of an epoch. Figure 8 presents the amount of time (in the Y axis) computing in GPU, CPU, and communication (colors) per epoch (the X axis), disregarding the first epoch. We also depict the time spent with communications between host and devices, even though NVIDIA GPUs can overlap data transfers and kernel execution. We intend to compare the total time per epoch spent with communication. Horovod uses almost all the time during an epoch performing operations in the devices. It spends few time with communication and presents differences in the total time per device, due to its asynchronous communication. Tarantella keeps a similar value per GPUs processing per epoch, resulting in less than half of the time per epoch spent inside the devices. It also presents a higher time performing communications than Horovod, which we can notice by the longer interval between epochs as shown in Fig. 7. We believe asynchronous communication in Tarantella could be explored so that it can increase the time using the devices. In the first epoch, Horovod spends ≈6 s outside of the devices and only ≈0.9 s computing in GPUs, while Tarantella spends 2.79 s outside and ≈0.5 in GPUs. However, the first epoch becomes rapidly absorbed by the total number of epochs that Horovod processes faster than Tarantella, which makes it train more quickly for most cases, as presented in Fig. 1.

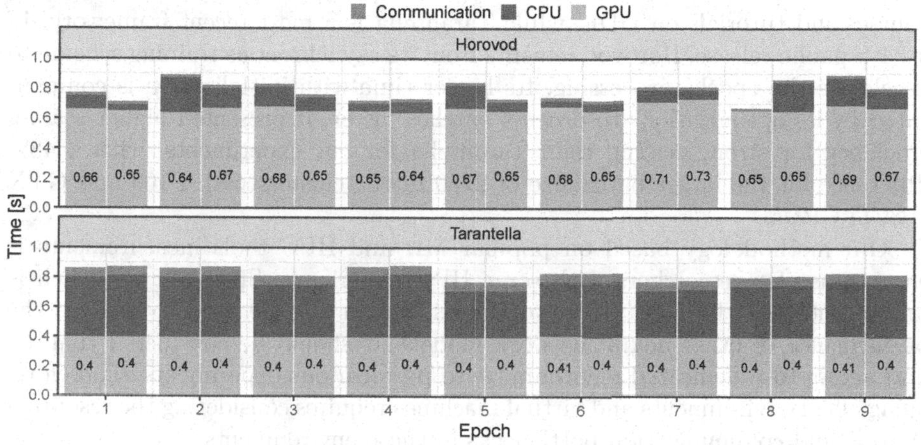

Fig. 8. Percentage of time computing in GPU and communicating between host and devices, device to device, or device to host. Time for each of 2 GPUs per epoch for 10 epochs for Horovod (top facet) and Tarantella (bottom facet).

7 Discussion

The presented results contribute to the performance analysis and comparison of DDL training, confirming that tracing events at the device level is complementary to the profiling at the high-level programming language only. Performing a temporal synchronization of the execution time of the Keras callbacks and NVProf reveals the time intervals performing the calculation. With a temporal aggregation, we can measure these results during the training steps (epochs and batches), and tracing at the back-end level reveals the standard's overhead for message passing.

For a small CNN and dataset, the GPU model is not significantly important to improve the training performance, but is enough to compare Tarantella and Horovod behavior. Both frameworks stop scaling after six GPUs, since the dataset is not large enough to enable further gains. Using a more complex model, with more layers requiring more matrix operations, we could benefit from Tensor Cores technologies present in recent devices and both NCCL and cuDNN usage.

Tarantella is a comprehensive tool for users starting in DDL. It requires even fewer configurations than Horovod to distribute a sequential code and provides complete documentation. However, it limited our performance analysis with state-of-the-art tracing tools as Score-P to get the communication time with the GASPI standard. It also limits command-line configurations for using TensorBoard and NVProf, for example, where we have to configure in its source code. Also, since it is a tool in development, there are no parameters to configure the network protocol used for communicating between nodes, for example.

Horovod is a more stable framework, in its 65th release, popular in several courses and tutorials on DDL, while Tarantella is a most recent framework, in its 4th public release. Horovod benefits from its asynchronous training scheme to accelerate the epochs processing. Its longer time with initialization is compensated by its optimizations to process batches faster. It presented higher scaling efficiency for strong scaling than Tarantella for our experiments, with a 48% difference for the larger batch size of 2250 in the clusters with P100 and GTX 1080Ti GPUs.

Our methodology based on popular ML and HPC tools measurements is easy to use for researchers with some HPC experience. Since our approach is implemented at the DDL framework level, it can also be used to analyze the performance of other neural network models. It should be considered that we had access to a dedicated environment to perform our experiments. Therefore, using cloud environments and virtual machines requires considering the resources sharing and communication bottlenecks in these environments.

8 Conclusion

DDL frameworks facilitate the usage by people without experience in distributed systems but hide details about their parallel strategy, wrapping the final code using high-level programming languages. For being very recent, there is a lack of studies comparing the performance of these frameworks and, even more, correlating information from different performance analysis tools from the HPC and the ML point-of-view for various hardware and parameters configuration. We compared and evaluated the performance of Horovod and Tarantella, modern DDL frameworks, using state-of-the-art ML and HPC tools. We presented a methodology to perform temporal analyses correlating information from different tracing and profiling tools and revealing potential improvement spots for both. As future work, we plan to create a more automatic methodology using a high-level programming language. Furthermore, we aim to evaluate Horovod, Tarantella, and other less user-friendly DDL frameworks. We will consider more complex models, larger datasets, and frameworks' features, such as using Tensor Cores and cuDNN during training.

Acknowledgments. We are thankful to the Tarantella, scorep-binding-python, and Score-P developers for the prompt replies that support our advances. This work was financed by the Coordenação de Aperfeiçoamento de Pessoal de Nível Superior - Brasil

(CAPES) - Finance Code 001, under grant no 88887.481194/2020-00. The experiments were executed on the PCAD at the Federal University of Rio Grande do Sul, and on the Grid'5000, supported by Inria, CNRS, RENATER and other organizations.

References

1. Abadi, M., et al.: TensorFlow: large-scale machine learning on heterogeneous distributed systems. arXiv preprint arXiv:1603.04467 (2016)
2. Abadi, M., et al.: TensorFlow: a system for large-scale machine learning. In: USENIX Symposium on Operating Systems Design and Implementation, OSDI 2016, pp. 265–283. USENIX Association (2016)
3. Ravikumar, A., Harini, S.: A comprehensive review and evaluation of distributed deep learning on cloud environments. J. Crit. Rev. **7**(19), 9519–9538 (2020)
4. Cappello, F., et al.: Grid'5000: a large scale and highly reconfigurable grid experimental testbed. In: The 6th IEEE/ACM International Workshop on Grid Computing, pp. 8–pp. IEEE (2005)
5. Competence Center for HPC: Tarantella: distributed deep learning framework (2020). https://github.com/cc-hpc-itwm/tarantella
6. Cunha, R.L.F., Rodrigues, E.R., Viana, M.P., Oliveira, D.A.B.: An argument in favor of strong scaling for deep neural networks with small datasets. In: 2018 30th International Symposium on Computer Architecture and High Performance Computing (SBAC-PAD), pp. 306 313. IEEE (2018)
7. Dai, J.J., et al.: BigDL: a distributed deep learning framework for big data. In: Proceedings of the ACM Symposium on Cloud Computing, pp. 50–60 (2019)
8. Gocht, A., Schöne, R., Frenzel, J.: Advanced Python performance monitoring with score-P. In: Mix, H., Niethammer, C., Zhou, H., Nagel, W.E., Resch, M.M. (eds.) Tools for High Performance Computing 2018/2019, pp. 261–270. Springer, Cham (2021). https://doi.org/10.1007/978-3-030-66057-4_14
9. Grünewald, D., Simmendinger, C.: The GASPI API specification and its implementation GPI 2.0. In: International Conference on PGAS Programming Models, vol. 243, p. 52 (2013)
10. Hasheminezhad, B., Shirzad, S., Wu, N., Diehl, P., Schulz, H., Kaiser, H.: Towards a scalable and distributed infrastructure for deep learning applications. In: Workshop on Deep Learning on Supercomputers, pp. 20–30. IEEE (2020)
11. Jäger, S., Zorn, H.P., Igel, S., Zirpins, C.: Parallelized training of Deep NN: comparison of current concepts and frameworks. In: Proceedings of the Second Workshop on Distributed Infrastructures for Deep Learning, pp. 15–20 (2018)
12. Jain, R.: The Art of Computer Systems Performance Analysis: Techniques for Experimental Design, Measurement, Simulation, and Modeling. Wiley, Hoboken (1991)
13. Jia, X., et al.: Whale: scaling deep learning model training to the trillions. arXiv e-prints arXiv:2011.09208 (2020)
14. Keras (2020). https://github.com/keras-team/keras
15. Kim, H., Nam, H., Jung, W., Lee, J.: Performance analysis of CNN frameworks for GPUs. In: International Symposium on Performance Analysis of Systems and Software, pp. 55–64. IEEE (2017)
16. Knüpfer, A., et al.: Score-P: a joint performance measurement run-time infrastructure for periscope, Scalasca, TAU, and Vampir. In: Brunst, H., Müller, M., Nagel, W., Resch, M. (eds.) Tools for High Performance Computing 2011, pp. 79–91. Springer, Heidelberg (2012). https://doi.org/10.1007/978-3-642-31476-6_7

17. Kurth, T., Smorkalov, M., Mendygral, P., Sridharan, S., Mathuriya, A.: TensorFlow at scale: performance and productivity analysis of distributed training with Horovod, MLSL, and Cray PE ML. Concurr. Comput. Pract. Exp. **31**(16), e4989 (2019)
18. LeCun, Y., Bottou, L., Bengio, Y., Haffner, P.: Gradient-based learning applied to document recognition. Proc. IEEE **86**(11), 2278–2324 (1998)
19. LeCun, Y., Cortes, C., Burges, C.: MNIST handwritten digit database (2010). http://yann.lecun.com/exdb/mnist
20. Liu, J., Dutta, J., Li, N., Kurup, U., Shah, M.: Usability study of distributed deep learning frameworks for convolutional neural networks. In: Deep Learning Day at SIGKDD Conference on Knowledge Discovery and Data Mining (2018)
21. Mahon, S., Varrette, S., Plugaru, V., Pinel, F., Bouvry, P.: Performance analysis of distributed and scalable deep learning. In: International Symposium on Cluster, Cloud and Internet Computing (CCGRID), pp. 760–766. IEEE (2020)
22. Mayer, R., Jacobsen, H.A.: Scalable deep learning on distributed infrastructures: challenges, techniques, and tools. ACM Comput. Surv. **53**(1), 1–37 (2020)
23. NVidia: Nvidia system management interface (2020). https://developer.download.nvidia.com/compute/DCGM/docs/NVSMI-367.38.pdf
24. NVidia: Nvprof, command line profiling tool (2020). http://docs.nvidia.com/cuda/profiler-users-guide
25. Paszke, A., et al.: Pytorch: an imperative style, high-performance deep learning library. In: Advances in Neural Information Processing Systems, vol. 32 (2019)
26. Python: the Python profilers (2020). https://docs.python.org/3/library/profile.html
27. Schnorr, L.M., Legrand, A.: Visualizing more performance data than what fits on your screen. In: Cheptsov, A., Brinkmann, S., Gracia, J., Resch, M., Nagel, W. (eds.) Tools for High Performance Computing 2012, pp. 149–162. Springer, Heidelberg (2013). https://doi.org/10.1007/978-3-642-37349-7_10
28. Sergeev, A., Del Balso, M.: Horovod: fast and easy distributed deep learning in TensorFlow. arXiv preprint arXiv:1802.05799 (2018)
29. Shi, S., Wang, Q., Chu, X.: Performance modeling and evaluation of distributed deep learning frameworks on GPUs. In: IEEE 16th International Conference on Dependable, Autonomic and Secure Computing, 16th International Conference on Pervasive Intelligence and Computing, 4th International Conference on Big Data Intelligence and Computing and Cyber Science and Technology Congress, pp. 949–957 (2018). https://doi.org/10.1109/DASC/PiCom/DataCom/CyberSciTec.2018.000-4
30. Van Essen, B., Kim, H., Pearce, R., Boakye, K., Chen, B.: LBANN: livermore big artificial neural network HPC toolkit. In: Proceedings of the Workshop on Machine Learning in High-Performance Computing Environments, pp. 1–6 (2015)
31. Wu, X., Taylor, V., Wozniak, J.M., Stevens, R., Brettin, T., Xia, F.: Performance, power, and scalability analysis of the horovod implementation of the candle Nt3 benchmark on the cray Xc40 theta. In: SC 2018, Workshop on Python for High-Performance and Scientific Computing, Dallas, USA (2018)

A Motivating Case Study on Code Variant Selection by Reinforcement Learning

Oliver Hacker, Matthias Korch, and Johannes Seiferth(✉)

Department of Computer Science, University of Bayreuth, Bayreuth, Germany
{oliver.hacker,korch,seiferth}@uni-bayreuth.de

Abstract. In this paper, we investigate the applicability of reinforcement learning as a possible approach to select code variants. Our approach is based on the observation that code variants are usually convertible between one another by code transformations. Actor-critic proximal policy optimization is identified as a suitable reinforcement learning algorithm. To study its applicability, a software framework is implemented and used to perform experiments on three different hardware platforms using a class of explicit solution methods for systems of ordinary differential equations as an example application.

Keywords: Reinforcement learning · Proximal policy optimization · Autotuning · Code variant selection · ODE methods · PIRK methods

1 Introduction

One of the major challenges for numerical software is utilizing the available, often cost-intensive, hardware resources as efficiently as possible. Typically, such software is used on different platforms during its lifetime. Its performance, however, strongly depends on the characteristics of the targeted platform, such as, e.g., the processor design or the cache architectures. Hence, the software needs to be optimized specifically for each individual platform, which requires a great deal of effort. Therefore, research is being conducted on how these steps can be automated using *autotuning* (AT).

Problem Statement. In general, implementing an algorithm involves taking multiple design decisions (e.g., order of loops or computations). Here, each decision path results in a different *code variant* with potentially widely disparate performance and runtime behavior. By application of sequences of correctness-preserving code transformations code variants can be derived from another. Depending on the algorithm at hand, for example, complex HPC simulations, this can result in a large candidate pool of possible code variants from which the best variant needs to be selected efficiently and reliably. It should be noted that some related works use a different definition of the term *code variant.*

A.-L. Varbanescu et al. (Eds.): ISC High Performance 2022, LNCS 13289, pp. 293–312, 2022.
https://doi.org/10.1007/978-3-031-07312-0_15

Classical AT approaches focus on tuning numeric parameters (e.g., block sizes). Here, known mathematical optimization methods (e.g., Nelder–Mead, simulated annealing) are applied to find near-optimal parameter values. Besides numerical parameters, non-numeric, so-called *nominal* parameters [13] can also have a big impact on performance. Their tuning, however, is not as well understood. Identifying the best available code variant, in the following referred to as *code variant selection problem* (CVSP), is an important use-case of nominal parameter tuning.

Main Contributions. In this work, we investigate whether the CVSP can be solved by *reinforcement learning* (RL) – a machine learning technique based on actions and rewards. Our main contributions are:

(i) Interpretation of the CVSP as a traversal of a code transformation graph.
(ii) Identification of RL as a suitable approach to solve the CVSP.
(iii) Identification of actor-critic proximal policy optimization (PPO) as a suitable RL method.
(iv) Design and implementation of a software framework which allows the evaluation of different RL methods.
(v) Experimental case study showing the applicability using a class of explicit solution methods for systems of ordinary differential equations (ODEs) as example application on different hardware platforms, including a comparison of PPO and deep Q-network (DQN).

Outline. The rest of this work is structured as follows. Section 2 presents an overview of related work, showing existing approaches to variant selection as well as existing applications of RL. After this, Sect. 3 introduces the application class used in our case study and its search space of code variants, thus motivating the importance of efficient variant selection algorithms. Section 4 describes the specific RL approach used in our study in detail, and Sect. 5 describes the framework in which this approach has been implemented. The experimental study and its results are presented and discussed in Sect. 6. Finally, Sect. 7 concludes the paper and discusses future work.

2 Related Work

A concept still under research for automating the optimization of performance knobs of numerical algorithms is AT. Typical performance knobs include implementation design decisions – leading to different code variants – as well as implementation parameters (e.g., blocking sizes) and system parameters (e.g., clock rate). Collectively, the selected knob values form a possible *configuration*. An important distinction needs to be made between *nominal* (unordered set with unordered codomain) and *non-nominal* (e.g., numeric) parameters leading to an (at least to some degree) smooth codomain of the search space, because they require different types of search strategies.

Early examples of AT include *ATLAS* [23] and *PhiPAC* [4] for dense and sparse linear algebra routines, respectively. They consider code variants (kernels) as well as implementation parameters (e.g., register and cache blocking). To decide which code variant to use, the available code variants are sampled based on expert knowledge hard coded into the tuner.

Modern AT frameworks which aim at being usable for different classes of applications, such as Active Harmony [20] and ATF [16], usually provide a set of different search techniques, e.g., exhaustive search, random search, simulated annealing, variants of Nelder–Mead or others. OpenTuner [2] even provides meta-techniques to run several strategies simultaneously. However, typically a single search strategy is applied to the whole search space. Hence, if the search space contains a nominal parameter, only strategies like the expensive exhaustive search or a purely random search can be used reasonably. Due to the large unified search space, this is either inefficient or unreliable.

To explore the unordered search space of nominal parameters efficiently, new approaches are required. To automatically select code variants, some works have successfully applied evolutionary techniques. For example, a previous version of the image processing framework Halide [15] used a genetic algorithm to select among possible pipeline schedules. However, since the genetic algorithm could take days, it was replaced by a tree search machine learning technique combined with a trained cost model [1]. Other works also suggest the use of machine learning techniques. For example, [12] uses multi-task learning for cross-architecture selection of code variants based on profiling data and device features. Tuning input-dependent code variants by machine learning is considered in [3,22]. A drawback of such machine learning techniques is that they require a separate training phase with a suitable large set of training data. A different approach is taken by [18], which ranks the possible code variants based on analytical white-box performance prediction of their kernels. In [13,14] a hierarchical tuning process which considers both non-nominal and nominal parameters is proposed. It separates the search spaces of non-nominal and nominal parameters so that different search algorithms can be used, e.g., ε-greedy for nominal parameters and Nelder–Mead for non-nominal ones.

In this paper, we consider RL as a possible new approach to variant selection. In contrast to other machine learning techniques, RL does not require a separate training phase, and is, thus, potentially suitable for a one-shot learning scenario as in online autotuning. RL has already been applied successfully in related areas. For example, [9] has used RL to optimize compiler passes, and [5] to select parameters for loop vectorization. [21] determines which code transformations to apply in order to target different computing hardware. Further, [6] uses a model-based RL approach to remove unused and unwanted code from programs and libraries, and [10] uses RL to find improved distributions of TensorFlow computations onto devices in heterogeneous systems.

1 **for** $l \leftarrow 1, \ldots, s$ **do** $\mathbf{Y}_l^{(0)} \leftarrow \mathbf{y}_\kappa$
2 **for** $k \leftarrow 1, \ldots, m$ **do**
3   **for** $l \leftarrow 1, \ldots, s$ **do**
4         $\mathbf{Y}_l^{(k)} \leftarrow \mathbf{y}_\kappa + h_\kappa \sum_{i=1}^{s} a_{li} \mathbf{F}_i^{(k-1)}$
5   with $\mathbf{F}_i^{(k-1)} \leftarrow \mathbf{f}(t_\kappa + c_i h_\kappa, \mathbf{Y}_i^{(k-1)})$
6 $\mathbf{y}_{\kappa+1} \leftarrow \mathbf{y}_\kappa + h_\kappa \sum_{i=1}^{s} b_i \mathbf{F}_i^{(m)}$

(a)

```
RHS_PRED•
for(int k=0; k<m; ++k){
  LC•
  RHS•
}
APRX
UPD
```

(b)

Fig. 1. (a) Computations required to implement the iterative one-step predictor-corrector process of a PIRK method. (b) A concrete implementation skeleton, named A, of possible code variants. The computations are covered by separate kernel templates (capital letters), which can have different implementation possibilities themselves. '•' denotes that synchronization is needed after a kernel.

3 Motivating Example

When writing code, the programmer's choices can greatly affect the performance of the program. For example, one might choose a specific data structure or a specific iteration order of loops explicitly. This results in a variability of programs on the code level which can be exploited through *code variants.*

As case study, we consider the CVSP on a specific class of explicit solution methods for initial value problems (IVPs) of systems of ODEs. In particular, we choose the class of parallel iterated Runge–Kutta (PIRK) methods [7]. Explicit ODE methods are simulation methods composed of evaluations of a mathematical model and linear algebra operations. In particular, we are interested in computationally intensive cases, where the ODE system is large. ODE methods can be used as time steppers in simulations of more complex mathematical models.

3.1 Mathematical Background

We consider IVPs of systems of ODEs defined as follows:

$$\mathbf{y}'(t) = \mathbf{f}(t, \mathbf{y}(t)), \qquad \mathbf{y}(t_0) = \mathbf{y}_0. \tag{1}$$

The numerical solution by PIRK methods [7] uses an iterative one-step predictor-corrector process to perform a series of time steps $t_\kappa = t_0 + \kappa \cdot h$ until the end of an integration interval $[t_0, t_e]$ is reached. Here, $\mathbf{f}$ denotes the right-hand-side function (*RHS*) and $\mathbf{y}_0$ the initial value of the ODE system. The corrector method used is a s-stage implicit RK method of order o which can be characterized by its *Butcher table* entries, i.e., coefficient matrix $A = (a_{ij}) \in \mathbb{R}^{s,s}$, weight vector $\mathbf{b} = (b_i) \in \mathbb{R}^s$ and node vector $\mathbf{c} = (c_i) \in \mathbb{R}^s$.

In each time step, a new approximation $\mathbf{y}_{\kappa+1}$ of the unknown solution $\mathbf{y}$ is computed from the previous approximation $\mathbf{y}_\kappa$ (cf. Fig. 1 (a)): First, the previous approximation $\mathbf{y}_\kappa$ is selected as *predictor* (line 1) for the stages $\mathbf{Y}_1, \ldots, \mathbf{Y}_s$. Next, the *corrector method* is applied a fixed number of $m = o - 1$ times (lines

2–5). After all corrector steps have been applied, the new approximation $\mathbf{y}_{\kappa+1}$ is computed (line 6).

Table 1. Search space of available PIRK method code variants

Kernel template (#Implementations)		Implementation skeleton							
		A (48)	B (48)	C (64)	D (64)	E (32)	F (32)	G (48)	H (48)
LC	(6)	×	×					×	×
RHS[a]	(2)	×	×	×	×			×	×
RHS_PRED[a]	(2)	×	×					×	×
RHSLC[a]	(4)			×	×	×	×		
RHSLC_PRED[a]	(4)			×	×	×	×		
APRX	(2)	×		×					
RHSAPRX[a]	(2)					×		×	
UPD	(1)	×		×		×		×	
APRXUPD	(2)		×		×				
RHSAPRXUPD[a]	(2)						×		×

[a]Contains evaluations of the RHS of the ODE problem.

3.2 Search Space of Code Variants

Implementing this iterative process and covering all its computations and dependencies requires a four-dimensional loop structure. By applying different code transformations to this basic structure, a large pool of code variants can be generated. Because of the large number of possible code variants, we use code generation based on *implementation skeletons* to systematically generate all the source codes of the variants. An implementation skeleton defines the processing order of so-called *kernel templates* – and, thus, of the computations – as well as required synchronization points. A kernel template is a generic loop kernel that can cover one or multiple computations. For each kernel template, different concrete kernel implementations might exist (e.g., several different loop orders).

One of the implementation skeletons, named *A*, is shown in Fig. 1b. Skeleton *A* covers a set of vector-oriented code variants which split all computations into separate kernels: *RHS_PRED* runs the predictor step (line 1). *LC* computes the linear combination (line 4). *RHS* evaluates the RHS functions (line 5). *APRX* and *UPD* compute the new approximation (line 6). Additional skeletons can be derived from skeleton *A* through code transformations. For instance, skeleton *A* can be transformed to *C* by fusing kernels *LC* and *RHS* to *RHS_LC*. More complex skeletons can be derived through sequences of transformations. E.g., fusing *APRX* and *UPD* to *APRXUPD* transforms skeleton *C* to *D* which consequently opens a transformation path from *A* to *D* through *C*.

Further, even more code variants can arise within the context of one skeleton by deriving additional kernel implementations of its kernel templates. A kernel template can potentially have multiple, different implementations with each enabling extra code variants. The three-dimensional loop structure of kernel LC, for instance, naturally leads to six different implementations (enabled by loop interchange) corresponding to the six possible permutations of loops i, j and l.

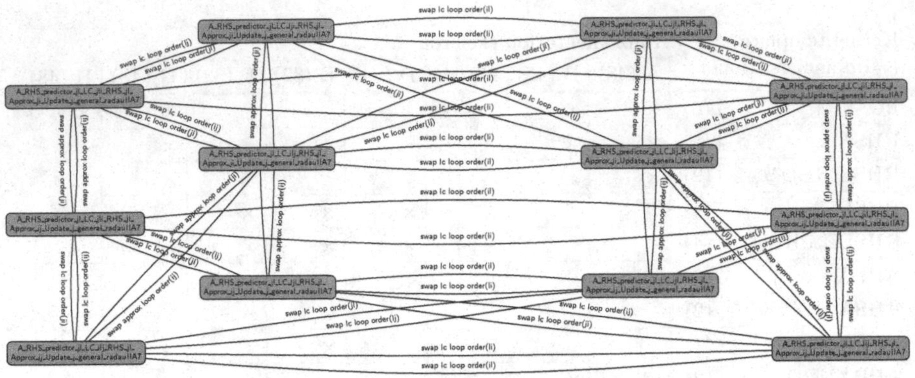

Fig. 2. A subset of the code transformation graph showing twelve code variants derived from skeleton A. Only transformations inside this subset are shown.

In total, we consider a pool of at least 384 different PIRK method code variants. As summarized in Table 1, these variants are derived from eight implementation skeletons and ten kernel templates. Each table column indicates the kernels required by a particular skeleton. E.g., skeleton B uses kernels *RHS_PRED*, *RHS*, LC and *APRXUPD* and leads to 48 different variants. If there are multiple implementation options for the kernels containing an evaluation of the RHS, e.g., different permutations of the equations, the total number of code variants even multiplies by the corresponding factor.

As the example of PIRK methods shows, the number of possible code variants of numerical algorithms can be quite large. While it is generally possible to reduce the search space by expert knowledge or preliminary manual performance analyses, an as high as possible degree of automatic tuning is desirable. For this, efficient heuristical search methods are needed which avoid an exhaustive exploration of the whole set of possible variants and make manual intervention unnecessary. However, classical optimization methods for numeric parameters of nonlinear functions are not applicable, because we cannot enumerate the code variants so that the resulting runtime function $T(i) \in \mathbb{R}_+$ of the variant number $i \in \mathbb{N}$ forms a sufficiently smooth shape with a locatable minimum without knowing $T(i)$ in advance. But computing $T(i)$ for all code variants i corresponds to an exhaustive search. The RL approach considered in this paper does not need to sample all variants. By learning about the reward of transformations, it can predict the performance even of unvisited variants.

3.3 Code Transformation Graph

Since the different code variants are the result of design decisions made by the programmer, there do exist relations between them, which we can try to exploit. Generally, one can derive code variants from another by applying a sequence of correctness-preserving code transformations such as loop interchange or fusion.

Thus, the search space of code variants and their relations defined by the code transformations can be represented by a graph where the nodes represent the code variants and the edges represent the code transformations. For our example, this leads to a complex transformation graph that contains a total of 384 PIRK code variants (nodes) and 84 code transformations (edges). Since the full search space is too large to be visualized, Fig. 2 shows an extracted subgraph of twelve code variants derived from implementation skeleton A.

4 Application of Reinforcement Learning

Human experts would tackle the CVSP by exploring the code transformation graph in a systematic way and, in this process, building an iteratively refined performance model in their mind. In other words, they would exploit the relations between the code variants and make use of their previously and newly learned experience to decide which code variant to investigate next. While other machine learning techniques usually require a separate training phase with suitable training data and evolutionary approaches often require a high number of individuals and generations and, thus, a high number of samples, RL is a machine learning technique that resembles the target-oriented approach of the human experts.

4.1 Principles of Reinforcement Learning

The formal principles of RL are captured by (finite) Markov decision processes (MDPs) [19]. A MDP is defined as a tuple $\mathcal{M} = (\mathcal{S}, \mathcal{A}, p, \mathcal{R})$ where $\mathcal{S}$ denotes the (finite) set of states, $\mathcal{A}$ the (finite) set of actions, and $\mathcal{R}$ the (finite) set of possible rewards. $p : \mathcal{S} \times \mathcal{R} \times \mathcal{S} \times \mathcal{A} \mapsto [0,1]$ is the probability distribution, often given as $p(s', r|s, a)$, determining for all $s, s' \in \mathcal{S}$, $a \in \mathcal{A}$, and $r \in \mathcal{R}$ the probability of going with action a from state s to state s' while receiving a reward r.

The goal is to find the state s_* or the action a_* in a given state s, from which the highest reward is to be expected. Most of the time, p is not – or only partially – known, necessitating solutions that are based solely on the experience gathered through interaction with the environment. This is the main problem RL algorithms try to solve.

4.2 Modeling Variant Selection as RL Scenario

The idea of interpreting the CVSP as an exploration of the code transformation graph directly leads to the notion of code variants as states and code transformations as actions. In the context of RL, the states consist of features, while the actions consist of changing the values of features. Therefore, a code variant is considered as a mapping from features of a general code template to their selected values. E.g., a feature may be some kind of loop kernel in the code, while the possible values for that feature are different iteration orders. Furthermore, the code transformations are considered as actions that take a code variant as input, modify some of its features, e.g., the loop order of a kernel, and deliver the resulting new code variant as output.

Applying this general idea to our case study results in 384 discrete states (one per PIRK variant) with 84 transformation actions. Each action can potentially be executed in each state. The maximum number of edges in a transformation graph is $|\mathcal{S}| \times |\mathcal{A}|$. In reality, not all actions are possible in all states resulting in the notation $\mathcal{A}(s)$ for the actions possible in a specific state s, i.e., the set of code transformations leading to/from this state.

Since there is no clear way to designate a state as a goal state without already knowing the best variant, we model our task as a continuing problem. At each step the action the agent takes returns a reward equivalent to the negative runtime of the new variant. Since reward is maximized, the runtime is reduced.

Finding a good variant requires the following general steps:

1. Select some initial variant s_0 randomly.
2. Let an RL-agent explore the transformation graph for a given time period.
   (a) Select one of the available transformations $\mathcal{A}(s)$ of the current variant.
   (b) Transform the variant into a new one.
   (c) Execute this new variant, measuring its runtime.
   (d) Update the values of variants and transformations.
3. Choose the state the agent stopped in as the result, or keep track of the best variant found.

4.3 Devising a Suitable RL Method

General RL is applicable to many problems, though choosing and implementing one of the many algorithms originating from the theoretical foundations depends on the properties of the problem at hand. In the following, we outline the methods and techniques chosen for the experimental study in this paper. An overview of the resulting RL algorithm is shown in Fig. 3.

The standard solution approaches like *TD(0)* or *Q-Learning* are the result of viewing the problem from a state-value or action-value perspective, i.e., they either approximate the value of a state $v_\pi(s)$ or of an action possible in a state $q_\pi(s,a)$. Here, π denotes the policy the reinforcement learning agent follows while trying to estimate the value. The governing equations are as follows [19]:

$$v_\pi(s) \stackrel{\text{def}}{=} \mathbb{E}_\pi[G_t|S_t = s] = \sum_{a \in \mathcal{A}(s)} \pi(a|s) q_\pi(s,a) \tag{2}$$

$$\begin{aligned} q_\pi(s,a) &\stackrel{\text{def}}{=} \mathbb{E}_\pi[G_t|S_t = s, A_t = a] \\ &= \sum_{s',r} p(s',r|s,a)(r + \gamma v_\pi(s')) \end{aligned} \tag{3}$$

Here, G_t is the return as a sum of discounted rewards under policy π at time step t, defined as

$$G_t \stackrel{\text{def}}{=} \sum_{k=0}^{T} \gamma^k R_{t+k+1}$$

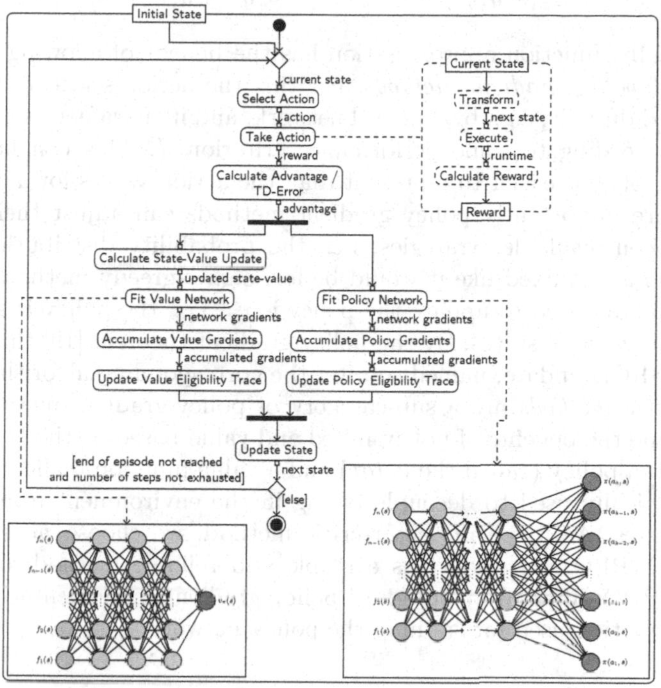

Fig. 3. Detailed depiction of the actor-critic approach to reinforcement learning, which is part of the learning process summarized in Fig. 4 as "Learning". Note, that the dashed nodes depend only on the concrete implementation of an action and not on the learning algorithm. They can therefore be replaced according to the current scenario. In addition to actor-critic methods like PPO [17], other methods such as DQN are supported by the learning process as well.

where T marks the end of an episode (i.e., T is the number of steps until a goal state is reached). $T = \infty$ and $\gamma < 1$ for continuing problems, i.e., T has to be chosen large enough for the approximate value functions to converge.

Evidently, there is a natural recursive relationship between both views and it is mostly an implementation choice, which one is used. Since both value functions depend on themselves, iterative methods have to be used to solve for a specific value. The aforementioned algorithms for example achieve this by updating the value function in each step they take in the environment (*online learning*) which also eliminates the need of knowing $p(s', r|s, a)$ since it is approximated by sampling. TD(0) and Q-Learning use a lookup-table to store the mapping from states (and actions) to their values, resulting in quickly growing memory consumption. Due to this, function approximation has had a growing interest in recent years [19], especially through deep neural networks [11]. For that reason we also use it in our study. In the case of function approximation, the value functions depend on parameter vectors $\boldsymbol{\theta}$ which describe the approximation:

$$v_\pi(s, \boldsymbol{\theta}_v) \qquad q_\pi(s, a, \boldsymbol{\theta}_q) \tag{4}$$

Additionally, function approximation has the benefit of allowing the implementation of *policy gradient methods*. For this the action-selection policy π is approximated directly, e.g., by a neural network, and its parameters are updated iteratively according to some performance criterion J. This can be advantageous if the policy is easier to represent than the action-values for a given problem, but more importantly policy gradient methods can adjust their randomization between available strategies, i.e., the probability distribution used to select actions is not fixed like it would be for, e.g., ε-greedy methods [19]. The objective function used to update the policy is v_π, i.e., the policy is adjusted to maximize the value of states. By the policy gradient theorem [19] this results in the REINFORCE update, named so after the corresponding algorithm.

Actor-critic methods are a sub-category of policy-gradient methods, which try to combine the benefits of policy-based and value-based methods by approximating both a policy (called the *actor*) and a value function (called the *critic*). They are typically used to decouple acting in the environment from assigning values to states. As a specific actor-critic method, we choose *proximal policy optimization* (PPO) [17], which is a stable and reliable method, but easy to implement. PPO differs from standard policy gradient implementations mainly in the loss function used for training the policy network.

5 Implementation of a RL Framework

To facilitate easy specification and implementation of reinforcement learning based solutions, we develop an extensible Java framework that models the concepts detailed in Subsect. 4.3. By extracting commonalities of learning algorithms, policies, states, actions, and concrete scenarios, it is possible to decouple the implementations using software design patterns like *strategy*, *template method*, and *observer*.

The framework offers multiple RL algorithms, based on tables as well as approximation through neural networks. Both value-based and policy-based solution methods are supported. None of these implementation details, however, matter for the particular specification of a learning problem but are completely transparent to it. The user only has to provide a concrete driver class which is responsible for setting up the current scenario and model elements (i.e., states and actions) and a corresponding implementation of the states and actions.

The same is true for learning algorithms: all they depend on is that states can be represented as some kind of feature vector and that actions take the current

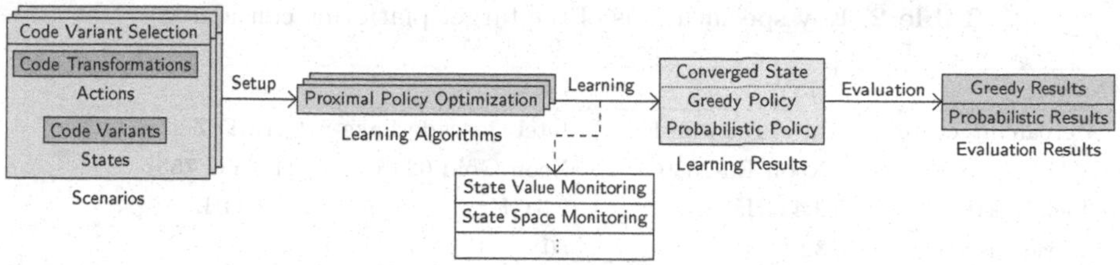

Fig. 4. Overview of the RL framework, following the learning pipeline from left to right. First, a scenario is defined which consists of specific actions and states. It then sets up any learning algorithms according to the user's configuration and starts the learning process which may result in a settled state, as well as a greedy and a probabilistic policy. The latter two can be run on unknown random starting states to evaluate the generalization capabilities of the learned policy.

state, returning a new state and the reward gained. This model is sufficient for all general reinforcement learning algorithms. To ease the configuration of algorithms with many hyperparameters, configuration files using the JSON format are used, further decoupling the implementation. For algorithms using function approximation, we employ DL4J [8] as our neural network library for building, training, and monitoring since it works within the Java ecosystem. It also allows defining new loss functions, which is needed for the implementation of algorithms like PPO where it is the main difference to other actor-critic algorithms.

A graphical overview of the framework is shown in Fig. 4, using the configuration chosen for our experimental study as an example. Only specific implementations for the classes on the left (scenario, action, state) had to be provided. Note, that each variant is represented by a state object as well as a corresponding executable on the file system. Code transformation actions take the current state (variant), apply their transformation logic to retrieve a new state, identify its executable via a filename convention, and execute it to get a runtime measurement. After this, a reward function is applied that turns the runtime measurement into a suitable reward which the action returns together with the new state. These steps are also shown in Fig. 3 as dashed nodes, since they constitute variability points of the learning algorithm.

6 Experimental Study

The main goal of our evaluation is to determine whether a learned policy can be used to select a well performing variant given an unknown environment (*criterion I*) while keeping the search time low (*criterion II*) The performance of our approach is assessed based on these two main criteria. It is worth stressing that our goal is not to find the best performing variant since this cannot be guaranteed. Instead, finding a near-optimal variant is sufficient for our purposes if the search speed outweighs the runtime penalty.

Since for the agent the only variables determining the performance of a variant are the parameters introduced in Subsect. 3.2, our problem setup falls into

Table 2. Key specifications of the target platforms considered

Name	HSW	CLX	ZEN
Microarchitecture	Intel Haswell-EP	Intel Cascade Lake-SP	AMD Zen2
CPU	Xeon E5-2630	Xeon Gold 6248	EPYC 7551
Clock speed	2.4 GHz	2.5 GHz	2.0 GHz
Threads used	32	80	64
SMT	enabled	enabled	enabled
Memory configuration	32 GiB, DDR4-2133	384 GiB, DDR4-2933	512 GiB, DDR4-2933

the category of partially-observable MDPs. This means there are other factors, unknown to the agent, that characterize the states (and, thus, influence the runtime). One such unknown, for example, is the configuration of the system the runtimes are measured on. Incorporating additional information about the machine would be possible but not required for the problem at hand. Instead, we rely on the agent approximating it during the learning process.

6.1 Experimental Setup

Our current setup requires the learning agent's process to be running on the same machine as the variant to be executed, so all communication happens using process pipes. The sharing of resources could potentially introduce noise in our measurements – however, we currently deem this interference minimal since the learning agent sleeps while a variant's binary file is executed, requiring only memory. If full independence is required a client-server architecture similar to existing approaches like [9,10] can be implemented. Also, if an online autotuning process is desired, the one-shot learning characteristics of RL allow to implement this by representing code variants using dynamically loadable libraries or function pointers instead of executable files.

Hardware Platforms. To investigate how different environments impact the resulting variant the learning agent chooses, we use three differently configured hardware platforms (Table 2) while all other parameters are kept the same. Load-adaptive frequency scaling is always deactivated.

PIRK Method and IVPs. In our experiments, we use the 4-stage ($s = 4$) method *Radau II A(7)* as corrector method and apply $m = 6$ corrector steps, unless noted otherwise. Three IVPs are considered. *IC* is a sparse IVP and describes a traversing signal through a chain of n concatenated inverters. As number of equations we used $n \approx 2.0 \cdot 10^6$ on HSW and $n \approx 1.6 \cdot 10^7$ on CLX and ZEN. *BRUSS2D* also is a sparse IVP, but models a chemical reaction of two substances with 2D diffusion. This leads to a 5-point stencil pattern with higher memory pressure than IC. Here, we use a mixed row-oriented, i.e., interleaved order of the equations. For BRUSS2D a system size of $n \approx 4.0 \cdot 10^6$ on HSW

Table 3. Key parameters of the neural networks used

Network	PPO		DQN
	Policy	State-value	Action-value
# inputs	38	38	38
# outputs	84	1	84
# hidden layers	5	5	5
# nodes in hidden layers	38	38	38
Output activation functions[a]	Softmax	Identity	Identity
Optimization epochs	64	80[b]	128

[a]The hidden layers use the ReLU activation function.
[b]with an additional maximum loss for PPO.

and $n \approx 16 \cdot 10^6$ on CLX and ZEN equations was used. In contrast, *STARS* is a dense IVP that models a naive n-body problem. We consider three implementations of STARS which use different orders of the equations (consecutive order of x-, y-, z-positions and x-, y-, z-velocities, interleaved order of positions and velocities, consecutive order of point positions and point velocities). The number of equations used were $n \approx 9.6 \cdot 10^3$ on HSW and $n \approx 2.4 \cdot 10^4$ on CLX and ZEN. Because of the dense structure, the RHS dominates the runtime. This property allows to evaluate whether the current RL approach can handle the case of a single dominant feature, or if a hierarchical approach is necessary. We used C as programming language and OpenMP for parallelization.

Features and Actions. A PIRK variant can be completely characterized using 38 features encoding the possible values for each defining parameter (8 skeletons, 27 kernel implementations, 3 IVP implementations for *STARS*) and there are at most 84 actions available to the agent which can modify these values.

Network Parameters and Hyperparameters. The network parameters of the neural network used for the function approximation components of PPO and DQN are summarized in Table 3. Further, hyperparameters were determined for both algorithms through manual optimization and testing. The results are shown in Table 4. Our goal was to find a set of hyperparameters that work well across all the tested systems, so almost no re-tuning should be required on other systems.

These parameters have been tuned with respect to both of our aforementioned evaluation criteria, i.e., the number of learning steps per problem has been chosen such that learning is considerably faster than an exhaustive search of all variants while still providing enough time to learn which variants are fast. We want to keep the number of steps as low as possible with a trivial upper bound being the total number of variants, above which simply testing each variant is a better option. Additionally, we searched parameter values that produce stable learning progress, i.e., during the learning process runtimes should decrease until a good variant is found and this should happen within the given number of steps. This also decreases the time the overall learning process takes since slow variants are mostly only encountered in the first few steps.

Table 4. Selected hyperparameter values for both RL algorithms

PPO		DQN	
Hyperparameter	Value	Hyperparameter	Value
Clip loss threshold ϵ	0.1	Discount factor γ	0.99
Policy trace discount λ_π	0.8	Replay memory size	32
Value trace discount λ_v	0.99	Mini batch size	16
Reward baseline step size $\alpha^{\bar{R}}$	0.8	Reset threshold C	16
# Learning steps		150	

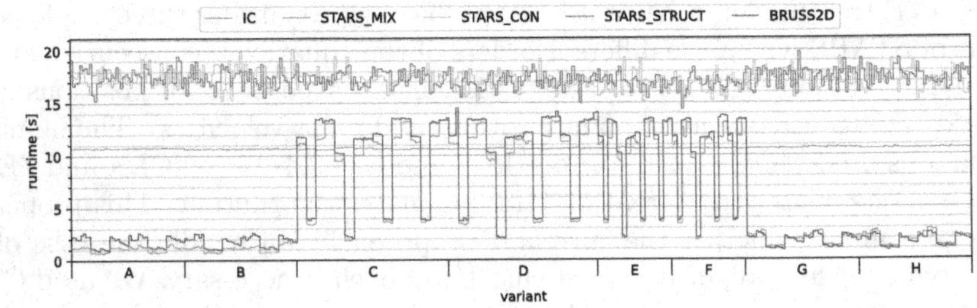

Fig. 5. Ground truth runtimes on HSW for the two different ODE systems used in our case study. Variants are shown grouped by skeleton. For IC and BRUSS2D there is a very clear distinction between the fastest and slowest code variants of the PIRK method, while for STARS the RHS dominates the runtime.

6.2 Results and Discussion

Ground Truth. Figure 5 shows the mean runtimes measured over multiple passes on HSW. Results for the other systems are similar and were omitted for clarity. This gives us an estimate on the hardness of either problem. While for the sparse problems IC and BRUSS2D we clearly see better and worse variants, this is not the case for the dense STARS. Different RHS implementations of STARS are, however, clearly distinguishable since they are slower by about a factor of two, resulting in what is basically a two step problem: First, the agent has to identify which RHS is fastest, then try to find the best in this subset.

DQN and PPO on Different Hardware Platforms. Figures 6a and 6b provide a comparison of DQN and PPO for the IC test problem by the median runtimes of multiple one-shot learning runs with random starting states on the three hardware platforms considered. While DQN performs relatively well on HSW, the other systems exhibit many deviations from the optimum (or near

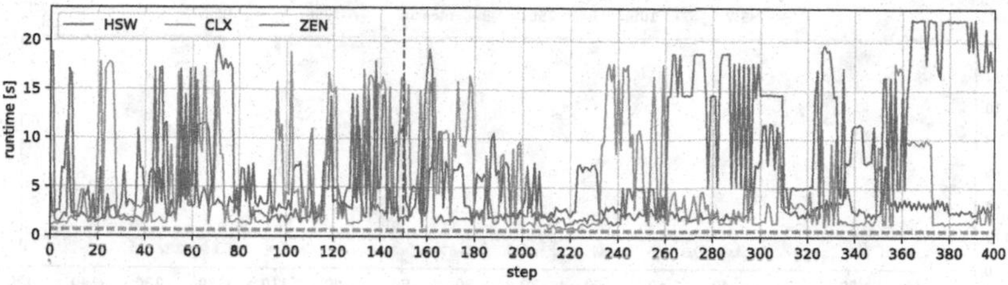

(a) DQN on IC

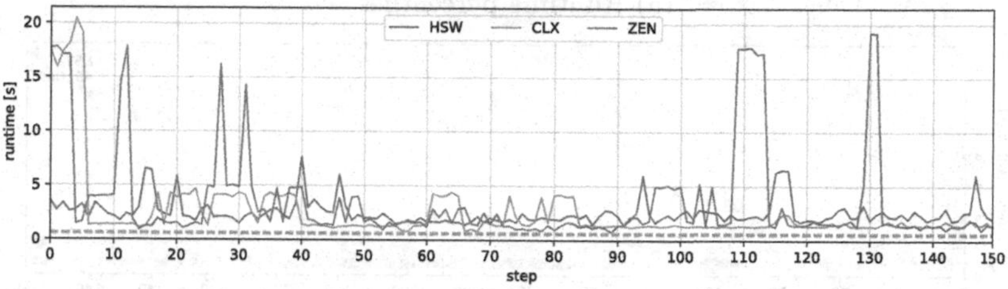

(b) PPO on IC

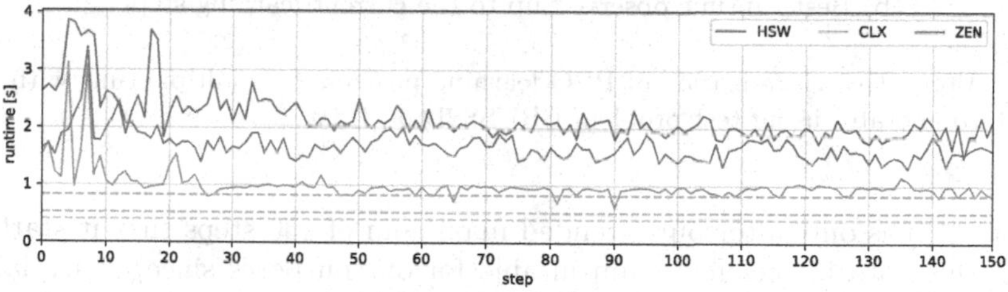

(c) PPO on BRUSS2D

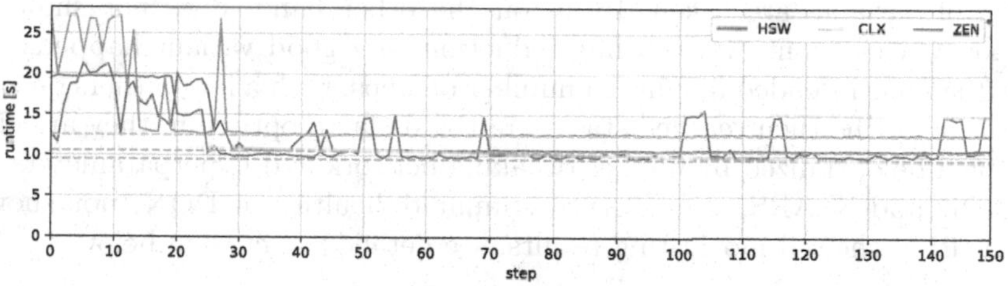

(d) PPO on STARS

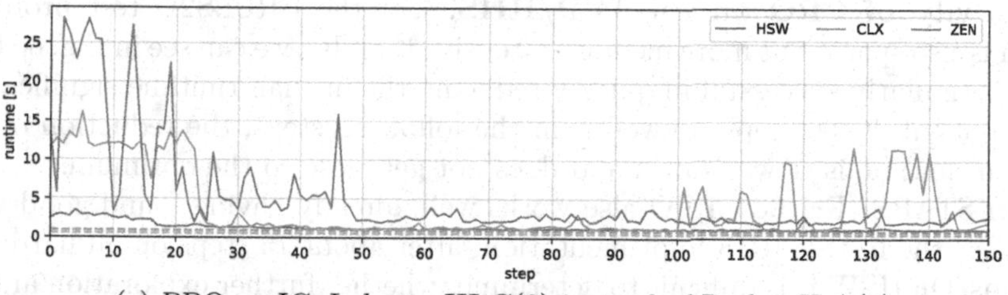

(e) PPO on IC, Lobatto III C(8) instead of Radau II A(7)

Fig. 6. Learning progress of DQN on IC and of PPO on different test cases. Shown are median runtimes of multiple runs with random starting states and in lighter color the corresponding optimal runtimes.

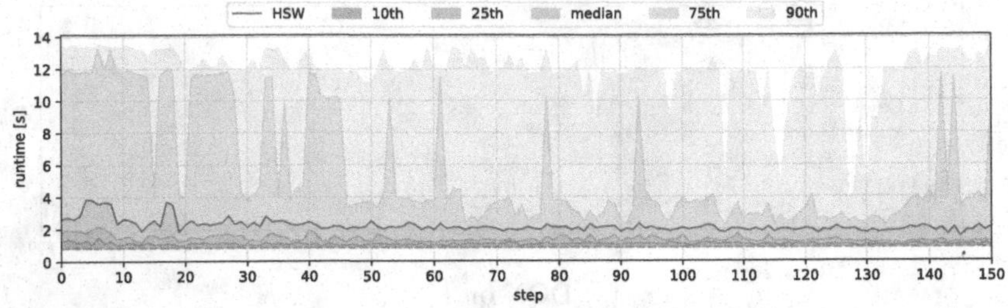

(a) Runtime percentiles

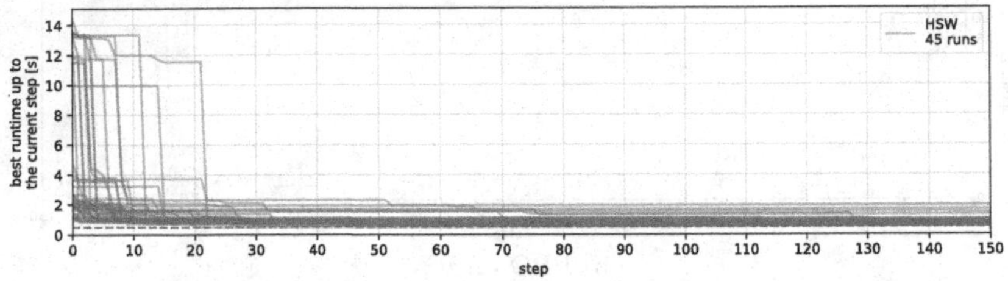

(b) Best runtime observed up to the current learning step

Fig. 7. Alternative visualization of PPO learning progress for multiple runs with random starting states using test problem BRUSS2D on HSW.

optimum). It is only after our intended maximum of 150 steps that it starts to settle. This data inefficiency is unsuitable for our purposes since, as explained earlier, the approach only makes sense if considerably less steps than the total number of variants are taken. PPO, on the other hand, does not show this behavior. On the contrary, runtime reduction to a good variant happens even earlier than our intended maximum number of steps, with a few outliers on ZEN. While none of the then reached states are the de-facto optimum, they are close. This could be optimized by further tweaking network and hyperparameters. For BRUSS2D and STARS, we observed similar difficulties of DQN (not shown), whereas PPO showed motivating results, see detailed discussion below.

Sensitivity of PPO on the IVP/RHS. For the BRUSS2D test problem, which is also sparse but more memory intensive than IC, we can see in Fig. 6c that PPO is similarly successful in quickly reducing the median runtime significantly within about 40–50 steps. However, in the following steps, the reduction of the median runtime is slowed down and does not get close to the optimum.

For STARS (Fig. 6d), PPO also works well, already having found good variants, i.e., the fastest RHS implementation, after about 75 steps on all hardware systems. On HSW it is difficult to determine, whether further exploration among the STARS_MIX implementations yields improvements due to the very similar runtimes. On CLX and ZEN however, the differences are more pronounced (around 1–2 s from the optimum). By closely examining the plot for ZEN in Fig. 6d one can observe small bumps in runtime, e.g., between steps 70 and 100,

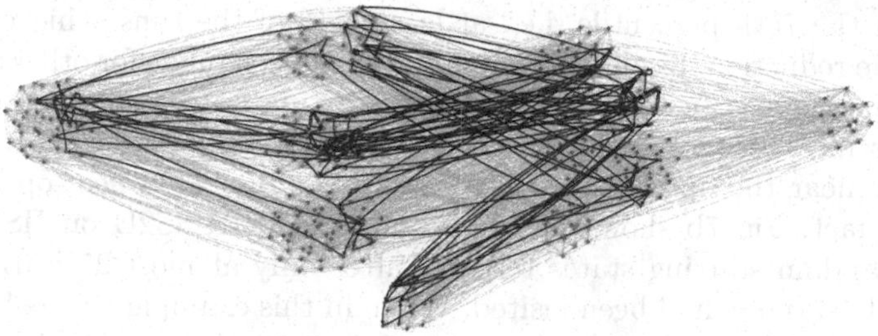

Fig. 8. Colored code transformation graph. Previous transformations are shown as black arrows, the current one is shown in cyan. Variants are represented as nodes whose color is related to the state-value as estimated by the learning agent.

corresponding to these differences. This shows, that exploration inside this subset of very good variants is still taking place, even resulting in going back to the worse categories by chance but quickly returning. On CLX this behavior is unfortunately less visible using median runtimes since one of the fastest variants is selected very early on in most cases, resulting in exploitation thereafter. It is, however, present in the 75th percentile.

Sensitivity of PPO on Input Data. What data are provided as input and which are already known at compile time depends on the use case of an ODE method. In some cases, the same IVP is simulated repeatedly using only different initial values, which usually has no influence on performance and, thus, on code variant selection. In other cases, the execution parameters, e.g., the number of threads, may change between executions. In the most challenging cases, even the IVP itself, including the RHS, may be part of the input, e.g., when the ODE method is started from a simulation environment with graphical model editor.

Since the one-shot learning starts from scratch each time, it can adapt to each current setting by learning a new policy. This includes not only the hardware platform, but also the input data. In the previous paragraph, it was already discussed that PPO works for different IVPs. As an additional use case example, Fig. 6e shows that PPO also works successfully for a different base method, Lobatto III C(8), which has one additional stage ($s = 5$) and uses one additional corrector step ($m = 7$), which leads to different working sets of the loop structure and, thus, to a different utilization of the memory hierarchy levels.

Sensitivity of PPO on the Starting State. Figure 6 already shows that the median runtime, can usually be improved by PPO as the learning process proceeds. However, since the median runtime appears to get not close enough to the optimal runtime in some cases, these figures do not exclude the possibility that some starting states are less successful than others.

To investigate this further, Fig. 7a includes additional percentiles for the example of BRUSS2D on HSW. Here, the runtime improvement can be best observed in the 75th percentile, i.e., at least 75% of the runs achieve a significant runtime reduction. Similar observations have been made for other examples, signaling that there is an improvement for all starting states in most experiments.

Another interesting question in that context is if PPO, even if it does not settle on or near the optimum, at least visits the best or a near-optimal code variant. In fact, Fig. 7b shows for the example of BRUSS2D on HSW that – for all 45 random starting states tested – after only at most 25 learning steps efficient code variants had been visited. While in this example – one of the worst cases observed – for a few starting states the minimal runtime achieved up to step 150 still was in some distance to the optimum, it is clearly visible that for most starting states near-optimal code variants had been visited. For IC and STARS on all hardware platforms, but also for BRUSS2D on CLX and ZEN, the maximum distance to the optimum at 150 steps is significantly smaller.

Insights Obtainable from the RL Models. The transformations chosen can be inspected easily. Also the values of the states (performance predictions) as estimated by the RL agent and the path it took can be shown in a colored visualization of the code transformation graph, see Fig. 8. This allows, e.g., identifying clusters of efficient variants. More in-depth analysis of the underlying neural networks would be required if one were interested in the impact of specific features, e.g., specific kernels or transformations.

Overheads of Offline and Online Tuning. We opted to generate code variants offline for ease of use and quicker testing of the framework. It is, however, possible to generate and compile code variants online. For this, the implementation of an RL action can be easily modified to call the generator/compiler in the same way as it calls the executable. Compiling on the fly on the one side has the benefit that only the sampled variants need to be compiled, but also the drawback of additional time required for compilation.

Currently, Figs. 6 and 7 show only the time it takes to execute the variants. The learning framework is not active while a variant is executed, and thus it does not impact its execution time. In total 56–97% of time is spent executing variants while the rest is spent in the framework. Hence, the overhead of an online tuning scenario is expected to be in this range as well. If the code variants were generated and compiled on-demand, the overhead would increase further. This overhead could be reduced significantly by switching from DL4J to a C-based framework and integrating it closely in the application.

Another type of overhead could be defined by the additional runtime of non-optimal code variants executed in the tuning/learning phase. Since efficient code variants are usually already visited after only a small number of learning steps (cf. Fig. 7b), the improvement of the best runtime observed so far would be a suitable termination criterion to keep this type of overhead small.

7 Conclusion

Selecting a well-performing code variant is a problem which is usually not approachable by classical mathematical function optimization. In this paper, we have shown by an experimental study using PIRK methods as example application that RL can successfully be used to explore the search space of code variants efficiently. The specific RL method chosen was actor-critic PPO, which outperformed DQN in the experimental study. The approach of modeling the code variants as states and the possible code transformations (e.g., loop transformations) as actions is expected to be adaptable to other applications. This will be considered as part of our future work, as well as tuning additional parameters, like the number of application threads, and investigating the possibility of explicitly incorporating machine-dependent features into the learning process.

Acknowledgments. This work has been supported by the German Research Foundation (DFG) under grant KO 2252/3-2.

References

1. Adams, A., et al.: Learning to optimize halide with tree search and random programs. ACM Trans. Graph. **38**(4), 1–12 (2019). https://doi.org/10.1145/3306346.3322967
2. Ansel, J., et al.: OpenTuner: an extensible framework for program autotuning. In: Proceedings of the 23rd International Conference on Parallel Architectures and Compilation (PACT 2014). ACM (2014). https://doi.org/10.1145/2628071.2628092
3. Beckingsale, D., Pearce, O., Laguna, I., Gamblin, T.: Apollo: reusable models for fast, dynamic tuning of input-dependent code. In: 2017 IEEE International Parallel and Distributed Processing Symposium (IPDPS), pp. 307–316 (2017). https://doi.org/10.1109/IPDPS.2017.38
4. Bilmes, J., Asanovic, K., Chin, C.W., Demmel, J.: Optimizing matrix multiply using PHiPAC: a portable, high-performance, ANSI C coding methodology. In: Proceedings of the 11th International Conference on Supercomputing (ICS 1997), pp. 340–347. ACM, July 1997. https://doi.org/10.1145/263580.263662
5. Haj-Ali, A., Ahmed, N.K., Willke, T., Shao, Y.S., Asanovic, K., Stoica, I.: NeuroVectorizer: end-to-end vectorization with deep reinforcement learning. In: Proceedings of the 18th ACM/IEEE International Symposium on Code Generation and Optimization. ACM, February 2020. https://doi.org/10.1145/3368826.3377928
6. Heo, K., Lee, W., Pashakhanloo, P., Naik, M.: Effective program debloating via reinforcement learning. In: Proceedings of the 2018 ACM SIGSAC Conference on Computer and Communications Security. ACM, October 2018. https://doi.org/10.1145/3243734.3243838
7. van der Houwen, P., Sommeijer, B.: Parallel iteration of high-order Runge-Kutta methods with stepsize control. J. Comput. Appl. Math. **29**(1), 111–127 (1990). https://doi.org/10.1016/0377-0427(90)90200-J
8. Konduit: DL4J: Deep learning for Java (2022). https://deeplearning4j.konduit.ai/

9. Mammadli, R., Jannesari, A., Wolf, F.: Static neural compiler optimization via deep reinforcement learning. In: 2020 IEEE/ACM 6th Workshop on the LLVM Compiler Infrastructure in HPC (LLVM-HPC) and Workshop on Hierarchical Parallelism for Exascale Computing (HiPar), pp. 1–11 (2020). https://doi.org/10.1109/LLVMHPCHiPar51896.2020.00006
10. Mirhoseini, A., et al.: Device placement optimization with reinforcement learning. In: Proceedings of the 34th International Conference on Machine Learning (ICML 2017), vol. 70, pp. 2430–2439. PMLR (2017)
11. Mnih, V., et al.: Human-level control through deep reinforcement learning. Nature **518**(7540), 529–533 (2015). https://doi.org/10.1038/nature14236
12. Muralidharan, S., Roy, A., Hall, M., Garland, M., Rai, P.: Architecture-adaptive code variant tuning. SIGOPS Oper. Syst. Rev. **50**(2), 325–338 (2016). https://doi.org/10.1145/2954680.2872411
13. Pfaffe, P., Grosser, T., Tillmann, M.: Efficient hierarchical online-autotuning: a case study on polyhedral accelerator mapping. In: Proceedings of the ACM International Conference on Supercomputing (ICS 2019), pp. 354–366. ACM (2019). https://doi.org/10.1145/3330345.3330377
14. Pfaffe, P., Tillmann, M., Walter, S., Tichy, W.F.: Online-autotuning in the presence of algorithmic choice. In: 2017 IEEE International Parallel and Distributed Processing Symposium Workshops (IPDPSW 2017), pp. 1379–1388 (2017). https://doi.org/10.1109/IPDPSW.2017.28
15. Ragan-Kelley, J., Barnes, C., Adams, A., Paris, S., Durand, F., Amarasinghe, S.: Halide: a language and compiler for optimizing parallelism, locality, and recomputation in image processing pipelines. In: Proceedings of the 34th ACM SIGPLAN Conference on Programming Language Design and Implementation (PLDI 2013), pp. 519–530. ACM (2013). https://doi.org/10.1145/2491956.2462176
16. Rasch, A., Gorlatch, S.: ATF: a generic directive-based auto-tuning framework. Concurr. Comput. Pract. Exp. **31**(5) (2019). https://doi.org/10.1002/cpe.4423
17. Schulman, J., Wolski, F., Dhariwal, P., Radford, A., Klimov, O.: Proximal policy optimization algorithms, July 2017. http://arxiv.org/abs/1707.06347
18. Seiferth, J., Korch, M., Rauber, T.: Offsite autotuning approach. In: Sadayappan, P., Chamberlain, B.L., Juckeland, G., Ltaief, H. (eds.) ISC High Performance 2020. LNCS, vol. 12151, pp. 370–390. Springer, Cham (2020). https://doi.org/10.1007/978-3-030-50743-5_19
19. Sutton, R.S., Barto, A.G.: Reinforcement Learning, 2nd edn. The MIT Press, Cambridge (2018)
20. Tiwari, A., Hollingsworth, J.K.: Online adaptive code generation and tuning. In: Proceedings of the 2011 IEEE International Parallel Distributed Processing Symposium (IPDPS 2011), pp. 879–892. IEEE, May 2011. https://doi.org/10.1109/IPDPS.2011.86
21. Vigueras, G., Carro, M., Tamarit, S., Mariño, J.: Towards automatic learning of heuristics for mechanical transformations of procedural code. In: Electronic Proceedings in Theoretical Computer Science, vol. 237, pp. 52–67. Open Publishing Association, January 2017. https://doi.org/10.4204/eptcs.237.4
22. Wang, T., Jain, N., Boehme, D., Beckingsale, D., Mueller, F., Gamblin, T.: CodeSeer: input-dependent code variants selection via machine learning. In: Proceedings of the 34th ACM International Conference on Supercomputing. ACM, June 2020. https://doi.org/10.1145/3392717.3392741
23. Whaley, R.C., Petitet, A., Dongarra, J.: Automated empirical optimizations of software and the ATLAS project. Parallel Comput. **27**(1), 3–35 (2001). https://doi.org/10.1016/S0167-8191(00)00087-9

Programming Environments and System Software

Remote OpenMP Offloading

Atmn Patel[1] and Johannes Doerfert[2(✉)]

[1] University of Waterloo, Waterloo, ON, Canada
atmn.patel@uwaterloo.ca

[2] Argonne National Laboratory, Lemont, IL, USA
jdoerfert@anl.gov

Abstract. OpenMP has a long and successful history in parallel programming for CPUs. Since the introduction of accelerator offloading, it has evolved into a promising candidate for all intra-node parallel computing needs. While this addition broke with the shared memory assumption OpenMP was initially developed with, efforts to employ OpenMP beyond shared-memory domains are practically non-existent.

In this work, we show that the OpenMP accelerator offloading model is sufficient to seamlessly and efficiently utilize more than a single compute node and its connected accelerators. Without source code or compiler modifications, we run an OpenMP offload capable program on a remote CPU, or remote accelerator (e.g., GPU), as if it was a local one. For applications that support multi-device offloading, any combination of local and remote CPUs and accelerators can be utilized simultaneously, fully transparent to the user. Our low-overhead implementation of *Remote OpenMP Offloading* is integrated into the LLVM/OpenMP compiler infrastructure and publicly available (in parts) with LLVM 12 and later. LLVM-based (vendor) compilers are expected to be compatible as well.

To evaluate our work, we provide detailed studies on microbenchmarks, as well as scaling results on two HPC proxy applications. We show scaling results across dozens of GPUs in multiple hosts with effectiveness that is directly proportional to the ratio of computation versus memory transfer time. Our work outlines the capabilities and limits of OpenMP 5.1 to efficiently utilize a distributed heterogeneous system without source, compiler, or language modifications, as opposed to solutions such as MPI.

Keywords: OpenMP · GPGPU · Distributed computing

1 Introduction

With the growing diversity of accelerator hardware, the number of competing programming models for intra-node computing, that is, multi-processor computing and local accelerator offloading has increased as well. For most single-node solutions, it is challenging, if not impossible, to orchestrate work across (accelerators in) multiple nodes. While various distributed programming models exist

A.-L. Varbanescu et al. (Eds.): ISC High Performance 2022, LNCS 13289, pp. 315–333, 2022.
doi.org/10.1007/978-3-031-07312-0_16

and thrive, they are usually developed separately from their intra-node cousins. Applications initially designed with a single node in mind cannot simply utilize remote hardware. In addition to infrastructure and software challenges, it would also require additional coarse-grained parallelism, i.e., exposed through a new domain-decomposition dimension. Thus, developers are historically in a tough spot if they outgrow single node capabilities but not in a way that justifies the expense of incorporating an additional model or framework. Even for applications that are early on expected to utilize significant resources, it makes sense to use a single coherent parallel programming model rather than a combination since the setup and maintenance cost increases dramatically per model and framework. While some newly developed languages, i.e., Chapel [10], try to bundle capabilities, their lacking adoption in various parts of HPC is still indicating that classic solutions need to step up and fill the void.

```
  if (N <= Threshold) {
#pragma omp target depend(out:A[0]) device(getDev()) map(tofrom: A[:N])
    sort(A, &A[N]);
  } else {
#pragma omp task depend(out:A[0])
    mergesort_rec(A, N/2);

#pragma omp task depend(out:A[N/2])
    mergesort_rec(&A[N/2], N - N/2);

#pragma omp target depend(in:A[0], A[N/2]) device(getDev())
     map(tofrom: A[:N])
    merge(&A[0], &A[N/2], &A[N]);
  }
```

Fig. 1. Schematic core of a parallel merge sort that uses OpenMP offloading. `getDev()` cycles round robin through the available devices and an outer OpenMP parallel region provides threads to execute the tasks concurrently.

Figure 1 illustrates the core of a parallel merge sort using the OpenMP tasking and offloading model. As target directives create implicit tasks they can interact natively with explicit tasks spawned for CPU utilization. If the code is employed on shared-memory system, i.e., if the offloading device is the CPU itself or a GPU that has coherent access to the host memory, the map clauses can be ignored by the compiler. However, if the host and the accelerator do not share the same memory space, these clauses will instruct the compiler and runtime on how to orchestrate memory transfers. This explicit denotation of necessary data transfers is common to offloading models but in OpenMP it is especially tightly integrated with the tasking and offloading runtime since each data transfer is kept as an explicit function call throughout compilation.

For this work we observed that the annotations and infrastructure introduced to deal with accelerators in the same system is sufficient to provide users with transparent and efficient access to remote compute resources. Neither the model nor the compiler need to be changed to scale the merge sort from a single multi-core application to a distributed program. The OpenMP-based source specialization shown in Fig. 2 make it even easier to specialize existing code to the heterogeneous remote hardware at compile time, all in the confinement of a single parallel programming model.

In the following, we outline the contributions and limitations of this work before we provide technical background in Sect. 3. After we discuss related approaches in Sect. 4 we dive into the details of our implementation in Sect. 5. An evaluation of our work based on a microbenchmark and two proxy applications run on Google Cloud as well as an HPC GPU cluster is presented in Sect. 6. We end with a discussion of the limitations of OpenMP 5.1 for remote offloading in Sect. 7, a future work section in Sect. 8, and conclude in Sect. 9.

```
void sort_x86(Ty *, int);
void sort_arm(Ty *, int);
void sort_gpu(Ty *, int);
#pragma omp declare variant(sort_x86) match(device={arch(x86)})
#pragma omp declare variant(sort_arm) match(device={arch(ARM)})
#pragma omp declare variant(sort_gpu) match(device={kind(gpu)})
void sort(Ty *, int)
```

Fig. 2. OpenMP variant declarations to provide specialized implementations in a diverse and heterogeneous computing environment.

2 Contributions and Limitations

The main contributions of this paper are:

- an OpenMP standard-conforming implementation of accelerator offloading which transparently exposes remote hardware as if it was local,
- an evaluation of the overheads of two distinct implementations of a remote offloading infrastructure for various offloading tasks,
- a scaling study with two HPC proxy applications executed on local and remote GPUs on the public cloud and an HPC GPU cluster,
- a discussion of required extensions to the OpenMP standard, or compilers, to make it more efficient to offload to multiple devices, local and remote.

We are aware of the following limitations of our work:

- local and remote accelerators are currently indistinguishable; this limitation will go away with the availability of the OpenMP 5.1 `interop` directive,
- we kept the host-centric model OpenMP is currently using which is why we expose a flat list of devices to "the host" instead of a hierarchical device tree,
- our two implementations for remote offloading via different network communication libraries do not fully utilize the advanced features of each library.

– our work does not aim to compete with MPI or other distributed programming models and attempts to improve developer productivity when beginning to extend OpenMP applications beyond a single node without any source modifications.

3 Background

Int this section, we review background information on LLVM's implementation of OpenMP. Specifically, we cover the Compilation Workflow and Runtimes used by LLVM's implementation to support target offloading. While we briefly introduce OpenMP target offloading support in LLVM, interested readers should consult the work [6] for further background information.

3.1 Compilation Flow for LLVM/OpenMP Offloading

OpenMP offloading directives (e.g., `omp target`, `omp target data`) are lowered by clang in the host code to calls to LLVM/OpenMP `libomptarget` runtime routines. In subsequent steps of the compilation process, the OpenMP target regions are compiled for all offload architectures into target-specific images. These images are embedded by clang into the host object file to support multiple accelerators from the same binary.

3.2 LLVM/OpenMP Offload Runtime Interactions

LLVM's target-independent runtime (`libomptarget`) handles OpenMP specific tasks with a set of target-dependent runtimes, also referred to as plugins, to facilitate the communication with the device. The target-independent runtime exposes synchronous and asynchronous APIs for data transfer and offloading tasks. The target-dependent runtime plugins (`libomptarget.rtl.ARCH`) provide primitive operations forwarded to a foreign device runtime, e.g., `libcudart`. An overview of how the runtimes interact is given in the top row of Fig. 3. In the figure, ① represents how that clang uses `libomptarget`, ② is the API that a new device plugin should implement to be supported for target offloading. ②' represents the new device plugin API and ⑤ represents the inter-node communication API we designed and implemented for our work. LLVM/OpenMP currently supports offloading to seven[1] architectures through plugins.

4 Related Work

The hybrid usage of OpenMP and MPI in HPC applications is complicated not only from an implementation perspective but also from a performance perspective. Approaches developed to ensure that a particular hybrid usage of OpenMP/MPI would be beneficial [15] are highly non-trivial since they are application and workload-specific.

[1] LLVM/OpenMP plugins: ARM, AMDGCN, CUDA, PPC, *Remote*, VE, X86. Others available: OpenCL [22], Virtual GPU [28].

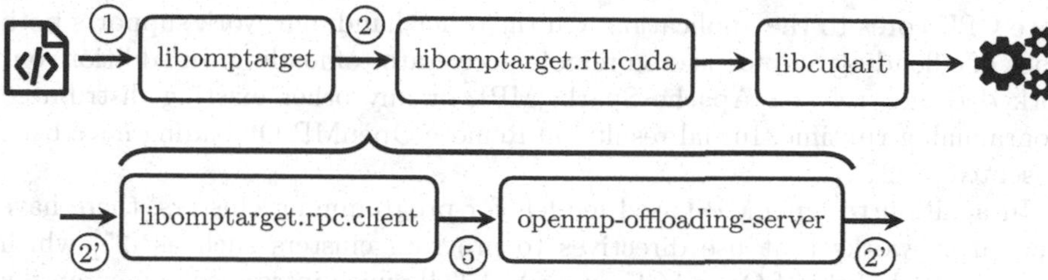

Fig. 3. Top row: Overview of LLVM's OpenMP offloading infrastructure for NVIDIA GPUs. Bottom row: Remote OpenMP offloading plugin design and its placement in the existing infrastructure. The circled numbers indicate different APIs, the boxes (shared) runtime libraries.

Attempts to use OpenMP to program multiple nodes predates OpenMP target offloading. An early approach [24] used the compiler to convert OpenMP to calls to a software distributed shared memory system (SDSM), here TreadMarks [21]. A later improvement [18] on the implementation used a modified TreadMarks that exploited the hardware shared memory in each SMP node and achieved performance within 7–30% of MPI. Iterations over the same concept resulted in the creation of HyComp [23] and Omni OpenMP [30]. HyComp contains a novel page-based SDSM that pre-fetches pages with help from the compiler and minimizes data consistency costs by tracking shared variable usage. The Omni OpenMP compiler implemented transformations to ensure efficient usage of the memory model in the SCASH SDSM.

Other than attempts to use OpenMP to program SDSM systems, there was also a source-to-source compiler that converted an extended OpenMP directly to MPI calls [13]. Other approaches were also considered in [19,35].

OpenMP has already been explored as an effective programming model in the conceptually similar environment of embedded SoC systems [9]. In this model, there are NUMA effects that arise from the slower inter-cluster communication. In this environment, the OpenMP teams and distribute construct were shown to effectively distribute work. Further explorations of OpenMP as an efficient programming model on many-core processors can be found in [5].

After the introduction of OpenMP target offloading in OpenMP 4.0, [20] also utilized the LLVM OpenMP target offloading runtime to program clusters. They evaluated their implementation with HMMER, a popular bioinformatics software, and with which they determined that there was a small constant-factor overhead to using their OpenMP remote offloading when compared to a baseline MPI implementation. A later implementation, OmpCloud [36] utilizes Apache Spark clusters to manage the communication, fault-tolerance, load-balancing, etc. because they were motivated by the prospect of running OpenMP target offloading applications at scale in the public cloud. This implementation utilized the Apache Spark runtime to expose the entire cluster of Spark nodes as a single OpenMP offloading device. Neither implementations were able to exploit accelerators, e.g., GPUs, on the remote nodes and instead focused on exposing more CPU cores to the application. On the other hand, our work supports both types of offloading and focuses on remote accelerator offloading. In addition, our work does not rely on Apache Spark, MPI, or any other existing distributed programming runtime. Initial results on Remote OpenMP Offloading have been presented in [27].

In addition to OpenMP-based models for programming clusters, there have been many works that use directives to program clusters such as [25] which introduced a hybrid of OpenACC and XMP, [34] which introduced an extension of OpenMP-based on MapReduce. An approach similar to ours was developed in [17] where CUDA kernels were annotated with data movements for remote multi-GPU execution. OmpSs [14] is another programming model developed that has also been extended [8] to also support GASNet [7], which is a high-performance networking middleware used to implement PGAS languages such as Chapel [3], Legion [4], UPC [1], UPC++ [2], etc.

Note that our work bears no relation to prior offloading work to accelerators through other models such as TornadoVM or rCUDA because of their focus on offloading paradigms in general, and GPU-level virtualization. Additionally, although this work is reminiscent of single system image (SSI) implementations, in our work this is an artifact of OpenMP's programming model, not our work in particular.

5 Implementation

The basic idea behind the *Remote OpenMP Offloading* implementation is to provide a transparent communication channel between the target-independent `libomptarget` library on the host with the target-dependent `libomptarget.rtl.ARCH` library on the remote system. This use case matches the well-known remote procedure calls (RPC) idiom. To facilitate communication, we added two new components into LLVM/OpenMP that build a tunnel from the host to the remote system through which all plugin API calls (② in Fig. 3) are forwarded. The first is a remote offloading plugin (`libomptarget.rtl.rpc`) which presents itself to the host `libomptarget` as any other plugin would, i.e., it looks no different than the NVIDIA GPU offloading plugin. The second is a server application that must be running on the remote system (`openmp-offloading-server`) that mimics `libomptarget` when it communicates with the remote device plugin, such as the one for NVIDIA GPU offloading. The bottom row of Fig. 3 illustrates their interaction with the existing infrastructure.

Previously there was only one instance of `libomptarget`, namely the one on the host, while we now have a "remote" `libomptarget` emulation via the server application. Since only the former has access to the binary and all the offload images (ref. Sect. 3.1), we needed to extend the original plugin API ②. Specifically, the new LLVM/OpenMP plugin API ②' matches ② but with two new optional plugin entry points. The new entry points are necessary as the remote `libomptarget` emulation cannot directly use the program binary to access the device image, for example, to pass the binary code of the target regions to the foreign device plugin. Thus, the new functions create a copy of the images embedded in the program binary on the remote host since the target code on the device is never explicitly copied (by OpenMP) otherwise. Note that this was the only modification we required to the existing system, and it has been in LLVM/OpenMP since version 12.

While the remote offload capability is encapsulated in a single runtime, it comes with two implementations for serialization (ref. Sect. 5.3): protobuf, and a custom serialization library, and two transport protocols (ref. Sect. 5.4): gRPC and UCX. To pick a non-default option, the user has to set the environment variables `LIBOMPTARGET_RPC_{SERIALIZATION,TRANSPORT}` at runtime. Note that not all options described are integrated into the community LLVM/OpenMP yet[2].

5.1 Remote Offloading Plugin

The remote offloading plugin (`libomptarget.rtl.rpc.so`) is loaded by `libomptarget` during the initialization of the OpenMP target offloading infrastructure. This plugin creates and manages connections with all remote offloading servers. The environment variable `LIBOMPTARGET_RPC_ADDRESS` takes a comma-separated list of network addresses to specify the remote host servers for offloading. After the initial connections, the remote systems determine how many compatible devices they can provide. The devices are determined by asking each plugin, similar to the host. To support multiple accelerators across multiple hosts, the remote offloading plugin has to keep track of the mapping from host device numbers to clients and their local device numbering. In addition, the plugin keeps maps to relate host pointers to remote system host pointers to simplify network communication and the processing on both sides. The plugin is responsible for handling all communication to all servers using whichever serialization and transport layer have been configured.

5.2 Remote Offloading Server

The server application (`openmp-offloading-server`) is started by the user and will wait for a single incoming connection by a client (`libomptarget.rtl.rpc`). Once such a connection is severed, that is, once the OpenMP offloading program has exited, the server shuts down. We do not reset to an initial state because not all LLVM/OpenMP offload plugins, e.g., the one for NVIDIA GPUs, can be reset safely at this point. If necessary, users can wrap the server start into a script that restarts it as needed.

The implementation is, as the OpenMP's offloading model itself, host-centric. A host application (client) can offload onto multiple servers at once, but a server is not yet able to receive offloading requests from multiple clients simultaneously. This limitation is not conceptual but merely was not required so far.

[2] Support for remote offloading in the LLVM/OpenMP community version is described here: https://openmp.llvm.org/docs/design/Runtimes.html#remote-offloading-plugin.

5.3 Serialization

As with other communication protocols, we have to serialize our data, including information about the API call from the host side, and deserialize it on the remote system. For this work, we compared two solutions: protocol buffers (protobuf) [16] and a custom serialization, one for each data structure and API call.

Protobuf is a library developed by Google for structured data that relies on interface definition `.proto` files. One of our transport layers (gRPC, ref. Sect. 5.4) integrates naturally with protobuf since the same interface definition can be used to generate serialization (host) and deserialization (remote) code. As an alternative, we also wrote specialized serialization and deserialization routines, free of external dependencies. In addition, a custom solution provides opportunities for optimizations. For example, protobuf does not permit random access, and its zero-copy semantics are lacking. Within the gRPC implementation, we use the protobuf arena allocator whose maximum size is set via an environment variable `LIBOMPTARGET_RPC_ALLOCATOR_MAX`.

Note that both solutions perform copies of the data during serialization. While one of our transport layers (UCX, ref. Sect. 5.4) provides an interface for sending non-contiguous data without an intermediate copy, this interface is still under active development.

5.4 Transport Layers

gRPC [11] is a universal remote procedure call framework that includes support for load balancing, tracing, authentication, compression, etc. Further, gRPC comes with a thread pool and handles concurrent connections out-of-the-box. However, due to the general-purpose nature of gRPC, it contains limitations that preclude it from being the optimal choice of transport for remote offloading on high-performance systems. For example, gRPC is optimal for small messages, so all individual messages are generally recommended to be under 2 MB in size. For large data transfers, the streaming approach introduces a large unnecessary overhead. At runtime, this maximum message size is configured via the environment variable `LIBOMPTARGET_RPC_BLOCK_SIZE`. On the other hand, it presents out-of-the-box support for compression that may help mitigate this overhead. gRPC is also limited to serialized protobuf messages as payloads. Due to the tight integration of all of its components, it is also impossible to introduce custom compression algorithms naturally such as nvcomp [26], which utilizes high-performance GPU (de)compressors on NVIDIA GPUs.

UCX [31] consists of three levels of frameworks: UCP for Protocols, UCT for Transport, UCS for Services. UCP utilizes the UCT framework to provide commonly used protocols needed by implementations of MPI, OpenSHMEM, and PGAS. UCP abstracts communication resources into *Workers* that are associated with *Endpoints*. Each Endpoint is associated with a single Worker object responsible for handling the communication on that Endpoint. These Endpoints are initialized directly with a socket address, in the case of IP over InfiniBand

(IPoIB), or with a UCP specific address object, in the case of generic TCP/IP addresses. For the latter, these addresses are constructed per worker, communicated by another mechanism (such as UNIX sockets), and then the Endpoints can be created to use UCX for the communication of future messages. Although UCX has support for generic TCP/IP, we did not explore implementing remote offloading over TCP with UCX, yet.

UCP provides various alternative interfaces for message transmission: remote memory access (RMA), atomic memory access (AMO), Tag Match, Stream, Active Message, and Collectives. We implemented remote offloading through the Tag Matching API, in order to maintain parallelism. Each tag encodes the message type (an enum corresponding to the plugin function being called) and a message ID to enforce ordering.

UCP Workers have several thread-safety options: single-threaded, multi-threaded serial access, and multi-threaded concurrent access. MPI implementations tend to simplify their implementation by providing each thread with its own worker. While we initially considered this, we wanted to avoid spawning a worker for each thread that will execute an OpenMP target region (on the host). This approach led to memory exhaustion on the networking devices while remote offloading onto 40 GPUs. Instead, we have one Worker and Endpoint for the whole program on the client-side and have a thread pool on the server to handle incoming requests in parallel. Depending on the number of concurrent offloading threads, the pool size should be adjusted to provide the best performance.

6 Evaluation

We used two benchmarking environments to evaluate our implementation: the Google Cloud and ThetaGPU cluster. Our Google Cloud (gCloud) benchmarking environment consisted of `n1-highcpu-16` instances that have 16 vCPUs of Intel Xeons (Skylake), 16 GB RAM, an NVIDIA T4 GPU, and a maximum egress bandwidth of 32 Gbps. For this setting, we were limited by the Google Cloud policies to 4 GPUs in total and the gRPC transport layer as we did not enable UCX over TCP/IP. Each node in ThetaGPU has 2 AMD Rome 64-core CPUs, 1 TB DDR4 memory, and 8 NVIDIA A100 GPUs. These nodes have 100GbE ports and are connected via InfiniBand. For this setting, we were limited to 15 nodes, 120 GPUs in total, due to the allocation policies of this cluster. Table 1 summarizes the evaluation environments.

All our Google Cloud results are presented normalized to execution without the remote offloading infrastructure, thus our baseline is *native* OpenMP offloading onto all GPUs on a single node. Our ThetaGPU results are presented normalized to execution on a single remote node to better display the scaling of Remote OpenMP offloading on HPC systems. In addition to tests using accelerators in remote systems, we run a *local* offloading configuration in which the host and the server application are running on the same system, again using all GPUs on the node. When remote systems were involved we did not offload onto the local GPUs of the host as the remote accelerators were always the bottleneck.

For notation, we adopt these acronyms to reduce the verbosity in the discussion that follows: $\mathcal{N}_d$ - native execution on the same system (no remote plugin) using d devices, $\mathcal{L}_d$ - local offloading onto the *same system* using d devices, and $\mathcal{R}_d^k$ - remote offloading onto k remote nodes with d devices in total.

Table 1. Evaluation environments summarized.

Name	# nodes	# GPUs per node	# GPUs	GPU model
gCloud	4	1	4	NVIDIA T4
ThetaGPU	15	8	120	NVIDIA A100

6.1 Benchmarks

To evaluate the performance of the remote offloading implementations we use two HPC mini-apps (RSBench [32] and XSBench [33]) and a microbenchmark for overhead analysis. Since there are essentially no existing OpenMP target offloading programs that utilize multiple GPUs (on a single MPI rank), we selected RSBench and XSBench as they were naturally portable to multi-device offloading.

Proxy Applications: XSBench/RSBench. RSBench and XSBench are proxy applications that serve as stand-ins for the Monte Carlo neutron transport code OpenMC [29]. They simulate only the most computationally intensive parts of OpenMC and are reported to represent 85% of its runtime. Both apps are in C with OpenMP threading in mind, but they are also available in CUDA, OpenCL, SYCL, and OpenMP offloading.

In our systems, the XSBench computation kernel is memory-bound as it performs semi-random memory accesses. RSBench is similar but uses a different method for computing cross-sections. This method trades memory efficiency for runtime and is compute-bound.

To target multiple GPUs we modified the source and introduced the outer loop illustrated in Fig. 4. To test the weak scaling of our setup, we increased the overall work by the number of available GPUs to keep the work performed by each OpenMP target region (`lookups_per_device`) constant. Both modifications were done after confirming their scientific meaningfulness with the authors.

Two parameters influence the memory requirement and runtime of RSBench and XSBench: the problem size (number of particles) and the number of lookups. Both benchmarks come in two problem sizes: small and large. The memory usages (as reported by the application) are in Table 2. At runtime, each device is sent identical arrays of roughly this size. The number of lookups is independent of the problem size, and for RSBench and XSBench, they are by default 1.02×10^7 and 1.7×10^7, respectively. In addition, we run experiments with as little as 10^3 lookups and up to 10^8. The number of lookups affects the runtime of the application by requiring more or fewer iterations of the Monte Carlo algorithm.

```
#pragma omp parallel for num_threads(num_devices)
for (auto K = 0; K < num_devices; K++) {
   #pragma omp target ... device(K)
   for (auto i = 0; i < lookups_per_device; i++) {
       seed = get_seed();
       energy = get_energy(&seed);
       material = get_material(&seed);
       compute_macro_cross_section(...);
   }
}
```

Fig. 4. Simplified kernel from RSBench/XSBench with our modifications to support multi-device offloading.

By changing the number of lookups, we explore how sensitive the scaling of remote OpenMP offloading is to different ratios of computing to data-transfer time.

Table 2. Memory usage of the proxy applications.

	Small	Large
RSBench	4.9 MB	25.5 MB
XSBench	38 MB	198 MB

Micro Benchmark. In addition to the proxy applications, we run the empty target region shown in Fig. 5 to determine introduced overheads. To this end, we compare local offloading $\mathcal{L}_1$, remote offloading $\mathcal{R}_1^1$, as well as $\mathcal{R}_{16}^2$ to native execution $\mathcal{N}_1$. To determine the effect of data movement we run the micro benchmark without a map clause (basically `N = 0`) and value for `N` between 2^{16} and 2^{23}.

```
int32_t *arr = ...
#pragma omp target map(arr[:N])
{ }
```

Fig. 5. Empty target region micro benchmark with variable data transfer.

6.2 Results

We ran RSBench and XSBench on Google Cloud and ThetaGPU, as well as a series of microbenchmarks on ThetaGPU. We ran weak-scaling experiments on the Google Cloud, and strong-scaling experiments on ThetaGPU. The Google Cloud experiments were only run with gRPC to test the efficiacy of Remote OpenMP Offloading in the public cloud, but the ThetaGPU experiments were run with both transports to test the scaling of the networking backends on HPC clusters.

gCloud Results. In this series of experiemnts, we kept the number of lookups constant for all runs and reported the difference for various configurations compared to native offloading $\mathcal{N}_1$. Figure 6 shows the scaling results for the compute-bound RSBench. Each program instance is denoted by the problem size and the number of lookups.

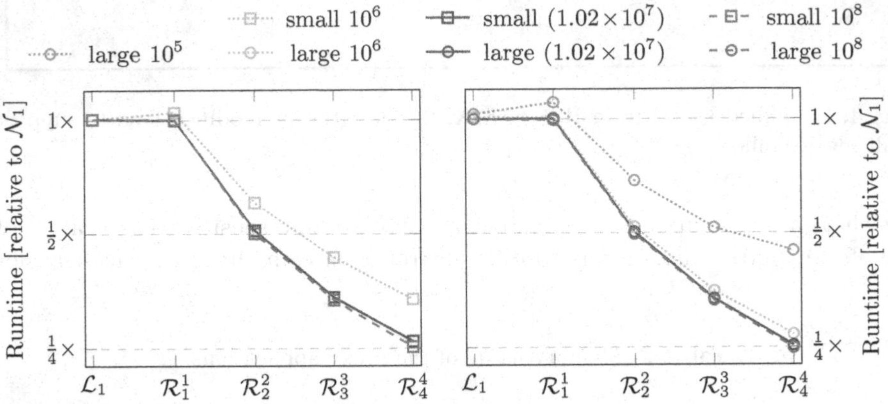

(a) Configurations running Small instance. (b) Configurations running Large instance.

Fig. 6. RSBench remote offloading performance for the gCloud environment.

In the worst case, the large instance with 10^5 lookups, we see an overhead of 10.7% for $\mathcal{R}_1^1$, and a maximum speedup of 2.23× for $\mathcal{R}_4^4$, that is, four remote systems with one GPU each. In the best case, we see that $\mathcal{R}_4^4$ improves performance essentially 4-fold. Although the case of perfect scaling can be engineered by increasing the number of lookups, we still see near-linear scalability for the default problem sizes where we achieve a 3.8× speed up for the small problem size and a 3.96× speedup for the large problem instance. The compute-intensive nature and low memory footprint of RSBench are certainly advantageous for our setup.

Figure 7 shows the result of the memory-bound XSBench. As expected, remote offloading performs overall much worse as the memory transfer to compute ratio is higher in this benchmark.

For the default number of lookups and the small problem size, we see an overhead of 18.6% for $\mathcal{R}_1^1$ and a speedup of 1.74× for $\mathcal{R}_4^4$. The performance of remote offloading expectedly improves with the number of lookups. For 10^9 lookups, we see a nearly linear speedup of 3.95× on $\mathcal{R}_4^4$. If we lower the lookups, we see slowdowns of more than 3-fold as the memory transfer times dominate the execution. For the large problem size and the default number of lookups, the performance decreases by 19.3% for $\mathcal{R}_1^1$ and improves by 1.97× for $\mathcal{R}_4^4$. Again, with a sufficient number of lookups, we see near-linear speedups, e.g., 3.87× for $\mathcal{R}_4^4$ with 10^9 lookups.

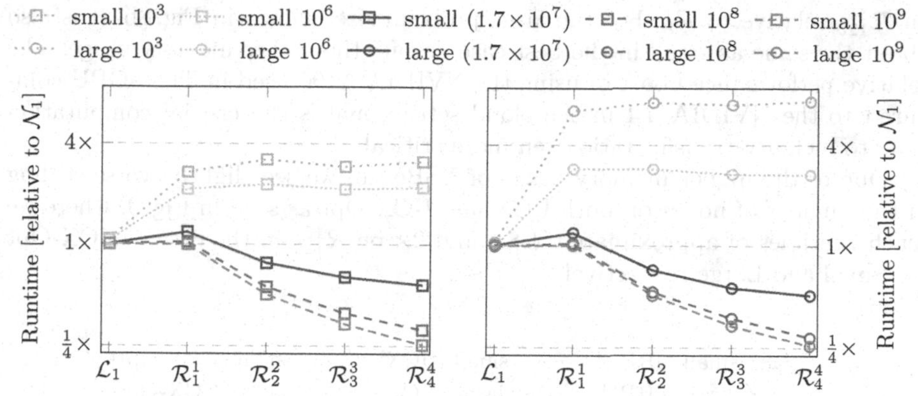

(a) Configurations running Small instance. (b) Configurations running Large instance.

Fig. 7. XSBench remote offloading performance for the gCloud environment.

ThetaGPU Results. On the ThetaGPU environment, we performed a weak scaling study with up to 15 remote hosts, each providing 8 GPUs using the default number of lookups. Thus, we kept the work per device constant as we added new nodes and devices. The best case is a flat line at 1× which would mean there is no overhead using 15× the number of remote resources compared to remote offloading onto one remote node with 8 GPUs ($\mathcal{R}_8^1$) using that networking backend. We compare against $\mathcal{R}_8^1$ rather than $\mathcal{N}_8$ to capture the scaling of remote offloading across multiple nodes in an HPC system.

To put the relative graphs into perspective, the average absolute runtimes across the networking configurations on a single ThetaGPU node are in Table 3.

Table 3. Absolute runtime on a single ThetaGPU node.

	$\mathcal{L}_8$ - Small	$\mathcal{L}_8$ - Large	$\mathcal{R}_8^1$ - Small	$\mathcal{R}_8^1$ - Large
RSBench	1.2 s	1.5 s	1.2 s	1.6 s
XSBench	1.2 s	2.8 s	1.2 s	2.7 s

To determine the potential effect of a hierarchical approach on the performance of our benchmarks, we performed an additional experiment. The UCX-Opt entry in Fig. 8 and Fig. 9 show the performance if the data replicated to all eight remote devices is sent to the remote host only once and are replicated locally. While a proper compiler analysis would be necessary to validate and guide such an optimization, we performed it manually as part of the runtime. Section 7 further discusses this limitation.

For RSBench with the small problem size, shown in Fig. 8a, we see the performance scaling across any number of remote nodes with only a 1.5× runtime on $\mathcal{R}^{15}_{120}$ relative to $\mathcal{R}^{1}_{8}$. For the large problem size, shown in Fig. 8b, it is also about the same as small in the best case despite the higher memory usage. The relative performance boost of using the NVIDIA A100 used in ThetaGPU compared to the NVIDIA T4 in the cloud setting makes the crucial computation time to memory transfer ratio even more critical.

Due to the higher memory usage of XSBench, we see slightly worse scaling in the number of nodes on both UCX and UCX-Opt as seen in Fig. 9, where we reach runtimes of approximately 1.8× and 2× on $\mathcal{R}^{15}_{120}$ in the case of UCX-Opt for Small and Large respectively.

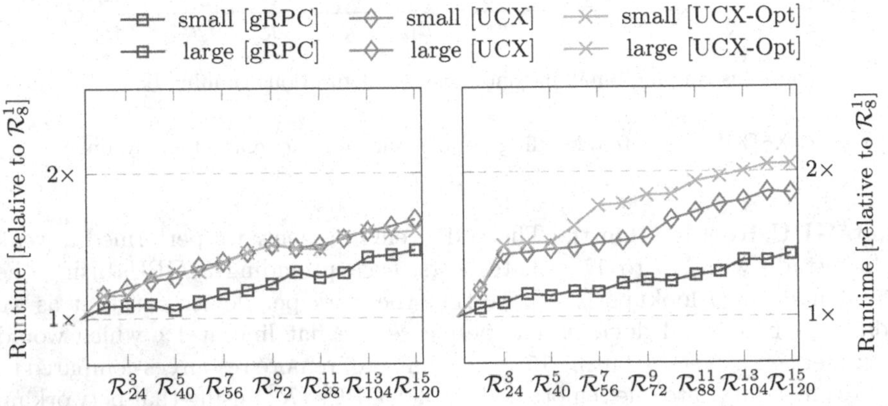

(a) Configurations running Small instance. (b) Configurations running Large instance.

Fig. 8. RSBench remote offloading performance for the ThetaGPU environment.

Microbenchmarks. The micro benchmarking results are shown in Figs. 10a to 10c. We see that UCX produces, as expected, significantly faster data transfers when compared to gRPC. Additionally, we see the effects of internal thresholds that UCX maintains for utilizing different UCT and UCS mechanisms at runtime through the drop in runtime for messages of size 1 MiB. For gRPC, due to issues known to occur with many large messages, we were unable to obtain results beyond 2 MiB for $\mathcal{L}_1$. Additionally, for $\mathcal{R}^{2}_{16}$, we were limited by the available memory for UCX and gRPC.

7 Limitations of OpenMP

In this work, we enabled transparent remote offloading in the confinement of the OpenMP 5.1 specification for target offloading. While the result shows promise when data transfer times are far lower than kernel computation times, there are conceptual limitations to the OpenMP model that would make distributed offloading simpler and more efficient.

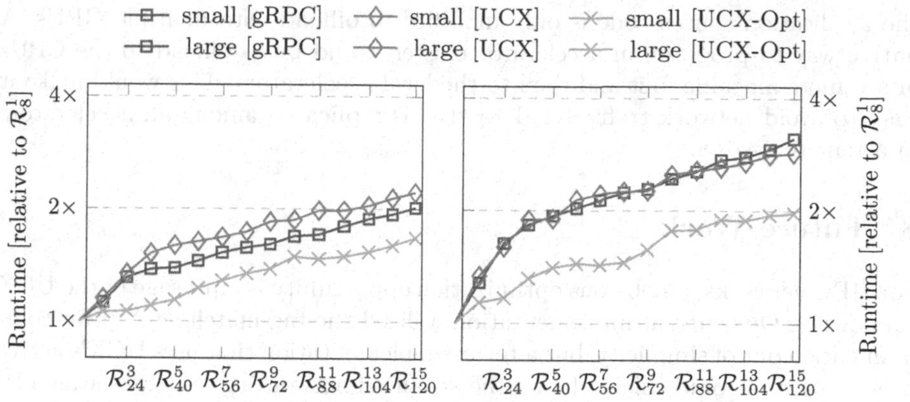

(a) Configurations running Small instance. (b) Configurations running Large instance.

Fig. 9. XSBench remote offloading performance for the ThetaGPU environment.

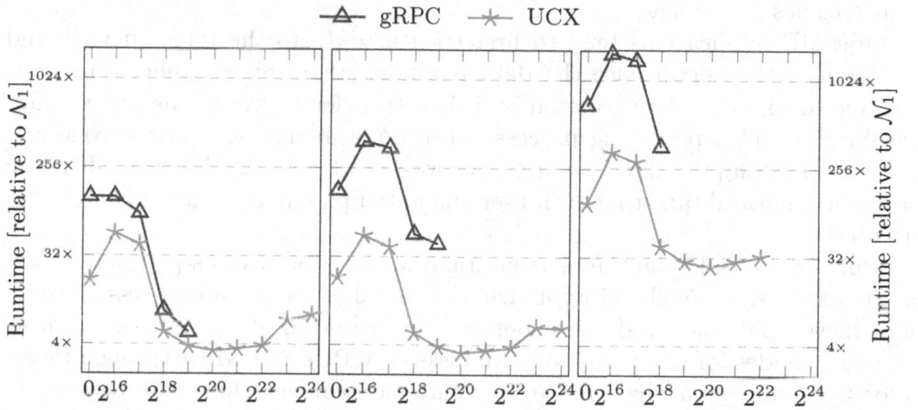

(a) Configuration: $\mathcal{L}_1$. (b) Configuration: $\mathcal{R}_1^1$. (c) Configuration: $\mathcal{R}_{16}^2$.

Fig. 10. Micro benchmarking results for the ThetaGPU environment of transferring `int[N]` where $N = 0, 2^{16}, \ldots, 2^{24}$.

One concern is the flat device model. Instead of enumerating all available devices from 0 to N, it would be preferable to expose a hierarchy to the user. This would not only benefit the distributed use case but also help divide GPUs into multiple devices and expose NUMA effects between accelerators. There are various ways to extend the current star topology, e.g., a more elaborate device identifier similar to the thread affinity format. For distributed offloading, it would be natural to allow hierarchical offloading, that is, nested target regions. While device-to-device copies are possible already, they were not considered for use in our proxy apps since they would require breaking our requirement that the application source code is only modified to offload onto multiple GPUs. A native way to program an accelerator cluster would be to offload to the CPUs of a remote machine first and then to the local accelerators. This would make it easy to avoid network traffic for data that is replicated among all accelerators in a remote system.

8 Future Work

For HPC networks, an obvious optimization opportunity is our usage of the UCX framework. Our current implementation utilized the tag-matching API for communication out of simplicity, but a future implementation that uses UCX's active messaging API could efficiently use the advanced networking resources available. In addition, we did not consider data compression, a promising endeavor for improving the overall performance of remote OpenMP offloading where we are network-bound. UCX also exposes RDMA and other advanced hardware features which could optimize the networking communication between nodes and reduce copies in the stack.

OpenMP applications tend to first transfer data to the target device, and then launch the kernel once the data is available. In many applications, it is possible to pipeline the execution and data transfer to avoid this unnecessary serialization. This pipelining process, when done manually, is error-prone and tedious, so a compiler directive approach was developed [12]. Remote offloading would be a natural target for such user annotated pipelining or a fully automatic approach.

Our remote offloading implementation has also been cross-platform tested on SmartNICs. Through our approach, easy parallelism in data processing could be achieved on network devices, before being received at the primary host or secondary nodes for compute-intensive tasks on CPUs and GPUs through target offloading - all within the same architecture-independent OpenMP program.

9 Conclusion

In this work, we extended the existing LLVM/OpenMP target offloading runtime to offload onto accelerators on remote hosts. Our OpenMP standard-conforming implementation transparently exposes remote accelerators as if they were local, removing the need for programmer intervention when extending an application to use multiple nodes. Our implementation is capable of using gRPC, a popular general-purpose RPC library, for offloading over TCP/IP networks, as well as UCX, a networking framework developed for HPC systems, for more advanced hardware such as InfiniBand. Given that our networking implementations are not finely tuned, our results serve as an upper bound for the overhead induced by remote OpenMP offloading. Our implementation was tested for different configurations on two HPC proxy applications, RSBench and XSBench. We demonstrated attractive strong scaling across four remote GPUs on the Google Cloud and attractive weak scaling across 120 GPUs on ThetaGPU. Specifically, we were able to offload onto 120 GPUs on 15 nodes with 1.5× the overhead of running on 8 GPUs in the single node for RSBench, and at 1.8× and 2× on XSBench Small and Large respectively. In the case of ThetaGPU, we experimented with a data transfer optimization mimicking hierarchical offloading for nodes with multiple devices.

In the future, we hope that with nested target regions hierarchical remote offloading can be introduced into OpenMP. Our bandwidth optimization, and many others, would become available natively to the programmer and through proper compiler analysis. We believe our work shows that OpenMP programs can be reasonably extended to multiple nodes without a redesign or the introduction of another programming model. Most parts of our implementations are already available in LLVM/OpenMP since LLVM 12, and the remaining parts will follow shortly.

Acknowledgements. We gratefully acknowledge the computing resources provided and operated by the Joint Laboratory for System Evaluation (JLSE) at Argonne National Laboratory. Part of this research was supported by the Exascale Computing Project (17-SC-20-SC), a collaborative effort of two U.S. Department of Energy organizations (Office of Science and the National Nuclear Security Administration) responsible for the planning and preparation of a capable exascale ecosystem, including software, applications, hardware, advanced system engineering, and early testbed platforms, in support of the nation's exascale computing imperative. Part of this research was supported by the Lawrence Livermore National Security, LLC ("LLNS") via MPO No. B642066.

References

1. Berkeley UPC - Unified Parallel C. https://upc.lbl.gov/
2. Upc++. https://bitbucket.org/berkeleylab/upcxx/wiki/Home
3. Chapel Lang (2021). https://chapel-lang.org/
4. Legion Programming System (2021). https://legion.stanford.edu/
5. Al-Khalissi, H.: Efficient Programming Model for OpenMP on Cluster-Based Many-Core System. Ph.D. thesis, Braunschweig University of Technology, Germany (2015)
6. Antão, S.F., et al.: Offloading support for OpenMP in Clang and LLVM. In: Third Workshop on the LLVM Compiler Infrastructure in HPC, LLVM-HPC@SC 2016, 14 November 2016. IEEE Computer Society, Salt Lake City, UT, USA (2016)
7. Bonachea, D., Hargrove, P.H.: GASNet-EX: a high-performance, portable communication library for exascale. In: Hall, M., Sundar, H. (eds.) LCPC 2018. LNCS, vol. 11882, pp. 138–158. Springer, Cham (2019). https://doi.org/10.1007/978-3-030-34627-0_11
8. Bueno, J., Martorell, X., Badia, R.M., Ayguadé, E., Labarta, J.: Implementing OMPSS support for regions of data in architectures with multiple address spaces. In: Malony, A.D., Nemirovsky, M., Midkiff, S.P. (eds.) International Conference on Supercomputing, ICS 2013, 10–14 June 2013. ACM, Eugene, OR, USA (2013). https://doi.org/10.1145/2464996.2465017
9. Capotondi, A., Marongiu, A.: On the effectiveness of OpenMP teams for cluster-based many-core accelerators. In: International Conference on High Performance

Computing and Simulation, HPCS 2016, 18–22 July 2016. IEEE, Innsbruck, Austria (2016)
10. Chamberlain, B.L., Callahan, D., Zima, H.P.: Parallel Programmability and the Chapel Language. Int. J. High Perform. Comput. Appl. **21**(3) (2007)
11. gRPC community: GRPC (2021). https://grpc.io/
12. Cui, X., Scogland, T.R.W., de Supinski, B.R., Feng, W.: Directive-based pipelining extension for OpenMP. In: 2016 IEEE International Conference on Cluster Computing, CLUSTER 2016, 12–16 September 2016. IEEE Computer Society, Taipei, Taiwan (2016)
13. Dorta, A.J., Badía, J.M., Quintana, E.S., de Sande, F.: Implementing OpenMP for clusters on top of MPI. In: Di Martino, B., Kranzlmüller, D., Dongarra, J. (eds.) EuroPVM/MPI 2005. LNCS, vol. 3666, pp. 148–155. Springer, Heidelberg (2005). https://doi.org/10.1007/11557265_22
14. Duran, A., et al.: OMPSS: a proposal for programming heterogeneous multicore architectures. Parallel Process. Lett. **21**(2) (2011). https://doi.org/10.1142/S0129626411000151
15. Gahvari, H., Schulz, M., Yang, U.M.: An approach to selecting Thread + Process Mixes for Hybrid MPI + OpenMP Applications. In: 2015 IEEE International Conference on Cluster Computing, CLUSTER 2015, 8–11 September 2015. IEEE Computer Society, Chicago, IL, USA (2015)
16. Google: Protocol buffers (2021). https://developers.google.com/protocol-buffers
17. Heldens, S., Hijma, P., van Werkhoven, B., Maassen, J., van Nieuwpoort, R.V.: Lightning: scaling the GPU programming model beyond a single GPU (2022). https://doi.org/10.48550/ARXIV.2202.05549, https://arxiv.org/abs/2202.05549
18. Hu, Y.C., Lu, H., Cox, A.L., Zwaenepoel, W.: OpenMP for networks of SMPs. J. Parallel Distributed Comput. **60**(12) (2000)
19. Huang, L., Chapman, B.M., Liu, Z.: Towards a more efficient implementation of OpenMP for clusters via translation to global arrays. Parallel Comput. **31**(10–12) (2005). https://doi.org/10.1016/j.parco.2005.03.015
20. Jacob, A.C., et al.: Exploiting fine- and coarse-grained parallelism using a directive based approach. In: Terboven, C., de Supinski, B.R., Reble, P., Chapman, B.M., Müller, M.S. (eds.) IWOMP 2015. LNCS, vol. 9342, pp. 30–41. Springer, Cham (2015). https://doi.org/10.1007/978-3-319-24595-9_3
21. Keleher, P.J., Cox, A.L., Dwarkadas, S., Zwaenepoel, W.: Treadmarks: distributed shared memory on standard workstations and operating systems. In: USENIX Winter 1994 Technical Conference, 17–21 January 1994, Conference Proceedings. USENIX Association,San Francisco, California, USA (1994)
22. Knaust, M., Mayer, F., Steinke, T.: OpenMP to FPGA offloading prototype using OpenCL SDK. In: IEEE International Parallel and Distributed Processing Symposium Workshops, IPDPSW 2019, 20–24 May 2019. IEEE, Rio de Janeiro, Brazil (2019)
23. Li, H., Liang, T., Lin, Y.: An OpenMP programming toolkit for hybrid CPU/GPU clusters based on software unified memory. J. Inf. Sci. Eng. **32**(3) (2016)
24. Lu, H., Hu, Y.C., Zwaenepoel, W.: OpenMP on networks of workstations. In: Proceedings of the ACM/IEEE Conference on Supercomputing, SC 1998, 7–13 November 1998, Orlando, FL, USA. IEEE Computer Society (1998)
25. Nakao, M., et al.: Xcalableacc: extension of xcalablemp PGAS language using OPENACC for accelerator clusters. In: Chandrasekaran, S., Foertter, F.S., Hernandez, O.R. (eds.) Proceedings of the First Workshop on Accelerator Programming using Directives, WACCPD 2014, 16–21 November 2014. IEEE Computer Society, New Orleans, Louisiana, USA (2014). https://doi.org/10.1109/WACCPD.2014.6

26. NVIDIA: Nvcomp (2021). https://developer.nvidia.com/nvcomp
27. Patel, A., Doerfert, J.: Remote OPENMP offloading. In: Proceedings of the 27th ACM SIGPLAN Symposium on Principles and Practice of Parallel Programming. pp. 441–442. PPoPP 2022, Association for Computing Machinery, New York, NY, USA (2022). https://doi.org/10.1145/3503221.3508416
28. Patel, A., Tian, S., Doerfert, J., Chapman, B.: A virtual GPU as developer-friendly OpenMP offload target. In: LLPP 2021: The First Workshop on LLVM in Parallel Processing (LLPP), August 9th, 2021, Chicago (Argonne National Lab), Illinois, USA. ACM (2021). https://doi.org/10.1145/3458744.3473356
29. Romano, P.K., Forget, B.: The OpenMC monte carlo particle transport code. Ann. Nuclear Energy **51** (2013)
30. Sato, M., Harada, H., Hasegawa, A.: Cluster-enabled OpenMP: an OpenMP compiler for the SCASH software distributed shared memory system. Sci. Program. **9**(2–3) (2001)
31. Shamis, P., et al.: UCX: an open source framework for HPC network APIs and beyond. In: 23rd IEEE Annual Symposium on High-Performance Interconnects, HOTI 2015, 26–28 August 2015. IEEE Computer Society, Santa Clara, CA, USA (2015)
32. Tramm, J.R., Siegel, A.R., Forget, B., Josey, C.: Performance analysis of a reduced data movement algorithm for neutron cross section data in monte carlo simulations. In: EASC 2014 - Solving Software Challenges for Exascale. Stockholm (2014)
33. Tramm, J.R., Siegel, A.R., Islam, T., Schulz, M.: Xsbench - the development and verification of a performance abstraction for monte carlo reactor analysis. In: PHYSOR 2014 - The Role of Reactor Physics toward a Sustainable Future. Kyoto (2014)
34. Wottrich, R., Azevedo, R., Araujo, G.: Cloud-based OpenMP parallelization using a mapreduce runtime. In: 26th IEEE International Symposium on Computer Architecture and High Performance Computing, SBAC-PAD 2014, 2–24 October 2014. IEEE Computer Society, Paris, France (2014). https://doi.org/10.1109/SBAC-PAD.2014.46
35. Yonezawa, N., Wada, K., Ogura, T.: Quaver: OpenMP compiler for clusters based on array section descriptor. In: Fahringer, T., Hamza, M.H. (eds.) Proceedings of the IASTED International Conference on Parallel and Distributed Computing and Networks, part of the 23rd Multi-Conference on Applied Informatics, 15–17 February 2005. IASTED/ACTA Press, Innsbruck, Austria (2005)
36. Yviquel, H., Cruz, L., Araujo, G.: Cluster programming using the OpenMP accelerator model. ACM Trans. Archit. Code Optim. **15**(3) (2018)

Hybrid Parallel ILU Preconditioner in Linear Solver Library GaspiLS

Raju Ram[1,2](✉), Daniel Grünewald[1], and Nicolas R. Gauger[2]

[1] Fraunhofer ITWM, Competence Center High Performance Computing, Kaiserslautern, Germany
raju.ram@itwm.fraunhofer.de

[2] Chair for Scientific Computing, Technische Universität Kaiserslautern, Kaiserslautern, Germany

Abstract. Krylov subspace solvers such as GMRES and preconditioners such as incomplete LU (ILU) are the most commonly used methods to solve general-purpose, large-scale linear systems in simulations efficiently. Parallel Krylov subspace solvers and preconditioners with good scalability features are required to exploit the increasing parallelism provided by modern hardware fully. As such, they are crucial for productivity. They provide a high-level abstraction to the details of a complex hybrid parallel implementation which is easy to use for the domain expert. However, the ILU factorization and the subsequent triangular solve are sequential in their basic form. We use a multilevel nested dissection (MLND) ordering to resolve that issue and expose some parallelism. We investigate the parallel efficiency of a hybrid parallel ILU preconditioner that combines a restricted additive Schwarz (RAS) method on the process level with a shared memory parallel MLND Crout ILU method on the thread level. We employ the PGAS based programming model GASPI to efficiently implement the data exchange across processes. We demonstrate the scalability of our approach for the convection-diffusion problem as a representative of a large class of engineering problems up to 64 sockets (1280 cores) and show comparable baseline performance against the linear solver library PETSc. The RAS preconditioned GMRES solver achieves about 80% parallel efficiency on 1280 cores. Our implementation provides a generic, algebraic, scalable, and efficient preconditioner that enables productivity for the domain expert in solving large-scale sparse linear systems.

Keywords: Sparse linear systems · Parallel ILU preconditioner · Domain decomposition · GASPI · METIS · Hybrid parallelism · Task-level parallelism

1 Introduction

The performance-critical part in many engineering simulations based on partial differential equation (PDE) models with implicit discretization is the solution of a set of linear systems which arise after the discretization. For large-scale

A.-L. Varbanescu et al. (Eds.): ISC High Performance 2022, LNCS 13289, pp. 334–353, 2022.
https://doi.org/10.1007/978-3-031-07312-0_17

problems of this type, the class of Krylov-subspace methods is the appropriate way to achieve a competitive performance on nowadays hybrid-parallel architectures. Preconditioners are used to accelerate their convergence and to reduce the turnaround time. As such, they are crucial for the overall productivity of the solver. However, the design and implementation of such iterative methods and their respective preconditioners is still far from being trivial, particularly on hardware possessing many levels of parallelism - clusters of computational nodes, consisting of several many-core CPUs. Therefore, simulation software with good scalability features is required to fully exploit the increasing parallelism provided by modern hardware. Scalability essentially measures the parallel efficiency of an implementation. The optimum is the so-called linear scalability. This corresponds to full utilization of the cores within a single CPU or the CPUs within a cluster which are interconnected by a network. Better scalability allows using the computational resources more efficiently, implying an abbreviated time to solution. Ultimately, better scalability allows for more detailed models, more precise parameter studies, and a more cost-efficient resource utilization.

Iterative solver libraries such as PETSc [5], Trilinos [17] or hypre [12] which are well adapted in the community are based on the Message Passing Interface (MPI). MPI is widely considered the de facto standard for communication on distributed-memory systems. Recently, fundamental limits of MPI concerning scalability have been investigated [6]. An in-depth analysis of the software shows overheads in the MPI performance-critical path and exposes mandatory performance overheads that cannot be avoided based on the MPI specification. These prevent MPI to push applications toward the strong scaling limit in which the ability to have efficient fine-grained communication is required. In contrast to that, the GASPI communication API [16,28] provides such fine-grained communication. The communication is single-sided, asynchronous, and is complemented by lightweight synchronization primitives. It aims to provide scalability for truly asynchronous data dependency-driven implementations with dynamic load balancing and maximal overlap of communication by computation. Explicit synchronization points can be avoided as much as possible. The GASPI communication API and its reference implementation GPI-2 [19] have proven to allow to implement scalable applications in many research fields [23].

The linear solver library GaspiLS [18] provides an abstract interface for basic linear algebra operations with matrix- and vector-classes, together with iterative methods to solve sparse linear systems whose implementation is based on top of the GASPI communication API. As such, GaspiLS is an effort to make an efficient and scalable GASPI based implementation easily accessible to a broad range of applications and to hide the complexity of the implementation from domain experts.

On top of the basic Krylov subspace solvers, scalable and efficient generic black box preconditioners that can be applied to a large set of problems and that reduce the turnaround time are crucial for the overall productivity of GaspiLS. Incomplete LU (ILU) decomposition is widely used as a preconditioner because of its robustness, accuracy, and usability as a black-box preconditioner for general purpose (asymmetric, indefinite) linear systems. Along with the ILU factorization, one essentially performs a Gaussian elimination process. Certain elements along the factorization may be dropped per a given dropping criterium. This allows limiting the preconditioning operation's size and complexity, which makes it very attractive from the numerical point of view. However, similar to Gaussian elimination, the basic ILU factorization algorithm is sequential. Additional parallelization strategies need to be employed to expose enough parallelism to the preconditioner to preserve the scalability of the underlying Krylov subspace solvers. At the same time, the approximation of the factorization, i.e. the quality of the preconditioner needs to be preserved. We aim to design an ILU-based preconditioner incorporating good concurrency and accuracy.

We propose a hybrid parallel Incomplete LU (ILU) preconditioner which is based on two-level (hybrid parallel) domain decomposition to mitigate the sequential algorithm's limitations and optimally fit the hardware hierarchies. Our hybrid parallel domain decomposition approach combines a restricted additive Schwarz (RAS) method [8] on the process level with a shared memory parallel MLND Crout ILU method on the core level [3]. While the RAS is easy to parallelize, the MLND Crout ILU method preserves the level of approximation even for higher degrees of parallelism. Our research exhibits the following contributions:

- We extend the MLND approach for symmetric positive definite (SPD) systems introduced in [3] to generic (non-SPD) problems.
- We use a data dependency-driven, task-parallel implementation using pthreads, which provides extremely fine-grained control over task-thread management for our algebraic ILU preconditioner.
- We show a hybrid parallel approach by combining the MLND based shared memory approach with Schwarz block preconditioners that use lightweight distributed programming model GASPI.
- Finally, we compare our hybrid solver and preconditioner in GaspiLS with methods in the most widely used linear solver library PETSc and demonstrate better scalability at high concurrency.

The paper is structured as follows. We review the related literature in Sect. 2. We describe the GASPI programming model and the linear solver library GaspiLS in Sect. 3. We introduce the hybrid parallel approach to ILU preconditioning in Sect. 4. We explain the shared memory-based MLND approach in detail in Sect. 5. Finally, we show the results of numerical experiments in Sect. 6 and conclude in Sect. 7.

2 Related Work

Crout ILU preconditioners are robust, accurate, and applicable to a broad range of problems, i.e., are useable as a black-box preconditioner. It is derived from the Crout version of Gaussian elimination. This version of ILU can be computed much faster than standard threshold-based ILU factorization [24]. Multi-leveling in combination with inverse-based pivoting and dropping can be used to make the Crout factorization more stable and accurate, as demonstrated by ILUPACK [7].

More recently, data structures have been described in the HILUCSI framework [9,14], that efficiently handle sparsity and provide optimal complexity ($\mathcal{O}(n)$). It takes advantage of the near or partial symmetry of the linear systems in a multilevel fashion by applying symmetric pre-processing at the top levels for nearly or partially symmetric matrices. It provides an efficient and robust implementation. However, the implementation lacks parallelism and may not be suited to solve extreme-scale large systems. To resolve that issue, fine-grained ILU preconditioners using an iterative algorithm have been described in [10]. The algorithm is based on a reformulation of ILU as the solution of a set of bilinear equations, which can be solved using fine-grained asynchronous parallelism. The nonlinear equations are solved using fixed-point iteration sweeps that are performed in parallel. This is different from the more common domain decomposition (DD) approaches which are usually used to expose some parallelism to the preconditioner. DD methods can be categorized into either overlapping or non-overlapping methods [15]. They differ in how the information is exchanged across the sub-domains along the solution process. For overlapping methods, the information is exchanged across the overlap region. They are iterative procedures and are easy to parallelize. Non-overlapping methods are Schur complement methods in which the information is exchanged across the interfaces. In principle, they are exact and do not require any iteration per se. However, since the Schur complement is expensive to construct, it is usually approximated and solved by an iterative method. To balance the parallelization effort with the quality of the preconditioner, we suggest using an Additive Schwarz method on the distributed memory level. In contrast, on the shared memory level, we use a Schur complement method based on the multilevel nested dissection (MLND) approach for SPD sparse matrices presented in [3]. We extend this approach to general-purpose (non-SPD) matrices. It uses the METIS library [20,21] to partition the graph corresponding to the sparse matrix A. For this, the METIS library takes the sparsity of $A + A^T$ as the input graph. Furthermore, [3] uses serial execution to partition the graph using METIS and only does the factorization and triangular solve in parallel. However, the graph reordering does not scale on the higher number of cores and becomes the bottleneck. Therefore, in our approach, we extend the recently developed multi-threaded version of METIS called MTMETIS [22] to extract the partitioning information in parallel. This is a domain decomposition on two levels which is not to be mixed up with two-level domain decomposition used in mathematics incorporating a coarse grid correction to stabilize the long-range decoupling effect across sub-domains. This domain decomposition is motivated by hybrid parallelism (to improve the scalability). There are other domain decomposition based preconditioners like e.g. IFPACK, IFPACK2 [25], HIPS, MaPhys [2], PDSLin [30] and ShyLU [26]. However, each of these solvers/preconditioners is different in the choices made at different steps and the domain decomposition. We are not aware of any of those codes to be hybrid parallel besides ShyLU. It uses an additive Schwarz method on the distributed memory level and an iterative Schur complement method on the shared memory level.

3 GASPI Programming Model and GaspiLS

GASPI is the specification of a Partitioned Global Address Space (PGAS) API [16] for inter-process communication in a distributed memory system. GASPI provides a compact yet powerful API which is maintained by the GASPI forum [13]. GPI-2 [19] is the reference implementation of the GASPI specification. It provides segments that allocate and pin some parts of the available process-local main memory for communication. These segments form a partition of the global address space. They are designed as a software abstraction to the hardware-provided memory hierarchies and can be mapped to CPU or accelerator memory like GPUs.

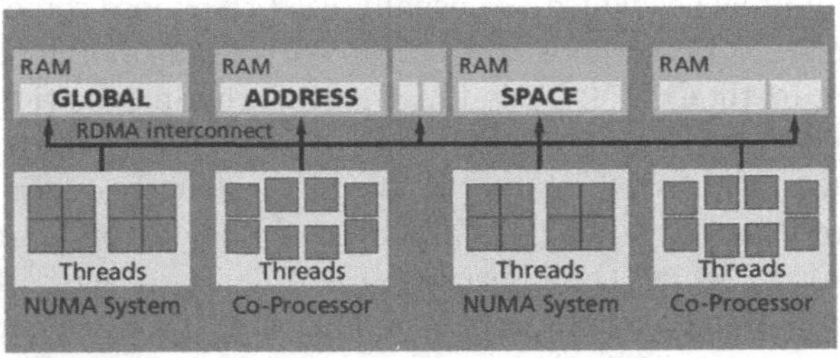

Fig. 1. GPI-2 allocates and pins one or more blocks of its local available memory for RDMA. Every thread can asynchronously read from or write to these so-called segments.

The primary communication mechanism provided by GASPI is single-sided communication. Every thread on a given process may directly access the memory segment of any remote process, bypassing the remote CPU and operating systems. Single-sided communication does not require the cooperation of the target whose memory is accessed. The Remote Direct Memory Access (RDMA) hardware performs the whole transfer without software interaction. As a consequence, the GPI-2 runtime system is lightweight. The network transfer is offloaded to the network interface. It is asynchronous to any computation on the source and target CPUs. The CPUs can be used for computation exclusively. Optimal overlap of communication by computation can be achieved. On top of that, GASPI provides a fine-grained synchronization mechanism, known as notification mechanism, which adds a remote completion notification to a message or a sequence of messages. This is a combined memory and process synchronization, i.e., it allows for detecting completion and memory visibility on the communication target. The critical path for communication in GASPI is a single transfer. The target process can use this notification for explicitly synchronizing local or remote accesses to the buffer. There is no implicit synchronization involved. As such, redundant synchronization steps can be avoided.

GaspiLS [18] is a linear solver library that is built on top of the GASPI programming model. It extends the proof of concept implementation of a GPI-2, and task-based parallel sparse matrix-vector multiplication [29]. The basic idea of GaspiLS is to make the scalability and performance of GASPI accessible for a broad range of applications like scientific or engineering simulations, which finally need to solve a system of linear equations. It provides a set of predefined hybrid parallel data structures for linear algebra, such as vectors and matrices. These data structures hide the complexity of a hybrid, fully asynchronous data dependency-driven task-based implementation, which incorporates a two-level domain decomposition and complete overlap of communication and computation from the domain expert. The guiding principles leverage the capabilities of GASPI the best. However, implementing them usually requires good programming skills and profound knowledge of the underlying hardware to perform well. This is usually a non-trivial task for the domain expert to manage. The provided hybrid parallel data structures are distributed row-wise across the processes on the first level. Furthermore, on the second level, the local parts of the data structures are assigned statically or dynamically to different threads. A thread is the elementary compute unit which is executing the tasks. Based on these data structures, GaspiLS provides several basic Krylov subspace methods like PCG, BiPCGStab, and GMRES.

4 Hybrid Parallel Approach

In general, the time to solution of a Krylov subspace solver is determined by the performance of a single solver iteration and the number of required iterations. GaspiLS provides a scalable hybrid parallel implementation of a sparse matrix-vector multiplication, and a dot product [29], which are the building blocks of a single solver iteration. However, generic and efficient preconditioners are required to decrease the number of solver iterations and runtime of the solver. At the same time, they need to provide the same level of hybrid parallel concurrency as the underlying solver to preserve the overall performance and scalability. Crout ILU preconditioners are known to be robust, accurate, and applicable to a broad range of problems, i.e., are useable as a black-box preconditioner. However, the Crout ILU preconditioner's factorization and subsequent triangular solve operations are sequential for sparse matrices in their original form. Additional graph reordering needs to be applied to enable parallelism. To expose some parallelism to the preconditioner, we propose a two-level domain decomposition (DD) approach following a hybrid execution model that fits the memory hierarchies of modern hardware architectures well. As such, our implementation is designed to preserve the quality of the preconditioner even for higher concurrencies.

4.1 Distributed Memory Parallelism

We use the Additive Schwarz (AS) method at the first level of DD and associate one sub-domain with each GASPI process. Thereby, the vertex set V of the graph corresponding to the matrix A is decomposed into N non-overlapping sub-domains V_i^0 such that $V = \bigcup_{i=1}^{N} V_i^0$ and $V_i^0 \bigcap V_j^0 = \emptyset$ for $i \neq j$. This decomposition may be augmented by a so called δ-overlap to generate partitions V_i^δ ($\delta \geq 1$), where $V_i^\delta \supset V_i^0$ is obtained by including all the immediate neighboring vertices of the vertices in V_i^0 up to distance δ. We select the sub-domains V_i^0 in accordance with the existing row-distribution provided by a distributed CSR matrix in GaspiLS. Restriction operators $R_i^\delta \in \mathbf{R}^{|V_i^\delta| \times |V|}$ and scaling operators $D_i^\delta \in \mathbf{R}^{|V_i^\delta| \times |V_i^\delta|}$ associated with each V_i^δ and can be defined such that a partition of unity $\mathbb{1} = \sum_{i=0}^{N} (R_i^\delta)^T D_i^\delta R_i^\delta$ is formed. Here, the transpose $(R_i^\delta)^T$ corresponds to the expansion operator. Then, AS decomposes the global problem $Ax = b$ into independent sub-problems $A_i x_i = b_i$, which can be solved in parallel on different subdomains and whose solutions are patched together a posteriori. The sub-domain matrix A_i is defined as $A_i := (R_i^\delta A (R_i^\delta)^T)$. Depending on the sub-domain partitioning, different preconditioners can be implemented:

1) AS preconditioner : $M_{AS}^{-1} = \sum_{i=1}^{N} (R_i^0)^T A_i^{-1} R_i^0$
2) Restricted AS (RAS) preconditioner: $M_{RAS}^{-1} = \sum_{i=1}^{N} (R_i^0)^T D_i^\delta A_i^{-1} R_i^\delta$. We use $\delta = 1$ in RAS, which is known to converge faster than AS method [11].

4.2 Shared Memory Parallelism

The global matrix A loses coupling information across sub-domains in the first level of the DD approach. This effect becomes severe with an increasing number of sub-domains. To prevent this, we introduce the second level of DD that partitions the distributed memory subdomain further using multilevel nested dissection(MLND) as described in [3]. This approach is extensively used in sparse direct solvers. MLND preserves the information in subdomain matrix A_i and allows for fine granular parallelism.

We use the multi-threading version of METIS [22] to generate the MLND permutation Π in our implementation. MLND reorders A_i into $A_{i,perm}$ such that $A_{i,perm} = \Pi^T A_i \Pi$. Independent local matrices are extracted from $A_{i,perm}$, which are then factorized in a task-parallel way. Similarly, we solve the triangular system using the same MLND task tree structure, exploiting the local dependency in the tasks. We provide a custom implementation for performance-critical sparse vector used during serial Crout ILU factorization. Our sparse vector implementation is significantly faster than C++ STL based data structures such as std::map and std::unordered_map [27].

5 Solving the Process-Level Sub-problem

In the preconditioning step, we aim to solve for u_i for a sub-problem matrix A_i and rhs vector b_i on a GASPI process

$$A_i u_i = b_i \tag{1}$$

at every iteration of the underlying Krylov solver. We solve this sub-problem using an incomplete LU (ILU) factorization based on the Crout algorithm as described in [24].

$$A_i = L_i U_i \approx \tilde{L}_i \tilde{U}_i = M_i \tag{2}$$

Here, M_i is obtained after dropping entries in the L, U factors of the matrix A_i such that $M = \tilde{L}_i \tilde{U}_i \approx L_i U_i = A_i$. For simplicity of notations, we omit the subscript i in A_i and b_i for a sub-domain and use the matrix A and the vector as b in the remainder of this section.

5.1 Graph Partitioning

The Crout ILU algorithm is sequential in nature, so we need to find a way to introduce parallelism in this method. We define a graph $G_A = (V, E)$ for the matrix A. The vertex of the graph V represents rows/cols of A, and the edge E represents nonzero sparse entries in the matrix A. The graph G_A reflects the nonzero pattern (excluding the diagonal) of A. The parallelization approach is algebraic, i.e., it is exclusively based on the information derived from the sparsity pattern of matrix A and does not depend on the domain/grid [3]. We use multi-threading variant of the METIS library [22] to generate the MLND permutation Π in our implementation. MTMETIS performs the graph reordering in parallel. However, it does not provide the information about the partitioning information of the vertices. We have extended MTMETIS implementation to extract the partitioning information. MLND transforms the matrix A into A_{perm} and the vector b into b_{perm} as

$$A_{perm} = \Pi^T A \Pi, \quad b_{perm} = \Pi b \tag{3}$$

To illustrate the MLND, we show two-level nested dissection of the graph G_A in Fig. 2. The graph G_A is recursively split into four sub-graphs G_0, G_1, G_2, and G_3, first using separator G_6 and then repeatedly by separators G_4 and G_5. Gaussian elimination applied to the corresponding reordered system matrix allows factorizing the diagonal blocks associated with the sub-graphs G_0, G_1, G_2, and G_3 independently in parallel. After that, the elimination proceeds with treating G_4 and G_5 in parallel until, finally, the separator G_6 is treated. The task dependency tree from this scheme is shown in Fig. 2b. Section 2.3 in the paper [3] contains more information about the algorithm doing the transformation from the graph to task tree.

Equation (3) for Fig. 2 can be represented as

$$\Pi^T A \Pi = \left[\begin{array}{cccc|cc|c} A_{00} & 0 & 0 & 0 & A_{04} & 0 & A_{06} \\ 0 & A_{11} & 0 & 0 & A_{14} & 0 & A_{16} \\ 0 & 0 & A_{22} & 0 & 0 & A_{25} & A_{26} \\ 0 & 0 & 0 & A_{33} & 0 & A_{35} & A_{36} \\ \hline A_{40} & A_{41} & 0 & 0 & A_{44} & 0 & A_{46} \\ 0 & 0 & A_{52} & A_{53} & 0 & A_{55} & A_{56} \\ \hline A_{60} & A_{61} & A_{62} & A_{63} & A_{64} & A_{65} & A_{66} \end{array}\right] \tag{4}$$

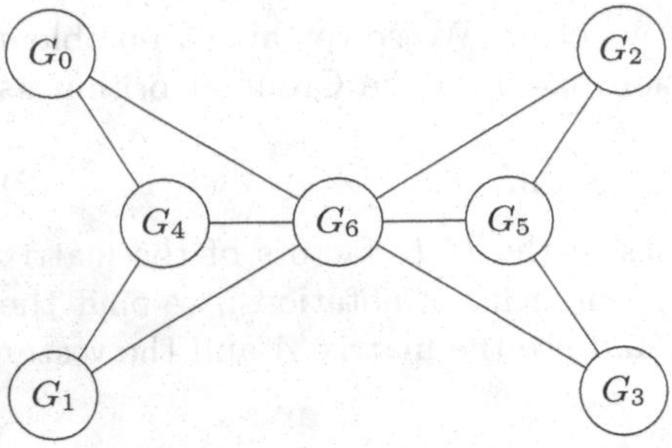

(a) Reordered graph after METIS

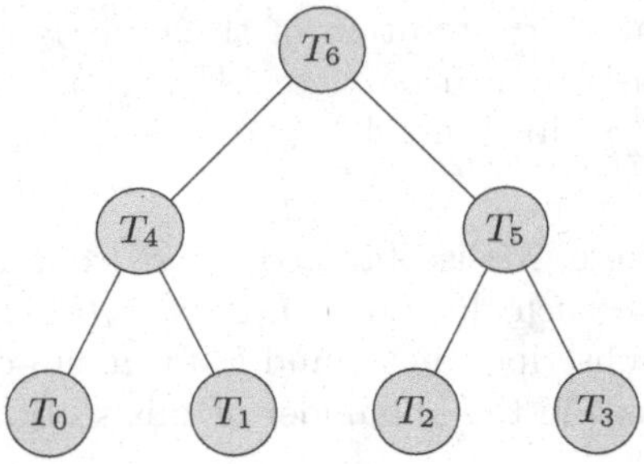

(b) Task tree

Fig. 2. Two level nested dissection applied on graph G_A

We can disassemble (4) into following independent matrix structures:

$$A_0 = \left[\begin{array}{c|cc} A_{00} & A_{04} & A_{06} \\ \hline A_{40} & A_{44}^1 & A_{46}^1 \\ A_{60} & A_{64}^1 & A_{66}^1 \end{array}\right], \quad A_1 = \left[\begin{array}{c|cc} A_{11} & A_{14} & A_{16} \\ \hline A_{41} & A_{44}^2 & A_{46}^2 \\ A_{61} & A_{64}^2 & A_{66}^2 \end{array}\right]$$
$$A_2 = \left[\begin{array}{c|cc} A_{22} & A_{25} & A_{26} \\ \hline A_{52} & A_{55}^3 & A_{56}^3 \\ A_{62} & A_{65}^3 & A_{66}^3 \end{array}\right], \quad A_3 = \left[\begin{array}{c|cc} A_{33} & A_{35} & A_{36} \\ \hline A_{53} & A_{55}^4 & A_{56}^4 \\ A_{63} & A_{65}^4 & A_{66}^4 \end{array}\right] \tag{5}$$

These independent sub-matrices can now be processed in parallel. Here, we choose $A_{44}^1 = A_{44}^2 = \frac{1}{2}A_{44}$, $A_{46}^1 = A_{46}^2 = \frac{1}{2}A_{46}$, $A_{55}^3 = A_{55}^4 = \frac{1}{2}A_{55}$, $A_{56}^3 = A_{56}^4 = \frac{1}{2}A_{56}$, $A_{66}^1 = A_{66}^2 = A_{66}^3 = A_{66}^4 = \frac{1}{4}A_{66}$ as described in [4].

5.2 Factorization

The task tree from Fig. 2b can be generalized such that it has L leaf nodes. Although our algorithm can be easily generalized for non-complete binary task trees, we assume for simplicity that we start from a complete binary task tree with L leaves of height $H = log_2 L + 1$.

$$A_{perm} = \sum_{i=0}^{l-1} P_i^T A_i P_i \tag{6}$$

In order to exploit parallelism, we extract the l independent sub-matrices from A_{perm}, similar to Eq. (5). The MLND permuted matrix A_{perm} is defined by summing these matrices A_i and using appropriate operator P_i as shown in Eq. 6. These matrices are factorized in parallel. We show here the decomposition of a matrix A_i at MLND task tree node i. The matrix A_i can be thought of containing the contribution from interior vertices (volume terms) denoted by A_i^v, and interface vertices (surface terms) denoted by A_i^s. The surface term includes entries of the separators nodes, starting from the parent of the node i until the root node of the tree. We capture the coupling information in the superscripts, for e.g. the sub-matrix depicting the coupling of volume terms to surface terms in A_i is denoted by $A_i^{(v,s)}$. Using these notations, A_i is represented in the Fig. 3. The matrix A_i is partially factorized using Crout ILU method as shown in Fig. 3b (black fill), such that $A_{ii} = L_i^{(v,v)} U_i^{(v,v)}$. The Schur complement matrix S_i is computed as $S_i = A_i^{(s,s)} - L_i^{(s,v)} U_i^{(v,s)}$.

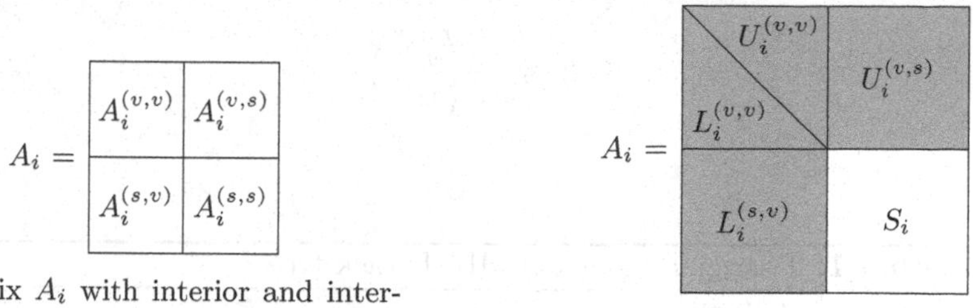

(a) Matrix A_i with interior and interface vertices

(b) LU factorization at tree node i

Fig. 3. Factorization of the matrix A_i

Once the leaf siblings have generated the Schur complements S_i and S_{i+1} after factorising A_i and A_{i+1} (where $i+1 \leq l$), their parent node in the tree can construct their local matrix by adding S_i and S_{i+1}. We define the local matrix A_i ($i \geq l$) for a separator node in the binary task tree as

$$A_i = S_{\text{leftChild}(i)} + S_{\text{rightChild}(i)} \tag{7}$$

Once the matrix A_i is set for the separator nodes, the Crout ILU factorization and Schur computation proceeds similarly as the leaf nodes (Fig. 3b). In this way we proceed the factorization for separator nodes, and finally reach the root node after traversing the tree from bottom to top. Since there are no separators above the root node (i.e. $A_i^{(s,v)} = A_i^{(s,s)} = \phi$ in Fig. 3a), the root node is factorized completely and no Schur complement matrix is generated. Once the entire MLND tree has been factorized, we obtain the lower triangular matrix $L_i^{v,v}$ and the upper triangular matrix $U_i^{v,v}$ at all the MLND nodes $0 \geq i < (2^H - 1)$. These matrices are later used in the triangular solve.

5.3 Triangular Solve

Although the triangular solve method is inherently sequential, we exploit the parallelism using the MLND tree structure in the same way as we did for the factorization. The MLND approach reorders the right hand side (rhs) vector b into b_{perm}. Thus MLND permutation transforms the preconditioning step from Eq. 2 into

$$M_{perm}\ x_{perm} = \tilde{A}_{perm}\ x_{perm} = b_{perm} \tag{8}$$

where $\tilde{A}_{perm}$ denotes the dropping in A_{perm}. The vector b_{perm} is used to generate the local rhs vector b_i similarly to Eq. (6) such that

$$b_{perm} = \sum_{i=0}^{l-1} P_i^T b_i \tag{9}$$

Here the vector b_i consists of the volume and surface terms and denoted as

$$b_i = \begin{pmatrix} b_i^{(v)} \\ b_i^{(s)} \end{pmatrix} \tag{10}$$

Algorithm 1. Triangular solve on MLND task tree i

Input : $L_i = \begin{pmatrix} L_i^{(v,v)} \\ L_i^{(s,v)} \end{pmatrix}, U_i = \begin{pmatrix} U_i^{(v,v)} & U_i^{(v,s)} \end{pmatrix}, b_i = \begin{pmatrix} b_i^{(v)} \\ b_i^{(s)} \end{pmatrix}, S_{parent(i)}$ at node i
Output : The solution vector $x_i^{(v)}$ at node i

procedure TRISOLVE($L_i, U_i, b_i, S_{parent(i)}$)
    Solve for $y_i^{(v)}$ in $L_i^{(v,v)} y_i^{(v)} = b_i^{(v)}$ using forward substitution
    if node i is not the root node **then**
        Compute $y_i^{(s)} = b_i^{(s)} - L_i^{(s,v)} y_i^{(v)}$
        Recursively solve for $x_i^{(s)}$ using the Schur: $S_{parent(i)} x_i^{(s)} = y_i^{(s)}$
        Compute $y_i^{(v)} = y_i^{(v)} - U_i^{(v,s)} x_i^{(s)}$
    Solve for $x_i^{(v)}$ in $U_i^{(v,v)} x_i^{(v)} = y_i^{(v)}$ using backward substitution

The triangular solve starts at the leaf nodes, where we solve for $y_i^{(v)}$ in $L_i^{(v,v)} y_i^{(v)} = b_i^{(v)}$ with forward substitution. Afterward, we prepare the rhs vector $y_i^{(s)}$ for the parent node to perform the forward substitution. We proceed in an upward direction in the MLND task tree until we have done the forward substitution at the root node. Then we solve for $x_i^{(v)}$ in $U_i^{(v,v)} x_i^{(v)} = y_i^{(v)}$ with backward substitution. The obtained solution vector $x_i^{(v)}$ is afterward sent to both the child nodes, which is used to prepare the rhs vector so that the backward substitution can be performed on the child nodes. We proceed in a downward direction in the MLND task tree until we have computed the partial solution vectors $x_i^{(v)}$ at all the leaf nodes. These partial solution vectors $x_i^{(v)}$ represent the solution x_{perm} to the MLND reordered preconditioning step Eq. 8. The permuted vector x_{perm} is then transformed into the original solution vector x using inverse MLND permutation. This vector x is the solution vector of the preconditioning step Eq. 2. It is important to note that the underlying Krylov solver is not affected by the MLND reordering done at the preconditioning step.

6 Numerical Experiments

We solve a stationary convection diffusion PDE as this is a representative of a large class of typical problems arising in computational science.

$$\Delta u + c_2 * x^2 (\frac{\partial u}{\partial x} + \frac{\partial u}{\partial y} + \frac{\partial u}{\partial z}) = f(x, y, z) \tag{11}$$

To make the linear system more challenging, we use high convection to diffusion coefficient ratio of $c_2 = 100$. We discretize the above 3D convection-diffusion PDE using second order finite differences on a regular rectangular mesh in an unit cube $(x, y, z) \in \Omega = (0, 1)^3$. We set $f(x, y, z)$ such that the solution $u(x, y, z)$ of the above PDE is equal to $exp(xyz) * sin(\pi x) * sin(\pi y) * sin(\pi z)$ and use Dirichlet boundary conditions as $u(\partial\Omega) = f(\partial\Omega)$. The coefficient matrix of the linear system is non-symmetric, so we use GMRES(30) solver to solve it. For orthogonalization, we use the modified Gram-Schmidt (MGS) method due to its superior numerical stability over the classical Gram-Schmidt method. We use a relative residual tolerance criterion of 10^{-6}.

We evaluate the scalability of our approach both for the shared memory parallel and full hybrid parallel implementation. The performance is evaluated on a cluster of 2.4 GHz Intel(R) Xeon(R) Gold 6148 CPU dual-socket nodes, each socket with 20 cores which are connected by EDR Infiniband interconnects. We run one distributed process on each socket. The code was compiled with the GCC 8.2.0 compiler using the optimization flag `-O3`.

6.1 Shared Memory Implementation

We evaluate the performance of the shared memory implementation. We solve the 3D convection-diffusion equation (11) on 200^3 grid (8 million unknowns). We use up to 20 available cores in one NUMA domain to use the full socket. We use MLND tree height of 6, which creates 32 leaf nodes, so every thread has at least one leaf task to start with.

In Fig. 4, we show that the serial graph reordering done using METIS becomes the bottleneck during the preconditioner setup phase even though the factorization scales well (see serial graph reordering S and factorization using 16 threads in Fig. 4). Therefore, parallel graph reordering becomes essential for scalability. Using MTMETIS instead of METIS reduces the preconditioner setup time by 6.7× and total time to solution by 2.8× on 16 cores. Thus, MTMETIS based parallel graph reordering eliminates the scalability bottleneck at higher degree of parallelism. This drastically improves the scalability of the preconditioner setup phase, which finally improves the overall scalability of the underlying solver.

6.2 Hybrid Parallel Implementation

We evaluate the performance of our hybrid parallel implementation. For this we choose a 400^3 grid (64 million unknowns) and solve the 3D convection-diffusion equation (11). We uniformly partition the grid along with the Z direction.

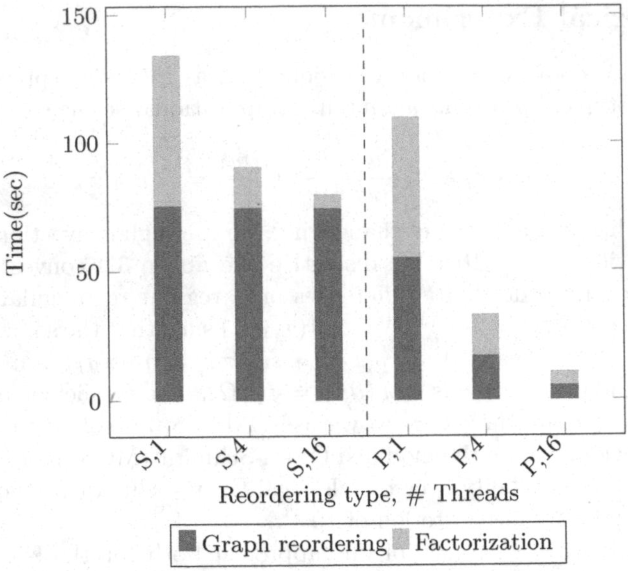

Fig. 4. Time distribution during the Crout ILU preconditioner setup phase; The first parameter in the x-axis denotes the graph reordering type: S denotes serial reordering using METIS, P denotes parallel reordering using MTMETIS; the second parameter in x-axis denotes the number of threads used.

Baseline Comparison with PETSc Library. To measure the baseline performance of our basic solver components (GMRES and Crout ILU), we compare it with the most widely used linear solver library PETSc [5] in its default configuration, i.e., an AS preconditioner using ILU(0) as subdomain solve in combination with an outer GMRES(30) Krylov subspace solver. Exactly the same algorithm, i.e. the same solver, the same preconditioner, and the same domain decomposition are used in GaspiLS. This allows having a fair comparison of GaspiLS with PETSc. We have followed the performance tuning hints provided by the PETSc online manual (https://petsc.org/release/docs/manual/performance/#performance-pitfalls-and-advice) in order to maximize the memory bandwidth (NUMA pinning) and to avoid performance pitfalls. We have compiled the non-debug PETSc version 3.16 with dependencies `fblaslapack` and `mpich-3.4.2`. We have used optimized build options `with-debugging=0` and `PETSC_ARCH=arch-opt`.

PETSc follows and suggests a FLAT MPI execution model in which one process is started per core [1]. This affects the number of sub-domains used along with the AS method. To mimic the PETSc domain decomposition in our hybrid parallel GaspiLS implementation, we use AS instead of MLND also on the shared memory level and further partition the process local subdomains into uniformly distributed thread partitions there. We refer to this as hybrid parallel AS + AS ILU(0) preconditioner in the following. For PETSc, we pin the

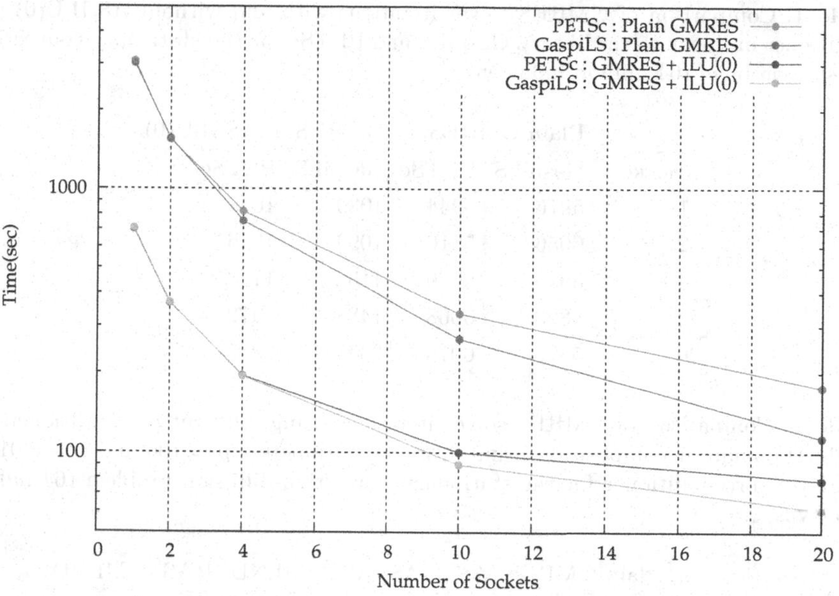

Fig. 5. Baseline comparison of GMRES runtime with and without preconditioner in GaspiLS and PETSc for the stationary convection-diffusion problem (64 million unknowns)

distributed processes on cores with options, `-bind-to=core` and `-map-by=numa` in mpich.

From Table 1, we observe that GMRES solver takes the same order of iterations for plain solver and ILU(0) preconditioner both in PETSc and GaspiLS. In Fig. 5, we validate the baseline performance: for the smaller number of sockets, both GaspiLS and PETSc take the same order of runtime. However, for the higher number of sockets, GaspiLS based solver and preconditioner runs faster than PETSc. On 20 sockets (400 cores), plain and ILU(0) preconditioned GMRES is 1.55 × and 1.34 × faster in GaspiLS than PETSc respectively.

GaspiLS Results. We now evaluate the performance of our proposed two-level hybrid parallel (R)AS + MLND ILU preconditioner and compare it to the AS + AS ILU preconditioner.

Table 2 shows for the different preconditioners, the number of required solver iterations as a function of an increasing number of sockets (subdomains). While the number of iterations increases significantly for AS + AS ILU preconditioned GMRES, this increase is mainly limited for (R)AS + MLND preconditioned GMRES solver. Figure 6 shows the runtimes as a function of an increasing number of sockets (subdomains) for the different preconditioners. On 64 GASPI processes (sockets), each having 20 cores, RAS+MLND preconditioned GMRES achieves a speedup of 54.44× which outperforms the AS+MLND preconditioned

Table 1. Comparison of GMRES solver iterations with and without AS ILU(0) preconditioner in linear solver library GaspiLS and PETSc for the stationary convection-diffusion problem (64 million unknowns)

	Plain GMRES		GMRES + AS ILU(0)	
#Sockets	GaspiLS	PETSc	GaspiLS	PETSc
1	5976	5944	1039	1058
2	6056	5816	1093	1086
4	5976	6040	1155	1143
10	5823	6068	1488	1472
20	5870	6076	2341	2355

Table 2. Comparison of GMRES solver iterations using different preconditioners for two-level domain decomposition using dropping parameters $p = 100$ and $\tau = 0.01$ for Crout ILU preconditioner for the stationary convection-diffusion problem (64 million unknowns)

# Sockets	Plain GMRES	AS + AS	AS + MLND	RAS + MLND
1	5976	481	310	307
2	6056	558	379	321
4	5976	715	373	325
8	5658	1077	383	321
16	6008	1826	384	320
32	5990	2336	443	329
64	5985	2254	599	388

GMRES's speedup of 47.88×. In total, we obtain 3.16× gain in GMRES runtime using RAS+MLND Crout ILU based preconditioner in comparison to no preconditioner on 64 sockets.

Figure 7 shows the parallel efficiency of different preconditioners as a function of an increasing number of sockets. The parallel efficiency is defined as the ratio of the speedup factor and the number of sockets used. For example, a parallel efficiency smaller than 50% means that more than half of the resources are wasted and not used productively.

The parallel efficiency for the AS ILU(0) preconditioner in FLAT MPI-based PETSc deviates strongly from the ideal parallel efficiency. It is less than 50% for 20 sockets. Therefore, we do not perform further experiments beyond 20 sockets for this preconditioner. The breakdown in parallel efficiency takes place due to a huge increase of iterations with increasing subdomains. This effect is reduced to some extent with the hybrid parallel AS + AS ILU(0) preconditioner in GaspiLS (c.f. column 3 in Table 2), since it allows to obtain the same degree of parallelism with fewer sub-domains at the distributed memory level. This can be improved drastically by using the MLND reordering instead of AS at the shared memory

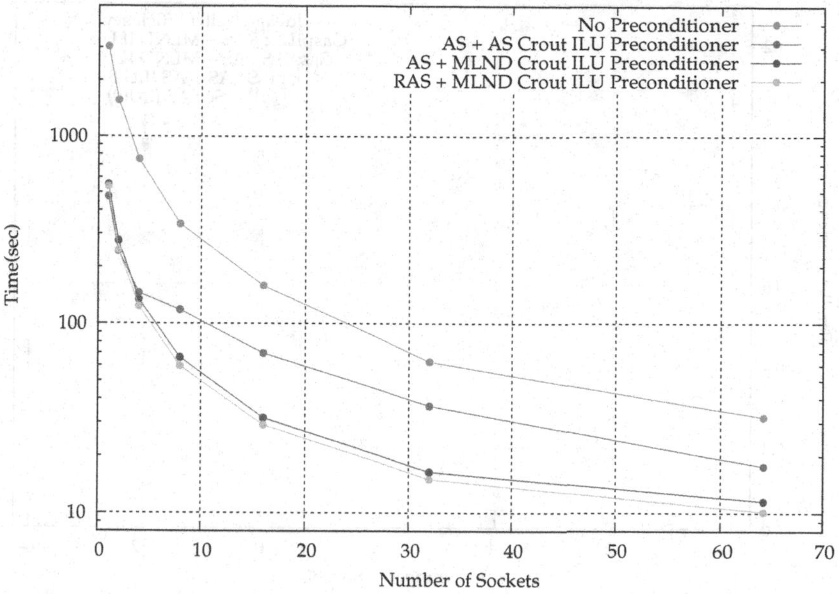

Fig. 6. GMRES runtime with different preconditioners in GaspiLS for the stationary convection-diffusion problem (64 million unknowns)

level, which reduces decoupling and still allows for the parallelism (c.f. column 4 in Table 2). We observe almost perfect parallel efficiency up to 32 sockets for (R)AS + MLND ILU preconditioner and it starts to decline afterwards. The remaining decoupling originating from the first level AS based partitioning can be further reduced by using RAS instead of AS (c.f. column 5 in Table 2). For RAS + MLND ILU preconditioner, our GMRES solver implementation achieves about 80% parallel efficiency on 64 sockets (1280 cores).

The evaluation of the convection-diffusion problem allows us to show the scaling and efficiency of the basic ILU preconditioner-based modules in GaspiLS such as factorization, triangular solve, etc. These modules are also required for more sophisticated problems. In our current research, we provide different dropping strategies and allow for diagonal pivoting with deferral in combination with equilibration techniques like MC64 in order to make the algorithm robust such that it is applicable to a broad range of ill-conditioned problems. Since we have demonstrated the effectiveness of basic modules in GaspiLS, other problems should also benefit from the scalability of these modules.

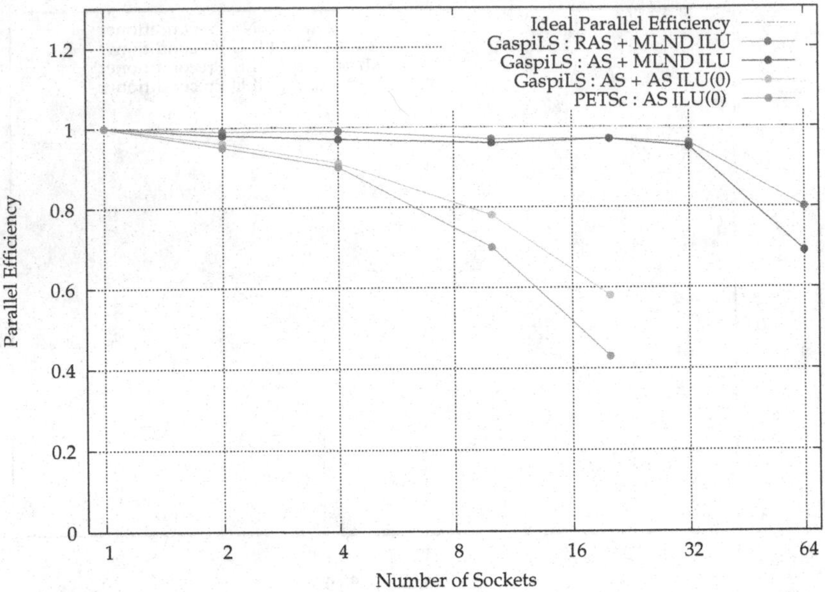

Fig. 7. Parallel efficiency of the GMRES solver with different preconditioners in GaspiLS and PETSc for the stationary convection-diffusion problem (64 million unknowns)

7 Conclusion

We have investigated a two-level domain decomposition approach that implements an ILU preconditioner for solving general purpose sparse linear systems arising from PDE-based simulations. In general, the solution of these systems is the most expensive part, and the performance of the preconditioner is crucial. The productivity for the domain expert can be directly related to it and is measured by the following factors:

- The methods can be applied to a huge set of problems (generic).
- The approach does not depend on the physics of the problem and the discretization method used (algebraic).
- The time to solution scales with the addition of resources (scalable).
- The methods are efficient in providing the solution (efficient).

To incorporate these features, we combine the restricted additive Schwarz (RAS) method on the process level with a shared memory parallel MLND Crout ILU method on the thread level.

Generic: We extend the MLND approach, presented in [3] for symmetric positive definite systems to generic (non-SPD) systems.

Algebraic: We provide a scalable black-box preconditioner that does not require specific information about the grid or domain and works directly on the matrices. As an input, it requires the discretization matrix and the rhs vector.

This allows solving the linear systems from different computational domains without specific domain knowledge.

Scalable: We employ MTMETIS, a recently developed multi-threaded version of METIS [22] which performs the MLND based graph reordering in parallel. This is essential to achieve better scalability during factorization and is accompanied by a data-dependency-driven, task-parallel implementation of the ILU preconditioner.

We demonstrate the scalability of our hybrid parallel approach by solving an ill-conditioned 3D convection-diffusion PDE, which represents a large class of typical problems arising in computational science.

The hybrid parallel RAS-based MLND Crout ILU preconditioner achieves 54.44× speedup on 64 GASPI processes running 20 threads when solving the 400^3 mesh. Thus, we provide a scalable implementation that optimally exploits the hardware using up to 1280 physical cores.

Efficient: We demonstrate the superior performance of our implementation against the default solver GMRES(30) and default preconditioner ILU(0) in the most widely used linear solver library PETSc.

As such, we have demonstrated generic, algebraic, scalable, efficient solvers and preconditioners that enables productivity for the domain expert in solving large-scale linear systems.

References

1. Threads and PETSc (2021). https://petsc.org/release/miscellaneous/threads/. Accessed 14 Dec 2021
2. Agullo, E., Giraud, L., Guermouche, A., Haidar, A., Roman, J.: MaPHyS or the development of a parallel algebraic domain decomposition solver in the course of the solstice project. In: Sparse Days 2010 Meeting at CERFACS (2010)
3. Aliaga, J.I., Bollhöfer, M., Martı, A.F., Quintana-Ortı, E.S., et al.: Exploiting thread-level parallelism in the iterative solution of sparse linear systems. Parallel Comput. **37**(3), 183–202 (2011)
4. Aliaga, J.I., Bollhöfer, M., Martín, A.F., Quintana-Ortí, E.S.: Design, tuning and evaluation of parallel multilevel ILU preconditioners. In: Palma, J.M.L.M., Amestoy, P.R., Daydé, M., Mattoso, M., Lopes, J.C. (eds.) VECPAR 2008. LNCS, vol. 5336, pp. 314–327. Springer, Heidelberg (2008). https://doi.org/10.1007/978-3-540-92859-1_28
5. Balay, S., et al.: Petsc users manual (2019)
6. Belli, R., Hoefler, T.: Notified access: extending remote memory access programming models for producer-consumer synchronization. In: 2015 IEEE International Parallel and Distributed Processing Symposium, pp. 871–881. IEEE (2015)
7. Bollhöfer, M., Saad, Y., Schenk, O.: Ilupack-preconditioning software package. Release 2 (2006). http://ilupack.tu-bs.de/
8. Cai, X.C., Sarkis, M.: A restricted additive Schwarz preconditioner for general sparse linear systems. SIAM J. Sci. Comput. **21**(2), 792–797 (1999)
9. Chen, Q., Ghai, A., Jiao, X.: HILUCSI: simple, robust, and fast multilevel ILU for large-scale saddle-point problems from PDEs. Numer. Linear Algebra Appl. **28**, e2400 (2021)

10. Chow, E., Patel, A.: Fine-grained parallel incomplete LU factorization. SIAM J. Sci. Comput. **37**(2), C169–C193 (2015)
11. Efstathiou, E., Gander, M.J.: Why restricted additive Schwarz converges faster than additive Schwarz. BIT Numer. Math. **43**(5), 945–959 (2003)
12. Falgout, R.D., Jones, J.E., Yang, U.M.: The design and implementation of hypre, a library of parallel high performance preconditioners. In: Bruaset, A.M., Tveito, A. (eds.) Numerical Solution of Partial Differential Equations on Parallel Computers, pp. 267–294. Springer, Berlin (2006)
13. Forum, G.: GASPI forum - forum of the PGAS API GASPI (2020). http://www.gaspi.de
14. Ghai, A., Jiao, X.: Robust optimal-complexity multilevel ilu for predominantly symmetric systems. arXiv preprint arXiv:1901.03249 (2019)
15. Giraud, L., Tuminaro, R.: Algebraic domain decomposition preconditioners. In: Magoules, F. (ed.) Mesh Partitioning Techniques And Domain Decomposition Methods, pp. 187–216. Saxe-Coburg Publications, Kippen (2006)
16. Grünewald, D., Simmendinger, C.: The GASPI API specification and its implementation GPI 2.0. In: Proceedings of the 7th International Conference on PGAS Programming Models, vol. 243 (2013)
17. Heroux, M.A., Bartlett, R.A., Howle, V.E., Hoekstra, R.J., Hu, J.J., Kolda, T.G., Lehoucq, R.B., Long, K.R., Pawlowski, R.P., Phipps, E.T., et al.: An overview of the trilinos project. ACM Trans. Math. Softw. **31**(3), 397–423 (2005)
18. ITWM Fraunhofer: GaspiLS - a linear solver for the Exascale Era (2020). https://www.gaspils.dc
19. ITWM Fraunhofe: GPI-2 - Programming next generation supercomputers (2020). http://www.gpi-site.com
20. Karypis, G., Kumar, V.: METIS: A software package for partitioning unstructured graphs, partitioning meshes, and computing fill-reducing orderings of sparse matrices. Technical Report; 97-061 (1997)
21. Karypis, G., Kumar, V.: A fast and high quality multilevel scheme for partitioning irregular graphs. SIAM J. Sci. Comput. **20**(1), 359–392 (1998)
22. LaSalle, D., Karypis, G.: Efficient nested dissection for multicore architectures. In: Träff, J.L., Hunold, S., Versaci, F. (eds.) Euro-Par 2015. LNCS, vol. 9233, pp. 467–478. Springer, Heidelberg (2015). https://doi.org/10.1007/978-3-662-48096-0_36
23. Leicht, T., Jägersküpper, J., Vollmer, D., Schwöppe, A., Hartmann, R., Fiedler, J., Schlauch, T.: DLR-project digital-X-next generation CFD solver 'flucs' (2016)
24. Li, N., Saad, Y., Chow, E.: Crout versions of ILU for general sparse matrices. SIAM J. Sci. Comput. **25**(2), 716–728 (2003)
25. Prokopenko, A., Siefert, C.M., Hu, J.J., Hoemmen, M., Klinvex, A.: Ifpack2 User's Guide 1.0. Tech. Rep. SAND2016-5338, Sandia National Labs (2016)
26. Rajamanickam, S., Boman, E.G., Heroux, M.A.: ShyLU: a hybrid-hybrid solver for multicore platforms. In: 2012 IEEE 26th International Parallel and Distributed Processing Symposium, pp. 631–643 (2012). https://doi.org/10.1109/IPDPS.2012.64
27. Ram, R., Grünewald, D., Gauger, N.R.: Data structures to implement the Sparse Vector in Crout ILU preconditioner (2019), Sparse Days 2019
28. Simmendinger, C., Rahn, M., Gruenewald, D.: The GASPI API: a failure tolerant PGAS API for Asynchronous Dataflow on heterogeneous architectures. In: Resch, M., Bez, W., Focht, E., Kobayashi, H., Patel, N. (eds.) Sustained Simulation Performance 2014, pp. 17–32. Springer, Cham (2015). https://doi.org/10.1007/978-3-319-10626-7_2

29. Stoyanov, D., Pfreundt, F.J.: Hybrid-parallel sparse matrix-vector multiplication and iterative linear solvers with the communication library GPI. WSEAS Trans. Inf. Sci. Appl. **11** (2014)
30. Yamazaki, I., Ng, E., Li, X.: Pdslin user guide. Tech. rep., Lawrence Berkeley National Lab. (LBNL), Berkeley, CA, USA (2011)

A Subset of the CERN Virtual Machine File System: Fast Delivering of Complex Software Stacks for Supercomputing Resources

Alexandre F. Boyer[1,2](✉), Christophe Haen[1], Federico Stagni[1], and David R. C. Hill[2]

[1] European Organization for Nuclear Research, Meyrin, Switzerland
alexandre.franck.boyer@cern.ch

[2] Université Clermont Auvergne, Clermont Auvergne INP, CNRS, Mines Saint-Etienne, LIMOS, 63000 Clermont-Ferrand, France

Abstract. Delivering a reproducible environment along with complex and up-to-date software stacks on thousands of distributed and heterogeneous worker nodes is a critical task. The CernVM-File System (CVMFS) has been designed to help various communities to deploy software on worldwide distributed computing infrastructures by decoupling the software from the Operating System. However, the installation of this file system depends on a collaboration with system administrators of the remote resources and an HTTP connectivity to fetch dependencies from external sources. Supercomputers, which offer tremendous computing power, generally have more restrictive policies than grid sites and do not easily provide the mandatory conditions to exploit CVMFS. Different solutions have been developed to tackle the issue, but they are often specific to a scientific community and do not deal with the problem in its globality. In this paper, we provide a generic utility to assist any community in the installation of complex software dependencies on supercomputers with no external connectivity. The approach consists in capturing dependencies of applications of interests, building a subset of dependencies, testing it in a given environment, and deploying it to a remote computing resource. We experiment this proposal with a real use case by exporting Gauss - a Monte-Carlo simulation program from the LHCb experiment - on Mare Nostrum, one of the top supercomputers of the world. We provide steps to encapsulate the minimum required files and deliver a light and easy-to-update subset of CVMFS: 12.4 Gigabytes instead of 5.2 Terabytes for the whole LHCb repository.

Keywords: Supercomputer · Software distribution · Automation · CVMFS · Monte Carlo simulation

1 Introduction

To study the constituents of matter and better understand the fundamental structure of the universe, HEP collaborations rely on complex software stacks

A.-L. Varbanescu et al. (Eds.): ISC High Performance 2022, LNCS 13289, pp. 354–371, 2022.
https://doi.org/10.1007/978-3-031-07312-0_18

and a worldwide distributed system to process a growing amount of data: the World Wide LHC Computing Grid (WLCG) [23]. The infrastructure involves 170 computing centers, 1 million cores and 1 exabyte of storage spread around 42 countries.

Delivering a reproducible environment along with up-to-date software across thousands of heterogeneous computing resources is a major challenge: Buncic et al. designed CernVM and CVMFS (CernVM-File System) [16] to tackle it by decoupling the software from the Operating System.

CernVM [20] is a thin Virtual Software Appliance of about 150 Mb in its simplest form. It supports a variety of hypervisors and container technologies and aims to provide a complete and portable user environment for developing and running HEP applications on any end-user computer and Grid Sites, independently of the underlying Operating Systems used by the targeted platforms.

CVMFS [20] is a scalable and low-maintenance file system optimized for software distribution. CVMFS is implemented as a POSIX read-only file system in user space. Files and directories are hosted on standard web servers and mounted on the computing resources as a directory. The file system performs aggressive file-level caching: both files and file metadata are cached on local disks as well as on shared proxy servers, allowing the file system to scale to a large number of clients [16].

This approach has been mainly adopted by the HEP community and is now getting users from various communities according to Arsuaga-Ríos et al. [3]. In a few years, it has become the standard software distribution service on Grid Sites of WLCG. Nevertheless, computing infrastructure and funding models are changing, and national science programs are consolidating computing resources and encourage using cloud systems as well as supercomputers, as Barreiro et al. explain [5]. CVMFS developers have extended the features of the file system and have provided additional tools to support clouds [36,46] and supercomputers [9].

Supercomputers are highly heterogeneous architectures that pose higher integration challenges than traditional Grid Sites. Many supercomputers do not allow a CVMFS client to be mounted on the worker nodes and/or do not provide external connectivity, which is critical to work with CVMFS. CVMFS tools designed to interact with High-Performance Computing sites are aimed at administrators of scientific communities that would like to integrate their workflows on such machines: they ease some steps of the process but may require additional efforts on behalf of the administrators.

In this study, we aim to automate the whole process and reduce these additional efforts by providing a utility able to extract, test and deploy parts of CVMFS on supercomputers not having outbound connectivity. Section 2 briefly introduces CVMFS and the ecosystem developed around it, in order to deal with supercomputers. Section 3 focuses on the design of the utility, the steps to extract software dependencies and to deploy them on a given supercomputer. Finally, Sect. 4 presents a use case and the obtained results in detail.

2 Context

2.1 CVMFS to Distribute Software on Grid Resources

At the beginning of 2021, CVMFS was managing about 1 billion files delivered to more than 100,000 computing nodes by (i) 10 public data mirror servers - called *Stratum1*s - located in Europe, Asia and the United States and (ii) 400 site-local cache servers [8].

To keep the file system consistent and scalable, developers conceived CVMFS as a read-only file system. Release managers - or continuous integration workers - aiming to publish a software release has to log in to a dedicated machine - named *Stratum0* - with an attached storage volume providing an authoritative and editable copy of a given repository [11]. Changes are written into a staging area until they are committed as a consistent changeset: new and modified files are transformed into a content-addressed object providing file-based deduplication and versioning. In 2019, Popescu et al. [43] introduced a gateway component, a web service in front of the authoritative storage, allowing release managers to perform concurrent operations on the same repository and make CVMFS more responsive (Fig. 1.1.b and 1.2.b).

The transfer of files is then done lazily via HTTP connections initiated by the CVMFS clients [43] (Fig. 1.3.b). Clients request updates based on their Time-to-Live (TTL) value, which is generally about a few minutes. Once the TTL value expires, clients download the latest version of a manifest - a text file located in the top-level directory of a given repository composed of the current root hash, metadata and the revision number of this repository - and make the updated content available. Dykstra et al. [27] provide additional details about data integrity and authenticity mechanisms of CVMFS to ensure that data received matches data initially sent by a trusted server. This pull-based approach has been proven to be robust and efficient, according to Popescu et al. [43], and has been widely used to distribute up-to-date software on grid sites for many years (Fig. 1.2.a). Figure 1 presents a simplified schema summarizing the software distribution process on grid sites via CVMFS.

Users may need to use various versions of software on heterogeneous computing resources implying different OS and architectures. To provide a convenient environment for the users, release managers generally provide software along with build files related to many architectures, OS and compilers. Framework for building and installing scientific software on heterogeneous systems can be used to supply CVMFS with build files. Easybuild [28], Spack [49], Nix [40] or Gentoo [33] are popular choices in this area [17,56,57].

2.2 Software Delivery on Supercomputers

Communities working around the Large Hadron Collider (LHC) [21] have extensively used WLCG and CVMFS to process a growing amount of data. This approach was reliable during LHC Run1 but has demonstrated its limit. According to the analysis of Stagni et al. [50] on the use of CPU cycles in 2016, all the LHC

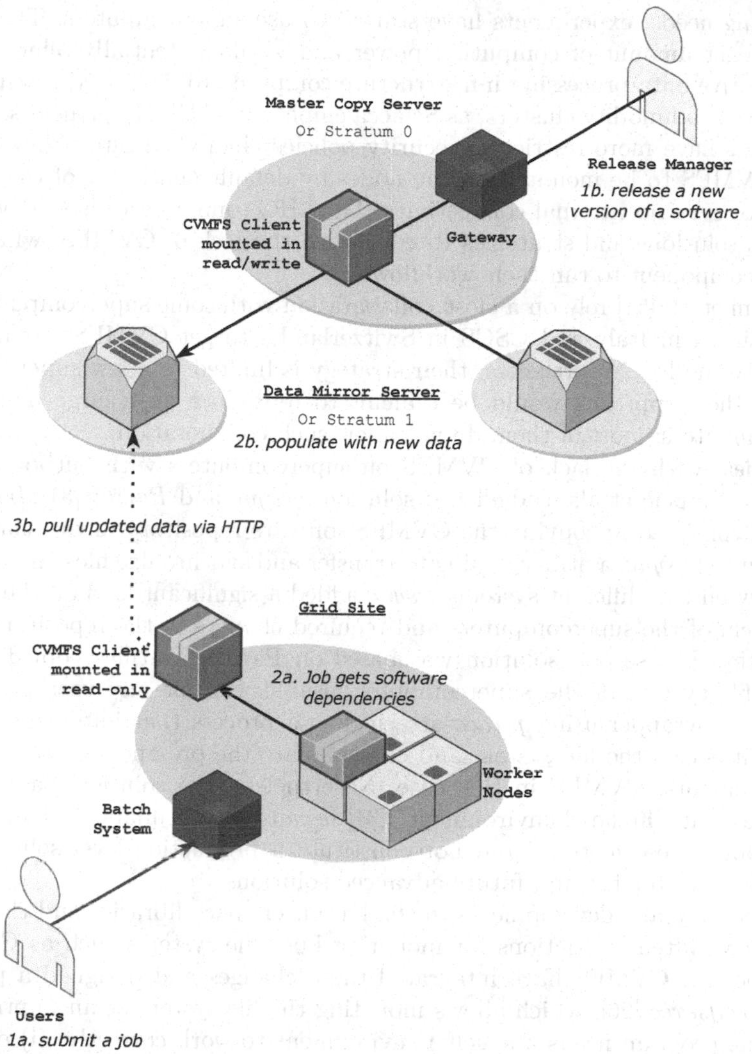

Fig. 1. Schema of the CVMFS workflow on Grid Sites: (a) the steps to get software dependencies from the job; (b) the steps to publish a release of a software in CVMFS.

experiments have consumed more CPU-hours than those officially pledged to them by the WLCG: they found ways to exploit opportunistic and not officially supported resources. Moreover, in the High-Luminosity Large Hadron Collider (HL-LHC) [2] era, experiments are expected to produce up to an order of magnitude more data compared to the current phase (LHC Run2). To keep up with the computing needs, experiments have started to use supercomputers. They offer a significant amount of computing power and would potentially offer a more cost-effective data processing infrastructure compared to dedicated resources in the form of commodity clusters, as Sciacca emphasizes [45]. Nevertheless, supercomputers have more restrictive security policies than Grid Sites: they do not allow CVMFS to be mounted on the nodes by default and many of them have limited or even no external connectivity. The LHC communities have developed different solutions and strategies to cope with the lack of CVMFS, which is a critical component to run their workflows.

Stagni et al. [51] rely on a close collaboration with some supercomputer centers - Cineca in Italy and CSCS in Switzerland - to get CVMFS mounted on the worker nodes. Nevertheless, their strategy is limited to a few supercomputers and their approach would be difficult to reproduce on a large number of supercomputers: most of them do not allow such collaboration.

To deal with the lack of CVMFS on supercomputers with outbound connectivity, Filipčič et al. studied two solutions: *rsync* and *Parrot* [31]. The first solution consisted in copying the CVMFS software repository in the shared file system using *rsync*: a utility aiming to transfer and synchronize files and directories between two different systems. *rsync* added a significant load on the shared file system of the supercomputers and required changes in the repository absolute paths. The second solution was based on Parrot: a utility copied on the shared file system of the supercomputer, usable without any user privileges. Parrot is a wrapper using *ptrace* attached to a process that intercepts system calls that access the file system and can simulate the presence of arbitrary file system mounts, CVMFS in this case. Nevertheless, the solution was "unreliable in a multi-threaded environment" [31] because it was unable to handle race conditions. These methods did not constitute a production-level solution but contributed to further and future advanced solutions.

In recent years, developments in the Fuse user space libraries and the Linux kernel have lifted restrictions for mounting Fuse file systems such as CVMFS. Developers of CVMFS have integrated these changes and designed a package called *cvmfsexec* [26], which allows mounting the file system as an unprivileged user. The program needs a specific environment to work correctly: (i) external connectivity; (ii) the *fusermount* library or unprivileged namespace mount points or a setuid installation of *Singularity* (efficient High-Performance Computing container technology). Blomer et al. provide additional details about the package [10].

Communities exploiting supercomputers that do not provide outbound connectivity cannot directly benefit from *cvmfsexec*: the package still needs to pull updated data via HTTP, which is not available in such context. We can distinguish two cases: (i) supercomputers that grant outside network or specific service access to a limited number of nodes and (ii) supercomputers that do not provide nodes with any external connectivity at all.

Tovar et al. recently worked on the first case [54]. They managed to build a virtual private network (VPN) client and server to redirect network traffic from the workloads running on the worker nodes to external services such as CVMFS. In this configuration, the VPN client runs on a worker node along with the job, while the VPN server is hosted on one of the specific nodes of the supercomputer and can interact with external services. Communities working on supercomputers from the second case cannot leverage the solution developed by Tovar et al.

O'Brien et al., one of the first teams to work with supercomputers in the LHC context, address the lack of external network access by copying part of it to the shared Lustre file system accessible by the WNs [41]. The approach (i) worked because the environment of the supercomputer was similar to a grid site one, (ii) required changes in the CVMFS files and (iii) degraded the performance of the software as Angius et al. described [42]. To tackle the latter issue on the Titan supercomputer, Angius et al. moved the software to a read-only NFS server [42]: this eliminated the problem of metadata contention and improved metadata read performance.

Similarly, on the Chinese HPC CNGrid, Filipčič regularly packed a part of CVMFS in a tarball. Filipčič provided a deployment script to install the software and fix the path relocation on the shared file system to the local system administrators: they were then responsible for getting and updating the CVMFS tarball on the network when requested [30].

To help communities to unpack a CVMFS repository in a file system, a team of developers designed *uncvmfs* [37]. The utility deduplicates files of a software stack: it populates a given directory with the CVMFS files that are then hard-linked into it, if possible. The program was used, in combination with Shifter [34], a container technology providing a reproducible environment, in the context of the integration of the ALICE and CMS experiments workflows on the NERSC High-Performance Computing resources [29, 38]. As a proof of concept, Gerhardt et al. used *uncvmfs* to deduplicate the ATLAS repository and copy it into an ext4 image - about 3.5 Tb of data containing 50 million files and directories -, compressed into a 300 Gb squashfs image; and Shifter to provide a software-compatible environment to run the jobs [34]. Despite encapsulating the files in a container reduced the startup time of the applications, the solution generated large images, long to update and deliver on time.

To cope with large images, Teuber and the CVMFS developers conceived *cvmfs_shrinkwrap* [52]. The tool supports *uncvmfs* features with certain optimizations and delivers additional features: *cvmfs_shrinkwrap* can extract specific files and directories based on specification files, deduplicate them, making them easy to export in various formats such as squashfs or tarball. In this way, the following operations remain on behalf of the user communities: (i) trace their applications - meaning, in this context, "capturing all their dependencies and their locations in the file system" -, (ii) call *cvmfs_shrinkwrap* to get a subset of CVMFS composed of the minimum required files, and (iii) export this subset in a certain format and deploy it on sequestered computing resources to run their jobs.

Douglas et al. already described such a project in an article [7], but the work remains specific to the ATLAS experiment. They use *uncvmfs* to produce a large image that has to be filtered afterward. In this paper, we aim at assisting various user communities in this process by providing an open-source utility that would take applications of interest in input and would output - with the help of *cvmfs_shrinkwrap* - a subset of CVMFS with the minimum required files to run the given applications, in combination with a container image if needed. To our knowledge, no paper has already covered the subject.

3 Design of the CVMFS Subset Builder

3.1 Input and Output Data

The utility takes a directory as input that should contain: (i) a list of applications of interest (`apps`): a command along with its input data in a separate sub-directory for each application to trace; and/or (ii) a list of files composed of paths to include in the subset of CVMFS (`namelists`). Additionally, user communities can embed a (iii) container image compatible with Singularity to get a specific environment to trace and test the applications; (iv) and a configuration file to fine-tune the utility with variables related to the deployment process, or information about repositories. A schema of the inputs is available in Fig. 2.

The expected output can take different forms depending on the utility configuration:

- The subset of CVMFS, generated as a standalone. In this case, administrators representing their user communities need to provide the right environment by themselves, which might also involve discussions with the system administrators.
- The subset of CVMFS embedded within the given Singularity container image. The utility merges both elements and submits the resulting image, which can be long to generate and deploy but may limit manual operations on the remote location.

3.2 Features

We break down the process into four main steps, namely:

- *Trace*: consists in running applications contained in `apps` and trapping their system calls at runtime, using *Parrot*, to identify and extract the paths of their dependencies. Applications can run in a Singularity container when provided, which delivers further software dependencies and a reproducible environment. Dependencies are then saved in a specific file `namelist.txt`. In this context, *Parrot* is only used to capture system calls and, thus, is not impacted by the issues mentioned in Sect. 2.2. If the step detects an error during the execution

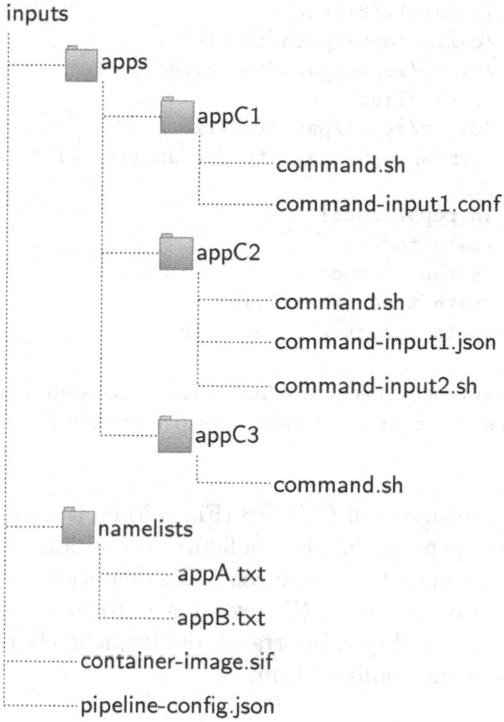

Fig. 2. Schema of the input structure given to the utility.

of an application, then the program is stopped. The step is particularly helpful for users of the utility having no technical knowledge of the applications of interest.

- *Build*: builds a subset of CVMFS based on the paths coming from *Trace* and the `namelists` directory. First, the step merges the namelist files to remove duplicated or non-existent path references, and then separates the paths in different specification files related to repositories. Finally, the step calls *cvmfs_shrinkwrap* to generate the subset of CVMFS. Figures 3 and 4.3 illustrate an example. The utility deduplicates the files, and hard-link data to populate a directory, ready to be exported in various formats as explained in Sect. 2.2 and shown in Fig. 4.3.
- *Test*: consists in testing certain applications - in the given Singularity container environment when provided - using the subset of CVMFS obtained during the *Build* step (see Fig. 4.4). By default, applications from `apps` are used but further tests can also be provided by modifying the utility configuration. All the applications have to complete their execution to go to the next step.

```
in namelist1.txt:
/cvmfs/repoA/path/to/file
/cvmfs/repoB/path/to/another/file
in namelist2.txt:
/cvmfs/repoA/path/to/file
/cvmfs/repoB/path/to/yet/another/file

in repoA.spec:
/path/to/file
in repoB.spec:
/path/to/another/file
/path/to/yet/another/file
```

Fig. 3. Transformation process occurring during the *Trace* step: CVMFS dependencies are extracted from `namelist.txt` and moved to specification files.

- *Deploy*: deploys the subset of CVMFS (Fig. 4.5) embedded or not within the container image depending on the configuration options. If such is the case, then the utility (i) generates a new container definition file that includes the files with the container image, (ii) executes it to produce a new read-only container image. The utility supports ssh deployment via *rsync*, provided the right credentials in the configuration.

3.3 Implementation

The utility is built as a 2-layer system. The first layer, *subcvmfs-builder* [12], is the core of the system and is self-contained. It takes the form of a Python package, which embeds the steps described in Sect. 3.2, and provides a command-line interface to call and execute steps independently from each other. The first layer is, and should remain, simple and generic to be easily managed by developers and used by various communities.

The second layer is the glue code: it consists of a workflow executing - all, or some of - the steps of the first layer. It contains the complexity required to generate and deliver a subset of dependencies according to the needs of its users. Unlike the first layer, the second one can take several forms and each community can tailor it for its software stack.

We propose a first, simple and generic layer-2 implementation calling each step one after the other: *subcvmfs-builder-pipeline* [13]. This layer-2 implementation is executed from a GitLab CI/CD [35], which provides a runner and a docker executor bound to a CVMFS client to execute the code (see Fig. 5) GitLab includes features such as log preservation to help debug the implementation and integrates a pipeline scheduling mechanism to regularly update a subset of dependencies. Even though this layer-2 solution is adapted for basic examples - implying a few commands to trace and test, having a small number of dependencies -, it might require further fine-tuning for more advanced use cases.

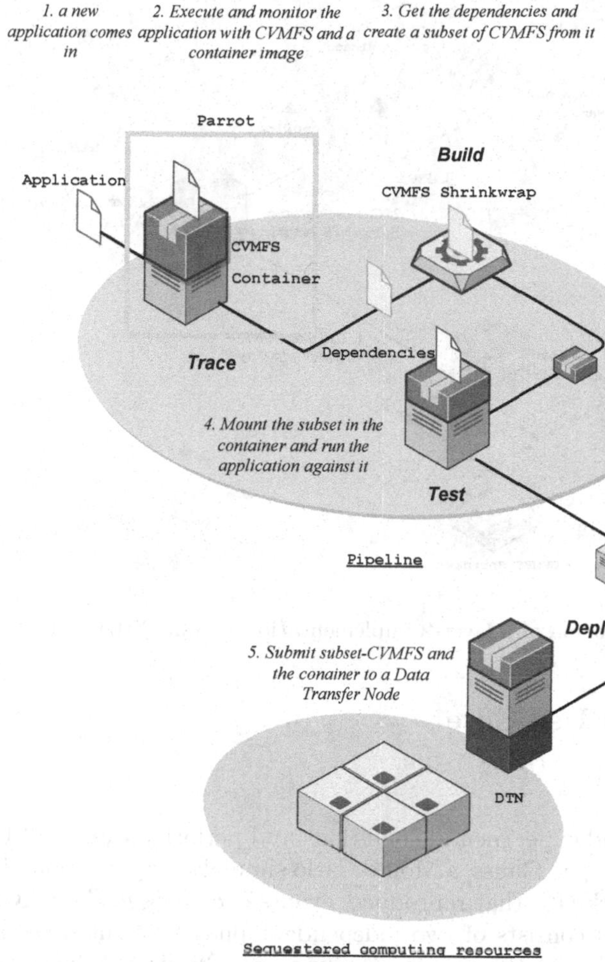

Fig. 4. Schema of the utility workflow: from getting an application to trace to a subset of CVMFS on the Data Transfer Node of a High-Performance Computing cluster.

Indeed, this generic layer-2 implementation is not scalable as it (i) is a single-threaded and single-process program, and (ii) requires manual operations to insert additional inputs in the process. This is not adapted to communities having to trace and test hundreds of various applications to generate large subsets of CVMFS. Two possibilities for such communities: building a new layer-2 implementation - able to automatically fetch applications and trace/test them in parallel - based on *subcvmfs-builder-pipeline* or creating one from scratch.

In the next section, we are going to study how the LHCb experiment [25] leverages *subcvmfs-builder* and *subcvmfs-builder-pipeline* to deliver Gauss [24], a Monte-Carlo simulation program, on the worker nodes of Mare Nostrum [55], a supercomputer with no external connectivity based in Barcelona, Spain.

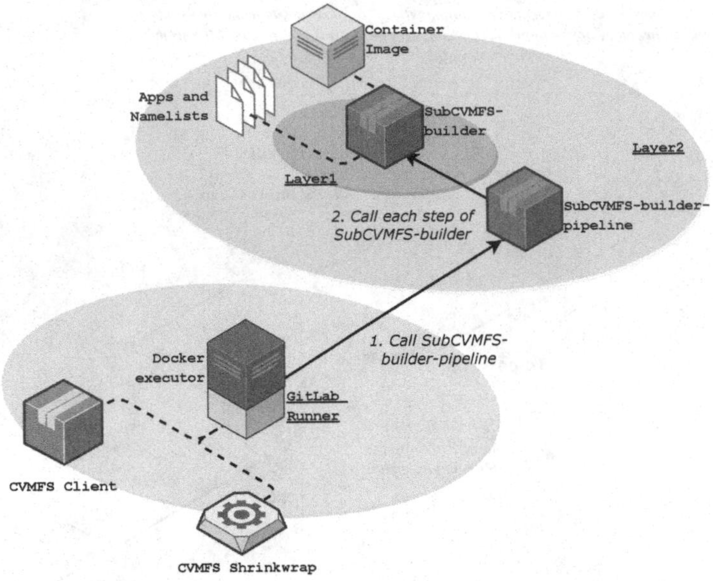

Fig. 5. Schema of a layer-2 implementation within GitLab CI.

4 A Practical Use Case

4.1 Gauss

To better understand experimental conditions and performances, the LHCb collaboration has developed Gauss, a Monte-Carlo simulation application - based on the Gaudi framework [4] - that reproduces events occurring in the LHCb detector. The application consists of two independent phases executed sequentially, namely the generation of the events [6] relying on Pythia [48] by default; the tracking of the particles through the simulated detector depending on Geant4 [1].

In 2021, Gauss represents about 70% of the distributed computing activities of the LHCb collaboration and 150 million events are simulated per day. The application has originally been tailored for WLCG grid sites: Gauss is a compute-intensive single-process (SP), single-threaded (ST) application, only supporting ×86 architectures and CERN-CentOS-compatible environments [19]. Gauss and most of its dependencies are delivered via CVMFS.

Gauss takes a certain number of events to process as inputs, as well as a "run number" and an "event number". The combination of both numbers forms a seed, which ensures repeatability during the generation and simulation phases. It mainly relies on packages such as Python, Boost and gcc to produce histograms and *ntuples* under the form of a ROOT [22] file.

Gauss is modular and highly configurable and constitutes a complex use-case: it can integrate extra packages such as various event generators and decay tools. Depending on LHCb production needs and the computing environments available, different versions of Gauss and its attached packages can be used. A plethora of option files can also be passed as inputs to the extra packages. Figure 6 describes the inputs, outputs and dependencies of Gauss as well as its interactions with some extra packages and their options.

4.2 Mare Nostrum

To start integrating their workflows on High-Performance computing resources, LHC experiments can benefit from a collaboration with PRACE [44] and GÉANT [18,32]. This collaboration gives them access to several European supercomputers such as Marconi in Italy and Mare Nostrum in Spain.

Managed by the Barcelona Supercomputing Center (BSC), MareNostrum is the most powerful and emblematic supercomputer in Spain [15]. MareNostrum was built in 2004 (MareNostrum 1), has been updated 3 times since then (Mare Nostrum 2, 3 and 4) and was ranked 63rd in the June 2021 Top500 list [53]. Each node composing the general-purpose block is equipped with two Intel Xeon Platinum 8160 24 cores at 2.1 GHz chips, and at least 2 GB of RAM: this configuration matches with Gauss requirements. Nevertheless, Mare Nostrum is more restrictive than a traditional Grid Site on WLCG: (i) no external connectivity at all; (ii) no service can be installed on the edge node; (iii) no CVMFS, and thus, no Gauss and its dependencies available.

4.3 Running Gauss on Mare Nostrum

Running embarrassingly parallel applications such as Gauss on a supercomputer can be seen as counterproductive. While it is true that the interconnect of the supercomputer partitions has not been designed for millions of small Monte-Carlo runs, it is better to use available, otherwise unused, cycles in agreement with the management of the supercomputer sites. In the meantime, developers are adapting software [39,47], but it remains a long process, requiring deep and technical software inputs.

To deliver Gauss on Mare Nostrum, LHCb can rely on (i) *subcvmfs-builder* to produce a subset of CVMFS containing the required files; (ii) a CernVM Singularity container to provide a Gauss-compatible environment and to mount the subset of CVMFS as if it was a CVMFS client.

Nevertheless, as we explained in Sect. 4.1, a Gauss execution can involve different packages, extra packages, options, data and versions. Encapsulating its ecosystem requires a good understanding of the application and/or a large amount of storage to encapsulate the right dependencies. Therefore, different options are available:

- Include the whole LHCb CVMFS repository: would not require any specific knowledge about Gauss and would involve all the necessary files to run any Gauss instance. However, this option would imply a tremendous quantity of storage - the full LHCb repository needs 5.2 TB -, long periods to update the subset and many unnecessary files.

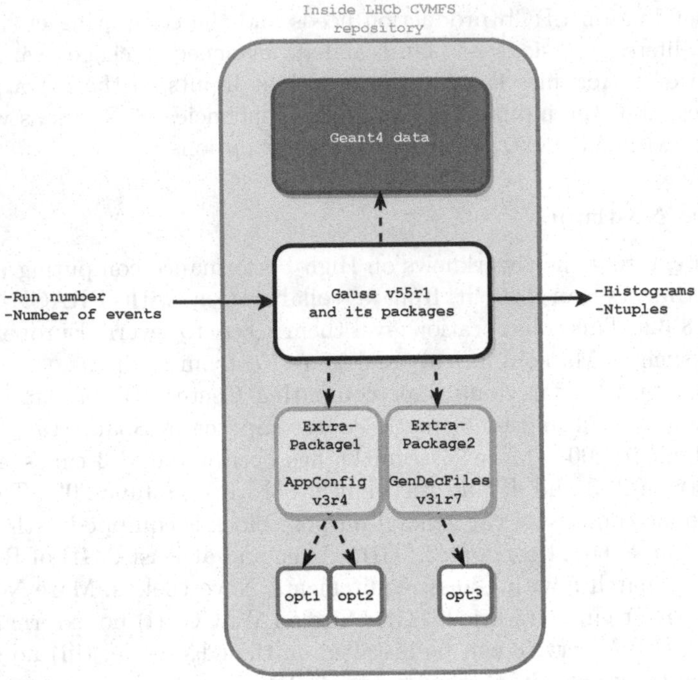

Fig. 6. Example of a Gauss instance, its dependencies and some interactions with extra packages and their options.

- Include the dependencies of various Gauss runs: as the first option, would not need any specific knowledge about Gauss and would include a few gigabytes of data. Nevertheless, such an option would not guarantee the presence of all needed files and would require a tremendous amount of computing resources to trace Gauss workloads continuously.
- Include all the known dependencies of Gauss: would require a deep understanding of Gauss and its dependencies to include all the required files in a subset of CVMFS. While this option would not involve many computing or storage resources, it would include human resources to update the content of the subset of CVMFS according to the releases of Gauss and its extra packages.

As the default storage quota on Mare Nostrum is smaller than the LHCb repository, we decided to reject the first option. LHCb has access to tremendous computing power: it interacts with hundreds of WLCG Sites to run Gauss workloads and could theoretically trace them and extract their requirements. In practice, tracing Gauss workloads in production could slow down the applications and their execution, which is not an option. Similarly, LHCb does not have human resources to update the subset of CVMFS according to the changes done. Thus, we chose to combine the second and the third options to propose a light and easy to update and maintain solution. The process consists in getting insights into the structure of the Gauss dependencies by running and tracing a small set of Gauss workloads and analyzing the system calls before including the structure in *subcvmfs-builder-pipeline*.

After analyzing 500 commands calling Gauss from the LHCb production environment and tracing 3 Gauss applications using *subcvmfs-builder* [14], we noticed that:

- 97% of the workloads studied were running the same Gauss versions (v49r20) with the same extra packages and versions. The versions of Gauss and its extra packages seem related to the underlying architecture.
- 846 Mb of files were needed to run 3 Gauss (v49r20) workloads. About 95% of the size is related to the Gauss version and the underlying architecture, and is common to the Gauss workloads traced, while the 5% left is bound to the options and Geant4 data used that are specific to a given Gauss workload.
- Integrating all the options and Geant4 data related to Gauss v49r20 would correspond to 1.8 Gb of files.

Based on these assumptions, we created a `namelist` file containing (i) the files shared by the 3 Gauss applications that we traced and (ii) all the options and Geant4 data in order to generate a subset of CVMFS able to run any Gauss workload targeting the v49r20 version. We used *subcvmfs-builder-pipeline* to build the subset of CVMFS, to successfully test it with 5 Gauss workloads - different from the ones we used previously - and to deploy it to Mare Nostrum. We fine-tuned the utility to disable the *trace* step and to deploy the subset separately from the container. Indeed, CernVM - the container that we use to provide a reproducible environment to the workload - does not need regular updates and merging it with the subset of CVMFS is a time-consuming operation.

This resulted in a CernVM singularity container occupying 6.4 Gb on the General Parallel File System (GPFS) of Mare Nostrum combined with a subset of CVMFS covering 6 Gb: dependencies occupies 3.2 Gb of space while 2.8 Gb are required for the *cvmfs_shrinkwrap* metadata. Thus, 12.4 Gb of space on the GPFS of Mare Nostrum is currently sufficient to run 97% of the Gauss workloads analyzed: 0.24% of the LHCb repository.

Even though this approach provides a light, easy and fast-to-update solution, LHCb developers need to keep it up to date to integrate new versions or structure changes. One way to proceed would consist in automating and repeating the analysis work regularly. One could also integrate the *trace* command of *subcvmfs-builder* within the LHCb production test phase, which consists in running a few events of upcoming Gauss workloads on a given Grid Site. LHCb developers could trace some of them during the process and store the traces in a database. An LHCb-specific *subcvmfs-pipeline-builder* could then periodically fetch the content of the database to build, test and deploy a new subset of dependencies to Mare Nostrum.

5 Conclusion

This paper presents a dependency delivery system based on CVMFS to provide complex software stacks on sequestered computing resources such as worker nodes of supercomputers not having external connectivity.

After introducing CVMFS (Sect. 2.1), a critical tool - especially for LHC communities - to supply workloads with complex dependencies on Grid Sites, we have described the context of this study (Sect. 2.2): several virtual organizations are exporting their workflow from WLCG to supercomputers, which have more restrictive policies than grid sites and generally do not allow to mount CVMFS on the worker nodes.

We have highlighted several solutions aiming to overcome the issue such as collaborating with the system administrators and using tools such as *Parrot* and *cvmfsexec*. Nevertheless, these approaches do not work when worker nodes have no external connectivity. Then, we have emphasized different ways to export parts of CVMFS to supercomputers with no external connectivity: *uncvmfs* and *cvmfs_shrinkwrap*. These solutions require several manual steps and therefore we have proposed a utility to assist communities in this process.

We have explained the different steps of the utility in detail (Sect. 3.2). It traces - captures the system calls of - applications of interest, builds a subset with the required files, tests the subset and deploys it to a remote computing resource. We also described the structure of the solution (Sect. 3.3), which is composed of two layers: a first one, generic with simple components, and a second one more complex, adapted to communities needs that can be fine-tuned.

Finally, we have provided a use case based on Gauss, a Monte-Carlo simulation application reproducing events occurring in the LHCb detector (Sect. 4.1). Gauss is highly configurable and can be coupled with different packages, extra packages, options, data and versions. It represents a complex bundle of dependencies, which makes it ideal to test our utility. We have proposed a method to encapsulate Gauss and its dependencies in a subset, which represents 12.4 Gb of space on the GPFS of the Mare Nostrum supercomputer (Sect. 4.3). The solution produced represents 0.24% of the full LHCb repository and, thus, is easier to update. We have successfully tested the solution with different Gauss workloads. Future work could focus on encapsulating further applications from different domains using this utility, and analyzing its performances to deploy subsets on various supercomputers.

References

1. Agostinelli, S., et al.: GEANT 4-a simulation toolkit. Nuclear Instrum. Methods Phys. Res. Sect. A Acceler. Spectrom. Detect. Assoc. Equip. **506**(3), 250–303 (2003). https://doi.org/10.1016/S0168-9002(03)01368-8, http://www.sciencedirect.com/science/article/pii/S0168900203013688
2. Apollinari, G., Béjar Alonso, I., Brüning, O., Lamont, M., Rossi, L.: High-Luminosity Large Hadron Collider (HL-LHC): Preliminary Design Report. CERN Yellow Reports: Monographs, CERN, Geneva (2015). https://doi.org/10.5170/CERN-2015-005, http://cds.cern.ch/record/2116337

3. Arsuaga-Ríos, M., Heikkilä, S.S., Duellmann, D., Meusel, R., Blomer, J., Couturier, B.: Using s3 cloud storage with ROOT and CvmFS. J. Phys. Conf. Ser. **664**(2), 022001 (2015). https://doi.org/10.1088/1742-6596/664/2/022001
4. Barrand, G., et al.: Gaudi—a software architecture and framework for building hep data processing applications. Comput. Phys. Commun. **140**(1), 45–55 (2001). https://doi.org/10.1016/S0010-4655(01)00254-5, https://www.sciencedirect.com/science/article/pii/S0010465501002545, cHEP2000
5. Barreiro, F., et al.: The future of distributed computing systems in atlas: boldly venturing beyond grids. EPJ Web Conf. **214**, 03047 (2019). https://doi.org/10.1051/epjconf/201921403047
6. Belyaev, I., et al.: Handling of the generation of primary events in gauss, the LHCb simulation framework. J. Phys. Conf. Ser. **331**(3), 032047 (2011). https://doi.org/10.1088/1742-6596/331/3/032047
7. Douglas, B.: Building and using containers at HPC centres for the atlas experiment. EPJ Web Conf. **214**, 07005 (2019). https://doi.org/10.1051/epjconf/201921407005
8. Blomer, J.: CernVM-FS overview and roadmap (2021). https://easybuild.io/eum/002_eum21_cvmfs.pdf. Accessed 26 May 2021
9. Blomer, J., Ganis, G., Hardi, N., Popescu, R.: Delivering LHC software to HPC compute elements with CernVM-FS. In: Kunkel, J.M., Yokota, R., Taufer, M., Shalf, J. (eds.) ISC High Performance 2017. LNCS, vol. 10524, pp. 724–730. Springer, Cham (2017). https://doi.org/10.1007/978-3-319-67630-2_52
10. Jakob, B., Dave, D., Gerardo, G., Simone, M., Jan, P.: A fully unprivileged CernVM-FS. EPJ Web Conf. **245**, 07012 (2020). https://doi.org/10.1051/epjconf/202024507012
11. Jakob, B., Gerardo, G., Simone, M., Radu, P.: Towards a serverless CernVM-FS. EPJ Web Conf. **214**, 09007 (2019). https://doi.org/10.1051/epjconf/201921409007
12. Boyer, A.F.: SubCVMFS-builder (2022). https://doi.org/10.5281/zenodo.6335367
13. Boyer, A.F.: SubCVMFS-builder-pipeline (2022). https://doi.org/10.5281/zenodo.6335512
14. Boyer, A.F.: SubCVMFS: gauss analysis (2022). https://doi.org/10.5281/zenodo.6337297
15. BSC: Marenostrum (2020). https://www.bsc.es/marenostrum/. Accessed 04 Oct 2021
16. Buncic, P., et al.: CernVM – a virtual software appliance for LHC applications. J. Phys. Conf. Ser. **219**(4), 042003 (2010). https://doi.org/10.1088/1742-6596/219/4/042003
17. Chris, B., Marco, C., Ben, C.: Software packaging and distribution for LHCB using nix. EPJ Web Conf. **214**, 05005 (2019). https://doi.org/10.1051/epjconf/201921405005
18. CERN: Cern, skao, gÉant and prace to collaborate on high-performance computing (2020). https://home.cern/news/news/computing/cern-skao-geant-and-prace-collaborate-high-performance-computing. Accessed 04 Oct 2021
19. CERN: Linux@cern (2020). https://linux.web.cern.ch/. Accessed 09 Feb 2021
20. CERN: CernVM-FS (2021). https://cernvm.cern.ch/. Accessed 19 May 2021
21. CERN: The large hadron collider (2021). https://home.cern/science/accelerators/large-hadron-collider. Accessed 27 May 2021
22. CERN: Root: analyzing petabytes of data, scientifically (2021). https://root.cern.ch/. Accessed 30 Sep 2021
23. CERN: Worldwide LHC computing grid (2021). https://wlcg.web.cern.ch/. Accessed 27 May 2021

24. Clemencic, M., et al.: The LHCb simulation application, gauss: design, evolution and experience. J. Phys. Conf. Ser. **331**(3), 032023 (2011). https://doi.org/10.1088/1742-6596/331/3/032023
25. Collaboration, T.L.: The LHCb detector at the LHC. J. Instrum. **3**(08), S08005–S08005 (2008). https://doi.org/10.1088/1748-0221/3/08/s08005
26. CVMFS: cvmfsexec (2021). https://github.com/cvmfs/cvmfsexec. Accessed 28 May 2021
27. Dykstra, D., Blomer, J.: Security in the CernVM file system and the frontier distributed database caching system. J. Phys. Conf. Ser. **513**, 042015 (2014). https://doi.org/10.1088/1742-6596/513/4/042015
28. EasyBuild: Easybuild: building software with ease (2021). https://easybuild.io/. Accessed 11 Dec 2021
29. Fasel, M.: Using nersc high-performance computing (HPC) systems for high-energy nuclear physics applications with alice. J. Phys: Conf. Ser. **762**, 012031 (2016). https://doi.org/10.1088/1742-6596/762/1/012031
30. Blomer, J., Ganis, G., Hardi, N., Popescu, R.: Delivering LHC software to HPC compute elements with CernVM-FS. In: Kunkel, J.M., Yokota, R., Taufer, M., Shalf, J. (eds.) ISC High Performance 2017. LNCS, vol. 10524, pp. 724–730. Springer, Cham (2017). https://doi.org/10.1007/978-3-319-67630-2_52
31. Filipčič, A., Haug, S., Hostettler, M., Walker, R., Weber, M.: Atlas computing on CSCS HPC. J. Phys: Conf. Ser. **664**(9), 092011 (2015). https://doi.org/10.1088/1742-6596/664/9/092011
32. GÉANT: GÉant (2021). https://www.geant.org/. Accessed: 04 Oct 2021
33. Gentoo: Gentoo linux (2021). https://www.gentoo.org/. Accessed: 11 Dec 2021
34. Gerhardt, L., et al.: Shifter: containers for HPC. J. Phys: Conf. Ser. **898**, 082021 (2017). https://doi.org/10.1088/1742-6596/898/8/082021
35. GitLab: Gitlab ci/cd (2021). https://docs.gitlab.com/ee/ci/. Accessed 23 Sep 2021
36. Harutyunyan, A., et al.: CernVM co-pilot: an extensible framework for building scalable computing infrastructures on the cloud. J. Phys. Conf. Ser. **396**(3), 032054 (2012). https://doi.org/10.1088/1742-6596/396/3/032054
37. ic hep: uncvmfs (2018). https://github.com/ic-hep/uncvmfs. Accessed 30 May 2021
38. Hufnagel, D.: CMS use of allocation based HPC resources. J. Phys: Conf. Ser. **898**, 092050 (2017). https://doi.org/10.1088/1742-6596/898/9/092050
39. Mazurek, M., Corti, G., Muller, D.: New simulation software technologies at the LHCb Experiment at CERN (2021)
40. NixOS: Nixos (2021). https://nixos.org/. Accessed 11 Dec 2021
41. O'Brien, B., Walker, R., Washbrook, A.: Leveraging HPC resources for high energy physics. J. Phys: Conf. Ser. **513**(3), 032104 (2014). https://doi.org/10.1088/1742-6596/513/3/032104
42. Oleynik, D., et al.: High-throughput computing on high-performance platforms: a case study (2017)
43. Radu, P., Jakob, B., Gerardo, G.: Towards a responsive CernVM-FS architecture. EPJ Web Conf. **214**, 03036 (2019). https://doi.org/10.1051/epjconf/201921403036
44. PRACE: Partnership for advanced computing in Europe (2021). https://prace-ri.eu/. Accessed 04 Oct 2021
45. Sciacca, F.G.: Enabling atlas big data processing on piz daint at CSCS. EPJ Web Conf. **245**, 09005 (2020). https://doi.org/10.1051/epjconf/202024509005

46. Segal, B., et al.: Lhc cloud computing with CernVM. In: 13th International Workshop on Advanced Computing and Analysis Techniques in Physics Research (ACAT2010) vol. 093, issue 4, p. 042003 (2011). https://doi.org/10.22323/1.093.0004
47. Siddi, B.G., Müller, D.: Gaussino - a gaudi-based core simulation framework. In: 2019 IEEE Nuclear Science Symposium and Medical Imaging Conference (NSS/MIC), pp. 1–4. IEEE, Manchester, United Kingdom (2019). https://doi.org/10.1109/NSS/MIC42101.2019.9060074
48. Sjöstrand, T., et al.: High-energy-physics event generation with pythia 6.1. Comput. Phys. Commun. **135**(2), 238–259 (2001). https://doi.org/10.1016/s0010-4655(00)00236-8
49. Spack: Spack (2021). https://spack.readthedocs.io/en/latest/. Accessed 11 Dec 2021
50. Stagni, F., McNab, A., Luzzi, C., Krzemien, W., Consortium, D.: Dirac universal pilots. J. Phys: Conf. Ser. **898**(9), 092024 (2017). https://doi.org/10.1088/1742-6596/898/9/092024
51. Stagni, F., Valassi, A., Romanovskiy, V.: Integrating LHCB workflows on HPC resources: status and strategies. EPJ Web Conf. **245**, 09002 (2020). https://doi.org/10.1051/epjconf/202024509002
52. Teuber, S.: Efficient unpacking of required software from CERNVM-FS (2019). https://doi.org/10.5281/zenodo.2574462
53. Top500: Top500 (2021). https://www.top500.org/. Accessed 04 Oct 2021
54. Benjamin, T., Brian, B., Michael, H., Kevin, L., Douglas, T.: Harnessing HPC resources for CMS jobs using a virtual private network. EPJ Web Conf. **251**, 02032 (2021). https://doi.org/10.1051/epjconf/202125102032
55. Vicente, D., Bartolome, J.: BSC-CNS research and supercomputing resources. In: Resch, M., Roller, S., Benkert, K., Galle, M., Bez, W., Kobayashi, H. (eds.) High Performance Computing on Vector Systems 2009, pp. 23–30. Springer, Heidelberg (2010). https://doi.org/10.1007/978-3-642-03913-3_2
56. l Valentin, V., et al. : Building hep software with spack: experiences from pilot builds for key4hep and outlook for LCG releases. EPJ Web Conf. **251**, 03056 (2021). https://doi.org/10.1051/epjconf/202125103056
57. Benda, X., Guilherme, A., Fabian, G., Michael, H.: Gentoo prefix as a physics software manager. EPJ Web Conf. **245**, 05036 (2020). https://doi.org/10.1051/epjconf/202024505036

Correction to: "Hey CAI" - Conversational AI Enabled User Interface for HPC Tools

Pouya Kousha, Arpan Jain, Ayyappa Kolli, Saisree Miriyala,
Prasanna Sainath, Hari Subramoni, Aamir Shafi,
and Dhableswar K. Panda

Correction to:
Chapter ""Hey CAI" - Conversational AI Enabled User Interface for HPC Tools" in: A.-L. Varbanescu et al. (Eds.): *High Performance Computing*, LNCS 13289, https://doi.org/10.1007/978-3-031-07312-0_5

In an older version of this paper, the name of the fourth author was missing. This has been corrected.

The updated original version of this chapter can be found at
https://doi.org/10.1007/978-3-031-07312-0_5

A.-L. Varbanescu et al. (Eds.): ISC High Performance 2022, LNCS 13289, p. C1, 2023.
https://doi.org/10.1007/978-3-031-07312-0_19

Author Index

Printed in the United States
by Baker & Taylor Publisher Services

Printed in the United States
by Baker & Taylor Publisher Services